ORGANIZATION THEORY

A PUBLIC PERSPECTIVE

SECOND EDITION

ORGANIZATION THEORY
A PUBLIC PERSPECTIVE

SECOND EDITION

HAROLD F. GORTNER
George Mason University

JULIANNE MAHLER
George Mason University

JEANNE BELL NICHOLSON
University of Maryland

Harcourt Brace College Publishers

Fort Worth Philadelphia San Diego New York Orlando Austin San Antonio
Toronto Montreal London Sydney Tokyo

Publisher	Christopher P. Klein
Senior Acquisitions Editor	David Tatom
Developmental Editor	J. Claire Brantley
Project Editor	Karen R. Masters
Production Manager	Jessica Iven Wyatt
Senior Art Director	Jeanette Barber
Production Services	York Production Services
Compositor	York Graphic Services
Text Type	Times Roman

ISBN: 0-03-019387-7

Library of Congress Catalog Card Number: 96-76555

To Sylvia, Cóilín and Llewellyn

Preface

The first premise of this book is that effective management of public organizations differs in key respects from the management of private organizations. Public agencies are administered in a demanding political, legal, and economic environment. They are charged with administering often ambiguous laws in a setting filled with well-organized opponents scrutinizing every action, zealous supporters, reluctant clients, and strict-but-often-conflicting guidelines for procedures. Legal constraints for equality and consistency of action dominate the design of programs and procedures. The political system drives public organizations. Change is a constant for both public and private organizations, but it is different in its manifestations. Managers in the public sector must work to develop organizational systems that respond to demands that change once the systems are in place; they must understand that the reasons for the change do not necessarily follow operational rationality. Agencies in currently popular policy areas are supported and well financed *regardless of past efficiency or effectiveness*. Likewise, those same agencies, faced with a public mood of cutback and reduction in government, find their programs diminished *regardless of past efficiency or effectiveness*. The "market" does not function for public agencies the way it does for private profit-seeking organizations. In consequence of the distinctiveness of the public mission and setting, public management differs from private management and requires a distinctive approach to the literature of organization theory and management behavior. Organization theory for public agencies must consider issues that do not appear in traditional, "generic" organization theory, or in management behavior texts.

The purpose of this text is to examine the basic topics of organization management from the perspective of public governmental organizations. The basic literature in the organization theory field is discussed from an applied management perspective. This text also highlights those aspects of theory and research that are important for the manager of public organizations. The revised edition attempts to recognize the increased importance, and managerial similarities, of not-for-profit organizations; however, the primary focus remains the public bureau.

This is not a new organization theory, but rather a selection from and interpretation of the existing literature. A special set of questions is asked about that literature and how each of the basic topics of organizational theory can best be applied to the problems of public administration. To do so, we must examine the requirements of, say, control systems in public organizations, and then discuss what the existing literature tells us about this organizational function that is relevant to the problems presented by public settings and purposes.

In addition to the material traditionally included in organization theory texts, there is considerable research in areas such as political science and economics that must be acknowledged and examined by students of public organizations. One cannot discuss leadership in public organizations, for example, without including material about chief executives that is not usually covered by most organization theory authors (much to their loss). Nor is it possible to understand leadership at the executive level in public organizations if one is ignorant of the fact that leaders rotate, and fluctuate in their ability and desires, relatively rapidly in most public organizations at the state and national level. In general, public administrators must have a special sensitivity to the political, social, and economic implications of their environment—both because of that environment's impact on the bureaus and because of the bureaus' influence on the rest of society.

The six readings and eleven cases that are included in this text are drawn from public sector experiences and writings. This additional source material will aid students in understanding the impact of the public and political arena on organizations. Each case raises several issues and can accompany various chapters in addition to the one it follows.

This book is geared toward students at the upper division of undergraduate school and those in the graduate programs of public administration across the country; therefore, the material is presented both pragmatically and theoretically. Only upon reaching the doctoral level is it likely that one studies organization theory primarily with the intent of focusing on the theory itself. Students at the bachelor's and master's levels are ultimately interested in the application of theory in the real world of the public bureaucracy.

For the reasons noted above, we feel that this text offers something special to the field of public administration around the United States, and perhaps in other Western countries as well. As one studies organizations, it is important to remember that in a liberal democratic society, bureaus are not the end for which society was established, but a means by which society can make its democratic institutions meet the needs of its citizens.

The revision and updating of this volume has been done by Harold F. Gortner. It has been my intention to follow the charge given those who perform surgery: First of all, do no harm. Much of what we co-authored in the first edition continues to be valid and dynamic—that remains. New material has been added, including some new cases and readings, and some reordering has occurred in those cases where such changes would improve the presentation of materials. Much of the material remains central to the understanding of public organizations, and I have tried to keep it in-tact. I have especially tried to retain the ease of reading and understanding that was one of the strong points of our original text. Every attempt is made to avoid jargon, obfuscation, and unnecessary complication in explaining the organizations in which we spend so much of our lives.

It is important to acknowledge several people who have contributed in a variety of ways to the development and completion of this revision. I especially appreciate the reviewers of the first edition—Nolan Argyle of Valdosta State University, Eugene Barrington of Texas Southern University, Bill Waugh of Georgia State University, and David Williams of the University of West Virginia—for their useful suggestions as I prepared the second edition. As would be expected, I did not heed all of their advice, so any errors in judgment or presentation are solely mine. The students in the master's and doctor's programs at George Mason University have consistently forced me to think "differently" about organization theory as it is applied to their public sector experiences and needs. They have also felt free to comment on the book and suggest ideas that have improved the current edition. Colleagues on the faculty, especially Russ Cargo, have given me thoughtful and helpful input regarding the presentation of many theoretical constructs. Although she was unable to help in this revision, Julianne Mahler has observed and commented from her busy vantage point, and I appreciate her help. Finally, I must thank my wife, Sylvia, who has contributed in innumerable ways (research assistant, moral supporter, motivator) as I have gone about this rather lengthy and nerve-racking task.

Harold F. Gortner

Contents

CHAPTER 7. Organizational Decision Making   222

CHAPTER 10. Organization Change and Development   357

List of Figures

Chapter 1

Varieties of Organization Research and Theory

INTRODUCTION

The subject of this text is organization theory for public organizations. We survey many of the most prominent explanations and theories of organizations as political, social, and economic phenomena; however, we interpret "political" more broadly than most theorists. Public bureaus have both an internal political nature—recognized by most organization theorists—and an external political environment that is not considered by generic theory. By adding the political environment, and its impact on inter- and intraorganizational functions, we hope to help public administrators devise their own effective and successful strategies for organizational management, informed by these theories.

We do not intend to offer a new theory of organization that is unique to the public sector; rather, our purpose is to integrate and highlight the existing body of research and theory around an understanding of public organization and the problems of public management. Such an effort is certainly long overdue, for, as we will note in the next chapter, there has long been a bias toward the problems and environments of the private sector in most of the field.

Thus, the emphasis here will be on the implications of the publicness of agencies along several dimensions. How do the demands of *constituencies and clients,* rather than markets, suppliers, and customers, affect what we know about designing organizational structures, communication networks, and systems of control? How do the legal requirements and the mission of public organizations affect power, authority, and leadership? What are the sources of organizational ethos, commitment, and motivation in public agencies? What are the pressures on intelligence and decision-making systems in public agencies as opposed to for-profit firms?

In this chapter, we will be concerned with some of the basic definitions, assumptions, and questions posed by organization theory as it is applied to public agencies. We will look at the contributions of various disciplines to the body of research and theory in the field, and we will introduce the wide variety of theories and explanatory perspectives that have emerged in the field. We hope to help the reader see organizations at many levels simultaneously and use the organization theories presented here as a set of conceptual tools for analyzing problems in public organizations and finding solutions to them.

1

WHAT IS AN ORGANIZATION?

In one sense, this is an easy and obvious question; we generally agree on what counts as an organization. A government agency or a private firm is an organization. Pillsbury, the Girl Scouts, and the Office of Management and Budget are organizations, but the people in line to buy stamps at the post office, the crowd at a soccer game, and this week's panel of reporters on a Sunday morning interview program are not. Not only size, but the ongoing interrelatedness of the people in the group contributes to the state we call organization.

The most common formal definition of an organization is a collection of people engaged in specialized and interdependent activity to accomplish a goal or mission. Typically, organization theorists further define their interest as "large, complex organizations" that are sizable, specialized, and highly interdependent collectivities. Size often allows specialization; specialization of function or division of labor permits efficiency; specialization creates interdependency and a demand for mechanisms that can coordinate these different but interdependent tasks. The activities in which members are engaged are typically not personalized or personally determined; rather, they are codified in job descriptions or roles, thus ensuring that the organization will survive even if the personnel change.

This definition, though acceptable, is a bit misleading. For example, the technology of some small organizations may be so simple that little specialization of work is necessary or possible. Perhaps an even more serious limitation is that not all the members of organizations (public or private) are there to accomplish some formal, perhaps intangible or abstract goal. They simply want to earn a living. Thus, questions of control, motivation, and supervisory style immediately become important.

Other limitations in the definition concern the desirability of nonpersonalized work roles, the lack of real freedom and democratic values, and what some see as an inappropriate focus on behavior rather than the culture of the organization and the intentions of the organization's members. A recent and interesting insight into the activity of organizing as opposed to whatever constitutes the organizational institution is provided by Weick, who suggests that:

> Organizing is like a grammar in the sense that it is a systematic account of some rules and conventions by which sets of interlocked behaviors are assembled to form social processes that are intelligible to actors. (1979, 3)

But once organizing has occurred, once routine and structure come into being, does it matter? There is certainly much railing about "the bureaucracy" in the political world, and in their campaigns many politicians "run against the bureaucracy." Other people make their living trying to move organizations from "the bureaucratic age" into the "post-bureaucratic age of the moment"—be that the information-age organization, the participative-democratic organization, or the learning organization.

At the same time, there is an underlying feeling among many that organization is not that important. James Q. Wilson comments that "only two groups of people deny that organization matters: economists and everybody else" (1989, 23). Economists, he argues, see people in organizations as individuals maximizing their utility under a set of market or political constraints—just another social phenomenon explained by marginal-cost economics. We will address this particular view occasionally as we discuss public choice theory (the ultimate economic explanation of organizational activity) and its impact on public organizations.

Other people, says Wilson, argue that the organization is unimportant, that it's the people in it who matter. He responds by saying there are two errors in the "only people matter" view. The first is that people are influenced by their membership and position in an organization just as they are affected by biological, social, and educational factors. Wilson quotes Herbert Simon, who says that a person:

> does not live for months or years in a particular position in an organization, exposed to some streams of communication, shielded from others, without the most profound effects upon what he knows, believes, attends to, hopes, wishes, emphasizes, fears, and proposes. (1976, xvi)

The second error in the "organization doesn't matter" argument is pointed out by simply noting that what people accomplish depends on their having the authority and resources with which to act (Wilson 1989, 24). Why cannot people accomplish the things they do *in* organizations *outside* organizations? Position, authority, and resources—available only in organizations—matter.

If organization matters, then it is important to understand how organizations come into being, develop structure, maintain resources and procedures, and accomplish their goals. Much of the debate about "bureaucracy" and its impact on society, politics, and individuals occurs in ignorance: Many of the individuals shouting the most shrill imprecations do so without any in-depth knowledge of the phenomenon against which they rail. Their debate would be greatly enlightened by an increase in knowledge about what they see as "the enemy." This book presents the knowledge needed to enlighten the debate; we cannot, of course, ensure that any of these critics will partake of the knowledge.

At the same time, serious discussions are occurring around issues related to the core meaning of the term *organization* and numerous concerns about how organization can be best utilized as a tool of society. In these cases, as noted by Gareth Morgan, our debate is based on our understanding of the phenomenon we study, and our understanding of "organization is always shaped by underlying images and ideas" (1986, 343). These images and ideas are broadened and deepened by coming to understand what has been learned about organizations through research over the last century. Of course, the concepts, theories, and models have raised new issues. These issues are raised by organization theorists and public administration theorists in their critiques of conventional approaches to organization theory. We will look briefly at some of these critiques in this chapter and throughout the text.

Public Organizations

It is necessary to distinguish public organizations, with which this book is concerned, from the whole universe of organizations. By public organizations, we mean government agencies, that is, organizations created to be agents of some unit of government, whether a local school district or the Executive Office of the President. Public organizations are part of government and have as their purpose the administration of law. This sets them apart from privately owned firms and nonprofit organizations, which are accountable to owners or boards of directors that are not government entities.

This is a purely legal distinction with implications concerning the purpose, require-ments, and character of the organization. Public oversight and accountability, for example, though a prominent and necessary feature of public organizations, is nonexistent, or limited and temporary, in firms and nonprofit organizations. The next two chapters will discuss both the characteristics of public agencies in contrast to other types of organizations and the implications of a focus on such organizations.

Over the last decade, a question of special interest to the study of organizations has arisen and needs to be briefly addressed here. As nonprofit organizations, often referred to as "the third sector," have grown in importance within society, it has become increas-ingly critical to decide where they fall on the "public–private" spectrum. Without spending a lot of time justifying the claim, it is our belief that third-sector organizations fall much closer to the public than the private end of that spectrum. Even though these organizations come into being outside government, they often exist to carry out social functions or to achieve specific social goals rather than to make a profit (which is the primary reason for business—see Chapter 2). If the claim that these organizations operate in a "quasi-public" fashion is correct, the material in this book should be especially applicable to them.

Bureaucracy

The term *bureaucracy* is used both to identify a particular type of organizational structure and to deride or criticize it (Downs 1967). The definition of bureaucracy offered by Max Weber (1947), the German sociologist who wrote from the turn of the century to the 1920s, is the most authoritative and still serves as the point of departure for contemporary organization theory. Based on historical and contemporary study of several great social and economic institutions—including the Prussian military, the Roman Catholic church, and the Chinese civil service—Weber identified a number of specific characteristics of organizational structure and personnel policy that set the bureaucratic institution apart from all other, less neutral, stable, and expert means of administering the law and coordinating the intricate activities of vast numbers of people in a predictable and efficient manner.

The characteristics of bureaucracy that Weber noted included the specialization of function; the requirement that the hiring and promotion of officials be based solely on expertise; that authority be exercised through a centralized, hierarchical chain of command; and the development of an intricate system of rules to cover all possible actions and to minimize discretion. In Chapter 3, we describe and analyze these and other characteristics of bureaucracies as an example of one prototype of public agencies.

Alternatively, Downs's formulation of the idea of bureaucracy highlights its economic foundations (1967). He distinguishes between bureaus and firms based on the bureau's lack of a market:

> Without a market that acts to set the value of the organization's work, managers rationally focus on obtaining a larger share of inputs, funds for expansion, or greater authority. The basic purpose and motivation of the bureau becomes not efficiency in the usual sense but greater recognition and support from funders.

All public bureaus, many nonprofit organizations, and some special offices in the private sector are therefore bureaus. The implications of the lack of a market are felt in many areas of the bureau's existence: growth, motivation, communications, control systems, leadership styles, and, especially, decision making. In the matter of the bureau's size and structural characteristics, Downs agrees with Weber.

Still other formulations of bureaucracy are offered by a number of contemporary theorists. Hummel (1994), who also begins with Weber's formulation, focuses on what Weber saw as the considerable dangers of bureaucracy for the personality of its officials and for society at large. Though Weber chronicled the rise of the bureaucratic form and was able to see its advantages for the control of far-flung enterprises, he was also extremely critical of the way bureaucracy destroys spontaneity, which, as one raised in the Romantic literary tradition, he equated with human freedom. The bureaucratic personality must always be oriented to the efficiency of any proposed course of action; thus, he or she loses the capacity to act in a spontaneous and fully human manner. Even worse, the trend Weber saw—and we continue to observe—is that more and more institutions, public, private, and even familial, have become bureaucratic, which makes us increasingly captive of the bureaucratic mentality and less able to see or to act on our plight.

Hummel notes that ultimately:

> Bureaucracy gives birth to a new species of inhuman beings. Peoples' social relations are being converted into control relations. Their norms and beliefs concerning human ends are torn from them and replaced with skills affirming the ascendancy of technical means, whether of administration or production. Psychologically, the new personality type is that of the rationalistic expert, incapable of emotion and devoid of will. Language, once the means of bringing people into communication, becomes the secretive tool of one-way commands. Politics, especially democratic politics, fades away as the method of publicly determining society-wide goals based on human needs: it is replaced by administration. (1994, 3)

Other definitions of bureaucracy, also highly critical and negative, derive from a variety of theoretical foundations. Some view bureaus as complex linguistic games, as cultural constructions rather than the objective realities we assume we perceive, or as "psychic prisons," or instruments of class domination (Burrell and Morgan 1979; Denhart 1981, 1993). We will look further at these characterizations in this and subsequent chapters.

The question of whether public organizations must have the negative characteristics associated with the bureaucracy is one that lies at the heart of most contemporary organization research, and one we hope to examine in this text. The effort to devise a better form of organization, one that balances the many and sometimes contradictory beliefs about what would be a better form, is a major occupation of the field. What are the alternatives to bureaucracy? What are the advantages and limitations of alternative organizational forms, in general and in particular, for public administration? What can the radical critics of bureaucracy teach us about the obligations of public agencies?

WHAT IS ORGANIZATION THEORY?

Organization theory is *not* a single theory. Rather, it is a loosely knit community of many approaches to organizational analysis. Its themes, questions, methods, and explanatory modes are extremely diverse. Dwight Waldo noted in a review of work in the field in 1978, "Organization theory is characterized by vogues, heterogeneity, claims and counterclaims" (597), and even greater differentiation in theory and practice have developed since then. Organization theory certainly cannot be described as an orderly progression of ideas or a unified body of knowledge in which each development builds carefully on and extends the one before it. Rather, developments in theory and prescriptions for practice show disagreement about the purposes and uses of a theory of organization, the issues to which it should address itself (supervisory style, organizational culture), and the concepts and variables that should enter into such a theory.

The interdisciplinary (really multidisciplinary) character of the field is probably the most important source of the diversity of questions, methods, and theories, and of the considerable energy in the field. Most of the social sciences contribute to organization theory. Psychology, and the more applied branch of industrial psychology, have contributed behavioral studies on such topics as leadership, motivation, group interaction, and conflict. Sociological research in the 1950s produced a small but important group of insightful case studies of the unintended consequences of official organizational rules and the effects of informal social relations. More recently, sociologists have studied organization structure and interorganizational coordination—to name only a few topics. Economic analyses of organizations have focused on the many theories of decision making, among other subjects. Anthropologists and communications analysts have studied the linguistic and cultural dimensions of organizational life. Systems analysts have provided applied mathematical models for planning and program management. Public administrators and political scientists have concerned themselves with policy analysis and have investigated the ways in which the political, professional, and technical characteristics of public organizations influence the making and execution of government policy. These disciplines study the relationships between public organizations and their political environments. Figure 1–1 gives examples of typical questions posed by the disciplines that contribute to the field of organization theory.

This variety of disciplines clearly contributes to the richness and complexity of theory in the field, as well as to the conflicts over theories, the absence of conceptual agreement on fundamental assumptions about the nature of organizations or the uses and purposes of organization theory. For some scholars and practitioners, the theories are expected to provide clear and direct guidelines for the selection of particular management styles or practices; for others, the purpose of theory is to explain phenomena; and for still others, its purpose is to activate resistance to the part the organization plays in political oppression.

There are, of course, many continuities in the field. Real interdisciplinary exchange results from the extensive borrowing of concepts, findings, and questions. Often, however, this borrowing is characterized by extensive reinterpretation and shifts in meaning and emphasis so that the result sometimes resembles piracy more than interdisciplinary cooperation in theory development. This state of affairs is fairly common in the social sciences generally (Kaplan 1964), but sometimes seems to reach new heights in organization theory because of its multidisciplinary nature.

Organization theory has also been open to the currents of political thought. Various organization theorists in the 1960s and 1970s advocated more democratic decision-making procedures and greater participation by citizens and officials, for example. Theoretical movements in the social sciences have also had an impact on the field. The behavioral revolution, the popularity of general systems theory, and the current re-emergence and acceptance of interpretive research on the intentions, meanings, and symbols of organizations rather than on behavior alone are some examples. Theory in the field has sometimes

---

FIGURE 1–1   Questions about Organizations Posed by Various of the Social Sciences

Anthropology: The social science concerned with the origins of humankind and its physical, social, and cultural development.

> **Questions:** What are the cultural norms of the organization, and how are they manifested in stories, rituals, and symbols? How are organizational norms related to the norms of the larger culture? How do they affect implementation of policies and the political strategies of the organization?

Sociology: The science of society, social institutions, and social relations; specifically, the systematic study of the development, structure, interaction, and collective behavior of organized groups of people.

> **Questions:** What is the relationship between the formal organization and the informal social life of the organization? How are organizational activities coordinated and controlled? What are the key social institutions, roles, and values in the organization? How are they related to external institutions and values? How do organizations interact? How are they linked?

Psychology: The social science that examines personality, cognition, emotional life, and behavior.

> **Questions:** How are we motivated? What attitudes or personality types lead to behavior that is valued in organizations? How do perception and learning influence organizational behavior such as work motivation and productivity? What are the processes of effective communication?

Social Psychology: The social science concerned with attitudes, cognitions, and behavior in social settings and the interactions of people.

> **Questions:** What is leadership, and what are the most effective forms of leadership behavior? How are attitudes formed in organizations, and how do they influence work behavior? How do cohesive groups form, how do members interact, and what are the implications for organizational functioning?

Economics: The social science concerned with the analysis of markets and the systems by which goods and services are produced, distributed, and consumed.

> **Questions:** What are the differences in market relations and economic motivation between public and private organizations? What economic conditions are necessary for the formation of a public agency? How is decision making linked to the economic characteristics of organizations?

Political Science: The social science concerned with the institutions and processes of government, public policy, and politics.

> **Questions:** What is the role of bureaus in government? What are the political responsibilities of bureaus? How are power and influence exercised within bureaus and in their relations with other actors, governmental bodies, and constituencies?

---

gone to extremes in its search for a conceptual wedge that can open the secrets of successful organizations.

All these currents have been combined in new "action theories" that attempt to create organizations with more sensitivity to internal and external changes, increased capability of learning and changing to meet constant challenges to existence, and, especially, greater chances for individual growth and fulfillment in conjunction with organizational success (Senge 1990; Heckscher and Donnellon 1994).

In sum, organization theory is a disorderly and fascinating field. To produce a useful overview of it is a difficult, almost presumptuous, task. But we feel that it is important to try because we believe that the field makes an important and useful contribution to the study of government and public management.

VARIETIES OF ORGANIZATION THEORY

The varieties of organization theory can perhaps best be understood by differentiating them at three levels. First, they differ in subject matter. Second, there are differences in their explanatory forms—that is, whether systems analysis, political economy, or some other approach is the basis for the explanation offered in the theory. Finally, theories can be differentiated in terms of their purposes. We will look briefly at each of these distinctions.

Essentially, the perspective taken here on the application of these theories might be called a multitheory approach in which the question is not which theory to accept and which to discard, but how to establish a basis from which managers, *informed* by theory, can pick and choose useful concepts and devise strategies for action. Concerning the application of the theories, we see them as a set of conceptual tools for diagnosing and acting on organizational problems. Within limits, the larger the number of theories and the more varied the conceptual tools at our disposal, the greater the likelihood that we will find an approach that suits the conditions we face. Thus, having a variety of theories at one's disposal makes one a more capable manager because one has the ability to see and conceptualize problems in alternative ways and to evaluate these alternatives.

Differences in Subject

Organization theorists study various phenomena and use different levels of analysis. Some research focuses on the individual, whereas other studies are concerned with groups or the organization as a whole. Studies at the organizational level include work on structures and hierarchies and on processes such as communication or decision making. In this way, four main subject areas in organization research and theory can be identified:

1. Theories of individual and group behavior

2. Theories of organization structure

3. Theories of organizational processes (such as communications and decision making)

4. Global or overall theories of organization

These topics do not, however, constitute unrelated or mutually exclusive categories. In fact, the *mutual use* of these theories in attacking organizational understanding and action is synergistic. For example, theories of structure focus on the formal chain of authority, but intelligence gathering and information processing also rely on some of these structures while also using other, nonformal aspects. Thus, the topics are related in ways we will discuss in detail later in this chapter.

At the level of *individual* behavior is, for example, research on motivation where inborn needs, attitudes, and perceptions are studied in relation to productivity or other desirable organizational outputs. However, groups, and the interaction of individuals with them, is an important part of understanding phenomena like motivation. The investigation of *groups and intergroup relations* encompasses such subjects as the dynamics and effectiveness of workgroups or decision-making groups, conflict management, and leadership. At the overall or *global* level of analysis are found research and speculative theory on such issues as what the reigning values of the organization should be; what its relations with outside clients or constituents should be; or what its means of motivation, coordination, or leadership are. A total picture is provided—usually at the speculative level—that energizes our efforts in theory and research at the other two levels. The "total quality" organization of Deming (Walton 1990), the "excellent" organization of Peters and Waterman (1982), the "Z" organization that reflects aspects of Japanese management (Ouchi 1981), and Orion White's "dialectical" organization (1969) are some examples.

Research on organizational structure and processes constitutes yet another distinction in the field's subject matter. *Structural* research is concerned with the organization's hierarchical pattern, centralization and decentralization, the shape of the organizational chart and its lines of authority, the formation of organizational subdivisions, and the coordination of those subdivisions. An important question in this area is how organizations adapt their structures to changes in the environment or technology. Organizational *processes* include the basic activities of the organization. We will discuss such topics as decision making and policy development, control and communication (key processes in policymaking and analysis), budgeting, evaluation, and program implementation.

These subjects are the basic topics that will be examined in this text. Differences in the types and purposes of theories, which we will describe next, will be discussed within this subject framework as we proceed.

Differences in Type

The type of theory, or the form of the explanation offered in the theory, is another distinction that can be made among organization theories. Some of the most common theories include systems theory, theories of political economy, public choice theory, theories of group politics and influence, theories of personality and attitude formation, theories of psychological humanism, theories of culture interpretation, and theories of social change. We will illustrate just a few of these to show the diversity of explanations used in the field. Usually, any one organizational subject is explained by several different types of theories, which makes for a great diversity of explanations and a richness in perspective on any single subject. Thus, each subject that is discussed in each chapter will typically be covered from several different theoretical perspectives.

Systems theories are used to explain many aspects of an organization. The technology for resource transformation, from inputs to outputs, and the influences of various environmental conditions are often described as particular patterns of activity called systems.

Systems theories point out how activities in the system are interrelated, sometimes in mathematical terms. Here events are explained as the product of natural, often unintended, patterns of interactivity. Organizational communication and control theories make frequent use of systems theory.

The political economy approach explains events in terms of the relations between political and economic systems (Wamsley and Zald 1976) and the nonmarket setting of bureaus (Downs 1967), and shows how these factors influence the choices of organizational actors. Incremental decision making, for example, is seen as the rational response when the costs of new information and reprogramming the rules and personnel are high relative to the value of a new, severely different policy for the organization (Allison 1971).

Differences in Purpose

Even though the most commonly accepted theories are diverse in explanatory content and topical focus, they share some basic assumptions about the nature of organizations and the purpose of organization theory. In general, the mainstream theories are empirical; that is, they are based on quantitative or qualitative observations, and they assume that there is a more or less objective reality that can become knowable through observation.

The theories also share the assumption that the purpose of organization research and theory is to uncover that reality and to use the knowledge of how to predict and sometimes control that reality to improve the functioning of organizations from the standpoint of the organization's "owners," including administrative professionals, the public, and the variety of governmental policymakers. Since these assumptions fit naturally with the assumptions and purposes of practicing administrators, the mainstream orientation to organization theory has generally been useful for practitioners.

Other responses to questions about the nature of organizational knowledge and the purposes of organization theory have been emerging in the past two decades in public administration. Although these theories, for the most part, lack the "scientific objectivity" of the theories previously mentioned, and therefore are centers of debate about their applicability to public organizations, they do show some noteworthy developments that are outside the mainstream theories, assumptions, and methods, as Burrell and Morgan (1979) note. Hummel's critique of the standard bureaucratic model of organization, based at least in part on phenomenology, is illustrative of one alternative model. According to this theory, what one thinks and perceives, the precepts and concepts of the mind, actually determine what is reality to the individual. And bureaucracy organizes the minds of most people because of the time spent in, and the impact on life of, bureaucratic organizations. According to Hummel:

> Unless a model can be found in bureaucratic policies of programs for a real individual trying to become a client, that individual can never come to exist for the bureaucracy as a client. Reality itself is defined according to ideal models. In bureaucratic speech, the client experiences this power to declare him or her existent, or a nullity, in terms of a number of demands by bureaucrats: Speak our language or get no help; answer our questions (according to some secret code unknown to you) or we will think you don't exist. (1994, 217)

In other words, phenomenology says bureaucratic organizations are mechanistic and depersonalizing; everyone in them and affected by them is forced into a category, a class, and treated with generic procedures and remedies to achieve universal goals. The painful and conflicting pressures that conscientious officials experience because of the bureaucratic system often have the effect of creating either loss of freedom or disobedience. Naisbitt (1982) refers to this phenomenon as the divided need for "high tech" and "high touch" in society. As more technology, bureaucracy, and "order" take over life, there is a corresponding need for connectedness and meaningful interaction with others as human beings. Some groups and nations have tried to escape bureaucracy by reverting to premodern existence and seeking charismatic guidance. The popularity of urban and rural communes in the 1960s and early 1970s, the desire of many people to leave large corporations and either work in or set up smaller businesses, and the emergence of charismatic and evangelical movements within mainline churches may be signs of this revolt.

For Hummel, a way to begin reforming organizational culture is to adopt what he calls an "intentionalist" position (a form of phenomenology), which focuses on the intentions and beliefs of workers, and on the perceptions and language that link one human being to another. We would then no longer treat workers or clients as objects to be motivated or manipulated. Instead, we would focus on our status as coworkers; use the discretion available to us as managers to increase interaction; and thereby enhance the power, capacity, and creativity of officials to perform their mission.

Other critiques of the ways in which bureaus and mainstream organization theory manipulate people and use them as objects include Denhardt (1981). Harmon (1981), like Hummel, emphasizes the subjectivity of organizational and social life, and suggests that attention be paid to the ways in which all officials try to make sense of their world by positing theories and engaging in linguistic and other symbol-sharing activities. As an outgrowth of this view, Harmon argues that cooperation and freedom of interaction will be more justice producing than the methods of social domination and control that are more commonly found in organizations and in society at large. Burrell and Morgan (1979) sketch a conceptual framework for describing and comparing these theories, and Denhardt (1993) reviews and critiques these and other organization theories as they apply to public administration.

Another theory, related to economics, that has gained attention over the last two decades is public choice theory and its application to bureaucratic actors (Tullock 1987). These theorists believe that people in public bureaucracies almost inevitably move away from dutiful behavior in carrying out the law or the goals established by their external masters—often the legislature or the chief executive. Instead, quoting Garvey:

> Drawing their premises primarily from the economic theory of the market, [public choice] theorists emphasize individual self-interest, not group goals. The appeal to an internalized sense of public trust may work partially or temporarily, but human egoism will eventually challenge the pattern of strict accountability that the machine model of bureaucracy implies. Bureaucratic actors have interests of their own to advance. Inevitably, these interests will come into conflict, at least to some degree, with the goals of the organization. The temptation of a conflicted employee to sacrifice the group goal for the personal one is likely to be irresistible. Thus, . . . if subordinates have any latitude for discretion, they will sooner or later abuse it. (1993, 29)

Public choice theory, if accepted, has strong explanatory and prescriptive power. It especially prescribes strong systems of control for decisions and actions of employees in any public bureau. This theory also speaks to the size of government: Proponents of this theory believe government should be minimal and the bureaucracy small.

Although we will discuss the insights and criticisms of these newer theoretical orientations throughout this text, we will not be advocates for one or another of them. Neither will we advocate any of the more conventional organizational theories. Rather, we hope to present a variety of theories organized around a fairly comprehensive set of topics in the field in a way that will permit and encourage readers to develop a way of using the insights from as many theories as possible.

OUR THEORETICAL PERSPECTIVE

As we noted earlier, the approach we are taking here is multitheoretical. From an application perspective, we see the theories we have outlined here and will discuss throughout the text as conceptual tools for diagnosing problems and assessing the potential of different solutions. The larger the number and variety of conceptual tools that we have to work with, the more facets of the organizational problem we can see, and the better and more intelligent our choice of action can be.

For example, in most organization theory classes, students confronting their first discussion of a management case will typically see all problems as personality conflicts and will try to find ways to get rid of the offending actor. After a few weeks of readings, however, they begin to see that the same case has other dimensions, such as problems in the form of the communication network or in the supervisory style of a manager. Reading organization theory helps us see organizations as multidimensional entities and allows us to identify alternative lines of analysis and action.

A variety of theories and research findings contribute to both understanding and action in organizations. Different theories are useful in different circumstances and for different kinds of managers. Although we are not suggesting that managers should simply "make up" a personal theory without recourse to the analysis and research in the field, we are suggesting that public managers can and do judge which dimensions of a problem are most critical, which aspect of the organization is in the most trouble, and what his or her own particular talents and predilections are. Based on these factors, the offerings of the field of organization theory should be studied and selectively used.

Some work has already been done on identifying the circumstances under which a particular theory or research finding would be most appropriate. What is called a contingency theory or metatheory (a theory about how or when to use other theories) has been developed in several subject areas of organization theory and will be presented in later chapters. These contingency theories prescribe different courses of action, depending on the circumstances in the organization. For example, one contingency theory of supervisory behavior leads to a recommendation of different styles of behavior, based on the psychological maturity and skill levels of the workgroup; another suggests that different decision-making models fit distinct situations. We will present a number of these theories wherein such factors as the environment of the agency, its program technology, and its political support influence our evaluation and selection of the available courses of action.

CHAPTER TOPICS FOR THIS TEXT

The chapters in this text are, for the most part, organized around subjects or themes central to organization theory. Two further introductory chapters follow this one, however. Chapter 2 discusses the differences between public and private organizations and how those differences affect the development of a public organization theory. Chapter 3 discusses some of the pivotal areas of interest to public administration and how various global theories of organization address or fail to address these issues. Our purpose in these introductory chapters is to identify some of the issues with which we are particularly concerned given our focus on public organizations.

Chapter 4 deals with theories of organization structure. It overviews traditional theories and presents a detailed review of the more contemporary research and theorizing on the design of organizations. This review takes into account the agency's needs for program support, its program technologies, and its environment.

Chapters 5 through 7 deal with the organization's intelligence system; communication, control, and decision making are the subjects covered. We consider the various types of formal and informal communications networks, their pathologies, and some partial remedies. The control system, of course, depends on the communication structure for the gathering and processing of information, which means that problems in one part of the system affect the other parts. Various forms of control using quantitative, behavioral, and social-psychological approaches to the subject are discussed. Finally, the variety of descriptive and prescriptive theories of decision making or policy making are described, and the prospects for a contingency theory of decision making are discussed.

The focus on individual behavior is covered in Chapters 8 and 9. Theories of motivation, largely borrowed from research on for-profit firms, are discussed in Chapter 8, and the alterations that would make them applicable to government agencies are considered. Leadership, managerial, and supervisory behavior are discussed in Chapter 9. We examine the traditional and behavioral approaches in terms of their appropriateness for different hierarchical levels and managerial settings. Chapter 10 concludes the book with a discussion of techniques of planned organizational change based on technological developments, behavioral research, and the human relations values mentioned earlier.

FOR FURTHER READING

At the end of each chapter are suggestions for further reading in that subject area. Here let us note some of the journals that are the source of the very latest information on research about, and application of, organization theory.

The latest in *behavioral research* is often presented in the *Administrative Science Quarterly.* Among the several journals in *public administration* that should be scanned for information about both research and current practice in government agencies is the main journal of the field, *Public Administration Review.* General management journals, such as the *Harvard Business Review* and the *California Management Review,* although usually focusing on the private sector, present valuable information on research in complex organizations. There is another set of journals, represented by *Organizational Dynamics,* that deal with the application of behavioral theory to current businesses or organizations. Each of the major disciplines involved in particular aspects of organizational research (psychology, sociology, economics, and so on) has journals that make contributions to the field of organization theory. And finally, there are journals dealing with each of the major subject areas covered in the latter chapters of this volume (communication, decision theory, leadership, and so on). This review of journals is very cursory and meant only to point the researcher in the right direction. A little effort will return great rewards in learning about the latest research about organizations and its application in the real world.

Another growing universe of potentially valuable information must be mentioned: the Internet. Most government organizations have "home pages" that offer increasing amounts of information to the public. Likewise businesses, universities, and many professional organizations with an interest in organization theory are sharing information about current research and activity through the Internet. Undoubtedly, this area of potential information will grow substantially each year and has the potential of being the most up-to-date source of information yet imagined.

REVIEW QUESTIONS

1. Think about what the goals are that you wish to achieve from reading this book. What do you want to know about organizations after this experience?

2. This book presents an introduction to the field, and it is possible to delve much deeper into every topic. How much more do you need to know about specific topics in order to accomplish the goals you have established for yourself?

3. As you read the following chapters, consider to what extent the materials presented as *particular* to public organizations also apply to not-for-profit organizations.

REFERENCES

Allison, Graham T. *Essence of Decision: Explaining the Cuban Missile Crisis.* Boston: Little, Brown, 1971.

Burrell, Gibson, and Gareth Morgan. *Sociological Paradigms and Organizational Analysis.* London: Heinemann, 1979.

Denhardt, Robert B. *In the Shadow of Organization.* Lawrence, Kans.: Regents Press of Kansas, 1981.

———. *Theories of Public Organization.* 2nd ed. Belmont, Calif.: Wadsworth, 1993.

Downs, Anthony. *Inside Bureaucracy.* Boston: Little, Brown, 1967. (Reissued, Prospect Heights, Ill.: Waveland Press, 1994.)

Garvey, Gerald. *Facing the Bureaucracy: Living and Dying in a Public Agency.* San Francisco: Jossey-Bass, 1993.

Harmon, Michael. *Action Theory for Public Administration.* New York: Longman, 1981.

Heckscher, Charles, and Anne Donnellon. *The Post-Bureaucratic Organization: New Perspectives on Organizational Change.* Thousand Oaks, Calif.: Sage, 1994.

Hummel, Ralph P. *The Bureaucratic Experience.* 4th ed. New York: St. Martin's Press, 1994.

Kaplan, Abraham. *The Conduct of Inquiry.* San Francisco: Chandler, 1964.

Morgan, Gareth. *Images of Organization.* Beverly Hills, Calif.: Sage Publications, 1986.

Naisbitt, John. *Megatrends: Ten New Directions Transforming Our Lives.* New York: Warner Books, 1982.

Ouchi, William. *Theory Z: How American Business Can Meet the Japanese Challenge.* Reading, Mass.: Addison-Wesley, 1981.

Peters, Thomas P., and Robert H. Waterman. *In Search of Excellence.* New York: Warner Books, 1982.

Senge, Peter M. *The Fifth Discipline: The Art and Practice of The Learning Organization.* New York: Currency/Doubleday, 1990.

Simon, Herbert A. *Administrative Behavior.* 3rd ed. New York: Free Press, 1976.

Tullock, Gordon. *The Politics of Bureaucracy.* Lanham, Md.: University Press of America, 1987.

Waldo, Dwight. "Organization Theory: Revisiting the Elephant," *Public Administration Review,* 1978, 589–597.

Walton, Mary. *Deming Management at Work.* New York: G. P. Putnam's Sons, 1990.

Wamsley Gary, and Mayer Zald. *The Political Economy of Public Organizations.* Bloomington, Ind.: Indiana University Press, 1976.

Weber, Max. *Theory of Social and Economic Organization.* Trans. A. Henderson and T. Parsons. Glencoe, Ill.: The Free Press, 1947.

Weick, Karl. *The Social Psychology of Organizing.* 2nd ed. Reading, Mass.: Addison-Wesley, 1979.

White, Orion. "The Dialectical Organization: An Alternative to Bureaucracy," *Public Administration Review* 1969: 29, 32–42.

Wilson, James Q. *Bureaucracy: What Government Agencies Do and Why They Do It.* New York: Basic Books, 1989.

Chapter 2

Bureaus Are Different

Organizations are an identifying characteristic of the world in which we live and work. Modern civilization probably could not exist without large, complex organizations—both public and private. Organizations are a part of some of the most significant events in our personal lives; for example, we are born in organizations, our marriages and deaths are documented by them, and we are educated in them. We practice our skills and crafts in them. We earn our livings and spend the greater portion of our waking hours in organizations. Our food is processed and delivered, our clothes are manufactured and sold, and our entertainment is provided by organizations. Organizations keep our peace and wage our wars. They are woven into the fabric of our social, economic, political, and even spiritual lives. Their accomplishments inspire our admiration and loyalty. And we feel fear and anger in the face of their power, inflexibility, and attention to petty detail (Blau and Meyer 1993).

This book is especially concerned with *public* organization theory and *public* management. Its principle assumption is that public and private management differ because public organizations are significantly and fundamentally unlike private ones. This chapter examines the treatment of public and private dimensions in organization theory and proposes a new emphasis. It also explores ways in which public bureaus are distinguishable from private firms. Finally, because of the increasing importance of third sector (nonprofit) organizations in the public policy arena, and the political pressure for privatization of many public functions, these two phenomena must be considered. Some understanding must be obtained as to how these relatively new emphases affect the definition of what is "public" and how the special interpretations of organization theory for the public sector apply to these new actors in the public process.

GENERIC THEORY AND PUBLIC ORGANIZATIONS

A basic premise of current organization theory is that all formal organizations share similar traits. Since some characteristics and processes are common to complex formal organizations, it is reasoned that a general theory of organization is appropriate. Most modern texts and collections of readings take this "generic" approach. A typical expression of this perspective, written by a public administration scholar, notes that:

> What is known about motivation, about behavior in small groups, or about organizing— all this knowledge is more likely to be applicable than not to both public and business organizations. (Golembiewski 1976, 5)

Similarly, management is presumed to be "a generic process with universal implications and with application in any institutional setting—whether a private firm or a public agency" (Murray 1975, 364). Institutional expressions of this viewpoint can be seen in the growth of management schools, university departments, and management programs built around the generic model. Concern about achieving organizational goals is the common thread in defining management, and as Hersey and Blanchard state in *Management of Organization Behavior:*

> This definition . . . makes no mention of business or industrial organizations. Management, as defined, applies to organizations whether they are business, educational institutions, hospitals, political or military organizations, or even families. (1993, 5)

Admittedly, some forms of human behavior and interaction retain their similarities under different organizational conditions and settings, but does this make a universalistic approach to organization theory valid? The answer is a qualified yes, but only on the broadest and most general levels of analysis and prescription. Does the generic approach provide a sufficiently useful basis for informing the action and choices of the public manager? The answer is no, often it does not. An approach to theory that is solely generic is premature. Haste and oversight mark any progression from the observation that a variety of organizations—such as bureaus and firms—are complex and formal to the conclusion that they are the same. Instead, there is an increasing recognition that:

> Although the elements of organizations have remained relatively constant, their purposes, structures, ways of doing things, and methods for coordinating activities have always varied widely. The variations largely (but not exclusively) reflect an organization's adaptation to its environment. Organizations are "open systems" that are influenced by and have an impact on the world around them. (Shafritz and Ott 1996, 2)

In actuality, public bureaucracies are different from private firms in ways that warrant their being treated separately—or at least that caution against an overweening and unexamined reliance on universalistic but incomplete theory. Yet books on organization theory and management concentrate almost exclusively on the private firm. Even a casual examination reveals that private firms form the substance of discussions, research, case studies, and exercises by most writers and researchers. Furthermore, despite the particularistic basis of much research, few attempts are made to indicate where the resulting theory is generic and where it is not. The absorption with the private firm, coupled with the near exclusion of public bureaus, violates the rationale behind generic theory building.

Organization Theory in a "Blurred" Environment

Another approach is being promulgated that may, if left unchallenged, have the unfortunate effect of stifling the development of public as well as truly generic organization theory. It begins with the observation that organizations are becoming less differentiated in terms of being either distinctly private or distinctly public. Increasingly, organizations display a blending or overlapping of "privateness" and "publicness." Dwight Waldo, dean of American public administration scholars, observes that "the separation of public and private has been one of the defining features of the modern world." But he cautions that this is changing: "In the United States—and I believe more widely—there is a movement *away* from a sharp distinction between *public* and private, and toward a blurring and mingling of the two" (1980, 164).

Many others have added to the gathering force of this theme. It is noted, for example, that the requirement that public administrators work within the law certainly constrains them, but "business is also subject to an endless variety of government rules that concern nearly every aspect of their operations" (Lorch 1978, 36). In fact, businesses vociferously complain that, through myriad regulations affecting all aspects of corporate life, the government constantly "lifts the skirts" of private firms that are expected to carry out public goals in addition to achieving their proclaimed business goals. At all levels of government, the lines between public and private functions are being blurred by privatization (through contracting-out work and by divestment of government organizations and functions). Likewise, the difference between national and subnational activities is being blurred by the use of grants and unfunded mandates. Sharp differences between the public and private spheres are also reduced by the trend toward public sector adoption of techniques associated with business (operations research, cost–benefit analysis, and productivity measurement) and "wholistic management systems" such as Total Quality Management (National Performance Review [U.S.] 1993).

From the standpoint of theory building, the observation that organizations increasingly have both public and private characteristics is not, in itself, disturbing. However, comments on this trend are usually juxtaposed with discussions endorsing the current generic approach to theory. Since public and private organizations increasingly share the same characteristics, it is reasoned that they should be treated the same. Such arguments are ill considered. Mingled characteristics do not justify muddled theory-building prescriptions. The coexistence of different dimensions in given organizations does not preclude the need to treat these dimensions as conceptually distinguishable from one another. Few concepts exist in a *pure* state in the *real* world.

To be truly generic, theory must embrace the entire range of its subject matter. The need to explore the nature and implications of "publicness" in organizations is especially compelling. To do less perpetuates theory building that fails to address public organizations. And any theory that is blind to public–private differences will be less relevant for those private organizations with hybrid features.

PUBLIC BUREAUS: HOW ARE THEY DIFFERENT?

We are interested in the type of organization that is governmental and clearly public, that is, the complex organization that is created by law and whose job it is to administer the law. The term *public bureau,* or simply *bureau,* will be used to describe this type of organization. More generic terms, such as *organization* or *agency,* will be used primarily for stylistic relief. We will examine how bureaus differ from firms, a type of organization that is clearly private. It is important to bear in mind that although publicness and privateness are analytically separable qualities (like most phenomena), these distinctions are admittedly less clear-cut in specific instances. Over a broad range, organizations can be characterized along a continuum of lesser or greater degrees of publicness, and not as a dichotomy. Nevertheless, differences between public and private organizations can be more clearly understood by first concentrating on organizations that are both empirically and analytically distinct. However, because of the increasing involvement of third sector and private organizations in governmental activities, we shall—in each major section of this book—address the applicability of "public organization theory" for these groups as they function in the public sector.

How then do bureaus differ from firms? Differences between public and private organizations have been approached in a variety of ways. Typologies have been constructed on the basis of ownership and funding (Wamsley and Zald 1976), and classified based on who benefits from the organization (Blau and Scott 1962). Public and private organizations have been arranged on a continuum according to the extent of outside interference they face in policy decision making (Gortner 1981). According to Anthony Downs, the distinguishing characteristic of a bureau is that it does not face an external market (1967). These approaches are useful and enlightening, but for the most part, they cover only specialized or partial aspects and do not provide a broad overview of public–private differences. Three public administration researchers achieved more comprehensive results by undertaking a survey of the literature on differences between public and private organizations (Rainey, Backoff, and Levine 1976). They summarize their review as a list of propositions about public agencies as compared to private organizations (see Figure 2–1).

Public bureaus are fundamentally unlike firms in their legal, economic, and political nature and roles. We will explore their differences at these three broadest and most general levels, as well as some of the consequences that flow from them.

Legal Differences: The Constitution, the Law, and Public Management

The Constitution and the law are major forces in determining the context and content of public bureau activities because the purposes and structures of public bureaus are set forth in the law, and the roles and resources of public agencies and their managers are significantly shaped by their legal framework.

Empowerment

Public organizations differ from private organizations in this most profound way: *It is the mission of public bureaus to administer the law.* Their function is authoritative in the deepest and most formal sense. Their role is as active and pervasive as the reach of law and governmental purpose. They are an intimate, integral part of constitutional and legal systems. Discussions about whether public and private organizations differ significantly overlook this fact, concentrating instead on the greater legal constraints placed on public agencies in our system. We will address these constraints in later discussions. The major point to be made here, however, is that *empowerment* is a distinguishing, even paramount, characteristic of public bureaus.

The significance of the empowerment of public bureaus cannot be overstated. Like other constitutional democracies, ours includes both a governmental system and a source of authority. Actions undertaken within the constitutional framework carry the formally sanctioned weight of the governmental system's legitimated force. This means that in our system, as in other representative democracies, those who exercise this formidable empowerment do so as governmental actors for publicly sanctioned purposes. Of course,

---

FIGURE 2–1   Summary of Literature on Differences Between Public and Private Organizations: Main Points of Consensus

This table presents a summary of the points of consensus by stating them as propositions regarding the attributes of a public organization, relative to those of a private organization.

Topic	*Proposition*
I. Environmental Factors	
I.1. Degree of marker exposure (Reliance on appropriations)	I.1.a. Less market exposure results in less incentive to cost reduction, operating efficiency, effective performance.
	I.1.b. Less market exposure results in lower allocational efficiency (reflection of consumer preferences, proportioning supply to demand, etc.).
	I.1.c. Less market exposure means lower availability of market indicators and information (prices, profits, etc.).
I.2. Legal, formal constraints (courts, legislature, hierarchy)	I.2.a. More constraints on procedures, spheres of operations (less autonomy of managers in making such choices).
	I.2.b. Greater tendency to proliferation of formal specifications and controls.
	1.2.c. More external sources of formal influence and greater fragmentation of those sources.
I.3. Political influences	I.3.a. Greater diversity and intensity of external informal influences on decisions (bargaining, public opinion, interest group reactions).
	I.3.b. Greater need for support of "constituencies" (client groups, sympathetic formal authorities, etc.).
II. Organization–Environment Transactions	
II.1. Coerciveness ("coercive," "monopolistic," unavoidable nature of many government activities)	II.1.a. More likely that participation in consumption and financing of services will be unavoidable or mandatory. (Government has unique sanctions and coercive powers.)
II.2. Breadth of impact	II.2.a. Broader impact, greater symbolic significance of actions of public administrators. (Wider scope of concern, such as "public interest.")
II.3. Public scrutiny	II.3.a. Greater public scrutiny of public officials and their actions.
II.4. Unique public expectations	II.4.a. Greater public expectations that public officials act with more fairness, responsiveness, accountability, and honesty.

FIGURE 2–1 *(continued)*

Topic	Proposition

III. Internal Structures and Processes

III.1. Complexity of objectives evaluation and decision criteria	III.1.a. Greater multiplicity and diversity of objectives and criteria.
	III.1.b. Greater vagueness and intangibility of objectives and criteria.
	III.1.c. Greater tendency of goals to be conflicting (more "tradeoffs").
III.2. Authority relations and the role of the administrator	III.2.a. Less decision-making autonomy and flexibility on the part of public administrators.
	III.2.b. Weaker, more fragmented authority over subordinates and lower levels. (1. Subordinates can bypass, appeal to alternative authorities. 2. Merit system constraints.)
	III.2.c. Greater reluctance to delegate, more levels of review, and greater use of formal regulations (due to difficulties in supervision and delegation, resulting from III.1.b.).
	III.2.d. More political, expository role for top managers.
III.3. Organizational performances	III.3.a. Greater cautiousness, rigidity. Less innovativeness.
	III.3.b. More frequent turnover of top leaders because of elections and political appointments results in greater disruption of implementation of plans.
III.4. Incentives and incentive structures	III.4.a. Greater difficulty in devising incentives for effective and efficient performance.
	III.4.b. Lower valuation of pecuniary incentives by employees.
III.5. Personal characteristics of employees	III.5.a.* Variations in personality traits and needs, such as higher dominance and flexibility, higher need for achievement, on the part of government managers.
	III.5.b.* Lower work satisfaction and lower organizational commitment.

*III.5.a and III.5.b. represent results of individual empirical studies rather than points of agreement among authors.

SOURCE: Hal G. Rainey, Robert W. Backoff, and Charles H. Levine, "Comparing Public and Private Organizations," *Public Administration Review* 36 (March/April 1976): 236–237.

Of Games and Gains . . .

Each game—Politics, Business, Governance—affects the lives of each of us as citizens in a capitalist democracy. Without attempting to weigh the relative strengths and weaknesses of the three or to equate them, it seems evident that their objectives are distinctly different—and so are their rules. It follows, then, that players who don't learn the rules, or assume there are no differences in the rules, are asking for trouble. For example, successful business people who enter government service for the first time, learn (sometimes the hard way):

1. That government organizations are not just another form of business corporation.
2. That the Constitution and its diffusion of power is the underpinning of government behavior.
3. That elected officials and political appointees are temporary policymakers who have been given an opportunity to establish and promote their points of view through new or modified laws and regulations.
4. That efficient use and control of public resources includes accountability for their use in conformance with the law.
5. That there is a double standard of ethical behavior which is far more stringent for public servants than it is for anyone in business or private life.

They also learn that Politics is the difference between public administration and business administration. . . .

[M]anaging a government organization is infinitely more challenging and complex than managing a business because public office is a public trust and government employees are:

1. Responsible for enforcing and implementing the laws as mandated.
2. Openly accountable to everyone—elected officials, appointed officials, news media, and the multiple publics (only one of which is the business sector).
3. Collecting and spending public money.
4. Using, preserving, and protecting public resources and property.
5. Responding to frequent shifts in policy as laws change and elected officials come and go.
6. Protecting the health, safety, welfare, and national security of all the people.
7. Carrying out their duties and responsibilities in conformance with their oaths of office, professional standards, official codes of conduct, and restrictions on their personal and political activities.

The Governance game, then, includes transitory amateurs at the very top, supported by career executives, technicians, and other professional staff who do the work and provide the continuity, institutional memory, and stability which is public administration. Do we need reminding that the first person on the moon was a federal bureaucrat—a GS-15?

Because careerists maintain the government's stability, they are experts in accommodating to periodic changes in administration philosophy and policy. When organizations and programs work well and apparently effortlessly, their products are taken for granted—what has been called the art of hiding the art. It is only when dysfunction occurs that citizens notice or care about systems or management problems.

SOURCE: Eileen Siedman, "Of Games and Gains . . . ," *The Bureaucrat* 13 (Summer 1984): 4–8.

private advantages may be furthered; however, governmental action requires and carries the force of formal sanction.

Compliance with private rules and regulations is voluntary: Compliance in the public sphere is mandatory because bureaus embody the power and authority of the state. In fact, it is this power that Blau argues we resent more than any supposed inefficiency on the part of the bureau. Therefore, legal empowerment raises other questions, especially questions of accountability and control.

Accountability

In a representative democracy, the scope of a public institution is very broad. "Its obligations extend not just to a particular group of share holders or sponsors," George Berkley points out, "but to the public at large." A government bureau, moreover, "is supposed to do what the public wants in ways which the public or its elected representatives have decreed" (Berkley and Rouse 1994, 11).

The writers of the Constitution were vitally concerned about assuring that government structures and processes focus on serving the public interest rather than the private interests of elected and appointed officials and their compatriots. The framers viewed human nature as essentially flawed; self-interest was the primary motivator. Theirs was not the modern view of self-interest as the mark of the rational gamesman; rather, self-interest was synonymous with invidious selfishness. The framers attributed the tendency to selfishness and greed to public official and common citizen alike, but it was in the governmental sphere that they saw its implications as most alarming.

Their solution was to divide and diffuse authority among the various levels and institutions of government, and even to divide and diffuse power *within* an institution (as they did in the bicameral legislature). As a further safeguard, power was to be shared as well as separated (for example, presidential veto of legislation, Senate confirmation of executive appointees, judicial review of statutes and of executive action). As Peter Woll points out:

> The Constitution, on the other hand, does not completely separate the powers of the three branches of government, but rather blends them so that each branch will be able to check the other branches by interfering with their functions. (1977, 18–19)

The authors of our Constitution sought mechanisms for accountability in the exercise of governmental authority by the president, the Congress, and the judiciary, but not for the scant bureaucracy contemplated at that time. This fact of history in no way diminishes the significance of the many consequences of a system of fragmented authority for today's public bureaucracy, a bureaucracy that is large and vigorous beyond the imagination of our constitution makers.

To whom and by what means are the public bureaucracy and its managers accountable? The fragmented system of authority created by the separation and blending of powers creates lines of authority that are both multiple and overlapping. In contrast to those for private firms, which are primarily internal and relatively clear, lines of authority for public bureaus are external as well as internal to the organization and are exceedingly unclear.

The Constitution states that "The executive power shall be vested in a President of the United States of America" (Art. II, Sec. 1), but leaves the power undefined. The president may and does initiate proposals to Congress, but it is through legislative action that government bureaus and programs become law and their legal empowerment is established. It is the legislature that authorizes the size of and funding for the personnel force of public agencies. Congress appropriates monies, though often at the request of the president and subject, of course, to executive veto. Top bureaucratic leaders are appointed by the executive but confirmed by the legislature.

Both Congress and the president oversee administrative actions. The judicial branch, in accordance with its own powers and procedures, also practices oversight. Courts may judge whether the statute or executive order under which an agency acts is legally valid. Chief executives, legislatures, or courts may all ask whether an agency is acting within the limits or intent of a statute or rule, or whether its administrative procedures are fair. All these institutions and actors charged with external control of bureaus have some power, but no single institution or actor has sufficient authority for control; thus, these actors often disagree and end up in conflict with one another.

Public bureaus are drawn into the processes by which chief executives attempt to influence legislators, and by which both branches of government seek to create public evidence of their responsiveness or the "rightness" of their position. Even the president cannot dictate major policy; his power has been aptly described as the "power to persuade" (Neustadt 1960). Lacking blanket formal power, the president must achieve cooperation and action by collaborating with others whose interests coincide with his. If collaboration fails, agreement is achieved in more overtly political ways—through persuasion, negotiation, bargaining, compromise, confrontation, and even threat. Similarly, Congress must obtain political support to supplement its formal power. In this dance of power, bureaucracies may be tools useful to everyone else.

These or similar patterns of fragmented authority, simultaneously external and internal, divided and overlapping, are found in state and local government as well. In fact, governmental authority at the state and local levels may be even more fragmented than at the national level. The chief executive's power over public bureaus is diminished by the practice in some states and localities of electing rather than appointing heads of government agencies. The prevalence of independent boards and commissions whose members have long and overlapping terms also dissipates the power of chief executives (governors, mayors, city managers) and legislators alike, and the problem of holding bureaus accountable is further compounded where they have a degree of fiscal autonomy through such means as charging fees for services or being recipients of earmarked funds. In countless ways then, the accountability of bureaus is complicated by fragmentation.

Administration Subordinate to Law

Accountability and control of government authority apply to all branches and officials in a democratic system. However, the bureaucracy, being unelected for the most part, is perceived as raising special problems. How is the power of public bureaus restrained and controlled? The answer is, in large part, related to the philosophy toward the role of law in determining administrative discretion.

Managers of private firms can generally take any action, establish any policy, or use any means of operation not specifically prohibited (a common law approach). Public managers, in contrast, may not do so in the absence of specific grants of authority (a Roman law approach). Private organizations can act unless proscribed or forbidden; public ones may act *only* if authority is granted.

The most general and important way in which law controls administration is that goals for public bureaus are both established and circumscribed by the law. But the role of law also extends to other crucial aspects of bureau management, such as the prescription of means and the provision and control of resources.

Policy implementation is often complicated, even thwarted, by lack of managerial control over budget and personnel resources. For example, passage of the national Freedom of Information Act resulted in a sudden high-volume increase of citizen requests for information disclosure by various agencies. But no additional money to carry out the policy was made available, agency personnel levels were not increased, and existing procedures made reassignment of personnel slow and difficult. In particular, the Federal Bureau of Investigation (FBI), which had engaged in widespread domestic surveillance during the turbulent 1960s and early 1970s, was deluged with requests. Thus, backlogs built up quickly and long delays resulted. Public ire was directed, of course, at the FBI and its administrators. Allegations of obstructive agency attitudes notwithstanding, it is difficult to see how the bureau's managers, saddled as they were with budget and personnel constraints, could have efficiently and effectively implemented the act.

State and local administrators face similar obstacles in implementation. In addition to the other limitations on taxes, budgets, and personnel created by state constitutions, state and local governments are told what they must do by higher levels of government. Unfunded mandates—programs created by law but with no concomitant financial support—often limit the alternatives of both state and local officials. For example, a policy of "mainstreaming" handicapped and disturbed students into regular classrooms has been mandated for school jurisdictions. At the same time, most local school administrators have not been provided with an accompanying increase in budget, teachers, or the special support personnel that this policy requires for effective implementation.

Entitlement programs such as unemployment compensation and Aid to Families with Dependent Children are in greater or less demand based on broad social and economic forces. However, the personnel levels of state and local agencies that administer these programs are not adjusted to correspond to these fluctuations in demand. Thus, caseworkers, who are typically overloaded under normal economic conditions, are swamped when the economy worsens.

The legal framework of the bureau, then, dictates that the public manager must accomplish the objectives set by others with resources that are often determined by still others, and must do so within a general organizational framework established by law and interpreted by political appointees. The objectives set by external forces may be unclear or unrealistic while resources and structures may be inadequate or inappropriate. The result may be goals that cannot be met, and inefficient, inflexible, or ineffective action by bureaus. Any change attempted by managers, however, must often be accomplished through the political process.

In contrast, private executives have the flexibility to adopt various courses of action with little external kibitzing. Procedures may be changed and the organization redesigned; projects may be reduced, canceled, expedited, or enlarged. New markets may be entered. Resources may be shifted from one purpose to another, workers laid off or additional ones hired. Admittedly, legal requirements or prohibitions are sometimes placed on private organizations, for example, affirmative action policies. The role of law for most private organizations, however, is relatively peripheral, and in no way is so central and pervasive to the private firm's management as to the bureau.

Economic Differences: Nature of the Bureau's Role and the Market

What is the nature of the economic role of government, and hence, public bureaucracies? The usual answer is articulated in terms of prescriptive, free market theory. This is an illuminating perspective as far as it goes, but it overlooks the place political values and processes occupy in our system in determining the nature of governmental roles—including those that are ostensibly economic.

Free Market Theory and The Role of Government

According to market theory, private firms are to seek economic enhancement. Their objective is to increase profitability through voluntary exchange and transactions, with government playing only a supplementary or, at most, complementary role. Government action is regarded as appropriate only when private resource allocation fails or operates very inefficiently.

Markets may fail as allocation mechanisms in a variety of ways. For example, some goods are public in that the benefits are held in common. Exclusion is not feasible. If the cost is high, the free or private market is especially unlikely to provide such goods. For instance, street lights increase safety for an entire area regardless of who pays and who does not; however, their cost is prohibitive for a single individual or firm. In such instances, action carried out by public bureaus is conceded to be an acceptable, or even indispensable, mechanism for providing public goods and is considered more efficient in ensuring that costs as well as benefits are shared—through compulsion and coercion if necessary.

Sometimes, actions or exchanges between individuals or firms result in costs to people not involved in a given transaction. Noise abatement, antipollution, and building height restriction laws are examples of governmental intervention in such circumstances.

Relevant markets may not emerge or exist under the usual workings of the private market system. As Stokey and Zeckhauser point out:

> In some areas the meagerness of private markets has been especially significant for public policy. One of these is insurance against income loss; government unemployment insurance and welfare programs may be thought of as efforts to remedy this market deficiency. Another is insurance against living too long after becoming disabled or retiring and thereby using up one's savings; the Social Security system serves as a response to such needs (1978, 300–301).

Even in free market theory, government bureaus are not linked to markets in the same way as private firms. By giving government the responsibility for tasks for which the market is inappropriate or for unprofitable services such as care of the poor, market theory implicitly recognizes differences in the economic roles of firms and bureaus. It does not go far enough, however, since the functions of government, and consequently of bureaus, are far broader than performing the passive or supplemental economic role left to it by market theory. More significant, market theory fails to recognize that the "economic" role of government basically is not economic in nature.

Rather than accepting classical market theory's artificial watertight categories of inviolate private and public spheres, we must recognize that "[p]ublic and private are not categories of nature; they are categories of history, culture, and law" (Waldo 1980, 164).

In other words, the line between public and private is not immutable; it shifts and changes in response to historical and political forces. The goals of public bureaus are products of the legal and political process and embody the values legitimated by these systems. Since the role of government is not determined solely by economic considerations, but by cultural and political forces as well, bureaus are charged with promoting and protecting both cultural and economic values.

Without question, the free market and economic competition are values with widespread acceptance in our culture; therefore, policies that reflect the values and ideas of the free enterprise system receive a great deal of government attention. In fact, our government's economic activities conform, to a large extent, to the role prescribed by market theory. Nevertheless, the important consideration here, especially where government bureaus are involved, is that economic policies are adopted not so much because of their desirability as economic theory, but because of political acceptability, demand, and expediency. Indeed, economic policy is adopted primarily as a means to achieve politically sanctioned ends. The long-standing Cuban trade restrictions, the freezing of Iraqi assets during and after the Gulf War, or a requirement that when states receive grant money the distribution formula must include "tax effort" are examples of the use of economic policy as means to political ends.

Public organizations certainly have functions that do not directly involve the economic system and that entail basically noneconomic objectives. Enforcement of affirmative action laws, protection of endangered species, and administration of elections are examples of such functions. Some may argue that even these policies have economic implications, but to do so is to miss the point. Unlike the goals of private firms, which are primarily economic and related to profit making, the objectives of public bureaus are varied; political, not economic, considerations are paramount.

Both market theory and organization theory have focused on the private firm to such an extent that the implications of political rather than economic values and goals for organizational behavior have been overlooked or dismissed. More puzzling is the fact that although market theory recognizes different markets and functions for government bureaus, it does not examine the significance of these differences.

Economic Versus Political Markets

Bureaus and firms exhibit marked differences in the nature of their markets and in their relationship to these markets. In an economic output market, each producer engages in voluntary transactions with buyers who exchange money for the producer's output. Anthony Downs points out the effects of output markets and discusses how the lack of such markets affects bureaus.

First, output markets provide a built-in tool for evaluating the work (output) of the organization. If the producer "can sell his outputs for more than his inputs cost . . . then he knows his product is valuable to its buyers" (Downs 1967, 29). If the market price does not cover the costs of producing the product, then the organization knows the output is not valuable enough.

Second, output markets are a means of allocating resources among organizations. A third function of the market is that of producing a standard for evaluating the individual performance of members of the organization; for example, when one salesperson sells more than another, he or she is more valuable to the firm. And as Downs explains, even

Run It Like a Business, No Matter How Much More It Costs

One of the most pernicious myths of Washington business is that the government—and virtually everything else—would be vastly improved if the people in charge would just "run it like a business."

Candidates have captured every office from dogcatcher to president of the United States by promising that the moral equivalent of the profit motive would become the guiding principal of their administration.

Worse yet, they've kept their promises, giving us such a stunning success as the U.S. Postal Service. Freed from the perils of politics and patronage and now "run like a business," the mail service costs more and delivers less.

Despite such self-evident shortcomings, the urge to "run it like a business" continues to flourish, infecting Washington with ill-thought initiatives like the plan to sell the Weather Bureau.

Neither rain, nor sleet, nor gloom of night would seem to be ingredients of a profitable enterprise. But no doubt a weather bureau run like a business could market the exigencies of nature with as much success as the postal service defies them. Like the mail, the weather forecast might not arrive when expected, but that would be a small price to pay for the ideological satisfaction of knowing the weather bureau is run like a business.

The run-it-like-a-business bug is even spreading into the private sector, where it is demonstrating the ability to transform perfectly adequate nonprofit institutions into bungled "businesses."

Ironically, the U.S. Chamber of Commerce was the first private, nonprofit organization to get burned by its business-like approach but now other Washington institutions have fallen victim, including National Public Radio.

. . . The U.S. Chamber has run up multimillion-dollar deficits. . . . Instead of using its magazine, *Nation's Business,* as a service to communicate with its members, the Chamber decided to run *Nation's Business* like a business. While the magazine vigorously expresses the Chamber's views, it has apparently been less successful as a business. In recent months,

individuals performing different functions can be objectively compared through cost accounting and related techniques.

Because bureaus do not have economic output markets, they cannot evaluate the costs of producing their output or its value on this external basis. The bureau's income is not directly related to the services it provides. As a result, the bureau's ability to obtain income in a market cannot serve as an objective guide to the appropriateness of the level of current expenditures. Nor can it aid the bureau in determining how to use the resources it controls, or in appraising the performance of individual bureaucrats. In short, the major yardsticks for decision making used by private firms are unavailable to those who run bureaus (Downs 1967, 30). The attempt to put profit-based criteria into a service context can, in fact, lead to disastrous results, as Jerry Knight reports in the above article.

the Chamber has had to explain why the magazine's circulation fell several hundred thousand subscribers short of what advertisers were charged for.

There is, perhaps, a certain justice in the Chamber of Commerce being seduced by its own rhetoric. It would be hard to find an organization that has preached the virtues of "running it like a business" more often than the U.S. Chamber.

But National Public Radio is no captive of corporate ideology. The likes of the Chamber of Commerce have been known to suggest that NPR is virtually socialized radio, the commercial-free antithesis of free enterprise.

So what did NPR do when government subsidies and corporate contributions ran short? You guessed it—they decided to go into business, forming profit-making partnerships that were supposed to finance nonprofit broadcasting. But now, just like the Chamber of Commerce, NPR is laying off people and canceling projects because its business ventures are proving to be something less than hoped for.

That's the first lesson that ought to be taught to people who believe government and nonprofit associations should be run like a business: Businesses can and do fail with predictable regularity.

Even well-run businesses fail, but more often, failure is the result of management mistakes.

More than just management style is involved. The reality is that weather forecasting, mail delivery, business advocacy and public broadcasting are not businesses. Their first and foremost goal is to deliver services, not to make a buck.

One of the marvels of the free market economy is that when services can be provided at a profit, somebody does it. The Mafia in several cities collects garbage cheaper and better than government employees; the National Geographic Society uses profitable publications to finance its educational activities; Federal Express and United Parcel Service make money competing with the mail.

But UPS doesn't want to deliver all the mail—just the profitable part—and there are services that even the Mafia couldn't make money on. The inescapable conclusion is that the goals of service and profit are often incompatible.

SOURCE: Jerry Knight, "Run It Like a Business, No Matter How Much More It Costs," *Washington Post* (March 21, 1983): 1B.

Bureau productivity can, of course, be ascertained. It cannot be evaluated in exactly the same way as firms, with their markets and objectively measurable standard—profitability. Bureaus do not lend themselves to a single, universal standard like profitability. Both efficiency and effectiveness must be measured, examining the functions and the goals of the particular agency, and leading to many separate and rather specialized measures of productivity. For example, a job-training program may record intake figures, attrition, number of applicants trained, number of trainees placed in jobs, training-to-placement ratios, and cost-of-training per placement to measure its productivity; most agencies use a variety of such measures. For example, the Federal Aviation Administration uses measures such as number of successful landings, number of airplane inspections, number of "near misses," and passenger miles-to-accident ratios.

Civil Service Turns 100, Burdened by Stereotypes

Since Federal Express has raised the question of postal efficiency, let us ponder it. It makes an especially good topic. Productivity measures are a lot cleaner at the Postal Service than they are at, say, the State Department.

The fact is the United States Postal Service delivers more mail, more efficiently, for less money than in any other nation on earth, and it is getting better.

It moves 110 billion pieces of mail per year, or some 161,879 pieces per employee, a productivity-per-worker rate that is 44 percent above that of the closest competitor, Japan.

The cost of mailing a first class letter in the United States is 12th lowest of the 14 industrialized nations surveyed last summer, with only Belgium, at an equivalent of 19.9 cents, below the Postal Service's 20 cents. Germany charges the equivalent of 33 cents. (Remember, these are 1983 prices.)

Rates here have been rising at a slower pace than inflation since 1974 and, in 1979 for the first time in four decades, the Postal Service operated in the black. It did again last year, and it is now operating on a fee basis. There are no subsidies anymore from Uncle Sam.

Speed-of-delivery is on the rise, too. In 1982, the Postal Service met its next-day-delivery standard for first-class mail traveling within a metropolitan area 95.5 percent of the time. In the two-day category, performance was 88 percent and in the three-day delivery, 90 percent.

Productivity measurements are difficult to apply to most of the federal government which produces policy, information and services, not widgets. But coarse standards have been devised for roughly two-thirds of the federal work force. And they show that since 1967, the average annual increase in productivity has been 1.4 percent among federal workers. This is a growth percentage that would make most sectors of the private economy envious, though comparisons are difficult because the standards of measurement vary.

SOURCE: Paul Taylor, "Civil Service Turns 100, Burdened by Stereotypes," *Washington Post* (January 16, 1983): A1.

Because different measures must be used to evaluate bureaus with different functions, the most reasonable approach to comparing organizations is to use those with similar functions and goals. Thus, bureaus of a given type should usually be compared with other bureaus of the same type, as Paul Taylor did in his commentary on the one hundredth anniversary of the civil service.

And, of course, in the political arena, criticisms of the bureaucracy do not go away because there will always be the case, the particular agency, or the specific region, where service and efficiency do not go as well as expected. This failure to please is partly caused by the "outrider" problem—the fact that there will always be some unit of the organization that does not meet the standards of the larger agency, as occurred with the Postal Service in the Washington, D.C., area during the 1993–1994 period, and the fact that the outrider will be highlighted by the news media rather than the successful service in the vast majority of cases. The failure to please is also caused by the natural tendency of customers to expect more once a specific level of service is achieved and maintained. Thus the displeasure with the U.S. Postal Service (a public corporation, not a government bureau) continues unabated over a decade after Paul Taylor's article, and in 1995, the new Republican Congress continued a call for postal "privatization." Such debates are an integral part of being in the public's purview and cannot be avoided.

Bureau–firm comparisons, when they are made, should be based on highly comparable functions. For example, Feller and Metzel compare public and private innovation rates in solid waste technology, a study that, incidentally, suggests that the stereotype of public sector inflexibility and inertia toward technology and change does not always fit (Figure 2–2).

Since bureaus do not have exclusively economic outputs, their "markets" and "consumers" are most often clientele, organized interest groups, and political elites. (However, their "customers" are the total population "in the public interest.") They engage in exchange relationships with these essential actors to achieve legitimacy and domain (Thompson 1967), as well as political support for resource allocations. Political exchange dominates a bureau's market or environmental transactions, and the evaluation or response to bureau outputs is political.

Further, bureau and firm outputs do not lend themselves to the same classifications. No attempt to classify businesses will be attempted here; however, one useful way of classifying bureau policies or outputs places them in three categories: distributive, regulatory, or redistributive (Lowi 1964). Each type of output is associated with different patterns "of consensus-conflict, group alignment, and breadth and intensity of group involvement" (Wamsley and Zald 1976, 35; Lowi 1964; Sharkansky 1965). For example, in distributive arenas, there is usually consensus in the environment that is supportive of the organization's output. In regulatory policy arenas, conflict marks bureau–environment

---

FIGURE 2–2   Diffusion of Technology: Public and Private Sectors

Below is a comparison of diffusion rates for technologies in the private and public sectors. Diffusion rates are a measure of the rapidity with which new ideas and innovations are adopted and spread from organization to organization. Columns one and two show the number of years before a new technology was adopted in the public and private sectors, respectively. Column three shows the percentage of cities, in a 220-city sample, in which the technology was used. It is generally assumed, though not always correctly as this table shows, that innovation is more rapid in the private sector.

Diffusion Rates of Four Solid Waste Technologies by Sector

	Public Sector (Years)	Private Sector (Years)	Extent of Diffusion as of 1975
Packer trucks	27	28	40%
Container trucks	18	20	20
One-man crews	13	21	10
Transfer stations	20	14	10

SOURCE: I. Feller and D. C. Metzel, *Diffusion of Technology in Municipal Governments*. Final report on NSF grant DA 44550. Pennsylvania State University Center for the Study of Science Policy, 1976.

The Continuing Debate—A Decade Later

One Side: Many Seek Postal Reform, But Few Agree on Agenda

As many of Washington's 302,000 federal workers fretted over the possible loss of their jobs last week, 5,000 government employees came to the city with a loud, angry message: They want higher pay and better benefits and they want them now.

They were postal workers, members of some of the federal government's strongest labor unions. As their noisy protest outside Postal Service headquarters Tuesday afternoon made clear, there are no fears about job losses inside the government's second-largest civilian agency. Instead, members of the American Postal Workers Union demanded the Postal Service avoid all efforts at privatization and agree to a new, costly labor contract. The rest of the federal bureaucracy may be shrinking, but the postal payroll is growing. That fact and the vision of chanting, unhappy postal workers, however, was reason enough for Rep. Dana Rohrabacher (R-Calif.) to call again last week for the government to privatize the Postal Service.

Rohrabacher and Rep. Philip M. Crane (R-Ill.) long have sponsored legislation to give the agency to its 748,000 career workers and let them run the nation's mail service as a private business in competition with other delivery services. Technology threatens to make the Postal Service "as obsolete as the Pony Express," so it has to change, Rohrabacher told a mail industry conference Thursday.

Until Republicans took charge of Capitol Hill in January, the Crane-Rohrabacher plan was given little chance of getting a hearing, much less moving forward. But with GOP majorities in the House and Senate and Postmaster General Marvin T. Runyon calling for major changes in the way his agency operates, the idea of revamping the 25-year-old independent Postal Service was declared the agency's top legislative priority. . . .

SOURCE: Bill McAllister, *Washington Post* (May 28, 1995): A12.

---

relationships—either between bureaus and the groups they regulate or among interest groups watching the regulatory process. This, at least, is a common pattern during the early life of a regulatory bureau. Older regulatory agencies are prone to developing accepted parameters of behavior and decisions with the regulated industries that lead to charges of cooptation. Conflict in redistributive arenas often touches on divisions among social classes and, consequently, tends to be broader than in the other policy arenas.

Whatever the classification, bureaus' internal characteristics also vary according to type of policy output. Lowi, for example, finds that the rules and procedures of bureaus in redistributive arenas will tend to be specific and detailed (1964). This is an organization's way of adapting to external political conflict and the widespread effects of bureau action. Once the procedures are detailed, the type of worker needed changes; thus, according to a study based on sixty-two government bureaus, a related finding is that the percentage of clerical workers is higher in redistributive bureaus than in other arenas (Willick 1970).

And the Response

Rep. John Kasich (R-Ohio), chairman of the House Budget committee, was recently quoted as saying, "We are going to privatize the Postal Service. That's on our agenda, not during the first 100 days, but we are going to do it." I believe this would be a serious mistake that would affect every household in the country.

The U.S. Postal Service has the lowest rates of any industrialized country in the world. The first-class rate in 1971 was 8 cents. Twenty-four years later, in 1995, the rate is a mere 32 cents. This computes to a penny-a-year increase. This rate allows a first-class letter to go from Florida to Alaska. The Postal Service is self-sufficient and receives no funding from the government. Postal workers are not subsidized by the federal government, as many would lead you to believe. We provide service to large metropolitan areas and small rural areas for the same low price. Do you think that elite privatizers would do the same?

The U.S. Postal Service also provides free forwarding of first- and second-class mail for up to 12 months after someone has moved. Again, would privatizers do the same?

Currently, the use to which the mailbox in front of one's home or business can be put is limited. This protects the public. Only U.S. Postal Service letter carriers are allowed to place mail into that mailbox. I'm sure no one wants strangers walking across his lawn to place anything and everything into that mailbox. That could range from ads to pornography to other unwanted materials.

The American public also enjoys protection from mail fraud and theft. The U.S. Postal Inspection Service is mandated to ensure Americans of that protection.

If the private express statutes are relaxed, we may all be subjected to a host of unwanted and unnecessary problems. The bottom line is that the U.S. Postal Service works. It remains the most affordable and most personal form of communication going. As postal workers, we deliver 550 million pieces of mail daily to 120 million households and businesses. We deliver. Don't privatize.

SOURCE: Dave Gibson, President American Postal Workers Union, AFL-CIO, The Northern Virginia Area Local, Merrifield, "Letter to the Editor," *Washington Post* (April 29, 1995): A16.

To summarize, unlike the primarily economic nature of the firm, the bureau's purposes and roles are more complex and are fundamentally political. And political factors, both within and external to bureaus, have an important influence on organizational structure and process in the same way that economic factors influence corporate organization and operation.

Political Differences: Internal and Environmental Politics of Bureaus

Probably the two best known and most frequently cited definitions of politics are Lasswell's statement that politics is the study of "who gets what, when, how" (1958) and Easton's phrase that politics is the process of society's "authoritative allocation of values" (1965). Bureaus, especially in their role of influencing *and* interpreting legislative choice, are integral to the authoritative process of determining who gets what, when, and how.

The process by which policies come about and the interests they promote or maintain (whether broad public interest, organized groups, elected or appointed officials, or even bureaus and their members) are political. The political process is, of course, not limited to the confines of government institutions. It is the process by which various individuals, groups, and institutions seek to influence public policy and government action or inaction. The boundaries of the political system are elastic and changeable; they encompass all interactions and activities that affect or seek to affect government action or inaction.

In what ways does the political context and purpose of the public bureau differ from that of the private firm? At first glance, the answer seems blurred and ambiguous. Certainly, firms often participate in the political process, and governmental policies sometimes address even the internal activities of firms. For example, private personnel practices, insofar as their effect or intent is discriminatory, are the object of equal employment opportunity requirements. Firms are also involved in the governmental-political system in a variety of other ways, such as environmental regulation, health and safety, and licensing requirements. Through activities such as participation in government job-training and employment programs, performance of government contract work, or the use of businesses as collectors of state or local sales taxes, firms may even be an instrument of public policy. Even these firms directly involved in government work, however, always exist to make a profit, and they may choose to contract with the government or to function in other areas of economic activity.

Public bureaus, on the other hand, are inherently governmental; they are pervasively enmeshed in the political process. *Every* public bureau is an object of the political process; *any* aspect of its goals, structure, and operation may be subject to that process. Bureaus exist for the purpose of implementing or enforcing public policy; thus, much of the time they are participants in the policy and political process. The differences between the political context and nature of bureaus compared to private firms dictates that different values come under consideration and different skills are needed in managing and leading public organizations. Bureaus differ from firms in important ways, some of which are relationships with clientele and interest groups, goal setting, goal ambiguity and diversity, and the role of the manager in all these.

External Groups and Public Bureaus

The nature of American public bureaus is political in great measure because of their ready accessibility to external influences—elected officials, political interest groups, and the like. Private businesses typically are more closed. Their access points (for example, boards of directors, marketing and customer service departments, stockholders' meetings) are fewer and more controlled.

Life in the fishbowl of public management means that legislators, chief executives, clientele, journalists, and hosts of others may legitimately scrutinize the actions of the public manager and other bureau employees. Based on his executive experience in both the public and private spheres, Frederick Malek writes:

> The corporate executive is accustomed to the usually informed and generally sympathetic scrutiny of his colleagues, his stock-holders; and, occasionally the public through annual reports and news releases. The government executive, however, lives in a fishbowl; depending on the level and nature of his job, he must expect to be exposed at any moment to the glare of publicity and notoriety. (1972, 64)

Nor is public scrutiny restricted only to what public bureaus do or how they do it. The spotlight of publicity lays bare ideas for future activity, however tentative and unformulated. Premature disclosure of programs or ideas is a public manager's occupational hazard. A given agency often has a contingent of journalists who specifically follow it, and who, because of their familiarity with the agency and their internal personal contacts, are often able to reveal agency matters that are merely under consideration. Such publicity can have a strong, troublesome effect; painstakingly laid plans may be disrupted. Equally distressing is the airing of proposals or suggestions that are at an exploratory stage, so early that commitment has not been made nor is expected. For example, Director of the Office of Management and Budget, Alice Rivlin, prepared for President Clinton a "preliminary think-piece" on balancing the budget that included some politically unpalatable suggestions, and this supposedly secret document became the centerpiece of a media feeding frenzy. The same kind of occurrence, perhaps on a lesser scale, is part of the essentially political burden that is imposed on every public manager.

> The glare of publicity and the concomitant power of public opinion make it important to gain public support and acceptance of a department's or agency's goals and essential to gain public understanding before proceeding with any major initiative or change of policy. This notion is unfamiliar to the average business executive. (Malek 1972, 64)

In varying degrees, agencies may also seek or receive broad public support, but such support comes with the problem of having both the intensity and direction of public opinion shift with events that may have little to do with the life and goals of the agency. Compared to general public opinion, attentive clientele and related special interest groups provide more stable support. Unlike the general public, their interests are tangible and direct, and typically both clientele and regulated groups have vested interests in a public bureau's actions (Rourke 1976; Wamsley and Zald 1976). However, the public manager also knows that as he or she works with the positive interest groups, and that is essential, opposites are created by the political system; the groups who are fighting the agency, policy, or program are often as troublesome as the positive groups are helpful.

Ties between bureaus and interest groups are reinforced in many ways. Bureau action or inaction affects the material interests and welfare of clientele and other related groups. The bureau provides a channel for political representation within the governmental structure. For their part, groups support agency requests to legislators and chief executives for empowerment and for resources; they oppose legislative and executive action that threatens the bureau's status, authority, and resources. Moreover, considerable movement among employees of bureaus and clients occurs in both directions, and frequent, long-term interaction breeds personal ties.

Similar professional training and experience further foster mutual identification between public administrators and related interest groups. This bond is not limited to public bureaus and private interest groups; it also exists between government organizations. Particularly in intergovernmental programs, bureaus at lower levels (state or local) have a clientele relationship to agencies at higher levels (national or state). Here, too, shared professional specialization and values lead to a joining of forces and political strength between subject matter specialists in bureaus at one level and their counterparts in bureaus at other levels.

Laws may grant interest groups access to the policy process, and even membership in public bureaus. Statutes mandating membership in or certification by professional groups as conditions for appointment as administrators are especially common at the state level for various boards, commissions, and other agencies.

Interest-group involvement is fostered by legal orders requiring that bureaus hold hearings, consult with, or secure the consent of these groups before they can enforce their regulatory power or adopt or change agency procedures. This situation in itself leaves public managers with considerable ambiguity about their own power in the decision processes, as well as uncertainty about what criteria are appropriate for the policy decisions they must make.

The general imperative to avoid "political" decisions is juxtaposed with the inconsistent expectation that bureaus be politically responsive to "the public," which in practice usually means a special and attentive public or set of organized interests. In the face of conflicting expectations of neutrality and responsiveness to adversarial groups, public agencies must, as part of their decision process, include achieving consensus or forming coalitions among diverse forces. As a result, the processes of organizational decision making in bureaus are certain to be slower and more disjointed than the more linear-type decision process favored by private management. Thus, greater conflict-resolving and consensus-building skills will be needed by the public manager.

Goal Making and Politics

Although firms depend on the environment for resources, consumption of their product or service, personnel, and so on, their means for obtaining these are primarily economic, not political, and decisions about their actions or exchanges are made internally, not externally. On the other hand, goals, available resources, and often basic procedures are determined for bureaus by legislation, executive order, court decisions, and with input from clients and interest groups.

Organizational decision making is often limited to interpretation of goals set externally and politically. Thus politics is inescapable in public management. When the context of decision making includes such an external element, other crucial organizational factors, such as power relations among individuals in the bureau, the role of the manager, the development of operating routines, and relationships with external groups are deeply affected.

Public goals that direct the bureau's efforts are typically a product of coalitional support and thus reflect a mixture of means and ends, often based on an uneasy compromise among conflicting claims for public benefits or recognition (Lindblom 1959). For example, various groups and officials might accept improvement of air quality as a goal, yet not agree on the means to achieve that goal. Some might want to create a new environmental agency that has considerable legal or economic power, whereas others might prefer that money be provided by one level of government to initiate the air-quality policy, but that it be administered by another level's agencies. Still others, of course, would oppose the basic goal or any governmental role in its achievement. Throughout the goal-setting process, both means and ends are pursued simultaneously through the political arts of persuasion, bargaining, and compromise; lacking these, no new program could be established since there would be a stalemate among the struggling forces (Braybrooke and Lindblom 1970; Gawthrop 1971).

The various means–ends conflicts that arise and the shifting coalitions of interest groups and politicians associated with them are kaleidoscopic. Bureaus and their managers enter into these conflicts either because of the needs and demands of other participants or because of organizational or personal values. The bureau's expertise and clientele support provide public managers with opportunities to initiate or shape (to a degree) the policies set by those outside the bureau. Through reports, studies, recommendations, and other forms of information, bureaus may play a role in shaping policy. In a more patently political vein, public managers sometimes leak information or indirectly mobilize interest group support.

The simultaneous and political nature of means–ends determination raises numerous problems for the public manager. For example, one result may be a poor match between ends (goals) and means (procedures to achieve goals), in which case the bureau's effectiveness is seriously hampered when it must work with—or around—inadequate and inappropriate means.

Just as goals are set externally, so too, is judgment about bureau actions. The public manager must answer in some fashion to the external standards of political acceptability. Although public managers play a limited though important role in evaluating the effectiveness and efficiency of the organizations they manage, bureaus are still extremely dependent on and vulnerable to the external environment. A police administrator, for example, might adopt a policy of blanketing high-crime areas with foot patrols. Crime may drop, but the overpowering presence of many uniformed police may be viewed as creating an oppressive and even racist climate, especially if mostly white police officers are used in a minority neighborhood. Protests by community groups and leaders may ensue.

The Problem of Goal Ambiguity

Statutes creating public bureaus or establishing programs usually set forth their goals in highly general and ambiguous terms. For example, the Interstate Commerce Commission is charged with regulating railroads in a "just" and "reasonable" fashion, as well as "in the public interest." Agencies at all levels of government receive equally undefined charges. In general, broadness and ambiguity in goals and purposes gives public managers responsibilities and opportunities for exercising power. As noted by Rourke:

> Control over the implementation of policy becomes especially important as a source of bureaucratic power when it includes the authority to exercise discretion in achieving policy goals. As used here, the term "discretion" refers to the ability of an administrator to choose among alternatives—to decide in effect how the policies of the government should be implemented in specific cases. (1976, 32)

Administrative discretion is extensive in the everyday, routine decisions of public bureaus. For example, the community health officer enforcing both state and local sanitary standards decides whether to give an informal reprimand, issue a warning notice, make a formal violation charge, or even invoke an order to close a restaurant. Police officers similarly decide whether to warn, charge, or arrest an individual. Of course, they are expected to do so within legal limits and in accordance with the norms of the organization in whose name they carry out their duties. For public administrators then, the exercise of authoritative political power is an everyday fact of life.

Public goals are general and ambiguous not only because legislators and others lack sufficient time and expertise to spell out every specific implication and application of legislation, but also because ambiguity and generality are useful in blurring the lines of conflict over both means and ends. This blurring promotes sufficient coalitional cohesion and support to get legislation passed, but the political struggle does not end; only its locus shifts. The Office of Coastal Zone Management, for example, was created with a charge both to protect the coastal environment and to foster orderly development in coastal areas because Congress had been unable to decide between these goals, to define them more specifically, or to set priorities between them. Such indecisiveness and lack of clarity explains why conflict among contending interests is transferred from a legislative to a bureaucratic setting.

Vague and general goals also mean that public bureaus have to make decisions on interpretation, activities, and means. Public administrators are expected, for the most part, to base their decisions on "professional" grounds. This prescription stems from the belief that using professional criteria removes political factors from administrative decisions. In theory, policy is to be made externally by politicians, and those inside the bureau are to be passive except for implementing externally prescribed goals. In real bureaucratic life, however, so passive a role is not possible given the generality and ambiguity of goals. This gives rise to the rationale that if public managers use professional criteria they will be prevented from making political decisions. But professional values are not apolitical. They may be nonpartisan, but they are political in the broader sense of benefiting some groups and not others and of advancing some values but not others. Ultimately, whether they are based on professional and technical criteria or on more obviously political considerations, the decisions of public administrators have basically political effects.

The emphasis on professional or technical values affects the internal organization in a variety of ways, particularly in the areas of internal conflict and power. Conflict between political appointees and professional bureau careerists is one dimension (Rourke 1976; Heclo 1977). Superior–subordinate conflict is rendered more complex. Conflict occurs among contending and different professionals at the same levels and among those at different levels. Likewise, in the fragmented world of government bureaus, conflict between professionals in different organizations or departments is also a fact of life.

In the process of interpreting and implementing vague legislation, public managers may increase political support for their bureaus and programs, but they may also risk political attack and loss of support. Client groups usually support aggressive action by the agency, and may make demands on a bureau for a broad interpretation of their eligibility to receive services. However, influential legislators or the chief executive may not have embraced a program even though it gained sufficient power to pass, or they may prefer a limited, even symbolic, program. A clientele that is regulated by a bureau may resist and oppose an assertive agency, whereas other groups and their elected officials may demand greater regulatory fervor. This was certainly the case for the Office of Coastal Zone Management discussed earlier. The agency's legal charges and goals placed it between conflicting pressures from coastal developers and environmentalists and their respective elected supporters. Local planning agencies constantly face pressure from these two conflicting community interests. For public managers, action may satisfy some interests but upset others, and inaction undoubtedly will have equally disparate results.

"Decisions usually involve risk."

© Wally Neibart

CONCLUSION

In summary, bureaus differ from firms in substantial and fundamental ways. Because of the political roles and ambitions of other major governmental actors and institutions, public bureaus and their managers are plunged into politics. Administrative agencies, principally because of their expertise and their access to the client groups they serve, are important political resources and allies to legislators and chief executives. Our governmental system creates an opportunity structure in which agencies are not only drawn into politics by others, but in which agency officials pursue and exercise political influence.

The climate and role of public bureaus are unlike those of the private firm. Clearly, the fact of external control, especially coupled with conflict among the overseers, creates a climate of uncertainty, hostility, and risk. Moreover, circumstances dictate an essentially political role for bureaus whether they are passive, defensive reactors, or active influence pursuers.

Organization theory, concentrating as it has on the private firm, has emphasized a relatively closed-system view. Stability, rationality, and efficiency have been stressed, whereas instability, power, and conflict have received short shrift. Organization theory that addresses the realities of public bureaus must look more to the interaction between bureaus and their environments, and must question more closely the ways their environments affect them.

FOR FURTHER READING

For an excellent summary of the literature about the differences between bureaus and private organizations, see Hal G. Rainey, Robert W. Backoff, and Charles H. Levine, "Comparing Public and Private Organizations," in James Perry and Kenneth Kraemer, eds., *Public Management: Public and Private Perspectives,* Palo Alto, Calif.: Mayfield, 1983. The major economic and market differences between private and public organizations are presented by Anthony Downs, *Inside Bureaucracy,* Boston: Little, Brown, 1967 (reissued, Prospect Heights, Ill.: Waveland Press, 1994). James Q. Wilson, in his book *Bureaucracy: What Government Agencies Do and Why They Do It,* New York: Basic Books, 1989, discusses the implications of the political nature of bureaus, or the inseparability of politics and public organizations. A serious and insightful investigation of the necessity to combine traditional managerial values with essential political functions and the complexity of administering public organizations is presented by Dwight Waldo, *The Enterprise of Public Administration,* Novato, Calif.: Chandler & Sharp Publishers, 1980. Finally, an excellent response to the antibureaucratic rhetoric that is so common in current politics and "scholarship" is Charles T. Goodsell, *The Case for Bureaucracy: A Public Administration Polemic,* 3rd ed., Chatham, N.J.: Chatham House Publishers, 1994.

REVIEW QUESTIONS

1. There is disagreement about the amount of difference, but there is general agreement that public organizations differ from private ones in some critical ways. What are those differences?

2. Given the political environment, how can structural change take place in public organizations?

3. Looking at the different characteristics of public organizations, how would these factors encourage and discourage change in behavior and productivity? How would these differences encourage and discourage employees to look at their clients—whoever and wherever those clients are—as "customers," as employees are told to do in current theories of "excellence"?

REFERENCES

Berkley, George E., and John Rouse. *The Craft of Public Administration.* 6th ed. Dubuque, Iowa: Brown & Benchmark, 1994.

Blau, Peter M., and Marshall W. Meyer. *Bureaucracy in Modern Society.* 3rd ed. New York: McGraw Hill, 1993.

———— and W. Richard Scott. *Formal Organizations: A Comparative Approach,* San Francisco: Chandler, 1962.

Braybrooke, David, and Charles E. Lindblom. *A Strategy of Decision: Policy Evaluation as a Social Process.* New York: Free Press, 1970.

Downs, Anthony. *Inside Bureaucracy.* Boston: Little, Brown, 1967. (Reissued, Prospect Heights, Ill.: Waveland Press, 1994.)

Easton, David. *A Framework for Political Analysis.* Englewood Cliffs, N.J.: Prentice Hall, 1965.

Gawthrop, Louis C. *Administrative Politics and Social Change.* New York: St. Martin's Press, 1971.

Golembiewski, Robert T. *Perspectives on Public Management: Cases and Learning Designs.* 2nd ed. Itasca, Ill.: F. E. Peacock Publishers, 1976.

Gortner, Harold F. *Administration in the Public Sector.* 2nd ed. New York: Krieger, 1986.

Heclo, Hugh. *A Government of Strangers: Executive Politics in Washington.* Washington: Brookings Institution, 1977.

Hersey, Paul, and Ken Blanchard. *Management of Organizational Behavior: Utilizing Human Resources.* 6th ed. Englewood Cliffs, N.J.: Prentice Hall, 1993.

Lasswell, Harold D. *Politics: Who Gets What, When, How.* New York: World Publishing, 1958.

Lorch, Robert. S. *Public Administration.* St. Paul, Minn.: West Publishing, 1978.

Lowi, Theodore. "American Business, Public Policy, Case Studies and Political Theory." *World Politics* 16 (July 1964): 677–715.

Malek, Frederick V. "Mr. Executive Goes to Washington." *Harvard Business Review.* (Sept./Oct. 1972): 63–68.

McCurdy, Howard E. *Public Administration: A Synthesis.* Menlo Park, Calif.: Cummings Publishing, 1977.

Murray, Michael A. "Comparing Public and Private Management: An Exploratory Essay." *Public Administration Review.* (July/August 1975): 364–371.

National Performance Review (U.S.). *Creating a Government That Works Better & Costs Less: Report of the National Performance Review,* Vice President Al Gore. New York: Plume/Penguin, 1993.

Neustadt, Richard E. *Presidential Power: The Power to Persuade.* New York: John Wiley & Sons, 1960.

Rainey, Hal G., Robert W. Backoff, and Charles H. Levine. "Comparing Public and Private Organizations." *Public Administration Review* 36. (March/April 1976): 233–244.

Rourke, Francis E. *Bureaucracy, Politics, and Public Policy.* 3rd ed. Boston: Little, Brown, 1984.

Shafritz, Jay M., and J. Steven Ott. *Classics of Organization Theory.* 4th ed. Belmont Calif.: Wadsworth, 1996.

Sharkansky, Ira. "Four Agencies and an Appropriation Committee: A Comparative Study of Budget Strategies." *Midwest Journal of Political Science* 9, no. 3 (August 1965): 254–281.

Stokey, Edith, and Richard Zeckhauser. *A Primer For Policy Analysis.* New York: W. W. Norton, 1978.

Thompson, James. *Organizations in Action.* New York: McGraw-Hill, 1967.

Waldo, Dwight. *The Enterprise of Public Administration.* Novato, Calif.: Chandler & Sharp Publishers, 1980.

Wamsley, Gary L., and Mayer N. Zald. *The Political Economy of Public Organizations.* Bloomington, Ind.: Indiana Univ. Press, 1976.

Willick, Daniel. "Political Goals and the Structure of Government Bureaus." Paper delivered at American Sociological Association, Washington, D.C., 1970. Cited in Wamsley, Gary L., and Mayer N. Zald. *The Political Economy of Public Organizations.* Bloomington, Ind.: Indiana Univ. Press, 1976: 35, 38.

Woll, Peter. *American Bureaucracy.* 2nd ed. New York: W. W. Norton, 1977.

READING 2–1   Mr. Executive Goes to Washington

(To succeed as a government executive, the businessman must acquire a politician's skills and learn to deal with the bureaucracy.)

When it assumed office . . . , the Administration of President Eisenhower was faced with the problem of restaffing the Executive Branch after 20 years of Democratic rule. It commissioned a study to be used as a guide. Concerning corporate executives in government, John Corson, who prepared the report, concluded:

> A majority of business executives are uncomfortable and unsuccessful in the federal government's top-most political, policy-making posts as department heads and assistant secretaries. They are unaccustomed to and sometimes resentful of the interest of the legislative branch in administrative affairs. They are unfamiliar with the necessity for clearance and coordination with numerous other departments. They are irritated by public scrutiny of their actions and by the rigid controls exercised over recruitment of personnel, budgeting of funds, and procurement of supplies and equipment. (as quoted by John McDonald, "The Businessman in Government," *Fortune,* July 1954, p. 69)

Nevertheless, President Eisenhower drew on the business community heavily in filling the top management posts of the federal government.

The conclusions of the report were reinforced a decade later, during President Kennedy's term. A foundation-supported study ranked businessmen a poor third after lawyers and educators in terms of likely effective public service (reported in *Business Week,* May 18, 1963, p. 120).

Success in business management does not necessarily assure or even imply success in government management, and businessmen who assume it does have found only frustration and disappointment in public service. In this article, I attempt to explain this phenomenon. First, I shall describe the differences between business and government in the ingredients for successful management. Then, I shall address myself to the qualities a corporate executive needs to succeed in government service.

Political Quicksands

The glare of publicity, Congressional power, and partisan constraints on action are basic and permanent facts of Washington life. They have an enormous impact on any person's effectiveness.

Glare of Publicity

The corporate executive is accustomed to the usually informed and generally sympathetic scrutiny of his colleagues, his stockholders, and occasionally, the public through annual reports and news releases. The government executive, however, lives in a fishbowl; depending on the level and nature of his job, he must expect to be exposed at any moment to the glare of publicity and notoriety.

Every department and agency has a cadre of newsmen whose primary job is to cover its activities. Competing for space and air time, these reporters constantly seek the controversy that is "newsworthy." As a consequence, they often reveal programs, plans, and projects before they are ready for public airing and cause actions or intentions to be grossly misinterpreted.

At the least, premature disclosure can be embarrassing. The government executive must be prepared to endure the discomfort of having his "discussion drafts" leaked and printed as if they were final recommendations. As long as he can follow through on his decisions, however, no harm is done—except perhaps to his ego or political future.

But premature disclosure can also disrupt carefully developed plans. A couple of years ago a Cabinet officer decided that one of his bureaus needed "shaking up" and to accomplish it he must replace three of its top-level managers. As he was proceeding carefully to arrange "transfers" that looked like promotions a newspaper report disclosed the plans in a way that made his action look extremely devious. Nevertheless, the Cabinet officer chose to proceed with the transfers. The morale problems that resulted in the bureau negated much of the positive effects of the management changes.

The glare of publicity and the concomitant power of public opinion make it important to gain public support and acceptance of a department's or agency's goals and essential to gain public understanding before proceeding with any major initiative or change of policy. This notion is unfamiliar to the average business executive, for whom a public image is either nonexistent or unimportant. His public support depends more on the law of supply and demand than on electoral laws. The adept businessman in government must quickly learn to develop in himself, or seek in others, the skills of a politician who is expert at sensing the mood of the public and at winning acceptance of his department's goals.

Secretary of Commerce Peter Peterson, who has spent most of his career in business—most recently as Chairman of Bell & Howell—has remarked, "In Washington, your ability to articulate your accomplishments in a way that is memorable and persuasive generally counts for more than the objective standards of efficiency and success as we know them in business."

Role of Congress

The Congress constitutes an extraordinarily active and sometimes dominant board of directors for the Executive Branch. Its influence and discretionary power extend from budget allocations to the content and direction of programs, to the number of personnel and their assignments, and even to questions of departmental organization. It is essential to devote considerable time and effort to informing, persuading, and gaining the confidence of members of Congress, particularly those who sit on the committees and those who address themselves to the constituencies relevant to the particular department's functions.

Most corporate executives are accustomed to giving orders and having them carried out without question. The act of influencing politicians is a mystery to them. The unaccustomed necessity of cajoling and persuading a large number of strong-willed and diverse men can prove to be a time-consuming, frustrating, and humbling exercise.

Partisan Constraints

Few things in the government-bureaucratic complex are above politics. Any initiative—no matter how nonpartisan, necessary, or high-minded it may seem to the department or agency—must run the gauntlet of partisan analysis in Congress, in the press, and among the public. Criticism of it will range from the highest to the lowest levels of rhetoric and imputation, from the most philosophical and detached to the most visceral and prejudiced. Whatever the motives behind it, such criticism means that no subject or proposal can be considered only on its own merits.

The significant consequence of this partisan dimension in government is that a government executive can never have complete freedom of action in framing or implementing a program to meet a perceived social need or purpose. The successful government manager realizes at the outset that the longest way around will often be the shortest and surest way home. The corporate executive going to Washington can learn much from him.

Bureaucratic Behemoth

The sheer diversity, complexity, and dispersion of government programs is a new experience for the former business executive. He is used to dealing with quantifiable data for a relatively small and definable segment of the market of the population.

Government organization often causes duplication and division of responsibilities—even within the Executive Branch—which makes accountability of any one person or agency difficult. The need to obtain a consensus from all affected agencies inhibits initiative.

For example, nine departments and twenty independent agencies are involved in education matters. Three different agencies deal directly with housing policy. In addition, since any housing decision is affected by monetary, fiscal, and wage-price policy and itself affects environmental conditions, residential relocation, tax losses, minority relations, and labor problems, consensus gathering in this area alone involves five departments (Treasury, HEW, Labor, HUD, and Agriculture) and four agencies (IRS, OEO, EPA, and VA). It is a staggering fact that at last count more than 850 interagency committees existed for coordination of matters affecting more than one agency.

Shortly after he was appointed Secretary of HUD, George Romney created a stir when he displayed a 30-inch high, 56-pound stack of paper that represented a single urban renewal application. A principal reason for the red tape, he decided, was the fragmentation of program administration in HUD. For example, one assistant secretary administered the public housing program while another administered the the subsidized housing programs, though the clientele overlapped. Each had his own staff of architects, engineers, inspectors, and other specialists, as well as his own set of regulations and specifications.

Secretary Romney reorganized the department on a functional basis, assigning responsibility for all housing production to one assistant secretary, all planning activities to a second assistant secretary, and all community development programs to a third. As a result, the department is processing applications more quickly and has significantly reduced overhead.

Pressures of Time

A characteristic of this vast and unwieldy government structure is the short time span available to achieve results, due to rapid turnover at the top levels and the inchwork pace of policy implementation at lower levels.

Changes in Administrations and the higher turnover of personnel in government, compared with business, require great efforts to learn rapidly, take hold quickly, and exert forceful leadership. Former Secretary of Commerce Maurice Stans, who has wide experience in both business and government, thinks that a business executive needs at least two years, and preferably more, in government before he can become effective. "Except in unusual cases," he has said, "a shorter tenure does not give the business executive enough time to know the intricacies of his programs and to make beneficial changes."

The average Cabinet or sub-Cabinet appointee, however, remains in office just 22 months. Since the nature of the bureaucracy is to resist major change, the new appointee must quickly gain an understanding of his job and win the cooperation of his career staff.

The corporate executive is accustomed to fast and purposeful action once a problem has been isolated and the solution agreed to. But the government executive must accept the fact that after he has done his homework and planning and gained the necessary support in Congress and in the nation, he still faces the long lead time needed for project completion.

Detailing of a budget justification, obtaining legislative authorization, and securing an appropriation can be frustratingly lengthy operations. In the Department of the Army, full implementation of a new directive at the troop level usually takes from 2 to 5 years. In the Bureau of Reclamation, 20 years may pass between conception of a project and the start of construction. Completion of it can take another 50 years.

Obstacles for Managers

The most fundamental problems confronting the business executive who enters government are the lack of management expertise among many career officials in top-level positions and the disinclination of many of them to accept new leadership willingly.

This problem is the result partly of a general inability to set precise goals—about which more in a moment. More important, however, is the predominant tendency to select persons to head major divisions or bureaus on the basis of technical expertise rather than managerial ability.

Furthermore, a study made a few years ago by the Committee for Economic Development showed that almost 70 percent of men and women in supergrade positions (GS-16 and above) in the federal government had spent their entire careers—an average of more than 20 years—in no more than two bureaus. This kind of career pattern reverses the maxim that experts should be on tap, not on top. It hardly encourages or nurtures the development of competent managers with broad-based skills.

To the extent that the executive from business fails to address himself to this problem, he will be ineffective. He will thereby lend visible support to the attitude of those career employees for whom "management" refers to the administrative and housekeeping activities for which they feel his MBA ideally suits him—just as they know their Ph.D.s enable them to plan, motivate, direct, and evaluate.

The business executive must also face a division of loyalties among his key subordinates. In recent years this phenomenon has been most visible in young employees in social action programs and agencies, who are not reticent about going to the press or into print about their struggles against the unsympathetic or unresponsive institutional establishment.

There is, however, a more deep-rooted structural and institutional problem here. As I have indicated, federal recruiting, promotion, and personnel development practices encourage civil servants to spend their entire careers within a single bureau or narrow specialty area. As the specialist progresses, he becomes increasingly involved with the relevant outside interest groups and Congressional staffs. These external groups determine his standing and prestige in the field, represent the major source of employment outside the government, and are long-lived relative to the political leadership. Consequently, many top career officials direct their loyalty more toward these groups than to the Administration in power.

Goals and Standards

Difficulty in setting precise goals and measuring the results of programs is probably the most serious obstacle to effective management in government. This phenomenon is generally what first strikes the executive from the private sector.

This difficulty stems primarily from government's inability to define long-range goals much beyond the general philosophical thrust it wants to project and encourage in the nation. The Demonstration Cities and Metropolitan Development Act of 1966, for example, calls on HUD "to improve the quality of urban life" through a combination of public and private efforts.

Sometimes these worthy but vague goals are stated in a manner that raises expectations to unwarranted levels. For instance, the law that created the Inter-American Social Development Institute in 1969 stated its purpose in this way: "to provide support for developmental activities designed to achieve conditions in the Western Hemisphere under which the dignity and the worth of each person will be respected and under which all men will be afforded the opportunity to develop their potential, to seek through gainful and productive work the fulfillment of their aspirations for a better life, and to live in justice and peace."

Translating these generalities into concrete, quantifiable objectives obviously is not easy.

Even where goals are precisely articulated, the standards used for measuring results are often not only unquantifiable but also uneven or arbitrary. How is it possible, for example, to determine whether improvement in a child's performance at school is due to some innovative government program, a different teacher, a subtle change in the learning environment, or an awakening in the child—some new maturity beyond the power of legislation or quantification? Inability to judge program results also makes it difficult to measure individual performance.

Unless the erstwhile corporate executive accepts this situation, he may fall back on allowing measures of activity to set their own kind of success standards. While this may appear to be an appealing alternative, in fact it is the line of least resistance. Thus some government managers adopt such superficial success criteria as lunch at the desk, long hours, whether all the appropriated funds have been expended, whether all new job openings have been filled, and whether Congressional correspondence has been handled properly.

Requiring specific objectives and implementation timetables can in part avoid this misdirection. At HEW for example, an objective can be changed from "make additional day care services available in two cities" to "develop day care services for 500 additional children in each of the Model City areas of Norfolk and Richmond." Obviously, setting precise objectives will not completely solve the measurability problem, but it can significantly improve the ability to evaluate performance.

Qualities Needed

It is obvious that success in the private sector is not automatically transferable to the public sector. In fact, to succeed in government, the businessman must develop some qualities that are almost the opposite of those he needed to succeed in business. Where he was persistent, he must now also be resilient; where he was guarded, he must be open; where he was arbitrary, he must be sensitive; where he viewed problems with a narrow focus, he must deal comprehensively with them; and where he was informed, he must be at least a little intuitive.

It is understood that he must be an exceptional manager, because all the traditional business tools are required in government. But beyond these, he needs certain personal characteristics and resources to meet the complex demands of the more highly convoluted government framework and more public-oriented and politically determined atmosphere of government service.

On the basis of my own experience and the frank observations of several men who have made the change from business to government with great success, I can pinpoint some of these critical qualities. I shall list them, beginning with the most important one.

1. Ability to Communicate

"Success in government depends upon the attitude of the people you deal with—the bureaucracy, the Congress, the media, the public," George Romney, who has had careers in both business and government, has said. "To shape this attitude there is a much greater need for the ability to communicate than exists in any business I can think of, including advertising."

Commerce Secretary Peterson has put it even more strongly: "In business, a man's ability to communicate, while important, is hardly the dominant consideration. If confronted with the choice between someone with a great track record or great ability to articulate, the businessman would take the track record. But in government, the choice might be different."

The department or agency with such a spokesman can use his persuasive profile to increase its impact and effectiveness. Such strong advocacy creates a feeling of purpose and purposiveness within the department, which further enhances both the leader's image and the department's effectiveness. The attention and spirit that former Secretary John Connally brought to the Treasury Department is a good example of the results of a leader's ability to communicate.

But his success was due to more than his communicative ability; it was also due to the force of his charismatic personality. The terrific impact of the news media on the operation of government has turned "charisma" into a household word. At the highest levels it has probably become a sine qua non for notable service.

Part of the ability to communicate is charismatic, inspirational leadership which can earn essential Congressional or public support for departmental programs and initiatives. It serves as a catalyst, mobilizing the force of a vast and unwieldy bureaucracy and moving it toward the Administration's goals.

2. Sensitivity and Empathy

A high degree of awareness is essential to sense and understand the real—often different from the apparent—motives, desires, and reactions of the public, the media, the Congress, and the special interest groups with which the government executive must deal. Most businessmen, who are conventionally concerned with restricted and more immediately ascertainable areas of thought and feeling, come into government lacking the required political instinct, savvy, or intuition.

However, the executive who possesses sensitivity and empathy to human situations can develop this astuteness quite naturally when placed in the context that depends on it. He will increasingly be able to judge in advance how people react to various actions and will factor this into his planning and decision making.

The executive without this sensitivity may be a competent manager, but he will never gain the support needed to get things done in government. And he can easily be carved up in the politically charged atmosphere of Washington.

3. Mental Toughness

Even the most charismatic, articulate, attractive, sensitive, and flexible business executive in government must steel himself to meet and cope with the sheer inertia of government. Dealing with the vagaries of the Congress, the slow movement of the bureaucracy, and the erratic turns of public concern, he must have the persistence and resilience to bounce back and pursue a target despite repeated diversions. This requires a determination to reach the goal by a variety of means and a grasp of how much one must accommodate to circumstances.

Secretary Stans' efforts to translate "black capitalism" into a meaningful program provide a good example. Recognizing that he could not win immediate approval for a full program, he settled for a small budget that included only salaries and expenses. Then he directed Office of Minority Business Enterprise personnel to concentrate on cajoling other departments and agencies into using their program funds to support minority businesses.

After a year of operating in this manner, Secretary Stans felt that he had sufficient grounds to request that OMBE should control its own program funds and thus provide grants directly to minority businesses. His initial proposals were rejected, but the Secretary persisted. He finally received the funding in late 1971—two and one-half years after receiving the responsibility.

4. Flexibility and Humility

These are difficult qualities for some businessmen whose success, public esteem, and even self-esteem are based on their ability to drive hard toward the solution they have decided is right and to resist compromise along the way.

Such rigidity fosters failure and frustration in government. Here, the executive must be willing to adopt or modify programs or shift direction to meet the changing needs of other agencies, the public, Congress, or different interest groups. He must realize that some progress is better than none and that he must at times move obliquely rather than straight ahead.

Above all, he must be willing to compromise. He must understand that few of his ideas will survive to completion in their original form, and that plans are seldom implemented without major adjustments somewhere along the line. He must realize from the outset that the process of compromise and trade-off comes with the territory in a vast popular government like ours.

Managerial Ability Plus

Too few top businessmen succeed or reach their fullest potential in government service. Some never perceive the importance of external forces—the Congress, the public, the media—and thus commit the error they would never commit in business: they misunderstand their market and do not orient their actions and organization to meet the market's needs.

But managerial ability—in the task orientation in which it is usually viewed—is not enough for effective government service. As Secretary of Labor James Hodgson, another former businessman, has put it: "The most general of the reasons for the failure of successful businessmen in government is a lack of breadth—an inability to conceptualize rather than merely achieve, an inability to understand and be effective in the *relations* elements of a governmental role, and an inability to deal with problems indirectly rather than through authoritarian line control."

The corporate executive turned government executive must be able to sense and accommodate to the peculiar nuances of government and avoid the pitfalls of pride I have discussed. He must be endowed with sensitivity and empathy to human motives and problems and have a flexibility of mind, a high tolerance for frustration and even abuse, and a good deal of humility. A sense of humor is no detriment either.

And he must have, in today's political setting, an abundant charisma and ability to communicate with all his constituent publics—including the Congress—forcefully and persuasively.

A major challenge to any President or Administration is to find and attract men and women who possess these extra dimensions. The degree to which they succeed will have a powerful influence on the effectiveness of government, and, consequently on the quality of life in the United States for decades to come.

SOURCE: Frederick V. Malek, *Harvard Business Review* 50 (Sept./Oct. 1972): 63–68.

Editor's Note

This classic article, written almost twenty-five years ago by a special assistant to President Nixon, focuses on the difference between the private and public environment and the impact of that difference on executives moving from business to government. Although the names of departments and other details have changed, the reality of the cultural variation, as well as the accompanying shock, still exists. As you review what you have read, consider the following questions:

1. We point to the Watergate scandal and the Iran-Contra scandal as examples of misdeeds by people who do not seem to understand the requirements of public service in a democracy. However, these same types of problems recur frequently in a not-so-historically-celebrated manner. To what extent might Mr. Malek have been describing some of the causes of the scandals mentioned—along with the resignations of secretaries of departments at the beginning of every new administration—and the inevitable accompanying crisis in the executive branch of the federal government?

2. Look at the "problems" (inertia, vagaries of Congress, erratic turns in public opinion, and so on) faced by an executive, and create an argument noting why these very problems may be positive or important to democratic government, whereas they are considered "bad" in business.

3. What accommodations are required of the public bureaucracy, and its managers, by the "problems" noted in question 2?

4. If the executive's world is so different, what does that say about the public bureaucracy that he or she is running?

5. After reading Chapter 9 "Leadership and Management in Public Organizations," you should refer to this reading and consider if or how the various theories about leadership and management help explain the phenomenon described by Mr. Malek.

Chapter 3

The Pivotal Controversies

As we pointed out in the first chapter, organization theory is a disorderly and fascinating field (Waldo 1978). Each theory starts with a unique set of assumptions, asks a different set of basic questions, and, not surprisingly, arrives at different—sometimes diametrically opposed—answers. Nevertheless, certain themes are constantly addressed as the frantic debate among "public" organization theorists goes on. These controversies about, or perspectives on, organization in the public sector can be categorized under the following four general headings:

1. *Law and legal authority.* Public agencies are established by law to administer the law, and all of society is affected by the result. Therefore, questions pertaining to the interpretation and implementation of the law as it applies to public organizations and about how these organizations fulfill their mandated functions are of central importance and are subject to constant debate.

2. *Rationality and efficiency.* The public's material resources are used by public organizations. Therefore, how efficiently and rationally those resources are used is of utmost importance to everyone, whether inside or outside those bureaus.

3. *Psychological and social relations.* Civil servants are human beings (even though some politicians might have us believe otherwise). Therefore, public managers must understand the psychological and sociological aspects of the organization if they are to accomplish good human resource management and achieve individual neutrality while maintaining high motivation and involvement among employees who cannot be rewarded in what are typical ways for the private sector. Psychological and social principles that apply to individuals and groups in organizations must be understood and then interpreted to fit the public milieu.

4. *Politics and power relations.* All public organization action takes place in a politically charged environment. Therefore, the decisions and actions of the principal actors in these organizations must be considered in a political context.

The second and third controversies noted are especially universal and must be considered in any discussion on organization theory although they must be interpreted in the context of the public sector. However, since public organizations exist for reasons (and have obligations) quite dissimilar to those in the private sector, the first and last of these pivotal perspectives assume a special significance that does not exist for organizations in the private sector. Although the reason for this emphasis on the law and the political

51

environment should be relatively clear after reading the last chapter, it may be worthwhile to comment briefly on the importance of these two areas.

In Chapter 2, the discussion centered on the way bureaus were involved in the formulation and interpretation of the law, but a further impact of the law must be noted: The law places serious limitations on the way public organizational structures and functions can be instituted and carried out. While striving for optimal efficiency and the best possible social and psychological arrangements in the bureau, the public manager must always be cognizant of "what the law will let one do." The following story, perhaps apocryphal but passed on to the authors as true, can best explain the difficulty faced in this area.

In a midwestern state, it was discovered that one particular employment office was extremely successful over an eighteen-month period in placing unemployed individuals in permanent jobs. In other words, not only were more than the usual number of people placed in available openings, but those people were remaining on the job longer than was usual compared with other offices in the state. When a state auditor made his biennial visit to the office to examine the files and validate the records, he found that the records were indeed correct. He also found that the director of the office was using a unique motivational system that apparently accounted for the tremendous record: She was rewarding the office employees with an extra day off after they had successfully placed X number of clients (determined by placement in a position where the client remained on the job for a predetermined period that was longer than the statewide mean). Despite the program's success, the auditor had to inform the director that she was in violation of state law and that she could not use such a reward system. One year later, the record of that particular employment office was slightly lower than the state average for both placements and length of time remaining in the new job. Everyone firmly believed that the unique reward system was the causal factor in the success of the office, and that removal of the system led to the immediate return to mediocrity, but all they could do was shake their heads, shrug their shoulders, and say, "It was a great idea, but it was against the law."

Public organizations must use existing theories in ways that meet the letter of the law. Solid proof that an experimental system works is not adequate justification for action (although such proof might be used to try to persuade the legislature to change the law). Therefore, public organization theory must include a consideration of the law as it relates to bureaus, its reason for existence, and the limitations that it places on freedom of action. Doing so creates a more complete and rational picture of "the real world" of public organizations.

When dealing with the fourth controversy noted, students of public bureaucracy need to be aware of the assumptions and thinking behind the questions asked about organizations. These questions and their answers are political; they often express, implicitly or explicitly, criticism of the political system and the predominant culture, and agendas for change. Therefore, they rest on a particular set of assumptions about authority, conflict, power, and the proper criteria for choice within organizations. Any organizational theory, when applied to bureaus in the public sector, should be examined for such assumptions when it is studied and, especially, before attempting to apply it in the hope of improving management or changing the operations of any group or agency.

Similarly, the politically charged environment is a prominent factor that must be considered as public organization theory is examined. How does the theory take into account the existing political system, which, in turn, helps explain why bureaus currently function as they do? And it must be considered whenever an attempt is made to apply organization theory to a bureau. How will actors in the political environment interpret what is attempted, and how will they react to that effort given their political philosophy, position within the political system, and the perception that both factors give them of the world? How will the reactions of the political actors affect the implementation of any change? It must be recognized that different types of rationality (that is, several types of political and managerial rationality) exist based on different sets of basic values and on whether substantive or instrumental rationality is being considered. (Rationality will be discussed later in this chapter.) These different rationality systems are being used simultaneously in defining the goals of public bureaus and in assessing how "rational and efficient" they are.

Thus, it is the inclusion of the four controversies in this particular combination that makes public organization theory unique, especially the heavy emphasis that must be placed on the first and last principles. If, when studying organization theory, such an emphasis is not included, there is no way to recognize the special problems faced by public organizations or the special interpretations that must be understood when the traditional theories are applied to this unique sector of our society; it is the addition of these issues that creates additional problems for nonprofit and private organizations when they are carrying out public policy functions.

In the next section, after presenting two models of organization that will help us focus the discussion throughout this chapter, we will examine the four pivotal themes of public organization theory, and, finally, we will take a special look at the influence of political history on the bureau, on public organization theory, and on public management practice.

MODELS OF ORGANIZATION

Let us briefly present two models of complex organizations and how to manage them, the first the more traditional model of bureaucracy presented by Max Weber and widely accepted as the norm[1] for public organization, and the second a currently popular model of how to organize the successful private sector business organization. Throughout the chapter, as we discuss the four controversies, we will refer to the two models. They will help us understand the larger field of organization theory and the application of its concepts to the workings of public organizations, and of equal importance, how the perspectives differ in importance within the private sector.

Probably the most influential model of organization ever presented is Max Weber's description of the internal characteristics of the "ideal type" bureaucracy. According to Weber, within the bureaucracy:

> The whole administrative staff under the supreme authority . . . consists, in the purest type, of individual officials who are appointed and function according to the following criteria:
> 1. They are personally free and subject to authority only with respect to their impersonal official obligations.

---

[1] The use of the term *norm* is solely descriptive. Weber's model describes the way public organizations look; it says nothing about how they should be structured or how they should operate. In fact, Weber decried such structure, but he described it in an objective and scholarly manner. Weber's use of the term *ideal type* means "the organization that most perfectly meets the criteria of bureaucracy," and not *the best* organization.

2. They are organized in a clearly defined hierarchy of offices.

3. Each office has a clearly defined sphere of competence in the legal sense.

4. The office is filled by a free contractual relationship. Thus, in principle, there is free selection.

5. Candidates are selected on the basis of technical qualifications. In the most rational case, this is tested by examination or guaranteed by diplomas certifying technical training, or both. They are appointed, not elected.

6. They are remunerated by fixed salaries in money, for the most part with a right to pensions. Only under certain circumstances does the employing authority . . . have a right to terminate the appointment, but the official is always free to resign. The salary scale is primarily graded according to rank in the hierarchy; but in addition to this criterion, the responsibility of the position and the requirements of the incumbent's social status may be taken into account.

7. The office is treated as the sole, or at least the primary occupation of the incumbent.

8. It constitutes a career. There is a system of "promotion" according to seniority or to achievement, or both. Promotion is dependent on the judgment of superiors.

9. The official works entirely separated from ownership of the means of administration and without appropriation of his position.

10. He is subject to strict and systematic discipline and control in the conduct of the offices. (1947, 333–334)

This model describes major aspects of the structure of almost all organizations, and in those cases where it does not, the organizations are generally categorized or specifically recognized by the extent to which their structure varies from the bureaucratic standard. Built into this model is a series of assumptions about the functions of an organization within the larger society, the goals of the organization and where they are established, and the individuals within the organization and how they think and act. For these reasons, the model may be described as "universal," or as an attempt to present facts and relationships that must be understood any time one talks about complex organizations, which has certainly been the case.

Over the last decade, total quality management (TQM) has swept through the business community. As American businesses felt the threat of foreign competition and the pressure for both efficiency and quality, the teachings of the "quality theorists," and especially W. Edwards Deming (1986), have been accepted by an increasing number of organizations and organization/management theorists. It is perhaps unnecessary to give much historical background to this movement; however, TQM is being "borrowed back" by Americans, after having been rejected earlier, and after it was developed and implemented during its first several decades by Japanese businesses.

There is a strong movement to bring TQM into government, with several state and local governments involved and the Federal Quality Institute working with agencies in the federal government. Elements of TQM appear in a variety of critiques of government organizations and operations, including but certainly not limited to Osborne and Gaebler's *Reinventing Government* (1992) and the report of the National Performance Review, *Creating a Government that Works Better & Costs Less* (1993).

Deming (1986) presents fourteen principles for successful total quality management (see Figure 3–1); however, the original principles were developed for manufacturing companies and need to be modified a bit to apply to governmental operations. According to

FIGURE 3–1   Deming's Fourteen Points for Management

1. Create constancy of purpose toward improvement of product and service, with the aim to become competitive and to stay in business, and to provide jobs.

2. Adopt the new philosophy. We are in a new economic age. Western management must awaken to the challenge, must learn their responsibilities, and take on leadership for change.

3. Cease dependence on inspection to achieve quality. Eliminate the need for inspection on a mass basis by building quality into the product in the first place.

4. End the practice of awarding business on the basis of price tag. Instead, minimize total cost. Move toward the single supplier for any one item, on a long-term relationship of loyalty and trust.

5. Improve constantly and forever the system of production and service, to improve quality and productivity, and thus constantly decrease costs.

6. Institute training on the job.

7. Institute leadership. The aim of supervision should be to help people and machines and gadgets to do a better job. Supervision of management is in need of overhaul, as well as supervision of production workers.

8. Drive out fear, so that everyone may work effectively for the company.

9. Break down barriers between departments. People in research, design, sales, and production must work as a team, to foresee problems of production and in use that may be encountered with the product or service.

10. Eliminate slogans, exhortations, and targets for the work force asking for zero defects and new levels of productivity. Such exhortations only create adversarial relationships, as the bulk of the causes of low quality and low productivity belong to the system and thus lie beyond the power of the work force.

11. a. Eliminate work standards (quotas) on the factory floor. Substitute leadership.
    b. Eliminate management by objective. Eliminate management by numbers, numerical goals. Substitute leadership.

12. a. Remove barriers that rob the hourly worker of his right to pride of workmanship. The responsibility of supervisors must be changed from sheer number to quality.
    b. Remove barriers that rob people in management and in engineering of their right to pride of workmanship. This means, *inter alia,* abolishment of the annual or merit rating and of management by objective.

13. Institute a vigorous program of education and self-improvement.

14. Put everybody in the company to work to accomplish the transformation. The transformation is everybody's job.

SOURCE: W. Edwards Deming, *Out of Crisis.* Cambridge, Mass.: Massachusetts Institute of Technology, Center for Advanced Engineering Study, 1986, pp. 23–23.

James E. Swiss (1992), the TQM model for a "successful" government organization includes seven primary tenets:

1. The customer is the ultimate determiner of quality. If the product does not meet the desires of the customers, it is bad quality, no matter how "perfectly" made.

2. Quality should be built into the product early in the production process (upstream) rather than being added on at the end (downstream). Proper early, upstream design

saves later redesigning or reworking and makes customers happier. TQM opposes mass inspections—quality is everyone's task, not someone's at the end of the process.

3. Preventing variability is the key to producing high quality. Quality slips when variation occurs. Therefore, process control charts that track deviation from the optimum are analyzed to prevent deviation in product or service.

4. Quality results from people working within systems, not individual efforts. The system usually creates quality slips, not individual. With committed people working together, it is a mistake to focus on individuals. The system should create intrinsic motivators that lead all workers to perform well.

5. Quality requires continuous improvement of inputs and processes. This continuous improvement should be in processes and inputs—not in outputs (defined as profits).

6. Quality improvement requires strong worker participation. The workers must do it right the first time, so managers and workers must work together "without fear."

7. Quality requires total organizational commitment. Managers must create an organizational culture where everyone focuses on consistently producing quality products and improving them constantly (Swiss, 1992, 357–358).

From these TQM principles comes a universal organizational and managerial model that the authors argue is the structure necessary for success in the competitive environment of capitalist free enterprise. This model, like Weber's, operates from a set of assumptions about the functions of organizations within the larger society, the goals of the organization and where they are established, and the individuals within the organization and how they think and act.

Both the Weberian and the TQM models more specifically address some, and de-emphasize others, of the four perspectives that we suggested are central to the study of public organizations. It is the thesis of this discussion that placing too much emphasis on any one of these perspectives is unproductive, whereas combining them creates a useful picture. After each perspective is examined separately, they must be brought together in a meaningful synthesis.

THE CONTROVERSY AROUND FOUR PERSPECTIVES

Law and Legal Authority

We take it for granted that bureaus operate on a legal basis, or according to the law. We also recognize that the purpose of the bureau is to execute the law. However, we may fail on occasion to recognize that the effort to execute the law according to structures and processes established by law may cause great difficulty for these agencies. The most obvious example of this difficulty is seen in law enforcement's attempt to control organized crime, where the strict limits placed on surveillance and collection of evidence and the broad interpretation of individual rights create problems for the police. Although *police departments* are derided for not doing a better job of controlling organized crime, *police officers* also work under procedural proscriptions, strongly ascribed to by most citizens, that limit their ability to control that crime. Law enforcement must find a way to meet the goals established for it by society while staying within the procedural limits placed on it by that same society.

In a similar vein, it is not uncommon for legislative adversaries, once aware that they cannot block passage of a new program, to attempt to place it in an already existing organization that is inimical or, at best, coldly neutral to that program. Another ploy regularly used by enemies of programs is to create, in the enabling act, procedures or structures that will hobble or make inefficient the delivery of the service or good in the hope that they may reopen the debate about the issue at a later date with "proof" that the decision to create the program was a mistake in the first place because of the problems that have been shown to exist in administering it.

That government and its bureaus should operate according to law is a widespread belief. Even in totalitarian states, the government and its agencies at least pay lip service to this idea and function under a constitution and laws that, though failing to guarantee some of the most important human rights, justify the legality of the imposed order to the citizenry. In our society, those few public organizations that we suspect may not always operate according to the law of the land (the Central Intelligence Agency, for example) cause considerable discomfort to interested observers because such activity, though perhaps necessary, is considered amoral. Even though it is endured, attempts are made to limit the amounts and types of covert activity, and various checks are created to oversee the organizations. As a result, leaders of such organizations sometimes complain of being hamstrung in their operations and of being unable to respond to, or counter, similar organizations elsewhere in the world or, as noted earlier, in organized crime.

The concept of the law as the basis of authority is relatively new in organization life. Authority, according to Max Weber, was based on charisma or tradition at earlier points in history. Although examples of increasing dependence on legal authority can be invoked from earlier times (the Athenian democracy, the Magna Carta, and canon law), the concept became fully developed and widely accepted only during the last few hundred years. Today, however, we take for granted Abraham Lincoln's statement that we have a government of laws, not of men. The public bureaucracy is the administrative or implementation and service arm of government, and it is based on laws. Laws establish the policy direction, or the goals, of bureaus, thereby spelling out what output or results are expected. Likewise, laws define proper organizational structure, due process, reporting procedures, and conflict of interest. In other words, the law clarifies both structural and procedural questions. It even establishes the system by which personnel are selected, rewarded, or punished within the bureau.[2] Public bureaucracy and dependence on the law grew together, as is noted by Herbert Spiro:

> Modern law and modern bureaucracy were created to fill the same needs. On the Continent, especially, the birth and growth of each cannot be conceived of without the other. Administrative law was designed to make responsible conduct possible for the ruler's new instruments, the bureaucrats, by giving them reasonable expectations of the probable consequences of their acts. . . . In the days of the youth of modern bureaucracy, the bureaucrat's accountability normally stood in fair proportion to his causal responsibility. He knew the extent of his accountability, i.e., it was explicit. What he should or should not do, and how he should go about his tasks, were laid down for him with greater exactness perhaps than for anyone else who acts politically. The statutes creating or regularizing his position told him from the outset what would happen to him if he committed "nonfeasance, malfeasance, or overfeasance." (1969, 86–87)

---

[2]Although the laws specify all the elements of organization mentioned here, it must be understood that the elements may not, indeed cannot, be complete, concise, and clear in many if not most cases.

The centrality of law and the concomitant responsibility for the execution of the law required the development of the modern public bureau. This is especially true if it is assumed that bureaus should *react to and fulfill* citizen desires and demands rather than *create* social objectives because the bureaucracy is geared toward objectivity, independence from personal pressure, and control over discretionary actions by bureaucrats. Looking back at Max Weber's model of bureaucracy, or at his description of the internal characteristics of bureaucratic organizations, one can see how these characteristics help guarantee that public agencies will "automatically" obey the law.

Weber argues that organizations of this type exist in both the private and public sectors—and this is certainly true; however, public organizations probably tend to match this model more closely than private ones. In the first place, public agencies, having been established by the legislature to achieve certain objectives through specified processes—all spelled out by the law—are creatures of the law.

A second aspect of the relationship between the law and bureaucracy becomes overwhelmingly apparent as we look at Weber's model and the ways in which it guarantees that the law will be the basis for bureau action. By examining Weber's criteria, we can clarify the way in which the bureaucratic system guarantees an inordinate focus by public employees on the law. Central to this point is the fact that each office has a clearly defined sphere of competence (criterion 3). And where is that sphere defined? In the law—if not in the enabling act, then in the rules, regulations, and other materials that are based on and interpret the inert law as it is put into action. Note also that bureaucratic officials are subject to authority only when it applies to their offices (criterion 1), these offices are at least their primary occupation (criterion 7), and the officials are entirely separated from ownership (criterion 9). These factors limit the possibility of conflict of interest; thus, employees of bureaus are under no other pressure except to know and obey the law. Furthermore, the fact that positions in the bureaucracy are filled by free contractual relationships (criterion 4) after being selected on the basis of technical qualifications (criterion 5) and are then paid fixed salaries in money (criterion 6) guarantees their loyalty. The officials are not forced to participate, and their rewards are fixed; therefore, no *person* has an undue claim on their services. They are not distracted by personal claims from the objective administration of the law. Finally, the hierarchical structure of offices (criterion 2) and the natural desire to advance in a career (criterion 8) mean that all officials are held accountable for their actions. Strict accountability breeds close adherence to the law, and deductive rules and rigorous control are the major objects of design and management.

What attention do the developers of total quality management pay to the law as they present their model for the successful business organization? Almost none. No time is spent in spelling out what the law says about the involved organization. It is assumed that the business will operate within the general parameters established by society (apparently an increasingly risky assumption) and that is all that matters. No further comment on the law is required.

Within the public sector, adherence to the law is central to all activities. Accountability and control, especially as spelled out in the law, are ensured by the structure of organizations. Structure, as portrayed in the organizational chart, is the formal aspect of organizational life, and if the chief executive or an external body such as the legislature wishes to have an impact on the operation of an agency, the primary line of attack is through changes in the law that force reorganization. Likewise, the easiest and most direct way for top officials to make an imprint on their agencies is through reorganization. The result is instantaneous and visual, whereas attempts to influence the informal portion of a bureau take an indeterminate amount of time and often cannot be concretely measured. Nor are these officials often able to get the enabling law changed to accomplish the shift in agency direction that they would like. In addition, appointed officials, bringing with them a portfolio of experience from their prior positions (often from the private sector), are convinced that by restructuring the bureau they can increase the efficiency and effectiveness of the public agency. Such changes and "improvements" always appear, ultimately, in formal rules and regulations or some similar "lawlike" format.

Interest in the effect of organizational structure on the success of public organizations as executors of law actually existed before the time of Max Weber, but no one had formalized the theory. Apparently, the structure of the governmental bureaucracy was not an issue of importance to the framers of the Constitution (Wilson 1887); little mention is made of such factors in records of the day, including the record of debates at the Constitutional Convention or the explanatory and laudatory *Federalist Papers* (Rossiter 1961). However, though the founders may not have recognized it, the civil service reformers who became active in the second half of the nineteenth century did. They argued that in order to improve the efficiency and effectiveness of government, a structural change was needed in public organizations and that such change had to occur through the establishment of law (the Civil Service Act and similar reform legislation). Interest in the public sector can then be traced through a series of reorganization commissions (the Brownlow Commission, the first and second Hoover Commissions, the National Productivity Commission/Gore Report), each of which led to new laws and, in some cases, to the reduction of laws and regulations.

Efficiency and Rationality

The principles of efficiency and rationality are grouped together here because many social theorists, especially during the first third of the twentieth century, used the terms almost interchangeably. Whether they realized the synonymity of the two concepts is unclear, but their recognition, or lack thereof, is not important to the major thrust of our argument. In the interest of clarity, we will first discuss the two principles separately. Then we will point out how they overlap.

Efficiency

In its simplest sense, efficiency equals maximization of productivity, or the greatest possible output for the least input. The founders of this school of administrative study came from both industry and public administration, with their ideas being adapted in both sectors. Let us look at the two approaches to this principle and then note the common assumptions from which the founders operated.

Frederick Taylor was interested in increasing productivity because everybody benefited from the result:

> It is perfectly clear that the greatest permanent prosperity for the workman, coupled with the greatest prosperity for the employer, can be brought about only when the work of the

establishment is done with the smallest combined expenditure of human effort, plus nature's resources, plus the cost for the use of capital in the shape of machines, buildings,
etc. (1947, 11)

Productivity was achieved by applying Taylor's interpretation of the scientific method to
the man–machine system in industry. Since little had been done up to that time by way
of systematically examining how men and machines interacted as a single task or process
(series of tasks) was carried out, Taylor zeroed in on this most obvious factor.

Industry had moved from the production of goods by tradespeople who made complete
items to production by specialization where items were produced by a combination of
machines and workers, each of whom performed part of a complex process that yielded
finished items more rapidly and in a more standardized form. The specialization occurred
somewhat randomly, however, and no careful scientific analysis of how jobs were done
was carried out. Machines were responsible for much of the improvement in productivity;
they would continue to account for much of the improvement because there appeared at
that time to be an almost infinite potential for technical development. However, little effort
went into examining how the weak link in the system—man—could be made to operate
more efficiently, either in conjunction with the machines he operated or in those jobs that
tended to require his attention without the aid of technology (because it either was not
appropriate to the job or was not yet developed).

Taylor's approach to the study of work soon became known as scientific management.
He best defines the central concepts of this approach at the end of his treatise when he
says that:

> It is no single element, but rather [a] combination, that constitutes scientific management,
> which may be summarized as:
> Science, not rule of thumb.
> Harmony, not discord.
> Cooperation, not individualism.
> Maximum output, in place of restricted output.
> The development of each man to his greatest efficiency and prosperity. (1947, 141)

By using his version of the scientific method, Taylor was convinced that it was possible
to discover the "one best way" to structure any job or process. With the discovery of the
one best way, the principle of efficiency was realized.

Another group of individuals was attempting to apply scientific principles to administration, which Luther Gulick defined as "the phenomena of getting things done through
cooperative human endeavor" (1937). Whereas politics is concerned with the process of
getting elected to office and setting objectives for the country, Gulick argues that "administration has to do with getting things done; with the accomplishment of defined objectives"
(1937, 191). If administration is removed from the value-laden field of politics, then a
science of administration becomes possible:

> In the science of administration, whether public or private, the basic "good" is efficiency.
> The fundamental objective of the science of administration is the accomplishment of the
> work in hand with the least expenditure of man-power and materials. Efficiency is axiom
> number one in the value scale of administration. (1937, 192)

The way to achieve that efficiency is by "scientifically" examining the structure of organizations, and this is what is done throughout Gulick and Urwick's *Papers*. Questions such
as what is the proper span of control for a supervisor, what should be the basis for as-

signing supervisors over workers, and what principles should control the division, or structure, of large organizations are analyzed throughout the book in one of the first attempts to find the "one best way" to structure organizations to guarantee efficiency in both administration and production of goods or services.

The followers of Taylor, Gulick, and the other expounders of the principle of efficiency are legion (including the proponents of TQM). Industrial engineering, which has as its goal improvement in efficiency and productivity, traces its beginning in the United States directly to Frederick Taylor (1911). Although the techniques that are used have become more sophisticated, industrial engineers still accept the basic premises postulated by Taylor at the turn of the century. Likewise, many current students of workflow and office design are convinced that there is one best way to establish the physical layout of a workplace so that all the tasks can be completed with optimum efficiency. On a larger scale, information scientists are striving to achieve the greatest possible efficiency in the flow, impact, and use of information; this requires an acceptance of the idea that there is, if not one best way, at least an optimal way to structure both organizations and information systems. The principle of efficiency lives on.

Rationality

The principle of rationality was accepted as an undisputed law by all the writers mentioned. When Weber defines the phenomenon that he calls bureaucracy, he is simply describing the organizational construct that has been established to guarantee rationality. Taylor, Gulick, Urwick, and the other proponents of scientific management and scientific administration prescribe rational procedures and structures. Both groups, whether descriptive or prescriptive, accept the idea that what organizations seek and need is rationality. Rationality (the quality or state of having or being based on reason) is central to all organizations in our modern, technological, interdependent world. Nowhere is this idea more alluring than in the public sector because of the government's influence on all of society.

However, these theorists are over simplistic in their definition and perception of essential elements. This simplicity is best understood by examining the term *rationality* and by recognizing the narrowness of their definition as opposed to the complexity that exists when a full explication of the concept is given.

First, there are two levels of rationality: substantive and instrumental (Weber 1947). Substantive rationality is concerned with the ends that an organization attempts to achieve—what are the right, appropriate, or best goals to be sought? Instrumental rationality is concerned not with ends, but means, or *how* an organization attempts to achieve a given end or set of ends. The two levels are both essential, but the types of logic and analytic tools that are involved differ dramatically. Second, Paul Diesing (1962) defines five types of rationality that currently exist in our society: technical, economic, social, legal, and political. He discusses the social conditions in which they exist, conditions that, as Diesing points out, they partially help create. Careful consideration leads to even more "rational systems" based on other premises (axioms) commonly accepted by major active sectors of society. For example, the major religious groups in our society have their own "rationalities" that determine both the substantive and instrumental decisions of their organizations.

Weber recognizes the need for rationality as one of the central causes for the development of bureaucracy. Bureaucracy is a necessary result of the development of modern technology, with its incredible level of interdependence among all parts of society. Technological interdependence creates a requirement for stable, strict, intensive, and calculable interactions, and "it [bureaucracy] is superior to any other form [of organization] in precision, in stability, in the stringency of its discipline, and in its reliability" (Weber, 1947, 339). Like them or not, bureaucracies are rational, and since that principle is central to our lives, bureaucracies will continue to exist until a form of organization is discovered that improves on the delivery of this particular characteristic. All this discussion, however, focuses on instrumental rationality—getting things done efficiently—rather than on "what should be done," which is determined by the superior powers (the legislature, courts, and so on) outside the bureaucracy. This is especially true in the public sector.

On the other hand, students of scientific management and administration prescribe rationality rather than describe it. It is significant that Gulick referred to efficiency as "axiom number one in *the value scale* of administration" (emphasis added). The use of the term *axiom* was not accidental. Axioms are a part of science and these people believed that by building a full set of axioms, or propositions regarded as self-evident truth, administration could become a part of science just as geometry became a part of mathematics. The axioms that were sought by the scientific administration group were related to the structures of organizations as those structures related to the functions of administration—or as Gulick referred to them, the functions of the chief executive—because all administrators simply fulfilled roles and exercised the powers delegated to them by the chief executive, either directly or indirectly. Through the use of axioms and rationality, many important problems could be solved by finding the one best way to organize, and the one best way was considered the most efficient way (a value judgment). A similar type of logic applied to the followers of Taylor.

The model presented by those advocating TQM also accepts much of the scientific management philosophy of Taylor; in their case, scientific methods are used to monitor performance and to identify points of high leverage for performance improvement. "TQM practitioners are expected to focus their attention on work processes rather than on outcome measures and to use scientific methods to improve those processes continuously" (Hackman and Wageman 1995, 325). Thus, although there is continuous improvement in performance, there is a "one best process" at any moment, arrived at rationally by teams of workers and managers through use of the scientific tools at their disposal, and it is to be followed by workers.

The goals behind this rational approach to work procedures ultimately do have a specific meaning for business organizations—a very special definition of rationality and efficiency—a "bottom-line" definition that says rationality and efficiency are measured by how successful the organization is in achieving the goals of profit, size, and growth. Although there is a strong argument against short-term measurement of these goals, they still exist over the long term, and the success of the TQM exercise is measured by the "strength" of the corporation within the total market.

Substantive rationality plays a role in the internal decision-making process in the private sector—corporations do care about what they make and what affect their product has on society; however, the decisions about "what ought to be" are biased by the basic assumptions about the goals of businesses. If the product makes a profit and it is not illegal, then it is okay to carry on that activity, maximize productivity, and reap the available profit. Such ends are usually not appropriate for the public manager. There may be a vociferous debate about the impact of alcohol and tobacco products on the society at large, but perfectly legitimate businesses will continue to make those products until they are specifically banned from doing so. Public agencies generally cannot be involved in such debatable activities unless there is believed to be a need for the activity despite its questionableness, and then the goals of the operations are specifically stated, and procedures are stringently regulated.

In order to achieve the bottom-line success that is assumed to be the goal of all organizations, TQM advocates accept structures and procedures that would be highly questionable in the public sector. For example, they argue that it is rational to break the employees of the corporation into small, independent teams (under management direction) to examine the work being done and to make changes once agreement is achieved on optimum procedures. This step, of course, accepts the basic tenet that the organization should cater to its customers. Both of these eminently rational suggestions for corporations may raise howls of protest if implemented by many of their public counterparts (Swiss 1992). It can also be suggested to private managers that they remain in the business the company knows best and that the administrative structure be kept lean and simple (Peters and Waterman 1982). Such a focus on quality often leads to success and growth for a private company.

However, public managers often do not have the luxury of deciding such matters; therefore, such advice may very well be useless to them. The public served, and the services to be rendered, are often decided before the public manager begins to get involved in the decision-making process. Rago (1994) also points out that public agencies often pay a price for being successful:

> Many companies in the industrial sector undertake TQM to improve their bottom lines by increasing market share by improving quality. Increased market share means new customers and new revenues. Conceivably, increased revenue enables companies to hire employees and purchase equipment as necessary to ensure that supply keeps up with demand. In many government service organizations, the order of business is opposite that of industry. That is, the more customers the organization has the less money is available to provide the service.
>
> As the government service organization gains efficiency in the delivery of services as a result of TQM, it expands its customer base by providing services to those citizens who needed services but who were too far down on the waiting list to obtain them. Typically, this expansion occurs without a correlated expansion in revenue. (63–64)

Public administrators may focus on process and improve it dramatically,[3] but that does not guarantee more resources or more satisfaction from "customers." Still procedural efficiency and rationality are the goals of TQM, and these two terms continue to dominate public organization debate even when in new rhetorical clothing.

---

[3]TQM assumes top management support, but political officials operate under a different concept of rationality than do business officials (see the section in this chapter on "Politics and Power"). TQM focuses, ultimately, on economic factors—in the long term, businesses increase profits or gain a larger segment of the market. Public officials focus on the short term—the next election. They must get reelected, or the politician who appointed them must. There are few incentives for public officials to focus on management. For example, Joseph Sensenbrenner, the mayor of Madison, Wisconsin, and a public official who was committed to TQM in the 1980s, enumerates the tremendous gains made in efficiency within the city. It gained him accolades from across the nation, "But this recognition was not enough to win me a fourth term. Other political factors were more compelling" (1991, 75).

Rationality-efficiency

By closely examining the two approaches to organization theory, and by probing for the more basic assumptions on which the approaches are built, it becomes clear that though different terms are used, they are used in almost identical ways. TQM searches for efficiency in procedures and uses scientific methods to achieve the one current best way of production. Other theorists—Weber, Taylor, Gulick, and others—consider only the instrumental level of rationality, and they define rationality and efficiency identically. According to these theorists, "The efficient achievement of a single goal is technical rationality (Taylor), the maximum achievement of a plurality of goals is economic rationality (Gulick; Weber), and no other types of rationality are admitted" (Diesing 1962, 1). Substantive rationality is irrelevant; goals are established somewhere outside the organization or the part of the organization being considered. Technical rationality, as developed by Taylor, was specifically geared toward increased output for the same amount of input; that equals efficiency. Gulick, Urwick, and the others who were scientifically examining administration were interested in *efficient* organization or structures that maximized the managerial functions; good management guaranteed efficiency in operation and maximum return for tax dollars spent. Weber argues throughout his writing that technical efficiency, a term he uses interchangeably with rationality, is the major benefit to be gained from bureaucracy and the reason that bureaucracy developed in the first place.

The issues of rationality, efficiency, or both, if they are in fact the same, are of great importance in the study of public organizations. Attempts to achieve rationality and efficiency must not be downplayed. However, focusing on such concepts inspires us to ask only some of the vital questions, and our horizons must expand, even when we are considering the place of reason or rationality in organizations. Both levels of rationality, and at least the five types of reason mentioned by Diesing, are required to understand or operate in a public organization.

Psychology and Social Relations

Interest in the social relations of organizations developed in part as a reaction to the formalistic approaches emphasized by the early students of management and organization and in part as the logical evolution of interest or curiosity by those who desired to examine all aspects of organizational life. The reaction to the formal emphasis and the ensuing recognition of the fact that informal relations within an organization are equal in importance to the structures and processes established by law or in writing occurred for at least three reasons. Some manager/scholars such as Chester Barnard (1938) began to point out that both a formal and an informal life existed side by side, if not intertwined, in the structure and functions of any organization, and that both aspects of organizational life had to be considered. At the same time, some of the programs attempting to reach the goals of increased productivity and rationality did not achieve the expected results (for example, the Hawthorne experiments, Roethlisberger and Dickson 1939). At least part of the reason for the failure of such efforts was the fact that after a certain point in the development of productivity programs and increasing rationality in structures, the individuals operating in the organizations began to resist further change. To comprehend the attitudes and reactions of employees, it became important to focus on both the individuals and groups in the organizations and how they interacted outside the formal structures and procedures. Finally, with the developing interest and skill in testing and evaluation of individuals, and to a certain extent groups, which was hastened and increased by the coming of World War II, it became obvious that the informal side of organization theory added a great deal to our knowledge about the total field.

The interest in the informal aspects of organization led to two major categories of theories: (1) those dealing predominantly with individuals and (2) those concerned with groups. The first can be considered the psychological approach and the second the sociological approach. Each obviously deals with an important aspect of the organization, and each has presented us with theories that try to explain and predict what has happened or will happen in organizations as different elements change. After examining both types of theories, we will go one step further and note how, by combining the two, a third level of theory appears that adds even more to our understanding.

Focus on Individual Behavior (the Psychological Approach)

The focus on individual behavior is, in many ways, a continuation of the interests noted by Frederick Taylor as he emphasized the study of individual jobs and how the "man–machine system" could be made to function more efficiently. However, the new focus on the individual recognized an aspect of human nature that Taylor tended to overlook even though students of psychology were emphasizing it. At the same time that Taylor was expounding on the principles of scientific management (which, in part, accepted as its basis the rationality of man), Walter Dill Scott, a psychology professor at Northwestern University, was arguing that man was not fundamentally a reasoning creature. Scott argued that the power of suggestion was very important in influencing human decisions and that it was therefore essential to study individuals for the purpose of understanding their personal makeup, which might, in turn, influence their habits.

The importance of examining the individual's skills and aptitudes (issues also important to Taylor) is recognized by everyone, but equally important is the study of individual traits and attitudes, with the second gaining major impetus from the "surprises" at Hawthorne. Central to the examination of individual skills and aptitudes is the area of testing and measurement. Personnel selection, for instance, has been one of the principle areas of interest to industrial and organizational psychologists since the field's earliest days. The goal of those involved in testing and measurement is to choose, from a larger group, the best individual or group of individuals to fill positions within an organization. These decisions are frequently based on tests that purport to measure one's ability to perform specified mental or physical tasks and to measure attitudes and personality traits or attributes that are believed to predict future success on the job. With the evolution of demands for equal employment opportunity, this field in the study of individual behavior has come under increased scrutiny and attack.[4] In this area, psychologists cannot lose for winning even though they cannot win for losing: The more tests—usually prepared with the help of psychologists—are challenged, the greater the demand for psychologists skilled in test validation to examine the testing procedures.

---

[4]In the public sector, an examination of the testing and selection process for either police or fire department employees will serve as a fine example of the development of, the complexity of, and the challenge to, the idea of tests and measurement as the chief tool for decisions about hiring.

Central to this issue is a series of questions, a sample of which are: What is the impact of the civil service system on recruiting top-notch individuals and then motivating them to do good work? How do bureau structures affect communication, decision making, and other functions? How do people interact with the new technologies being introduced into bureaus? Organization structure, job design, and even the physical layout of offices have an impact on the way that individuals interact and carry out their tasks. All these factors then must be considered as organizational managers decide what is appropriate job preparation for applicants, and, for those already in the bureau, what kinds of preparation, training, and knowledge and skills are required for the new jobs being created by technological change or for promotion to higher positions.

The researchers at the Hawthorne experiments, who set out to examine the impact of the immediate physical surrounding on worker productivity, came to the conclusion that one of the most important factors influencing individual behavior was the morale or motivation of the subject workers; in other words, the most important factor influencing the workers was not the physical environment, but the attitudes that resulted from the workers seeing themselves as important to the ongoing experiment. Even though the Hawthorne research is methodologically suspect in retrospect (Carey 1967; Roethlisberger 1941), it started a line of inquiry that continues today. In the ensuing decades, a variety of theories about motivation and the impact of motivation on productivity have been developed. Indeed, a great deal of work continues in this area and is the theme of a later chapter. The relationships between job satisfaction, material rewards, productivity, the physical and psychic environment of work, and numerous other factors associated with individual attitudes have been found to be correlated with the success of organizations, but in varying ways and degrees. In addition, the unique aspects of public organization environments create peculiar challenges for those interested in this sector of society.

The focus on the individual extends to the examination of the functions or processes of organizations. The functions of management are described in numerous ways, but however described, it is essential that one understand how an individual thinks, acts, and reacts to the various stimuli that constantly bombard him or her. When a public official, whether Attorney General Janet Reno or City Auditor Henry Smith, has to make decisions, he or she normally goes through a series of steps, and a variety of individual factors determine how he or she sees the problem, what alternatives are possible, which ones are acceptable, and which one is ultimately chosen. These and other issues are examined by psychologists, economists, decision scientists, and others. Indeed, Herbert Simon, whose intellectual roots are in public administration, has been awarded the Nobel Prize in Economics because of his work in decision theory which, in part and in a very sophisticated way, deals with the issues just noted. The role of the individual in other management activities, such as communication, coordination, planning, and objective setting, also plays an important part in the theory of the individual in the organization.

Finally, the study of leadership focuses much attention on the individual; considerable effort has gone into the attempt to discover the personality characteristics or traits of leaders. Do individuals who become leaders have certain traits in common? Are certain traits always necessary in particular types of situations? These and similar questions are examined by students of leadership. When one examines history, it appears that some individuals were destined to become leaders, whereas others would never have risen to the top, no matter how hard they tried. This phenomenon has piqued the interest of all those who examine the leadership role.

Focus on Group Behavior (the Sociological Approach)

The common thread in every preceding case is the researchers' interest in the individual. A parallel interest exists in the role of the group and how it affects and is affected by the organization. The informal organization, which comprises groups that form outside or despite the formal structure, plays a significant part in determining the perceptions and attitudes of group members, as well as in establishing the values and norms of behavior. One of the early discussants of the importance of the informal aspects of organization was Chester Barnard (1938), who argued that informal organization preceded the formal in existence. Barnard also pointed out that each type of organization needed the other if both were to continue existing for a significant time because each fulfilled functions that could not be accomplished by the other.

Of course, the recognition of the importance of informal groups meant that a new fact of organization life had to be examined if we were to be fully cognizant of *all* the forces that influence organizations. The most inclusive term for this study is *group dynamics,* which is defined by Cartwright and Zander as "a field of inquiry dedicated to achieving knowledge about the nature of groups, the laws of their development, and their interrelations with individuals, other groups, and larger institutions" (1968, 4). From this research came numerous explanations of and theories about group behavior.

Of special interest is the recognition of the importance of informal groups in establishing values, norms, roles, and status. *Values,* the ideas that are considered to have intrinsic worth or desirability and that are the basic standards and principles that guide action, are greatly influenced by groups (Gortner, 1994). Individuals do not create their values in a vacuum; instead, values are developed in a group context. Thus, the result is inevitably different from what it would be if an individual did not interact with numerous groups of varying persuasions. *Norms,* the social rules or authoritative standards or patterns against which attitudes and behavior can be measured, are directly related to group interactions. Without groups, norms could not be developed. *Roles,* the behavior that is expected from an individual by the others in the group, are assigned to the person or position by the other group members. Although a formal role may be spelled out by the official organizational chart, job description, and official pronouncements, there is just as assuredly an informal role established by the group or groups with which the individual interacts and the two roles may or may not coincide. Likewise, groups develop roles that they play in the larger institutional setting and that develop both formally and informally. Finally, the whole idea of *status,* one's position or rank in relation to others, is again possible only as a concept in a group setting.

These and other similar concepts help describe the workings of the informal side of an organization, which is essential since it has become apparent that formal structures and processes are always matched by informal systems. When, for example, an agency establishes a hierarchy that spells out who an employee is to seek help from and who is to evaluate that employee's work (usually an "immediate supervisor"), a second system develops that allows an employee to go to selected peers for help and advice—usually people with recognized expertise (Blau 1955). Peer evaluations of work performance are often considered just as important as or more important than the opinions of the boss. This type of informal structure is apparent in a factory setting or a government office and is a key element in such matters as job satisfaction and morale, as well as efficiency and productivity. These kinds of factors are especially important for public managers because of the limitations placed on them by formal rules and regulations. One of the ways that public managers can motivate their employees is by using the informal system that exists in every agency to foster esprit de corps and reinforce appropriate behavior.

The recognition of this "group" side of organizational life led to the development of the Human Relations School, which emphasizes the importance of employee morale in productivity. The keynote theme of the school is that successful organizations generally have satisfied employees, or employees who are happy with and challenged by the organization's environment. The applied approach to the field is organization development (OD), in which behavioral scientists use the findings about organizational culture in an attempt to make changes so that bureaus will be "better" (more satisfying) places to work and more effective in serving the public. Behind the theories of OD lie a complex set of values that can only be summarized here by using Robert Simmons's phrase, "humane organization," about which he says:

> The first essential step in provisioning humane organization is to confront the full meaning of groups, organizations and bureaucracies in the context and fabric of our political, social and personal lives. . . . The attainment of humane bureaucratic organizations is crucial for the full achievement of human dignity in industrial urban society. The social "payoff" is creative and producing human beings fulfilling their own capabilities, contributing to stable social institutions, and challenging the unknown horizons of human existence and understanding. (1981, 241)

Closely related to the idea of organization culture and its impact is the understanding of leadership in the group context. Success in changing the attitudes and habits of individuals and groups usually depends on the commitment of the leaders: If they support change, it has a chance; if they do not support change, it probably will not occur. The relationship between groups and their leaders has become an increasingly important aspect of organization theory. Social exchange theory, for example, bases leadership effectiveness in a group not on formal position, but on the benefits the leader can generate for the group in return for his or her acceptance in the position (Jacobs 1971). In other words, leadership is a role or position granted by the group in exchange for services rendered. This and other similar theories point out the difference between management and leadership, the first being based on one's position in the bureaucratic hierarchy and the second on power relationships in a social situation (French and Raven 1958).

Group behavior is also a major focus when examining the processes of organizations. Much effort has gone into noting how decisions are influenced by groups. Irving Janis (1972), for example, has looked at what he refers to as the dangers of groupthink, whereas other students of decision making, attempting to find productive ways to use groups, have promoted the use of group decision-making techniques, such as synectics, brainstorming, and Delphi. Likewise, all the processes (POSDCORB) discussed by Gulick (1937) or other writers about public management have a group aspect to them. Only by understanding the group aspects of these processes can anyone claim to be knowledgeable about the theory of organizations or about how to apply that theory to group management.

Combining the Individual and the Group

Our understanding of organizations increases immensely by examining the individual or the group and how he or she or they interact with the organization. Perhaps even greater progress has been made by combining the various theories into a more comprehensive network. When one looks at theories about individuals in organizations, then adds the element of individuals in informal groupings that also are operating within the formal organization, and finally recognizes that the formal organizations themselves operate in larger environments where each organization may be thought of as an individual within the larger system, the complexity of organization theory is brought home rather forcefully. The results of such a "Weltanschauung" create an incredibly rich tapestry that allows great detail to be developed at multiple levels. It also enables one to see the interrelationships between numerous factors that, when considered singly, do not provide an appropriate or adequate explanation for how or why they occur.

In looking back at the two models presented at the beginning of the chapter, we find that Weber seems to separate consideration of the individual and the group (although he docs look at both). This separation occurs because of the strictly formal view he takes of bureaucracy. Social relations—at least the formal ones—within the bureau are spelled out by the criteria of each job and the structure of the organization, whereas the informal side of the organization is ignored.

On the other hand, advocates of TQM take a broader view of both individuals and organizations that recognizes both formal and informal relationships. They encourage a formal structure that serves as the instigator and modulator of group process—both formal and informal—that flourishes as work teams focus on production processes. Management's job is to guarantee that the total organization, formal and informal, is focused on the major value of the firm (which is to guarantee satisfied customers). By recognizing that productivity occurs through people, this model emphasizes the importance of motivating employees. Demming, Juran, and the others recognize that a broad and multifaceted view of the psychological and social principles operating in any organization is necessary. The problem becomes one of figuring out what parts of their ideas can be applied in the public sector and how, and then using them.

A good example of this more inclusive approach to organization theory is presented in the systems theories of Kenneth Boulding (1956), an economist, and Talcott Parsons, a sociologist. Parsons, for example, argues that:

> Like any social system, an organization is conceived as having a describable structure. This can be described and analyzed from two points of view, both of which are essential to completeness. The first is the "cultural/institutional" point of view which uses the values of the system and their institutionalization in different functional contexts as its point of departure; the second is the "group" or "role" point of view which takes suborganizations and the roles of individuals participating in the functioning of the organization as its point of departure. (1956, 67)

Other scholars, notably March and Simon (1993), Katz and Kahn (1982), and Thompson (1967) also use the systems approach in their consideration of complex organizations.

Finally, the much-touted area of "organization development" is based on an attempt to apply all the theories in a way that will open communication channels, increase trust, and create a more democratic environment in organizations. Although there is a fierce debate about the feasibility and propriety of the objectives and about the methods used to achieve them, the debate is one that includes all the various aspects of organization theory. In a similar manner, TQM includes a broad interpretation of organization theory—that sometimes disagrees with commonly held ideas about motivation and reward, for example—and attempts to maximize quality in performance through the combination of human understanding and scientific methods. Therefore, these theories about organizational change and improvement encourage a scope of integration that is beneficial to those wishing to improve their understanding of how public bureaus work, regardless of what happens to the ideas generating the debate.

Politics and Power

Public organizations, which we refer to as bureaus, are unlike most others in one important way: The difference is the political setting in which public organizations function. In this area, most of the generic or universal models have failed; they simply do not deal with the issue of politics, and they interpret power as an internal phenomenon usually related to the area of leadership. Weber, when describing bureaucracy, spends little time in discussing power, and to the extent that he does discuss it, internal power relations are defined by the law and its formal interpretation in the hierarchy and in individual spheres of competence. Ultimate power and the relationship of each bureau with the others in society are determined either totally outside the organization or are considered by only those few in formal positions at the top of the hierarchy where such matters fall within their sphere of competence.

The adherents of TQM also ignore the subject of power and politics. Power relationships within the corporation remain basically the top-down system traditional to American industry. Since "quality is ultimately a management responsibility . . . attempts to improve quality must begin at the top" (Hackman and Wageman 1995, 315). The success or failure of the TQM program depends on the wholistic implementation of the principles noted earlier, and this implementation is seen as an internal process. Nothing is said about the political environment within which the organization operates.[5]

Public employees operating at lower levels of bureaus, especially those in nonboundary-spanning positions, may not recognize or care much about the political environment because the way they work may be somewhat similar to the way an employee in the private sector works. However, when one examines positions at higher levels of the bureau, or when the behavior of the public organization as an entity is the focus of attention, the political environment becomes an essential element in the equation. In this case, it is necessary to note the development of theories related to political values and power, which in turn have an impact on resource distribution, coalition building, and political goal setting

---

[5]Private organizations also must pay attention to the political setting. An example that shows the difficulty that may be caused when two sociopolitical systems are involved is the case of international corporations giving bribes to government officials in foreign countries to gain contracts. Such behavior is a common practice in some countries, but the practice—even though taking place in another country and in an environment that accepts the behavior—causes an uproar in the United States and has been declared illegal by law. Businesspeople, therefore, must be politically sensitive and astute in their actions. Industries that are regulated by government or that depend on government for much of their business are naturally much more cognizant of the principles of politics and power; however, these are generally seen as external factors, only peripherally affecting internal operations. Review the discussion of the political environment of bureaus in the last chapter.

and decision making. A grasp of these theories is essential to an understanding of the political factors that profoundly influence public organization.

The oldest of the continuous studies of politics—political philosophy—has much to say that is relevant to students of organizations. Herbert Kaufman (1960) points out that organization theory and political theory have produced findings and inferences that are "closely parallel in many important respects." (See Reading 3–1 at the end of this chapter.) The values espoused by the political system also have a dramatic impact on the way that bureaus' structures actually operate. Basic premises about the state and the citizen vary significantly depending on whether organizations with identical structures are located in an authoritarian-communist state, an authoritarian-fascist state, a democratic-socialist state, or a democratic-capitalist state because their objectives will operate quite differently.

Just as one must consider political philosophy when examining public organizations, so must one look at the "culture" of government. Included in culture are such factors as (1) the history of government, or how it developed; (2) the role of government as perceived by members of society; (3) the structures and processes considered proper to government; and (4) the values, mores, and habits of the primary actors, especially the elected and appointed officials and the bureaucrats working beneath those officials. All these factors help "define reality" for public officials, employees, and the organizations they represent. Even relatively small differences in political culture may create important variations in the way bureaucrats perceive the world and the way they operate in it.

The impact of political culture on perceptions and actions can be seen by comparing the views toward the civil service in Canada and the United States. Even though Canada and the United States both have a representative democratic form of government, a history that is predominantly related to Great Britain, and much in the way of a common cultural heritage, the structures and practices of the two governments vary substantially. It is doubtful that two geographically contiguous countries anywhere else in the world are so culturally alike, but there are still major misunderstandings (or a lack of understanding) between the two governments and the people who work in them. For example, when one of the authors spoke with Canadian civil servants who were attending an international conference on the future of public administration held in Quebec City during 1979, the Canadians were mystified by the strict enforcement of the Hatch Act, which limits political activities of federal employees in the United States. Canadian civil servants simply could not understand the necessity of such strict adherence to the act by their southern counterparts. In Canada, despite the clear prohibition of political activity in Section 32 of the Public Service Employment Act:

> Federal employees are in practice much more active than the Act allows. Yet, complaints about the political activity of public servants have been negligible. The political parties seem to have adopted an informal "live and let live" arrangement whereby no party complains about political activity by public servants. (Kernaghan 1975, 29)

If such differences exist in perceptions about what is necessary legal protection and proscription for public employees and the way those proscriptions are administered, it is obvious that the way public servants operate within the bureaucracy will also differ.

Likewise, political culture plays a major role in attempts to resolve the problem of acid rain in the northeastern United States and eastern Canada. While Canadian officials urge the United States to take firmer action against the industrial air pollution that is responsible for a major portion of the problem, members of the U.S. Congress bitterly complain that Canada should go home and strengthen its own laws. One of the major causes of this controversy is the different ways in which government agencies are expected to behave as they enforce laws. In the United States, government agencies are expected to enforce rules to the letter of the law, but no more,[6] and even then they are often opposed, often in the courts, by private corporations that, for whatever reason, wish to drag their feet concerning compliance. On the other hand, Canadian officials argue that their government agencies tend to operate in such cases through persuasion and gentlemen's agreements, and that, therefore, the overall level of compliance with air-pollution abatement goals is superior in Canada. Needless to say, the U.S. congressmen are hard to convince. Much of the difficulty here is not related to the blindness of political expediency; it is simply hard for U.S. legislators to believe that attitudes toward the legitimacy of government regulation vary that much and, therefore, that organizations can operate that differently on opposite sides of an arbitrary line on a map. To understand the relevant public agencies, their objectives, and their processes, it is necessary to understand the political culture in which they operate.

Political culture may lead to results that are the opposite of the objectives stated in the law. Weisband and Franck (1975) note that top officials in the United States are guaranteed by the Constitution the right to resign and use whatever nonclassified information is available to them to fight policies proposed by the president if they are convinced those policies are wrong. On the other hand, in Great Britain, cabinet officials operate without a formal guarantee of protection if they release information that is damaging to the government. However, in almost every case, officials in the United States resign quietly, without taking up the battle against the policy that caused them to resign. In the few cases where these officials have protested publicly, they have tended to be viciously attacked and their public careers ruined, if not their private careers as well. In Great Britain, on several occasions where officials not only resigned but also released information damaging to the government's cause, the officials were not punished for the infraction, and in fact, they often found themselves at a later date holding equal or higher posts in the cabinet (Weisband and Franck 1975, 95–98). By looking only at the law or the formal rules and by not understanding the structural and cultural context in which the law and the relevant public organization operates, an observer would be totally bewildered.

The culture of a political system is inextricably bound up with the existing governmental structure. A mayor–council or a council–manager form of government exists in a city not by chance, but because of the size of a community, the heterogeneity of its population, and the political values of the citizens in the community. (Smaller and middle-sized communities that are socioeconomically homogeneous tend to have manager–council governments, whereas larger and more socioeconomically heterogeneous communities tend to have mayor–council systems.) To a great extent, the structure of local government is a formalized statement of the citizens' values as they relate to such vital issues as political empowerment and decision making, communication, conflict resolution, and control. The

---

[6]There is much disagreement on what the letter of the law is. The constant debate over affirmative action and equal employment opportunity shows the drastic differences that can exist between politicians, civil servants, and the interested public in interpreting the law.

structure, in turn, influences the procedures around and in the bureaus established to carry out city policy. Therefore, theories about how the political system works, who has access where, and what is considered "proper" within the political sphere are vital to understanding how public structure develops and is maintained.

There are two major theories of democratic politics: the pluralist and the elitist. Although there is some disagreement on which offers the best description of the political process, there is no doubt that both theories are useful in examining how bureaus attempt to operate as actors in the political system.

The pluralist or group theory of politics[7] presents a systematic statement of the role of interests and interest groups in the U.S. governmental system. In a definition commonly accepted by all pluralists, David Truman says, "An interest group is a shared-attitude group that makes certain claims upon other groups in the society. If and when it makes its claims through any of the institutions of government, it becomes a political interest group" (1951, 37). These groups create a mosaic of actors who influence governmental policies and processes, with a balance developing as the power and influence of the groups become known. But that balance is never static:

> The moving pattern of a complex society such as the one in which we live is one of changes and disturbances in the habitual subpatterns of interaction, followed by a return to the previous state of equilibrium or, if the disturbances are intense or prolonged, by the emergence of new groups whose specialized function it is to facilitate the establishment of a new balance. (1951, 44)

Sometimes bureaus are the recipients of group action; at other times they become actors attempting to influence the policies or processes of other parts of the government— other bureaus, branches of government, or levels of government. In fact, the departments in the national government have been established around a set of related interests, and it is easy to identify the roles played by the Departments of Labor, Housing and Urban Development, Agriculture, Energy, and Transportation in the policymaking free-for-all. To the extent that the pluralist theory describes reality in our political process, it helps explain how public organizations decide who to listen to, what to hear, and how to use information. It also explains many of the tactics used by bureaus as they try to influence other agencies or other parts of the government.

The elitist theory of politics[8] contends that the prominent actors in the political arena are a few powerful individuals or groups, often outside formal positions in government, who control the rules of the political game as well as the resulting politics and activities of government. Briefly summarized, the elitist theory argues that:

1. Society is divided into the few who have power and the many who do not. Only a small number of persons allocate values for society; the masses do not decide public policy.

---

[7]The pluralist school of politics traces its beginnings to Bentley (1908). Other major contributors include Truman (1951), Dahl (1961), and Dahl and Lindblom (1953).

[8]The elitist theory of politics is as old as history, but the first presentation of it as a model of local government in the United States can be traced to Hunter (1953).

2. The few who govern are not typical of the masses who are governed. Elites are drawn disproportionately from the upper socioeconomic strata of society.

3. The movement of nonelites to elite positions must be slow and continuous to maintain stability and avoid revolution. Only nonelites who have accepted the basic elite consensus enter governing circles.

4. Elites share a consensus on the basic values of the social system and the preservation of the system. They disagree only on a narrow range of issues.

5. Public policy does not reflect demands of masses but the prevailing values of the elite. Changes in public policy will be incremental rather than revolutionary.

6. Elites may act out of narrow self-serving motives and risk undermining mass support, or they may initiate reforms, curb abuse, and undertake public-regarding programs to preserve the system and their place in it.

7. Active elites are subject to relatively little direct influence from the apathetic masses. Elites influence masses more than masses influence elites (Dye and Ziegler 1993, 5).

To the extent that elites do control politics and government in the way described here, theories about individuals, groups, and formal organizations in the public sector must reflect the realities of the situation. Public agencies will fall into a hierarchical arrangement based on such factors as which bureaus serve members of the elite, receive the elite's attention and accolades, or in some other way gain the support or fulfill the programmatic desires of those who control the political environment. The tactics used, even the goals perceived as feasible and appropriate, will match the perception if there is agreement that power rests in gaining the ear and influencing the decisions of an elite rather than in coalition and majority building.

A more recent development in the field is known as public choice theory. This is a political theory that attempts to combine parts of organization theory, especially decision theory, and economics to improve the "scientism" in the study of public organizations, which means that both explanations and predictions can be improved. According to this theory, founded by James Buchanan and Gordon Tullock (1962), public organizations—and individuals within those organizations—should be considered rational decision makers who carefully weigh the costs and benefits of all actions where they have a choice. Both organizations and individuals will make choices in their own interest (see Figure 3–2). According to Harmon and Mayer, "for public choice theory, the rational bases for voluntary cooperation are deducible from, to put it baldly, people's selfish nature" (1986, 246). For public choice theorists, individual interests are given a priori legitimacy, and the individualistic postulate "goes beyond the scientific concerns of prediction and explanation because it influences their theory of values, as well" (246). They reject a "collective good" and argue that important values:

are not found in moral codes and philosophies, but are instead synonymous with the private wants or interests of individuals. Insofar as collective values can even be considered, they are derived from the coincidence of people's shared interests. These are empirically identifiable, rather than postulated in advance on the basis of metaphysical speculation. Thus "private gain" should be the goal of institutions and legal constraints (Harmon and Mayer 1986, 247).

FIGURE 3–2   Public Choice Theory's Assumptions About Individuals (and Organizations) in a Democracy

Individuals:

- Are motivated mainly by considerations of self-interest
- Are rational in the sense that they are able to rank alternative choices known to them
- Have varying amounts of information regarding the probable consequences of pursuing those alternatives
- Prefer an orderly context within which to engage in those pursuits
- Will choose strategies that will maximize their interests

SOURCE: Vincent Ostrom, *The Intellectual Crisis in American Public Administration*, rev. ed. University, Ala.: University of Alabama Press, 1974: 51.

There is much debate about the applicability of public choice theory,[9] and the success of this marriage may be in doubt; still it is an interesting effort that is a portent of future theoretical efforts. To the extent that public choice theory is successful in describing the way in which bureaus operate—at least in their choice of policy—a valuable addition will be made to our understanding of how public organizations interact within the political system.

A technocratic theory has also been espoused recently that argues that experts, through their professions and their positions of authority in both public and private organizations, actually make most of the important political decisions (Fischer 1990). This theory could be considered a specific derivation of the elite theory. Technocrats use their expertise and positions of power to dominate in the policy formulation and implementation process. This occurs for two reasons: (1) the increasing complexity and interdependence of society (technologically and economically, nationally and internationally) create a need for expertise and attention to both broad and specific effects that are beyond the time—and perhaps intellectual capacity—of much of society; and (2) at the same time, technocrats are aware of their monopoly on information and use this very powerful tool to make their positions secure. Technocrats find it relatively easy to interact, whether in public or private positions, and to "arrange" public policy to suit their technological needs.

---

[9]George Garvey represents at least a major segment of those attacking public choice theory when he makes a special plea to reject it in *Facing the Bureaucracy* (1993). He believes that self-interest is a dangerous tool to use when attempting to guarantee the *public interest* in a society. He argues that our culture, including its democratic underpinnings, developed as a product of *human experience in society*, a group, a larger collectivity than that portrayed in the egoistic model of public choice; therefore, individuals can be inspired to identify with larger values related to that society and culture.

> No one doubts that worker self-interest may be harnessed to move a public agency, like a private firm, toward efficiency. But more than efficiency is involved in public service. . . . [I]n any large technically based bureaucracy, organizational distance and increasing information costs limit a supervisor's ability to monitor subordinates. To try to remedy this deficiency with a self-regarding rewards-and-punishments calculus would be to reaffirm precisely the wrong values among our public servants. For this reason, I would [give] a nod . . . of approval for the progressives' ideal—an internalized standard, an *ethic of public service*. (218)

This approach to politics, which postulates an elite theory based on technological training rather than socioeconomic position in society, is further defended by its supporters, who point at the decreasing levels of participation by the citizenry-at-large in the political process. The steadily declining portion of citizens who vote or take part in any electoral activities is offered as proof of this growing lack of citizen interest. According to one group of theorists, the citizenry has lost interest because it recognizes that it is being "manipulated" by the technocrats; according to theorists viewing the phenomenon from the other side, citizens cannot comprehend the complex issues that they are inappropriately asked to settle through a single vote in an election. In either case, political decisions are ultimately made by the military–industrial complex, the Madison Avenue marketing and advertising group, or by an "international conspiracy" made up of bankers and industrialists.

There is often a tendency to dismiss the technocratic theory completely because of the pejorative and sensationalistic nature of those at the fringes of this theoretical group. But such a response fails to recognize the elements of truth in the theory. It is easy to miss, or at least fail to give enough credence to, the important questions that are raised by this group of theorists as one attempts to understand how organizations operate everywhere, especially in the public sector. For example, do public bureaucrats place their loyalty in their bureaus or in their professional associations? Do bureaucrats make their decisions based on bureau or professional perspectives and information? Are people with technical training and experience able and willing to look beyond their specialties and recognize the social and political consequences of their decisions and actions? It is impossible to comprehend the impact of bureaus and of the many specialists within those bureaus without understanding the power of technology in society, and hence, of the technocrats in public organizations.

The Impact of The Political Setting on Public Organization Theory

Undoubtedly, some readers are not convinced that the political setting is important to a discussion of organization theory. It may be impossible to convince those who do not wish to agree, but a brief history of the interaction between the political arena and public organization theory may help make the point. What is important to note in the following review is that every time a new historical development occurred, a concomitant new perspective of public organization was introduced. No attempt to prove a cause-and-effect relationship is made here. The authors simply wish to note that the two factors—political developments and public organization theory—were and are interconnected.

At the very beginning of the formal study of organizations, for example, the two major theories (those of Weber and Taylor) melded perfectly with the major thrust of the reformers.[10] Reformers were trying to remove the "business of government," as Woodrow Wilson referred to it, from the political arena, at least to the extent that decisions and

---

[10]Although Weber's writings were not translated from German to English until the 1940s, it is probable that the intellectual leaders of the reform movement were familiar with his writings and those of his intellectual predecessors. Wilson, for example, notes the import of German sociologists on the Progressives of his day. It is not possible at this point to debate the questions of intellectual causality and to attempt to decide whether the reform movement was a result of the developments in the social sciences or if the two developed coterminously but independently.

actions could be made independent of politicians. Second, a major claim of reformers was that, by separating politics and administration, efficiency and neutrality could be dramatically improved. The theories of Wilson and Taylor gave rational and powerfully persuasive support to the reform movement, which, in turn, gave impetus to the development of the civil service system, the anchor point of the reform movement. If one examines the merit personnel system from beginning to end, it is obvious that it almost perfectly matches the bureaucratic system as described by Weber—even if the reformers were not aware of Weber's writings. The structure also allowed the specialization and development of expertise as defined by Taylor. Despite temporary setbacks, such as the refusal of civilian naval employees to allow stopwatches in the armories, the technological complexity of society led to an increasing acceptance of specialization and its focus on efficiency.

With the arrival of President Roosevelt's New Deal, two major political facts of life (the Great Depression and World War II) influenced the development of organizations and the way scholars thought about them in government. For the first time, government was expected to be responsible for the state of the economy and to help those people who were out of work or had other chronic or serious economic needs. The increased charge led to two phenomena, the first of which was the general growth of government and new agencies. Government could not take on all the new functions that became part of its sphere without growing immensely; therefore, the magnitude of public organizations became increasingly important as a part of the total society. Along with growth came an influx of new people into public service, many of whom were well-educated and highly specialized individuals who would obviously be leaders of public organizations for the next two generations. Second, many of these people had been trained in political science, economics, history, and other disciplines by scholars who wholeheartedly accepted the politics–administration dichotomy as presented by Woodrow Wilson, Frank Goodnow, and numerous others writing between 1880 and 1930.

The storm of World War II, which broke over the United States with the Japanese attack on Pearl Harbor, also attracted many highly talented and well-trained individuals to federal government positions. After the war, many of these people either continued their careers in government or began a routine of moving regularly between government and academic or private sector positions. Not only did the government benefit from the infusion of intellectuals, but scholarly understanding of public administration was expanded dramatically because many of these intellectually inclined individuals, on returning to the more objective and neutral environment of the university, took advantage of the opportunity to thoughtfully consider their experiences as practitioners.

From this group, a quite different view of the public organization emerged, a view that included the bureau and its top managers as active participants—by necessity as well as desire—in the overall public policy process. The idea that politics and administration were separate and autonomous functions was put aside and a more viable theory that recognized the overlap of the two fields became the standard doctrine of public administration. The concepts of efficiency and effectiveness and the belief that public bureaucracies were just like private ones were rethought and enriched by the addition of political theory, both in philosophical terms and in terms of "political system mechanics" and the roles of public organizations and administrators in that process.

The demands of the cold war, space exploration, and technological development in general required a larger and more sophisticated public bureaucracy to carry out the government's work. Even the social programs needed greatly expanded capabilities in information science to keep pace with increased demands for record keeping, much less for any planning or decision making based on the most rudimentary models of facts, trends, and potential outcomes. Thus, when examining public organizations, the theories of the information and decision sciences firmly established themselves as a major component of a required knowledge base.

As the bureaucracy grew in size and scope, and the growth replicated the impact of government on everyone's life, the inevitable occurred: People became distrustful of the organization for which they had clamored. To carry out the functions that the citizens demanded of government, it grew; and as it grew, there was increasing fearfulness of big government. Of course, the same phenomenon was occurring throughout society. Even though most organizations were becoming larger and more bureaucratic, people saw largeness in the government as a threat to their everyday lives because government played such a central and visible role, especially at the national level.

The complaints are almost legion, but perhaps three themes can illustrate, in a simplified way, the attitudes of the citizenry. First, the public bureaucracy lacks "humaneness." Ralph Hummel describes this attitude with the proper rhetorical inflection when he recites the following litany:

> The bureaucrat has to be a truncated remnant of a human being. Bureaucrats are allowed to feel emotion, but only those emotions specified in the work orders. They are allowed to be responsible for their actions and in fact will be held responsible, but only if the action performed falls within their jurisdiction. The bureaucrat is not officially responsible and will not be held responsible for the action or nonaction of another bureaucrat in a different and independent part of the bureaucracy. The bureaucrat has a will, but it is an officially limited will: it cannot transcend his or her role. It is a will whose origins lie, not in personal conscience, but in machinery set in motion by a superior, the work rules, or the understanding of one's jurisdiction. (1982, 5–6)

Although not everyone expresses their feelings about bureaucracy quite as negatively and passionately as does Hummel, we can all remember times when the bureaucracy treated us as if we were dehumanized objects. We also tend to forget the overwhelming number of things that the bureaucracy accomplishes and remember only those occasions when something goes wrong.

Because of this universal phenomenon of selective memory, bureaucracy developed the highly negative image of being inhumane to both its members and clients. To change this situation, several new administrative remedies were proposed. Among these were (1) representative bureaucracy, which argued that public employment patterns should mirror, or represent, the composition of the general population because they then better serve all the people; (2) affirmative action, which argued that to achieve a representative bureaucracy it was necessary to go beyond strict neutrality, to actively recruit minorities and then discriminate in their favor during the selection and promotion process to make up for systemic and societal discrimination that had worked against them in the past; (3) the new public administration, which advocated active participation by public administrators in the policy process, with a special emphasis on their being surrogate representatives for those parts of the population not currently represented in the political system, (4) community participation in public agency decision making and implementation of policies, which insisted that the public could be served well only if they had input into the interpretation and implementation of public policy because only those being served could know what they wanted and needed; and (5) organization development, which was internal to the public bureaucracy and attempted to apply behavioral science to bureaus in a way that would increase openness, trust, and sensitivity so that public agencies would be more humane and democratic in dealing with their employees.

Even though there are relatively vociferous advocates for each of the particular approaches to bureaus mentioned, there are also those who see these steps as overreaching by government to the detriment of the greater society. The debates about such approaches to public administration continue, and none of them have been totally adopted into the mainstream of public organization theory. On the other hand, each has had some important influence in the public sector in that many of the basic premises have been accepted and some efforts have been made in individual organizations or in the larger public administrative system to accomplish at least part of the goals of the groups. This again is typical of the political arena, for as Woodrow Wilson noted nearly a century ago, "Wherever regard for public opinion is a first principle of government, practical reform must be slow and all reform must be full of compromise" (1887, 9).

The second change is related to control. Many people feel that the public bureaucracy has gotten completely out of control. According to these complaints, departments have become the equivalent of independent agencies. Civil servants, who are appointed by the merit system, which operates well in guarding entree to a position but has serious shortcomings in attempting to maintain high working standards, do their work with little guidance from elected officials. The merit system is a complex set of formal rules that has the effect of forcing job performance evaluations of both marginal and superior employees into a vast body of "satisfactory" workers with significant financial protection. Since the employees have special knowledge and expertise about their programs and processes, and since there are so many programs that it is impossible for the general public to watch over them, agencies tend to become their own power base. The public perceives the agency as independent and powerful when it is frequently the private special interest group that has power, with the public agency that serves this interest as the visible proof.

Many attempts have been made to increase control over the public bureaucracy and its pluralistic set of interests; some are primarily political (usually on the part of Congress or competing interests), whereas others attempt to use the new systems of information science (usually appointed top officials and technically oriented interest groups or clients). A major attempt at increasing control by appointed officials over the merit civil servant, while hopefully improving morale and motivation, was carried out by the Carter administration when it sponsored the Civil Service Reform Act and the establishment of the Senior Executive Service. A more current attempt at controlling bureaucracy while improving efficiency and effectiveness is carried out in the Clinton administration's National Performance Review (1993). The framers of these studies and programs were affected by modern organizational theories—theories about motivation, competition (economic and social), and employee empowerment, for example. Obviously, they were also influenced by current political theories. It may also be arguable that some important discoveries of organization theory were downplayed in these cases, again by design or default, much to the detriment of the final outcome and its effectiveness. Nevertheless, it is impossible to believe that the academics and practitioners who designed these efforts were not influenced by their intellectual background.

The third complaint against the public bureaucracy, and government generally, is that it is too large. When all levels of government are considered together, they compose by far the largest single portion of our economy. By 1980, the rebellion against the size of government was consummated in the election of Ronald Reagan, which brought into the national government people with attitudes that were already having an impact at the state and local level. In 1994, the Republicans gained power in Congress, at least in part, on a platform of reducing the size of government. As a result of this groundswell of public opinion, a new type of question is being faced by government at all levels. How do we cut back on services, employees, and revenues? To achieve this new demand made by the citizenry and still maintain employee morale and overall program effectiveness, it is necessary to call on every bit of knowledge that has been developed and then to discover innovative ways of applying it. In fact, one of the major charges against the Reagan administration was that as programs were cut back, public employee morale and program effectiveness were decimated either by failure to recognize the impact of policies or by deliberate design. In order to avoid some of the negative factors existent in such an endeavor, those implementing the National Performance Review in the Clinton administration are attempting to achieve wide participation by the public and by the government bureaucracy in discussing and carrying out the goals of the study.

PUBLIC ORGANIZATION THEORY TODAY

All the forces just discussed have led to an intense interest in organization theory as it applies to the public sector bureaucracy, and this discussion is a greatly simplified review of the environment in which both scholars and managers have to work. It is no wonder that a large number of theories has appeared, given the multitude of perspectives from which to examine organizations. In most cases, we have a situation similar to that of the group of blind men who examined an elephant. Any one theory about public organizations may appear to be wrong, even ludicrously wrong, at least in part because the theory focuses too closely on one particular aspect of the organization at the expense of the others.

By examining the full range of theories, we can move toward the creation of a set of perspectives useful to public administrators and students of public management. Most readers of this book are primarily looking for a basis of knowledge that will help them accomplish the daily task of managing public organizations. To accomplish this task, all four perspectives presented in this chapter must be considered, and it is the fourth dimension—the political environment of public management—that is usually missing as organization theory is studied. Likewise, the legal dimension is downplayed in the private sector. Although we focus on rationality and efficiency, it is important to recognize that managerial, political, and economic definitions of these terms may be, and in fact usually are, dramatically varied. An understanding of these differences and how to either bring them together or accept the impossibility of doing so, and discovering ways to survive in the resulting conflictual environment is essential to managing public organizations.

In a similar vein, it is not enough for public managers to know all about the psychological and sociological theories related to complex organizations. When any attempt is made at application of these theories (and that is the prevalent goal), it is essential to understand the legal and political environment in which that attempt is being made. For example, public managers cannot use all the methods of motivation that are open to managers in the private sector. Likewise, many other theories about organization, when applied in the public sector, must be adjusted to meet the demands of the general political culture and the specific political actors that are relevant to the bureau in question. Public organization theory must address all four perspectives in the controversy to develop a comprehensive picture of the bureau and how it works.

FOR FURTHER READING

Obvious first reading for any serious student of organization theory is Max Weber, *The Theory of Social and Economic Organization,* translated and edited by A. M. Henderson and Talcott Parsons, New York: Oxford University Press, 1947, (especially Section 111, "The Types of Authority and Imperative Control," and within it, pages 329–341, which deal with "Legal Authority with a Bureaucratic Administrative Staff"). Alongside Weber, in order to understand the political world of the public administrator, one should read James Q. Wilson, *Bureaucracy: What Government Agencies Do and Why They Do It,* New York: Basic Books, 1989. As a presentation of modern, popular thoughts about management that differ greatly from Weber, see David Osborne and Ted Gaebler, *Reinventing Government, How the Entrepreneurial Spirit is Transforming the Public Sector,* Reading, Mass.: Addison-Wesley, 1992; and Peter M. Senge, *The Fifth Discipline: The Art and Practice of The Learning Organization,* New York: Doubleday, 1990. For a presentation of the classic view of public administration and the rules governing it, see Lyndall Urwick and Luther H. Gulick, eds., *Papers on the Science of Administration,* New York: Institute of Public Administration, 1937. For a justification of public administration in an administrative law context, especially one that deals with due process, see James O. Freedman, *Crisis and Legitimacy,* New York: Cambridge University Press, 1978. The best presentation of the psychological and sociological aspects of generic organization theory is found in Daniel Katz and Robert L. Kahn, *Social Psychology of Organizations,* 2d ed., New York: John Wiley & Sons, 1978. An interesting discussion of (especially internal) political aspects of organizations in which is presented the sources and uses of power in management and decision making occurs in Jeffrey Pfeffer, *Power in Organizations,* Marshfield, Mass.: Pitman Publishing, 1981.

REVIEW QUESTIONS

1. What are the major theses of each of the four pivotal approaches to organization theory? What impact does the fourth (politics and power) have on each of the other three?
2. Given the differences described in the prior chapter, how would the interpretation of these four theoretical foci vary in their application to public and private organizations?

REFERENCES

Barnard, Chester. *The Functions of the Executive.* Cambridge, Mass.: Harvard University Press, 1938.

Bentley, Arthur F. *The Process of Government; A Study of Social Pressures.* Chicago: University of Chicago Press, 1908.

Blau, Peter M. *The Dynamics of Bureaucracy.* Chicago: University of Chicago Press, 1955.

Boulding, Kenneth E. "General Systems Theory—The Skeleton of Science," *Management Science* 2, 1956: 197–208.

Buchanan, James M., and Gordon Tullock. *The Calculus of Consent.* Ann Arbor, Mich.: University of Michigan Press, 1962.

Carey, Alex. "The Hawthorne Studies: A Radical Criticism," *American Sociological Review* 32, 1967: 403–416.

Cartwright, Dorwin, and Alvin F. Zander. *Group Dynamics: Research and Theory.* New York: Harper & Row, 1968.

Creech, Bill. *The Five Pillars of TQM: How to Make Total Quality Management Work for You.* New York: Truman Talley Books/Dutton, 1994.

Dahl, Robert. *Who Governs? Democracy and Power in an American City.* New Haven: Yale University Press, 1961.

———, and Charles E. Lindblom. *Politics, Economics and Welfare: Planning and Politico-Economic Systems Resolved into Basic Social Processes.* New York: Harper, 1953.

Demming, W. Edwards. *Out of the Crisis.* Cambridge, Mass.: MIT Center for Advanced Engineering Study, 1986.

———. *The New Economics for Industry, Government, Education.* Cambridge, Mass.: MIT Center for Advanced Engineering Study, 1993.

Diesing, Paul. *Reason in Society: Five Types of Decisions and Their Social Conditions.* Urbana: University of Illinois Press, 1962.

Dye, Thomas R., and Harmon Ziegler. *The Irony of Democracy: An Uncommon Introduction to American Politics.* 9th ed. Belmont, Calif.: Wadsworth, 1993.

Fischer, Frank, ed. *Technocracy and the Politics of Expertise.* Newbury Park, Calif.: Sage Publications, 1990.

French, John R. P., and Bertram Raven. "The Bases of Social Power." In *Studies in Social Power,* ed. Dorwin Cartwright. Ann Arbor, Mich.: Institute for Social Research, 1958: 150–167.

Garvey, Gerald. *Facing the Bureaucracy: Living and Dying in a Public Agency.* San Francisco: Jossey-Bass Publishers, 1992.

Gortner, Harold F. "Values and Ethics." In *Handbook of Administrative Ethics,* ed. Terry L. Cooper. New York: Marcel Dekker, 1994: 373–390.

Gulick, Luther H., and Lyndall Urwick, eds. *Papers on the Science of Administration.* New York: Institute of Public Administration, 1937.

Hackman, J. Richard, and Ruth Wageman. "Total Quality Management: Empirical, Conceptual, and Practical Issues." *Administrative Science Quarterly* 40, 1995: 309–342.

Harmon, Michael M., and Richard T. Mayer. *Organization Theory for Public Administration.* Boston: Little, Brown, 1986.

Hummel, Ralph. *The Bureaucratic Experience.* 2nd ed. New York: St. Martin's Press, 1982.

Hunter, Floyd. *Community Power Structure: A Study of Decision Makers.* Chapel Hill: University of North Carolina Press, 1953.

Ishikawa, Kaoru. *What is Total Quality Control? The Japanese Way.* Englewood Cliffs, N.J.: Prentice Hall, 1985.

Jacobs, T. O. *Leadership and Exchange in Formal Organizations.* Alexandria, Va.: Human Resources Research Organization, 1971.

Janis, Irving L. *Victims of Groupthink.* Boston: Houghton Mifflin, 1972.

Juran, Joseph M. *Juran on Planning for Quality.* New York: Free Press, 1988.

Katz, Daniel, and Robert L. Kahn. *The Social Psychology of Organizations.* 2nd ed. New York: John Wiley & Sons, 1978.

Kaufman, Herbert. *The Forest Ranger.* Baltimore: The Johns Hopkins University Press, 1960.

Kernaghan, Kenneth. *Ethical Conduct: Guidelines for Government Employees.* Toronto: Institute of Public Administration, 1975.

Lens, Sidney. *The Military Industrial Complex.* Philadelphia: Pilgrim Press, 1970.

March, James, and Herbert A. Simon. *Organizations.* 2nd ed. Cambridge, Mass.: Blackwell, 1993.

Mosher, Frederick C., and Richard J. Stillman, eds. *The Professions in Government.* New Brunswick, N.J.: Transaction Books, 1982.

National Performance Review (U.S.). *Creating a Government that Works Better & Costs Less: Report of the National Performance Review.* Vice President Al Gore. New York: Time Books, 1993.

Osborne, David, and Ted Gaebler. *Reinventing Government: How the Entrepreneurial Spirit is Transforming the Public Sector.* Reading, Mass.: Addison-Wesley, 1992.

Ostrom, Vincent. *The Intellectual Crisis in American Public Administration.* Rev. ed. University, Ala.: University of Alabama Press, 1974.

Parsons, Talcott. "Suggestions for a Sociological Approach to the Theory of Organizations." *Administrative Science Quarterly* 1, 1956: 63–85.

Peters, Thomas J., and Robert H. Waterman, Jr. *In Search of Excellence: Lessons from America's Best-Run Companies.* New York: Harper & Row, 1982.

Rago, William V. "Adapting Total Quality Management (TQM) to Government: Another Point of View." *Public Administration Review* 54, 1994: 61–64.

Roethlisberger, Fritz J. *Management and Morale.* Cambridge, Mass.: Harvard University Press, 1941.

_____, and W. Dickson. *Management and the Worker.* Cambridge, Mass.: Harvard University Press, 1939.

Rossiter, Clinton, ed. *The Federalist Papers: Alexander Hamilton, James Madison, John Jay.* New York: New American Library, 1961.

Scott, Walter Dill. "How Suggestion Works on the Prospect's Brain." *Advertising & Selling* (May 1914): 11, 59.

Senge, Peter M. *The Fifth Discipline: The Art and Practice of The Learning Organization.* New York: Doubleday, 1990.

Sensenbrenner, Joseph. "Quality Comes to City Hall." *Harvard Business Review* 69, 1991: 64–75.

Simmons, Robert H. *Achieving Humane Organization.* Malibu, Calif.: Daniel Spencer Publishers, 1981.

Spiro, Herbert. *Responsibility in Government; Theory and Practice.* New York: Van Nostrand Reinhold, 1969.

Stokey, Edith, and Richard Zeckhauser. *A Primer for Policy Analysis.* New York: W. W. Norton, 1978.

Swiss, James E. "Adapting Total Quality Management (TQM) to Government." *Public Administration Review* 52, 1992: 356–362.

Taylor, Frederick W. *Principles of Management.* New York: Harper & Row, 1911.

_____. *Principles of Scientific Management.* New York: W. W. Norton, 1947.

Thompson, James. *Organizations in Action.* New York: McGraw-Hill, 1967.

Truman, David. *The Governmental Process; Political Interests and Public Opinion.* New York: Alfred A. Knopf, 1951.

Waldo, Dwight. "Organization Theory: Revisiting the Elephant." *Public Administration Review* 38, 1978: 589–597.

Weber, Max. *The Theory of Social and Economic Organization.* Trans. and ed. A. M. Henderson and Talcott Parsons. New York: Oxford University Press, 1947.

Weisband, Edward, and Thomas M. Franck. *Resignation in Protest.* New York: Grossman Publishers/Viking Press, 1975.

Wilson, James Q. *Bureaucracy: What Government Agencies Do and Why They Do It.* New York: Basic Books, Inc., 1989.
Wilson, Woodrow. "The Study of Administration." *Political Science Quarterly* 2 (June 1887): 197–222. In *Classics of Public Administration,* ed. Jay M. Shafritz and Albert C. Hyde. Oak Park, Ill.: Moore Publishing, 1978.

READING 3–1   Organization Theory and Political Theory

If two men of similar talents, identical training, shared values, and common interests were to study the same phenomena it would not be at all remarkable if they approached the phenomena in the same way, described them in the same terms, employed the same logic in analyzing them, drew the same conclusions from them, and formulated the same theories about their causes.

If, however, two men of similar talents but of rather divergent training, professing differing objectives, and displaying varied (perhaps even conflicting) concerns were to pursue studies of phenomena each believed to be quite distinct from the other's field of inquiry, it would be most astounding if their findings and inferences should turn out to be closely parallel in many important respects, particularly if there were little evidence of communication between them.

That is why the parallels between political theory, probably the oldest of the social sciences, and organization theory, perhaps the newest such discipline, are so totally unexpected. If there is any conscious agreement between the two fields, it is on their separateness from each other: political theorists and organization theorists alike seem to take for granted the impossibility of encompassing within a single theoretical framework propositions about states—that is, the relation of governments to subjects, and the relations of governments to each other—and propositions about other forms of human association. In the literature on organization theory, one rarely finds references even to contemporary political theorists and almost never to those who wrote in the past. By the same token, political theorists rarely seem to find anything relevant to their interests in the work of students of organization. Measured by the acknowledged exchange of information between the disciplines, the gulf between them is wide and seldom bridged.

Perhaps such a gulf is inescapable. Political theorists draw heavily upon history, philosophy, and personal experience for their ideas and evidence; organization theorists rely heavily upon sociology, social psychology, economics, and, when possible, on controlled experimentation. Political theorists are frankly normative; organization theorists generally believe their work is value-free. Political theorists deal willingly with the intangible aspects of human associations, for it is difficult to measure the outputs of governments and governmental agencies; organization theorists are more at home with organizations producing tangible products and measuring their performance ultimately in terms of profit. The fields do seem to have quite different traditions, methods, goals, and subject matters.

But all this merely makes the similarities in the problems they investigate and in their findings more surprising and intriguing.

I

For example, both organization theorists and political theorists encountered the same enigma: in order that the human systems may come into being and continue, men often have to do, at the behest of others, tasks that are unpleasant or even hazardous (such as working on assembly lines or going to war), and must refrain from doing what they would greatly enjoy (such as helping themselves to the property of others or saying whatever they please wherever and whenever the spirit moves them). What accounts for obedience and docility entailing such self-sacrifice, self-restraint, self-denial, without which neither states nor other associations could long survive?

Political philosophers and organization theorists have offered essentially the same range of explanations: the rationality of men and the conditioning of men's minds.[1]

Because men are rational, they can calculate what they would lose if everyone were to follow his own impulses and preferences without restraint. They can also see that collective action will be taken against individuals who disobey. Out of fear of the consequences, they submit. They can calculate, too, the advantages they may gain from organized life and activity. They can see that the gains usually outweigh the costs. Out of hope for the benefits, then, as well as out of fear, rational men yield to the will of others.[2]

At the same time, according to many political and organization theorists, men obey because obedience to certain commands from certain sources is a conditioned reflex. Even in infancy, every individual is introduced to the exercise of authority; maturation is in many ways a process of learning when to obey, whom to command, and under what circumstances to do either. That is, from his social environment generally, and also by virtue of the deliberate drill and indoctrination to which he is subject, every man is prepared for his social roles. He comes to yield to others because he learns it is right and proper to do so, and he may even come to cherish his submission. The will to obey is implanted in him; depending on the discipline one draws upon for appropriate language, he is educated, indoctrinated, trained, socialized, acculturated, programmed, or brainwashed.

Interestingly enough, political theorists have from the very beginning made more strenuous efforts to incorporate the non-rational (i.e., the conditioned) elements of men's behavior into their hypotheses than have the organization theorists. For men are born into

---

[1]A third explanation, offered initially by political philosophers of classical antiquity, was that some men are by nature followers and others are by nature rulers. The followers obey because it is their nature to do so, just as leaders command because that is their nature. This argument has few defenders among contemporary political theorists, and it is seldom articulated by organization theorists. But one may wonder whether the batteries of personality and aptitude and intelligence tests used for selecting executives do not rest ultimately on the assumption that there are "natural" leaders who should be identified, separated from the "naturally" subservient mass, and elevated to their "natural" managerial roles.

[2]This reasoning underlies most social-contract philosophies of the origins of civil and political society. The emphasis was placed in some cases on escape from the risks and uncertainties of anarchy (as in Hobbes and Locke), in others on ascension to a higher, richer, distinctively human and civilized life (as in Rousseau, whose logic, in turn, parallels that of classical political theory). The hypothesized reasoning in men's decisions to form or join groups in which they must then submit to others is not far removed from the analysis by J. G. March and H. A. Simon (1957, chapter 4) of individual calculations regarding "the decision to participate" in organizations. See also Simon's assertion that a distinctive feature of organization theory is its treatment of joining an organization as an "all-or-none choice of participation or nonparticipation" (1957, 74; chapters 10 and 11).

political systems, and the possibilities of withdrawal are much more limited. It is not clear that joining or remaining in a political system is really a matter of rational choice at all, except in isolated instances. Organization theorists, on the other hand, deal more extensively with associations that men presumably choose to enter and may leave at any time. To explain membership and all it entails, students of organization lean toward a rather literal application of social-contract theory and utilitarianism; many eighteenth- and nineteenth-century political philosophers, who employed these concepts as metaphors to aid in understanding the rational component of behavior, would find little in most modern organization theory with which to quarrel. And some organization theorists would doubtless be surprised to discover how many political philosophers in ancient and medieval times were aware there were social norms and group loyalties that a ruler dared not violate without risking extensive disobedience.

At any rate, more or less independently of each other, drawing in different ways on different bodies of experience, political theorists and organization theorists have dealt in very similar fashion with the obedience of man to man.

II

They have also dealt similarly with organizational structures for the achievement of coordination. For purposes of this discussion, coordination means ordering the direction, volume, and timing of flows of activities, goods, and services so that the functioning of one element in a system at least does not prevent or negate or hamper the functioning of other elements, and at best facilitates and assists the functioning of other elements. Coordination is not always a goal of system designers; the separation of powers, for example, encourages some contradictions and deadlocks in order to protect other values. But it is often among the principal values, and practically never is a matter of total indifference. And when political theorists and organization theorists discuss methods of promoting coordination, they end up in much the same positions.

Fundamentally, coordination is accomplished by two processes: central direction, which means that the activities of the elements of a system respond chiefly to cues and signals from some common source, and reciprocal relations, which means that the elements respond to cues and signals from each other. Every system employs some blend of the two processes. Moreover, the systems are not mutually exclusive; an increase in reliance on one does not necessarily produce a decrease in the other. On the contrary, effective central direction often permits a higher degree of reciprocal cueing, as in a well-trained platoon, and vice versa. Whatever the blend of modes of coordination and whatever the general level of coordination in any system, these may be explained in terms of the relative weight assigned to each of the two underlying processes.

Political theorists who believe men are inclined to take advantage of one another tend to stress central direction as the best means of coordinating them. Without an overriding central figure, according to them, any system breaks down in disorder, confusion, and internal warfare. Hobbes, of course, presented this argument in its purest, most logical form. On the other side, philosophers who assume the interests and tendencies of men are harmonious emphasize the possibility and desirability of coordination through reciprocity, and regard central direction as an exploitative or disturbing factor in what would otherwise be a highly coordinated system distributing maximum satisfaction to all its members. The anarchists; both Marxist and non-Marxist, pushed this reasoning to its logical extreme. It matters little for this discussion whether the extremists on both sides meant their doctrines to be taken literally or as analogies for the sake of clarity and vigor of statement. They bracketed the range of possibilities. In the history of political thought, not only the extremes, but virtually all conceivable intermediate positions, have at some time or other been advanced or defended.

During most of the short history of organization theory, few theorists seriously questioned the premise that central direction (expressed structurally as a hierarchy of authority because of the need of leaders to delegate formal powers and because of the assumed inability of men to supervise directly more than a small number of colleagues) is the primary method of achieving coordination; indeed, hierarchy and organization were sometimes treated as almost synonymous. Yet very early some questioning voices were heard, particularly after experimental studies in the sociology of industry drew attention to the responsiveness of workers to cues and signals emanating from sources other than (and sometimes hostile to) the designated managers of the firms examined. Mary Parker Follett, a political scientist of Pluralist persuasion, became well known to students of organization for her advocacy of "power with rather than power over" and for her criticism of "the illusion of final responsibility." Later on, Argyris and Thompson and others would search explicitly for a pattern of organization that is nonhierarchical. . . . It would be grossly inaccurate to equate these organizational analysts with the anarchists, but there can be no question that organization theory has begun to display an awareness of a range of positions on the central-reciprocal scale that political philosophers have explored extensively for centuries.

I do not intend to imply that political philosophy is somehow superior to organization theory, or that organization theory is a mere branch of the history of political thought. My object in pointing out similarities between their treatments of coordination is simply to demonstrate that these seemingly unrelated disciplines confront common problems in common ways.

III

Another such problem is the reconciliation of individual or other narrow objectives with the objectives of the collectivity. Political theorists discuss it in terms of special interests as against the general or public interest. Organization theorists speak of personal or subgroup goals via-à-vis organizational goals. But the issues are the same.

In both fields, the dominant opinion seems to be that every collectivity is in some sense goal-seeking, or purposive. That is, there is some general interest or organizational goal shared or at least acknowledged by nearly all the participants in the system, and although the over-arching purpose is accomplished by the labor of individuals, it is distinct from the goals or interests of individuals; rather, it is viewed as an attribute of the system as a whole. There is little agreement on the specifics of the general interest, and even a given commentator may switch from one to another interpretation as conditions change. (Implicitly, however, one goal can be discerned in every interpretation: the survival of the system.) Yet, although students of states and of organizations may never arrive at a consensus on exactly what the shared interests of human associations are, many of them tend to take it for granted that one exists for every human association.[3]

A substantial number of political theorists, on the other hand, have taken the view that virtually every definition of the public interest is but a reflection of the personal interests of the definer, and consequently, the only realistic way to understand the performance of a system is to construe its output (or its policies) as nothing more than the resultant of the interplay of many special interests. The representatives of each interest may invoke the symbol of the public interest as an honorific, perhaps even with sincere conviction that the actions they espouse are better for the system and all the members of the system, but what is actually decided and done is the product of negotiations and understandings among specialized groups and individuals.

Among organization theorists, the counterpart to this point of view is seldom advanced even tacitly, let alone explicitly; it is distinctly a minority position. Barnard, however, comes close to it. Although he discusses organizational purposes at length, and attributes great importance to them, they are not central to his analysis. He defines formal organizations without referring to goals, and he describes them largely in terms of individual motivations and objectives coordinated with each other through an "economy of incentives." The "absolute test" of efficiency is survival of the organization. An organization is thus portrayed as a kind of marketplace in which each man pursues his own goals by offering a contribution in return for those inducements (selected from the range of inducements provided, consciously or unwittingly, by the system) that appeal to him. The enterprise is an arena in which each participant offers his wares and services in exchange for what he can get. From the elaborate network of agreements, accommodations, and behaviors come products, wages, salaries, profits, prices, dividends, interest, taxes, working conditions, and all the other outputs of a complex system. Managers, workers, suppliers, customers, stockholders, creditors, competitors, government regulators, consultants, academics, and others may all see different transcendent purposes in the undertaking, so that its ends are in a sense the sum of all the special purposes. To this extent, this view resembles in many respects the view of the state espoused by the political theorists mentioned above. What is sometimes referred to as a collective purpose is merely the resultant of a constantly shifting adjustment among individual and subgroup purposes.

---

[3]Plato and Aristotle, for example, saw as the purpose of the city-state the promotion of the highest moral development of its citizens. For Hobbes, the end of government was the preservation of order. For Locke, it was the protection of "natural rights," such as the right to private property. For the Utilitarians, it was to produce the greatest good for the greatest number. For the early liberal economists, it was to furnish just enough service and regulation to permit the reciprocal processes of the marketplace to operate effectively. In all these instances, selected haphazardly from the broad array of goals postulated in political thought, the existence of a common purpose and interest is axiomatic.

The same is true of most contemporary organization theory, although the specification of common interests is rarely articulated as explicitly as in political philosophy. Rather it is assumed that every human association has some goals shared by all its members, and can be understood only in terms of those common purposes, e.g., in H. A. Simon, D. W. Smithburg, and V. A. Thompson, purpose and cooperative action are described as the "two basic processes of what has come to be called administration. . . . Administration can be defined as the activities of groups cooperating to accomplish common goals" (1950, 3). Similarly, P. M. Blau and W. R. Scott declare that what organizations "all have in common is that a number of men have become organized into a social unit—an organization—that has been established for the explicit purpose of achieving certain goals" (1962, 1). And C. Argyris hypothesizes "that organizations are intricate human strategies designed to achieve certain objectives," and that the objectives of any organization include "achieving its goals (intended consequences)" (1960, 10–11).

Over the relationship of private interests to the general interest, organization theorists and political theorists have divided into similar camps. Again, the resemblances between the fields are impressive.

IV

The foregoing illustrations do not exhaust the parallels between organization theory and political theory. But they are probably sufficient to establish the point of departure for this discussion, namely, that striking similarities have developed in two disciplines that seem to be quite different in their interests and methods.

Why should this occur? Why should two fields of study with such discrepant premises and perspectives converge?

Perhaps it is because the discrepancies are, after all, merely the distinctions between different species of the same genus. When all is said and done, they both treat a phenomena that encompass vast areas, if not all, of human life. We are all members of at least several organizations, and organizations give characteristic content and general form to our lives. Moreover, states, governments, the branches and agencies of governments, political parties, and interest groups are organizations like other organizations even though they have their unique attributes. What aspect of civilized existence then lies outside the scope of organization theory?

At the same time, every organization is sometimes construed as a political system, with all the problems of leadership, policy formation, succession, strategy, rivalry, resistance, revolution, and influence that this implies. If organizations are an all-embracing subject of inquiry, politics is an equally comprehensive theme. To be sure, organization theorists tend to avoid political institutions in searching for data, and political philosophers tend to concentrate on those institutions immediately associated with public governments. But they may end with strong similarities because they are both addressed to phenomena permeating the whole of human affairs. Fields that take so much for their province must have far more overlap than is immediately obvious.

Furthermore, they both start from normative bases. Political theorists were historically engaged in a quest for the ideal political system; organization theorists began by seeking "the one best way"—e.g., the most efficient way—to organize production and distribution. There are probably some in both disciplines who still believe such ideal arrangements, superior to all alternatives under any conditions and at any time, are attainable; most contemporary theorists, I believe, now adopt a relativist position, holding that the definition of the ideal changes as circumstances change, and perhaps even that a wide variety of organizational and political patterns may satisfy equally well these requirements of any particular definition. At any rate, men in both fields set out to discover the "laws" or "principles" governing social behavior so as to formulate proposals for improvement consonant with the constraints imposed by reality. Sometimes they try to sharpen their thinking by reasoning from admittedly oversimplified hypotheses, such as man in a state of nature or completely rational man. Eventually, however, they complicate their models by adding variables that render the hypotheses better approximations of the real world. (Such variables are more often discovered by non-normative research of an historical or experimental kind than by intuition.) Conceivably, the fields may come to resemble each other because they have parallel normative underpinnings.

But the explanation of the resemblances may not lie in the character of the disciplines at all; perhaps it is to be found rather in the nature of the world the disciplines purport to describe. The convergence could result from the existence of such pronounced and persistent regularities in large-scale human associations that no matter which such associations one examines and what approach one adopts, the sum of the findings of each set of observers will inevitably be much the same as those of any other set. When all the blind men compare their notes, they do end up with a description of an elephant, and the description by each team of blind men will not differ materially from the description produced by any other team, because, after all, it *is* an elephant they are studying. The consensus of two relatively insulated fields, when the whole range of their content is reviewed, lends corroboration to the impression that our ideas about organizations and politics have a substantial degree of validity. . . .

SOURCE: Herbert Kaufman, *American Political Science Review* 58 (March 1964): 5–14. Copyright 1964 by The American Political Science Association. Only selected footnotes have been included, and citations have been changed to the format used in this text. If interested, the reader should look at Kaufman's numerous citations supporting his argument in the original essay.

References

Argyris, Chris. *Understanding Organizational Behavior.* Chicago, Ill.: Dorsey Press, 1960.

Blau, Peter M., and William R. Scott. *Formal Organizations.* San Francisco: Chandler & Sharp Publishers, 1962.

March, James G., and Herbert A. Simon. *Organizations.* New York: John Wiley & Sons, 1957.

Simon, Herbert A. *Models of Man.* New York: John Wiley & Sons, 1957.

———, Donald W. Smithburg, and Victor A. Thompson. *Public Administration.* New York: Alfred A. Knopf, 1950.

Editor's Note

In the essay, Herbert Kaufman argues for a position shared by the authors (although we do not necessarily agree with all the points that he makes). The argument seems to be especially true when one is looking at public organizations, which must operate in a political environment. When reading any such essay, however, it is important to understand the perspective from which the author proceeds when writing; therefore, it is important to consider the following questions:

1. What basic assumptions and political values are accepted by Herbert Kaufman as he argues for the overlap of political and organizational themes?

2. How do Kaufman's assumptions about people in organizations differ from those of behaviorists such as Fiedler, Hersey and Blanchard, Porter and Lawler, or Vroom?

Chapter 4

Organization Structure and Design

INTRODUCTION

> We trained hard . . . but it seemed that every time we were beginning to form up into teams we would be reorganized. . . . I was to learn later in life that we tend to meet any new situation by reorganizing, and a wonderful method it can be for creating the illusion of progress while producing confusion, inefficiency, and demoralization.

This quote is attributed to Petronius Arbiter, who died in 66 AD, but it could also be the comment of most government workers in the 1990s. Reorganization is one of the basic facts of organizational life. It is regularly used to serve political ends or to improve organizational operations. A reorganization may be largely cosmetic, designed to portray agency leaders or policymakers as hard-working administrators in search of solutions to intractable problems. Centralizing the structure consolidates authority in the hands of a few, whereas decentralizing can expedite and make more visible the work of particular offices. Mergers of previously specialized offices can highlight, dilute, or conceal their work. Placing program implementation authority in a weak, low-profile office essentially determines the program's fate. On the other hand, it may be used to co-opt critics of the bureau's activities by placing them in newly created offices where their power is only illusory.

A case that illustrates many of these points is the move to reorganize the human services agencies in many states. During the 1970s, the formerly independent departments of health, mental health, and various social services were merged into one superbureau, usually termed the Department of Human Services. The official purpose of this reorganization trend was to improve efficiency by removing duplicative offices and to improve the level of coordination in human services policy. In reality, however, the evidence suggests that the object of reorganization was to allow the governors or legislatures to control human services programs more closely as the budgets in that area began to rocket upward (Lynn 1980; Owens 1985). This is not an unusual case.

If we are to have a realistic understanding of the motivations and results of government reorganization, it must be comprehended as a political art. But organization structures serve more than political ends. First and most often, administrators analyze and choose structures based on technical considerations. Structures differ in this capacity to adequately coordinate task activities, in their degree and form of specialization, and in their capacity to permit bureaus to respond adequately to changing environments and program technologies. To look only at the political characteristics of reorganization, however, is to underemphasize the efforts that managers make to improve the functioning of the bureau based on their professional judgments about administrative needs.

The literature on the technical advantages and disadvantages of various structural arrangements has long existed in the field. For most of this century, public administrators have relied on classical principles of proper structure as the key to sound management; these principles have been called the "proverbs of administration" (March and Simon 1993) and include concepts such as the unity of command and the six-person span of control. Although the more traditional principles are well entrenched and still widely used, newer models of organization, which reflect structural adaptations to the technical and environmental characteristics of the bureau, are beginning to supplant the conventional structures.

The purpose of this chapter is to examine both the traditional and contemporary models of organizational structure from the literature in the organization theory field. Thus, the primary emphasis will be on the technical as opposed to political uses of organization structures. In some cases, as we have noted, the rationale behind a reorganization will be political. But when reorganization can follow what writers in the field have called "rational" organizational designs, working administrators should be aware of the considerable and well-developed body of research and theory on the advantages of different types of structures. We will also include a discussion of the impact of political considerations on the design of structures. In the end, we hope to offer a set of alternative designs and concepts for assessing the particular structural needs of bureaus, as they attempt to satisfy technical, programmatic, and political objectives.

The topics in this chapter will include, first, an exploration of the political and technical sources of organizational structural arrangements; in other words, who designs structures in public agencies and how? We will then consider the most basic of the traditional structural concepts, those that most often influence decisions about structure. Finally, three contemporary schools of thought regarding how best to design innovative and responsive organizational structures will be described.

SOURCES OF STRUCTURE IN GOVERNMENTAL ORGANIZATION

The formal structure of any organization is the officially prescribed distribution of authority and task responsibility among its offices and officials. The authority of officials to decide, to act, or to delegate responsibility is prescribed in the structure, and there is often some further specification of the conditions or bases for action. Command and intelligence-gathering structures specify how new policies and procedures are to be communicated from the top to the bottom of the bureau, or laterally. They also prescribe the manner in which reports of results, problems, or conflicts are to be communicated upward to the appropriate level for official action. Formal structures prescribe how the bureau's work is to be divided into individual tasks and grouped into departments, offices, and other subdivisions. The relationships among all the subdivisions, their specific responsibilities, and their coordination are prescribed in the structure.

Merger/Reorganization in County Government

In the second stage of a government reorganization promised to go on four years, Montgomery County Executive Douglas M. Duncan proposed yesterday creating a single public works and transportation department from two existing departments and part of a third.

If approved by the County Council, the change will eliminate 22 jobs and save $1 million a year, according to Duncan. "This consolidation will allow us to provide essential services at an affordable cost, which is what local government is all about," Duncan said at a news conference.

Half of the lost jobs would be managers and the rest clerical workers. The plan cuts the number of divisions from 11 to seven.

Council member Isaiah Leggett (D-At Large) said he expected the council to approve the move.

"I'm optimistic that we can realize some saving," said Leggett, chairman of the council's Transportation and Environment Committee. "I'm not sure they'll be as great as projected."

But the head of the affected union complained that Duncan had not given adequate notice of the change.

"He continues to give us false assurances that he will not make final decisions without consulting the unions," said Gino Renne, president of the Montgomery County Government Employees Organization, the United Food and Commercial Workers local that represents about half of the 7,000 county employees.

"The morale of this work force is at an all-time low," Renne said. "There is not confidence in [Duncan's] leadership as an employer."

The new department would be headed by Graham Norton and replace the Department of Transportation, which Norton currently heads, and the Facilities and Services Department. The directorship of Facilities and Services is vacant.

The trash collection and recycling functions of the Department of Environmental Protection, which were transferred to the transportation unit in the budget year that began July 1, also would come under the new department.

In March, Duncan announced the consolidation of four departments into a new Health and Human Services Department, saving $4.4 million while eliminating 163 jobs.

The council approved that consolidation, but only after restoring programs for the homeless and working poor that trimmed about $1 million from the projected saving. Leggett suggested the council might do the same with the public works department.

Under county personnel rules, any employee whose position is eliminated becomes eligible for a comparable or lesser vacancy elsewhere in the government. Renne said that no union member has been laid off so far as a result of the Health and Human Services consolidation.

SOURCE: Karl Vick, "Duncan Urges Merger of 2 Montgomery Departments; Public Works, Transportation Functions Would Be Combined in 2nd Stage of County Restructuring," *Washington Post* (July 27, 1995): C6.

The prescriptions that define structure are a product of legal, managerial, and professional decisions, all tempered in many cases with a strong dash of political strategy. The legal document, the legislation or court decision authorizing the bureau and its programs, usually contains some structural and procedural requirements, for example, the initial size of the bureau and the structure of its upper echelons may be spelled out. Some statutes and resolutions are purposely left vague on these points, however, to avoid the political implications of a choice. In other cases, often those involving hotly contested proposals to reorganize a bureau or reformulate a program, statutes may spell out structures in excruciating detail, as was the case in the creation of the Department of Energy. The Department of Energy was formed from offices taken from several departments, including Interior and Commerce and some independent agencies such as the Energy Research and Development Agency. There was, of course, great opposition from the agencies and their constituencies over this loss of program control, so the highly detailed proposals for the new department included some complex power-sharing arrangements as well.

Internally, and often incrementally, executive and midlevel managers develop structures; some examples are rules of procedure for initiating new projects, routing activity reports, and monitoring compliance. Professional program specialists develop the codes, regulations, and procedures for programs that determine specific reporting and generate command structures for program implementation. Written rules of all kinds are normally collected in manuals that constitute the standard operating procedures of the bureau. Job descriptions, and thus indirectly even the civil service laws of a jurisdiction, specify the division of task responsibilities. Altogether, these procedures and rules determine the specific activities of the bureau and how its structure will operate.

What models are used in the creation of these structures? What principles of "good" structure, or at least of useful structural forms, guide the original design and subsequent reorganizations over the life of the bureau? These are the questions to which the rest of this chapter is devoted.

TRADITIONAL STRUCTURAL PRINCIPLES

The most readily identifiable characteristic of the traditional approach to organizational structure is the idea that there exists an ideal structure to which all organizations should conform to be maximally effective. This approach, known as the Administrative Science School, assumed that finding the set of universal principles of structure would be the key to successful management and that a well-structured organization would nearly manage itself. The search for universal principles that could be applied to all, or almost all, organizations occupied the analysts, managers, and researchers who worked under the traditional approach.

Max Weber's definition of the ideal-type bureau (discussed in the previous chapter) set the stage for the analysis of structures. Three key structural elements of the ideal-type bureaucracy are its *hierarchy,* the *delimited authority* of officials, and the principle of *specialization* or division of labor (Weber 1947). The idea of hierarchy is that the authority of offices and officials is rank ordered on a descending scale of subordinate relations. Officials at the top of the ordering have the greatest authority, perfectly matched in the *ideal* bureau to their knowledge and expertise in office operations. Almost everyone would agree that few real agencies, and certainly not the ones they work for, reflect this ideal today. But most bureaus here and abroad are probably closer to this ideal model now than they were 100 years ago.

Specialization of function enhances the efficiency of bureau operations. It enables officials to become highly proficient in a relatively narrow professional task, and it generally allows workers to become more productive since organizing complex work into simple repetitive tasks increases the speed of production. For the ideal-type bureaucracy, there is to be a professionally designed, technically rational order to positions and tasks, and this order produces the stability, consistency, and efficiency that are hailed as the hallmarks of traditional bureaucratic structure.

Specialization, and the stability it brings is a mixed blessing in public bureaus, as many have noted. We want and need this degree of predictability in a law-enforcing institution, but we regret the rigidity that is the seemingly inevitable side effect. Although specialization brings expertise, it may also lead to a kind of unwillingness or inability to see alternative solutions to, or divergent points of view about, what a program should mean or how it could be implemented.

The traditionally oriented Administrative Science School of organizational theory worked to expand on these structural prescriptions and to refine them into more explicit principles that were intended to represent universal organizational laws based on an analysis of the experiences of successful administrators. However, the status of these principles as scientific laws, or even as coherent statements of practice, was seriously called into question by Simon (1965) and March and Simon (1993), who criticized them as vacuous and inconsistent. Contemporary research on organization design supports the usefulness of only a few of the principles.

Nevertheless, probably because of their apparent simplicity, the principles retain a surprising degree of influence on organization design: They still represent the conventional, though not the latest, administrative wisdom. For that reason, we identify some of the more basic of the traditional structural principles in Figure 4–1.

Three issues in particular are still important parts of contemporary debate and research in organization design, however, and we will consider them in some depth. They are the centralization–decentralization issue, the relationship between differentiation and integration, and the ongoing debate over the advantages of various bases for the departments in an organization. These issues introduce some of the basic concepts of organization structure.

Centralization and Decentralization

The terms *centralization* and *decentralization* refer to the degree to which decision-making authority is confined to the top echelons of the bureau or assigned to the lower echelon offices and officials.[1] Centralization is used to achieve greater control, to monitor operations, and to clarify policymaking and communication channels. All these uses can, in

---

[1]In practice, these terms are sometimes applied in a different and less useful way. Centralization is sometimes used to describe situations in which all offices are located in one place (in contrast to branch or regional offices) and to refer to the merging of some management functions from program departments to a unified office, as in a "centralized personnel office." However, these are not analytically useful applications of the term.

FIGURE 4–1 Some Principles of Administrative Science

Unity of command: An official should receive commands from and be responsible to only one supervisor to avoid confusion, unfair expectations, divided loyalties, and uncoordinated action.

> **Comments:** Henri Fayol, one of the earliest and most prominent of the administrative scientists, maintained, "For myself, I do not think that a shop can be run in flagrant violation of [unity of command]" (Fayol 1949, 69). As we will see, however, many contemporary organization designs, such as the matrix organization, do not follow this principle.

Line staff: An unbroken chain of command should be carried by line officers from top to bottom in the organization. Technical support and advisory staff should be attached to the offices with decision-making authority and command responsibility without disrupting the line of command.

> **Comments:** The distinction between line and staff is based on the difference between decision-making authority and advisory or support work, but this distinction is not always easy to maintain in practice, especially in bureaus where technical analysis is at the core of the mission.

Span of control: The optimal number of subordinates that can be successfully commanded by a supervisor.

> **Comments:** Working on the problem as a question of the mathematical combinations of possible relationships among superiors and subordinates, administrative scientists arrived at the conclusion that five or six was the optimal span (Urwick 1943). But little agreement on the ideal span ever emerged. Each branch of the military, for example, had its own scheme.

The functional and scalar principles: The search for the optimal basis for determining the appropriate type and degree of specialization in subordinate offices, and the optimal point at which to add another level in the hierarchy.

> **Comments:** Firm conclusions about the optimal point for either type of expansion are, not surprisingly, rare (Scott, Mitchell, and Birnbaum 1981, 36–37).

---

some cases, be critical to the survival and effectiveness of the organization. For example, demands for greater centralization often go with political claims that an agency (such as the Central Intelligence Agency or the Internal Revenue Service) is exceeding, misinterpreting, or failing to achieve its mission—or abusing its powers.

Decentralization is clearly the popular trend in structure, at least in part because of today's emphasis on responsiveness to clients and participatory management (National Performance Review 1993). Decentralized structures, by definition, permit greater autonomy in the bureau's subdivisions and make broad participation in some decisions possible. Decentralization can also increase the visibility of lower-level offices and emphasize their importance. Greater flexibility in dealing with external demands and faster decisions are also associated with decentralization.

Decentralization may, however, make it harder to determine program accountability and to establish consistent policies throughout the organization because more officials are active decision makers. The cooperative use of scarce resources may generate conflict in decentralized organizations since there is less central assignment of resources. Planning new projects may also take a back seat to developing existing ones. In an extremely decentralized structure, there may be no one watching for new opportunities for the *whole* organization or for new activities requiring cross-program coordination.

The search for guidelines about adopting centralized or decentralized structures is an ongoing issue in organization theory. Alfred Sloan, longtime president of General Motors, used a model of "centralized control of decentralized functions" that offered a mixed strategy. Key control activities were centralized for the corporation, while the auto subdivisions were given considerable discretion and room for initiative in design and marketing (Sloan 1964). Contemporary research uses the contingency approach, showing the effectiveness of each model to be dependent on certain technical and environmental conditions. Even so, there is disagreement among current management models since total quality management supports centralized authority more than do some of the other models emphasizing participative and democratic processes in organization.

Differentiation and Integration

Closely related to centralization and decentralization are two basic theoretical concepts of organizational structure that underlie contemporary organization design—differentiation and integration. The addition of specialized offices or subdivisions at a single hierarchical level and the evolution of new levels in the hierarchy both have the effect of differentiating the organization, that is, making finer lateral and hierarchical task distinctions. *Differentiation* refers to the degree of specialization, both vertical and horizontal, in the organization. The more differentiated the organization, the more complex its structure. Specializing the work of an office to distinguish between clientele groups in an affirmative action program or merging project offices to reduce the degree of specialization are examples of ways in which specialization has policy implications as well as technical consequences.

The greater the level of differentiation, the more formidable the task of integrating or coordinating all these distinct specialized tasks within and among the subdivisions of the organization. The integration process includes all the mechanisms and procedures by which the differentiated tasks are coordinated and ordered to achieve the organization's purpose. *Integration* is achieved through the hierarchical command and communication system and also through the processes for task coordination specified in rules, program regulations, plans, and schedules. Staff meetings, program task forces, procedures for circulating memos about policy changes, informal consultations, and even the departmental grapevines all contribute to organizational integration.

Balancing differentiation and integration is the key to designing effective organizational structures. The greater the level of differentiation, the greater the need for integration. External political forces often demand more specialized services for specific clientele or greater specialization in regulation; yet they complain about the amount of money spent on administration and the bloated midlevels of management. What is not understood by those making such requests is that the structure of any organization is a series of tradeoffs. Different levels and patterns of differentiation require corresponding levels and types of integration mechanisms. Administrative costs, technical requirements, and professional assumptions all affect what will be the most appropriate choices for matching differentiation and integration. Alternative structural forms exhibit different solutions to the balancing of differentiation and integration. The literature on organization design presented in the second half of this chapter illustrates the application of these analytic terms.

The Bases of Departmentalization

Many of the distinctions traditionally made about structural forms refer to the type of specialization on which a given structure is based. Division of labor at the individual level results in specialized tasks that then must be grouped together to form departments, offices, and other subdivisions. But on what basis should tasks be grouped? By professional specialty? By jurisdiction? Traditionally, bureaus have formed departments on one of four bases: (1) policy area or program, (2) management function, (3) client type, and (4) geography.

Departments that are based on similarity of *programs and policy* area are probably the most familiar; the federal executive departments are structured in this way. Fire departments, health departments, and natural resource departments share the fact that they are organized around a goal, a set of policies, and a group of programs. The idea behind the program-based structure is that all the bureau's resources, its professional specialties, its command and communication structure, and its management procedures are focused on the administration of policy and program goals. Each department is a self-contained administrative unit devoted to the program, which permits program-oriented problem solving and experimentation to proceed as a top priority. Normally, specialists in the most prestigious field associated with a program become executives in the bureau (Mosher 1982), which further protects established program goals and inhibits change. Thus, physicians traditionally manage health agencies, and lawyers dominate in regulatory agencies. These are some of the traditional rationales for program-based departments, but the reality may be quite different. The drawbacks of this form of organization are not hard to imagine. Since each department is self-contained, all management functions and support services, such as budgeting and personnel, must be established on a small scale. This situation creates duplication of effort among program departments and may be inefficient from the standpoint of any economies of scale that are possible in management function. Therefore, when a government priority is new program development, program-based departments are a means of responding to that priority, but this choice carries high management costs (Filley, House, and Kerr 1976, 363).

F.D.R.'s strategies for establishing his New Deal programs illustrate an extreme case of program development through structure. Roosevelt often created new agencies whose jurisdictions overlapped those of existing agencies. Doing so ensured the loyalty and responsiveness of the agencies and generated competition among them for survival as agents of the New Deal (Schlesinger 1959, 534–536). This was an effective but administratively costly strategy that would probably not be tolerated today.

Departments based on management *functions* solve some of the problems of program departments, but introduce others. In functional departments, officials are grouped into offices based on their management specialty, such as program management, policy evaluation, personnel, budgeting, or planning. For example, a functionally based health department would create major subdivisions based on management functions that would cut across programs or patient types. The bureau's divisions would no longer be self-contained from the program standpoint, and the administration of each program would require the coordinated effort of officers in different divisions. Here management efficiency becomes the first priority, and management specialists, such as finance experts, will generally hold the high-level departmental posts.

The advantages of this form of structure are clearly detailed by Filley, House, and Kerr (1976, 630–650). Functional departments allow officials to become specialized in particular management functions, some of which (budgeting, planning, and so on) have become highly technical fields; in contrast, the smaller numbers of technical specialists in program-based departments must spread themselves over a wider range of activities. The opportunity for professional camaraderie in functional departments may improve morale, and the chance to work with professionals in the same technical field and to climb the professional career ladder within the department may also be a motivating factor for these professionals. Finally, functionally based departments permit optimal use of resources and eliminate unnecessary duplication of personnel, equipment, or other facilities. In some cases, the larger operations of functional departments may also be more efficient because of the existence of economies of scale.

Again, drawbacks are associated with this structure. The coordination of program parts necessary to achieve the program goals can be exceedingly difficult and time consuming, and the administrative costs associated with some types of complex coordination can be very great, as we will show later in this chapter. Program goals may even be lost in the effort to optimize the efficiency and quality of management functions; client services may be subtly altered as managerial priorities affect program procedures; and budget-control procedures may slow claims processing or client intake. Research and development may be hampered by coordination requirements for sign-offs from specialists in wholly different fields. These and other effects can be anticipated and avoided.

Thus, the choice of program-based versus function-based departments presents a series of tradeoffs. It is generally proposed that bureaus placing the higher priority on program development use program-based departments, whereas those whose higher priority is re-source conservation use the functional approach. However, this rule of thumb, and the advantages claimed by each approach, should be considered hypotheses rather than laws. They assume all other things to be equal when, in fact, political, technical, and professional factors always intrude to complicate the application of such tidy rules.

The last two bases of departmentalization are less common organizational schemes though they are often used to define subdivisions *within* departments. An example of a department organized on the basis of *client type* is the Office of Human Development Services in the Department of Health and Human Services. It has created subdivisions for each of its major clientele—the elderly, children, and so on.

Geography-based departments are also relatively uncommon, though planning districts and some environmental management bureaus are organized on this basis. The Agency for International Development exhibits this form, with four of its main bureaus organized by host-country geographic areas. The regional offices of the federal executive departments also illustrate the use of geography as a basis for organization though at a lower than departmental level.

Mixed Forms of Organization

Actually, the issue in departmentalization is not which type to use—functional, geographic, and so on—but which types will be combined in some hybrid form. In other words, we usually do not choose between program or functional bases; rather, we decide which form to use to define departments and which to use to define the offices within the departments. Most large bureaus are organized on the basis of program or function and use the other forms at lower or subdivision levels. The police department of a large city is a good example of how these different rules for organization may apply in a single bureau: It is an agency, created within the city to deliver a general set of activities related to public safety, which then uses management functions (personnel and budget), law enforcement specializations (traffic control, homicide, and criminalistics), and geography (neighborhood precinct houses) as factors in its overall structure. This hybrid form attempts to combine the advantages of the program- and functional-based schemes while avoiding the weaknesses of each. Nevertheless, coordination between large functional departments and the programs that depend on them for critical program components may still present difficulties. Some method for managing this coordination must be devised. The federal Office of Management and Budget (OMB), for example, has an elaborate sign-off procedure for new departmental regulations to ensure their conformance with OMB cost–benefit analysis requirements.

Some other mixed-type forms of organization have recently emerged, especially in bureaus whose missions require interdisciplinary teamwork and project research and development. Team-based organization and matrix organization are two examples. In a matrix organization, staff are grouped into functional departments, often based on professional specialties. But they are also assigned, for varying lengths of time, to program or project groups. Each program group, therefore, comprises an interdisciplinary collection of specialists selected to fit the needs of the project. These project groups can be visualized as cutting across the functional or disciplinary departments to produce a matrix in which the columns represent projects and the rows represent functional departments (planning, finance, and so on) or discipline-based departments (a hospital setting, physicians, nurses, paraprofessionals) (see Figure 4–2). Each project is headed by a director, usually from the lead functional department involved in the project. Depending on the size of the project group, each disciplinary or functional subgroup may also have its own supervisor to direct and control its functions and to act as liaison with the permanent functional department.

This is a fairly complex form of organization and is generally both costly and time consuming to administer because of all the crosscutting lines of authority and accountability that must be coordinated. A great deal of time must be spent by the functional or discipline-group heads, the heads of project teams, and even the professionals themselves negotiating who will work on what parts of what projects. Every official works under two superiors, so the structure violates the principle of unity of command. In general, it sacrifices simplicity of form for the advantages of cross-disciplinary teamwork and professionally based departments.

The extra expense and personnel needs of this form of organization have most often been justified by pressing project development needs in which cost, within some limit, is not as high a priority as program goals. Some NASA projects have used this form, negotiating released time for specialists from functional departments as new projects develop

FIGURE 4–2   Matrix Organization

Number of Employees in Task Force

	Project 1	Project 2	Project 3	Project 4
Legal Dept.	2		1	3
Finance Dept.	1	1		1
Personnel Dept.		1	1	
Service Delivery Dept. I		2	2	3
Service Delivery Dept. II	3		3	

In this simple organization, five different departments are working on four special team projects.

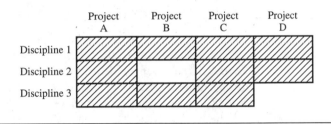

and needs change (Delbecq and Filley 1976, 8). Peters and Waterman, stressing the excessive costs and the heavy paperwork and control requirements of the model, noted that almost none of their "excellent" organizations used a matrix (1982, 307).

Project organization is a term used to describe a similar but more temporary organizational arrangement. Here, the ties of the functional departments are more strongly maintained. Teams of this nature are central to the process of total quality management (TQM). TQM advocates argue that:

> organizations are systems of highly interdependent parts, and the central problems they face invariably cross traditional functional lines. . . . [Therefore] Deming and Juran are insistent that cross-functional problems must be addressed collectively by representatives of all relevant functions. (Hackman and Wageman 1995, 311)

TQM requires managers and workers to collectively examine the processes of the organization to look for possible improvements and then to gain their acceptance within the total establishment. This means that both managers and workers:

> need to work "without barriers"—using matrix-like structures and quality circles to break down communication barriers between hierarchical levels and between functional units. (Swiss 1992, 368)

Team organization is another related form in which members of different functional departments work together in small, but more or less permanent, teams headed by the member from the most professionally prestigious specialty; medical teams and team policing are well-known examples. Members maintain their ties to the functional departments for personnel, training, promotion, and other such matters, but they work face to face principally with members of other departments to achieve the level of coordinated expertise demanded by their tasks.

Other forms of organizational structure are constantly evolving in response to new managerial experiences and program requirements. Cost reduction, new technical requirements for programs, and unanticipated consequences from implementation also motivate the search for alternative structural arrangements. In 1970, for example, Frederickson described forms of local government organization that had grown out of the demands for citizen participation, joint programs, and contracted services; Agranoff (1976) noted the ways in which organization design aided in interagency program development and service delivery; and Osborne and Gaebler (1992) described numerous attempts by state and local governments to change both structure and process to achieve what they call "entrepreneurial government."

General Concerns of the Traditional Approaches

The traditional approaches to organizational structure placed high value on stability, symmetry, clarity of lines of command, and on fully rationalizing the structure of the bureau. The universal principles of structure and management sought by the Administrative Science School still guide some management practices, and their questions are important ones as far as they go. But the search for a set of universal rules of thumb for structures forced managers to be oversimplistic in their analysis of alternative forms of organizations. New programs and rapid changes in the political and cultural environment of bureaus place more complex demands on today's bureaus; new structural forms are one kind of response to these changes.

Current research and theory on organization structures look at these and other factors in offering more complex prescriptions for organizational forms. The current approaches attempt to create an organizational form that is responsive to circumstances rather than to find a form that will be applicable everywhere. The idea that a structure can be crafted to support the specific workflow of the agency and its complex exchanges with its environments is reflected in the name of the newer trend—organization design.

ORGANIZATION DESIGN PERSPECTIVES ON STRUCTURE

The questions posed by current perspectives on structures are, simply, how to design organizations that can adapt to changing environmental demands and that are supportive of increasingly complex program goals and procedures in bureaus. As noted, these questions reflect an important departure in purpose and research focus from the universalistic principles of the Administrative Science School.

The design approach recognizes the internal and external complexities of program management. It offers alternatives to the hierarchy assumed in the traditional administrative science approach, and in the long run it may well support alternative approaches to program development. For now, to the extent that public bureaus have failed in their missions because of their operational rigidity, their inability to coordinate their efforts, or the absence of communication channels for discovering and acting on evidence of failure, the newer design approaches hope to promote more effective administrative practices (Levine et al. 1975).

One important characteristic of the design approaches is that they are, for the most part, contingency theories; that is, instead of offering one structural prescription for all bureaus, they argue for the use of *different* forms depending on the environment, technology, and program development needs of the bureau. Thus, they are strategic rather than global approaches to the problem of design. The result is that a varied and complex set of factors must be considered, including legal and political ones. This orientation, then, forces us to systematically raise questions that are particularly important for implementation and program management.

For the purpose of this discussion, we will divide current research on design into three approaches: (1) designs based on program technology, (2) designs based on environmental circumstances, and (3) designs that facilitate a continual reexamination of current arrangements and encourage organizational learning. These approaches do not represent mutually exclusive design strategies; rather, it is important to note the underlying links among them. And it is useful to point out their implications, their uses, and their limitations for bureaus.

No literature has been developed specifically to instruct and inform managers about the design of politically or legally responsive structures. However, each of these three rather well-developed approaches to design does shed light on how organizations might use structural changes to better cope with their complex and rapidly changing political environments.

Technology-Based Designs

One of the most widely researched design approaches focuses on the technology of the organization. The main thesis of this approach, termed the *technological imperative,* is that in effective organizations, structure reflects technology. In this context, technology means the process for transforming raw materials into finished products. More broadly stated to include the types of work done in most public bureaus, technology refers to the programs and procedures designed to respond to situations and to process cases to achieve the results specified in law and public policy. For example, agency activities for collecting and auditing tax returns, for planning and implementing foreign assistance, or for delivering social services each comprise a complex set of activities that constitute the technology of the bureau.

Technology in this sense refers not just to machines or the use of the most advanced findings of applied science, but to the programs and performance routines of the bureau. The more simple, controllable, and predictable these work routines are, the less complex the technology is said to be.

The interpretation of the technological imperative as it applies to public agencies is that programs are technologies, and these technologies are based on complex political and professional values as ratified by legislatures and agency rule making. The message here is that to be effective, bureaus must establish structures that match their program technologies.

It is important to bear in mind while perusing the research and theory in this section that the field is still very much in a developmental stage. Thus, the literature does not offer a simple blueprint for redesigning an agency; rather, it offers a new set of concepts with which to assess the workflow of the agency and the structure that is supposed to support it. The categories of technology that we will discuss and the prescriptions for structure that the theories offer are not fixed: Administrators in various policy fields may well discover types of technology that are more useful than the ones noted here. The general structural forms and types described here should serve as the foundation for the design of many specific structures, each created for particular circumstances. In sum, the material in this section should be used as a starting point for the analysis of structural problems and the design of more adequate structures.

Types of Technology

Specific types of program technologies for the work of bureaus have not yet been developed. But we can identify agencies with routine technologies in which the work is specialized, repetitive, and almost wholly defined by rules. Similarly, we find agencies engaged in research or in some kinds of regulation in which their work is not generally subject to established rules. For example, regulation that proceeds on a negotiated, case-by-case basis would require more discretion by officials than regulation based on enforcing highly codified standards and criteria. Until we have a typology of public program technologies, we must build on more general types.

Large complex bureaus are involved with more than one technology. Agencies with responsibilities for several programs, such as research and grants administration, may have several technologies, each housed in separate structural components. The activities of different hierarchical levels may also required different technologies (Perrow 1967). Most of the research in this area is concerned only with the "core" technology, but more recent research is beginning to recognize the structural consequences of multiple technologies.

The first task for design research is to find a way to classify technology that clearly distinguishes and explains the structural needs of each type. The simplest typology distinguishes only between routine and nonroutine technology. A series of repetitive tasks performed on an unchanging set of cases or situations would be the most routine technology. Hage and Aiken (1969) found that the routine technologies in organizations were associated with highly developed rules and procedures manuals, centralized decision making, and a high degree of task specialization. This is, of course, a fair description of the traditional bureaucratic structure, with its emphasis on stability and reliability through rules and the chain of command. Less routine work, with varying tasks or cases, requires more discretion and would find an elaborate body of rules an impediment.

Research using more sophisticated categories of technology was done by Joan Woodward (1980); it produced similar findings. Woodward found a reasonably strong association between a firm's technology, its structure, and its economic success. The more routine technologies tended to have more traditional structures, whereas the less routine technologies had more discretionary and decentralized structures. The importance of Woodward's findings is not only that differences in structure are generally associated with differences in technology, but that we find this pattern only in successful firms. The implication here is that managers who match structures to technology are more successful.

Charles Perrow's (1967) typology tries to answer questions about why technology and structure are related. His research has become highly influential both in academic and practitioner circles (Gerwin 1981). But his argument is complex, so it is essential to begin with a quick overview. Perrow classifies the technology of an organization according to four types, ranging from a highly routine, rule-governed technology to a highly nonroutine, problem-solving technology. He then prescribes a basic structural model for each type. That structure is prescribed on the basis of the need for autonomy, discretion, and coordination in the workflow of each technology. Different structural arrangements provide autonomy to different portions of the organization and use different mechanisms to coordinate the work of offices and people.

Perrow's analysis begins with a way to classify technologies along two dimensions. The first reflects the degree to which the cases or inputs for the organization are either uniform or diverse. Are the people or situations the agency encounters similar in the agency's eyes, or are they seen as individual, diverse entities? The greater the diversity of cases, the more complex the technology. On this basis, the technology of a general hospital is more complex than that of a nursing home.

The second dimension in Perrow's scheme is the process used to find solutions for the exceptional or variable cases. This is the knowledge technology. The issue here is whether the cases encountered can be handled with the existing program and routines or if new programs must be created. If the organization has fully codified procedures for dealing with cases in its standard operating procedures, the technology is said to be analyzable; that is, the transformation process is so well understood that even new types of cases and situations can be classified and analyzed using known techniques. The mission of some bureaus, however, is to create new program technologies. Their work rests on professional judgments and cannot therefore be codified or rule bound. Research bureaus are the prime example of this type, but planning offices and intelligence agencies may also fall into this category.

Combining Perrow's two technological dimensions produces a fourfold table for classifying organizational technologies, as Figure 4–3 illustrates. Quadrant 2 is the least routine, most complex technology, characteristic of the core technologies of research and development organizations such as NASA and NIH. Perrow notes also that elite service institutions such as some schools or hospitals employ this technology. Quadrant 4 is the most routine technology and is exemplified by the post office, parts of the IRS, and other form-processing agencies and custodial service institutions.

Quadrants 1 and 3 constitute the middle range of routineness, but for different reasons. For quadrant 1, even though the cases encountered are generally uniform, no routine or formally codified procedures exist for processing cases; thus, professional judgment and artistry are necessary. Some courts, higher education, and case-by-case adjudication in regulatory agencies illustrate this technology.

The technology classified in quadrant 3 is well adapted to handling exceptional cases or situations. Many are encountered, and their processing requirements are clearly understood. A large repertoire of procedures for classifying and processing them has been worked out in advance so that problem solving consists of putting together the proper set of responses and activating the relevant subunits. Examples of this type of technology (in which Perrow includes engineering-type operations) might include some social and public services, active military units, and some aspects of law enforcement.

FIGURE 4–3   Classifying Organizational Technologies

| | | Uniformity of Cases and Situations | | | |
		Uniform			*Variable*
	Must search for new procedures; process not codified	Treatment based on professional judgment			Nonroutine work
Analyzability of cases within existing procedures and knowledge		Decentralized structure	1	2	Flexible, polycentric structure
	Standard procedures exist; technology is codified	Routine work	4	3	Combine programs to fit cases
		Centralized structure			Flexible, centralized structure

SOURCE: Charles Perrow, "A Framework for the Comparative Analysis of Organizations," *American Sociological Review* 32, 1967; 33–34.

Structural Prescriptions

The structural prescriptions for each of these technological types are derived from the requirements for coordination and discretion under each technology. For the agencies with the least routine technologies (in quadrant 2, Figure 4–3), Perrow recommends a "flexible, polycentric" structure that provides the maximum autonomy for professionals at the operations level, such as a matrix or project form. Research institutes at universities and multidisciplinary policy research teams might be some examples. Matrix or project forms of organization would be examples of structures with multiple, quite autonomous, professional workgroups.

For bureaus with the most routine technologies, those in quadrant 4, such as highly standardized form-processing offices and claims processing, Perrow prescribes the traditional mechanistic bureaucratic form. This form offers some of the most effective ways to achieve consistent compliance with the rules and to limit discretion, both of which are critical for this technology, which requires great standardization of action.

Organizations with engineering-type technologies (quadrant 3-types) may handle varying and novel conditions by recombining the parts of a set of well-established procedures. The structure prescribed in this case is a flexible centralized structure, which allows middle managers to rearrange program components to meet new situations. Examples here are the use of hand-picked investigatory teams in law enforcement agencies or the shuffling of combat units to cover a series of changing tasks.

The technologies that rely on professional judgment, (quadrant 1) are best handled in a decentralized structure in which professionals are given the needed decision-making authority. Examples are the collegial, nonhierarchical structure of some regulatory commissions and the delegation of pedagogical and personal decisions to the departmental level in universities.

Theories of Technology-Based Design

Perrow's prescriptions for these structural forms are based on an analysis of where discretion is needed in each technology and how the work of offices is to be coordinated. Figure 4–4 illustrates two links between technology and structure.

The need for discretion at different hierarchical levels of the organization is the first of the links between technology and structure. The more routine the technology, the less autonomy and flexibility are required by the officials processing the cases. Thus, the most routine technology needs discretion only at the upper echelons, and a traditional centralized hierarchy is quite satisfactory. The least routine program technology, however, requires much more discretion for professionals at the operations level since they must exercise judgment. Semiautonomous, highly participatory work teams or project groups in what Peters and Waterman (1982) refer to as "skunk works" are more supportive of this work than a traditional hierarchy could be. Even in the scientific and research world of air fighter development, the stealth fighter could be produced only in the even more participatory, open, and accepting environment of such a skunk works.

The second linkage between technology and structure is more complex. Each technology presents its own patterns of dependencies among offices or individuals. The most complex and nonroutine of the technologies requires the most flexible and elaborate ways of coordinating the interdependent work of people and offices such as direct feedback through meetings, sign-offs, and so forth. This is the case because their work is relatively unpredictable, and it is hard to know much in advance what will be required by way of mutual adjustments to keep the operation flowing smoothly. For example, members of a research project may have primary responsibility for different parts of the project, but if an individual assignment does not turn out as anticipated, most or all of the work of the rest of the team may have to be adjusted or redesigned. For the most routine technologies, the most mechanistic bureau model is prescribed, the one that makes use of the least costly and least flexible coordination devices: rules and schedules. In general, Thompson (1967) notes that organizational actors in pursuit of rationality would select the least expensive coordination device adequate for the degree of unpredictability in the work process.

The foregoing analysis can make an important contribution to improving coordination within public agencies, but the requirements of accountability within the agency and to

---

FIGURE 4–4　Two Links Between Technology and Structure

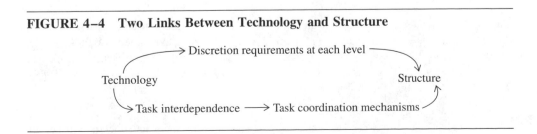

external policymakers complicates the issue. Many task forces or committees are far too large and inefficient from a design viewpoint, but they serve symbolic as well as coordinative purposes; they show that all interested groups are being heard and have a role in program direction. The symbolic functions of organization structures can be as critical as their coordinative functions. Some other coordination mechanisms, such as the use of feedback when rules would be as useful and less costly, serve social and political purposes by demonstrating openness and the desire to be responsive and participative. Finally, some types of feedback may include actors to whom the work team is formally or informally accountable so that the feedback cannot be optimally constructed according to Thompson's principles. In all these cases, the efficiency of the coordination system is sacrificed for the requirements of external accountability, political responsiveness, and organizational cohesiveness—other important values in public agencies.

It must also be noted that in most bureaus there is a tendency to make programs as routine as possible. Several organizational analysts describe the rigidity of bureaus as the result of efforts to prevent deviant cases and situations from disrupting established routines (Allison, 1971; March and Simon 1993). The "sunk costs" of trained personnel, procedures, and other resources in existing programs make administrators reluctant to alter routines (Downs 1967). In military organizations, for example, a limited number of combat scenarios are well established and "built into" the procedure manuals and the training regimes. These scenarios represent a huge investment in planning, training, and coordination. Thus, only with great reluctance will the organization discard this investment and establish new scenarios. The same investment in procedures characterizes most bureaus, and their preference for routines and control may help explain why bureaus seldom depart from the traditional hierarchical form.

To summarize this rather complex theory of design, the technology in use in an organization creates a pattern of task interdependencies, coordination requirements, and needs for discretion. The most appropriate structure for each technology will be the one that supports these requirements at the least cost. The model implicit in this thesis is that technology leads to task interdependencies, which, in turn, lead to coordination requirements, which, in turn, define the structure. If this is true, mismatching the structure and the technology will result in a wasteful level of discretion and communication for activities that could be more reliably and economically planned or scheduled in advance. Alternatively, hierarchies with centralized decision making and planning could seriously impede the ability of professionals engaged in nonroutine technologies to proceed with their work. The attempt to impose standardized procedures on uncertain discovery or production processes is a common complaint of both officials and clients of bureaus.

Criticisms of Technology-Based Design

Criticisms of the technology approach are of two sorts: (1) research that does not find an association between technology and structure, and (2) conceptual problems with the model itself. A serious challenge to the evidence for this thesis is the Aston research conducted in Britain by Pugh, Hickson, and Hinings (1969) and Hickson, Pugh, and Phesey (1969). They did not find that technology predicted *overall* structure, but rather that:

> Structural variables will be associated with operations technology only when they are centered on the workflow. The smaller the organization the more its structure will be

pervaded by such technological effects; the larger the organization, the more these effects
. . . will not be detectable in variables of the more remote administrative and hierarchical
structure. (Hickson, Pugh, and Phesey 1969)

Current research on technology and structure, in acknowledgment of these findings,
focuses on a refinement of the technology thesis that looks at the link between structure
and technology at the workgroup level rather than the larger organizational level. This
version of the thesis has been supported by a number of studies (Gerwin 1981). These
findings suggest that more complex organizational structures with different forms in different divisions might be the most rational in the absence of other political and legal
constraints.

A more damaging series of criticisms of the thesis are conceptual in nature. The first
is that its assumptions about cause may be in error so that in reality existing structures
determine technology (Robey 1994). The argument here is that the bureaucratic form itself
influences the perception and choice of what the most appropriate technology for the
organization is, and this, in turn, influences the design of new programs and routines.
Thus, tasks that might not be properly subject to division of labor and serial production,
for example, are set up in this manner anyway. If this is true, very few organizations
would ever break out of the routine technology and hierarchical model, as in fact, relatively
few bureaus have.

This criticism leads to a further conceptual problem already implicit in Perrow's research (1970). In one of the case studies he uses to support his theory, he describes two
schools for juvenile offenders. One uses a routine technology in which students are treated
in a regimented fashion; the other tries to individualize the students' programs based on
the assumption that their problems and potentials are different and that changing them is
not a standardized process. Wilson (1989) describes two prison systems that also operate
with these two differing assumptions about the inmates, and argues that most measures of
success support the regimented system. Although it is true that the differences in technology in this case are associated with differences in structure, the case also suggests that
technology itself is a matter, at least in part, of perception and choice. In addition to goals,
technology, and process, assumptions about organizational culture (discussed later in this
chapter) influence perceptions and choices of those involved in deciding the structure of
the organization. If this is true, on what basis is the appropriateness of a structure to be
judged? Does one use the objectively appropriate technology, if such a thing exists, or the
technology chosen by the bureau's administration, even if it is inappropriate by some
professional or political standards for program technology? Implicitly, theorists have assumed that only when the technology is "appropriate" and the structure supports it will
the bureau be successful and effective. But questions about the appropriateness of the
technology raise new and thorny problems for research into public agencies, problems that
have not yet been addressed directly.

A question raised by both of these criticisms of the technology thesis, and of particular
importance for bureaus, is how and where these technologies are established. By professionals? By legislatures? How is it determined whether a situation or case fits the existing
routine? On what basis are these choices made? When professional program specialists
and managers make such decisions, they do so on the basis of traditions, sometimes conflicting professional values and beliefs, and at least for appointees, on the basis of overt
political loyalties as well.

Further, the dominant professional coalition within a bureau has been shown to exert a strong influence on the interpretation and implementation of policies, even when program mandates are quite explicit (Montjoy and O'Toole 1979). F.D.R. understood this well when he established new program agencies for his new policy initiatives rather than entrusting them to bureaus with entrenched interests and established routines.

Acknowledging technology as an important factor in the design of bureaus in no way implies that administration is therefore a wholly technical scientific task. On the other hand, if organizational design is to fulfill the promise of creating a smoother and more efficient workflow by matching structure and technology, we cannot ignore questions about the appropriateness of the technology itself.

Environmental Change and Organizational Design

A second approach to organizational design might be called the environmental imperative. The thesis here is that under conditions of rapid environmental change, successful organizations adopt less formal, more decentralized, and professionally specialized structures that can adapt more quickly and effectively to change. The traditional centralized hierarchical structure, with its long chain of command and pattern of downward communication, is not designed to either discover or respond to change rapidly. In fact, as Weber observed, its stability was counted as one of the bureaucracy's chief advantages. Contemporary theorists no longer consider it a virtue, however, and argue that in an age of constant change in demands, program knowledge, and levels of expectation, organizations that cannot adapt will not survive.

There are two caveats to bear in mind in interpreting the environmental design thesis. First, the theory and research should not be conceived of as final, but rather, as emerging. The thesis probably works best when thought of as a series of suggestions for assessing the organization's work processes and methods of coordination, and not as a rigid plan of action.

Second, no organization; public, private, or nonprofit, can use the design principles as their sole basis for structure. Political, social, professional, and traditional factors all intervene to temper the capacity of the organization to adopt what might, all things being equal, be the most efficient and effective structures. Public organizations provide abundant evidence of this, illustrating again and again the legal and political constraints on structures. Nevertheless, we should be aware of the possibilities for structures that facilitate environmental responsiveness, and in fact many of the structural adaptations described in the literature generally have commonly been used to respond to the constantly changing political environments in which agencies must survive.

Bureau Environments

The principal components of bureau environments are policymakers, clients and constituency groups, and other organizations. Policymakers who authorize and fund bureau activities include elected and judicial officials and high-level executive appointees. Bureaus are not only responsible to these actors, but usually also seek to influence them directly or indirectly in an effort to control threats to their autonomy and growth. Clients and interest groups who support or oppose bureau actions are also important elements in a bureau's environment. Clients must be identified, and their demands and complaints must be channeled into appropriate programs. Supportive groups must be mobilized on the bureau's behalf to speak to policymakers about their shared interests; nonsupportive groups must be neutralized. Other agencies, public and nonprofit, may operate as competitors for program authority and funds. Especially in an era of political pressures for downsizing (reductions in force) and outsourcing (privatizing or contracting out), bureaus are forced by external forces to reexamine all aspects of organizational structure and process.

The sources of rapid and ongoing change in the bureau's environment are myriad. For example, changes in the economy and their concomitant impact on revenues and deficits have led to changed societal perspectives about and expectations of public organizations. These changed perspectives and expectations have led, in turn, to drastic cuts in funds and changes in program authority for bureaus at every level of government. Changes in national views on federalism shift program responsibilities from the federal to the state level or from the local to the federal level, as has been occurring in welfare and health policies. Grass-roots action or the emergence of widespread public awareness of the danger of ecological pollution, drunk drivers, airline maintenance, product safety, or nuclear power plants causes the rise of new pressure groups that launch hard-hitting legal and political attacks on program and regulatory agencies. And periodically, cries for "more protection for the average citizen" are replaced by complaints of "too much regulation" and "government interference in our daily lives." The only constant seems to be change; the environmental factors will change, often in a cyclical manner.

The theoretical characteristics of rapidly changing environments have been described by a number of authors. Emory and Trist (1965) describe organizational environments at four levels of complexity, depending on the number and predictability of other actors in the system. The simplest level is placid and relatively free of other cooperating or competing organizations. In this environment, organizations can plan and act independently, without concern for the reactions of other organizations. The most complex level is an environment so unstable and densely populated with other actors and organizations that the consequences of independent action by any one organization are no longer predictable, and strategic action must of necessity be replaced by joint action and merger. Thompson (1967), after reviewing a number of earlier typologies, argues that the most important environmental dimension for the structure of organizations are the stability and homogeneity of the organization's task environment. (Stability and homogeneity refer to the uniformity of the demands and resources from the environment over time and the similarity among the groups with which the bureau deals.)

Responses to Changing Environments

How do agencies respond to changes in their political and program authority environment? In several ways at once. Program goals may be adjusted up or down, or reworded, to give the necessary signals about what the agency is doing. When the mood of the environment is to cut back and reduce government's role, the agencies may attempt to reduce their programs in an effort to show they are responsive and to keep some control over the cuts that are made in bureau programs and structure. On the other hand, the agency may pursue a new program authority if some policy area appears ripe for expansion and the agency has support. The emergence of programs to aid cities became part of the mission of many program agencies in the 1960s, whereas energy and environmental missions were founded in the early 1970s. The agency may cope with environmental pressures by working with constituency or pressure groups to create support. The EPA was credited, during the 1970s, with having created nationwide grass-roots support for its clean-water regulations by establishing local boards to determine the level of water purity required based on the uses determined for a body of water. In the 1990s, the EPA is fighting a defensive battle, rallying its supporters against political forces that wish to reduce water purity standards.

Establishing linkage mechanisms for policymaking or service delivery with other agencies is a way of coping with limits on program growth imposed by the political environment. This tactic rests on the assumption that if programs are better coordinated, they will be more effective and require fewer new resources. This was a major priority in health and human services programs in the 1970s. With the rising costs to society of health care, reorganization of the health care industry still remains one of the alternatives being considered in the 1990s because structural and procedural changes are often preferable—to most sides in the debate—to basic, radical changes in the philosophy behind such a system. Usually the first organizational adaptations to changes in the environment are structural.

Research on the relationship between environmental change and structure, like the research on the technological imperative, is rather mixed, but as with the technology approach, it does appear to point to a consistent trend: Organizational success is enhanced when the complexity of the environment is matched by the complexity of structures. One of the most important early studies of this relationship was conducted by Lawrence and Lorsch (1967), who studied private sector firms, but whose findings have interesting implications for public agencies. They found that in the more successful firms, the rate of market change was matched by the complexity of the firms' internal structures. The structural variables studied were the degree and type of differentiation and the integration mechanisms for coordination within and among departments. Firms in three industries—plastics, food processing, and container manufacturing—were chosen to reflect differences in environmental conditions.

As predicted, the plastics firms, which had the most unstable environment, showed the greatest structural complexity, with a relatively large number and diversity of subdivisions. Further, the subdivisions that interacted most with external groups, the research and sales divisions of the plastics firms, were less hierarchically structured than the relatively isolated and routine production divisions. These facts imply that the structural differences were not global matters of style in these firms, but choices designed to meet environmental uncertainties.

Integration mechanisms also differed among the industries, with more complex task coordination methods used in the plastics firms than in the others. Special liaison units were created, for example, to improve interdepartmental coordination between research and production because their divergent goals and work processes resulted in frequent conflicts. The relationship between environmental change and structure was stronger for successful than for unsuccessful firms, echoing the contingency theory findings of the Woodward study.

Hage and Aiken (1970) conducted research that also supports the relationship between environment and structure. They identified seven structural characteristics of adaptive or "dynamic" organizations, firms that were able to change in response to changes in environmental conditions. Their findings are based primarily on case studies of organizational change, including examples of bureaus and service organizations. These characteristics, and the rationale behind their association with responsiveness and change are as follows:

1. Organizational complexity, defined as the number and professionalism of occupational specialties in the organization, is positively associated with the ability of the organization to respond to external change because professionals are often externally oriented to the developments in their fields and bring them to the agency.

2. Centralization of authority in the upper echelons of the bureau slows the rate of change because decision criteria are static, and lower-ranking personnel, who often see the need for change, are most directly excluded from decisions.

3. Formalization, the degree to which tasks are highly codified into rules and standard operating procedures, slows the rate of program change. When large portions of program and management activities are rule governed, change is delayed and perceptions of the possibility of substantial change are limited. Extreme formalization also slows the process of implementing a change since a whole set of new rules must be developed and coordinated with existing ones.

4. Stratification, the differentiated distribution of rewards among employees to emphasize rank, decreases the rate of change. Stratification creates insecurities and fears of loss of status. It also discourages negative reports on organizational performance and open discussion of problems with superiors.

5. Emphasis on a high volume of production lowers the rate of change since change, almost of necessity, disrupts production.

6. Greater emphasis on efficiency delays change because new program ideas are usually oriented first to improvements in quality, not efficiency. Thus, program changes will be adopted only when they have developed to the point of high operating efficiency.

7. Higher levels of job satisfaction are also associated with greater rates of change since satisfaction increases commitment to organizational success and enables the organization to overcome the strains involved in change.

What is missing from this research is a comparative analysis of the state of the environment and the subsequent success or failure of the organizations studied. Nevertheless, their work is important in that it offers some explanations for the relationship between structural characteristics and the capacity to change.

Thompson's (1967) analysis of structural responses to environmental conditions helps us further explore this issue for bureaus. In Thompson's view, organizations comprise offices, activities, and roles that contribute to two key functions: (1) the core professional technology of the bureau, that is, its basic work processes and management procedures, and (2) the "boundary-spanning" units, whose job it is to manage the interaction between the bureau and its environment. The boundary spanners, which are roles played by individuals or a whole office, are supposed to buffer this core technology from outside interference. On this point, Thompson proposes: "Under norms of rationality, organizations facing heterogeneous task environments seek to identify homogeneous segments and establish structural units to deal with each" (1967, 70).

This proposition is in accord with the findings of Lawrence and Lorsch (1986) and is illustrated by the plethora of public information offices, legislative liaison offices, hot lines, interagency task forces, ombudsmen, and other offices established in an agency to deal with important external groups. The larger the number and diversity of groups in the bureau's environment—governmental bodies, interest groups, media investigators, and so on—the greater the number of specialized boundary-spanning units we expect the "rational" bureau to create. A further implication is that the greater the proliferation of these specialized boundary-spanning units, the more elaborate the integration mechanisms must be to coordinate their activities with each other and with the technological core. Thompson helps explain why we should expect bureaus in tumultuous environments to have more complexity of specialization and integration than bureaus in more placid environments.

Although little systematic research on this point has been done for bureaus, Thompson's proposition squares with considerable experience. As the public becomes more involved—through citizen participation requirements, freedom of informations laws, increased oversight by Congress or other interested groups, or by demanding the addition of programs such as the Inspector General offices to the ongoing functions of an agency—the agency must respond by creating structures to deal with these additional duties or demands; and if all the demands apply, as is frequently true, the added complexity is compounded.

Complex ongoing relations with other bureaus and private organizations may be part of the boundary-spanning activities of an agency as well, whether the agency is attempting to cooperate and coordinate with another agency or is in competition for resources or program jurisdictions. Awareness by administrators of a real interdependency among agencies can lead to voluntary cooperative adjustments among agencies and a more stable, effective, interorganizational system (Litwak and Hylton 1962; Benson 1975; Lindblom 1965).

Another of Thompson's propositions suggests a rationale for the link between environment, technology, and structure. Although environments that include many diverse external bodies and groups create greater numbers of boundary-spanning units, the stability and predictability of the actions of external groups and actors determine the degree of routineness in the boundary-spanning units' responses. The greater the predictability of environmental activities, the more routine the bureau can be in handling them. Thompson notes: "The organization component facing a stable task environment will rely on rules to achieve its adaptation to that environment" (1967, 71).

The routine application of rules is, of course, less costly and time consuming than direct feedback, negotiation, or an elaborate planning process. But unstable, unpredictable demands, complaints, or opportunities cannot be effectively handled by rules. Negotiation between the agency and an outside group must be used instead. Uncertainty and the possibility of departure from standard operating procedures in a boundary-spanning unit will have a ripple effect on the rest of the organization, imposing greater uncertainty and even departures from rules in the core technology. If, for example, a regulatory or benefit agency makes an exception to some requirement in a particular case, other internal procedures will have to be altered to allow the case to proceed through the system. In general, according to Thompson's prescriptions, the more dense, heterogeneous, and unpredictable the environment, the greater the number and complexity of boundary-spanning units, the more elaborate the means of integrating them to the core, and the more complex the core technology.

One final model based on environmental design has been developed by Burns and Stalker (1994). In an argument that is by now familiar, they propose that we are moving into a postindustrial phase of development in which high technology and rapidly changing organizational environments make the traditional pairing of routine operations technology and bureaucratic administrative technology obsolete. A new ideal type of administrative form is now needed to provide a supportive setting for the high-technology workflow, with flexibility and the milieu for professional creativity needed to keep pace with rapid market changes and the growth of knowledge. By implication, all organizations do, should, or will find themselves in such an environment and thus require the organismic form. Burns and Stalker's version of the thesis is less a contingency theory than a global prescription for change, and it is supported by new models of "learning organizations" (Senge 1990) and parts of the TQM movement that require teamwork and constant change in procedures (Walton 1990)

Key elements of the new organizational systems are that their structures emphasize a network rather than a hierarchy of authority and control relations, with open, lateral, and upward communications based on consultation, not just downward commands. Furthermore, tasks and workflow are flexible and subject to continual redefinition on the basis of new information (as in quadrants 1 and 2 of Perrow's typology). Expertise, regardless of rank, is openly acknowledged and used, jurisdictional disputes and rivalries are subordinated to open professional commitments. Members are loyal to their work and their professional communities, but not necessarily to a single firm. Career migration is common. It might be noted by way of contrast, that these characteristics are accepted by TQM advocates, and by those attempting to develop "learning organizations" (organizations that can enhance their capacity to realize constant improvement in order to achieve their highest aspirations), but loyalty to the firm is viewed as very important to success.

Applying the environmental design theories to public agencies and environments gives rise to a wealth of hypotheses and questions, very few of which have been systematically tested. How should we classify and measure environmental density, stability, and homogeneity? Is the capacity to change evidence of organizational effectiveness in public agencies? In what policy fields or level of government is environmental change most common, and under what conditions is interorganizational density and interaction the greatest? How are agencies such as the Office of Management and Budget or the Office of Personnel Management structurally adapted for their interagency roles? How do the environments of federal departments, for example, vary with congressional relations or the administrative programs of presidents? Can we compare regulatory agencies to find structural patterns that are linked to the variety of their clientele and constituency groups? Are there consistent structural patterns in municipal governments that are contingent on the size and complexity of their citizenry and interagency environments? In general, the literature suggests that we can improve the functioning of agencies by self-consciously considering adaptations to the environment.

Self-Designing Bureaus

A third, and still developing, approach to design is one that creates structures that are self-designing or that "learn" over time. The principal thesis is that organizational structures and technologies, or key operational parts of them, should evolve uniquely and impermanently in response to emerging knowledge of program development needs rather than in response to traditions or excessive needs for internal security and control.

In a sense, this thesis is critical of abstract design before program development experience. The "blueprint" approach (Korten 1980) in which structures and technologies are planned from the top down as part of mapping out an implementation strategy (Elmore 1979) and are then frozen and formalized is responsible for much of the wasted effort and ineffectiveness in program administration, according to advocates. Instead, they argue, we should place top priority on developing the really important program procedures, and only later design the organizational structures to support those programs. This strategy allows organizations to adjust structures later, without trying to reorganize a large, already entrenched, system. It also requires restraint and a willingness to start small, begin slowly, and experiment before expanding and formalizing the organization. Advocates argue that all projects and programs should learn to be effective before becoming large, but the approach is nonetheless a contingency theory because ultimately structures should be tailor-made to program needs.

Korten's (1980) study of development programs in the Third World offers concrete advice for applying this approach. After identifying five particularly effective programs, and noting the diversity of goals, sponsorship, size, and funding among them, he argues that what sets them apart from less effective efforts is the way in which they were developed and institutionalized. For Korten, a successful program development process depends on the learning capacity of the implementing organization. Three key attributes of learning organizations are, first, that "The learning organization embraces error" (1980, 498). Rather than denying that a program is failing, or insisting that some other set of actors is responsible for the failure, the learning organization looks for problems, corrects those it can, and seeks change from other quarters when necessary to remedy other problems. Thus, for example, pilot projects and field experiments are the first step in program development.

Second, the learning organization takes advantage of existing local knowledge and the technology of those who have been coping with the problems the program seeks to remedy. The examination of existing technologies, even those that have been inadequate, allows program developers to understand the priorities and constraints of the target group.

Finally, the learning organization links knowledge to action so that the implementing organizations are "built up from the teams that created the original program" (1980, 499). Peters and Waterman (1982) also see this as a way to ensure that the initial dedication and enthusiasm of project founders and "champions" are used and rewarded. Pressman and Wildavsky (1979) offer similar advice—that policymaking should not be separated from implementation. In the programs Korten identifies as successful, the initial organization structure comprised teams of clients, researchers, and administrators, which allowed for the "rapid, creative adaptation" necessary to build new knowledge into the developing programs. In contrast, the traditional blueprint approach treats programs and organizations as entities that exist independent of the people who created them. Characterizing this approach, Korten says:

> What remains is an idea reduced to paper while the operating organization—the vibrant social organism which encompasses the skills, commitment, knowledge and systems required to give the idea life and adapt it to the local circumstances as required—has been discarded. (1980, 499)

In some respects, Korten's model may be too straightforward for the program development process in this country, where clients rarely present a unified set of demands, and multiple constraints on program procedures, staffing, and funding are the norm. What Korten's study may also be saying is that client support, which is so important to program success, can be built through participation in program development. Some of the features of learning organizations have been and continue to be tried here, however, such as pilot projects and citizen participation. Learning problems in bureaus are not the only problems contemporary programs face, but they are important.

Other criticisms of bureaus as being unable to learn offer different remedies. Landau (1973) argues for self-correcting organizations, committed more to the core value of the Weberian bureaucratic model, which he identifies as the exercise of technical knowledge rather than power. In essence, to be self-correcting, bureaus must be more rational, more empirical, and much more open to continuous reexamination. Too often in bureaus, Landau claims, "rationalization replaces verification" (1973, 540), a phrase closely resembling Korten's idea of embracing error. The ways to bring about self-correction are periodic program audits, the use of operations research, and cost analysis in the context of searching for error rather than trying to rationalize it. Interestingly, these self-examination techniques are explicitly rejected by Korten, who argues for interpretive case narratives over statistical analysis. The reasons for this may be that quantitative analysis so often is used to disguise failure and tends to close citizens out of the examination process.

Argyris and Schon's analysis of organizational learning (1978), though not specifically focused on structure, points out another of the hurdles associated with change—learning to tell how deep organizational change must go. What these authors refer to as single-loop learning means recognizing that the organization is not effective because it has departed from its own procedures and goals; how quickly and adequately the organization reestablishes its routines will determine its success. But when the routines and goals of the agency are no longer adequate for the problems faced, returning to them will only make the problem worse. This is where double-loop learning enters—learning not only that the organization is off course, but that its very conception of how to reach its goals is outmoded and must be replaced. This more radical learning requires much different tactics than a good control system, and it typically involves deep organizational conflict.

Yet another version of the self-designing organization thesis is offered by Hedberg, Nystrom, and Starbuck (1976). They focus on designing ongoing organizational search processes (as Landau does), but their approach is based on creating tensions and incentives for search rather than on establishing new control procedures. The processes they advocate are supposed to force organizations to be flexible and to redesign themselves continuously in response to new opportunities and knowledge. Although this sounds to some extent like Perrow's nonroutine structure or Burns and Stalker's "organismic" system, these three researchers are less concerned with structural prescriptions than with suggesting organizational decision-making processes that will prevent rigidity and force continuous reappraisals. Their thesis—that processes create structures—turns on its head the traditional administrative science assumption that structures control processes.

The processes that drive continuous self-design are basically those that prevent complacency. Hedberg, Nystrom, and Starbuck (1976) offer the following six remedies for complacency.

1. Acting on minimal consensus rather than waiting for unanimity.

2. Striving for only minimal contentment among personnel, which sharpens their desire for change and their search for alternatives.

3. Working toward only minimal affluence since even though a "small buffer of flexible resources is an asset" (1976, 59), too much affluence breeds complacency and contempt for new opportunities.

4. Placing only minimal faith in plans or goals. Even though they are needed to direct immediate action, they should be discarded easily.

5. Attempting to be only minimally consistent since total consistency impedes the pluralistic bargaining process that produces incremental changes, thereby forcing a delayed and destructive revolution to achieve any change.

6. Aiming only for minimal rationality in procedures. Even though basic managerial processes must be established, highly coherent and fully rationalized structures convey a false sense of control and prematurely define new problems and opportunities rather than encouraging their exploration. Some structural and procedural ambiguities will keep the organization in a state of readiness for change.

In his recent work describing "learning organizations" as they are developing in the American business community, Peter Senge adapts the principles mentioned by these authors, but adds another dimension to the discussion because he argues, in essence, that learning organizations must have a different culture than the traditional, hierarchical, authoritarian one of the past. This concept of "culture"—the perspectives, values, beliefs, myths, behavior patterns, and so on *commonly held within an organization*—is an important addition to the understanding of learning organizations.

Senge describes five component technologies or disciplines that must converge in order for businesses[2] to develop a culture that will tap the expertise and commitment of every member at every level. When that is accomplished organizations "can truly 'learn,' . . . can continually enhance their capacity to realize their highest aspirations" (1990, 6). The five technologies that Senge says are critical to success as a learning organization are:

1. Systems thinking. The ability to contemplate the whole of a phenomenon instead of any individual part of the pattern.

---

[2]The basic assumption behind learning organization theory, of course, is that organizations, or the people in them, are committed to the improvement of the processes and products in a way that guarantees the success of the business—whatever it is. Senge admits that his model may be harder to apply outside the business world, for he notes that:

> business has a freedom to experiment missing in the public sector and, often, in nonprofit organizations. It also has a clear "bottom line," so that experiments can be evaluated, at least in principle, by objective criteria. (1990, 15)

Organization Charts: Rigor Mortis

They have uses: for the annual salary review; for educating (individuals) on how the organization works and who does what.

But draw them in pencil. Never formalize, print, and circulate them. Good organizations are living bodies that grow new muscles to meet challenges. A chart demoralizes people. Nobody thinks of himself as *below* other people. And in a good (organization) he isn't. Yet on paper there it is. If you have to circulate something, use a loose-leaf table of organizations (like a magazine masthead) instead of a diagram with the people in little boxes. Use alphabetical order by name and by function wherever possible.

In the best organizations, people see themselves working in a circle as if around one table. One of the positions is designated chief executive officer, because somebody has to make all those tactical decisions that enable an organization to keep working. In this circular organization, leadership passes from one to another depending on the particular task being attacked—without any hang-ups.

This is as it should be. In the hierarchical organization, it is difficult to imagine leadership anywhere but at the top of the various pyramids. And it's hard to visualize the leader of a small pyramid becoming temporarily the leader of a group of larger pyramid-leaders which includes the chief executive officer.

The traditional organization chart has one dead give-away. Any dotted line indicates a troublemaker and/or a serious troubled relationship. It also generally means that an unsatisfactory compromise . . . has been worked out and the direct solution has been avoided.

SOURCE: Robert Townsend, *Further Up the Organization* (New York: Alfred A. Knopf, 1984): 159–60.

2. Personal mastery. The discipline of continually clarifying and deepening one's personal vision, of focusing one's energies, of developing patience, and of seeing reality objectively.

3. Mental models. The process by which individuals learn how to surface and challenge other individuals' mental models (deeply ingrained assumptions, generalizations, pictures, or images) that influence how one understands the work and, therefore, takes action.

4. Building shared vision. The skill of unearthing a shared "picture of the future" that binds people together around a common identity and sense of destiny, therefore fostering genuine commitment and enrollment rather than compliance.

5. Team learning. The skill of sharing "dialogue," the capacity of members of a team to suspend assumptions and enter into a genuine "thinking together," and learning how to recognize the patterns of interaction in teams that undermine learning (1990, 6–10).

The existence of these five characteristics, or disciplines as Senge calls them, obviously means that many of the traditional structures and patterns of behavior are radically changed.

In general, the idea behind the self-designing organization is to maintain a state of dynamic tension: It is similar in many ways to the organismic model described earlier. But the self-designing organization differs from this model in the strategies it uses to create and maintain the dynamic state. Self-designing organizations make satisfaction with the status quo difficult by permitting some degree of dissatisfaction and by adopting decision-making rules that make change easier to achieve. This kind of dynamic, constructive tension exists also in much of the TQM process, so the two ideas might work in synergistic ways.

There may be many arguments about the applicability of self-designing, learning, quality-enhancing theories to public organizations, or to nonprofit organizations that so often are involved in the public policy process. Does the political environment, which is interested in efficiency and accountability, allow such procedures? Is it possible to develop such organizations when those filling the top leadership positions turn over rapidly and often see the public employee as "the enemy"? Can a clear set of goals be envisioned in the tug and pull of interest groups? Whatever the debate and difficulty, these theories help point out the importance of structures in the overall flexibility and responsiveness of bureaus as they work in the public interest, and they create new visions of organizational structures and processes that can be examined for potential benefits.

CONCLUSIONS

In this chapter, we have surveyed a variety of approaches to designing organizational structures from the traditional, universalistic prescriptions of the Administrative Science School to the antidesign theories. Our purpose in doing so has been to indicate the variety of factors to be considered in designing or reorganizing bureaus, and the range of alternative structural forms that bureaus may take.

Although issues such as control and unity of command have traditionally been uppermost in the minds of administrators considering reorganization, these are not always the only, or even the most useful, terms in which structures can be analyzed. Consideration of technology and task interdependency focuses attention on structures that can be efficiently tailored to support workflow. Consideration of environmental conditions focuses attention on the flexibility required of boundary-spanning units and on various ways to integrate them with the rest of the organization. Program development considerations, as described by the antidesign advocates, raise questions about the point at which programs should be institutionalized and expanded.

The traditional assumptions about reorganization have been that it changes the bureau's internal processes and thus is a suitable remedy for many kinds of management and program development problems: Study of the organization design literature reviewed in this chapter raises some serious questions about the adequacy of that assumption. Especially in the context of examining the structure–technology link, we are forced to acknowledge that structures can support or impede the efficient coordination of work processes, but they do not define those processes. On the other hand, careful attention to matching structures to technology, environments, and program development can help produce structures that reinforce rather than thwart program administration.

In general, the examination of the program design literature alerts us to the alternative organizational structures and their limitations, and offers usable, analytic guides to the design of efficient and supportive structures.

FOR FURTHER READING

Daniel Robey provides a good overview of the basic contemporary research and theory of organization design in *Designing Organizations,* 4th ed. Burr Ridge, Ill.: Richard D. Irwin, 1994. A review of the research on technology as a basis for structure is offered by Donald Gerwin in "The Relationship Between Structure and Technology," in ed., Paul Nystrom and William Starbuck, *Handbook of Organization Design: Volume 2—Remodeling Organizations and Their Environments,* New York: Oxford University Press, 1981. David Korten raises an interesting discussion of the possibility of organizational learning and structure in "Community Organization and Rural Development," *Public Administration Review* 40 (1980): 480–511. The impact of political agendas on design efforts is described in Lawrence Lynn, *The State and Human Services,* Cambridge, Mass.: MIT Press, 1980. Finally, Karen Hult and Charles Walcott, in *Governing Public Organizations: Politics, Structure, and Institutional Design,* Pacific Grove, Calif.: Brooks/Cole, 1990, discuss decision models as they relate to organizational structure and different forms of contract.

REVIEW QUESTIONS

1. What are the basic values and goals behind the traditional structural principles of organization?

2. How do the traditional principles, and their values and goals, fit with the principles, values, and goals of the democratic political system?

3. How do the traditional structural principles of organization deal with the questions raised in relation to the four pivotal controversies discussed in Chapter 3?

4. How do the basic values and goals of the new organizational design perspectives vary from those of the traditional principles?

5. How do these new design perspectives fit with the values and goals of the democratic political system?

6. How do the new design perspectives address the issues raised in the four pivotal controversies? Do they do it better than did the traditional organizational structure principles?

REFERENCES

Agranoff, Robert. "Organization Design: A Tool for Policy Management." *Policy Studies Journal* 5, 1976: 15–23.

Allison, Graham. *Essence of Decision: Explaining the Cuban Missile Crisis.* Boston: Little, Brown, 1971.

Argyris, Chris, and Donald Schon. *Organizational Learning: A Theory of Action Perspective.* Reading, Mass.: Addison-Wesley, 1978.

Benson, Kenneth. "The Interorganizational Network as a Political Economy." *Administrative Science Quarterly* 20, 1975: 229–249.

Burns, Tom, and Gerald Stalker. *The Management of Innovation.* Rev. ed. Oxford: Oxford University Press, 1994.

Delbecq, A., and A. Filley. "Program and Project Management in Matrix Organization: A Case Study." Monograph 9, Graduate School of Business Research and Service, University of Wisconsin, 1974. Quoted in Alan Filley, Robert House, and Steven Kerr. *Managerial Process and Organizational Behavior.* 2nd ed. Glenview, Ill.: Scott, Foresman, 1976: 375–378.

Downs, Anthony. *Inside Bureaucracy.* Boston: Little, Brown, 1967. (Reissued, Prospect Heights, Ill.: Waveland Press, 1994.)

Elmore, Richard. "Backward Mapping: Implementation Research and Policy Decisions." *Political Science Quarterly* 94, 1979: 601–616.

Emory, F. E., and E. L. Trist. "The Causal Texture of Organizational Environments." *Human Relations* 18, 1965: 21–32.

Fayol, Henri. *General and Industrial Management.* Trans. Constance Storrs. London: Pitman, 1949.

Fellmeth, Robert. *The Interstate Commerce Commission.* New York: Grossman, 1970.

Filley, Alan, Robert House, and Steven Kerr. *Managerial Process and Organizational Behavior.* 2nd ed. Glenview, Ill.: Scott, Foresman, 1976.

Frederickson, H. George. "The Recovery of Structure in Public Administration." Washington: Center for Governmental Studies, 1970.

Gerwin, Donald. "Relationship Between Structure and Technology." In *Handbook of Organizational Design: Volume 2—Remodeling Organizations and Their Environments,* ed. Paul Nystrom and William Starbuck. New York: Oxford University Press, 1981: 3–38.

Hackman, J. Richard, and Ruth Wageman. "Total Quality Management: Empirical, Conceptual, and Practical Issues." *Administrative Science Quarterly* 40, 1995: 309–342.

Hage, Jerald, and Michael Aiken. "Routine Technology, Social Structure and Organizational Goals." *Administrative Science Quarterly* 14, 1969: 366–376.

––––––. *Social Change in Complex Organizations.* New York: Random House, 1970.

Hedberg, Bo, Paul Nystrom, and William Starbuck. "Camping on Seesaws: Prescriptions for a Self-Designing Organization." *Administrative Science Quarterly* 21, 1976: 41–65.

Hickson, David, Derek Pugh, and Diana Pheysey. "Operations Technology and Organization Structure: An Empirical Reappraisal." *Administrative Science Quarterly* 14, 1969: 378–397.

Korten David. "Community Organization and Rural Development." *Public Administration Review* 40, 1980: 480–511.

Landau, Martin. "On the Concept of a Self-Correcting Organization." *Public Administration Review* 33, 1973: 533–542.

Lawrence, Paul R., and Jay W. Lorsch. *Organization and Environment: Managing Differentiation and Integration.* Rev. ed. Boston: Harvard Business School Press, 1986.

Levine, Charles, Robert Backoff, Allan Calhoon, and William Siffin. "Organizational Design: A Post-Minnowbrook Perspective for the New Public Administration." *Public Administration Review* 35, 1975: 425–435.

Lindblom, Charles. *The Intelligence of Democracy.* New York: Free Press, 1965.

Litwak, E., and L. Hylton. "Interorganizational Analysis: A Hypothesis on Coordinating Agencies." *Administrative Science Quarterly* 6, 1962: 397–420.

Lynn, Lawrence. *The State and Human Services: Organizational Change in a Political Context.* Cambridge, Mass.: MIT Press, 1980.

March, James G., and Herbert A. Simon. *Organizations.* 2nd ed. New York: John Wiley & Sons, 1993.

Montjoy, Robert, and Lawrence O'Toole. "Toward a Theory of Policy Implementation: An Organizational Perspective." *Public Administration Review* 39, 1979: 465–476.

Mosher, Frederick C. *Democracy and the Public Service.* 2nd ed. New York: Oxford University Press, 1982.

National Performance Review (U.S.). *Creating a Government That Works Better & Costs Less: The Report of the National Performance Review,* Vice President Al Gore. New York: Plume/Penguin, 1993.

Osborne, David, and Ted Gaebler. *Reinventing Government: How the Entrepreneurial Spirit is Transforming the Public Sector.* Reading, Mass.: Addison-Wesley, 1992.

Owens, Julianne Mahler. "Some Limits on the Uses of Reorganization." *International Journal of Public Administration* 7, 1985: 21–50.

Perrow, Charles. "A Framework for the Comparative Analysis of Organization." *American Sociological Review* 32, 1967: 194–208.

_____. *Organizational Analysis: A Sociological View.* Belmont, Calif.: Wadsworth, 1970.

Peters, Thomas, and Robert Waterman. *In Search of Excellence.* New York: Warner, 1982.

Pressman, Jeffrey and Aaron Wildavsky. *Implementation: How Great Expectations in Washington are Dashed in Oakland.* 3rd ed. Berkeley: University of California Press, 1984.

Pugh, Derek, David Hickson, and Christopher Hinings. "The Context of Organizational Structure." *Administrative Science Quarterly* 14, 1969: 91–144.

Robey, Daniel. *Designing Organizations.* 4th ed. Burr Ridge, Ill.: Richard D. Irwin, 1994.

Schlesinger, Arthur. *The Coming of the New Deal.* Boston: Houghton-Mifflin, 1959.

Scott, William, Terence Mitchell, and Philip Birnbaum. *Organization Theory: A Structural and Behavioral Analysis.* 4th ed. Homewood, Ill.: Richard D. Irwin, 1981.

Senge, Peter M. *The Fifth Discipline: The Art and Practice of The Learning Organization.* New York: Currency, Doubleday, 1990.

_____, et al. *The Fifth Discipline Fieldbook: Strategies and Tools for Building a Learning Organization.* New York: Currency, Doubleday, 1994.

Simon, Herbert. *Administrative Behavior.* New York: Free Press, 1965.

Sloan, A. P., Jr. *My Years with General Motors.* Garden City, N.Y.: Doubleday, 1964. (Reprinted in 1990 by Currency, Doubleday.)

Swiss, James E. "Adapting Total Quality Management (TQM) to Government." *Public Administration Review* 52, 1992: 356–362.

Thompson, James D. *Organizations in Action: Social Science Bases of Administrative Theory.* New York: McGraw-Hill, 1967.

Urwick, Lydall. *The Elements of Administration.* New York: Harper, 1943.

Walton, Mary. *Deming Management at Work.* New York: G. P. Putnam's Sons, 1990.

Weber, Max. *Theory of Social and Economic Organization.* Trans. A. Henderson and T. Parsons. Glencoe, Ill.: The Free Press, 1947.

Wilson, James Q. *Bureaucracy: What Government Agencies Do and Why They Do It.* New York: Basic Books, 1989.

Woodward, Joan. *Industrial Organization: Theory and Practice.* 2nd ed. Oxford: Oxford University Press, 1980.

CASE 4–1 Public Safety Deconsolidation

Editors' note: In September of 1983, the police, fire, and code enforcement functions of the city of Alexandria, Virginia, were consolidated into a public safety department. The consolidation was initiated by the former city manager in an effort to:

- Maintain and enhance services where possible.
- Improve coordination within the units of the department.

- Consolidate inspection functions.
- Enhance emergency disaster planning.
- Reduce expenditures.
- Reduce the number of departments reporting to the city manager.

The initial decision to implement the public safety consolidation in September, 1983, did not go to council because the city attorney advised the city manager that under the charter, the organization of city departments was his prerogative. (At the national level there is a specific law dealing with executive reorganization, but at local levels the handling of this matter varies greatly.) Because of the lack of clarity about who must be involved in administrative organizational decisions, there were questions raised by some members of the council in 1983 about whether the consolidation needed their approval before implementation.

In 1985, the new city manager decided that the consolidation should be reversed; however, because of the questions raised when the former manager took his action, the large number of city employees involved (564 in fiscal year 1985–86), the size of the budget for the Public Safety Department ($27,680,633), and the publicly sensitive nature of the services involved, she originally put deconsolidation in the form of a recommendation to the city council for their approval or disapproval. She quickly found from background checking that the mayor and the council preferred that she take the action, and the attorney again confirmed that she had the legal power. Therefore, she gathered the appropriate data and advice from her administrative staff and outside consultants, and then she took the action herself after "conferring with council" in an executive session. The consultant's memorandum (which follows) was titled "Advice to the Council on the Merits of the Choices."

TO: The Honorable Mayor and Members of City Council
THROUGH: Vola Lawson, City Manager
FROM: Wayne F. Anderson, Consultant
SUBJECT: Public Safety Consolidation

City Manager Lawson and Director of Public Safety Strobel, assisted by his Deputy Directors, are submitting separate reports to you that . . . recommend deconsolidation—that is, reversal of the 1983 consolidation action. I concur in the City Manager's recommendation, and this report from me is a supplement to theirs. . . . It was the City Manager's desire that I write a separate report, even though theirs will convey the updated facts and even though we all share in the central conclusion. My perspective and degree of detachment are different, and I will be trying to evaluate the consolidation/deconsolidation alternatives quite comprehensively, though not exhaustively.

The City Manager's Recommendation

As was already mentioned, the City Manager is recommending that the Council approve deconsolidation—that is, return to separate Fire and Police Departments. Each department would once again have its own administrative capability; communications would remain combined in the Police Department.

From the first meeting of the staff team, the City Manager and I knew that the Director of Public Safety and the three Deputies were unanimously and overwhelmingly convinced, on the basis of their 27 months of experience, that the Department should be deconsolidated. In fact, questioning of them then, and over subsequent weeks, uncovered no strong arguments whatsoever for staying with consolidation.

Notwithstanding the fact that the case for deconsolidation seems to us very strong, the City Manager decided against transmitting a quick, bare-bones report for your consideration. Instead, our three reports, taken together, provide the City Council with what we believe is a fully adequate basis for the consolidation/deconsolidation decision, and pin down understandings concerning future actions to be taken by the Fire and Police commands, as well as future staffing requirements and budgets. . . . My primary purpose is to evaluate consolidation on its merits as briefly as possible and without unnecessary duplication of facts in the reports from the City Manager and Public Safety Command group.

Evaluation of Public Safety Consolidation and Alexandria's Experience with It

Public safety consolidations come in several primary types. The variant installed in Alexandria in September 1983, provided for (1) a Director of Public Safety, who serves as the Director and Police Chief; and (2) three bureaus—Fire, Police and Administrative Services. The Fire Bureau includes the code enforcement function which conducts most, but not all, of the City's inspectional activities.

Alexandria's consolidated Department of Public Safety has not embodied the public safety officer (PSO) or any of the other "integration" or "cooperation" approaches. Under the PSO approach, a city has only one type of officer who performs both fire and police duties. Under other integration and cooperation approaches, policemen usually are assigned some fire duties, and firemen are usually assigned some police duties. . . . Hence, Alexandria's consolidation is of the least far-reaching type and affects mainly the top command structure and administrative services and code enforcement operations.

In evaluating Alexandria's public safety consolidation, I will address the following questions:

- What should the Director of Public Safety's responsibilities include?
- Would planning and coordination be strengthened under consolidation?
- Is consolidation less expensive?
- What are the effects of consolidation on employee morale and performance?
- How is consolidation related to public safety integration?
- Does consolidation improve service to the public?

What Should the Director of Public Safety's Responsibilities Include?

Alexandria, in establishing its consolidated Public Safety Department, faced, and continues to face, a choice pertaining to the Director's responsibilities which . . . affects service effectiveness, employee perceptions, and costs. The choice is between a Director of Public Safety who functions as both Director and Police Chief, or a Director of Public Safety who has only the department head responsibilities and separate Police and Fire Chiefs reporting to him. Whether this choice can be resolved in a satisfying way is one factor that bears on whether consolidation should be retained. Each of the choices entails certain problems, and neither represents a satisfying arrangement to me.

To date, Director of Public Safety Strobel has served as both the Department Director and Police Chief, but he has recently reiterated his request that a separate Police Chief be appointed if consolidation is to continue. His Police Chief duties preempt his time and energy and leave too little time for planning and coordination of the three Bureau's operations, or for the fire and code enforcement decisions that must be reviewed or made at his level under the consolidated organization.

It is my sense that the Police Chief position in Alexandria is very demanding and that it would be difficult for any Police Chief to free ample time through delegation to others. Operating at two levels and balancing one's attentions so as to do justice to both jobs and three bureaus is always difficult. Such arrangements calling for one individual to serve simultaneously as department head and bureau chief are usually transitional or otherwise temporary, even where the operations are much smaller and less sensitive than is true of the Department of Public Safety and Police Operations Bureau.

On the other hand, appointing a separate Police Chief would generate a new question or problem—that is, would the Director of Public Safety then have enough to do? He certainly would during any shakedown period but how about after that?.

Planning and coordination of Fire and Police operations and related administration activities would be the Director's primary responsibilities. [However] it is my opinion that over the long run a community of Alexandria's size and composition cannot justify having both a Director of Public Safety and Police Chief. A Director of Public Safety, backed up by a fully competent Police Chief, Fire Chief, and Administrative Services Chief, would not be fully and productively occupied. He would be tempted to oversupervise, overcentralize decision making, and cover areas of work that should be undertaken and controlled by the Chiefs reporting to him. Predictably, if not audibly, the Fire and Police Chiefs would experience some frustration. Their place in the organization chart and in the sun would be diminished, as the Fire Chief's already has been, and both the City Manager and these Chiefs would chafe because lines of authority precluded direct, frank, and unfiltered contacts and relations. In any future situations where the City decides to consider applicants from the outside for the Fire Chief or Police Chief positions, these "third level down" positions would attract fewer talented applicants than would be true if the chief reported directly to the Manager.

The Director of Public Safety position . . . would almost always be occupied in the future, as it is now, by a person from the police profession. The police function is the most multifaceted, complex, sensitive, and largest of the functions assigned to the Department, and psychologically is the most dominating. It is conceivable that a superior Fire Chief would be appointed to the position, but such appointments would occur rarely, if ever. Appointment of a "civilian" generalist public administrator possessing some public safety background is also within the realm of possibility, but a new set of strains would be introduced. In general, American cities still prefer to go with specialists when filling department head positions.

The likelihood that the Director of Public Safety would almost always be a former police officer . . . institutionalizes the subordination of the Fire Service and, therefore, has a negative effect on the atmosphere there. Hopes that their sense of inferiority and resentment would wither away are doomed to disappointment, experience shows.

Would Planning and Coordination Be Strengthened under Consolidation?

It ought to stand to reason that consolidation under a single head would strengthen planning and coordination of Fire, Police, and Code Enforcement operations; . . . however, two points need to be made. The first was stated in the previous section—namely that a Director of Public Safety who is also the Police Chief will have to fight for time to concentrate on planning and coordination of the four functions. All municipal department heads must be trained, disciplined time managers if they are to prevent daily fires from crowding out the charting of future improvements, so a combination Director of Public Safety-Police Chief in charge of the City's largest department faces a double difficulty.

The second point is . . . more conclusive. Separate fire and police departments typically do a creditable job of planning and coordinating operations that are repetitive in nature. . . . Why wouldn't this be true when fire and police departments build on years of experience and have hundreds of incidents each year that require coordination and therefore are opportunities to learn and further perfect procedures?

However, as one authority observed to me, fire and police departments, in combination with all the other municipal departments that should contribute, often do not plan carefully and perform in a coordinated manner when their communities suffer major disasters or emergencies that present threats they haven't coped with before or recently. He, however, went on to say that this generality hardly applies to Alexandria. Alexandria's emergency planning and operations are considered by peers to be very advanced, and Alexandria's procedures are used as training models by the Federal Emergency Management Agency. Alexandria is one of relatively few communities that regularly puts itself through mock emergencies involving a variety of potential disasters.

Given Alexandria's excellent record in this area, the prospect of marginal improvement in planning and coordination is . . . a weak argument for consolidation.

Is Consolidation Less Expensive?

If comparisons . . . assume for each of the organization options, continuation of present service levels, shift strength levels, company sizes, and the other parameters that determine total personnel requirements, no savings is gained under either plan. . . . There is next to no difference between the personnel requirements under consolidation and under the deconsolidation or separate department option.

Significant personnel reductions have been achieved under consolidation, but comparable savings could have been made under the prior separate departments and would not be reversed by a return to separate departments. The savings essentially are not attributable to consolidation except in the sense that the deliberations on consolidation shone the spotlight on these cutback opportunities and led to a commitment to move ahead.

What Are the Effects of Consolidation on Employee Morale and Performance?

Reactions to consolidation vary within each unit, but the net effect is a minus. The Police have not lost status or any part of their identity or anything else of much significance, so most of them have taken the reorganization pretty much in stride, but without enthusiasm.

Firemen, however, have lost their "independent" chief and, therefore, have lost a good deal of the decision-making latitude on budget, personnel, and other matters, and the relatively unfettered right and responsibility to speak out for the fire function, that a fire chief of department head rank has traditionally had. Predictably, firemen see the fire function as having been subordinated to police, and their service as having been downgraded. None of the top command officers believe that these hurts to morale have hurt performance, which is the ultimate test of an organization, but they have some concern about the long-run effects.

How Is Consolidation Related to Public Safety Integration?

If consolidation had been entered into as a well-planned first step leading to some form of public safety integration or the PSO approach, this fact alone might have justified the consolidation, but this was not the case. Public safety integration was viewed as no more than an intriguing idea that might become politically and managerially feasible at some time in the indefinite future.

Having lived for 14 years in Evanston, Illinois, with responsibility for one of the lesser forms of police-fire cross training and cross operations, I can attest that seeing this approach through to maturity is a long, enervating, somewhat bumpy journey.

Is there a case for retaining consolidation so as to be "ready" for public safety integration? No, not in my opinion, not even if the Council were to desire immediate consideration of the alternative public safety integration approaches. In a community of Alexandria's size, at least two years of work should be expended in studying the alternatives, developing detailed operational plans, and preparing the community and employees for changes to come. Implementing such an integration blueprint would be no more difficult if you were starting from separate departments than it would be from the present consolidated department.

Does Consolidation Improve Service to the Public?

Of paramount importance is whether the consolidated Department of Public Safety can provide better protection to the people of Alexandria and their property than separate fire and police departments can. The effectiveness of these vital services even outweighs their costs in the minds of most citizens. The answer appears to be "No, service has not been significantly changed, or harmed, by the current consolidation, and I would expect that service levels can be maintained at relatively effective and equivalent levels in the future by either the consolidated or deconsolidated organizations."

Summary

Alexandria's public safety consolidation has not produced net benefits or service improvements and does not promise to do so in the future. Personnel levels and costs will be about the same under consolidation or deconsolidation. Any marginal improvement in planning and coordination will be more than counter-balanced by the greater bureaucratization of decision making that is inevitable when you add an organizational level, and by negative effects on employee attitudes, particularly in the fire service.

SOURCE: Wayne Anderson, has been Distinguished Professor of Public Administration at George Mason University, the City Manager of Evanston, Illinois, and Alexandria, Virginia, directed the Advisory Committee for Intergovernmental Relations, and served as Secretary of Administraton for Virginia's Governor Robb.

Editor's Note

This is a condensation of a consultant's report to a city council. As you reexamine the facts in the report, consider the following questions:

1. What importance to this case is the fact that a new city manager, who has been in office less than a year, took this deconsolidation action?

2. What gains and losses could be expected in moving to a public safety department?

3. What kind of research should go into consideration of a structural change such as the one discussed in this case?

4. To maintain good communication and coordination after deconsolidation, what techniques or theories of management might be applied by the city manager?

5. After reading the appropriate chapters later in this text, refer to this case and consider the impact of a public safety department and of deconsolidation on the morale and motivation of the affected employees, on decision-making processes within and between parts of the organization(s), and on communication and control.

CASE 4–2 Dilemma in Juvenile Court

The people of Tidewater County take pride in the fact that their county has ranked very high nationally in population growth for the past 20 years. Since 1950, the county has grown approximately eightfold.

The Juvenile Court of Tidewater reflects this growth. In 1952, the juvenile section was merely a branch of the Tidewater County Criminal Court. It then consisted of one counselor, Ellen Mann, who handled all juvenile cases that were not handled informally by parents or small-town police officers. In 1954, newly enacted state statutes set up a system of separate juvenile courts. A judge was elected in Tidewater, and Mann was made his sole assistant. In 1958, Mann hired Harry Barnes to assist her in processing the increasing number of juvenile referrals. The court grew steadily with the county and currently employs 20 counselors (see Exhibit 1).

Bill Jones comes to work for the court as a counselor after obtaining his degree in criminology and corrections in 1972. He is appalled at the backward operation at Tidewater, one of the larger juvenile courts in the state. He finds that almost all other counselors share his evaluation, and he soon becomes their spokesperson. After much griping and

EXHIBIT 1   Present Organization of Tidewater County Juvenile Court

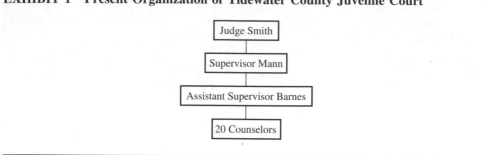

complaining among the younger counselors, Jones drafts a recommendation and takes it directly to the judge (see Exhibit 2). Jones and his contemporaries are convinced that if the recommendation is adopted, the efficiency of the court will improve markedly.

Judge Smith is shaken when he reads the recommendation in Exhibit 2. He is surprised that Jones had brazenly brought the information directly to him instead of sending it up through Barnes and then Mann, as the structure in Exhibit 1 provides.

Judge Smith feels a lot of questions need answers. Is it true that all the new counselors are as upset as Jones claims? Why hadn't someone told the judge that his employees are so unhappy? It seems as if he is always the last to know. If this situation should leak to the press, he might have problems in next year's election. The judge is a lawyer, not a social scientist or an administrator. What had Mann or Barnes been doing to rile up these youngsters so much?

EXHIBIT 2   Recommendations from Counselors

Dear Judge Smith:

Your court is unhappy. The procedures followed here were outdated 10 years ago. All of the younger counselors agree with me; vast changes are needed.

The change that is needed most drastically, and could be instituted at very little cost, is a simple reorganization. The current counselor system stinks. As nearly as I can tell from observing it for a year, it works (or is supposed to work!) as I have depicted it in the attached chart (see Exhibit 3). The counties around us gave up this system some time ago. It simply places too much work on individual counselors. When counselors have to fool around with the police departments and running down parents for the first time, they let their probation work slip. If counselors concentrate on probation work (as they should!), the incoming cases stack up. This system would be fine if we only had three or four cases each to worry about. My current case load is 47 and growing every day.

I propose the system shown in the next two charts (see Exhibits 4 and 5). This new system provides for a better division of work, specialization of counselors, and a more favorable span of control for the supervisors.

Respectfully yours,
Bill Jones

Exhibit 3, showing how Jones thought the court was currently running, looks accurate enough. The judge does not get involved in the process until the counselor handling the case brings him the pretrial investigation and discusses it with him. This usually occurs just prior to the hearing. The judge is a little surprised at how complex Jones had made the process seem, but it does appear to be completely accurate.

It appears to the judge that Jones was right in his statement that it will not cost much to institute the proposed change. Moving a few desks and throwing up a few wall partitions in the main office building should do it.

Jones's approach is brash, but his plan does appear to have some merit. If the kid went singing to the press, Smith also muses, he could stir up a lot more trouble than he is worth.

Judge Smith is leaning toward trying the plan but decides to get Mann's view on it before making his move. "Ellen," the judge requests, "I want you to to take a look at this recommendation Jones handed me. I think the lad makes some good points, but I want your opinion before I make my decision."

Ellen Mann has her own questions as she scans Jones's recommendation. Why is Jones concerned about "flows" when he has so many cases that demand his time? Why hadn't Jones brought this thing to Mann in the first place instead of bothering the judge with it? Didn't Jones know that Mann was the supervisor?

Mann is certain about two things. First, she knows for a fact that the new counselors are unhappy. The Supreme Court has really messed up the works. Imagine, juveniles now have all the same rights as adults. That isn't right. The delinquents are all getting lawyers

EXHIBIT 3 Present Flow of Cases

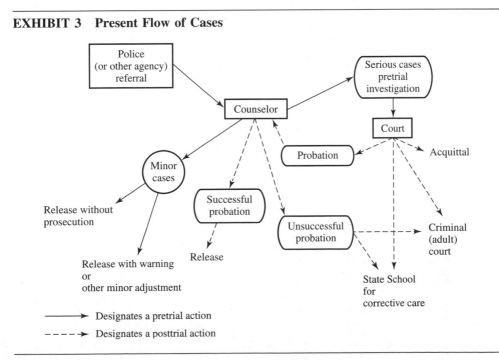

and beating the charges against them. Mann has seen the discontent grow among the newer counselors after recent Supreme Court rulings. Mann also reflects that President Nixon is cleaning up the Supreme Court, so the young counselors should be better satisfied in the near future.

Second, there is no way Mann's schedule and work habits will allow her to make any reasonable sense of Jones's proposal. She calls on her assistant, Barnes. "This gobbledy-gook gets worse every year, Harry," she says. "Decipher it, and give me a reading on it in the morning, will you?"

Barnes cannot believe what he reads. The kid has gone and done it. He has submitted an asinine proposal to Judge Smith. Barnes wonders why he had not advised Mann against hiring that wise ass a year ago. As assistant supervisor, it would have been easy for Barnes to convince Mann not to hire Jones in the first place.

Things had been smooth before Jones started as a counselor, Barnes fumes. Until Jones arrived, there were no radical troublemakers stirring up animosity in the court. The court functioned perfectly well for the 15 years Barnes worked for it. The old system functioned well with two employees, and it was functioning well with 20 counselors. Time had proven its effectiveness. Under this old system, each child referred to the court has a single counselor appointed, depending on the district in the county where the child resides. This one counselor receives the referral from the police, conducts the pretrial investigation (when necessary), and is the child's probation officer if the judge decides on probation.

The beauty of this system is its simplicity, Barnes believes. The same counselor works with the same child from the time he is first reported to the court until he is released from

---

EXHIBIT 4   Proposed Flow of Cases

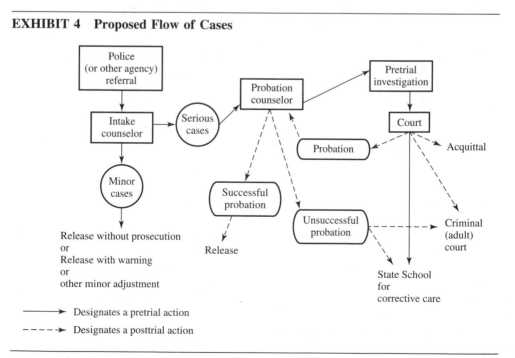

EXHIBIT 5   Proposed Organization of Tidewater County Juvenile Court

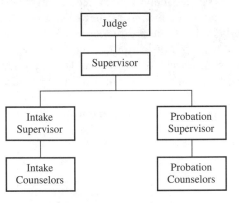

probation or confined. Every counselor has the opportunity to really get to know each child assigned to him.

As a former counselor, Barnes does know what a headache the "intake" process is. The police report is usually full of errors. The court records have to be screened to see if the child has ever been before the court. The child's school performance also has to be reviewed.

Moreover, letters have to be prepared requesting the parents to bring the child in for an initial interview. Finally, the parents have to be hunted down if they don't show. No doubt, intake processing is the worst job in the court.

But Barnes knows it can be done. In fact, he is the best intake counselor the court has. He knows the police and school officials, and he knows how to get parents and their children in for initial interviews.

Despite his competence in it, however, Barnes hates the intake process. He hates to have to run all over the county. He does not like to drive, and he does not like being out in the weather. As assistant supervisor, he is able to supervise the secretaries, run the office from inside, check the progress of cases, keep the court docket flowing, and devote a great deal of attention to his favorite area, probation counseling. Barnes is not about to casually threaten this personally comfortable situation.

In any case, Barnes considers the main goal of the court to be straightening out youngsters through probation. The probationers come in twice a month, report their grades and difficulties to the probation counselor, and are on their way. The counselor will make a little note as to what was said, and this will be entered into the child's file. The same counselor processes the intake, trial, and probation phases of each case. What could be more logical?

True enough, the adjacent counties had split their juvenile courts into intake and probation sections in the way Jones recommended. Any fool could see, though, that the rash reorganizations clearly had a disasterous effect on the morale of the personnel who were made intake counselors. Faced with the deluge of all the referrals in their respective counties, the relatively few intake counselors were unable to keep up. Four of them in other counties left to go to other courts or agencies. It appeared strange to Barnes that, in spite of this, the governor's blue-ribbon Committee on Juvenile Delinquency praised the action of these adjacent courts in adopting the newer system.

Barnes takes an early and definite position, as Jones learns when their paths accidentally cross as they are leaving the office on the very afternoon that the memo made the rounds. Jones had never seen Barnes so angry. The words are not merely spoken; Barnes spits them out at Jones. "So you thought things used to be miserable around here? Just wait. . . ."

Several colleagues observe the encounter; the word gets quickly back to Judge Smith.

SOURCE: Robert Golembiewski and Michael White, *Cases in Public Management,* 3rd ed. (Chicago: Rand-McNally, 1980).

Editor's Note

Reflect on the following questions about the events in the case and the proposal for reorganization. Take Judge Smith's point of view, but consider the perceptions and motivations of the other actors too.

1. In traditional structure terms, describe the original structure and the proposed change.

2. Consider the proposal as a problem in organizational design under the more contemporary theories. How would you analyze the situation and the proposal?

3. How is the organizational technology changed under the new proposal? Are operating goals or agency policies altered in any important ways?

4. Considering the situation in purely technical structural terms, what do you think is the best solution? Why?

5. What are some of the nonstructural issues raised in the case? Considering the case as a whole, what would be the best course of action? Why?

Chapter 5

Communication

Communication and organization are inseparable. Chester Barnard held that "in any exhaustive theory of organization, communication would occupy a central place, because structure, extensiveness, and scope of organizations are almost entirely determined by communication technique" (1938, 8). Three decades later, Katz and Kahn stated no less emphatically that communication is the essence of a social system or an organization (1978).

Given its ubiquitous place in organizations, communication is a central force in defining the structure, processes, and culture of the bureaus, just as those three forces help shape the communication network. As information technology has increased in sophistication and power, organizations have been influenced by those in charge of the specialists in that field—often without recognition of the views of those individuals. Child et al. (1987), for example, found that managers often turn decisions about information technology and communication implementation strategies over to the specialists in those departments, and the views of these specialists, about organizations and the available technology, become critically important in determining what systems are chosen and how they are adopted. Most important, the researchers determined that these technicians still adhered to a classical Tayloristic model of organizations. Thus they placed emphasis on specialization, standardization, and formalization—the classic concepts of the assembly line. Needless to say, the strategies recommended and implemented by these specialists were often suboptimal in solving organizations' problems; the very people most committed to new technology were also most responsible for its lack of impact.

Certainly, communications and organization structure are powerful influences on each other. Behavior and communication take on new dimensions when they occur within an organizational structure; they are "patterned" by it. That is, organization structure introduces considerable predictability and stability into interaction. Major structural characteristics of bureaucracies include (1) a hierarchy of formal positions and authority, (2) the specialized division of tasks, and (3) rules and procedures. Members of this type of formal organization must accept direction from some individuals but not others, perform certain tasks (often in specified ways) but refrain from others, and work and interact with some individuals rather than others. Their behavior, including communication, is different than it would be without the organization's structure.

Communication, in turn, has a significant influence on organizational structure and its functioning. Organizational structure is differentiated in a variety of ways—hierarchical levels, departments, task specialization, and so on—and must be integrated to achieve the organization's goals. Information about goals, rules, the functioning of the organization's human and other resources, and its environment must be exchanged. Different activities and tasks must be coordinated. As noted in Chapter 4, the greater the organizational differentiation and complexity, the greater the need for integration. And an organization's communication system is a key mechanism for achieving integration and coordination.

Important as integration and coordination are in all organizations, the role of the communication system of public organizations is more complex: It is a political process as well. Policy and the distribution of power are affected. In this process, expertise and control of information are major sources of bureaucratic political influence (Rourke 1984).

Interpersonal communication is an interactive process exchanging information between sources and receivers for the purpose of conveying meaning. This communication may be instrumental, consummatory, or incidental (Zajonc 1966). Instrumental communication is purposeful or goal directed; the sender intends to have an effect (related to knowledge, attitude, and behavior) on the receiver. Consummatory communication arises and is emitted from the emotional state of the sender (for example, enthusiasm, fear, uncertainty). Incidental communication imparts information without the sender being aware of having done so.

The focus here is on instrumental communication but with the understanding that emotional and unintended meanings may be present also. Because the purpose of communicating may be to exercise influence rather than simply to transmit information, we will be concerned here with distortion in ways that depart from its usual treatment in organization texts.

Discussions of communication often assume that its only purpose is the accurate transmission and reception of information between senders and receivers. Accuracy in communication promotes greater organizational efficiency and productivity. Distortion, which is generally assumed to be unintentional, is dysfunctional, then, because it reduces the accuracy and completeness of the communication. But distortion may in fact be intentional, as in the distinction between *mis*information or error and *dis*information, in which a message includes a true factor to make a story credible and then adds deliberate distortion or untruth. Whether distortion is intentional or not, its significance in public organizations lies either in its political intent or in its programmatic consequences.

After introducing an interactive model of the communication process, we turn to the focus of this chapter: organizational communication. We will discuss formal and informal communications and network research, followed by an examination of directions of communications and communication roles in organizations. Finally, we will explore some types of distortion and interference, along with several techniques for coping with distortion.

INTERPERSONAL COMMUNICATION: AN INTERACTIVE MODEL

Models of the communication process date back at least to Greek antiquity. Aristotle identified the speaker, the speech, and the audience as the principal features of communication. Although the terminology of our century's more complex and abstract theories may vary somewhat, these basic elements persist.

Ride a Pale Horse

The meeting was ended.

Not yet, thought Karen. I have been doing some thinking. On disinformation. I could write two articles at least on that subject—if I had some solid facts as a basis.

"Disinformation?" That had caught his attention. He dropped the pen back on the desk.

"It's important—something we all ought to be aware of. Most of us don't really know the difference between misinformation and disinformation." "But you know now—since Prague?" He was amused but interested. "Give me an example of that difference, Karen. No fancy language: just a simple explanation that any ignorant layman—like myself—can understand."

He is challenging me, she told herself. All right, let's show him this isn't just a Prague-inspired notion. "The scene is Paris. An attempt to shoot Mitterrand as he was entering his car. The actual facts are that he wasn't hit, his driver was wounded, and the two assailants escaped.

"An early press report of the incident said that Mitterand was wounded and his chauffeur was killed; two, possibly three, terrorists had done the shooting. That report is a case of misinformation.

"Another press report starts appearing. It says that an attack on Mitterrand took place; he wasn't hit, but his driver was wounded. The two assailants have been identified as gunmen used in previous killings by a West German intelligence agency. A reliable source states that the assassination of Mitterand was to have been followed by a right-wing coup, establishing in power a French general favored by fascist elements in Germany." Karen paused. "And that report is pure disinformation."

She knew what she was talking about. Schleeman nodded his approval. "It includes a fact or two to make a story credible, then adds the distortions."

SOURCE: Helen MacInnes, *Ride a Pale Horse* (New York: Ballantine Books, 1984): 42–43.

Human communication is an ongoing, interactive process. Each element in the process influences the others. In particular, the role of receiver perception and acceptance of messages must be recognized if the interpersonal dimension of organizational communication is to be more fully understood and more effectively put into practice.

David Berlo, in a reference both historical and lyrical, compares the concept of process to Heraclitus's observation five hundred years before Christ that "a man can never step into the same river twice; the man is different and so is the river" (1960, 23). Process, so conceived, leads us to "view events and relationships as dynamic, on-going, ever-changing, continuous" (1960, 24). Everett Rogers and Rekha Agarwala-Rogers share this dynamic view of change and continuity intertwined:

> Communications is a *process*—that is, a continuous sequence of actions through time. It is not meaningful to talk about a beginning or an end of communication, because, like all other processes, communication flows like a stream through time. Someone has suggested that all processes should always begin and end with the word "and." (1976, 17)

The classical model of the interpersonal communications process includes the basic elements of source-encoder, message, channel, and receiver-decoder plus feedback (see Figure 5–1). Since the model is exclusively concerned with human communication, the source and receiver are individuals or groups of individuals.

Before proceeding to the separate elements of the model, some difficulties in communicating about communication warrant attention. The strength of this model lies in its recognition of interpersonal communications as an interactive process. The concept of process as interactive is one of considerable subtlety and complexity, however, and cannot be fully depicted in a diagram. If arrows were pointing to and from each element to all the others in Figure 5–1, it would give a greater sense of the multiplicity of directions between and among elements; even then, however, the diagram falls short of conveying the complexity of an interactive, ongoing process. Perhaps this is one of those rare times when a thousand words is better than a picture.

Even so, talking or writing about communication is difficult since, as linguist Michael Reddy points out, English as a language about communication is "its own worst enemy" (1979, 286). Metaphors, symbolic representations of one thing in terms of something else, pervade language. Our language injects what Reddy calls "a conduit metaphor" into a discussion about communication. It is, in fact, almost impossible to avoid language that lacks this metaphor. It explains communication as a process in which (1) language transfers thoughts and feelings from person to person, (2) speakers or writers insert thoughts and feelings in words, (3) words contain thoughts and feelings, and (4) people extract thoughts and feelings from the words (Reddy 1979; Axley 1984).

Our thoughts, and even our behavior, are influenced by metaphors. The idea of a "conduit" oversimplifies our thinking about communication. In truth, people do not transfer meanings to one another since the receiver creates meanings in his or her own mind, and words do not have meanings aside from those in people's minds. The conduit metaphor, by encouraging the assumption that communication is easy or requires little effort, obscures

FIGURE 5–1 Classic Interactive Communication Model

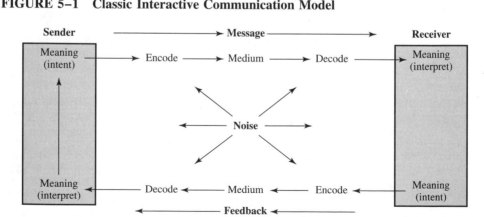

SOURCE: Richard M. Steers and J. Stewart Black, *Organizational Behavior,* 5th ed. New York: HarperCollins, 1994, p. 437.

the magnitude of the effort required for successful communication. A crucial point to remember, both for practitioners in and students of organization, is that communication is more receiver than speaker dominated. The classic communication model should be considered with these constraints about communication in mind.

The *sender-encoder* has a purpose or reason for engaging in communication. An individual encodes a message that is intended to produce some desired result. In person-to-person communication, encoding is usually accomplished through speaking and writing. Speaking and writing are examples of encoding skills; listening and reading are examples of decoding skills. Thought and reasoning apply to both decoding and encoding.

Communication behavior is affected by the sender's attitudes toward self, the subject matter, and the receiver. The expectations that sources have for themselves and others, the position they hold, and the role they play in the organization help determine the nature of the communication. The assumed knowledge about the subject matter on the part of the receiver also affects the language and style of communication. For example, a professional will communicate with other professionals quite differently than with clients. Thus a variety of social–cultural influences are a final factor in determining the communication process.

The *message* is the actual physical product of the source-encoder. The message may be spoken or written; if the communication is between visible actors, one's posture, body movement, or facial expression may also deliver an important message.

The *medium* is the means by which the message is physically transmitted from sender to receiver. To be effective, channels of communication must take into account not only the encoding skills of the sender, but the sensory and decoding skills of the receiver. Can or will the receiver be more attentive to a written memo, an announcement over a public address system, or a personal chat or phone call? Should only one channel be used, or should the message be given in more than one way—and if so, should it be given simultaneously or not? For example, when an instructor lectures while showing overheads on a screen, two channels are being used at the same time. Books frequently include pictorial and mathematical representations of the written text.

The *receiver-decoder* is, according to many contemporary theorists, the most important link in the communication process. Much that has been said about senders applies to receivers as well. The receiver's communication behavior, like the sender's, is affected by communication skills, attitudes, knowledge level, and social–cultural background.

In still another sense, the receiver is central to the communication process; this has to do with differences between meaning and message. Messages are transmitted, but words and other symbols have no meanings in themselves. Meanings are assigned by both the source and the receiver, and those meanings may not be the same. In particular, the role of receiver perception, comprehension, and acceptance of messages must be recognized if organizational communication is to be more fully understood and more effectively used.

It is the interdependence of sender and receiver that is critical to understanding communication as a process. Up to a point, it is useful to talk about senders and receivers separately, but doing so can create one of the difficulties of thinking about communication as process: Calling one individual a sender and another a receiver implies a single finite act that stops at a given point, but often communication is a process with no beginning (sender) or end (receiver). In interactive communication, a source at one moment may be a receiver at another; the same rapid change of role is true for a receiver.

Feedback, the final element in the model, is the receiver's response to the source's message. It provides the source with information about the degree to which an intended effect was achieved. Feedback, certainly in interpersonal communication, is a reciprocal process. The action of the source affects the receiver's reaction; the receiver's reaction affects the subsequent reactions of the source. Each can make use of the reactions of the other in a continuous, ongoing fashion. But feedback is more than a simple action–reaction concept; it is part of a dynamic and mutual interdependence.

> People are not thermostats or furnaces. They have the capacity to make trial responses within the organism, to use symbols, to anticipate how others will respond to their messages, to develop expectations about their own behavior and the behavior of others. The concept of expectations is crucial to human communication. (Berlo 1960, 16)

People bring their own expectations to interpersonal encounters, and they also have expectations about the expectations of those with whom they communicate (Thayer 1986). These expectations have an ongoing effect on the communication process between sender and receiver. Human interaction is designated as the highest level of interdependence and mutual role taking because of the complexity of the human being. Successful communication between individuals requires that the two people put themselves into each other's shoes, perceive the world as the other person perceives it, and predict how the other will respond.

Finally, this process must occur in an environment where there is *noise,* or unanticipated factors that cause a lack of clarity on the part of the source, garble the message during transmission, or distract the receiver. Noise may come from other actors in the area, technology, simultaneous social and political occurrences, or innumerable other factors. The danger of noise interrupting or distorting communication is constant; thus, feedback becomes exceedingly important because it is the primary way to find out if the communication occurred as desired.

Thus interpersonal communications attempt to bridge the gap—in experience, knowledge, feelings—between two individuals through messages that are meaningful to both. However, there is many a slip between message and meaning. Distortion in communication is of increasing concern to communication scholars. Most often, it has been dealt with as an unintended aspect of the process; however, the capacity of humans to anticipate the expectations and reactions of others, and thereby to deliberately shape the meanings that others will draw from messages, introduces the ability to either reduce or introduce distortion into the communication process. Looked at in this way, distortion has important implications in public bureaus, especially for the gaining of influence or avoidance of control.

FORMAL AND INFORMAL COMMUNICATION NETWORKS

Organizations have both formal and informal communication systems. Formal and informal communication are discussed separately here for purposes of definition and description. In reality, however, they coexist and are relatively inseparable.

An organization's formal structure, which was defined in Chapter 4, is the officially prescribed distribution of authority and task responsibility among its offices and officials.

Formal communication networks coincide with the organization's formal authority structure. The formal communication system consists of those interactions among the organization's members and its subdivisions that are prescribed by the formal structure. Formal communications, such as organizational charts, standard procedures, formal policy directives, orders, correspondence, reports, and so on are regarded as official by the bureau (Downs 1967, 113). It is impossible to design formal channels in a manner that can meet all the communication needs of the organization and its members. Informal channels emerge when there is a need for organization members or officials to communicate and no formal channel exists (Downs 1967, 113)—or the use of formal channels poses risks to personal or policy interests.

All organizations have informal communication networks. Informal communication is interaction that is not prescribed by the organization's formal authority structure or official procedures (although, over time, certain patterns can gain implicit official approval). Informal communication is highly significant in organizations, and it is ubiquitous, sometimes overlapping with and sometimes existing outside the formal structure. Not only wide ranging and flexible, informal communication patterns are also more dynamic and unpredictable than formal ones. This is not to imply that informal organization is random or without form, or that all individuals in the organization are linked to others in the same way. Informal communication may be either task related—but not official even when it flows along formal channels—or personal or social. The face-to-face nature of much informal communication facilitates trust, social support, informal learning, and feedback. The results can be useful to the organization in increased satisfaction to and motivation of members (for example, filling in gaps in the formal communication system), or it can be dysfunctional (for example, growth of loyalties and norms that are at odds with formal goals and rules). Interestingly, recent research indicates that informal communication channels are more effective for implementing change when risk and complexity are characteristics of that change. Informal channels provide those adopting innovations with social support. Informal communication is also more likely to meet the specific needs and questions of the adoption unit because of the immediacy of feedback and the situational specificity of the communication (Fidler and Johnson 1984).

From the perspective of bureau members and officials, unofficial communications have great advantages; they "can be withdrawn, altered, adjusted, magnified, or cancelled without any official record being made" (Downs 1967, 113). In this way, new ideas are encouraged. Policy alternatives can be generated, program implementation problems anticipated, and support cultivated and marshaled without anyone being "locked into position." It is still possible to change positions, because of new information or opposition, without having to explain the inconsistencies of formal statements. Internal control is also affected since subordinates can avoid or delay exposing their ideas or problems to superiors.

Just as informal communication can be a boon, it can also create a variety of problems. This becomes especially true when dealing with individuals outside the organization. Organization leaders often attempt to restrict informal communications about sensitive topics, especially with journalists or officials outside the bureau. In these areas, specific officials may be designated agency spokespeople.

Network Research

Network analysis provides a fruitful approach to the study of the human communication process in the organization. The unit of analysis in network research is the recurrent communication interactions that are evidence of communication networks. In other words, network analysis studies the structure of the organization's communication, not the structure of the organization. Such study is especially helpful in revealing the structure of informal communication networks. Unlike formal communications channels, which are rather explicitly set out and known, informal systems are more elusive and ephemeral.

Each of us knows from our our experience that every individual in a large organization cannot interact continually or even frequently with every other member. Within the formal organization, some individuals and groups become linked through more or less regularized channels of interpersonal communication. Communication scholars term such a set of individuals, interconnected by a patterned communications flow, a *network*. The size of networks is intermediate—somewhere between the individual and the organization. In other words, a network includes some, but rarely all, individuals or groups in an organization. In any sizable organization, many networks may exist and can be linked to other networks. From these patterned though often informal networks, an organization's communication structure emerges.

In their investigations of work and informal group communications, researchers have used two approaches: small-group laboratory experiments and network analysis. Their principal concerns have been the patterns of communication flow and how these patterns affect individual and group functioning.

Small-Group Experiments

Communications researchers of the 1950s and 1960s conducted laboratory experiments with small-group networks. The structure of a network, that is, the pattern of communication flow, was predetermined and controlled by the researcher. In this way, communication structure served as an independent variable, along with several others such as group size and task complexity. In the controlled laboratory setting, these variables could be manipulated to determine their effect on dependent variables such as task performance, member satisfaction, and leadership. The principal types of communication networks studied were chains, circles, and wheels. All-channel and Y networks were also investigated. Each type is characterized by a different communication flow (see Figure 5–2).

Sociologists Alex Bavelas pioneered the technique of laboratory experimentation with small communications structures or networks. Group members in Bavelas's experiments were placed in separate cubicles and allowed to communicate via written messages. Different types of networks were imposed on each group. In each type of network, an individual could communicate only with those to whom he or she was connected; these communication patterns are indicated by the solid lines in Figure 5–2. Information given to each member of a group had to be shared for an assigned task to be completed, and the "solution" to the task had to be conveyed back to all members.

The findings of this research revealed several interesting relationships between communication structure and task performance. For simple, routine tasks, a centralized network (wheel) is more effective (Bavelas 1950; Leavitt 1951). For more complex problem solving that requires pooling information, a decentralized network is superior. Decentralized net-

FIGURE 5–2   Small-Group Experiment Networks

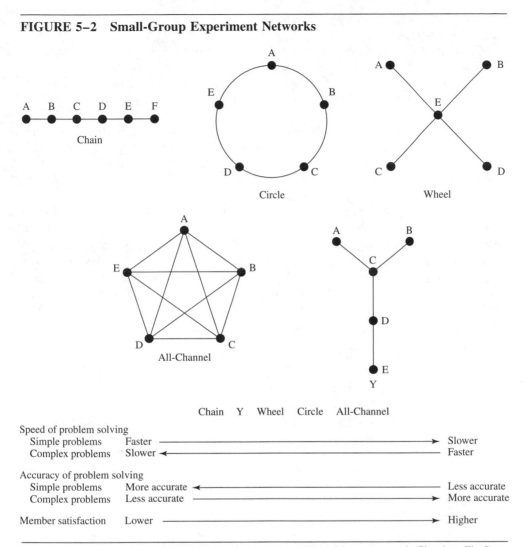

	Chain	Y	Wheel	Circle	All-Channel	
Speed of problem solving						
Simple problems	Faster ──►					Slower
Complex problems	Slower ◄──					Faster
Accuracy of problem solving						
Simple problems	More accurate ◄────────────────────────────────					Less accurate
Complex problems	Less accurate ────────────────────────────────►					More accurate
Member satisfaction	Lower ──►					Higher

SOURCE: Adapted from R. Daft and R. Steers, *Organization: A Micro/Macro Approach* (Glenview, Ill.: Scott, Foresman, 1986): 534. Copyright © 1986 Scott, Foresman and Company.

works may also be preferred if accuracy is important since it was found that centralized groups, although faster, had a higher error rate.

Position in the network was found to be related to leadership and satisfaction. Bavelas, for example, devised an index of relative centrality: The more persons with whom an individual could interact, the more central he or she would be. In Figure 5–2, the most central person is individual E in the wheel; next is individual C in the Y followed by individual C in the chain. The circle and all-channel networks do not differentiate among member centrality. The more central an individual was in the communication structure, the more information he or she was likely to have compared to other members. And those individuals who were more central were regarded as leaders by other members of the group (Bavelas 1950; Leavitt 1951).

Centrality and satisfaction are linked (Bavelas 1950). In highly centralized networks like the wheel, the most central (therefore independent) person is also the most satisfied person (Shaw 1954). In networks that are decentralized and allow the most independence or freedom to interact, satisfaction is more equally experienced by all members of the group.

The negative effects of centrality were also explored. Saturation, to use Shaw's term (or information overload in today's terminology), can occur. For example, in Figure 5–2, the information input and output requirements are highest for individual E in the wheel group or individual C in the Y group, and saturation is highest for these positions. Overload lowers performance in group tasks.

The small-group experiments yielded considerable information about communication flows and their effects, but their methodology was not without flaws. Critics pointed out important limitations in the approach (Becker 1954; Starbuck 1965; Collins and Raven 1969; Rogers and Agarwala-Rogers 1976). The experiments brought together individuals who were strangers, and there was no expectation that their relationships would continue. Tasks were artificial, not real. Perhaps the greatest flaw was that of setting or context: Interaction occurred in a vacuum of sorts, devoid of the larger structure or system in which organizational communication—formal and informal—actually occurs.

Organization Network Analysis

When research on networks moved into real-life organizations, studying communication networks required changes in research procedures. The general approach that is used for identifying the communications structure within an ongoing system—whether group or organization—is network analysis. By means such as questionnaires, interviews, and observation, researchers gather sociometric data on interpersonal communication relationships (basically who interacts with whom and how frequently). In this way, networks and communication flows can be identified, and relationships between formal and informal structures can be determined. Moreover, network analysis has assisted researchers both in recognizing specialized communication roles performed by individuals and in assessing certain systemwide variables.

Most individuals have personal networks of other individuals with whom they interact frequently—at least about certain types of concerns. A personal network may be radial or interlocking in structure. In a *radial network,* a person interacts directly with others, but these people do not interact with one another. In an *interlocking network,* the people with whom a person interacts interact with one another as well (see Figure 5–3). It is useful to regard these terms (radial and interlocking) as descriptive of a quality rather than as designating categories. To some degree, personal networks are more likely to be both radial and interlocking; that is, some individuals in a personal network may interact with one another, whereas others may not. On balance, however, personal networks tend to be more interlocking than radial (Granovetter 1973; Rogers 1973).

Communication occurs quickly and easily within interlocking personal networks, but the closed nature of such a network reduces its informational strength. Although the ties among individuals may be weaker in radial networks, communication researchers have noted what they term the "strength of weak ties" (Granovetter 1973). That is, communi-

FIGURE 5–3 Personal Networks: Radial and Interlocking Types

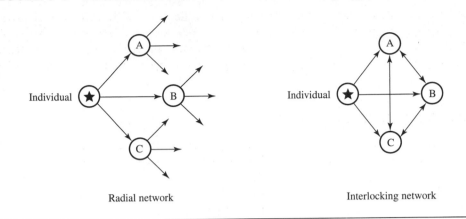

Radial network   Interlocking network

cation is unlikely if there are no ties or links among individuals, but weak sociometric ties (which are more characteristic of radial networks) promote the exchange of more information that is new to members of a network. For example, imagine a network that is almost completely interlocking. Its members communicate only with one another, except for one individual who communicates with people outside the group. That individual, then, has weaker ties to the interlocking network than its other members, yet he or she can be an important conduit for new information. Through such links, information passes from one network to another.

DIRECTIONS OF ORGANIZATION COMMUNICATION

Organizational structure influences both the direction and substance of communication. The authority hierarchy provides a vertical axis for the flow of communications. *Vertical* communication occurs between superiors and subordinates; it may flow downward (from superior to subordinate) or upward (from subordinate to superior). Vertical communications are often formal in that their substance is in some sense official. In general, the greater the degree of formalization or status and power differences, the higher the proportion of vertical communications, and the more likely the direction will be downward.

   Horizontal communication links related tasks, works units, and divisions of the organization. Some horizontal communication is formal but to a lesser extent than that within vertical channels. Two structural factors, task specialization and the diversity of organizational structure, stimulate internal horizontal communication. Organizational diversity is interpreted as complexity and sheer number of occupations and professions, and not as the microdivision of labor implied by task specialization (Thompson 1961). Task specialization increases the need for coordination and integration. Similarly, the proportion of horizontal task communication is greater as the occupations in an organization increase in number and become more professional (Hage, Aiken, and Marrett 1971).

Most organization theory concentrates on communication *within* the organization. But public bureaus, because of greater visibility and accessibility due to their political environment, are tied to outside actors and forces to a degree beyond that of most private firms. Therefore external communication must also be considered. Moreover, whereas the study of internal communication dictates an emphasis on interpersonal behavior patterns, external communication includes a macro perspective—that is, bureau-to-bureau patterns as well.

Downward Communication

Downward communication provides a mechanism for the policy command process in bureaus, which is essential to their central function of implementation. Downward communication generally furnishes information about why and how tasks should be done, and it also helps create the ideological framework within which workers go about their activities. Thus downward communication includes at least:

1. Information of an ideological nature to foster a sense of mission—inculcation of ends or goals
2. Information about organizational procedures and practices—explanation of organizational means to ends
3. Specific task directives—job definition
4. Information designed to produce understanding of the task and its relation to other organizational tasks—job context
5. Feedback to the subordinate about his or her performance—job evaluation (Katz and Kahn 1978)

Job instructions are communicated to subordinates in a variety of ways—oral directions, training sessions, manuals, and written directives—and often with great specificity. Information about organization procedures may pertain to job tasks (and how they fit into the larger organizational functions) or to the rights and obligations of members of the organization such as salary, promotion, and vacation. Too often, communication around tasks and procedures is given priority while ideological information and feedback about job performance, including the impact of the workers' activities on the larger system, are neglected. Why do these patterns occur, and how is the organization and its membership affected?

Strong emphasis on job instruction and organizational procedures is understandable in light of the requirement for managerial and supervisory individuals to direct and control those below them in the hierarchy. But overemphasis on directives can foster the kind of authoritarian atmosphere that leads to problems in control. If the organizational climate is repressive, subordinates may "go by the book" and meet minimum requirements when allowing them to exercise greater individual discretion would do more for task performance and the achievement of organizational goals. Or, rather than becoming passive, subordinates may react with resentment and respond to organizational rigidity by subverting organizational control. Either way, an insidious spiral may be set in motion—new directives and efforts at control followed by more subversion or passivity followed by more new directives, and so on.

Unfortunately, managers usually give less attention to communication about job rationale. Yet an understanding of the importance of one's job can increase motivation and commitment; similarly, individual decision making may be improved. Helping workers understand how their job is related to organizational goals can promote better overall coordination. On the other hand, organizational control may not be as well served if the organizational goals are understood but not the interactive process. Katz and Kahn point out that workers who think they understand why they are doing something may attempt to do it in other than the specified fashion, and the organization's leaders may not want to have the variability of behavior this introduces into the system (1978).

Despite its motivational and control significance, feedback to subordinates about their individual performance is another type of downward communication that is often overlooked and poorly handled. Some reasons for neglecting such feedback stem from general cultural values. American ambivalence toward authority, emphasis on self-determination and individual freedom, and generally egalitarian principles may inhibit superiors— especially when negative evaluations are involved. The psychological tendency to avoid conflict and discomfort also explains to some degree the unpopularity of supervisory evaluation for superior and subordinate alike.

Other, more organizationally related considerations may diminish the use of performance appraisal. For example, the external accountability of government bureaus, coupled with the expectation that the citizens they serve or regulate will be treated impartially and equally, leads to rigid standardized procedures and limited discretion and variability. The size of many government bureaus may also encourage detailed and complex rules constraining both internal and external interaction. If supervisors and managers have little control over the use of resources for rewarding or punishing job performance, there is lessened incentive for either superior or subordinate to pursue authentic and complete feedback on performance.

Superior–subordinate communication has as one of its purposes the promotion of organizational goals. Leaders can impart a sense of mission and commitment to followers. This type of communication has particular significance for public bureaus since it can be done particularly effectively in organizations that make major contributions to social welfare (Katz and Kahn 1978). On the other hand, certain factors inhibit such downward communication in public organizations. The commonly held idea that public bureaucrats should be politically neutral creates one constraint. Almost all public issues, and programs, have both proponents and opponents. Bureaucrats often fear that strong and overt identification with ideological positions and goals will endanger their career progress and job security.

Unlike the internally set goals of firms, external and often shifting political processes are determinants of bureau goals. For example, one administration may actively pursue antidiscrimination goals through vigorous class-action suits and by appointing activist advocates to top agency posts. A change of goals and ideological emphasis occurs when the next administration appoints antidiscrimination opponents and weaker advocates, preferring to curtail the government's adversarial role by changing from a class-action to an individual, case-by-case approach. When one administration is succeeded by another, an administrator who has advocated and is identified with an ideology and goals that are no longer in favor is open to attack by new forces and actors inside and outside the bureau. This occurs at one time or another at all governmental levels.

Upward Communication

Upward communication functions as a reporting and control system for the organization. It also functions as an adjunct to decision making to the extent that higher officials use or need information from lower ones in making decisions and setting policy. A subordinate's upward communication may contain various types of information about personal actions, performance, or problems; actions and problems of his or her peers or subordinates; and actions and problems about the operations of the organization.

Upward communication is necessary to organizational functioning, but it is faced with numerous difficulties. Some are structural, but others stem from the desire of subordinates to influence policy and to protect themselves from the actions or control of their superiors.

The hierarchical structure of organizations in particular discourages open and free upward disclosure of information. Because of authority relationships and reward systems, subordinates (especially those with strong aspirations for upward mobility and promotion) are likely to distort or omit information that will reflect adversely on themselves, or lead to decisions they do not favor or that their bosses do not want to hear (Wilensky 1967, 42–48; Sinetar 1988).

Sometimes an immediate supervisor deadheads the message, that is, does not transmit any part of it upward. A tragic instance of this type occurred moments before the attack on Pearl Harbor.

> At 7:00 A.M. the army shut down its five mobile radar units, as it did every morning at that time. When an army private turned on one radar set for practice, he saw a huge flight of planes. He telephoned his lieutenant, who told him to forget it. The Japanese "surprise" attack began at 7:55. (McCurdy 1977, 209–210)

In an effort to improve upward communication (in fact, communication in all directions), an emphasis was originally placed on increasing personal authenticity and openness,

SOURCE: *Issues and Observations* 4, no. 3. (August 1984): 1. Center for Creative Leadership, 5000 Laurinda Drive, P.O. Box P-1, Greensboro, NC 27402-1660.

as well as the disclosure of feelings and thoughts in communication. Techniques such as transactional analysis (James and Jongeward 1971) and Johari windows (Luft 1970), along with group exercises that increased self-worth, empathy, and openness were stressed in the 1960s. In addition to fostering personal growth, and satisfaction, it was assumed that the skills learned in these exercises would foster openness in communication within organizations. However, the belief that such training would open communication, remove hierarchical barriers, reduce conflict, increase worker morale and motivation, and therefore increase productivity, was only partially realized.

Despite its appeal and the advantages it offers, the personal authenticity approach proved to be of limited utility in communication situations governed by power and influence considerations. In fact, this approach can lead to the manipulation of those individuals who practice it by those who do not—and those who do not, whether inside or outside the bureau, are likely to be legion in number in the public arena. Inside the organization, even if there is an honest attempt to develop open communication, organizational specialization and diversity create impediments that require strenuous efforts to overcome.

Therefore, emphasis has now shifted to an attempt to create a "learning organization," where the total membership communicates openly *with understanding*. As described by Luthans et al.:

> Every complex organization has a variety of subcultures—departments, divisions, levels of management, and the like. Each has its own special interests, mental model of how the (organization) works, and, quite possibly, its own language (jargon). Dialogue,[1] as the discipline is now emerging, is a technique for helping individuals recognize and put aside these basic differences. Consequently, higher levels of collaboration are possible. (1994, 13; see also Schein 1993 and Isaacs 1993)

The emphasis in much of this activity is aimed at reducing the impact of hierarchical status and power on organizational communication. Especially in organizations working in the public arena, this is quite difficult. The "power game" is played by subordinates as well as superiors, and the constant presence of outside forces wishing to have an influence on organizational decisions and processes makes the possibility of achieving a "learning" state even more difficult for bureaus. Other factors such as size and structure also have a significant impact on the methods employed, success, and outcomes in upward communication activity.

As in downward communication, the size of the communication loop affects information transmitted upward. In general, the higher the organizational level, the more constricted the upward feedback tends to be. Some constriction or filtering is needed to prevent

---

[1]*Dialogue* is quite different from the common discussion that goes on in organizations because in discussion the goal of the participant is "to win," or to get one's views accepted by the group. According to Senge (1990), the discipline of team learning starts with dialogue, in which "people become observers of their own thinking" (242) and "individuals gain insights that simply could not be achieved individually" (241). Bohm (1965) created the concept, which has three basic conditions:

1. All participants must "suspend" their assumptions, literally to hold them "as if suspended before us."
2. All participants must regard one another as colleagues.
3. There must be a "facilitator" who "holds the context" of dialogue (Senge 1990, 243). (This means that the facilitator understands and practices the process of dialogue so faithfully that he or she can "influence the flow of development simply through participating.")

information overload but a byproduct, isolation of the organization's leaders, can be harmful.

Messages that must pass through many individuals or through numerous hierarchical levels tend to be distorted at each level in the hierarchy. The effects of distortion on information are aggregated as messages pass from one level to the next. The greater the length of the communication loop and the more levels it involves, the greater the likelihood that significant distortion will occur. Conversely, communication loops may be too small. Typically, the upward communication loop terminates with the immediate supervisor who may choose to transmit some part of the message upward, but usually in a condensed and modified form (Katz and Kahn 1978).

Horizontal Communication

A substantial amount of communication flows laterally in organizations. These lateral flows connect individuals within the same work unit, span diverse but interrelated divisions and levels, or even link different organizations. Horizontal communication serves important purposes for the organization: task coordination, problem solving, information sharing, and conflict resolution. Most horizontal communication connects peers rather than superiors and subordinates, but even when officials of different ranks are involved, variations in status are likely to be played down (Downs 1967; Blau and Scott 1962, 116–139).

Horizontal flows, which are thought to be more frequent than vertical flows, are subject to less distortion. For various reasons, organization members are more comfortable in using lateral channels and have less cause to restrict, withhold, or distort messages. Research shows that the more threatening a message, the more likely it is to be ignored or distorted. Unlike the authoritative (downward) or control-related information on per-

SOURCE: *Issues and Observations* 4, no. 3 (August 1984): 2. Center for Creative Leadership, 5000 Laurinda Drive, P.O. Box P-1, Greensboro, NC 27402-1660.

formance (upward), horizontal messages are often concerned with coordination and are therefore less threatening. Further, lateral communication is more likely to be interactive than unilateral, informal rather than formal, and face to face or oral rather than written. As a result, feedback occurs rapidly and often, and distortion is reduced. Because peers have a common frame of reference, their meanings are shared and similar. A degree of openness and personal authenticity is easier and less risky to sustain in horizontal communication.

Communication between peers provides emotional and social support as well as task coordination. Socioemotional support is needed by individuals whether in organized or unorganized groups. The question is whether the organization benefits from peer communication of this type. The answer is "probably" or "yes, but. . . ." Katz and Kahn caution, for example, that if there are no problems of task coordination left to a group of peers, the content of their communication can take forms that are irrelevant or destructive to organizational functioning (1978). Of course, total quality management and learning organization theorists view horizontal communication as a serious part of improving quality and learning about problems and possibilities facing the organization. Horizontal communication is as important, in these approaches to management, as either upward or downward communication.

Horizontal communications are a check on the power of an organization's top leaders, so leaders often have to learn to accept this and use the communication tool to achieve other management or leadership styles (see Chapter 9). In authoritarian organizations, information is used to control members at lower levels, and controls and restrictions are placed on the horizontal flow of information. If members cannot communicate with one another, they will be unable to engage in any coordinated efforts not sanctioned by the leadership. On the other hand, new techniques of organizational improvement require communication skills in all directions.

The fact remains that horizontal interaction is inevitable. Organizations need task coordination, and the functions performed by horizontal communication will be increasingly important as organizational tasks become more complex and professionalism rises because individual members will continue to seek the stimulation, support, and identity with peers that come with lateral and informal interaction.

External Communication

Bureaus are extremely permeable; information easily passes through in both directions. Bureaucrats at all levels, responding to a variety of situations and for a variety of reasons, communicate with those outside their agency. Their external and largely informal communication has wide-reaching implications for the bureau. Networks of interest groups, politicians, clients, and bureaucrats develop around programs and policy fields. For example, civil servants who wish to maintain support for superiors or for specific programs can make positive information available to outside sources. On the other hand, government employees who disagree with the substantive policies of their organizational superiors may appeal and supply information to powerful actors outside the agency.

In some instances, the bureau's accountability or its responsiveness are improved by such external communication; in other cases, damage may be done to agency programs and policies. In either case, bureau processes—the vertical authority system, managers' control over subordinates, and the organization's decision processes—may be disrupted. For the organization, the greatest significance of boundary-spanning activity depends on whether it results in favorable exploitation or containment of environmental factors.

One way that an organization can make its environment more predictable and favorable is by coordinating information and actions with the relevant actors in that environment. Seitz (1978) gives interesting models, simple and complex, of the form these linkages take (see Figure 5–4). The channels of power and communication among fragmented policymakers, target clientele, and multiple bureaucracies are complex. Sometimes these complex channels among policymakers, bureaus, and clientele are considered benign—as with most pluralist political theory. Other students of politics and administration have referred to the results, with mixed feelings, as "iron triangles" (Heclo 1977) of administrators, politicians, and interest groups, or as the "military-industrial complex," a phrase coined by President Eisenhower to describe the coalition that included the relevant politicians and bureaucrats in addition to business and defense organizations.

For a variety of reasons, power channels also open among multiple bureaucracies. Bureaus compete with other bureaus for the scarce resources that policymakers allocate, especially in a period of budgetary cutback. They also compete for programs and target clientele. At the same time, the need to cooperate with other bureaus in providing more comprehensive or better clientele services also arises.

The structures of channels linking bureaucracies to one another take several basic forms (see Figure 5–5). In the hierarchy model, one bureau at the top is related to the other bureaus in the pyramid through a formal chain of command. In general, messages sent from the top agency would be commands, and messages coming from the lower

---

FIGURE 5–4   Power Channels

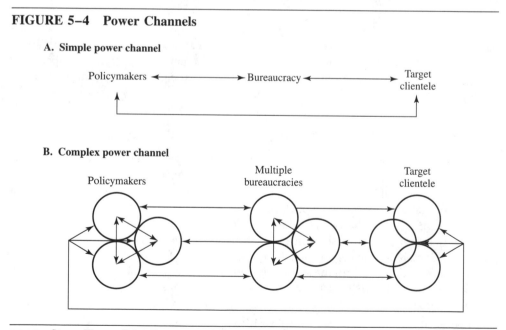

A. Simple power channel

Policymakers ⟷ Bureaucracy ⟷ Target clientele

B. Complex power channel

Policymakers   Multiple bureaucracies   Target clientele

SOURCE: Steven Thomas Seitz, *Bureaucracy, Policy, and the Public* (St. Louis: C. V. Mosby, 1978): 91.

FIGURE 5–5   Models of Interorganization Channels

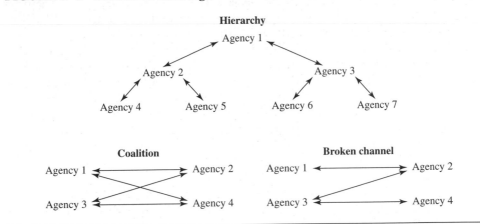

SOURCE: Steven Thomas Seitz, *Bureaucracy, Policy, and the Public* (St. Louis: C. V. Mosby, 1978): 93.

bureaus would contain information and reports desired by the top agency. With this model, interagency cooperation in delivering services, for example, ought to follow the formal structural arrangement, usually bolstered by formal rules, contracts, and the like.

The hierarchy model implies that the top bureau would have authority over lower bureaus. Political resistance to this arrangement from bureaus and their separate clienteles is a certainty. The existence of multiple jurisdictions in our government system is another source of resistance. If bureaus are averse to being placed under other bureaus' control, clearly jurisdictional aversion is equally strong. For example, in the 1982 crash of an Air Florida jet into the Potomac River in Washington, D.C., emergency units from numerous local jurisdictions were needed. Rescue operations were plagued by lack of effective interagency communication and coordination. The hierarchy model offers a structural approach to such a problem, but from an interjurisdictional as well as interagency viewpoint, reservations had to be accommodated. Only after months of task force meetings, studies, and much formal and informal conferring among agency and political leaders could a plan be adopted to improve communication and the direction of future emergency and catastrophe operations. More streamlined and effective interagency communication channels were instituted, but the resulting design was considerably less pyramidal than a pure hierarchy. This outcome is common, given the resistance from bureaus, clientele, and officials in different jurisdictions and levels of government, and is one that can be expected when organizational design must take political actors and factors into account.

In the coalition network, a complex set of channels links the bureaus to one another. Direct channels exist among some bureaus in the broken-channel model, but no agency is linked directly to all the others, and none has power over all the others by virtue of a formal chain of command. In coalition and broken-channel models, coordination occurs but is less centralized and systematic.

Coordination in these coalition and broken-channel models rests on how participants use power to achieve mutual adjustment. There are three approaches to mutual adjustment and power relationships among these types of sets (Seitz 1978, 95–101). First, agencies might agree to accept the current balance of power and to respect the turf of the other bureaus. Second, bureaus may agree to actively coordinate their activities and facilitate each others' activity. This would imply more systematic coordination, usually to accomplish more complete and better quality service delivery to clientele. The third approach is active competition among bureaus. The relationship between competing agencies and cooperation is somewhat surprising. "Under conditions of competition in the organization set, each agency must seek information about its competitors and must seek to match any improvements made by one agency with similar improvements of its own" (Seitz 1978, 96). Competition is now one of the central tenets among current "reinvention of government" proponents (Osborne and Gaebler 1992), and one of the arguments is that it increases communication about goals, processes, tasks, and efficiency and effectiveness. At the same time, because of the increased communication, competition in public goods (as in capitalist markets) increases standardization of goods, services, and knowledge.

Power in interorganizational networks is beginning to be investigated. A recent study was conducted of client referral networks in seventeen communities. It concludes that the communication strategies of an organization (such as joint programs, formal and informal communications, advisory boards) are more important than environmental constraints (such as low administrative autonomy, mandated ties) in determining an organization's centrality and influence in interorganizational networks (Boje and Whetten 1981).

INDIVIDUAL COMMUNICATION ROLES

Organizational communication, as we have seen, can be differentiated in numerous ways: the channels and the content may be formal or informal; the direction of communication may be upward, downward, horizontal, or external; a variety of networks may develop among individuals and groups; and some individual communication roles are established within the organization's communication system.

It is of immense importance for everyone, from organization theorist to public manager to citizen, to understand that bureaus are not some "mass of sameness." In organizational communication as in other areas of life, individual differences count. Researchers have identified specialized communication roles and functions that certain individuals may fulfill. Four of these individual roles deserve particular attention: (1) gatekeeper, (2) liaison and bridge, (3) opinion leader, and (4) boundary spanner or cosmopolite (Rogers and Agarwala-Rogers 1976, 132–140) (see Figure 5–6).

Public managers and citizens also can deal more effectively with bureaus when they can identify individuals in terms of communication roles, recognize the behaviors associated with different roles, and understand the effects of those behaviors on organizational functioning. Some roles are political in specific cases; some are not explicitly political. Yet all have program and public management consequences. *Gatekeepers* can often determine who delivers messages and what messages get through; *liaisons* contribute to internal coordination; *opinion leaders* frequently have policy influence inside the agency and in the larger political process; *cosmopolites,* or boundary spanners, strengthen coordination between agencies—and between agencies and other groups in the political environment of our fragmented governmental system. Organizational adaptability and change may be significantly influenced by individuals playing all these roles.

FIGURE 5–6   Individual Communication Roles in Organizations

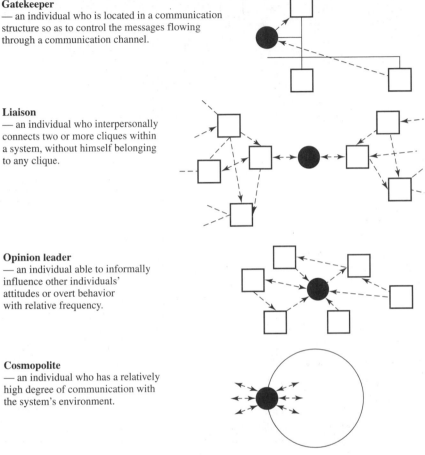

Gatekeeper
— an individual who is located in a communication structure so as to control the messages flowing through a communication channel.

Liaison
— an individual who interpersonally connects two or more cliques within a system, without himself belonging to any clique.

Opinion leader
— an individual able to informally influence other individuals' attitudes or overt behavior with relative frequency.

Cosmopolite
— an individual who has a relatively high degree of communication with the system's environment.

SOURCE: Everett M. Rogers and Rekha Agarwala-Rogers, *Communication in Organizations* (New York: Free Press, 1976): 133.

Gatekeepers

Gatekeepers control the flow of communication through a given channel or network— formal or informal. Any individual in a position through which messages must pass plays the role of gatekeeper to some extent. For example, any individual in a chain network is a gatekeeper (see Figure 5–2). In Figure 5–7, individual B is a gatekeeper in the formal structure, but under certain conditions, individual C (or D or E) may be in an informal gatekeeping position. Individuals C and A may confer unofficially within the organization. Or they may share some extraorganizational membership or activity (professional association, recreation, carpool, church, and so on) in which they interact and share organizationally relevant communication.

FIGURE 5–7   Formal and Informal Gatekeeping Patterns

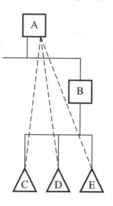

SOURCE: Adapted from Everett M. Rogers and Rekha Agarwala-Rogers, *Communication in Organizations* (New York: Free Press, 1976): 134.

Since they act as a filter for message flows, gatekeepers perform an important function in reducing information overload, especially in upward communication. For example, voluminous proposals are reduced to two- or three-page memoranda for approval by the president. Whether this is accomplished without harmful distortion and omission depends on the criteria used by gatekeepers in regulating information flows.

The selection criteria used by gatekeepers in public organizations are critical to organizational intelligence and responsiveness. Information can be advanced or withheld by gatekeepers, but their power becomes most noticeable when they cause problems. In fact, inspectors general and ombudsmen in government organizations can be seen as structural responses to the vulnerability of communication within the usual hierarchy to distortion, omission, or suppression of information.

Not all gatekeeping is negative. Most of us have had reason to appreciate the helpfulness and responsiveness of gatekeepers, public and private. The sympathetic university secretary who suggests that a shy freshman talk with the department head or a professor about a scheduling problem and, by briefly accompanying and introducing the student, ensures his or her ease is a benevolent gatekeeper. So too is the welfare worker who in dealing with an applicant unfamiliar with programs and bureaucratic procedures provides not only program information, but also assists the client in mastering bureaucratic terminology and required paperwork.

Liaisons and Bridges

Liaisons and bridges (also called "linking pins") are individuals who connect communication subsystems or networks in the organization. These roles can be formal or informal and can link networks both vertically and horizontally. A bridge is a member of one of the connected subsystems, but a liaison does not belong to either of the subsystems he or she connects. The coordinating function of liaisons and bridges is crucial to effective functioning of the organization. For simplicity, only the term *liaison* will be used in our discussion.

Liaisons may expedite the flow of information between groups and subsystems or serve as a bottleneck (Rogers and Agarwala-Rogers 1976, 136). Serious organizational consequences result from the loss or removal of liaisons; they have been called the cement that holds the organization's structural parts together. In a study of communication patterns among officials in the U.S. Office of Naval Research, researchers found that if liaisons were removed, organizational disintegration followed and continuity was destroyed. The affected organization networks fell apart into disconnected and separate subsystems (Jacobson and Seashore 1951).

"The distinctiveness of liaisons stems . . . from their unique communication-bridging function in the organization network" rather than from differences in personal attributes (Rogers and Agarwala-Rogers 1976, 138). In fact, research indicates that there is little difference between liaisons and other organization members although there is some evidence to suggest that liaisons possess qualities or norms intermediate between those of the groups they link (Yadav 1967). Research also generally indicates that individuals in the upper management of organizations tend to be liaisons.

The structure and stability of organizational networks and individual roles are important from both theoretical and applied perspectives. Even though a small percentage of members usually play such a role, it is a matter of strategic importance that an organization consider—in terms of its tasks—its need for liaisons and where that need is located. In some instances, liaison roles may need to be created formally if they do not exist informally. Even where a liaison role is informally filled, it may be advisable to make the position formal if that is necessary to coordinate important organizational activities.

Mobility of personnel may render performance of the liaison role unreliable. In public organizations, the rapid turnover of appointed officials can reduce the stability of networks in which there are liaisons, yet their positions in the organization or the information and influence they have often make their existence important to organizational functioning. Bureau leaders must constantly calculate the costs and advantages to the bureau's communication systems of using a career bureaucrat instead of a political appointee in a particular liaison position.

Opinion Leaders

Opinion leaders are people who have "the ability to informally influence other individuals' attitudes or behavior in a desired way with relative frequency" (Rogers and Agarwala-Rogers 1976, 138). An opinion leader may hold a formal position in a work group, but most research findings conclude that opinion leaders are generally part of the informal structure of their organization, and that they can be expected to be distributed throughout all status and hierarchical levels (Redding 1972; Carroll and Tosi 1977). Opinion leaders have high credibility with other group members. Their influence is not based on formal authority; rather, it stems from their greater expertise and experience or their greater knowledge of and conformity to the norms of their group (see Figure 9–2).

Opinion leadership based on conformity to norms promotes the socialization of members to group norms, which enhances coordination and control through organizational culture. Members are more motivated to achieve the organization's goals if the informal group norms correspond to the organization's formal goals. When this is not the case, normative leadership poses difficult problems for the organization's formal leaders.

Opinion leadership based on substantive knowledge facilitates informal decision making in the group. The wider knowledge and information of leaders on certain topics or issues is passed on to their followers. Radial networks appear more suited to knowledge-based opinion leadership, whereas the opinion leader in a tightly cohesive group may be part of the group's interlocking network (see Figure 5–3). Acceptance of their leadership may be limited to a specific topic, or it may embrace a wide range of concerns. The importance of opinion leadership in organizations is probably enhanced by the growing importance and numbers of professionals in public bureaus.

Boundary Spanners

Boundary spanners, also called cosmopolitans or cosmopolites, are individuals whose interactions include numerous contacts in the external environment (Rogers and Agarwala-Rogers 1976). In the sense that they control or filter the flow of communication and information coming into or going out of the organization, they are like gatekeepers. Organizational openness, the degree of information exchange between an organization and its environment, is provided to a considerable degree by boundary-spanning communications. Not surprisingly, the personal networks of boundary spanners are open or radial rather than closed and interlocking (see Figure 5–3).

Boundary-spanning activities are an essential feature of interaction between bureau and environment. "Adjustment to constraints and contingencies not controlled by the organization is the crucial problem for boundary-spanning components" (Thompson 1967, 81). They significantly affect the organization's ability either to adapt to or to exploit and control its environment.

Boundary-spanning jobs vary in the types of action and rewards they entail depending on the stability of the environment. The potential is greater for power and upward mobility in heterogeneous and somewhat unstable environments. Boundary-spanning jobs in such environments require the exercise of discretion to meet changing and unpredictable contingencies. This, in turn, furnishes the individual in a boundary-spanning job with opportunities to learn through experience and provides for visibility inside and outside the department; jobs that are routinized do not offer comparable opportunities for favorable visibility. The worker with standardized tasks is likely to be noticed only if he or she goofs, and will generally have poorer or slower chances to learn the contents and requirements of other better jobs in the organization (Thompson 1967, 107–111).

Boundary-spanning communication is part of the job of top officials and those with formal external liaison roles such as public information officers or congressional liaisons. Individuals at the top of the organization obtain different kinds of information than is gathered by lower-level members. Higher bureau administrators and political appointees may gather intelligence, that is, information of strategic importance. Such information is usually about changes in the larger system—the economic outlook, political alliances, legislative climate with respect to the bureau, or potential policy initiatives by elected officials. These environmental changes, although seemingly remote from the organization, are likely to affect it in the future.

Lower bureau members who directly serve the bureau clientele also occupy boundary-spanning positions. Boundary spanners—like police dispatchers, license clerks, and welfare evaluators—who also function as external gatekeepers can affect the access and treatment of clientele. Lower-level bureaucrats also handle a large part of the agency's incoming contacts or correspondence, as well as its material and equipment. Their information is likely to be related to changes in clientele demands and needs, the increase or decline in acceptance of bureau activities, and the adequacy and quality of materials or services received by the bureau. Information and observation about the effectiveness of operational activities is also gathered by lower-level boundary spanners.

External communication is not confined to bureau members whose formal roles and positions require it. Some individuals engage in extensive external communications because of a strong professional identity that goes beyond their organizational position. They maintain contacts with fellow specialists, membership and affiliation with professional organizations and groups, and read the publications of their fields. These boundary spanners, who may also be opinion leaders, are interested in exercising their special skills and knowledge (Mosher 1982; Rourke 1984).

The cosmopolitan boundary spanners whose identification with their specialized fields (education, law, accounting, and so on) outweighs their organizational identification and loyalty can present problems of organization control. Their policy objectives or preferences and the program designs they develop may reflect professional values and standards that are not consistent with those of elected officials or the public. In addition, a recent study concluded that informal ties between boundary spanners can constrain an administrator's choice of strategies for establishing linkages with other actors in interorganizational networks (Boje and Whetter 1981, 391). The greater mobility of this type of boundary spanner can add to organizational turnover and instability. On the positive side, their expertise is valuable in stimulating program development, innovation, and adaptability, and in maintaining organizational ethics.

In summary, individual communication roles perform numerous functions for the organization—coordination, filtering, socialization, and innovation. In many ways, they make communication more accurate and effective. They are also sources of distortion and interference. In any event, like other variables in public organizations, their ultimate significance lies in their impact on policy and power in bureaus.

DISTORTION AND INTERFERENCE IN BUREAU COMMUNICATION

Accurate exchange of information is a goal of communication. Distortion is dysfunctional to this end. However, in public bureaus, communication often has goals other than transmitting information. Its purpose is to influence. Distortion here, rather than being dysfunctional, may be an influence tool.

Ambivalence is strong about attempts by unelected officials to influence policy—even without distortion. One concept of public accountability in our system holds that officials who make policy should be accountable to the public they represent. Elections provide one such mechanism. Bureaucrats, according to this reasoning, are not elected and therefore not accountable to the public, so they should not have policy roles, however inadvisable or impossible this may be in practice. Intentional distortion of information by a bureaucratic official causes even greater accountability concerns.

Not all the types of distortion discussed in this section and elsewhere in this chapter are intentional: Sometimes distortion is intentional, sometimes it is unintentional, and sometimes it is both. But all distortions have the potential to affect policy implementation and control.

Distorted Perception

Each of us lives in a world fashioned in large measure by our own individual perceptual processes. Many factors affect our perceptions. Motivations, personality, and past learning determine both what we perceive and what we fail to perceive. Individual differences add richness to both our internal and social worlds, but they also introduce complexities and obstacles into interpersonal communication.

Perception is selective. Although we constantly engage in selective perception, we are only occasionally aware of its effects. In communication situations, our perceptions and attention facilitate our ability to receive some messages and distort or block others. For example, participants in a meeting become less attentive as the time for lunch approaches; discussion lags, questions decrease. But if someone asks whether the group prefers to break for lunch or begin consideration of a lengthy matter, the response will be instantly energetic and clear. The word *lunch* or *eat* will be heard—and responded to. Motivation or need, in this example, hunger, affects the participants' perception.

Different individuals interpret the same message or behavior in different ways. Take the example of an employee who has been directed to prepare a report. At the time the report was assigned, the boss emphasized its importance and set a short but mandatory deadline. The employee completed and handed in the report before the deadline. The boss made no comment at the time she was given the report, and after three weeks there is still no feedback, good or bad. An experienced and secure employee may find this behavior acceptable and routine though some praise would be welcome. However, instead of perceiving that the absence of feedback stemmed from other demands on the manager's time and attention, or to a lapse in good human relations practices, an insecure and inexperienced employee may perceive it as disapproval.

Our mental set determines our perceptual readiness, "the tendency to perceive what one expects or wants to perceive" (Haney 1979, 63). For example, the expertise and dedication of professionals to their special field may focus their attention on the achievement of objectives with little thought about cost (Rourke 1984). They tend to regard administrative rules and procedure as stifling the effectiveness of policy implementation. Administrators, on the other hand, are more concerned with the efficient use of resources and with the need to compromise and moderate policy objectives in light of competing political forces in and out of the bureau. Professionals are inclined to disregard procedures and avoid routines and channels established by administrators, whom they regard as "paper shufflers." The same kind of conflict occurs between line and staff employees in most organizations.

Communication research also confirms that individuals normally perceive and recall those messages that reinforce prior images (Sebald 1962, 149). This phenomenon conditions what we attend to and what meaning we attach to it (March and Simon 1993). First impressions, as we all know, are hard to shake. So strong is the impulse to self-perpetuate our mental set that "the tendency to distort messages in the direction of identity with previous inputs is probably the most pervasive of the systematic biases" (Campbell 1958, 346).

Researchers have described how we go about sustaining our existing perceptions and mental set: "When confronted with a fact inconsistent with a stereotype already held by a person, the perceiver is able to distort the data in such a way as to eliminate the inconsistency. Thus, by perceiving inaccurately, he defends himself from having to change his stereotypes" (Zalkind and Costello 1962, 227). In a similar vein, Salvatore Maddi's research indicates that longer exposure to threatening as opposed to nonthreatening stimuli is required even to recognize or register awareness of them (1972, 195–205, 641).

In no other respect is the tendency to selective perception so strong as when self-image is involved. S. I. Hayakawa asserts that "the fundamental motive of human behavior is not self-preservation, but preservation of symbolic self" (1961). And according to Haney, "The peculiarity of the self-image is that it is 'threatenable' by *change*—sudden, dramatic, uncontrolled change (even if the change is favorable)" (1979, 101).

This selective perception lends stability to our internal state, but it frequently introduces distortion into our perceptions and communication. Likewise, organizational communication, therefore control and responsiveness to change, may be complicated by perceptual distortion and resistance to change—depending on the nature of the stimuli or message. And this distortion, or misunderstanding of information, is doubtless an ingredient in both internal and external organizational conflict.

Erroneous Translation

In this type of miscommunication, the sender and receiver miss each other's meaning. Errors in translation come about in several ways. The same words may have a different meaning for one person than for another. Sometimes confusion occurs when sender and receiver use different words but mean the same thing. In either case, their actual position may be concealed until clarification of meanings is achieved. The discovery of differing meanings for the same word can be unpleasant. In an organization, the result of such an "error" can be conflict, mistakes, and unproductive action. When actual agreement is concealed by apparent disagreement, the effect is equally disconcerting. Distortion occurs because of the mistaken assumption that words have a single usage or meaning. Another prevalent fallacy is that words have meaning in themselves.

Abstraction and Differentiation Errors

Whenever we talk, write, listen, or read, we necessarily abstract; that is, we select some details and omit others. Our language by its very structure uses abstracting. If you say of someone, "She is my coworker," you have abstracted. You selected only one of numerous characteristics: she is a marathon runner, loves pistachio ice cream, speaks Spanish, majored in history, or whatever.

Several types of differentiation errors contribute to miscommunication. *Indiscrimination* is neglecting differences while overemphasizing similarities. Linguists note that English-speaking persons are particularly inclined to perceive and speak in terms of similarities and to generalize instead of differentiate. Our language has numerous general nouns and verbs; other languages have proportionately fewer of these terms, but numerous specific ones. For example, the Eskimo language has many words for specific types of snow but no general word. The Navaho language distinguishes specific stages and manners of going but has no general word for this verb (Haney 1979).

Polarization is a form of differentiation failure that occurs when "contraries (situations involving graded variations, middle ground) are treated as if they were contradictories (strictly either-or affairs)" (Haney 1979, 435). To say that people are either over six-feet tall or not is a genuine contradictory. But saying that people are either short or tall is polarization since people of medium height are, of course, neither short nor tall. *Frozen evaluations* also cause differentiation errors: When we do not take the possibility of change into account, both thinking and communication suffer.

Public policy, of necessity, must be general. It must satisfy a variety of similar individual circumstances. Yet its design should allow implementation to adequately reflect differences and varieties of people and situations. Those carrying out public policy must, therefore, be especially sensitive to balancing the overall goals of legislation with the individual circumstances of those for or about whom the law is written.

Lack of Congruence

Some messages lack congruence; that is, their meaning is ambiguous or even ambivalent. This is often true because more than words are involved in communication; we communicate through nonverbal cues and behavior as well.

When verbal and nonverbal communication are inconsistent, "it seems that receivers generally give greater weight to the nonverbal elements. These are seen as more reliable indicators of the sender's feelings and emotional state" (Hayes 1977). "Action speaks louder than words" is a succinct summary of how we usually resolve behavioral versus verbal discrepancies. Moreover, consistent discrepancy in a person's verbal and nonverbal language leads to higher tension and ambiguity in others than when there is high congruence in communication (Carroll and Tosi 1977, 243).

A manager may claim to have an "open-door" policy. Members of the organization may be told to come in at any time to talk over what is "really on their minds." But if the workers meet with resistance from the outer office or experience excessive delays, the open-door message becomes incongruent. If the manager frets, glowers, or reads during the exchange or reacts defensively or unsympathetically when problems are brought up, the overall message becomes ambivalent. For most workers, the manager's verbal message is "the door is always open" but her behavioral message is "don't bother me, I'm busy with more important things."

Distrusted Source

Receivers evaluate sources or senders and judge messages accordingly. All other elements in the communication being equal, higher source credibility leads to greater acceptance of communication (Zimbardo and Ebbesen 1970).

Communication researchers report an interesting paradox concerning the effect of distrusted sources. If the sender is thought to have biased attitudes, greater weight is given to unintended than to intended communication because receivers' defenses are not aroused by communication that they don't believe was intended for them (Allyn and Festinger

1961; Festinger and Maccoby 1964; Jones and Davis 1965). Perhaps the importance given to information received through the organization's informal grapevine or leaked to the outside is related to this phenomenon. Rumor may engender less defensiveness and skepticism since it will be seen as unintended or unguarded in a sense.

Distrust of the source can lead to distortions of the message. For example, John McCone, director of the Central Intelligence Agency during the Kennedy administration, reported his suspicions that the Soviets were preparing to put offensive missiles into Cuba; it was the message the president least wanted to hear. Moreover, according to Graham Allison, "Kennedy heard this as what it was: the suspicion of a professional anti-Communist" (1971, 190). The president did not share the stance and outlook of such types. Later, however, other information was to verify the presence of offensive weapons, thus changing the course of administration action in dealing with this greater danger than it had anticipated. The tendency to evaluate the sender, which we all share, is basically rational—as long as we are aware of how our own biases can distort our judgment.

Jargon

The notion of specialization in knowledge is relatively new. In the past, specialization referred to separate task components in organizations. But modern scientific knowledge has expanded beyond the capacity of the minds of single individuals and has therefore become fragmented into separate disciplines and bodies of knowledge. Thus, specialized vocabularies develop within discrete technical and professional areas. Communication gaps arise between those who have specialized knowledge and vocabularies and those who do not.

Expertise, Influence, and Jargon

The fragmentation of knowledge creates a situation in which those who need but do not have a particular kind of expertise depend on those who do. This phenomenon gives rise to the tendency to defer to experts in technical matters and to follow the advice of experts in policymaking. The vocabulary and jargon used by individuals with specialized knowledge serves to identify them as experts—and thereby, to enhance their power. Jargon erects communication barriers, but it also reinforces the tendency to follow the advice of experts in policymaking.

Because of the notion in Congress, for example, that technical matters should be left to professionals and experts, bureaucratic specialists frequently have great influence on policy. There are, of course, constraints on the experts' influence in shaping public policy. For example, the balance of power between elected officials and bureaucratic experts depends in large measure on whether these officials perceive an issue as technical or not and to what extent the politicians can call on their own staff experts.

Because of both pressure groups and their own personal values, legislators and executives are unlikely to perceive certain issues as technical. Communication between politicians and experts, the influence of specialists, the distribution of influence, and policy outcomes are altered accordingly. Public health specialists, like some other experts, are frequently in control of presenting the alternatives from which elected politicians choose. Yet, the influence of these specialists is limited. For example, elected officials at national, state, and local levels have initiated and enacted various abortion-related policies quite independently of public health or medical experts. For those who define an issue in terms of their personal religious or moral views, technical or expert perspectives are not relevant. Similarly, local and state legislators may perceive no-smoking ordinances from a variety of perspectives, including political, safety, economic, and the proper role of government in regulating personal behavior.

Since Congress feels dependent on experts, who are often out of their control, they try to counter the expertise of outside sources. The Congressional Budget Office was created because Congress did not trust the figures given to them by the Office of Management and Budget; however, individual members of Congress refute or refuse the figures of the CBO when its figures do not match the policy desires of that congressperson and he or she can present more favorable figures—usually prepared by his or her staff economic expert. Likewise, issues like environmental regulation are often left to the experts in the Environmental Protective Agency; however, countering expertise has been developed through interest groups on all sides of the issues, and the EPA is now challenged much more regularly on its decisions. In other cases, such as the closing of military bases at the end of the cold war, decisions are turned over to "experts" by Congress primarily because the politicians realize the issue is so volatile that (1) they do not want to have to handle it, and (2) it needs to be handled by a group that can claim expertise and objectivity in its deliberations.

If their specialized knowledge and vocabularies are sources of power for experts in their relationships with elected officials, experts are also dependent on officials. The relationship between officials and experts is best described as one of mutual dependence. Experts are not always right, nor are they always in agreement. Politicians often lack the technical knowledge that would be necessary to choose from conflicting expert advice and thus base their choice on other grounds. Thus experts recognize the need for trust between politician and advisor. Successful professional and expert advisors are scrupulous about the veracity of their information; they then understand that the politicians often will use that information that they find most satisfactory from their personal political perspective. Top-level organizational leaders, as generalists, may do the same thing. A city manager, in reporting an ingenious refinement of this strategy to the authors, noted that he always kept two attorneys in his legal office. One was inclined to react to the manager's ideas and initiatives with positive recommendations and legal approaches for implementing them. The second and more cautious attorney tended to focus on legal obstacles and ambiguities. The manager generally acted on the first attorney's recommendations while taking precautions against the pitfalls pointed out by the other.

Expertise, already fragmented by specialization, is further fragmented by multiple bureaucracies. Separate bureaucracies with their different perspectives provide policymakers with the opportunity to shop for opinions—usually those consistent with their own career or policy goals (Seitz 1978, 89). The power relationships among bureaus may also determine which expert advice will be selected. This occurred, for example, in 1963 when Robert McNamara, as secretary of defense, succeeded in squelching the reports of Lew Sarris, an intelligence expert at the State Department (Halberstam 1969, 257–258). Seitz suggests that if Secretary of State Dean Rusk had been more forceful, Presidents Kennedy and Johnson might have received better information, with a more realistic Vietnam policy as the result (1978, 89). In the budgetary and economic arenas during the Reagan and Bush presidencies, policymakers similarly chose to rely on experts whose optimistic reports told them what they wanted to hear. A basic distrust of one another's economic projections is a major factor in the battles between the congressional Republicans and the Clinton Whitehouse as attempts are made to correct the budgetary deficit.

Clientele and Jargon

In addition to fragmentation and specialization of knowledge, other factors foster bureaucratic miscommunication. On the one hand, bureaucrats are expected to be responsive to their publics. This could reasonably include communicating in ways familiar and understandable to their clientele. At the same time, norms of impartiality and equal treatment create pressures that sometimes have unintended effects on communication. Language becomes depersonalized. Bureau members use passive expression or style; standardized terminology is coined that does not correspond to ordinary usage. One of the most frequent complaints of outsiders about public bureau communication is the use of jargon—or worse, of "bureaucratese" or gobbledygook.

Some public bureaus "ration services by manipulating the nature and quantity of information made available" (Lipsky 1980, 91). Street-level bureaucracies, those whose workers directly dispense benefits or sanctions, usually have inadequate resources. Confusing jargon, especially in conjunction with elaborate and obscure procedures, is a barrier to many clients. The bureau limits client access and demand as a way of coping with its resource problem.

Inflated Style, Euphemism, and Evasion

As George Orwell points out in his classic essay on politics and language in the British public service, language is "an instrument which we shape to our own purposes" (1956, 355). Frequently those purposes are political, especially in public bureaus. Pretentious diction "is used to dress up simple statements to give an air of scientific impartiality to biased judgements" (Orwell 1956, 358). Speakers also use inflated style to keep their political intentions and alternatives unclear. For example, George Orwell notes that:

> The inflated style is itself a kind of euphemism. A mass of Latin words falls upon the facts like soft snow, blurring the outlines and covering up all the details. The great enemy of clear language is insincerity. When there is a gap between one's real and one's declared aims, one turns as it were instinctively to long words and exhausted idioms, like a cuttlefish squirting out ink. (1956, 363)

Even more alarming to Orwell is the use of meaningless words or euphemisms. These are used to make the unpalatable palatable. Sometimes, political communication is the attempt to defend the indefensible, or things that can be defended "but only by arguments that are too brutal for most people to face" (Orwell 1956, 363). Instead, we turn to "euphemism, question-begging and sheer cloudy-vagueness":

> Defenseless villages are bombarded from the air, the inhabitants driven out into the countryside, the cattle machine-gunned, the huts set on fire with incendiary bullets: this is called *pacification*. Millions of peasants are robbed of their farms and sent trudging along roads with no more than they can carry: this is called *transfer of population or rectification of frontiers*. People are imprisoned for years without trial, or shot in the back of the neck or sent to die of scurvy in Arctic lumber camps: this is called *elimination of unreliable elements*. (Orwell 1956, 363)

Thank God the Government Would Never Do This. Would It?

The first rule of communication is that different groups and different people can speak the same language and thereby understand one another. This lesson should be easy enough to grasp, particularly for consultants who are paid highly to improve communications in a company. But when some world-renowned consultants came to our utilities company several months back, few of us were prepared for the communication breakdown that was about to hit.

The problem started small: a word sprinkled here or there in managers' conversations. Someone felt "empowered"; someone else was breaking free of "paradigms."

Then it spread. Managers started speaking in tongues. You'd round a corner and you'd hear a manager say: "Through virtual leadership, I took the cultural determinants and broke through."

Not that my company was innocent to begin with. Most aren't. Managers typically avoid strong verbs and "utilize" words. And corporations thrive on acronyms. I once met an employee who proudly announced to me that she had STD. I beat a retreat, unsure of what sexually transmitted disease she had. Later, I discovered she meant short-term disability.

Luckily, we had always had our line workers to keep our corporate lingo simple and direct. Whenever they dropped a tool, they yelled "headache" to warn people below. To "hang a pot" meant to install a new meter. To "hook up a buggy" meant to hook up a portable generator. And to "torch your shorts" was a clever phrase for receiving a mild electric shock.

Then the consultants came in droves, dragging their charts and graphs and their *vocabularies!* Our company became completely jargonized. The words slithered everywhere.

The magic word seemed to be "strategic." A feeling grew among managers that if you attached the word "strategic" to anything, it would get approved. I even saw a memo discussing "strategic dreaming."

Oh, there were a few brave managers who strategically resisted by wearing earplugs and nodding happily at everything the consultants said. Unfortunately, nodding happily translated into approval for a new consulting project. So they stopped wearing earplugs and the jargon seized them too.

It was insidious. You couldn't sit in the cafeteria without hearing about "excellerated" cultural change, cultural "interventions," three-stream models, architectural rigor and disci-

Manipulating and Withholding Information

Members of the bureaucracy have longevity in office, expertise, familiarity with issue communication networks, and control of information as power bases that make political officeholders dependent on them for information and advice. This allows bureaucrats to shape the flow of information in favor of the policies and decisions they prefer. They do this by use of selective information and structuring or choosing "appropriate" channels through which to release information so that it will present the best possible face on the issue.

pline, people value, integrated strategic change and core efficiencies. Managers would chat happily for hours, a glazed, contented look on their faces, while they chowed down their "cultural vitamins."

But one day, barricaded in my office, wearing a copy of Strunk and White's "Elements of Style" around my neck like a protective charm, I had a thought. Surely the consultant psychobabble hadn't seduced our line workers. Surely common sense survived among the line crews and customer service representatives.

I ventured forth. There was hope! The line employees gave me these quotes:

"It's really frustrating. This consultant language has developed into a language of its own. It really alienates us. I have to get out my dictionary just to understand my manager."

"I feel we should pay someone to translate for us."

"My manager is indoctrinated in this language. He doesn't speak English anymore. He doesn't even have to think what it means. He just types it in and there it is."

"It's like they're some elite group that speaks French, when the rest of us speak American."

"If someone walked into this company, they'd be thinking we speak Martian."

"You start thinking you should know what these terms mean, so you don't say anything."

Perhaps the light at the end of the tunnel wasn't a consultant brandishing a flashlight. The frontline was still holding out, waiting for common sense or at least clear English to return to the management ranks.

They were also delivering a message that none of us should ever forget: If you want to change your company's culture, speak the employees' language, not the consultants'.

I returned to corporate headquarters refreshed. But images of "energizing visions" and "vision congruences" still darted through my head.

I thought I could hold out. Then "empowerments" and "visions" started creeping into my own conversation. I had to get someone to listen to the line employees! I searched the hallways for a sympathetic manager.

But the empty hallways only echoed my running feet. I stumbled into a large meeting room. The managers were kneeling on the floor, bowing before a large icon of the letters spelling out the name of a famous consulting firm.

I yelled, but they couldn't hear me. Their chant of "Strategic, Strategic, Strategic" drowned out my screams.

SOURCE: Phil Theibert, "Manager's Journal: Eschew That Paradigm! Drop the Jargon," *The Wall Street Journal*, August 1, 1994: A13.

The first strategy for controlling information is selectively releasing information. Bureau administrators find that one way of doing this is by requesting studies from those who will give the desired conclusion. The strategy is further bolstered by preparing careful detailed studies that present facts in an authoritative fashion. Facts may even be intentionally distorted if necessary—although this strategy is extremely dangerous in a world of multiple information sources.

In his memoirs, President Eisenhower wrote that he had been assured that the American U-2 spy aircraft would destroy itself on impact so that the plane's advanced technology and the evidence of its espionage activity would not fall into Soviet hands (Eisenhower 1965, 554–559). This passage in the president's account caused Gary Powers, the U-2 pilot who, along with the plane, was captured by the Soviets, to comment: "If Eisenhower was told this he was deceived" (Powers 1970, 353). Since experts and administrators in charge of programs may distort or fail to report unfavorable information because they want to win or maintain approval of a program or system, a variety of information sources have been developed by countervailing forces (lobbyists, interest groups, congressional staff, and the like) who are often attempting to present that same information in a way that best represents their particular slant on the subject.

Selective presentation of facts also includes the tactic of *not* reporting all the information if some of it reflects poorly on the wisdom of the bureau's preferred policy or procedure. Likewise, reporting of information can be structured to ensure that senior officials or policymakers see only what bureaucrats want them to see. Information conveyed in routine reports from lower-level members usually does not reach top officials in its original form; the information is synopsized or rewritten for digestion by superiors—often at their request because of information overload and limitations on time. Bureaucrats, and higher organization officials, have long been acquainted with the obscuring technique of supplying too much information and thus creating information overload. However, that screened and condensed information may be biased or intentionally limited if such action appears beneficial (for whatever reason) to those preparing it. Finally, techniques for structuring channels to control information flow include circumventing formal channels, informally exposing "target" officials to those who hold the correct views, and keeping sources away who might report preferably suppressed facts.

COPING WITH DISTORTION

Various sources of distortion in communication—perceptual, social, structural, and political—have been raised. No single answer exists to the problem of distortion, and it must be kept in mind that remedies can introduce new problems along with solutions. Nevertheless, bureau administrators and political officials outside the bureau can adopt strategies to reduce distortion, whether that distortion was intentional or not.

Leaders too can shape the flow of information they receive from bureau members. At least five types of strategies are available to bureau leaders, political officials, and others for obtaining better information and constraining the power of bureaucratic actors: (1) creating alternative sources, (2) encouraging divergent views, (3) eliminating middlemen, (4) using distortion-proof messages, and (5) counterbiasing.

Creating Alternative Sources

Administrators and leaders can check distortion and achieve better verification of the information they receive by creating alternative sources. A fuller and more accurate picture emerges from a wider range and amount of information. Several independent groups can be set up within the bureau to work on the same policy question (Downs 1967, 119–120; Janis 1972; 211–212). This technique introduces an element of competition combined with each group's lack of information about the reports and actions of the other groups and individuals. Officials can also create overlapping areas of responsibility in different bureaus.

Informal ties and friendships within the bureau are alternative sources. In part this is "learning to use the grapevine productively." Sources outside the bureau are useful also; these include the press, clientele, social acquaintances, reports of other agencies, and even gossip.

Encouraging Divergent Views

Certain leader behaviors and communication styles encourage divergent views. Leaders can surround themselves with individuals of differing views and still not achieve divergence in views and openness in communication of those perspectives. Much of the "learning organization" theory is built around the development of openness and sharing of knowledge, information, and perspective. Senge (1990), for instance, notes that there must be more than just "participative openness," which allows the freedom to speak one's mind. In order to learn from our environment and our experiences, we must also practice "reflective openness," which leads to looking inward:

> Reflective openness starts with the willingness to challenge our own thinking, to recognize that any certainty we ever have is, at best, a hypothesis about the world. No matter how compelling it may be, no matter how fond we are of "our idea," it is always subject to test and improvement. Reflective openness lives in the attitude, "I may be wrong and the other person may be right." It involves not just examining our own ideas, but mutually examining others' thinking. (277–278)

The kind of reflective openness needed for encouraging and utilizing divergent views requires the skills of:

- Reflection (slowing down our own thinking processes so that we can become more aware of how we form our mental models)
- Inquiry (knowing how we operate in face-to-face interactions with others, especially in dealing with complex and conflictual issues)
- Dialogue (the examination of assumptions and willingness to play with new ideas)
- Dealing with defensive routines (breaking through perspectives and routines that form a protective shell around our deepest assumptions and defend us from pain or embarrassment)

In order for such a system—encouraging divergent views—to function successfully, a strong sense of trust must exist as part of the organization's culture (see Chapter 6), and this is exceedingly hard to create in public organizations. Constant turnover of political appointees at the top of the organization, and the seemingly unavoidable tension between those appointees and merit system employees, limit the development of trust. Thus it is difficult to create communications systems that do *not* soft-pedal disagreements or suppress bad news. Difficulty, however, does not let managers off the hook—divergent views are still necessary for successful operation in the public interest.

Eliminating Middlemen

Opportunities for distortion and omission increase with the number of organizational levels communication must pass through. A structural approach to this problem is to flatten the hierarchy by having fewer levels. This approach is popular now, but for reasons primarily of economy. That does not, however, keep administrators from taking advantage of this opportunity to improve communication channels at the same time. A more informal technique for overcoming these structural sources of distortion is "by-passing"—that is, for officials to contact individuals considerably above or below themselves in a hierarchy.

Using Distortion-Proof Messages

When accuracy of reporting is critical, one way to make sure that information does get forwarded in its original format, and with its complete content, is to use forms of communication that cannot be distorted because they are forwarded without screening or condensation. Standard forms and statistical reports are a couple of these communication devices. The National Aeronautics and Space Administration, after the explosion of the Challenger shuttle, found that critical safety information had not been passed forward to higher-level officials, so they changed their reporting system so that conflicts had to be reported to the next higher level in all cases. This meant that distortion could not occur, nor could the information simply be withheld.

Counterbiasing

If administrators have experience in the organization they lead, or if they have professional insight into the goals and processes, they can often counterbias information. They can estimate the distortion that occurs during communication and then make an appropriate adjustment in their interpretation of the information. For example, a line administrator, who knows the tendency of the bureau's staff lawyers to include all remotely possible legal pitfalls as well as the more likely ones, can conduct his or her operation with more latitude than if he or she regards all the legal warnings as equally imminent or likely. By "reading between the lines," the bias in information can be corrected. However, other sources of correction are critical because it is always dangerous to depend too much on personal experience.

CONCLUSION

Communication is essential in all organizations. It is a process through which organizations inform and clarify goals for members. Internally, communication provides a medium for organizational coordination and control and, more informally, for social support among members. External communication is especially vital to bureaus to (1) maintain political responsiveness and accountability, (2) foster coordination with other agencies and levels of government, and (3) promote external support. In this chapter, we have discussed accountability and power as well as communication. The two are closely related for public bureaus because communication is a primary medium for exercising power. Bureaus and their members can raise smoke screens to evade accountability. Information can be withheld or its timing and content manipulated to protect the bureau's operating routines and policies from external scrutiny. By shaping the flow of information, bureaus and their members attempt to maintain or increase their power and resources, to avoid the control of others, and to reduce undesirable environmental turbulence. Policy outcomes and power relationships inside and outside the organization are affected.

Before organization and communication theory can fully encompass public bureaus—and their important differences—much future research and integration of public–private perspectives will be needed. For now, we can point to some issues of special interest for communication and public bureaus. In particular, the political nature of government organizations and their communications should be acknowledged and understood. We also need to understand the importance of organization–environment relationships and the external communications of public bureaus.

FOR FURTHER READING

A useful reference to earlier communication theorists, and an attempt to present a model of interpersonal communication as a dynamic process is David K. Berlo, *The Process of Communication: An Introduction to Theory and Practice,* New York: Holt, Rinehart & Winston, 1960. A lucid and concise presentation of communication research in an organizational context appears in Everett Rogers and Rekha Agarwala-Rogers, *Communication in Organizations,* New York: Free Press, 1976. Anthony Downs, in *Inside Bureaucracy,* Boston: Little, Brown, 1967 (reissued, Prospect Heights, Ill.: Waveland Press, 1994), discusses the interaction between the communication process and bureaucratic structure and processes. He also looks at communication as one element in other functions such as decision making, motivation, and coordination and control. A particularly significant contribution to communication theory is made by Steven Seitz in *Bureaucracy, Policy, and the Public,* St. Louis: C. V. Mosby, 1978, because he includes external communication as an important element in the total managerial process. Seitz explores the influence of (especially external) communication patterns on policymaking and implementation. For an emphasis on sources of unintentional distortion in interpersonal communication, see William V. Haney, *Communication and Interpersonal Relations: Text and Cases,* 6th ed., Homewood, Ill.: Richard D. Irwin, 1992. On the other hand, George Orwell, "Politics and the English Language," in Richard Rovere, ed., *The Orwell Reader,* New York, Harcourt Brace Jovanovich, 1956, and Morton Halperin, "Shaping the Flow of Information," in Halperin (with the assistance of Priscilla Clapp and Arnold Kanter), *Bureaucratic Politics and Foreign Policy,* Washington, D.C.: The Brookings Institution, 1974, both look at *intentional distortion* and its political significance.

REVIEW QUESTIONS

1. Note the differences between formal and informal communication. Considering the "noise" that occurs within and around communications, how can the formal and informal channels of communication help correct any distortion or information loss?

2. How does communication differ when moving upward, downward, or laterally in the bureau? What impact will the structure of the organization have on how communication flows in each direction?

3. Given the political environment of public bureaus, how important is communication to the leaders (or managers, or workers) of the organization? What political factors must be taken into account when the leader talks to those outside the organization, or those inside the organization? Will the message and the medium be different in those two situations?

4. Looking at the roles individuals play in the communication network, how many roles can a single individual play? How (and why) would people's behavior, and their power in the organization, change as they shifted roles?

REFERENCES

Allison, Graham T. *Essence of Decision: Explaining the Cuban Missile Crisis.* Boston: Little, Brown, 1971.

Allyn, J., and L. Festinger. "The Effectiveness of Unanticipated Persuasive Communications." *Journal of Abnormal Social Psychology* 62, 1961: 35–40.

Argyris, Chris. *Interpersonal Competence and Organizational Effectiveness.* Homewood, Ill.: Dorsey Press, 1962.

Axley, Stephen R. "Managerial and Organizational Communication in Terms of the Conduit Metaphor." *Academy of Management Review* 9, 1984: 428–437.

Barnard, Chester. *The Functions of The Executive.* Cambridge, Mass.: Harvard University Press, 1968 (originally published in 1938).

Bavelas, Alex. "Communication Patterns in Task-Oriented Groups." *Acoustical Society of America Journal* 22, 1950: 727–730.

Becker, Howard. "Vitalizing Sociological Theory." *American Sociological Review* 19, 1954: 383–384.

Berlo, David K. *The Process of Communication: An Introduction to Theory and Practice.* New York: Holt, Rinehart & Winston, 1960.

Berne, Eric. *Games People Play; The Psychology of Human Relations.* New York: Grove Press, 1964.

Blau, Peter M., and W. Richard Scott. *Formal Organizations.* San Francisco: Chandler, 1962.

Bohm, David. *The Special Theory of Relativity.* New York: W. A. Benjamin, 1965.

Boje, David M., and David A. Whetter. "Effects of Organizational Strategies and Contextual Constraints on Centrality and Attributions of Influence in Interorganizational Networks." *Administrative Science Quarterly* 26, no. 3 (1981): 378–395.

Burke, Kenneth. *A Grammar of Motives.* Berkeley: University of California Press, 1945. In "Managerial and Organizational Communication in Terms of the Conduit Metaphor," Stephen R. Axley. *Academy of Management Review* 9, 1984: 428–437.

Campbell, D. T. "Systematic Error on the Part of Human Links in Communication Systems." In *Information and Control* 1, 1958: 334–369.

Carroll, Stephen J., and Henry L. Tosi. *Organizational Behavior.* Chicago: St. Clair Press, 1977.

Child, J., H. D. Gunter, and A. Kieser. "Technological Innovation and Organizational Conservatism." In *New Technology as Organizational Innovation: The Development and Diffusion of Microelectronics,* eds. Johannes M. Pennings and Arend Buitendam. Cambridge, Mass.: Ballinger, 1987.

Collins, Barry E., and Bertram H. Raven. "Group Structure: Attraction, Coalitions, Communication, and Power." In *Handbook of Social Psychology,* Vol 4, eds. Gardner Lindzey and Elliot Aronson. Reading, Mass.: Addison-Wesley, 1969.

Dexter, Lewis A. "Congressmen and the Making of Military Policy." In *New Perspectives on the House of Representatives,* 2nd ed., eds. Robert L. Peabody and Nelson Polsby. Chicago: Rand McNally, 1969: 175–194.

Downs, Anthony. *Inside Bureaucracy.* Boston: Little, Brown, 1967. (Reissued, Prospect Heights, Ill.: Waveland Press, 1994.)

Eisenhower, Dwight D. *Waging Peace, 1956–1961: The White House Years.* Garden City, N.Y.: Doubleday Publishing, 1965.

Festinger, L., and N. Maccoby. "On Resistance to Persuasive Communications." *Journal of Abnormal Social Psychology* 68, 1964: 359–366.

Fidler, Lori A., and J. David Johnson. "Communication and Innovation Implementation." *Academy of Management Review* 9, 1984: 704–711.

Flash, Edward S., Jr. *Economic Advice and Presidential Leadership.* New York: Columbia University Press, 1965.

Goldhaber, Gerald M. *Organizational Communication,* 6th ed. Madison, Wis.: Brown & Benchmark, 1993.

Granovetter, Mark S. "The Strength of Weak Ties." *American Journal of Sociology* 78, 1973: 1360–1380.

Hage, Jerald, Michael Aiken, and Cora Bagley Marrett. "Organization Structure and Communications." *American Sociological Review* 36, 1971: 860–871.

Halberstam, David. *The Best and the Brightest.* New York: Random House, 1969.

Halperin, Morton H. "Shaping the Flow of Information." In *Bureucratic Politics and Foreign Policy.* With the assistance of Priscilla Clapp and Arnold Kanter. Washington, D.C.: The Brookings Institution, 1974: 158–172. Reprinted in *Bureaucratic Power in National Politics,* 3rd ed., ed. Francis E. Rourke. Boston: Little, Brown, 1978: 102–115.

Haney, William V. *Communication and Interpersonal Relations: Text and Cases,* 6th ed. Homewood, Ill.: Richard D. Irwin, 1992.

Harris, Thomas. *I'm OK–You're OK: A Practical Guide to Transactional Analysis.* New York: Harper & Row, 1969.

Hayakawa, S. I. "Conditions of Success in Communication." From an address presented to the Twelfth Annual Round Table of the Institute of Languages and Linguistics, Edmund Walsh School of Foreign Service, Goergetown University, Washington, D.C., April 22, 1961. Cited in William V Haney, *Communication and Interpersonal Relations: Text and Cases,* 4th ed. Homewood, Ill.: Richard D. Irwin, 1979: 234–235.

Hayes, M. A. "Nonverbal Communication: Expression without Words." In *Readings in Interpersonal and Organizational Communication,* 3rd ed., eds. Richard C. Huseman, Cal M. Logue, and Dwight L. Freshley. Boston: Holbrook Press, 1977: 55–68.

Heclo, Hugh. *A Government of Strangers: Executive Politics in Washington.* Washington, D.C.: Brookings Institution, 1977.

Isaacs, William N. "Taking Flight: Dialogue, Collective Thinking, and Organizational Learning." *Organizational Dynamics,* Fall 1993, 24–39.

Jacobson, Eugene, and Stanley Seashore. "Communication Patterns in Complex Organizations." *Journal of Social Issues* 7, 1951: 28–40.

James, Muriel, and Dorothy Jongeward. *Born to Win.* Reading, Mass.: Addision-Wesley, 1971. (Reprinted 1991.)

Janis, Irving L. *Victims of Groupthink.* Boston: Houghton Mifflin, 1972.

Jones, Edward E., and Keith E. Davis. "From Acts to Dispositions: The Attribution Process in Person Perception." In *Advances in Experimental Social Psychology,* Vol. 2, ed. Leonard Berkowitz. New York: Academic Press, 1965: 219–266.

Katz, Daniel, and Robert L. Kahn. *The Social Psychology of Organizations,* 2nd ed. New York: John Wiley & Sons, 1978.

Leavitt, Harold J. "Some Effects of Certain Communication Patterns on Group Performance." *Journal of Abnormal and Social Psychology* 46, 1951: 38–50.

Lipsky, Michael. *Street-Level Bureaucracy: Dilemmas of the Individual in Public Services.* New York: Russel Sage Foundation, 1980.

Luft, Joseph. *Group Processes: An Introduction to Group Dynamics,* 3rd ed. Palo Alto, Calif: Mayfield, 1984.

Luthans, Fred, Richard M. Hodgetts, and Sag M. Lee. "New Paradigm Organizations: From Total Quality to Learning to World Class." *Organizational Dynamics,* Winter 1994, 5–19.

Maddi, Salvatore. *Personality Theories: A Comparative Analysis,* 6th ed. Pacific Grove, Calif.: Brooks/Cole, 1996.

March, James B., and Herbert A. Simon. *Organizations,* 2nd ed. Cambridge, Mass.: Blackwell, 1993.

Martin, John Bartlow. "The Blast in Centralia No. 5: A Mine Disaster No One Stopped." In *Public Administration: Concepts and Cases,* 5th ed., ed. Richard J. Stillman II. Boston: Houghton Mifflin, 1992: 19–35.

McCurdy, Howard E. *Public Administration: A Synthesis.* Menlo Park, Calif.: Cummings, 1977.

Merton, Robert K. *Social Theory and Social Structure.* New York: Free Press, 1968.

Mosher, Frederick. *Democrary and the Public Service,* 2nd ed. New York: Oxford University Press, 1982.

Orwell, George. "Politics and the English Language." In *The Orwell Reader,* ed. Richard Rovere. New York: Harcourt Brace Jovanovich, 1956: 355–366.

Osborne, David, and Ted Gaebler. *Reinventing Government: How the Entrepreneurial Spirit is Transforming the Public Sector.* Reading, Mass.: Addison-Wesley, 1992.

Powers, Francis Gary. *Operation Overflight: The U-2 Spy Pilot Tells His Story for the First Time.* New York: Holt, Rinehart & Winston, 1970.

Presthus, Robert. *The Organizational Society.* New York: St. Martin's Press, 1978.

Redding, William C. *Communication within the Organization.* New York: Industrial Communication Council, 1972.

Reddy, Michael. "The Conduit Metaphor—A Case of Frame Conflict in Our Language about Language." In *Metaphor and Thought,* ed. A. Ortony. Cambridge, England: Cambridge University Press, 1979: 284–324. Cited in "Managerial and Organizational Communication in Terms of the Conduit Metaphor," Stephen Axley. *Academy of Management Review* 9, 1984: 428–237.

Ripley, Randall B., and Grace A. Franklin. *Congress, the Bureaucracy, and Public Policy,* 5th ed. Pacific Grove, Calif.: Brooks/Cole, 1990.

Rogers, Everett M. *Communication Strategies for Family Planning.* New York: Free Press, 1973.

————, and Rekha Agarwala-Rogers. *Communication in Organizations.* New York: Free Press, 1976.

Rourke, Francis E. *Bureaucracy, Politics, and Public Policy,* 3rd ed. Boston: Little, Brown, 1984.

Schein, Edgar H. "On Dialogue, Culture, and Organizational Learning." *Organizational Dynamics,* Fall 1993, 40–51.

Schilit, Warren K., and Edwin A. Locke. "A Study of Upward Influence in Organizations." *Administrative Science Quarterly* 27, no. 2 (1982): 304–376.

Sebald, Hans. "Limitations of Communication: Mechanisms of Image Maintenance in Form of Selective Perception, Selective Memory, and Selective Distortion." *Journal of Communication* 12, 1962: 142–149.

Seitz, Steven Thomas. *Bureaucracy, Policy, and the Public.* St. Louis: C. V. Mosby, 1978.

Senge, Peter M. *The Fifth Discipline: The Art and Practice of the Learning Organization.* New York: Doubleday/Currency, 1990.

Shaw, M. E. "Some Effects of Unequal Distribution of Information upon Group Performance in Various Communication Nets." *Journal of Abnormal and Social Psychology* 49, 1954: 547–553.

Sinetar, M. "Building Trust into Corporate Relationships." *Organizational Dynamics,* Winter 1988: 73–79.

Snow, C. P. *Science and Government.* Cambridge, Mass.: Harvard University Press, 1961.

Starbuck, William H. "Mathematics and Organizational Theory." In *Handbook of Organizations,* ed. James G. March. Chicago: Rand McNally, 1965.

Steers, Richard M., and J. Stewart Black. *Organizational Behavior,* 5th ed. New York: Harper-Collins, 1994.

Thayer, Lee O. *Communication and Communication Systems: In Organization, Management, and Interpersonal Relations.* Lanham, Md.: University Press of America, 1986.

Thompson, James D. *Organizations in Action.* New York: McGraw-Hill, 1967.

Thompson, Victor A. *Modern Organization.* New York: Alfred A. Knopf, 1961.

Tullock, Gordon. *The Politics of Bureaucracy.* Lanham, Md.: University Press of America, 1987. (Originally published in 1965.)

Westley, Bruce, and Malcolm A. MacLean, Jr. "A Conceptual Model for Communication Research." *Journalism Quarterly* 34, 1957: 31–38.

Wilensky, Harold L. *Organizational Intelligence: Knowledge and Policy in Government and Industry.* New York: Basic Books, 1967.

Yadav, Dharam P. "Communication Structure and Innovation Diffusion in Two Indian Villages." Ph.D. thesis, 1967. East Lansing, Mich., Michigan State University. Cited in Everett M. Rogers and Rekha Agarwala-Rogers, *Communication in Organizations.* New York: Free Press, 1976.

Zajonc, Robert B. *Social Psychology: An Experimental Approach.* Belmont, Calif.: Wadsworth, 1966.

Zalkind, S. S., and T. W. Costello. "Perception: Some Recent Research and Implications for Administration." *Administrative Science Quarterly* 7 (September 1962): 218–233.

Zimbardo, P., and E. B. Ebbesen. *Influencing Attitudes and Changing Behavior,* 2nd ed. Reading, Mass.: Addison-Wesley, 1977.

READING 5–1   Listening Tips

Effective listening can make you more efficient and more productive. People who improve their listening skills are worth more to their companies. And they enhance their chances of advancing in their careers.

In fact, listening is so important that Lee Iacocca, the chief executive officer of the Chrysler corporation, once said that it can make "the difference between a mediocre company and a great company."

And Robert L. Montgomery, president of a major business consulting firm, said that business efficiency would double, if employees could be taught to listen correctly.

Unfortunately, most people are only 25 percent effective as listeners.

Yet, they can improve their listening skills by following a number of simple techniques. And when they do, they will become more valued employees—and more effective human beings. . . .

The Benefits of Listening
Want to increase your self-confidence? Handle conflicts better: solve more problems? Relieve stress and tension?

According to Madelyn Burley-Allen, author of *Listening: The Forgotten Skill,* these are just some of the benefits she received after improving *her* listening skills.

Some other benefits of listening:

- People will respect and like you more because you have shown that you care about them and what they have to say.
- You'll be better informed, because when you actively listen, you learn more.
- You'll be better able to get things done, because you'll understand how to motivate people when you pay attention to what they're *really* saying—and thinking.
- People will listen to what you're saying, because they realize that you have made them feel important—and they will want to please you.

Things You Should Know

- Many people—especially managers—spend 42–45 percent of their time listening, 30–31 percent talking, 15–16 percent reading, and 0–11 percent writing. Yet our schooling has failed to prepare us to be good listeners.
- Hearing and listening are not the same things. Hearing is a physical process that takes place naturally. Listening is a mental process that requires effort. You have to muster a willingness to concentrate, to interpret, to evaluate, and to react to what you hear. Yes, it works. And it's well worth the effort.

What Poor Listeners Do
Poor listeners are inattentive, and their minds often wander. They tend to interrupt speakers and finish thoughts and sentences for them. Too often poor listeners change the subject of a conversation or jump to improper conclusions.

Attentive listeners, however, often question speakers to clarify points. They don't rush or interrupt people speaking.

What Good Listeners Do

- Look at the person who's speaking.
- Question the speaker to clarify what's being said.
- Repeat some of the things the speaker says.
- Don't rush the speaker.
- Pay close attention to what the speaker is saying.
- Don't interrupt the speaker.
- Don't change the subject until the speaker has finished his or her thoughts.

Why We Listen Poorly
Here are some reasons why we listen poorly:

- We get bored. When we lack interest in a subject or in the way it's presented, we fail to listen.
- We refuse to put forth the energy to really concentrate. Concentration requires effort, and we prefer not to exert ourselves to that extent.
- We take our mind off the message and place it on the speaker. We focus our attention on how a speaker is dressed or on what mannerisms he or she exhibits.
- We become impatient with the speaker and want him or her to get to the point.

■ We fail to wait long enough to find out if a subject has any benefit for us. We conclude too early that it doesn't—and we stop paying attention.

■ We are tired and can't put forth the energy to listen attentively.

How to Listen Better

Studies conducted at the former Sperry Corporation uncovered these keys to good listening:

■ Listen for ideas, not just for facts. When you listen only for facts, you may not grasp the ideas or themes of the speaker. Here are some questions you might ask yourself when listening:

   Why am I being told this information?
   What does it lead to?
   If that's true, what does it prove?

■ Judge what the speaker says, not how it is said. Don't let the speaker's delivery get in the way of your understanding the message. Ignore any peculiar mannerisms or speaking problems the speaker may exhibit.

■ Be optimistic when you listen. Try to find something of interest in the subject no matter how dry it may seem at first. Open your mind and try to find out what attracted the speaker to the subject.

■ Don't jump to conclusions. Don't listen to the beginning of a sentence and try to fill in the rest. Wait and keep listening. Clear your head of your own ideas and listen to those of the speaker.

■ Be a flexible listener when you're taking notes. Determine as soon as possible how the speaker puts forth his or her ideas, and gear your note-taking style to the speaker's style. *Example:* Ask yourself, "Is the speaker concise or does he or she take a while to make a point?"

■ Concentrate. Remain relaxed but attentive. But don't become tense, or you'll make any distractions more pronounced. *Your best bet:* Try to remove as many distractions as possible. *One way:* When going to a meeting, get there early and sit up front where there will be fewer distractions.

■ Remember that you can think at least four times as fast as someone can talk. This means that your thoughts will race ahead of the speaker's words—and you can become so detached that you'll have a hard time catching up with what was said. To stay on track, try to summarize what was said, or interpret the speaker's ideas, or evaluate the speaker's logic. You'll have time to do these things because your thoughts move so swiftly.

■ Work at listening. Try to listen alertly and enthusiastically. Strive to "be alive." *How:* Respond to the speaker by giving feedback. *Examples:* Come up with an appropriate comment, smile if appropriate, summarize what the speaker just said.

■ Keep your mind open—and restrain your emotions. Don't be distracted by strong words that may offend you. Train yourself to note the presence of emotional words—but to let them pass without an emotional reaction on your part. Work on interpreting and evaluating what the speaker is saying.

■ Practice mental exercises. Use every opportunity to sharpen your listening skills. Work on your attitude. And practice, practice, practice.

A Few More Tips

Try these two valuable tips, which will help you develop rapport with the speaker. They were suggested by Joseph De Veto in *The Interpersonal Communication Book* (Harper and Row).

- Accept the speaker's feelings. Show that you have empathy for the person and his or her problems. For example, you might offer a comment, such as "You must have felt terrible when he corrected you in front of others." This will help you become a partner in the communication transaction.

- Ask questions to let the speaker know you are paying attention to him or her. People realize you're listening to them when you ask a question, wait for an answer, and follow up with a related question.

AIM to Listen

Try this simple formula, from *The Secretary* magazine, that will help you remember three vital listening concepts. It's called AIM.

A—Attention. Don't fake paying attention. If the person is important enough to listen to, then try to resist distractions.

I—Interest. Try to maintain interest even if you don't think the topic or person is interesting. Tell yourself that the content might prove useful to you someday.

M—Motivation. Try to motivate yourself by going over all the reasons you should pay attention. Be sure to list motives that offer you the greatest benefits.

SOURCE: From the editors of *Communication Briefings,* 110 King Street, Suite 110, Alexandria, VA 22314. 703-548-3800.

Editor's Note

When discussing communication, the emphasis is usually on projecting your own ideas in a clear and concise manner so that they can be understood by others. Increasingly, however, there is a recognition that everyone is a listener as well as an initiator, and that listening skills are as important in guaranteeing quality communication. As you review these tips on listening as a central part of interpersonal communication, think about the following issues:

1. When we speak of listening, we usually think of face-to-face, usually informal, communication. Do any recommendations presented here apply to aspects of formal communication?

2. Throughout these "listening tips" there is constant referral to a variety of aspects of organization theory. Note the different concepts, theories, and models of organization theory (for example, related to motivation or decision making) that the writer assumes you understand, and discuss how these elements of organization theory are important in each case. Many of these theories and models are discussed in later chapters of the book, so come back to this reading after completing each chapter to see how the concepts introduced in the chapters apply to the ideas presented in this reading.

CASE 5–1   Documentary Evidence

It was an exciting moment for Royfield Puckett as he drove his Volkswagen into the Deep Valley Children's Center parking lot with its sign: Doctors and Administrative Staff Only. Before him stood the 65-bed hospital of which today he would become the chief administrator—a modernistic structure of glass, concrete, and steel.

Only thirty-five years old, Puckett had a feeling of accomplishment as he viewed the hospital and its landscaped grounds. Only a few years before, after receiving his master's degree from Howard University, he had joined the staff of a 250-bed hospital and worked his way up to assistant director. Now he had assumed the responsibility of operating an institution serving about eight hundred disabled children across the state, providing physical, occupational, and speech therapy; social services; and dental, recreational, and dietary programs.

Yet he also felt apprehensive. Was he really qualified by experience for the top administrative post in such a center? It looked open and welcoming as he approached the entrance, but more from instinct than from knowledge he suspected it was not all it seemed to be—a happy place providing humanitarian services to young people.

His predecessor, Lester Morton, had resigned unexpectedly upon his father's death to manage a family business, Puckett had been told when interviewed by the hospital board. Puckett felt, however, that he had heard only part of the story. The guarded manner in which staff members talked with him when he was taken on a tour led him to feel that below the surface problems lurked. Or was their attitude, he asked himself, because he was black? Well, he was in charge now, he thought as he entered the building, and he would soon find out.

In his first few days Puckett devoted his efforts to familiarizing himself with hospital policies and procedures, its printed rules and regulations, and the minutiae of day-to-day operations, and to getting acquainted with staff members. All those he conferred with were friendly but hesitant in talking about the two-year administration of Lester Morton. Puckett decided that he might find out more if he read the minutes of staff meetings and of the hospital board of directors.

The minutes of the Morton staff meetings were contained in a single manila folder, and it did not take Puckett long to review them since only eight had been held, each one featuring a guest speaker or theme. Morton appeared to dominate the sessions, his remarks being reported in full. He concluded the meetings with exhortatory pep talks devoted to platitudes about the need for teamwork and good public relations. The staff was seldom consulted about policy matters and problems and there appeared to be little general discussion.

In contrast to Morton's staff meetings, those of his predecessor, Alfred Kahn, had been held weekly. Kahn would summarize any hospital news, training programs, or developments and then ask department heads to discuss their projects or problems. Puckett disliked cliches, but he decided that under Kahn the administrative staff was a team, whereas under Morton it was always being urged to become one.

Puckett also researched the rate of turnover during the Morton and Kahn administrations. He asked the personnel department to draw up a list of all positions vacated during the last three months of the Morton administration, the reasons employees gave their supervisor for leaving the center, and the reasons they gave in an anonymous questionnaire.

Meanwhile Puckett sought more information from department heads about their operations and problems. Among the first he interviewed was Martha Ritter, director of public relations. He found her friendly but somewhat cynical. After they had chatted a few minutes, Puckett asked, "Well, Martha, I'd like to know what you think we can do to improve the hospital."

Ritter looked surprised and then, stifling a giggle, replied: "Excuse me, it's just that, well, I wouldn't know where to begin."

"Don't worry," Puckett said. "Please feel free to tell me what is on your mind."

"Well, my latest nightmare is the donor list—you know, the list of four thousand people who have made contributions to the hospital," Ritter said. "It's gone."

"Gone?"

"Gone. I called up the computer center and the woman who used to run the list for me said she doesn't even work with the computer any more since they put in a new machine. 'New computer?' I said. 'No one told me about changing computers.' Needless to say the list is gone. Oh, if I'd only known we were going to change systems. But who was going to tell me? No one ever saw Mr. Morton. We rarely had staff meetings."

Ritter looked out the window and adjusted her glasses. "No, Mr. Puckett, things started going downhill the first week Mr. Morton was here and especially after he put in the time clocks. It doesn't seem to matter any more how much you actually work so long as you're not two and a half minutes later in checking in."

Chats with other department heads confirmed what Ritter had told Puckett—Morton's administration had been a disaster. The best description of the situation came from Hester Wilson, head of nursing services: "We were a team, or better still, more like a family before Mr. Morton became the administrator. I suppose things were going too smoothly. Have you ever been in a boat, Mr. Puckett, on a calm sea? Well, you'd swear the boat is just standing still. The fact is the current below the surface is moving you right along. It must have looked to the Board of Directors like we were moving too smoothly to be making progress. They wanted a new administrator with—what's the word—pizazz, somebody who could get the center known in the state. Well, he was a good advertisement—for himself. Our duty is to handicapped children, and our services to them suffered."

Returning to this office after talking with Wilson, Puckett found a report on his desk prepared by the Department of Personnel on the employees who had left the center in the last three months. (See Exhibits 1 and 2 at the end of this case.) He studied the reasons given supervisors for leaving and the reasons given in the anonymous questionnaire. Here was documentary evidence of a situation not fully revealed in his interviews. He faced a difficult administrative problem, and it was not race-related.

EXHIBIT 1.   Item 1 of the Supervisors' Report on Employee Separation

Item 1.   Information concerning the separation of this employee is necessary for the purpose of processing unemployment insurance claims. Please obtain information from the employee concerning his or her reasons for termination. Involuntary terminations must contain information supporting the reasons for termination. Voluntary terminations must include information as to why the individual has terminated and what the individual is going to do after termination. If he or she is separating to accept other employment, information is necessary indicating the type of new employment.

Reasons for Termination

Employee 1

"Lack of job satisfaction. Frustration due to discrepancies in administrative practices. Some personal problems, but for the most part Mary was the first counseling therapist to tackle some of the demanding tasks associated with intake diagnostics. Nothing could have been done to prevent her from leaving."

Employee 2

"Henry was asked to resign for failure to obey a direct order given to him by a supervisor. He left the area telling the ward staff to call the supervisor's office telling them that he refused to work in the area. He left without reporting in with the supervisor's office."

Employee 3

"Mr. Jones left to accept a position in the private sector with greater promotion possibilities and a higher starting salary."

Employee 4

"Leaving due to better employment opportunities in the city and an opportunity to work on a special-education certification."

Employee 5

"This counselor was terminated for unnecessary roughness with the patients, agitating children by teasing them and unacceptable work performance while on duty."

Employee 6

"Mary came into my office tearful, stating that she felt that she was not able emotionally to continue her work in caring for clients in the area to which she was assigned. She said the center was becoming a depressing place to work and she needed a little time to think about where she was going with her career."

Employee 7

"Herriott drives 56 miles to work a day and is finding that with the cost of gas it is terribly expensive. In fact, it is so expensive that she has to resign. She also is planning on the foster care facility which she has been working on for the past few months in her home, and will be providing some meals, housing, etc., for elderly persons."

Employee 8

"It was my understanding that she requested to transfer to the 8:00 A.M. to 4:30 P.M. shift. I was also informed it might be beneficial for her to work in a more closely supervised situation due to questionable job practices. Also, she needs to improve her communication skills. She generally complied to what was requested of her, but frequently voiced discontent with numerous center policies, procedures, management, personnel, etc. She did not convey a genuinely sincere, enthusiastic, and motivated attitude. In turn she tends to function in a rather regimented, authoritarian manner and will continue to need to strengthen her communication skills. With added experience she has the potential of becoming a more effective counselor."

Employee 9

"Voluntary termination. She stated that she only wanted to work during the week so that she would have more time to spend on extracurricular affairs."

Employee 10

"The employee is leaving because he said he cannot do this type of work."

Employee 11

"Found a better-paying job at the VA Hospital. Nothing could be done to keep her from leaving Deep Valley Center."

Employee 12

"Terminated because she found other employment. Also, she would have been terminated because she had taken leave without proper notification and because the grant she was working on is being discontinued."

Employee 13

"Conflict with supervisor over work schedule. Employee seems to be unable to compromise when the need arises. Employee can be easily replaced since he performs janitorial services."

Employee 14

"Terry Nichols seems to have serious personal family problems and it is affecting her attendance and quality of work. She is a single parent with two very young children and feels a strong responsibility to her family. Unplanned absences and chronic tardiness, however, cause serious work disruptions and have adversely impacted on the services that Deep Valley renders. Her position will be a difficult one to fill."

EXHIBIT 2.   Item 8 of Employee Notification of Separation Form

Question 8.   Please provide a brief statement of your reason(s) for termination from Deep Valley Children's Center. Your response will remain anonymous.

Employee 1

"I have been assigned to night duty for the greatest share of my employment at the Center. I have to work alone constantly and need to have regular daytime hours where I can have at least *some* contact with people."

Employee 2

"The suggestions that I made and those which other people made to improve patient care either took too long to be implemented or were never made. The day the center starts paying people and promoting them according to their abilities, it will be able to retain employees rather than losing them."

Employee 3

"I don't feel that I'm accomplishing anything due to some conflicts of procedures and attitudes among personnel."

Employee 4

"I'm being offered my previous job and I have decided to take it. This way I'll also be able to further my education. I have no complaints toward this facility.

It has progressed very much since I was here as a student four years ago. I enjoyed working with the people and the majority of them are definitely interested in their clients."

Employee 5

"Too much bureaucracy. Too many fingers in the pot. Lack of interest for advancement of fellow workers, so that they can become better qualified for their positions and provide better care and counseling to the children."

Employee 6

"Poor personnel management procedures, and poor training coordination. Overall, poor working conditions and low morale!"

Employee 7

"When I would tell Mr. Morton, the administrator, about the girls and boys sneaking into the lounge at night or being late for activities, he would tell me, 'What can I do about it?'"

Employee 8

"I think the separation questionnaire missed the point. I think the various units of Deep Valley Center need constant assessment of goals and objectives with restatement in clear, concise manner, and leadership responsive to ideas and suggestions of employees. Opportunities for professionals to exercise judgement in completing their job assessment are becoming fewer, thereby resulting in less motivation."

Employee 9

"I want to spend more time in a newly built home, spend more time on outdoor activities and craft work, hobbies, etc. I do think that the salary for this particular position, and similar positions in the center, is too low for the amount of work involved. After working 10 years at this position the salary was very poor in comparison to the counselor positions with the Feds. One woman left here to work with the Feds for more than I was making after 10 years. That is embarrassing and disgusting."

Employee 10

"I feel that I couldn't handle this kind of work and of taking care of these kind of people. I guess I overestimated my own capabilities when taking the position."

Employee 11

"Direct care nurses have the most responsibility toward patients, yet they receive the lowest pay. Too many bureaucrats who are sitting on their cans, they won't understand this statement. 'Taxation without representation' law should go into effect immediately!"

Employee 12

"I was told that the grant program under which I was working was terminated and that there was no place for me in the center. In effect, I was asked to resign under threat of adverse action. Someone had better recognize the fact the center is about to go quickly down the tube!!!"

Employee 13

"The job itself was misrepresented to me by Mr. Morton. It stated that the job
was 8 to 5 Monday through Friday. It did not state that nightwork or weekend
duties would be required."

Employee 14

"Unfair treatment toward me for the thing that I did. A follow-up letter will be
sent to the Board of Directors, State's Attorney, and the Governor."

SOURCE: C. Kenneth Meyer and Charles H. Brown, *Practicing Public Management: A Casebook*, 2nd ed. (New
York: St. Martin's Press, 1989): 141–148.

Editors' Note

This case is not an unusual situation for a program executive to discover on arrival at a
new appointment. The following questions are a few of the problems that must be faced
in such a circumstance. Assuming the role of Mr. Puckett, answer the following questions:

1. How would you describe the current state of affairs at Deep Valley Children's
   Center, both in relation to the staff and the hospital board?

2. Understanding that there may still be more to learn about the total situation, what
   would you assume to be the major causative factors for the specific problems that
   you see? How does the information in the exhibits help clarify what is going on
   in the center?

3. What kind of communication system(s) would you try to create within the total
   organizational structure?

4. Besides the communication problems, what other issues must you deal with in
   order to firm up the operations of the center?

Chapter 6

Bureaucratic Control

INTRODUCTION

Control is a fundamental management task in all organizations. Some system for monitoring and redirecting, if necessary, the diverse and specialized activities of large complex organizations is necessary if the organization is to be effective. In bureaus, where accountability is a political and legal necessity, control systems become more complex, and even cumbersome, leading to charges of inertia and red tape. The idea of organizational control, the variety of control systems that are in use, and the threats to the integrity of control and accountability in public bureaus are the subjects of this chapter.

Organization control is the "means used by an organization to elicit the performance it needs and to check whether the quantities and qualities of such performance are in accord with organizational specifications" (Etzioni 1965, 650). Viewing control as an ongoing cycle of monitoring and correcting organizational activity, Downs identifies seven steps in the process from issuing an order to collecting information about the performance of subordinates to evaluating the adequacy of performances and issuing corrective orders (Downs 1967, 144). Generally, the emphasis in these definitions and in the literature is on gathering information about performance and evaluating that performance against some kind of standard. Both of these aspects of control involve complex political and technical issues.

There are a great variety of control systems in any large complex organization. Direct supervision through the hierarchy, time clocks, personnel evaluations, program evaluations, "spies," quality circles, statistical quality control, and many types of management information systems (MIS) are all designed to provide upper management with qualitative and quantitative information on performance. Using this information to redirect organizational efforts so as to improve or correct agency activities involves major program development responsibilities and is at the heart of public management.

Indirect methods of control are also important in bureaus. Both socialization to professional values in graduate schools and socialization within the bureau to the mission, norms, and the bureau's sense of identity are vital to organizational control. These indirect methods rely on the development of internalized controls and are an important component of contemporary management theories, including models of Japanese management (Ouchi 1981), the "excellent" organization (Peters and Waterman 1982), and "quality control" in total quality management (Creech 1994).

Such indirect methods are aimed at eliminating one of the many sources of resistance to control: the human desire for autonomy. Anthony Downs describes this desire in his "Law of Counter Control" which states that "The greater the effort made by a sovereign or top-level official to control the behavior of subordinate officials, the greater the efforts made by those subordinates to evade or counteract such control" (1967, 147).

Organizational processes for control are linked to communication and decision making. These three interrelated processes form the "intelligence" system of the organization, the system that enables the organization to monitor its internal and external state and correct its course. The monitoring aspects of the control system rely on the formal, and less often informal, lines of communication to collect and route information upward to actors who can interpret and use it for making new policy or program choices. Each type of control system relies on different aspects of the communication system. Any inaccuracies or distortions in communication and information processing make effective monitoring nearly impossible.

There are also serious limitations in our knowledge of how to interpret and use the information collected and how to make decisions that will effectively redirect the organization. Too often, we collect mountains of data without having a very good idea of what to do with it, how to use it to "diagnose" the state of the organization or its program or to devise a set of remedial actions. Under these circumstances, monitoring managerial or program indicators becomes an end in itself without clear ties to future choices. The uncertainty of program technologies in the public sector, their necessarily exploratory or unprofitable character, make control both especially difficult and especially desirable. As we will note in the conclusion to this chapter, the development of increasingly sophisticated controls implicitly encourages us to define management almost solely in terms of control systems. Doing so may be counterproductive, however, since we are prematurely attempting to institutionalize unproven program technologies (Landau and Stout 1979). Yet many pressures for greater control surround the manager.

Layers of Control Systems

Public bureaus function within complex layers of control systems. The most commonly acknowledged system and the one discussed so far here is the system that is oriented toward control *within* the organization. But the bureau as a whole is also subject to control by the larger environment of external government policymakers, including elected officials, legislative bodies, courts, and client and interest groups. To the extent that these bodies closely monitor and enforce their standards on the bureau, control is a matter of politics and public agenda setting. External critics, supporters, and interest groups may organize and press for the imposition of standards that they believe are needed as part of the broader struggle to control policy goals. And *external* policymakers, preparing for an election, may impose tougher performance standards on a bureau, which, in turn, can lead to changes in the *internal* control systems.

Bureaus also establish control systems over other organizations, as in the case of regulatory agencies and agencies implementing policy by administering grants and contracts in conjunction with other units of government or with firms. The responses and pressures of these outside bodies create demands on the bureau's internal control system. Antinuclear groups and consumer groups, for example, demand strict monitoring and en-

---

Federal, State Mandates Erode Local Flexibility

A county hospital in Maryland is required by state law to keep its hot water temperature at no less than 100 degrees. That same hospital is mandated by federal law to keep that very same water no more than 110 degrees. The hospital was forced to purchase highly sophisticated water heaters—$20,000 more expensive than ordinary ones—to keep water temperature maintained at 110 degrees.

San Bernadino County California was forced to move a stone wall 50 yards at $50,000 cost to local government because of a federal requirement dealing with historical preservation.

"It's called mandate madness," Roy Orr, a Dallas County Commissioner and the new president of the National Association of Counties (NACO) told President Carter, Congress, and federal agency heads September 17.

"Mandates erode local decision-making power and shrink already limited tax revenues," Orr said. "And if this mandate madness continues, local county officials will lose the control necessary to deal with complicated local issues." Compliance with state and federal mandates eats up as much as 80 percent of some county budgets.

SOURCE: Effie Cottman, *Public Administration Times* 3, no. 19 (October 1, 1980), American Society for Public Administration staff.

---

forcement of regulatory standards for industries. Industry groups and those using public lands may demand more flexible regulation, reduced oversight, and less paperwork.

These layers of control systems, their operation, and their influence on one another are an often-ignored aspect of organizational control. However, the question of control systems in bureaus raises complex interbranch and intergovernmental issues.

The Theory of Control

The theory of organizational control for public bureaus comes in two basic forms: a systems theory (cybernetics) and a political theory. The theories, though not always incompatible, emphasize different values and attend to different phenomena. The cybernetic theory of control is based on an analogy between the organization and the idea of an automatically self-correcting system. The system maintains itself at a point of equilibrium of activities and resources that is conducive to survival. The point of equilibrium may change over time if the system's various components can jointly and smoothly adapt to changes. For example, an agency could survive and continue to be effective even if its size, funding levels, or the scope of its programs were to change from year to year. The cybernetic model is concerned with the operation of the self-controlling mechanisms that evaluate information on the state of the system and its environment, and adjust the system's activities to achieve equilibrium.

The role of information (feedback) in this theory is crucial. Information that is evaluated as showing an acceptable system state (positive feedback) dictates a continuation of current policies. Information evaluated to show a threat to system survival (negative feedback) indicates a need for change in policies. A further refinement on the feedback notion is feedforward; here information that is known or theorized to be an index of the *future* state of the organization is used to prepare for, rather than react to, changes (Filley, House, and Kerr 1976, 441–447). In a cybernetic system, mechanisms for monitoring feedback and feedforward and routines for taking corrective action are automatic, as in a thermostat, so that the system is self-maintaining.

The idea of a self-maintaining organizational system is the dream of system designers, including management information analysts (Cyert and March 1992). If we could learn to recognize the information about personnel, budgets, constituencies, or performance that is necessary to diagnose the need for corrective change, we could design a program for organizational self-management. Total quality management is the latest effort to develop such a system. By defining the customer as the ultimate determiner of quality, the system attempts to reduce variation in processes by involving everyone in the organization in the collection and analysis of data about inputs and processes. As Swiss notes, this emphasis on inputs and processes rather than outputs "directly contradicts the rationale of all recent government management reforms" (1992, 357); it flies in the face of the political theory of control, thus creating a tension between those interested in procedural efficiency and those interested in political control.

The political theory of control is concerned with the bureau's accountability to policymakers. Weber notes that although the "ideal-type" bureau may be accountable to democratic as well as socialist regimes, externally generated laws form the basis of rational bureau activity. In the United States and in most Western democracies, executive-branch agencies at every level of government are subject to numerous legal and political checks based on the principle of separation of powers. The duties of the bureau are delimited in its authorizing legislation and appropriations, and agency heads are held responsible to political officials, elected or appointed; thus, a bureau is subject to control by outside authorities, and internal control is maintained by the chain of command leading to a politically accountable executive. The exceptions, such as commissioners of independent regulatory agencies, compromise the accountability principle only to achieve another bureaucratic imperative—impartiality of judgment.

These requirements for political and legal accountability leave their mark on the control systems of bureaus. To ensure that bureaus perform in the consistent, equitable, and stable manner mandated by legislation and case law, control systems closely monitor program procedures. Thus, the control system in an unemployment office, for example, commonly goes into much less detail about client results than one would expect in a service agency, but establishes elaborate standards for daily procedures. Without such controls, the legal and ethical requirements for consistency of action in bureaus could not be met; with them, of course, the irksomeness and density of red tape increases.

Both the cybernetic and the political theories of control guide the design of control systems in bureaus. Some procedures stress the chain of command, whereas others emphasize the design of more accurate information systems. Even though these two theories emphasize different components, in practice bureaus have devised monitoring and correction systems that derive from both models. Problems continually appear, however, because of an inability to agree on what is relevant information, how data should be collected, how it should be interpreted, and how to devise corrective action based on such information. Evaluation studies, for example, try to incorporate both theories, but often fail as an accountability device because data are collected for purposes of management improvement and thus serve the interests of the internal system rather than the needs of funders trying to decide which programs to cut. Similarly, productivity measures in the internal management information system may be "hidden" from public view to avoid criticism or interference. A more elaborate version of this was the navy's use of a sophisticated management information technique (PERT) as a public relations device to placate critics and ward off interference in the Polaris submarine project. The management information shown by the technique had virtually nothing to do with the real progress and problems of the project's development (Sapolsky 1972).

Types of Control Systems

There are a number of ways to classify and analyze control systems. The distinction between internal control systems and those in which the bureau is the recipient of commands and monitoring is an important one for bureaus. Most attention here will be paid to internal control, but external control will be considered later in the chapter.

Several typologies for distinguishing among internal control systems are offered in the organizational literature. Etzioni's (1965) theory of organizations rests on the sources of control in organizations: These are physical, material, and symbolic bases in which coercion, self-interest, or identification with certain values motivate compliance. Robey (1994) contrasts control based on measured work outputs with that based on behavior or activity levels that are only indirectly or indeterminately linked to organizational outputs. As substitutes for control, Robey considers those compliance techniques based on identification that Etzioni describes. These techniques, such as selection and socialization, are also important as bases of control in Weber, who considered professional training to be the backbone of a disciplined professional bureaucracy.

Relatively new to the list of typologies are the rapidly emerging techniques of participative control, such as workers' councils or quality circles. Total quality management, and the other systems of employee involvement in service delivery, take full advantage of these participative techniques in addition to using many of the tools developed earlier— such as performance data, statistics on problems and failures of products or services, and scientific examination of variations from the norm. To encompass the full range of contemporary approaches to control, we offer the following typology of methods of control:

1. Controls using quantitative measures of work outputs for review.
2. Controls based on quantitative and qualitative reports of activities and behaviors.
3. Controls that rely on the active participation of the workers themselves for monitoring and, in some cases, corrective action.
4. Controls based on a worker's identification with the organization, its mission, or a profession within it.

Of these techniques, the most established are the first two. Quantitative measures for control, such as management information systems and program evaluation, have received the greatest attention and have been most developed in the past decade. Techniques to generate identification with the bureau or its work have long been in use though particular techniques such as "mentor relationships" become more popular from time to time. Participative control may sound like a contradiction in terms, but the contemporary emphasis on participation and unionization has made these models more prominent. We will now consider each of these types, their operations, and their limitations.

CONTROLS BASED ON QUANTITATIVE MEASURES OF OUTPUT

Control systems based on measures of program output or project milestones are currently receiving a great deal of attention and have become increasingly sophisticated and accessible. Some of the techniques to be considered include the variety of work output data (often referred to as efficiency or productivity measurement), management by objectives, evaluation research, and project management systems. As a group of techniques, their strength lies in their concreteness and in the clarity of the link between the measures and at least the presumption of organizational effectiveness.

Less positively, this approach to control is generally difficult, costly, and time consuming to administer. It may suffer from problems of inaccuracy and invalidity and from ambiguous or conflicting standards for evaluating results. The accuracy of the output measurements may be compromised by the kinds of intentional and unintentional distortion common to organizational communications of all kinds, such as the filtering that results from messages passing through a long chain of command, the intentional alteration of emphasis and content to further the political and personal interests of the senders, and the misinterpretations that result from information overload or too much jargon.

The validity of control measures refers to the degree to which they measure what they purport to measure. Thus, validity is compromised whenever there is uncertainty or conflict over the definition of the organization's program outputs—and there is some disagreement in almost all bureaus on such definitions because of the pluralistic nature of goals in public bureaus. The level of serious disagreement determines the feasibility of using program output measures as the basis for organizational control.

Finally, control systems based on output measures may run into difficulty when standards for determining what constitutes appropriate levels or types of outputs become the subject of controversy among professional groups or political factions within or outside the organization. Given this context, it is clear how much power resides in the ability to design the control system; setting the standards for evaluating outputs allows the person who does so to define what will count as satisfactory performance, which, in turn, affects the way in which a program is interpreted and implemented.

Productivity and Workload Measures

The most typical work output measures are workload, efficiency, and productivity. Workload measures express the raw number or units of work completed, such as the number of cases processed or the number of pounds of food distributed. Measures of productivity and efficiency present output levels relative to costs or some other input measure. Examples of productivity measurement in state government include staff–client ratios in schools and health institutions and maintenance costs per mile of roadway or cost per accident investigated in transportation (The Urban Institute 1975, 1981). Interest in work-

Measuring Outcomes

Outcome-based management is new in the public sector. Some U.S. cities have developed it over the past two decades; some states are beginning to; and foreign countries such as Great Britain, Australia, and New Zealand are on their way.

Sunnyvale, California, a city of 120,000 in the heart of the Silicon Valley, began the experiment 20 years ago. In each policy area, the city defines sets of "goals," "community condition indicators," "objectives," and "performance indicators." "In a normal political process, most decision-makers never spend much time talking about the results they want from the money they spend," says City Manager Tom Lewcock. "With this system, for the first time they understand what the money is actually buying, and they can say yes or no" (Osborne and Gaebler 1992, 144).

Sunnyvale measures performance to reward successful managers. If a program exceeds its objectives for quality and productivity, its manager can receive a bonus of up to 10 percent. This generates pressure for ever-higher productivity. The result: average annual productivity increases of four percent. From 1985 to 1990, the city's average cost of service dropped 20 percent, in inflation-adjusted dollars. According to a 1990 comparison, Sunnyvale used 35 to 45 percent fewer people to deliver more services than other cities of similar size and type.

At least a half-dozen states hope to follow in Sunnyvale's footsteps. Oregon has gone farthest. In the late 1980s, Governor Neil Goldschmidt developed long-term goals, with significant citizen input. He set up the Oregon Progress Board, comprising public and private leaders, to manage the process. The board developed goals and benchmarks through 12 state-wide meetings and written materials from over 200 groups and organizations. "Oregon," the board stated, "will have the best chance of achieving an attractive future if Oregonians agree clearly on where we want to go and then join together to accomplish those goals" (Osborne and Gaebler 1992, 145).

The legislature approved the board's recommended 160 benchmarks, measuring how Oregon is faring on three general goals: exceptional individuals; outstanding quality of life; and a diverse, robust economy. Seventeen measures are deemed short-term "lead" benchmarks, related to urgent problems on which the board seeks progress within 5 years. They include reducing the teen pregnancy rates, enrolling people in vocational programs, expanding access to basic health care, and cutting worker compensation costs.

Another 13 benchmarks are listed as "key"—fundamental, enduring measures of Oregon's vitality and health. These include improving basic student skills, reducing the crime rate, and raising Oregon's per capita income as a percentage of the U.S. average.

Barbara Roberts, today's governor, has translated the broad goals and benchmarks into specific objectives for each agency. This year, for the first time, objectives were integrated into the budget—giving Oregon the first performance-based budget among the states.

Great Britain has instituted performance measurement throughout its national government. In addition, the government has begun writing 3-year performance contracts, called "Framework Agreements," with about half its agencies. These agencies are run by chief executive officers, many from the private sector, who negotiate agreements specifying objectives and performance measures. If they don't reach their objectives, the CEOs are told, their agencies' services may be competitively bid after the 3 years.

SOURCE: National Performance Review (U.S.). *Creating A Government That Works Better & Costs Less: The Report of the National Performance Review*. Vice President Al Gore. New York: Plume/Penguin, 1993; 114–116.

Monitoring by Computers
Sparks Employee Concerns

The mechanical arm seizes envelopes and shoves them onto a conveyer, then moves relentlessly in front of Patricia Johnson's keyboard on the midnight shift at Washington's cavernous main post office.

At a rate of 50 letters a minute, Johnson, in a split second, must remember all the thousands of addresses within the 20017 and 20018 zip codes of Northeast Washington and must punch, by memory, the proper two-digit code to route each piece of the morning's mail to one of 70 letter carriers.

In the past, supervisors would measure her performance by watching her or examining a batch of her work. But now, her supervisor sits at a video screen, punches a computer keyboard and can immediately see how many mistakes Johnson is making. If her accuracy falls below 95 percent for an extended period, Johnson can be fired.

Computers can provide management with unusually detailed performance reports—monthly, weekly, even hourly—that not only tabulate an employee's speed, but also compare it with his fellow workers' or with his office average or even with his past performance.

Some computer systems also keep track of how many times the employee leaves the work site, for bathroom visits or other breaks, and can monitor how long the breaks took and how long the worker actually spent working.

In many cases, computer-generated performance reports are being used to structure "piece-rate" pay systems and to form the basis for disciplining, demoting or even firing the slow or underskilled employee.

Large businesses and computer firms tout computer monitoring as an effective means of improving productivity, speeding the flow of information and giving customers faster and better service. Precise standards, they say, also provide an objective measure of efficiency that many workers welcome, especially if the system is used for rewards such as merit pay.

load and productivity measures has increased, especially with the recent reduced growth trend in the public sector (see Figure 6–1).

The deficiencies in output measures as viewed by state budget officers include insufficiencies in the techniques for performance measurement, problems in the quantity and quality of routinely collected data, lack of staff capacities and expertise in productivity measurement, too little attention to performance measurement, and organizational constraints such as inconsistent data collection and analysis methods among agencies in the state (The Urban Institute 1975, 169–171). These problems are commonly encountered in studies of state and local government (Finz 1980, 142–146): What is rather surprising is the apparent lack of effort to correct them (The Urban Institute 1975, 180).

One often-expressed concern behind many of these and other problems is that even when data are correctly collected and analyzed, they will not be used in agency decision making (The Urban Institute 1975, 169–170). Similar criticisms of the *real* use to which evaluation research and other expensive information are put are common. When information that is difficult and costly to collect is not used for personnel evaluation or program

But the critics contend that computer monitoring represents the intrusion of "Big Brother" into the workplace, a development that they say increases stress dramatically, and may cause illnesses such as hypertension, migraine headaches and stomach maladies among workers who suffer "technostress" from having a computer constantly watching and from being evaluated by a sometimes unseen supervisor.

Moreover, opponents of monitoring say that computer-paced employees often provide poorer, slower and even less courteous service to customers because they are forced to work in an "electronic sweatshop" where speed is at a premium, according to labor organizations, academic critics and other skeptical observers of computer tracked work places.

Time-and-motion studies of industrial workers are nothing new in the American work place. In the 1890s, industrial engineer Frederick W. Taylor meticulously observed the movements of laborers hauling pig iron and factory workers toiling on assembly lines. He perfected a method of stopwatch observation of workers' movements in a process that came to be called Taylorism, which evolved into the modern concept of "scientific management."

But the computer and its programs have far surpassed Taylor's stopwatch in giving management a virtually unlimited capability to assess each worker's productivity and in minute detail.

Although the issue has not yet been fully studied, preliminary research suggests that the health effects of computer monitoring can be severe, according to Michael Smith, an industrial psychologist at the National Institute of Occupational Safety and Health, the government's job safety arm.

"It is quite clear from the literature that employer monitoring of computers creates a dehumanizing work environment in which the worker feels controlled by the machine," Smith wrote in a recent study of video display terminal operators. Smith said in an interview that the machine-monitored worker often feels a "loss of control" that is a key cause of stress.

SOURCE: Peter Perl, *Washington Post*, September 2, 1984: A1, A18.

development, the whole control effort is delegitimized in the eyes of most staff and becomes a meaningless exercise in paperwork generation. The cost of data collection and analysis is too great to relegate the whole process to the status of a symbolic gesture toward political accountability.

Management by Objectives

Although productivity and workload measures easily describe the routine and repetitive tasks in a bureau, many bureaus are project oriented and nonroutine, and their staff have workloads that are highly specialized. Greater flexibility in output measurement is needed for these bureaus, and this is provided by the technique known as management by objectives (MBO). MBO was designed not only to provide flexibility, but also to serve as a way of establishing a clear and motivating work target for each individual. Under MBO, each organizational subunit from the top down establishes concrete, quantitative work objectives that may also include time and cost estimates. Objectives are set at each level

FIGURE 6–1   What to Measure?

	General Definition	*Street Sweeping*	*Welfare: Job Training*
Output (or process)	Volume of units produced	Miles swept	Numbers of people trained
Outcome (or result)	Quality/effectiveness of production: degree to which it creates desired outcomes	Cleanliness rating of streets	Numbers of people placed in jobs, working, and off welfare after six months, one year, and beyond. Impact on their lives
Program Outcome	Effectiveness of specific program in achieving desired outcomes	Cleanliness rating of streets as a result of sweeping	Numbers placed in jobs, working and off welfare after six months, one year, and beyond. Impact of their lives
Policy Outcome	Effectiveness of broader policies in achieving fundamental goals	Measures indictating how much litter citizens leave on streets	Percentage of potential work force unemployed, on welfare, and in poverty; percent of welfare population on welfare more than one year, five years, etc.
Program Efficiency	Cost per unit of output	Costs per mile of streets swept	Cost per job trainee; placement; retained job; etc.
Policy Efficiency	Cost to achieve fundamental goals	Cost for X level of street cleanliness	Cost to achieve desired decrease in unemployment, poverty rate, welfare caseload, etc.
Program Effectiveness	Degree to which program yields desired outcomes	Level of citizen satisfaction with cleanliness of streets	Numbers placed in jobs, working and off welfare after six months, one year, and beyond. Impact on their lives
Policy Effectiveness	Degree to which fundamental goals and citizens needs are met	Do citizens want to use their money this way, e.g., would they rather spend it on repaving streets?	Effect on larger society: e.g., poverty rate, welfare caseload, crime rate, later spending to remediate poverty, etc.

SOURCE: David Osborne and Ted Gaebler, *Reinventing Government: How the Entrepreneurial Spirit is Transforming the Public Sector*. Reading, Mass.: Addison-Wesley, 1992: 356–357.

that will contribute to the fulfillment of objectives at the next higher level. Specific quantitative objectives for projects and self-development are then set for individuals in each of the subdivisions, ideally in a manner that permits some participation, negotiation, or consultation between the individual and the supervisor. Having a very clear work target has itself been found to contribute to worker performance (Carroll and Tosi 1973, 16); in addition, participative management techniques are usually associated with greater motivation. Review sessions between individual staff and their supervisors are arranged yearly or at more frequent intervals. These sessions may focus more on guidance and learning than on appraising, especially when the motivational uses of the technique are being emphasized.

The MBO process works from the top down to ensure that the objectives are formulated in an integrated fashion that is consistent with the agency's overall mission (Morrisey 1976, 17–24). However, as Swiss (1991) notes, management systems of this type are not centralizing tools in the classical sense; "they entail power sharing between top administrators and subordinate line managers" (120). He argues that in smaller, hierarchical agencies, MBO can lead to subordinates sharing in power; however, for the large government bureaucracies, where most of the power is held by subordinate managers (the bureau heads), MBO can shift power up to top departmental officials. By clarifying accountability, documenting successes and failures, and reducing interest group influence by speeding up implementation, the officials whom the citizens can see—and whom the citizens believe to be "the boss"—can gain some control over actions. Although there is no such thing as total executive control—nor is it desirable—this system helps achieve the modest premise that:

> Top political executives should have a major voice (along with the legislature, its committees, and affected interest groups) in public policy. In some sectors of (government) these top executives have lost virtually all their power to an alliance of interest groups, career civil servants, and legislative committees. In such cases, MBO can help put the executives back into the game from which they have been excluded. (Swiss 1991, 120)

The uses of this technique as a control device are clear. It provides a forum for in-depth review of performance against a concrete standard. In addition, it provides the flexibility needed for assessing professional tasks and individualized projects, and it permits early corrective action or advice. On the other hand, the technique is very time consuming to administer, especially at the outset, because of the conferences and paperwork involved (Carroll and Tosi 1973, 15). Moreover, the record of MBO as a control or motivational device is mixed. Some departments and city governments have made use of the natural link between the MBO process and performance budgeting to foster a real performance-oriented management style. However, anecdotal evidence suggests that initial optimism may also sour under the burden of paperwork, and the process may become a symbolic exercise without any of the advantages of performance management.

According to Sherwood and Page (1976), other limitations on the use of MBO in public organizations are (1) that work assigned to the public sector is typically not well understood or is too uncertain for private firms to undertake, which also means that it will be extremely difficult to set clear and feasible objectives for bureaus, (2) that the stated and the "real" program objectives may be quite different, reflecting the ambiguities of both the policy and the agency charged with its implementation, and (3) that there are few accepted standards for monitoring and measuring performance of public objectives because programs themselves may not be well defined or are subject to professional controversies.

Finally, advocates of TQM believe that MBO should be dropped altogether. They argue that when quality slips, it is because of systemic, not individual, problems (Carr and Littman 1993; Walton 1986, 92). Merit pay and other individually oriented reward systems are misguided; since they focus on individual measures of productivity, they lead managers astray from the true systemic problems that reduce productivity and quality.

Evaluation as Control

Evaluation research is concerned with measuring program results and comparing them with the intentions of the program framers to improve, or in some cases to cull, the program. Program evaluation has become an important technical innovation in public administration in general and in control and accountability systems in particular. Evaluation is now a legal requirements for many programs and is well entrenched in contemporary ideas of professional management. The rise of evaluation is linked both to the larger professional concerns with quantitative analysis of policy and the need for greater efficiency and control in an era of little or no growth in the public sector.

There are several types and uses of evaluation. Suchman offers one typology that includes the evaluation of effort, performance, adequacy, efficiency, and process (1967, 60–66). Effort evaluations measure the direct activities and outputs of agency staff; performance measures the extent to which the results are those intended in the legislation or authorization; adequacy measures the degree to which the size and scope of the program are appropriate to the size of the problem; and efficiency focuses on the existence of less costly ways to achieve similar or better results. Each of these evaluation types articulates a dimension of control. Only process evaluations (important in total quality management), which are concerned with program design, technology, or management questions, are not clearly linked to output measuring.

Ideally, each type of evaluation would be used to meet the specific needs of program administrators, outside funders, or policymakers. In reality, however, there are serious questions about whether evaluation results are, in fact, well used. Controversy over research design and data interpretation, motivated by technical and often political considerations, may block the use of evaluation results in policymaking or program development. The controversy over a national health care policy is one example of how different parts of the government and each interest group can prepare greatly differing evaluations and interpret the same data in dramatically different ways. Technical questions about the design or interpretation of evaluations are not always the basis of problems, however. In general, the methods used in evaluation range from traditional management case studies to sophisticated, large-scale field experiments.

Other impediments to both the conduct and use of evaluations derive from fears of program managers or advocates that evaluations will result in the loss of autonomy, funds, or program authority. The possibility that evaluations will be used to justify political support or opposition by outside groups is another source of tension. Program managers may become especially concerned when external, and thus likely unsympathetic, evaluators are called in (Weiss 1972, 98–120).

In general, recent research shows that often little use is made of evaluation findings, whether use is defined as prompting specific policy changes, leading to a reconceptualization of policy, or providing "political ammunition" for policy supporters or opponents. Factors associated with higher levels of evaluation utilization include (1) the direct relevance of the findings to policymakers or managers, especially with information about allocations or implementation; (2) the direct communication of results to policymakers or managers, unfiltered by interested intermediaries; (3) the clarity of findings and the awareness by users of the implications of those findings for policy decisions; (4) the credibility of the findings or the degree to which they jibe with other information policymakers have; and (5) the existence of a strong political advocate for the findings (Leviton and Hughes 1981). Patton's analyses of the impediments to the uses of evaluations and strategies for fostering their use are similar (1986).

It is interesting to note that it is just those characteristics of evaluation that make it a valuable control device that also make it controversial and diminish its use in practice. This illustrates again the pervasive ambiguity about the nature of bureau control: Should it serve the information needs of internal systems adjustment or the requirements of political and legal accountability?

Project Management Systems

Project management techniques are a family of models that fall under the general rubric of systems analysis. The models help us make projections about the time and other resources needed for a program and help monitor departures from those projections. The most widely used models are the project evaluation and review technique (PERT) and the critical path method (CPM).

In general terms, these models break a project down into discrete tasks, each with a time estimate and sometimes other resource allocation estimates. The sequence of the tasks, including simultaneous activities, is set out in a table, and a diagram is constructed to show the network of activities in the project from start to finish. In CPM, time estimates for project completion are calculated, as is the sequence or "path" of tasks whose timely completion is necessary (critical) if the project is to be completed on schedule. The probability of completion on time, late, or early to some degree can also be determined by using more complex original time estimates and by the assumption of one of the theoretical probability distributions. This is the PERT model (Ackoff and Sasini 1968; Welch and Comer 1988). In addition, the models can be used to determine which tasks could be rushed given the extra costs of rushing and the rewards of early completion. Ongoing frequent monitoring of work in progress against the project diagram or calendar allows project managers to catch delays or unexpected advances and perhaps to realign resources for greater efficiency.

The uses of these techniques as control systems are obvious, and they are slowly coming into greater prominence. These models come the closest of all the techniques discussed so far to the theoretical notion of control as a cybernetic system with automatic correction. Especially when the process is computerized so that frequent updates can be made and the project plan reevaluated on the basis of new information, the monitoring and correction process becomes almost automatic. Management has thus provided itself with the tools to discern the state of the system and with the knowledge of how to correct it to reach a new equilibrium point.

These project management techniques are being used with greater frequency, especially in building and the production of concrete products, at every level of government, but not without complications. The use of PERT and CPM as window dressing in the Polaris project was noted in the introduction. A group of department heads in Alexandria, Virginia, introduced PERT and CPM to city government, applying them to the city budget and to the monitoring of contractors' work on a renovation project. However, the city's more ambitious goal of coordinating personnel, plans, and budgeting through the system did not materialize. Although no systematic study of reasons for the slow acceptance of the models is available, they are probably similar to those found to impede the use of productivity monitoring: a relative lack of expertise, especially computer expertise, with the models at this stage; lack of awareness of the availability and uses of systems models; and the costliness or unavailability of the detailed kinds of data needed to apply the techniques, especially to service functions. As with the productivity measurement movement, increased use may follow as work accounting becomes necessary to cope with scarcer resources and as we become more aware of the cost of delays.

Summary

The ostensible purposes of organizational control systems are to assist in the management process and to guide and correct the bureau's diverse efforts to achieve its mission. Yet we have also noted the numerous political and technical problems that arise, especially it seems with the most sophisticated control efforts. The accuracy of the data may be questionable because of collection problems or distortion, and it may be difficult to get agreement on what constitutes good program output measures. Often data for control are collected but not used because of the political or professional sensitivity of those data or because the knowledge of how to correct or redirect organizational efforts is missing. Having a management information system, as we have discovered, does not necessarily provide that wisdom.

CONTROL THROUGH BEHAVIOR MONITORING

Monitoring behavior, processes, or activities within a bureau to determine compliance is markedly different from output monitoring both in the techniques used and in the standards against which the information is evaluated. Either quantitative or qualitative (for example, historical) observations may be made, but in either case the focus is on behavior or actions without a specified relationship to the bureau's outputs.

Measures of activity or behavior may include simple tracking of hours worked, personnel evaluations, more elaborate and exotic lie-detector tests, or the medical tests designed to monitor undesirable behavior such as drug use. More common, however, are activity reports describing the efforts, successes, or problems experienced by an office or by individuals in the course of their work with a program. Activity reports may be open-ended, allowing the description to be shaped by staff, or they may be highly formatted and require standardized quantitative measures of events and activities that are less subject to distortion (Downs 1967, 145). Direct observation by supervisors and indirect observation of behaviors through time clocks, informants, monitoring agencies, or the grapevine are other common methods.

Monitoring activities and behaviors have advantages and limitations. When programs have vague outputs or there is disagreement about what the proper output measures should be, reports of staff activity are often used instead as the basis of a control system. The link between staff activities and outputs may also be vague, as in agencies where the desired outputs are elusive or not easily defined; research and policy development agencies are examples. In these cases, activity monitoring, rather than output monitoring, is necessary.

The limitations of these approaches to control will be described in detail later, but in general, variations in the perceptions of behavior and the evaluation standards are common. The validity of measures of behavior may be questioned when the link between the monitored activities and goals is not clear. For example, what are we really monitoring when we collect reports on regulatory hearings? What is the relationship between these control activities and the goal of a more competitive price structure in a regulated industry? Intentional distortion of activity reports deriving from self-interest or a desire to promote a favored program is also a common problem with some forms of behavior monitoring. Finally, activity reports, in contrast to output reports, are generally evaluated against procedural rules and regulations. Since these are rarely quantitative, staffs' expectations about

© 1986 Wasserman for the Boston Globe. Los Angeles Times Syndicate, Reprinted by permission.

their evaluations may not be clear. More important, when evaluations are ultimately based on rule compliance, rule following may become the real goal, thereby displacing the original service goal. This is the phenomenon that Merton (1957) identified as goal displacement. In sum, there are numerous potential problems with activity monitoring as a means of control even though in many cases it is the only alternative possible because of the agency's program goals.

Time Controls

The simplest and most direct form of activity monitoring is automatic reporting devices that create the needed information; time clocks or sheets and sign-in boards are examples. These devices allow supervisors to directly observe job activities in a relatively rapid, low-cost, objective, and consistent manner. In cases where an individual's time is charged against specific accounts or cost centers, a breakdown of time by set increments is necessary for control and for other accounting purposes. Although such devices are found in bureaus, many professionals consider them irksome because they do not regard hours in the office or at a desk to be a good measure of the amount of work they perform. Some flexibility in hours and work location is expected. In motivational terms, we would expect that such devices may also have the effect of implicitly condoning a minimal standard of performance, in this case, merely being present (Katz and Kahn 1978, 408).

Direct Observation

The prime control method built into the bureaucratic model is direct day-to-day supervision through the hierarchy. Ongoing observation and correction are such common managerial tasks that they may not be thought of as requiring any special skills. Yet perceived inequities in treatment by supervisors and controversies over the methods and results of personnel evaluations that are not carefully designed and executed are a source of serious conflict. Further, research in motivation and human relations shows that supervision that is considered too close breeds discontent, at least among professional workers (Filley, House, and Kerr 1976, 385–386). Perceived inequities are also difficult to eliminate; this was an important reason why quantitative output measures such as MBO were introduced.

The standards used to evaluate behaviors vary widely and are more often considered subject to arbitrariness or manipulation than the output-monitoring techniques described in the last section. In principle, of course, behavioral standards should be linked to current policies or program commands. But how clear is this link? The relative importance of different activities to the success of the organization's mission may be a matter for debate. What are the best behavioral measures of a good teacher or regulator? The standard for "appropriate" behavior may be set outside the agency by the staff's professional association, as is common in health fields, for example. Behavioral standards for promotion may reflect the choices of the upper echelon's empire builders or conservers (Downs 1967, 92–110). Control over the standards is important to controlling the bureau. Intense dissatisfaction is created when staff perceive that they are being appraised on bases they do not consider professionally appropriate, as when college teachers are monitored for attendance at some kinds of meetings.

**TLS Industries had a tendency to
overmanage its employees.**

© 1996 John McPherson/Dist. by Universal Press Syndicate

Standards based on the procedures of the bureau constitute another basis for behavior evaluation. Compliance with rules may improve the consistency of actions taken by officials, but it may also lead to goal displacement—the displacement of service goals by procedural rules (Merton 1957).

Activity Reports

Reports on the experiences, successes, or failures of officials working with existing programs are another means of control. These reports may be periodic, reactive, or even unsolicited although the last may not be well received by policymakers. This is an area that is often affected by pressures to cut budgets and reduce middle management because requirements for frequent or extensive reporting generate large staffs in the reporting parts of the bureaus and in the office in which the reports are read. The personal, professional, and political interests of the reporting staff all influence the selection and interpretation of reported circumstances, including intended or unintended distortion of information.

The reports are, of course, highly subject to manipulation and distortion by their author or those through whom they are conveyed. Morton Halperin, in a discussion of intentional distortion in foreign policy reporting, described a menu of tactics for preparing reports to influence the outcome of policy (1974, 158–172). One such tactic is reporting only those facts that support your position. An advocate may also select communication channels to delay or "lose" information that he or she wishes to suppress and to speed and highlight the importance of information that supports his or her position. These and other tactics appear in a variety of bureau settings.

Downs, as noted in Chapter 5, is also concerned with distortion in the bureau's control and communication channels. Downs suggests several antidistortion devices. One is redundancy, using several different sources of information as a check on accuracy. Using sources with different interests in the case also improves accuracy. Alternatively, officials can discount known biases in reports, though this tactic may backfire if reporters change or biases are misunderstood. Upper echelon officials may also cut through the normal channels of communication, bypassing possible sources of distortion. Franklin Roosevelt practiced this technique for getting accurate information (Schlesinger 1958). Frequent use of bypassing, however, could lead to a breakdown of the regular communications and reporting channel. Finally, requirements for report preparation themselves may limit distortion. Report forms that specify exactly what data are required and how any calculations are to be done, such as those the Internal Revenue Service provides, reduce discretion in the selection of information to report. Report forms that require quantitative data on activities or conditions also limit "imaginative" reporting. None of these techniques is foolproof, however, illustrating Downs's Law of Counter Control (1967, 147), noted earlier in this chapter.

Informants

Informants or spies are used to report on subordinate behavior in institutions ranging from schools to intelligence agencies. The advantage of a network of informants is that it provides officials with specific information, uninfluenced by the perspectives of the office or the individual being monitored. Often, the loyalty of informants is based simply on pay, the expectation of a better position, or the desire to be an "insider" and confidant. Downs notes too that hiring relatives (nepotism) further ensures their loyalty as informants though some relatives may become empire builders in their own right (1967, 156–157).

Information on the operations of programs can also be gleaned from site visits and from the informal agency grapevine. Care should be taken, however, in any interpretation of what is heard because of the universal desire to "look good" and to please in such circumstances.

Summary

All these types of behavior or activity monitoring are common and important as control devices for bureaus, in large part because of the difficulty of defining or agreeing on valid output measures or even goals. Activities rather than routinely produced outputs are the norm in public bureaus, and most government work is more likely to be described as a process than as a product. Therefore, control systems based on activities or behavior reports will continue to be necessary despite their flaws.

PARTICIPATORY CONTROL SYSTEMS

There are many forms of participation in control systems and almost as many theoretical justifications for them. In general, participatory control refers to an organizational program in which members, directly or through representatives, take an active role in monitoring and establishing standards for their work. In some cases, work processes, personnel matters, and decisions about price may come under review by the participatory body. Participation in control may be as limited as a job-enrichment program, which adds quality control and some self-management responsibilities to existing jobs. At the midrange, participation is a central function of total quality management, with teams made up of members from throughout the organization working to analyze and solve production problems while the hierarchy remains in place for coordination of work toward the establishment goals. At the upper limit, participation may be broadly interpreted to include power sharing, as in the various forms of workers' councils in Europe.

The objectives and theoretical justifications for these participatory schemes are varied. The workers' councils of Western Europe rely on a mixture of trade unionist, egalitarian, and socialist perspectives. In the United States, humanistic psychology and the human relations approach to organization theory generally promote participation as a way to increase motivation and commitment to the organization, eschewing any political reasons for fostering participation as a means of real power sharing (Strauss 1963). Finally, quality control circles (usually considered a feature of Japanese management) and the monitoring and analysis teams established in TQM stress group-based control stemming from a cultural commitment to group responsibility and decision making (Ouchi 1981; Walton 1986).

Participatory control has seemed like the answer to Downs's Law of Counter Control. If control could be linked to a sense of commitment and motivation through participation or self-direction, some of the problems of control would be eliminated. In practice, however, for bureaus there is still cause for resistance to control because of their accountability to external bodies and because legal constraints permit only partial autonomy of judgment.

The conceptual problem in at least some formulations of participatory control is illustrated in recent research on the question of whether increased participation in management decisions leads to any change in the amount of control perceived by workers. Past research and theory led researchers to hypothesize that the total amount of perceived control would increase—and that is what they found. However, the meaning of control that they use is simply influence in general, without a more particular focus on monitoring performance against policies or other standards and without providing a means of performance correction. Workers' councils, under various national plans (Tannenbaum et al. 1974), establish participation and increased self-control in many areas of work life, yet such councils do not fulfill the entire control function. The fact that control can be a source of influence does not mean that all forms of influence contribute to the organization control function.

One form of participatory control that seems to meet the requirements of a control system is the quality circle. Quality circles are voluntary groups of employees who meet regularly to "enhance the quality of goods and services . . . ; solve work place problems; develop a closer identification with the goals of the organization; and improve communication between supervisors and workers" (Bryant and Kearns 1982, 144). In a navy application of the technique, groups met to identify and analyze possible causes of work problems using systems analysis aids. They were taught brain storming and systems analysis techniques to help them find solutions. Pay incentives were available for solutions, but the workers interviewed said, "Participation in the program, contact with top management and resolving work related problems were satisfaction enough" (1982, 149).

The motives and dynamics created by this control technique are exceedingly complex—both sociologically and politically. The possibility that the motivational benefits from the technique stem from a form of cooptation is an issue that requires further research. Not all quality circle attempts in the navy program were successful; groups may not produce any usable solutions or may disband from lack of interest or poor leadership. Furthermore, white- and blue-collar workers appear to adapt to the system better than professional staff. Overall, however, the navy program's ratio of benefits to cost on the project was four to one.

Another issue concerning the use of participatory control techniques, though not necessarily a restriction, is that bureaus are generally required to firmly fix responsibility for actions in reporting to external governmental bodies. To the extent that participatory control in the public sector really does allow officials to establish and monitor their own professional performance standards for public programs, this requirement could be interpreted as interfering with external accountability channels. In fact, however, many legislative and judicial policymakers give bureaus wide discretion in defining programs. In general, as experience with them in the public sector grows, participatory control systems offer much promise as a way of increasing acceptance of and commitment to control systems.

INTRINSIC CONTROLS

Intrinsic controls may be considered alternatives to control, as we normally construe the term. The principle here is that the bureau, or some other agent of society, succeeds in inculcating conformance with the goals, rules, and performance expectations in the bureau's members. Intrinsic controls produce conformance without monitoring and correction of work by relying on the fact that the goals of the individual and the organization have become the same. Whether based on personal loyalty, professional socialization, socialization to the norms of a particular organization, careful screening of job applicants, self-selection, or strong ideological beliefs in the bureau's mission, intrinsic controls fulfill many of the functions of the control systems described so far.

The idea of intrinsic controls is not a new one. In describing the ideal-type bureaucracy, Weber noted the importance of socialization to professional norms of impartiality, competence, and a career commitment to the bureau (Weber 1947, 329–341). Likewise, Gulick argued that if everyone shares an idea, that fact alone will often serve as the primary motivation for cooperative effort—this he referred to as "leading through an idea" ([1937] 1973, 37–38). More recently, Burns and Stalker's (1994) model of the "organismic" form of organization relies largely on professional interest and commitment to the technology used in an organization though not necessarily to the specific organization. Etzioni's analysis of the reasons for compliance with orders in organizations includes norms or the "identitative" power of the organization, that is, shared beliefs in the organization's goals, as one finds in voluntary religious or "ideological-political" groups (Etzioni 1965). The greater the basis of identitative power in the organization, the greater the likelihood that an individual's loyalty and compliance will be strong enough to reduce the need for the overt forms of control. The problem for bureaus, of course, is that only part of their attraction as a place in which to work is based on identification; money also plays a significant role. Further, Etzioni notes, identitative power varies with environmental conditions, such as the strength of public support for an issue (like environmentalism or equal employment), the number of organizations competing for a member's loyalty, or the economic conditions affecting the funds available for such organizations (Etzioni 1965, 654).

The conditions for intrinsic control that exist in bureaus can be identified as personal loyalty, professional or organizational socialization, selection, and ideological commitment to the organization's policies. Personal loyalty to a leader can be based, as Downs notes (1967, 156), on nepotism or long-standing trust and friendship. Charismatic leaders also gain loyalty because of their ability to sway those around them. Loyalty can also be created and may be the result of mentor relationships. The strength of these relations lies in the confidence that the mentor or leader can have in the cooperation and loyalty of the staff. Reliance on such personal relationships also has its drawbacks. If the mentor leaves or becomes alienated and no longer adheres to the bureau policy line, the followers may well also "defect," thereby compounding the loss. A series of strong personal loyalties can also disrupt other organizational command functions, especially if the followers begin to develop a distorted view of their own authority, as distinct from their leader's authority. White House staff are said to have fallen into this pattern in many instances (Reedy 1987), and such a misreading of personal power may have led to actions that resulted in the Watergate and Iran-Contra scandals. Intense personal loyalties can also be a sign of immaturity in leaders or followers, which can disrupt core management functions.

Socialization refers to the learning or orientation the individual goes through on entering a profession or an organization, and is another way of trying to ensure that members hold the appropriate values and goals. Socialization can occur "on the job," in orientation sessions, or through a longer process of observation and imitation—or it may be accomplished in the professional schools. Professional school socialization usually occurs at the graduate levels and consists of both technical information about the state-of-the-art professional standards and the values that the profession considers appropriate.[1] Though the technical information comprises the formal curriculum, the inculcation of values is of great importance too. The professionalism of the members' values is ensured both by the careful selection of students for the program based on their existing values and by subtle training through exposure to successful role models at conferences, seminars, and informal discussions with professors and peers. In general, Etzioni (1965) notes that there is a relationship between selection and socialization such that the more selective an organization can afford to be (for example, the air force or medical schools), the more screening for technical competence and for values before entry into schools can be done, and the less emphasis need be placed on socialization in school. At least in the past a relatively high proportion of West Point graduates (25 percent) came from families of West Point graduates or officers (Janowitz 1960, 98), indicating the importance of existing values in selection.

---

[1]For an in-depth discussion of the impact of professional socialization on values, see Harold Gortner, *Ethics for Public Managers*. New York: Greenwood Press, 1991, chapter 7, "Professions, Professionalism, and Ethics."

The object of "on-the-job" socialization in the bureau is to orient new officials, regardless of past professional training, to the bureau's norms and values. Teaching the rules of the organization and the more subtle ideas of the bureau's mission and ethos is done through department handbooks, orientation sessions, periodic retreats, and briefings. Common but less obvious methods of teaching include the banter at staff meetings and the folklore of the bureau, which generally focuses on points of crisis or stories of departed "characters" who become more bizarre and mythic each year. Much about the organization's sense of its real mission, importance, and character can be learned in informal gatherings and conversations; new members must listen carefully.

Myths and symbols, which embody the emotional content of our responses toward organizations or political events generally (Edelman 1964; Elder and Cobb 1983), are an important means of expressing and teaching organizational norms and the bases of commitment. Myths interpret and express the meanings of events and actions from the actors' viewpoint, and unify members around some self-conception, often a professional identity. Important events are retold, embellished, and selectively recalled in the form of myths, with heroes, quests, and magical incantations. In one agency that was studied, foreign service officers described themselves in heroic terms, bringing scientific advances to cultures in need (Mahler 1988). Other studies of organizational myths show how stories of computer-design coups or legends of sophisticated new machines being built in garage workshops by young geniuses are told in heroic terms, and the heroes serve as a point of identity for the organizational members (Kidder 1981; Pondy et al. 1983).

Symbols of the organization's identity and spirit have been studied in several settings. Kaufmann's study of the Forest Service (1967) describes the ways in which paramilitary training, uniforms, and procedures are used to create internalized controls in the extremely isolated and dispersed officials in the service. Similarly, when the regional planning concept behind the TVA was new and untried, a sense of clearer mission and direction was created when a concrete identity—administration through the grass roots—was developed (Selznick 1966). The idea of grass-roots administration, loosely linked to ideas of democratic administration, became a symbol of the legitimacy and energy of the agency. In 1966, the Economic Development Administration in the Department of Commerce developed for itself an image of an innovative and nonbureaucratic organization capable of moving quickly and effectively to forestall urban riots. It would lead, and other agencies would be pulled along (Pressman and Wildavsky 1984). The identification with the organization and its mission in these instances was critical to the level of contributions and control that was needed to undertake new projects.

Ideological commitments by officials to bureau policies is another basis of organizational control though a rather inconstant one. Officials may decide to work with a department or agency because they believe in the administration's objectives. Some departments' policy arenas are more likely to elicit such commitments than others. The CIA, the EPA, the FBI or the Department of Energy, for example, probably have higher levels of policy commitment than the IRS or the U.S. Postal Service since the former administer programs that are more clearly visible, controversial, or exciting though no research on this is available.

The value of policy or ideological commitments, like professional commitments, lies in the willingness of officials to exert energy and imagination to accomplish the programs' goals. Yet if policies or administrations change, the commitments that were self-controlling may lead officials to thwart a new policy. This is certainly the fear of new administration officials, who see the civil servants as the enemy. Both ideological and professional commitments, focused as they are on factors outside the bureau's chain of command, are effective agents of control only when ideologies or professional norms coincide with the bureau's policies. Such commitments are uncertain bases of control regardless of their considerable importance in intelligent policy debate and development.

EXTERNAL CONTROLS

As noted earlier, the bureau may control other bureaus and firms, and it may be controlled by external policymakers, interest groups, and other bureaus. The control relations that the bureau imposes and that are imposed on it are complex and affect the requirements of the internal control systems.

The situations in which bureaus are controlling agents are familiar ones: the bureau as regulatory agency and as implementor and enforcer of policies and regulations. Bureaus are also, however, influenced by the firms or groups they regulate, and several theories seek to describe the consequences of this situation for regulation. The most extreme thesis regarding these influence relationships is the "capture theory" in which the regulatory agency is seen as dependent on the regulated firms for political support and the private decision makers conspire to use the government agency as a tool of their own self-serving intentions (Garvey 1993, 25–34; Brandl 1989). The more moderate thesis, the political economy thesis, is that regulatory agencies must find a balance of support and opposition among their clients and organized interest groups to survive (Noll 1971). The Environmental Protection Agency, for example, cannot police every environmental hazard and therefore must cultivate the cooperation of firms, but it also needs the support of the environmental lobby to offset the fundamental opposition of the regulated firms. Conversely, professional links with external groups may lead to pitting one part of the agency against another so that aggressive regulators may encourage or even assist in suits against the agency to achieve compliance with regulations by recalcitrant staff. The common pattern of negotiated regulations and implementation similarly shows the ambiguous position of the regulatory agencies (Katzman 1980).

Implementing agencies also must compromise and negotiate. The failure of the intended targets of a policy to comply with unpopular regulations can stalemate an implementing agency (Pressman and Wildavsky 1984). Low levels of support for a program among those whose cooperation is needed can force an agency to relax its requirements for a time, reestablishing them only when the program gains momentum (Mahler 1976). Competition among bureaus for clients or interest-group support may also lead to a relaxation of monitoring requirements.

Of course, politicians can control programs through oversight and purse strings. For both regulators and implementors, controls, especially limitations in action, can be created by politicians who wish to limit governmental actions even though they may not be able to do away with agencies and programs. The IRS cannot make extremely large returns without approval of Congress; thus, both how the law and the agency work can be observed by the Ways and Means Committee. The Reagan administration controlled government agencies through inaction as well as active budget cutting. During the first two years of the Reagan administration, the productivity of agencies, in writing and enforcing regulations and implementing programs, was dramatically decreased through a series of budget impasses, budget cuts, and reductions in force that threw the organizations into turmoil, reduced morale dramatically, and in general created an environment that led to reduced productivity. Most observers believed that this was a deliberate ploy by the Reagan administration to reduce the level of government activity in many of the affected areas.

Not only are the standards of bureau performance compromised by influential clients and constituencies, but the control process itself is affected. To the extent that the regulatory or implementing agency must adjust programs or negotiate regulations to obtain a degree of cooperation, that agency cannot use a routine program to process cases. Discretionary problem solving and an enlarged staff must be used instead of a relatively efficient routine. Special boundary-spanning units must be established (Thompson 1967, 70–73). As we noted in Chapter 4, all this also implies a more highly differentiated and intricately coordinated structure to deal with the more heterogeneous and unstable set of environmental actors.

Under these circumstances, as case results become more variable and with policies uncertain or shifting, the internal control process will also become more complex and less routine. Measures of performance become more complex as the work becomes more variable and discretionary. Thus, the degree of clients' influence and their ability to insist that regulations be negotiated will affect the routineness of operations and the complexity of the internal management and control systems.

The actions of the external policymakers and organized interest groups also affect the structure and operations of the bureau's control system directly. External policymakers mandate programs, but they also determine, by the type and detail of their own monitoring, what the scope of the bureau's control system will be. In general, bureaus may be forced to adjust internal controls to the level of external surveillance to which they are subject. Opposition interest groups or groups seeking expanded or revised services may also be on the watch for lapses in procedure or any instance of misfeasance. Some public interest research groups have proved to be diligent watchdogs of consumer and environmental affairs; for example, consumer and patient groups closely follow rule making and licensing decisions of the Food and Drug Administration. Bureau growth in an environment that includes hostile elements requires that bureaus accumulate evidence of their effectiveness to head off criticism. As external critics become more vigilant, the internal control system must become more rigorous to prevent or limit the damage caused by a slip from policies that the bureau must justify. The Food and Drug Administration, for example, must constantly be ready to defend itself against critics, some of whom claim that the procedures for approving drugs are too slow, and some of whom want greater care and time taken to guarantee that no drug is allowed on the market that might have serious unanticipated consequences for individual health and well-being.

It should not be overlooked, however, that the intensity of controls may be motivated by internal factors. Executives who fear loss of authority and staff who fear criticisms of their judgments may wish for intensified controls. Programs that do not have the support of professional staff may also be judged to require tight controls to ensure the correct implementation. Montjoy and O'Toole (1979) point out the obstacles to this approach, as noted in Chapter 4.

The external control systems in which every public bureau is enmeshed, as controller and as the object of control, put great pressure on the bureau's internal operations, including its control systems. External critics and supporters in the form of policymakers and interest groups create demands for a level of internal control that matches the level and type of scrutiny to which the bureau is subject. The role of bureaus as implementors or regulators in control of other bureaus, units of government, or groups often requires the bureau to compromise and negotiate to achieve compliance and avoid serious opposition. These procedural complications, in turn, make internal controls of the implementation and regulatory process more complex, as they try to accommodate discretionary judgments.

QUALIFICATIONS AND CONCLUSIONS

The emphasis in this chapter on management control systems has been the logic of the various techniques for control. There is growing concern in both public and private management, however, that some of the emphasis on control as the core management function is misplaced, and that the availability and accuracy of techniques such as management information systems or evaluations are distorting the role of management and hampering organizations. The assumption has been that as control systems become increasingly sophisticated, management will become a more certain and automatic process—an applied science.

Downs argues against this view in his Law of Counter Control, based on the intractability of human nature. Landau and Stout take their criticism further. "Control is a function of knowledge, and in uncertain environments knowledge often does not exist" (1979, 148). They liken the management error of overcontrol in bureaus to a type II statistical error, that is, to prematurely establishing strict program rules or prematurely rejecting a potentially promising thesis or course of action. The source of their criticism is that the technology of public policies and the management of human and material resources in pursuit of those policies is a process rife with uncertainties or unknowns. To say, therefore, we have "diagnosed" a problem and applied corrective action is more a hopeful analogy than a statement of fact. In truth, program technologies are often experiments. We may be unsure if a program is really doing well, and even less sure how to "treat" a problem in a program once diagnosed. Given the knowledge that the program is not operating as intended, we are often left with little or no idea of how to alter existing procedures. We simply lack the knowledge of how to change society, the economy, or international politics to our liking. Alternatively, changes in the environment or mutations in the programs themselves may change the effectiveness of a formerly workable solution. Program managers who overrely on control systems may focus too much on reestablishing controls and restoring previous levels of outputs, without considering alternative program ideas, or even more important, without encouraging the political and professional debates and negotiations that constitute public management.

Perhaps the most serious consequence of the overreliance on control systems is that management becomes defined as a narrow technical process of control rather than as the experimental process it really is. Management control systems play an important role in the ongoing process of clarifying the success of program technologies, but they cannot be substitutes for the judgments of managers and professionals about the timing and direction of program development. These remain political and professional decisions.

Implicit and participatory controls also reduce the level of direct control and may, therefore, reduce overreliance on control systems as a means of management. These approaches are still being explored, but despite their promise, more research is necessary to help evaluate the extent to which they can replace or supplement the more direct methods of control. Thus, the field continues to change rapidly.

FOR FURTHER READING

Daniel Robey, in *Designing Organizations,* 4th ed. Burr Ridge, Ill.: Richard D. Irwin, 1994, outlines the basic purposes and mechanisms of organizational control in straightforward terms. An earlier classic view of control, which considers the role of professional training and organization indoctrination in control, is offered by Amitai Etzioni in "Organization Control Structure," in the *Handbook of Organizations,* ed., James March, Chicago: Rand McNally, 1965. A case study in the use of intensive training and socialization as a substitute for direct control is illustrated in Herbert Kaufman's classic research on *The Forest Ranger,* Baltimore: Johns Hopkins Press, 1967. Anthony Downs, *Inside Bureaucracy,* Boston: Little, Brown, 1967 (reissued, Prospect Heights, Ill.: Waveland Press, 1994), considers the use of conventional quantitative and qualitative monitoring systems for control and such things as spies in bureaus in his political economy view of organizations. A more exclusively quantitative approach to performance monitoring in public agencies is offered by Susan Welch and John Comer in *Quantitative Methods for Public Administration,* 2nd ed. Chicago: Dorsey Press, 1988. Martin Landau and Russell Stout outline the dilemmas of public managers who must establish clear standards for control with programs that are less than clear in their article, "To Manage is Not to Control: Or the Folly of Type II Errors," *Public Administration Review* 38, 1979: 148–156. Donald Chisholm, in his book *Coordination Without Hierarchy: Informal Structure in Multiorganizational Systems,* Berkeley: University of California Press, 1989, uses a case study of the public transit system in the San Francisco Bay Area to show how coordination can occur between peer organizations and without formal hierarchies. Finally, James E. Swiss gives an overview of current control systems used in government in *Public Management Systems: Monitoring and Managing Government Performance,* Englewood Cliffs, N.J.: Prentice Hall, 1991.

REVIEW QUESTIONS

1. To what extent is the choice of control systems limited by the political environment within which public administrators operate? Would the choice be broader for those in the nonprofit sector or the private sector? Why or why not?

2. Studies have shown that control systems usually cannot work in isolation; more than one must be used in order to avoid unanticipated consequences in the behavior of workers. Consider what unanticipated consequence might arise from an emphasis on

each of the individual control systems related in this chapter, and note what other control systems might be used to help overcome those unproductive behaviors or procedures.

3. What communication systems (see Chapter 5) would be depended on by each of the control systems noted in this chapter?

4. What impact would control systems have on decision making (see Chapter 7) and motivation of employees (see Chapter 8)?

5. Would the control systems in place have any impact on the way supervisors and subordinates interact (see Chapter 9)?

REFERENCES

Ackoff, Russell, and Maurice Sasini. *Fundamentals of Operations Research.* New York: John Wiley & Sons, 1968.

Brandl, John. "How Organization Counts: Incentives and Inspiration." *Journal of Policy Analysis and Management* 8, 1989: 489–493.

Bryant, Stephen, and Joseph Kearns. "Workers' Brains as Well as Their Bodies: Quality Circles in a Federal Facility," *Public Administration Review* 42, 1982: 144–150.

Burns, Tom, and Gerald Stalker. *The Management of Innovation,* rev. ed. Oxford: Oxford University Press, 1994.

Cain, Glen, and Harold Watts. "Problems in Making Policy Inferences from the Coleman Report." In *Evaluating Social Programs: Theory, Practice and Politics,* ed. Peter Rossi. New York: Seminar Press, 1972.

Carr, David K., and Ian D. Littman. *Excellence in Government: Total Quality Management in the 1990's,* 2nd ed. Arlington, Va.: Coopers and Lybrand, 1993.

Carroll, Stephen, and Henry Tosi. *Management by Objectives: Applications and Research.* New York: Macmillan, 1973.

Coleman, J. S. et al. *Equality of Educational Opportunity.* Washington, D.C.: U.S. Government Printing Office, 1966.

Creech, Bill. *The Five Pillars for TQM: How to Make Total Quality Management Work for You.* New York: Truman Talley Books/Dutton, 1994.

Cyert, Richard, and James March. *A Behavioral Theory of the Firm,* 2nd ed. Cambridge, Mass.: Blackwell Publishers, 1992.

Downs, Anthony. *Inside Bureaucracy.* Boston: Little, Brown, 1967. (Reissued, Prospect Heights, Ill.: Waveland Press, 1994.)

Edelman, Murray. *The Symbolic Uses of Politics.* Urbana, Ill.: University of Illinois Press, 1964.

Elder, Charles, and Roger Cobb. *The Political Uses of Symbols.* New York: Longman, 1983.

Etzioni, Amitai. "Organizational Control Structure." In *Handbook of Organizations,* ed. James March. Chicago: Rand McNally, 1965.

Filley, Alan, Robert House, and Steven Kerr. *Managerial Process and Organizational Behavior,* 2nd ed. Glenview, Ill.: Scott Foresman, 1976.

Finz, Samuel. "Productivity Measurement Systems and Their Implementation." In *Productivity Improvement Handbook for State and Local Government,* ed. George Washnis. New York: John Wiley & Sons, 1980.

Garvey, Gerald. *Facing the Bureaucracy: Living and Dying in a Public Agency.* San Francisco: Jossey-Bass, 1993.

Gortner, Harold F. *Ethics for Public Managers.* New York: Greenwood Press/Praeger, 1991.

Gulick, Luther. "Notes on the Theory of Organization." In *Papers on the Science of Administration,* eds. Luther Gulick and Lyndall Urwick. 1937. Reprint, Clifton, N.J.: Augustus Kelley, 1973.

Halperin, Morton. *Bureaucratic Politics and Foreign Policy.* Washington, D.C.: The Brookings Institution, 1974.

Janowitz, Morris. *The Professional Soldier.* New York: Free Press, 1960.

Katz, Daniel, and Robert Kahn. *The Social Psychology of Organizations,* 2nd ed. New York: John Wiley & Sons, 1978.

Katzman, Robert. *Regulatory Bureaucracy:* The Federal Trade Commission and Antitrust Policy. Cambridge, Mass.: MIT Press, 1980.

Kaufman, Herbert. *The Forest Ranger.* Baltimore: Johns Hopkins Press, 1967.

Kidder, Tracy. *The Soul of a New Machine.* Boston: Little, Brown, 1981.

Landau, Martin, and Russell Stout, Jr. "To Manage Is Not to Control: Or the Folly of Type II Errors," *Public Administration Review* 39, 1979: 148–156.

Leviton, Laura, and Edward Hughes. "Research on the Utilization of Evaluations." *Evaluation Review* 5, 1981: 525–548.

Mahler, Julianne. "Politics and Professionalism: A Bargaining Analysis of the Implementation of the Community Mental Health Centers Act." Ph.D. diss., SUNY Buffalo, 1976.

————. "The Quest for Organizational Meaning: Identifying and Interpreting the Symbolism in Organizational Stories." *Administration & Society* 20, 1988: 344–368.

Merton, Robert. "Bureaucratic Structure and Personality." In *Social Theory and Social Structure,* rev. ed. New York: Free Press, 1957.

Montjoy, Robert, and Laurence O'Toole, Jr. "Toward a Theory of Policy Implementation: An Organizational Perspective." *Public Administration Review* 39, 1979: 465–476.

Morrisey, George. *Management by Objectives and Results in the Public Sector.* Reading, Mass.: Addison-Wesley, 1976.

National Performance Review (U.S.). *Creating a Government That Works Better & Costs Less: The Report of the National Performance Review.* Vice President Al Gore. New York: Plume/Penguin, 1993.

Noll, Roger. *Reforming Regulation: An Evaluation of the Ash Council Proposal.* Washington, D.C.: Brookings Institution, 1971.

Osborne, David, and Ted Gaebler. *Reinventing Government: How the Entrepreneurial Spirit is Transforming the Public Sector.* Reading, Mass.: Addison-Wesley, 1992.

Ouchi, William. *Theory Z.* Reading, Mass.: Addison-Wesley, 1981.

Patton, Michael. *Utilization Focused Evaluation,* 2nd ed. Beverly Hills, Calif.: Sage, 1986.

Peters, Thomas, and Robert Waterman, Jr. *In Search of Excellence.* New York: Warner Books, 1982.

Pondy, Lewis, Peter Frost, Gareth Morgan, and Thomas Dandridge, eds. *Organizational Symbolism.* Greenwich Conn.: JAI Press, 1983.

Pressman, Jeffrey, and Aaron Wildavsky. *Implementation,* 3rd ed. Berkeley, Calif.: University of California Press, 1984.

Reedy, George. *The Twilight of the Presidency,* rev. ed. New York: New American Library, 1987.

Robey, Daniel. *Designing Organizations,* 4th ed. Burr Ridge, Ill.: Richard D. Irwin, 1994.

Sapolsky, Harvey. *The Polaris System Development: Bureaucratic and Pragmatic Success in Government.* Cambridge, Mass.: Harvard University Press, 1972.

Schlesinger, Arthur, Jr. *The Coming of the New Deal.* Boston: Houghton Mifflin, 1959.

Selznick, Philip. *TVA and the Grass Roots.* New York: Harper, 1966.

Sherwood, Frank, and William Page. "MBO and Public Management." In *Public Management: Public and Private Perspectives,* ed. James Perry and Kenneth Kraemer. Palo Alto, Calif.: Mayfield, 1983.

Strauss, George. "Some Notes on Power Equalization." In *The Social Science of Organizations,* ed. Harold Leavitt. Englewood Cliffs, N.J.: Prentice Hall, 1963.

Suchman, Edward. *Evaluative Research: Principles and Practice in Public Service and Social Action Programs.* New York: Sage, 1967.

Swiss, James E. "Adapting Total Quality Management (TQM) to Government." *Public Administration Review* 52, 1992: 356–362.

Tannenbaum, Arnold et al. *Hierarchy in Organizations.* San Francisco: Jossey-Bass, 1974.

The Urban Institute, State and Local Government Research Program. *The Status of Productivity Measurement in State Government: An Initial Examination.* Washington, D.C.: The Urban Institute, 1975.

The Urban Institute. *Developing Client Outcome Monitoring Systems.* Washington, D.C.: The Urban Institute, 1981.

Thompson, James D. *Organizations in Action.* New York: McGraw-Hill, 1967.

Walton, Mary. *The Deming Management Method.* New York: Praeger, 1986.

Wamsley, Gary, and Mayer Zald. *The Political Economy of Public Organizations.* Bloomington: Indiana University Press, 1976.

Weber, Max. *The Theory of Social and Economic Organization,* ed. and trans. A. M. Henderson and Talcott Parsons. New York: Free Press, 1947.

Weiss, Carol. *Evaluation Research: Methods for Assessing Program Effectiveness.* Englewood Cliffs, N.J.: Prentice Hall, 1972.

Welch, Susan, and John Comer. *Quantitative Methods for Public Administration,* 2nd ed. Chicago, Ill.: Dorsey, Press, 1988.

CASE 6–1 Performance Evaluation and Organizational Rigidity

It is 10 A.M., and Jim Daniels has already had four cups of coffee and attended three meetings. His desk is still piled high with paperwork, and tomorrow will be Friday, his last workday before the start of two weeks of long-awaited vacation. He puts aside the report he is reading and reflects upon some of the problems in his organization that have arisen or intensified during the past month. He thinks for a few minutes and then says to himself: "How can I afford to go away at such a critical time?"

Most people would agree that Jim Daniels had started a brilliant military career. He had performed well in every assignment given to him from the very beginning and had been awarded outstanding ratings on all past performance evaluations. Twice he had been promoted ahead of his contemporaries, and he now holds the rank of lieutenant colonel.

In his present assignment Jim is commander of a selectively staffed Air Force squadron that flies aircraft with a unique mission. When Jim was a captain six years ago, he had applied and competed for an assignment in this prestigious unit; like many other members of the squadron, he was promoted early and sent to a military school for promising command and staff officers. Following the one year of school, he spent two years on the headquarters staff before assuming his present duties. Since he had previously served at this Air Force wing, Jim was already aware of most of his responsibilities when he arrived at the squadron. Equally important, he knew most of the people and tasks connected with the operation of his unit. All along the way, he had looked forward to this job and to working with high-caliber personnel. But a lot of things had changed since he had left for school, especially. . . .

The phone rings. It is another young captain interested in applying for the unit's flying program. Jim only half listens to this enthusiastic pilot tell about his background, but he does manage to give some answers to questions concerning the program scope and the duties and responsibilities that each new candidate will encounter. Jim's mind is still wandering back across the events of the morning when one last question from his caller brings him back to the phone conversation: "What sort of performance evaluation might I expect during my first year with your squadron?"

Performance evaluations! Performance evaluations! Everybody now seems concerned about performance evaluations! Most of Jim's problems of the past week involved performance evaluations in some respect, in fact. Jim's first meeting of the day had been with the wing commander, the director of operations, and the director of training—a meeting dealing with past performance evaluations of new applicants for the unit flying program. The staff had prepared a personal folder for each candidate containing his personnel, flight, and physical records, letters of recommendation, and evaluation reports of the applicant's personal interviews with various members of the staff. The personnel records seem to have the most influence since they contain personal data, previous duty assignments, and the individual's previous evaluations.

During the meeting with the wing commander, each participant studied every folder, asked questions of the staff, and completed a rank ordering of the most qualified candidates. Jim feels that the others gave too much weight to the performance evaluations and not enough attention to the other data available, especially the records of flight evaluations. The performance evaluations are too general for the purpose of evaluating flying accomplishments and skills and are perhaps better suited to evaluating promotion and career potential. Jim wants to maintain the high personnel standards of his unit, but he needs more reassurance that those applicants with high performance evaluations are also highly skilled aviators. Moreover, he is concerned because he sees a trend developing—the number of highly qualified applicants has been decreasing over the past year since the Air Force instituted a new method of conducting performance evaluations for all officers. A few candidates chosen for the unit program had reconsidered accepting the assignment when they learned that they would be competing against other members of the elite squadron for ratings, according to the new system, and it would not be possible for everyone to receive a top performance-evaluation score.

In the second meeting, Jim got much data that reinforced his concern. He conferred with the unit personnel officer about finding replacements for the operations officer and the maintenance officer. These positions are about to become vacant due to personnel reassignments, and Jim was amazed to learn that nobody from the unit had volunteered for these two choice jobs. In his day, he would have jumped at the chance to gain additional experience in either of these two areas. Of course, it would have meant starting at the bottom again in a new organization, but the opportunity to learn new skills was tremendous. Jim was also surprised when the personnel officer told him that no one from his unit had made an application for a future assignment. During further discussion of the matter, Jim learned that better than half of his squadron had four or more years in their present assignment. Still more important, he learned that some people had turned down special assignments or schools. It looked as if some of the squadron members had staked an organizational claim and were in the process of homesteading their assignment.

Jim's third meeting was with the wing administrative officer. The time was drawing near for completing performance evaluations for each of his squadron officers, and the administrative officer gave him a listing of pertinent data for each member to be evaluated plus a detailed briefing on the new evaluation procedures.

The wing administrative officer stressed one point about the performance-evaluation procedures, a point that troubled Jim because he thought it would cause over-cautious and shortsighted behavior among young officers: No more than 50 percent of the unit members would be able to receive the top two rating scores. The ratings assigned by the unit commander would be reviewed at two additional levels, and could be changed at either one or both levels. First, Jim would write the performance evaluation for each officer in his squadron and assign a rating. Second, the director of operations would review evaluations from his squadron, along with others from related units, and would assign a second rating which could differ from the first. Finally, the wing commander would review and rate all the performance evaluations from all of the units. But the wing commander is still bound by the same quota constraints as are Jim and the director of operations: no more than 50 percent of those rated can receive the top two ratings, and no more than 20 percent of those rated can receive the top rating.

Jim picks up the report he was reading before the phone rang. He notes that better than 90 percent of the people who were eligible for promotion last cycle, and who received the top rating on their last performance evaluation, were in fact promoted. Additionally, almost 75 percent of those with the second-highest rating who were eligible for promotion were promoted. But less than 50 percent of those who received the third-highest rating were promoted; and less than 10 percent of the remaining eligibles were promoted. There is little doubt that high performance evaluations are necessary for promotion, and the new system instituted throughout the Air Force makes virtual losers of 50 percent of the officers.

A knock on his door interrupts Jim's thought, and he answers cheerfully; "Come in." Captain John Douglas walks in and closes the door behind him. His face looks a bit strained, but his manner is calm and pleasant. Douglas is undoubtedly the best pilot in the organization, being charged with instructing other pilots as well as training new members. He does his job extremely well and otherwise keeps to himself. Jim knows that this is no casual visit to shoot the breeze. After exchanging the pleasantries of the day, Douglas gets right to the point:

> Sir, we've got a big problem in our unit, and I don't know what to do about it. There used to be a great spirit of cooperation here; we would all help one another. Now people don't discuss much about their problems—I mean problems about how they fly or do their job. Maybe you've noticed the lack of exchange we've had lately at our crew meetings. It seems everyone is becoming secretive about what experiences they've had recently or about mistakes they might have made. They don't discuss much at all with the new trainees. Everybody seems to be running off doing their own little projects or blowing their own horn about their accomplishments. We just don't have the morale we used to have. I'm beginning to feel like a stranger in my own outfit.

Jim listens intently, for Douglas is usually in tune with what is going on in the unit. As the commander, Jim knows that declining morale is a recurring theme. Also, communications have occasionally been strained during the squadron meetings, and it is true that the unit sometimes acts as cliques or as individuals rather than as a team. For example, some tend to guard information that is valuable to others in the unit. On the surface, however, things seem to go well. For the most part, everyone is amiable. All the crew members did very well on their last flying evaluations, and the squadron received an outstanding rating on a no-notice inspection recently from headquarters. All the officers are professionals and perform their jobs in an exemplary fashion.

After Douglas leaves, Jim begins to think more about the upcoming performance evaluations of his unit which will be due shortly after he returns from vacation. Somehow he will have to justify assigning less than a top rating to 80 percent of his officers— officers who had competed for this assignment and who were handpicked after careful consideration of their records. Jim begins to see the scope of the problem and once again thinks "How can I leave at a critical time like this?"

SOURCE: Robert Golembiewski and Michael White, "Performance Evaluation and Organizational Rigidity," in Golembiewski and White, eds. *Cases in Public Management,* 3rd ed. (Chicago: Rand McNally, 1980): 217–220.

Editor's Note

This case illustrates several issues in organizational control and personnel management, but there are also other dimensions to the problems facing Daniels. Consider the following questions:

1. Is this is a classic case of "overcontrol"? What is the purpose of the new performance evaluation guidelines establishing the proportion of people who may be given the top rankings?

2. Why do you think Daniels believes that too little emphasis is being given to aviation skills? What are the issues in professionalism here?

3. What could Daniels do about the morale and motivation (see Chapter 8) consequences of the trends in performance evaluation and promotion? The promotion picture?

4. What are the unintended consequences of the new guidelines?

5. What is the link here between the performance evaluation patterns and organizational rigidity? Are the purposes of control fulfilled or confounded in this case?

CASE 6–2   When an Accident Isn't: Arsenal Managers Ignore Ills to Keep Safety Mark Going

Radford arsenal officials say their plant is one of the safest industries in Virginia, despite the deaths of three workers in explosions in the past 3½ years.

Until a worker bruised his knee earlier this month, the plant had recorded 8 million hours worked without a lost-time injury. Before that, the plant recorded 18 million hours worked without a lost-time injury, going back to 1982.

Behind the safety records is another story.

While the two most recent safety records were being compiled, dozens of workers received injuries at the arsenal that required them to miss work. Arsenal officials overlooked broken bones, torn ligaments, burns and other disabling injuries, that occurred on the job over the past 3½ years.

The safety record was maintained by the arsenal despite rulings by the Virginia Industrial Commission that the plant had to pay employees for work-related injuries that kept them off the job.

The record was maintained even though some employees were required to report to work to avoid lost time after being seriously injured.

The record was maintained even as some employees were required to have job-related surgery on their days off in order to avoid lost time.

In fact, until the worker bruised his knee earlier this month, the only time in the past 3½ years that the arsenal has acknowledged a lost-time, on-the-job injury, was when employees were killed in explosions at the ammunition plant.

Officials of the Radford Army Ammunition Plant are proud of the safety record and say it helps motivate workers. They also defend the record, pointing to a complex set of government and industry standards they must follow in determining a lost-time injury.

"You need to remember that the rule book we use for making these kinds of judgements is about three-quarters of an inch thick," said Charles Gardner, the director of safety and plant operations.

"It gets quite complicated, and there is a very delicate matrix that we have to reach before we can say that we have that record," he said. Gardner said the plant must meet state safety standards, Army rules, National Safety Council standards and Hercules rules.

Plant officials acknowledge that there have been injuries at the arsenal while the safety record was being compiled.

In 1985, 42 injuries were reported to the state Occupational Safety and Health office, but plant officials maintain that none was serious enough to warrant lost time, based on the safety record standard.

Union officials have speculated that Hercules maintains the safety record to impress the Army, which pays the company $185 million a year to operate the plant.

Part of the contract includes a $250,000 safety incentive fee. If there are no lost-time injuries in one year, Hercules gets the entire amount.

"Companies are looking for the best overall performance record they can get because that's where they earn their extra dollars," said Nolan Hancock, a national representative for the Oil, Chemical and Atomic Workers International Union. The union represents most workers at the arsenal.

Arsenal officials often used the government and industry standards to determine that a disabling injury that happened while the employee was performing normal duties was not work-related thus exempting it from harming the safety record.

When that happens, employees often are denied workers' compensation.

At least 50 employees were denied workers' compensation in the past four years after Hercules decided their injuries were not work-related, Don Strock, the workers' compensation chairman for the union local, said.

Most of those employees took their cases to the Industrial Commission, a state agency that decides contested compensation cases, Strock said.

The union and Hercules disagree exactly how many times the Industrial Commission has ruled in favor of the employees. The union says the workers won 75 percent to 80 percent of the cases; Hercules acknowledged that it had to pay benefits in 21 cases, or slightly fewer than half the contested cases.

(The Industrial Commission said the records that would prove who is right could not be released because they are private.)

Even in those 21 cases Hercules admits were won by the workers, the safety record remained intact after the Industrial Commission ruled the injuries had been job-related. Hercules said that because different standards are used for workers' compensation and compiling the safety record, the two should not be compared.

Union officials failed to see the difference.

"Out of all the cases that we've won, we've never seen them take any hours off the board," Strock said.

John "Chip" Craig, a Radford lawyer, said he has represented at least 30 injured employees who were denied workers' compensation by Hercules after missing work in the past three years. Of those cases, he said he has won a "vast majority." The union supports his numbers.

Hercules disputes Craig's figures. Jack Kelly, who handles workers' compensation cases for Hercules, said Craig has represented 15 plant employees and Hercules has won most of those cases.

"That's a crock," Craig said when informed of Kelly's estimates.

Hercules voluntarily pays workers' compensation to a large majority of employees who are hurt on the job, Kelly said.

Not true, Strock said.

He says the plant voluntarily pays workers' compensation to about "one in 10" of the workers injured at the plant.

Strock keeps records of all the injuries involving union employees. Those records— like Craig's—indicate that Hercules often refuses to pay workers' compensation until ordered to by the commission.

"We have to go to the Industrial Commission to win a lot of these cases that never should have been brought up in the first place," Strock said.

'Almost Laughable'

Commission officials declined to discuss Hercules' method of dealing with workers' compensation, citing the privacy of records involving individual industries. But Craig provided these examples of cases he has handled in the past 3½ years.

—An employee fell down a flight of steps while on the job and tore ligaments in his knee. Hercules denied workers' compensation, and said the injury was not work-related because it was a "reactivation of an old football injury." The commission reversed the decision.

—A worker strained her back while leaning over a large pipe to tighten a bolt. The injury was not work-related, Hercules maintained, because it could have happened "in the ordinary course of life." The commission reversed the decision.

—Another employee ruptured a disc in her back when boards that covered a large drain broke under her weight. Hercules ruled the injury was not work-related. The commission reversed the decision.

"It's almost laughable," Craig said.

Kelly declined to elaborate on his decisions about specific employees, saying the cases involved privileged medical information.

Craig said many employees are at a disadvantage in contested workers' compensation cases because they often are uninformed about their rights under the law, and do not receive proper instruction from Hercules officials.

"It's not my obligation to school 4,000 people about workers' compensation laws," Kelly said. The nearest workers' compensation regional office is in Lebanon, 100 miles away.

Working in Pain

Other workers whose injuries were judged as job-related by Hercules officials have been required to keep coming to work, they said, to preserve the safety record—even if it meant working in pain or doing no work at all.

A half-dozen workers who were interviewed said they had been involved in these practices. Another dozen said they had heard of them. Most of the employees asked that they not be identified out of concern for their jobs.

Sherman Williams of Pembroke, who ruptured a disc in 1982 while lifting a 40-pound bucket of paint, said he was told by plant officials to keep reporting to work after a plant doctor diagnosed the injury as a pulled muscle.

"They didn't want to have a lost-time injury, so they said 'You come in tomorrow, it doesn't matter what you do once you get here,'" Williams said.

Plant officials acknowledge that it is company policy for injured employees to keep reporting to work, but only when they can be assigned useful or productive work.

Williams later stopped going to work on the advice of his private physician and underwent a back operation. He still is unable to work.

Hercules denied his request for workers' compensation, saying the injury was not work-related. The Industrial Commission ruled in Williams' favor.

'Just Sitting Around'

Other workers recounted similar experiences:

—A former plant employee, who asked not be identified, said he spent most of a month in 1985 after injuring his knee "just sitting around" in an office. Plant officials say he was doing useful and productive work.

—Some workers who have been injured on the job said they were not asked to do any work during their normal shifts. Others said the limited work given them was not enough to keep them busy for an eight-hour shift.

—Strock, the workers' compensation chairman for the union, said that in some cases injured workers have been asked to report to work when even getting there was a problem. He said there was one case in which an employee who injured his shoulder needed help getting dressed so he could go to work.

—In some cases, Strock said, Hercules has required workers who need surgery to have it on their days off—so they can return to work in time to preserve the safety record.

The employee who tore ligaments in his knee said his surgery was scheduled for a Friday afternoon so he could be back on the job Monday morning.

Plant officials acknowledged such situations have occurred, but only when the surgery is minor and the employee has agreed to the arrangement.

Public Relations

Plant officials stand by the safety record as an accurate indication of working conditions. The record helps motivate workers to follow safety guidelines, they said.

Other people had different opinions.

"We feel like a lot of the accidents that are work-related are held non-occupational because they (Hercules) are trying to make a good showing with the government," Strock said.

A statement from the plant's headquarters, the Army Material command in Northern Virginia, said the Army is aware of the safety record and program at the plant.

"Radford and all other AMC installations use the same set of guidelines to establish classification of injuries that occur," the statement said.

But union officials wonder if the Army is fully aware of the way Hercules officials have been using the guidelines to make classifications of injuries.

Hancock, the national union representative in Washington, said he is not aware of the specifics of Radford's safety record. But he acknowledged it is a "fairly common" method used at Army ammunition plants. There could be other reasons behind Radford's apparent efforts to preserve its safety record, Hancock said.

One is good public relations.

"Rather than really instituting a good safety program, they are instituting a false public relations program," Hancock said.

In the past, plant officials have issued press releases whenever a new safety milestone has been reached.

"There's a lot of difference between working hard to build a good safety record and working hard to cover up a safety program that has some problems," Hancock said.

In addition, Hercules' contract with the Army includes the $250,000 safety incentive fee. Hercules gets the fee if there are no lost-time injuries or other accidents at the plant in one year.

SOURCE: Laurence Hammack, *Roanoke Times and World-News*, March 30, 1986: A1, A6.

Editor's Note

Consider the following questions related to the safety program of the Radford Arsenal and its impact on the organization:

1. Recalling that the purpose of the program is prevention, assess the logic and success of the safety program as a control device. What kinds of monitoring and corrections devices seem to exist?

2. What sorts of cooperation, resistance, and evasion would be expected from the employees in this kind of a safety program?

3. What other negative and positive effects might the program have on overall performance?

4. Suggest ways to alter the program to gain employee acceptance. What are the pitfalls?

5. Does the operation of the safety program give any clues to how communication (see Chapter 5), motivation (see Chapter 8), and leadership (see Chapter 9) occur in this organization? Would the current operation of the safety program suggest some changes in these areas that might help the overall performance of the organization?

Chapter 7

Organizational
Decision Making

INTRODUCTION

Decision making is one of the most complex and overtly political activities in organizations. Although most basic policy decisions are formally made by elected officials and courts, administrative decisions about program implementation, staffing, and budgets have significant and lasting effects on public policy. Even apparently minor decisions about the day-to-day operating details of a program can have important consequences for how effective a program is or who it reaches. The classic statement in public administration about the separation of politics and administration has become a debate concerning the proper domain of decision making in bureaus.

The methods or procedures that bureaus employ for decision making also have important political consequences. The decision method affects who participates, how agendas are established, which alternatives are considered, how they are compared and analyzed, and which values will dominate in the final selection. As we will see, the *procedures* of administrative decision making affect the *substance* of choice. Therefore, the method of decision making, like the domain, has important political consequences. Which method is best? On what grounds? For what problems or in what situations? Because of its importance:

> For many public executives, perhaps most, the exhilaration of choice is the primary reward for service and the chief ingredient in "morale." (Cleveland 1980, 183)

Organization theory is primarily concerned with the *methods* of decision making rather than the *domain*. For some time, the organization theory field has focused on two decision-making methods and their variations: rational and incremental. The first is the classic model of rational choice among well-researched options. It is the implicit bureaucratic model of decision making in an expert hierarchy, and it has also been the classic model for economics and business decision making. The model has long been criticized as unrealistic, but it has more recently become linked to policy analysis, and as analysis has become more important, the rationalist method has gained new support and interest.

The incremental-bargaining method is the basic model of politics: conflict resolution through negotiation. Controversy surrounds this method. Many would agree that the method accurately describes decision making, but fewer support or condone choices made on this basis. We will look further at the criticisms of the model in this chapter.

A third method is currently emerging in organization theory and administrative practice. The Delphi process and related techniques are termed here *aggregative* methods of decision making; they appear increasingly as consultant-assisted methods for policymaking and program development with staff or external governing boards. Consensus and equal participation are hallmarks of the methods. An understanding of the political and technical implications of these methods is critical to successful use.

The fourth model, called by March and Olsen (1979a) the *garbage can* or nondecision-making model, is an attempt to devise a descriptive model of choice that rejects even the limited rationality of incrementalism and focuses on the expressive character of decision making in organizations. In this model, attention is drawn to the ways in which discussions drift from the agenda and encompass a variety of personal and social issues as well as, or even instead of, the problems before the group. Some decisions emerge only by default, and can almost be described as unintended. Perhaps most important, the decision-making process is viewed as uncovering and articulating goals in the process of the discussion of alternatives rather than evaluating the best way to achieve those goals. The process poses a serious challenge to conventional views of how governmental decisions are reached.

We will compare these methods by focusing on three elements of decision making: the search for alternatives, the analysis of alternatives, and the choice criterion by which one alternative is finally selected. Thus, the final act of choice is only one element in the complex decision-making process, where the search for alternatives and the techniques for examining those alternatives are critical. Taken together, the three elements provide a general definition of decision making: an elaborate process by which alternative courses of action are identified and analyzed in preparation for the final selection.

Search is concerned with the bureau's techniques for generating alternatives to improve current operations; the methods differ radically in their search procedures. Brainstorming to identify innovations is a key feature of the aggregative method, whereas, by design, few really novel alternatives emerge in the incremental method. The *analysis* element also clearly differentiates the methods. The rational method is quantitative and uses an array of analytic techniques from economics and engineering. Incrementalism also uses a sophisticated calculus, but it is political calculus and is therefore based on determining how the benefits from each alternative are distributed among the contending interests. Finally, the *choice* criterion differentiates the methods. The rationalist's criterion is to select the alternative that provides the optimum return for the resources expended, whereas in the aggregative method, the selection is done by having participants vote to rank order the alternatives. Figure 7–1 highlights the differences among the methods based on these three elements.

However, before looking at these three elements of decision making, a few words need to be said about one other aspect of decision making that influences the process and is often out of the control of the administrator, especially if the process deals with important policy issues. *Definition* influences search, analysis, and choice. How the problem gets defined often places limitations on the later processes, for example, disallowing search in certain areas of possible alternatives because of values, political beliefs, or the tactics of the administrators' political "bosses." Likewise, analysis is influenced by the definition

FIGURE 7–1   Elements of the Decision Process

	Search	*Analysis*	*Choice*
Rational	Preselected	Quantitative	Optimize gains
Incremental	Linked to status quo	Resource distribution	Group agreement
Aggregative	Brainstorming	Participation of experts	Group ranking
Garbage can	Personal agendas	Sequential comparison	Choice is an artifact

of the problem, as is choice of an alternative to put into effect. Many times the definition is determined by the setting of the organization in the public sector.

The Setting of Decision Making in Public Organizations

Several aspects of the settings for decisions in public agencies influence decisions. First, the domain or level of decision determines the degree to which administrators can act autonomously (at least under some constitutional arrangements) in making decisions. Second, a number of theorists argue that the bureau setting limits the search for alternatives and thus narrows the options for choice. Third, the decision-making process in the organization is affected by the organization's communications, information-processing, and control systems. Finally, the bureau's political setting, its external relations, and the strength of its supporters and detractors influence the decisions made and perhaps the methods used as well since, in part, methods are linked to the substance of solutions.

As we noted earlier, questions about the proper domain of administrative decision making have been the subject of lengthy and intense debate in public administration. Kraemer and Perry (1983), in one of many portrayals of the various domains of organizational choice, suggest three levels of problems for organizations: operational, programming-management, and development or planning decisions. The appropriate type of analysis for problems at the day-to-day operational level is said to be the quantitative techniques such as operations research. These are choices where efficiency is the foremost concern and administrative autonomy in analysis and choice is most clearly appropriate. Kraemer and Perry further argue that decisions about program design are more appropriately made with a mix of qualitative and quantitative methods such as simulations of the specific social or economic system under analysis. Planning or development choices that involve organization goals are seen as susceptible to qualitative analysis, such as the Delphi process.

Organization theory has not been particularly concerned with the link between the level of decision and the method of choice used to make it since the primary concern of the field as a whole has been with firms where such differences are usually matters of internal policy. We must be concerned about this link, however, because of the political and legal constraints on administrative authority over policymaking. We will consider these issues further when we examine the various decision-making models, and we will reexamine the assumptions behind this schema at the close of the chapter.

Another characteristic of decision making in bureaus that has frequently been commented on, especially by theorists writing from an economic perspective, is that the search for alternatives in bureaus is typically extremely limited; genuinely new options and innovations from which to choose are rare. A reason for this phenomenon, which is attributed to organizational factors in bureaus, is their reliance on standard operating procedures, scenarios, or what March and Simon (1993) term *performance programs*. What this term means is that the ways in which officials come up with alternatives is specified or programmed in advance. Most of what we call routine or programmed decisions are fully codified with respect to both the identification of options and the method and criterion for choice. This high degree of programming serves to make the bureau stable, consistent, and predictable, as required of an agent of law, but it also makes the bureau rigid and reduces the possibility for innovation. The incrementalists are especially concerned with this constraint on decision making and discuss it at some length.

Decision making in any organization is also influenced by the control and communication processes. As noted earlier, the communication system is the backbone of most types of organizational control because it is through communication that monitoring of compliance with past program and policy choices is conducted. Communication is critical to the integration of the specialized structures in the organization. It is also important in decision making because, regardless of the type of decision method used, some kind of information about the needs and opportunities of the organization, its resources, internal conflicts, and concentrations of influence are used as a basis for choice. If some information is suppressed or highlighted, and this is common (as described in Chapter 5), this distortion may be reflected in the decision. The timeliness of information, the extent to which the control system "notices" and can report departures from programs, the credibility and legitimacy of the information in the control system for professionals, and the degree to which we understand how to use the information in the control system to reform or improve the agency's programs all influence decision making. Each method of decision making has a different sensitivity to the weaknesses of communication and control systems, and we will consider these in our discussions of each of the models.

The political setting of decision making has a direct bearing on the specific choice made, and each model describes a different approach to incorporating political preferences—whether of officials or external actors—into the choice. For some policy analysts, these questions are not broached, at least overtly, and issues are examined on the basis of economic factors. In other models of decision making, political factors are openly considered, and choice involves a form of political calculus. The aggregative methods attempt to shun politics and eliminate it as an element in choice. We will note these assumptions about the role of the political setting in each model—even though some models purport to ignore political issues.

The purpose of this chapter, then, is to describe and contrast the various methods of decision making and to raise questions about the techniques and assumptions of each one. After considering some of the commonly raised criticisms of each method, we will contrast the methods in terms of search, analysis, and choice in an effort to set the stage for the development of a contingency theory that links the methods to different conditions of choice.

THE RATIONAL-POLICY ANALYSIS METHOD

The rational method of decision making was long considered the ideal choice process in both the public and the private sector. With an emphasis on analyzing a broad range of alternatives and a goal of optimizing efficiency and return on investment, the rational method was the ideal model for decision making. The emphasis on efficiency in achieving policy or goals set by external policymakers was well suited to the bureaucracy's role— at least in principle.

With the advent of research on administrative behavior, however, the rational method was criticized more and more for what were considered its unrealistic idealized assumptions, and it was overshadowed by the more empirically descriptive models, such as incrementalism and satisficing. The rational method has taken on new importance, however, in the context of policy and systems analysis. Modified forms of the classic rational model are now practiced as policy analysis though they are used selectively owing to their costliness and elaborateness. (See Figure 10–3, p. 364, for an example of systems analysis techniques that are often used in rational-analytic decision models.)

The rational-policy analysis method is rational in only one of two senses of the term. What we call rational choice is rational in that it attempts to select the most efficient means or instrument to realize a given purpose or goal; hence, it is sometimes called instrumental rationality. It is concerned with identifying the alternative that produces the most of a desired effect or the greatest level of return. Efficiency is the only value that is promoted. In contrast, substantive rationality is concerned with many kinds of values, with the "goodness" of the goal or purpose itself. The questions posed by substantive rationality are is it desirable, and should we want it if we are rational? What is substantively rational is generally debated by political philosophers, and in more immediate terms, by the legislative bodies, courts, and other policymakers in government. In general, we expect that administrative agencies will be more occupied with instrumental than substantive rationality, more with means than ends. As we will see, however, the distinction between policymaking and choosing the most efficient means or programs for the policy is not easily maintained in practice.

Instrumental rationality as a decision-making process is generally characterized by four steps (March and Simon 1993). First, the goal or end of the policy is considered a given for the situation under consideration; that is, it is assumed that goals are set by external policymakers. It is also usually specified that all feasible alternatives or means to accomplish the goal are givens. Thus, in *principle,* search, the process that determines which alternatives will be considered, is not in the hands of administrators. This is one of the model's assumptions that is commonly found difficult and unrealistic. In fact, administrators usually determine the pool of alternatives to be analyzed, and political and technical considerations typically enter into the selection.

In the second step, the alternative programs or procedures are subjected to a thorough analysis to identify all the consequences, desirable and undesirable, intended and unintended, that are associated with each alternative. These consequences may be known with certainty or may involve an element of uncertainty or risk. The analysis of these alternatives usually involves forecasting on the basis of experience.

The third step, a critical one, is to rank these alternatives according to a consistent ordering of preference for the set of consequences associated with each. Since each alternative has a different set of consequences, we must rank the consequences as steps toward ranking the alternatives. For example, among the alternatives under consideration, some may have economic and environmental consequences, others educational consequences. The importance of these consequences to the decision maker must be ranked before he or she can make an instrumentally rational choice.

— In the fourth step, the alternative with the greatest amount of the most-valued consequences is chosen. The requirements of optimal efficiency have been met. The choice criterion is to optimize benefits or to select the alternative with the highest value. The simplicity of the final step is possible only because of the complexity of the preceding steps.

Instrumental rationality was long used as the normative standard against which to judge decisions in administration and elsewhere even though by far the majority of decisions did not follow this method. Renewed interest in designing methods to improve instrumental rationality has sprung up with the advent of policy analysis and systems analysis in administration. Policy analysis is also concerned with examining the consequences of proposed alternative policies, programs, and operating procedures; it uses various economic and mathematical methods of analysis.

The rational decision method can be applied at any level of decision making. It is typically viewed as advisory to the policymaking process when goals and policies are at stake. The method is of direct and immediate administrative use for identifying efficient programs and operating procedures, however. Although this distinction between decisions about means and ends is maintained in principle, it is not so clearly maintained in practice. This raises questions, of course, about the uses of the method.

Criticisms of the Rational-Policy Analysis Method

Questions have been raised about this decision-making method in terms of both its general feasibility and its use by public administrators. James March and Herbert Simon (1993) look at decision making as the core administrative activity and identify three unrealistic assumptions in the rational model. First, it is not clear how or by whom the alternatives to be analyzed and ranked are identified. Clearly, not all possible alternatives are examined; imagination is limited, and selective perception is common. What sample of options is identified and studied, and on what basis are they selected? The model does not specify this or assumes that the alternatives are selected by policymakers. In essence, the research process, which is critical in determining the findings, is left unspecified. This may leave the way open for arbitrary or nonanalytic selection to start. The objectivity of the search process and its fidelity to the principle of efficiency are called into question if political considerations determine which possible programs will be analyzed.

The second of March and Simon's criticisms is that the rational method assumes the consequences of each alternative can be known, even if not with certainty. That is, the method assumes that the degree of risk or uncertainty will be known. This is a questionable assumption at best, as illustrated by such errors of planning and forecasting as the swine flu epidemic that never was, the aborted Iranian hostage rescue effort, the overestimation of the rate of increase in demand for electricity from nuclear power, and the underestimation of costs for programs like Medicare. Not only do we over- or underestimate consequences, we also miss whole categories of consequences known as "*unanticipated consequences.*" This is not a criticism of the often considerable talents of forecasters and planners, but a counter to the too grandiose claims made for the rational method and its comprehensiveness.

Finally, March and Simon criticize the classical rational method for its assumption that the decision maker, whether an individual or a group, has a consistent preference ordering for the consequences of the alternatives. The difficulty here is that few real options for new programs, for example, have only one *kind* of consequence; usually many consequences, desirable and undesirable, accompany a program. To fulfill the requirements of the rational method, we must not only make comparisons among a set of alternatives on the basis of one type of consequence (environmental effects, for example), but also compare all the various consequences of the alternatives. Do we, for example, prefer alternative A, which has some good but unlikely health consequences and some desirable environmental consequences, or alternative B, which as a better chance of producing good health consequences but worse environmental and economic consequences? The problem is to establish a *consistent* ordering of preferences across the different alternatives being compared: This is an immense task even for a single individual, and the problem of finding such an ordering for a group is even greater. Economist Kenneth Arrow has shown that there is no unambiguous procedure for measuring and combining the preferences of two or more individuals to provide a ranking of total social preference (Stokey and Zeckhauser 1978, 276).

The problem of finding a consistent preference ordering for the various consequences of different alternatives was an important theoretical stumbling block for policy analysis. The way analysts have coped with this difficulty is to transform all types of consequences into one—money. Cost–benefit analysis is a key form of policy analysis. It is based on comparing the monetary value to society of all costs and all benefits of each alternative: then only one kind of consequence—financial—must be compared to find the optimal solution. The alternative that maximizes net benefit to society is the "best" and thus the one that is selected.

The rationale for this practice is found in two decision criteria. The Pareto criterion, named after the Italian economist and sociologist, states that a change should be made if at least one person benefits by it and none are any worse off. This, of course, is a rare occurrence. More commonly applied is the Kaldor–Hicks criterion, named after two British economists, which argues that if a policy change makes the "gainers" so much better off that they can compensate the "losers" and still come out ahead, the policy should be undertaken. There is no requirement that this compensation actually take place, so in practice this criterion simply recommends that we maximize net benefits, that is, benefits minus costs. This apparently undemocratic principle is justified on the grounds that in the long run the various program advantages will even out among the groups (Stokey and Zeckhauser 1978). Recent analysis does in some cases look carefully at the specific distribution of a program's benefits to ensure that it will have the intended effect though doing so does not address the problem of equity in distributing compensation.

There are some commonly noted drawbacks to the cost–benefit method that point up further weaknesses in the rational-policy analysis method. First, there is considerable disagreement over the ways in which intangible benefits and costs are assigned monetary worth. This debate raises questions about race, gender, and other "human" political

The Results of Absolute Efficiency

a la Frank Herbert

(Are "efficiency" and "rational decision making" appropriate goals in and of themselves? Writers often test concepts and ideas by carrying them to their ultimate conclusion: Science fiction author Frank Herbert examines these two concepts in his series of books about Jorj X. McKie, Sabateur Extraordinary, and arrives at one possible outcome of such development. In his version, absolute efficiency and rationality are so dangerous that they must be stopped at any cost.)

McKie began reflecting on his role in the affairs of sentiency. Once, long centuries past, consentients with a psychological compulsion to "do good" had captured the government. Unaware of the writhing complexities, the mingled guilts and self-punishments, beneath their compulsion, they had eliminated virtually all delays and red tape from government. The great machine with its blundering power over sentient life had slipped into high gear, had moved faster and faster. Laws had been conceived and passed in the same hour. Appropriations had flashed into being and were spent in a fortnight. New bureaus for the most improbable purposes had leaped into existence and proliferated like some insane fungus.

Government had become a great destructive wheel without a governor, whirling with such frantic speed that it spread chaos wherever it touched.

In desperation, a handful of sentients had conceived the Sabotage Corps to slow that wheel. There had been bloodshed and other degrees of violence, but the wheel had been slowed. In time, the Corps had become a Bureau, and the Bureau was whatever it was today— an organization headed into its own corridors of entropy, a group of sentients who preferred subtle diversion to violence . . . but were prepared for violence when the need arose.

SOURCE: Frank Herbert, *Whipping Star*. New York: Berkeley Pub. Corp., 1969, p. 11.

issues about which there is intense disagreement. In the area of prevention of injury or diseases, how should life or the absence of disability be valued monetarily? Clearly, different people expend different amounts of money and effort to preserve health; whereas some jog and eat broiled fish, others enjoy steaks and cigarettes. A measure of the value of health that has been widely used is the amount of lost productivity to the economy caused by illnesses of various kinds. Income losses for workers of different types, for example, are taken as an estimate of lost productivity. The problem with such an estimate is that it places the highest value on preserving the health of young white males at the expense of women, minorities, and older people. Although correction factors are now used with such data, their use illustrates the biases that can enter into efforts to monetize intangible factors.

Another drawback of cost–benefit analysis as the cornerstone of a decision-making method is that it substitutes judgment based on economic factors or technical efficiency for professional judgment. Cohen (1980) argues that the use of cost–benefit analysis in the area of weapons systems makes it impossible to consider the value of flexible or multiple uses and strategies of some systems. The analysis asks instead what is the most cost-efficient means to fulfill a particular policy or mission. Cohen argues that this question places economists and engineers in the position of assessing the capacity of various weapons systems to fulfill some narrowly defined functions without considering the political or psychological factors associated with war or the need for flexibility. For example, a nuclear-powered ship costs much more than a conventionally powered one; therefore, if both can perform the same mission, it is only rational to select the conventional ship. However, the psychological deterrence capacity of a nuclear-powered fleet may be greater than that of a conventionally powered one, and a nuclear ship may respond better in unanticipated conditions, so a military judgment would favor nuclear power. Thus, Cohen shows, military judgments are overshadowed by the technical requirements of the choice process. In general, there is concern that using the cost–benefit technique as the principal method of choice will result in a far too heavy emphasis on the measurable quantitative aspects of the alternatives under analysis and too little attention to professional judgments and intangibles.

These criticisms are countered by advocates who note that some analysis is better than none and certainly better than politically motivated efforts to obscure differences among policies. Even flawed analyses improve our choices by forcing us to examine our assumptions and their consequences. For example, problems in monetizing intangibles often merely reflect current social practices that should be scrutinized and changed. In sum, even problematic analyses can not only be remedied, but can lead to greater awareness of inequities in prevailing social and political practices.

Finally, the issue of the political impact of the cost–benefit method has been the subject of some debate. In general, advocates of the method argue that it is objective and apolitical in any partisan sense, and that in the realm of policymaking, its role is advisory rather than determinative. Thus, they do not overstep the distinction between policymaking and administration. Critics of the method argue that since it reflects a change in who makes decisions and how, changes in the political system are inevitable. Further, Gawthrop argues, "There are no neutral tools of administration, . . . and if, as some have contended, the analytical approach knows no politics, it will learn in short order if it is to survive" (1971, 75).

Illustrations of the political uses of some analyses include the finding by Merewitz and Sosnick (1971, 118) that program agencies, beneficiaries, and Democrats tend to favor low discount rates, a component of cost–benefit analysis that makes projects appear more efficient, whereas budget agencies, taxpayers, and Republicans tend to favor higher rates. Agencies may also place very different discount rates on the same project, showing the degree to which the analysis is subject to differences of opinion. When debating a major political policy like health care, the same data is used by the president, congressional Republicans and Democrats, the Congressional Budget Office, and various interest groups to produce literally dozens of different "results" showing the impact of any particular set of programs, procedures, charges, and taxes. Thus, both the possibility and the desirability of a wholly objective and apolitical stance for the rational-policy analysis decision process is questionable. Perhaps political questions require political processes to solve them. The incremental method is the most clearly political method.

THE INCREMENTAL MODEL AND RELATED METHODS

The 1950s brought behaviorism to the study of decision making and a concern for descriptive accuracy not met by the prescriptively oriented rational model in its original form. Decision making became an important focus of organization theory, perhaps because it was a relatively easily studied behavior. Decision theorists of that era developed several models that attempted to be empirically accurate, in particular, the incremental and satisficing methods.

In general, the incremental model portrays decision making as a bargaining process among interested participants, each of whom attempts to achieve some improvement in resources such as budgets, personnel, program authority, or autonomy. The "best" alternative is the one on which participants can agree. For the solution to be acceptable, each party must be better off by some increment of benefit. The classic description of the method was provided by Lindblom (1959).

Incrementalism is characterized by compromise—decisions that change programs or policies in small steps—and thus never depart far from the status quo. This is explained by the fact that incremental decision making is a bargaining process in which persuasion, debate, and negotiation, not analysis as the rationalist uses the term, are the key features. Proposals and counterproposals are exchanged until a mutually acceptable solution is found. The immediate vicinity of the status quo is a good source of such solutions because only a renegotiation of any new or changed resources and needs is required rather than a comprehensive renegotiation of all resources. Such a renegotiation would be lengthy and conflict ridden. The incremental process strives to minimize conflict and allow the gradual testing of new ideas.

The incremental solution generally focuses on tangible programs and projects rather than on more abstract goals and policy statements. It is, Lindblom (1959) notes, much easier to compromise over concrete project components, such as the features of an educational grant or a highway project, than it is to bargain over ideology, principles, and goals. Program components can be apportioned among participants as part of the bargain, but goals and abstract policy statements are not so easily parceled out. Compromises about program size and resource share can be resolved without reopening the much more basic but intense issues of whether or not the goals are appropriate and the program should exist in the first place. In consequence, decisions made by the incremental method tend to be crisis oriented, internally fragmented, and even contradictory, and are characterized as a series of changes in program activities rather than a specific statement of policy or organizational outcome.

Although the incremental method is well suited to describing the activities of political decision-making groups such as legislatures, it also allows for a good description of budget and policy decision making in bureaus, where multiple levels and divisions are involved in program development. In the case of administrative decision making, persuasion and bargaining occur among officials linked to professional, organizational, and constituency interests.

In summarizing the incremental over the rationalist method, Lindblom (1959) characterizes the incremental method as follows. First, clear value preferences are rare despite what the rationalist model claims. Generally, decision makers can attach preferences only to specific proposals that may reflect abstract goals and values only indirectly. This is why incremental decision makers bargain over programs. A second characteristic deriving from this is that means (policies and programs) are not distinguishable from ends (goals and values). Third, the test of a "good policy" is that the actors agree on it even though they may not be able to agree on its underlying values. Fourth, the analysis of alternatives is limited both in number and depth by considering only a few alternatives that depart marginally from the status quo. This means that some important new policy directions will be ignored and some legitimate values will not be heard, but Lindblom argues that the range of interests represented among the decision makers in the whole cycle is so broad that a nearly comprehensive range of realistically possible issues and options are, in fact, considered. Thus, what appears as a fragmented process, is really the working out of a decentralized pluralistic system that automatically coordinates itself as actors compete for support. The pluralistic assumptions of the method are a major justification for it; the method reflects the political system. Last, decisions reflect a series of successive approximations to multiple desired ends or values. This is necessarily a political rather than an empirically analytical process because we do not have the theoretical understanding of how to achieve policy success. Thus, the incremental method of successive approximations avoids costly or lasting mistakes and moves gradually toward the multiple goals of a complex pluralistic society.

Innovation and Incrementalism

The search processes associated with the incremental method are very limited for several reasons. Lindblom (1959) argues that the bargaining process favors limited change. But other theorists see bureaucratic organization itself as responsible for limited search that favors options close to the status quo. The search for new programs and approaches requires planning, research, and professional development, all of which are costly and take personnel away from their ongoing work. Incremental changes are easier to correct if found to be wrong. The tendency of administrators to spend time on immediately pressing projects and to react to crises rather than to plan is commonly observed. The high degree of organizational and program specialization in most bureaus, especially the older, more entrenched ones, also works against the pursuit of novel programs (Downs 1967).

Another interesting and well-developed thesis about the causes of narrow search is that new decision options are limited by the bureau's standard operating procedures. March and Simon (1993) characterize standard operating procedures as a series of organizational performance programs composed of an elaborate and more or less rigid set of prescribed routine activities. These programs are the product of program development and reflect operating improvements added over a period of years to make program mechanisms operate smoothly, reliably, and efficiently. When a problem is encountered, the bureau with highly codified procedures will be able to deal with the situation in an efficient, programmed way, choosing the routine that dovetails with other established routines. Although this process is very efficient, it limits the development of innovative alternatives to deal with problems. Graham Allison (1971) illustrates the drawbacks of highly codified performance routines in his study of the U.S. response to Soviet missiles in Cuba; the routine procedures for classifying and acting on certain military situations virtually blinded military advisors to other alternatives.

Comments on Rulemaking: They Measure Pressure, Seldom Change Minds

There is more ado to interpret interpretations than to interpret the things and more books upon books than upon all other subjects; we do nothing but comment upon one another.

Michel de Montaigne

The people in the Office of Adolescent Pregnancy Programs, with 80,000 written comments sitting in front of them, know what the 16th century French philosopher was talking about.

When the Health and Human Services Department moved this spring to require doctors to notify a teen-ager's parents before dispensing contraceptive devices, the agency, thanks to a 1946 law, had to publish its proposal in the Federal Register and solicit public reaction. As a result, four staffers have been opening, sorting, analyzing and summarizing comments for nearly six months.

Except in emergencies and special cases, the federal government must announce its intensions and invite response every time it tries to make or change a rule. This often means a time-consuming, exasperating and predictable ritual for everyone involved—regulators, lobbyists and citizens alike, according to those familiar with the procedure. Yet a recent effort to short circuit the process has met with a strongly negative response by some of the same people who find it most exasperating.

Why does this procedural issue matter so much to so many people? According to lobbyists, government officials and experts in administrative law, there are a variety of reasons, both theoretical and practical.

Philosophically, "its important for the legitimacy of government to say, 'We will listen to anybody about this issue,'" said a former Carter administration regulatory expert. "I think it is fundamental that people have a chance to participate in decisions, however marginal that participation may be."

That's the theory. In practice, according to one lawyer-lobbyist who often drafts comments for a variety of regulatory agencies, "comments rarely change minds."

Groups . . . who use a comment period as a political referendum, usually give regulatory officials few facts to consider but effectively convey the volatility of an issue. "This sort of thing is far more influential in terms of indicating the strength of the opinions held than giving us a particular view of the state of the world and answering the substantive questions we've asked," said Richard Wilson, an FERC official who has analyzed many of these comments.

Mike Roudemeyer, a staffer at the Federal Trade Commission, agrees. As a procedural device, he said, the comment period works to the benefit of lobbyists who object to something an agency proposes to do.

"Using comments as a referendum, a vote, that's not really very effective," Roudemeyer added. Yet when a friend suggested that he write HHS's Office of Adolescent Pregnancy Programs protesting the proposed rule on parental consent, he was tempted.

"I saw it as a political rule," Roudemeyer said, "and in that situation you should bring political pressure to bear."

SOURCE: Felicity Barringer, *Washington Post*, October 6, 1982: A23.

James Q. Wilson, though agreeing that the use of standard operating procedures does limit choice processes, argues that the limitations come from the political environment and not from within the organization. First, the constraints that limit choices, which are said to be the result of the "bureaucracy's love of red tape," do not come from the bureaucracy at all. Most of the rules producing this complexity would not be generated by the bureaucracy if it had a choice, "and many are as cordially disliked by the bureaucrats as by their clients." These rules are imposed on the agencies by external actors, chiefly legislators. The rules are not bureaucratic but political ones. Legislators—whatever they may claim—value "fairness" over effectiveness (Wilson 1989, 121–122).

Second, the government bureaus develop standard operating procedures to reduce the chance that an important contextual goal or constraint is not violated. The bureau cannot serve a single, primary goal, for example, "making a profit." In addition to its primary goal, any government agency:

> must serve a large number of contextual goals—that is descriptions of desired states of affairs other than the one the agency was brought into being to create. For example, a police department not only must try to prevent crime and catch criminals, it must protect the rights of the accused, safeguard the confidentiality of its records, and provide necessary health services to arrestees. These other goals define the context within which the primary goals can be sought. (129)

Whatever the cause of the development of standard operating procedures, once established these routines are not easily altered. Because they represent great "sunk costs" with respect to training, personnel, and the specialization of facilities and equipment, the most rational (efficient) response to a novel situation is to redefine the situation to fit the routine, or to modify in some small way an existing routine, or to combine existing programs. Only if protests or damaging failures result will new routines and new alternatives be created, usually at considerable cost. Other conditions associated with gaining extended search are new funds especially allocated for it (Montjoy and O'Toole 1979) and such things as allowing a long time for decision making, bringing many and diverse people into the decision process, increasing the number of highly skilled people in the process, and isolating decision makers from other (especially short-term) responsibilities (Downs 1967, 185).

In sum, for the incrementalist, two lines of reasoning explain why final decisions and even the options for choice do not depart much from the status quo in bureaus. First, the bargaining process requires the distribution of limited resources to a coalition large enough to gain adoption of the alternative. Generally, the easiest way to ensure such support is to distribute new resources on the basis of past resource distributions rather than confronting fundamental questions of value. The latter course of action could result in conflict and deadlock. Second, the search process is limited by the standardized operating procedures that make the bureau consistent and efficient.

Satisficing

An alternative formulation that resembles the incremental method in several ways is the satisficing method of organizational decision making offered by March and Simon (1993). Compared with the rational method, both search and the process of analyzing alternatives are simplified, but these steps are somewhat more rational than the process in the incremental model. Satisficing takes the perspective of a single decision maker or a unified group and attempts to optimize, rather than maximize, the return or results from the choice among possible alternatives. The first step in this process, after agreeing on a goal, is for the decision maker to choose the desired level of response to be sought as the available alternatives are screened. The desired level is seldom, if ever, the best possible response, but instead is a choice aimed at what would appear to be a reasonable improvement given what is known about the current situation. It is an educated guess based on imperfect knowledge and, if a group is involved, it may be a choice based on agreement over which step is to be taken without agreeing on the ultimate end of the policy. The agreement on a goal for "improvement," however, means that the decision maker is attempting to reach beyond the first alternative that shows any improvement in the situation to a predetermined level of improvement. This adds one level of rationality in the form of forethought about desired goals related to this decision.

Once the level of improvement is agreed on, the first alternative encountered that meets or exceeds the decision maker's expectations or demands will be chosen. If, after search, such alternatives are not found, the decision maker's expectations and the minimum standard will decline. Thus, the standard is flexible over time since experience with the environment informs the decision maker's expectations.

In contrast to the incremental model in which various alternatives are examined simultaneously, satisficing examines alternatives sequentially, being content with the first one to meet the minimum standard. Search is likewise sequential and is limited to the vicinity of the status quo for the same reasons we identified earlier. March and Simon contrast their method with the rationalist one as "the difference between searching a haystack to find the sharpest needle in it and searching a haystack to find a needle sharp enough to sew with" (1993, 162).

The differences between Lindblom's incremental model and the satisficing model are interesting. Satisficing assumes a preestablished standard rather than a group negotiation process. In this way, satisficing is closer to the rational model. Further, the sequence in which alternatives are discovered is much more important in the satisficing model so that the search process, current environmental events, and professional interests are likely to have more of an impact with satisficing than with incrementalism. Both models reveal the dynamics of organizational decision making, however, and they may be related. Satisficing appears to describe how individual decision makers act, whereas the incremental model more often describes group or interactive decision making in larger, perhaps more political, settings.

Mixed Scanning

Mixed scanning is another variation on the incremental model, and one that attempts to rectify some of that model's limitations. Etzioni (1967) describes mixed scanning as a dual method of search and decision making that does not fully accept either the rationalist model, which is expensive and slow, or the incrementalist model, which is biased toward status quo groups and issues. Rather, a cursory review of all alternatives is followed by a detailed analysis of the most promising options. In this way, innovations have a chance to be noticed, but a full-scale search need not be done each time.

The decisions are also of mixed types. For example, a series of incremental decisions may follow a more fundamental choice of values. To focus on either type to the exclusion of the other is unwise and unrealistic.

Thus, the mixed scanning method is offered both as a description and a prescription. It is descriptive in that fundamental change is more common than can be accounted for by the incremental method; it is prescriptive in its criticism of incrementalism and in its emphasis on the importance of fundamental, value-ordering decisions.

Criticisms

The incremental model is subject to criticisms on both technical and political bases. Technical criticisms include the fact that, without systematic planning and analysis, decisions assume a short-term perspective, neglect basic social innovations, and lead to policy drift (Etzioni 1967). Available research and experience may not be effectively incorporated into new choices. Conflict may become a major problem, sapping the energy of the decision process and leading to stalemate and costly delays in action. Innovation, as noted earlier, is not a common result of incrementalism, and this may retard program development as promising new alternatives are rejected, or more likely, never even considered.

Criticisms of the political consequences of the method include the charge by both Gawthrop (1971) and Etzioni (1967) that it disenfranchises significant portions of the population. Etzioni further notes that the method is set to reflect only well-organized powerful interests that have influence with legislative and administrative decision makers; only those who have the skill and resources to "play the game" can participate. The pluralism claimed for the model is seen as providing only very limited access to decision making. Further, Gawthrop argues that the process is dominated by intense regional interests to the detriment of less well-organized national interests. Finally, both Gawthrop and Etzioni note that the model is pro inertia and serves, in fact, as a justification for responsiveness only to influential interests. Intangible values, such as equity, are also generally ignored since they cannot be adapted to piecemeal distribution. In sum, incrementalism rests on a pluralistic model of American politics but cannot fully live up to the demands of that political model. At least partly in response to these criticisms, an attempt to eradicate influence from decision making is seen in the aggregative method.

AGGREGATIVE METHODS OF DECISION MAKING

Over the years, a third method of group decision making has emerged in public and private sector organizations. The techniques included under this method are prescriptive, that is, we are urged to use them to solve problems. Examples of the method include such consultant-assisted processes as the Delphi technique and the nominal group technique (NGT). We will examine the nominal group technique in detail to study this form of decision making.

In general, with these techniques, group members are coached on how to generate a wide range of alternatives. One alternative is finally selected through some type of voting or consensus process. The final choice is said to be an accurate composite (or aggregation) of individual preferences rather than a negotiated synthesis of preferences as emerges in the incremental method. The aggregative methods seek to avoid the political conflict and stalemate that may arise under incrementalism. Advocates argue that the aggregative methods allow groups: (1) to generate a broader, more diverse, and more innovative set of alternatives than either the rationalist or incrementalist methods; (2) to avoid the stifling influence of status and claims of expertise by some participants; and (3) to avoid the constraints of overroutinized standard operating procedures. Brainstorming is encouraged, and premature criticism of new ideas is avoided. The hallmark of these techniques is that they attempt to maintain a healthy, well-balanced level of group interaction without imposing excessive conformity or allowing excessive conflict, as is found in some bureaus and elected bodies.

The groups using these techniques include agency staff, external expert advisory councils, and elected boards and councils. Often the techniques are used for planning, for identifying and setting priorities among problems and projects, for identifying future needs and resources, and for goal setting. Implementation tactics and timetables may also be included in their process.

The Delphi technique is typically used as a planning or forecasting method in which experts in a field are assembled and asked to individually generate a list of future states regarding some problem in the field. For example, the International City Management Association might want to know "What will be the top priorities of city managers in the year 2010?" These lists are collated and fed back to the group for discussion and another round of list making, ranking, and feedback. This process may be repeated several times to narrow the alternatives under consideration and reach some consensus about priorities or future probabilities.

Although the Delphi process affords much less interaction than the incremental method, the nominal group technique (NGT) allows less interaction than either the Delphi or incremental methods and illustrates the procedures and assumptions of the increasingly popular aggregative method of decision making. The name of the technique, nominal group, tells us its orientation. The participants form a group in name only. Interaction of any kind, but especially political exchange, is kept to a minimum. Expressing individual ideas and preferences free from the influence of others is the technique's chief characteristic. In their description of the NGT, Delbecq, Van de Ven, and Gustavson note, for example, that it is important to "reduce status barriers among members, encourage free communication, and decrease the tendency for high status individuals to be unduly verbal" (1975, 42). Each phase in the NGT shows its emphasis on minimizing interaction that could confound the natural inclinations of the participants.

The first stage in the process is establishing a clear question or problem for the group to work on. This is the consultant's job. The question should be clear, direct, and specific enough so that the results will readily translate into action. Coke and Moore illustrate a good and a poor question:

> *Poor question*: "What are the goals to be achieved and the projects and programs to be undertaken in the city's community developments?"
> *Good question*: "What obstacles do you anticipate to carrying out the city's housing rehabilitation programs?"
> (n.d., 3)

The decision process itself begins with the "silent generation of ideas in writing" (Delbecq, Van de Ven, and Gustavson 1975, 44) in which each participant in a group of five to nine people works as an individual on a list of goals, projects, or whatever is needed. The purpose of this individual exercise is to maximize the variety of views expressed at the outset without inhibition from group criticism. The next step is to have each participant read off the items on his or her list until all lists have been read and recorded. This simple step is important because it demonstrates to participants the breadth of possible solutions and the degree of consensus that already exists. It also prevents the group from prematurely settling on one definition of the problem (Delbecq, Van de Ven, and Gustavson 1975, 49).

Discussion of the items is not permitted until all have been recorded so as not to inhibit ideas. After recording is completed, however, as the third step in the process, each item is given a limited discussion, which serves to clarify its meaning and logic. Lobbying for an item or arguments are seriously discouraged, however, and group leaders are urged to intervene nondirectively and move the discussion along to the next item if conflict occurs. The intention here is to prevent high-status members from dominating the group "even though other members still disagree with his or her logic" (Delbecq, Van de Ven, and Gustavson 1975, 52).

The final steps in the process are concerned with voting to select the goal or program or to rank order the items that were generated. First, to reduce the number of items to be ranked, each participant is asked to select his or her highest priorities, generally five of them, which are then combined into a joint list for the group. From this list, the group then votes or uses some other ranking technique to identify the most favored items. Various voting procedures are used. For example, each participant may use a one through five numerical scale to rank his or her items. The item with the highest ranking is given top priority and so on. Having each participant use the more traditional system of voting for only one item is believed to underrepresent minority views and open the door to the kind of conflict and influence peddling that the technique is designed to avoid.

The object of the technique is to foster the expression of individual judgment. Consensus based on the true preferences of group members is thought to be fostered by having a preliminary round of rank ordering followed by discussion aimed at clarification of the pros and cons of each item. Computer-assisted ranking procedures have also been used to identify the group's choice. With these techniques, the actors vote their preference on a comparison of each pair of items, which yields an overall rank ordering (Ostrowski, White, and Cole 1984).

Questions and Criticisms

Research on the uses and results of the group process poses several questions that must be considered when the process is used. First, to what extent will the process be considered legitimate in an agency and by clientele? The incremental bargaining process is so ingrained in political life that a decision that eliminates negotiation and avoids the real, known distribution of influence may not be accepted. If the legitimacy of the process is questioned, the results will probably never be implemented.

A second question concerns the assumption by NGT advocates that the process gives the truest reading of group preference. Every step in the process is designed to eliminate the influence or persuasiveness of high-status or politically skillful leaders. The assumption that politics always acts to distort rather than articulate genuine preferences or interests should not go unquestioned: It rests on the broader unspoken judgment that politics serves only to manipulate unwary participants into acting against their real interests. This is a very narrow view of politics and one that rejects the possibility that politics can be a vehicle for articulating broad social interests and principles, and can provide an alternative to the strictly economic allocation system. Persuasion, as the first art of politics, can clarify as well as obscure interests. And bargaining, as the incrementalists show, is an effective way of resolving conflicts over goals and resources.

Yet group process advocates' desire to rid group decision making of seemingly useless conflict and delay is understandable, and the techniques described are effective for that purpose. Group members, as well as the external constituencies who depend on the group, become frustrated when stalemate and delay result from obstructive behavior. The incrementalists may consider these behaviors part of the process of partisan negotiation, but from the social-psychological perspective (refer to Chapter 3) of group process, they appear pathological and fruitless. At times, stalemate also appears politically purposeless, though, of course, it represents the blockage of unacceptable action by one group against another.

THE GARBAGE CAN OR NONDECISION-MAKING MODEL

March and Olsen's garbage can model of decision making (1979a) is an attempt to accurately describe decision making in organizations. It goes beyond the incremental model in identifying the limits in rationality, and suggests finally that the incremental and satisficing models posit a level of clarity of intentions, understanding of problems, and predictability in the relationship between individual and organizational actions that is unrealistic for most organizations. In actuality, they argue, decision making is a rather unreliable and ambiguous process for selecting courses of action. However, it does serve as a forum for individual and group expression of conflict, values, myths, friendships, and power. In important ways, decision making in organizations is more expressive of social and personal needs than it is strictly instrumental.

Rejecting the standard models of rational decision making that assume the consideration of differing means to a single, well-defined goal, the garbage can model views:

> a choice opportunity as a garbage can into which various problems and solutions are dumped [sic] by participants. The mix of garbage in a single can depends partly on the labels attached to the alternative cans; but it also depends on what garbage is being produced at the moment, on the mix of cans available, and on the speed with which garbage is collected and removed from the scene. (Cohen, March and Olsen 1979, 26)

In nonmetaphorical terms, decision making is viewed as an expressive activity that provides an opportunity for fulfilling roles or earlier commitments, for defining virtue and truth, interpreting events and goals, distributing glory and blame, reaffirming or rejecting friendships and status relations, expressing or discovering self-interest or group interest, socializing new members, and enjoying the pleasures of a group choice (March and Olsen 1979b, 11–12).

From the standpoint of this model, the rational and incremental models err in assuming too much certainty and knowledge in decision making. In reality, most decision-making situations are plagued with ambiguities of many sorts: Objectives are ambiguous; there is no clear set of preferences that represent the organization's intentions; causality is obscure;

technology is difficult to define, and environments are not easily understood; past events are interpreted differently by participants; and the attention and participation of key actors is uncertain since other activities and other decisions compete for their time (March and Olsen 1979b, 12).

The consequences of these factors are that decision making is not seen as a single-minded method for goal attainment in which the optimal means to the end is selected. Instead, decisions reflect shifts in the goals, beliefs, and attention of participants. Goals are defined—to the extent that they are ever clearly specified—only in the process of considering particular proposals and debating whether to accept or reject them. This pattern is shown in some of the case studies in the March and Olsen volume (Olsen 1979; Rommetveit 1979) and, with some adjustment in theory, by Anderson (1983) in his analysis of the Cuban missile crisis.

Anderson found no evidence that a set of alternatives was considered and an optimal one selected in that case (as the rational or even the incremental model would have us believe). Rather, he found that the decision was made through a series of binary (yes–no) choices on specific proposals. The goals that were eventually said to be served by our actions in the crisis were not mentioned in early sessions and were "discovered," Anderson suggests, in the course of deliberations (1983, 211). For very difficult problems, the decision makers did not necessarily select choices they thought would solve the problems, but ones that had reasonably predictable consequences and were not expected to produce either very dangerous or successful results—what Anderson, after March and Simon (1993), terms a bland alternative. All these characteristics of decision making support aspects of the garbage can model though evidence of the expressive uses of the decision-making process was not studied in this case.

A variation on the garbage can model is the artifactual or nondecision model, which focuses on the unconscious and unintentional aspects of decision making. What we think of as decisions, Olsen suggests (1979), are often just a socially acceptable reconstruction of what has occurred. Calling something a decision does not necessarily mean that there has been an act of deliberative choice. This view of decision making illustrates a phenomenological perspective on organizations in which what we ordinarily think of as reality is largely a social construction. Decisions here are interesting fictions.

Questions and Criticisms

This model has not been as widely discussed and studied as the others, and its particular application in bureaus has not been given much attention though it appears that it is implicitly a model of bureaucratic decision making. The garbage can model is meant to be descriptive, but the circumstances in which it would tend to be more accurately descriptive than the incremental model have not yet been well explored. Olsen suggests that the nondecision model will be most accurate under conditions of change, that is, when organizational goals and opportunities are most ambiguous (1979, 83–85), but the case studies that accompany his essay do not necessarily bear out his generalization. The model is also said to apply under conditions of organized anarchy, but it is not clear what the limits are of that state.

Much is yet to be done with the model to explore its policy implications. It is an interesting model, however, that reflects the field's emerging concerns with socially constructed realities and the ways in which organizations integrate and socialize their members.

These four models of decision making—the rational, incremental, aggregative, and garbage can—will next be compared to assess their relative advantages and limitations, especially for decision making in public organizations.

SUMMARY AND CONTRAST OF THE METHODS

The four methods show some interesting differences with respect to the elements of the decision-making process discussed in the introduction: search, analysis, and choice. We will consider these differences after introducing some assumptions about culture—especially those parts of culture related to participation, accountability, and organizational setting—behind each method. Finally, in the last section of this chapter, we will discuss the importance of these differences for a contingency theory of administrative decision making.

Culture

The everyday operations of an organization are affected by its culture. As described by Gareth Morgan, "organization is now seen to reside in the ideas, values, norms, rituals, and beliefs that sustain organizations as socially constructed realities" (1986, 14). Organizations are minisocieties that have their own way of looking at the world, and therefore, of perceiving problems and establishing ways to resolve them.

> Thus one organization may see itself as a tight-knit team or family that believes in working together. Another may be permeated by the idea that "we're the best in the industry and intend to stay that way." Yet another may be highly fragmented, divided into groups that think about the world in very different ways, or that have different aspirations as to what their organization should be. Such patterns of belief or shared meaning, fragmented or integrated, and supported by various operating norms and rituals, can exert a decisive influence on the overall ability of the organization to deal with the challenges that it faces. (Morgan 1986, 121)

The culture of the organization, therefore, affects the way individuals operate, how the decision process is carried out, which of the various methods so far discussed in this chapter are acceptable, and what the probable outcomes or choices will be when resolving problems and opportunities. The composition of the membership, and the values and beliefs held by those individuals, will influence the choice of rational or incremental decision processes—or some method that falls between these extremes.

Search

The search process refers to staff activities, at all levels of the organization, to identify ways of improving the bureau's policies, programs, and operations. Search is an ongoing process in that we are always looking for ways to improve management and program administration. But as Downs notes, recognizing a "performance gap" and making a decision to change a basic program component meets with a great deal of resistance since it disrupts the elaborate standard operating procedures that surround managerial and administrative activities. The need for some fundamental change may only be recognized with difficulty after a turnover in personnel, or when a change in technology or in the power of the bureau forces a reappraisal of the bureau's performance (Downs 1967, 192–193). Inertia and the costliness of change battle against the desire by officials to make a revision so that they can do a better job, to fend off forced change from external actors, or to improve their own position in the bureau. Thus, even though search is ongoing, decision making is not.

In general, we would expect that the search process would be most exhaustive, systematic, and detailed under the rationalist method. The agenda of options would include policies, programs, or operational solutions that are new in the field, that have worked well elsewhere, or that seem, based on reason and experience, to offer some promise of success. These methods are most likely to be used where administrative staff with training in quantitative and economic analysis methods are the key participants and have major responsibilities for identifying the projects to be subjected to analysis.

In many discussions of the theory behind the rationalist-policy analysis method, little or no attention is paid to the search process. The identification of the alternatives to be analyzed is assumed to be part of the task of policymaking and therefore done by political actors outside the bureau. This limitation on the administrative analysts' role is an attempt to keep them from setting the agenda and thus essentially determining the outcome of political decisions.

In practice, however, the specific alternatives are typically selected by the analysts so that the distinction between politics and administration is not maintained in the strict sense. Advocates of a clear demarcation between politics and administration find much to criticize, therefore, in the rationalist-policy analysis method (Goldwin 1980). Some view the method as a threat to the other branches of government by the bureaucracy.

In contrast, the incremental method's search process is characterized as limited, unsystematic, and perhaps too much controlled by outside political actors. Search in this method is generally not comprehensive, and innovative alternatives are usually not sought. Further, with incrementalism, since the emphasis is on minimizing conflict and fostering negotiation, the precise goals of a program and the differences among programs and policies may be obscured.

The breadth of the search and the number of options included depends on the diversity of interests represented by the participants. The greater the number, interest, and expertise of participants, the greater the number and variety of alternatives that will be considered (Downs 1967, 185). Incremental search processes will be used, in general, when participation is not limited to experts of one or another kind, but rather depends as much on the political as the technical capabilities of the staff.

Search in the aggregative method is less developed as a process or procedure than in the other methods. The focus of the process is as much on participation as it is on any particular kind of result. The breadth of the search and the depth of knowledge about a particular alternative depend on the expertise of the individual participants. Because the presentation of options occurs spontaneously in the group setting, detailed background research into the feasibility or consequences of an alternative, such as that found in policy analysis, is not possible. Nor are the political consequences of the alternatives always well known at this early juncture, as they would be in the incremental method where the distribution of benefits is an important attribute.

The aggregative method does, however, do much to encourage innovation in the design of alternatives. By training participants in the art of brainstorming—where the expression of untested ideas is encouraged—and by permitting only clarifications—not criticisms or debates on the merits of a proposal—the method fosters new ideas. What is lost in the method's capacity to critically assess alternatives is perhaps gained in its capacity to generate new ideas for programs or operations.

The search for new alternatives in the garbage can model is not systematic, but it may admit to more creativity and a broader set of alternatives than the incremental view of search. Search is not separate from the actual process of discussing and choosing. The rejection of an existing alternative or the discovery or articulation of a goal may open the way to the consideration of an option previously thought to be outside the realm of possibility or not imagined at all. Moreover, however, the discovery of a new option may lead to the articulation of a new goal, so the process works both ways with this model. Search is clearly ongoing in the choice process and is not a separate prior activity.

Analysis

Analysis is concerned with examining alternatives in light of particular attributes such as feasibility, cost, and who the beneficiaries of the alternative will be. An alternative's feasibility is both a political and technological matter, and the technique used to search for and evaluate alternatives is determined by the value placed on qualitative and quantitative data. In addition to simple efficiency and effectiveness, administrators must be concerned with the passage and funding of programs and with gaining support for (and from) the administrative actors who will be needed to implement the plan. Questions of program technology and how to achieve the desired change in society, the economy, or foreign affairs are increasingly seen as issues for social science since they require considerable scholarly expertise.

Each method attacks the problem of analysis in a different fashion. The rational method uses policy analysis techniques to examine alternatives and identify the most cost-efficient ones. Policy analysis encompasses a variety of analytic techniques, including cost–benefit analysis, some of the operations research models that project the cost and output of projects, and evaluation studies of the effectiveness and efficiency of programs. An enormous consulting industry has grown up around the use of these analyses at all levels of government as the rational-policy analysis method becomes more prominent.

The culture surrounding the decision process must accept the value of the scientific method, however. The analytical requirements of the rationalist method impose heavy costs because of the time, professional expertise, and organizational support needed; major decisions requiring substantial research can consume months or even years, lots of money, and huge amounts of human resources. Decisions regarding relatively small operational changes also consume the time of extremely well-trained experts. In some cases, the expense of the analyses may have the effect of limiting the number of alternatives that can be compared. The expectation, however, is that the quality of the decision and the money saved by selecting the most efficient alternative will make up for these costs. This assumption is rarely tested.

Gawthrop (1971) notes that the rational-policy analysis approach is associated with centralized organizational structures in which decision-making authority is reserved for the upper executive levels. Centralization is required here to provide a clearinghouse for co-ordinating the large amounts of information used in decision making. The coordination and information-processing function needed for the rational-policy analysis method adds to the cost as well. The incremental method, by contrast, requires a decentralized structure, which permits the local autonomy needed to conduct negotiations.

In contrast, the analysis process of the incremental method is much less systematic and much less likely to be quantified. The basis on which an alternative is examined is the way it dispenses benefits, including intangible, symbolic resources to participants in the decision. This kind of analysis requires a combination of political and technical ex-pertise. Judging the support potential for a proposal from other agency actors, profession-als, and appointees, and from the external constituents of the agency is an important aspect of analysis under the incremental method.

The aggregative method depends on the individual judgments of participants, so sys-tematic prior research or analysis of alternatives is not generally done. Participants may, of course, be experts, and thus could use any research they wish in deciding whether to recommend an alternative, but since debate is not permitted, other participants would not be influenced. In general, the method does not encourage in-depth analysis, political or technological, and for that reason might best be used to generate ideas rather than decide among them.

The view of analysis offered by the garbage can model is notably different from that described in the other models. Analysis is not separate from the decision process; rather, it is one of the things that happens in the course of discussion and debate. In the obviously fragmented environment (probably with many cultures interacting) where the garbage can model is useful, the reasons for rejecting or accepting alternatives (that is, the bases for analyzing the "goodness" of an alternative) are especially complex because of the expres-sive, personal, and social nature of the decision process. Objections can be raised to a proposal to solidify a friendship or to play out a ritual, as well as to articulate a political or technical difficulty. Another distinctive characteristic of analysis in the garbage can model (at least according to Anderson [1983]) is that comparisons are not generally made directly between competing alternatives, but sequentially, as in the satisficing model. In consequence, an alternative that is rejected early may not be considered again later when goals have changed and other interests or social needs are uncovered even though these objectives might be well served by the rejected option. Thus, the order in which alternatives are considered is critical to the kind of analysis that occurs.

Choice

The choice criterion of a decision-making method is the basis on which one alternative is selected over another. The criterion reflects the organizational and political values assumed in the method and what they consider to be the best basis for making decisions for society. Economic, professional, and personal standards are also reflected in the methods.

The formal criterion of the rational-policy analysis method is the Kaldor–Hicks cri-terion, which as noted earlier, recommends the adoption of projects for which total social benefits exceed total social costs. With this criterion we choose, by definition, the program that is most efficient. Such a choice seems appropriate for administrative decision making since the primary value in a bureaucratic organization is efficiency. Efficiency may be less appropriate as a criterion for decisions about society in general, however, where there are competing values such as equity and justice.

The rationalist method portrays the bureaucrat as an analyst without any discretion who works within the guidelines of goals established by the external policymakers. In principle then, the bureau official is not really a decision maker under the rationalist method, but performs analyses for, and is accountable to, the legislative, judicial, and elected officials who do make policy. The reality is more complex. Often policy statements are vague, and analysts have considerable autonomy in interpreting them. Furthermore, the control policy analysts have over search and analysis gives them considerable latitude in defining the options policymakers really have. Thus, policy analysts can act as decision makers, but unlike their colleagues operating under the incremental method, no compromises among competing claims can be negotiated (at least not openly) because nonanalytic issues are not overtly recognized.

The criterion that operates in the incremental method is selection of the policy or programs that can claim the support of a group of participants. This group must be large enough to fulfill the system's voting requirements, which may in some cases require less than a strict majority and in others total consensus. These requirements may be formal or informal. What the criterion reflects, however, is that the best alternative is the one that can gain the support needed for adoption. The criterion is a very pragmatic one that puts the highest value on pluralism, the belief that tradeoffs among diverse values are inevitable (Dahl 1991). Thus, programs and policies arrived at by the incremental method are characterized by the satisfaction of many specific interests simultaneously, with a plan reached by bargaining among participants in a stable slow-changing system.

The aggregative methods select an alternative based on the number of supporters as well, but its criterion is different from that of the incrementalists. There is no mechanism for compromise or coalition building. The grounds for preference may or may not be scrutinized under NGT. Even when the group is made up of experts, the method is still not investigatory.

The choice criterion in the aggregative method seems to be based on a rather naive belief that majority rule will produce the best solution for all, and a fear that bargaining will lead to political manipulation. Because advocates of the method see themselves as rejecting political decision-making methods, they do not discuss, and may even be unaware of, the political values that underlie their procedures.

The final choice in the garbage can model is not necessarily an optimal one, as Anderson noted. Nor will it necessarily be the one expected by the participants or based on the goals established at the outset of the process (Rommetveit 1979). The basis on which the final choice will be made apparently varies in this model, and in some ways what we call decisions are only arbitrarily identified as such. Olsen, for example, in describing nondecision making, characterizes decisions as post hoc interpretations (1979, 83). According to Olsen, our ability to theorize and interpret events is greater than our capacity to actually make "goal oriented decisions" (1979, 83). The meetings, debates, and discussions that constitute the garbage can process continue until the agenda of instrumental and expressive items has been dealt with.

Public vs. Private Management

In the government no one has the power to decide that this is the policy he wants to develop, these are the people who are going to develop it, this is how it's going to be decided, and these are the folks who are going to administer it. No one, not even the President, has that kind of power.

Take . . . the framing of a U.S. economic policy toward Japan. If the President said to me, you develop one, Mike, the moment that [it] becomes known there are innumerable interest groups that begin to play a role. The House Ways and Means Committee, the Senate Foreign Relations Committee, the oversight committees, and then the interest groups, business, the unions, the State Department, Commerce Department, OMB, Council of Economic Advisors, and not only the top people, but all their people, not to speak of the President's staff and the entire press.

So it's assigned to me, but I can't limit who gets in on the act. Everyone gets a piece of the action. I'm constantly amazed when I have the lead responsibility to find two people talking to each other and negotiating something—when I haven't assigned them any responsibility. They're not in the loop. But everybody wants to be in the loop.

Therefore, to control the development of a policy, to shape out of that cacophony of divergent interests and dissonant voices an approach that eventually leads to a consensus and can be administered in a coherent fashion is an entirely different task in the government than it is for the chief executive of a company. There you can control the process and tell group executive A, you're not involved, stay out of it. And he will, and he must. In government that's simply unworkable. So you have to learn to become one of a large number of players in a floating crap game, rather than a leader of a well-organized casino that you're in charge of. I should emphasize that this is not a complaint—that the diversity of interests seeking to affect policy is the nature and essence of a democratic government.

SOURCE: W. Michael Blumenthal, "Candid Reflections of a Businessman in Washington," *Fortune*, January 29, 1979. Reprinted in *Public Management: Public and Private Perspectives*, eds. James Perry and Kenneth Kraemer (Palo Alto, Calif.: Mayfield, 1983): 22–33.

The differences among the methods on all three elements of the decision-making process are important for determining the particular strengths and weaknesses of each method. On the basis of these differences, we can begin to explore the possibility of a contingency theory.

THE POSSIBILITY OF A CONTINGENCY THEORY

A contingency theory of decision making would specify the conditions under which each method would be most effective. These conditions might include at least the type of decision to be made; the costs involved; the degree of disagreement over known options; the supportiveness or homogeneity of the bureau's constituency; the level of ambiguity and change in the system; and the availability of data.

The type of decision to be made appears to be a promising basis for a contingency theory. In the introduction to this chapter, we discussed three levels of decisions: (1) decisions about the broad policies or plans for the bureau; (2) decisions about the programs and projects to undertake in pursuit of those goals, and (3) decisions about the operations of the programs and the bureau's management system. If we could link the methods of decision making to these decision levels, we would have the beginnings of a contingency theory though one in need of refining and testing.

The rational method appears to be most appropriate at the level of operating decisions, such as determining the most efficient way to staff a program or design a bridge; these are the most common and immediate questions for bureaus. The operations research and quantitative analyses that are at the heart of the rationalist method are designed especially for these types of questions. The principal concern of the rational method is efficiency, and that is precisely what is desired at the level of operating decisions. On the other hand, questions of goals and values other than efficiency do not seem appropriate for this method.

The incremental method, alternatively, is not particularly well suited to making operations-level decisions because, by comparison with the rational method, it uses little quantitative analysis. The advantage of the incremental method is not that it identifies the most efficient solution, but that it mediates conflict among officials who hold different values and must find an acceptable compromise. In doing so, the method produces program packages rather than policies. Thus, it is appropriate for creating compromise programs that will be widely accepted, but not for deciding basic values about which there is generally no compromise.

The aggregative method may best be reserved for creating an initial rank-order list of goals or programs to be subjected to further analysis and final selection under one of the other methods. Without a more developed capacity for technical analysis and without the legitimizing effect of political negotiations and compromise, the use of the method to make final choices is questionable. In practice, we may find that the aggregative technique is also used as a last resort (attempting to change perceptions) when negotiations result in stalemate.

According to Olsen (1979, 85), the garbage can model is more likely, though not necessarily more desirable, where participants, goals, and issues are highly uncertain. This ambiguity is a characteristic of goal setting and planning decisions rather than operational decisions. At the planning and program levels, the political decisions at stake require the type of open expressive debate over the clarification of basic values that the garbage can model describes.

A difficulty in developing a contingency theory is that the advantages and limitations of each method are matters of political importance and, therefore, subject to disagreement. Devising a contingency theory of decision making is not simply a technical matter of collecting research findings, but involves political choices about who will control what kinds of decisions. The appropriate use of each method may, therefore, remain a matter for political debate.

CONCLUSIONS

The prescribed decision-making process in bureaus has undergone a good deal of change in the last three decades from the classic rational model to incrementalism and satisficing

Franklin Roosevelt: Strategies of Choice

Roosevelt . . . evidently felt that both the dignity of his office and the coherence of his administration required that the key decisions be made by him, and not by others before him. He took great pride, for example, in a calculation of Rudolph Forster's that he made at least thirty-five decisions for each one made by Calvin Coolidge. Given this conception of the Presidency, he deliberately organized—or disorganized—his system of command to insure that important decisions were passed on to the top. His favorite technique was to keep grants of authority incomplete, jurisdictions uncertain, charters overlapping. The result of this competitive theory of administration was often confusion and exasperation on the operating level; but no other method could so reliably insure that in a large bureaucracy filled with ambitious men eager for power the decisions, and the power to make them, would remain with the President. This was in part on Roosevelt's side an instinct for self-preservation; in part, too, the temperamental expression of a restless, curious, and untidy personality.

SOURCE: Arthur M. Schlesinger, Jr., *The Coming of the New Deal* (Boston: Houghton Mifflin, 1958); 527–528.

to the reincarnation of rationalism as policy analysis, and now to the group process method and expressive model. These changes are probably due to more than shifts in theory and new research findings. Rather, they reflect new popular and political views on what constitutes a legitimate role for the bureaucracy in policymaking and what constitutes a legitimate process of choice. There appears to be a cyclical pattern in these changes in method as well, from the earlier view of bureau decision making as a matter of deferring to hierarchical authority and expertise to the acknowledgment of an overtly political role for bureau decision makers to the recent efforts to erase politics from the process, replacing it with analytic expertise and a leveling of power differences.

The reasons for the recent shift to analytic and purportedly apolitical methods of decision making in bureaus are not easily identified. One possibility may be that suspicion of the pluralist-bargaining method generally grows from a disillusionment with interest group liberalism and pork barrel politics in an era of budgetary restraints. The move from acknowledging a political method to the interest in the more technically deliberate methods may also be part of the larger recent interest in high technology and futurist thinking. Attempts in the past two decades to adopt more quantitative and analytic criteria of policy effectiveness may also be related to changes in decision processes.

These shifts in decision-making methods, in theory and practice, illustrate that the bureau's most fundamental processes are not static; they respond to a variety of internal and external political and technological changes. The search for a single best decision-making process in bureaus may, therefore, be based on an unrealistic assumption about the stability of bureaus.

FOR FURTHER READING

A good overview of organizational decision making is Bernard Bass, *Organizational Decision Making,* Homewood, Ill.: Richard D. Irwin, 1983. The rational model of choice is clearly presented by Edith Stokey and Richard Zeckhauser in *Primer for Policy Analysis,* New York: W. W. Norton, 1978. Charles Lindblom, in "The Science of Muddling Through," *Public Administration Review* 19, 1959: 79–88, sets out the incremental-pluralist model. Louis Gawthrop analyzes the political and structural implications of the rational and incremental-pluralist models in *Administrative Politics and Social Change,* New York: St. Martin's Press, 1971. Structured group choice models are introduced in Andre Delbecq, Andrew Van de Ven and David Gustavson, *Group Techniques for Program Planning: A Guide to Nominal Group and Delphi Processes,* Glenview, Ill.: Scott, Foresman, 1975. The unpredictability of the choice process and its resemblance to a garbage can is described by James March and Johan Olsen in "Organization Choice Under Ambiguity," in their *Ambiguity and Choice in Organizations,* 2nd ed., Bergen, Norway: Universitetsforlaget, 1979. In their later work, *Rediscovering Institutions: The Organizational Basis of Politics,* New York: Free Press, 1989, March and Olsen discuss the relationship between choices and values. Finally, James G. March and Roger Weissinger-Baylon discuss the garbage can model further in *Ambiguity and Command: Organizational Perspectives on Military Decision Making,* Marshfield, Mass.: Pitman Pub. Inc., 1986. Kenneth Kraemer and James Perry propose a means for linking the method of decision making and the level or type of decision to be made in "Implementation of Management Science in the Public Sector," in *Public Management: Public and Private Perspectives,* James Perry and Kenneth Kraemer, eds. Palo Alto, Calif.: Mayfield, 1983. Gareth Morgan discusses various metaphors for organizations and decision making in his *Images of Organization,* Beverly Hills, Calif.: Sage, 1986.

REVIEW QUESTIONS

1. What are the values, goals, and assumptions behind each of the decision methods described in this chapter?

2. Given the different methods, what would be the probable results if each of the methods was used in dealing with the same problem?

3. Would the structure or design of a bureau have any impact on what decision methods would be used, or be successful? Why?

4. Would there be a different *emphasis* (one method used more than another or given more legitimacy than another) on the decision methods used in private, public, and nonprofit organizations? Why?

5. How would politicians and public administrators differ in their opinions about the value of the different models, and which would each group be more likely to use? Why? What kinds of conflicts might that cause between politicians and administrators?

REFERENCES

Allison, Graham. *Essence of Decision: Explaining the Cuban Missile Crisis.* Boston: Little, Brown, 1971.

Anderson, Paul. "Decision Making by Objection and the Cuban Missile Crisis." *Administrative Science Quarterly* 28, 1983: 201–222.

Cleveland, Harlan. "The Future Executive." In *Professional Public Executives,* ed. Chester Newland. Washington, D.C.: American Society for Public Administration, 1980.

Cohen, Eliot. "Systems Paralysis." *The American Spectator,* November 1980: 2227.

Cohen, Michael, James March, and Johan Olsen. "People, Problems, Solutions and the Ambiguity of Relevance." In *Ambiguity and Choice in Organizations,* 2nd ed., eds. James March and Johan Olsen. Bergen, Norway: Universitetsforlaget, 1979.

Coke, James, and Carl Moore. *Guide for Leaders Using Nominal Group Technique.* Washington, D.C.: Academy for Contemporary Problems, n.d.

Dahl, Robert. *Modern Political Analysis,* 5th ed. Englewood Cliffs, N.J.: Prentice-Hall, 1991.

Delbecq, Andre, Andrew Van de Ven, and David Gustavson. *Group Techniques for Program Planning: A Guide to Nominal Group and Delphi Processes.* Glenview, Ill.: Scott, Foresman, 1975.

Downs, Anthony. *Inside Bureaucracy.* Boston: Little, Brown, 1967. (Reissued: Prospect Heights, Ill.: Waveland Press, 1994.)

Etzioni, Amatai. "Mixed Scanning as a 'Third' Approach to Decision Making." *Public Administration Review* 27, 1967: 385–392.

Gawthrop, Louis. *Administrative Politics and Social Change.* New York: St. Martin's Press, 1971.

Goldwin, Robert, ed. *Bureaucrats, Policy Analysis, Statesmen: Who Leads?* Washington, D.C.: American Enterprise Institute, 1980.

Kraemer, Kenneth, and James Perry. "Implementation of Management Science in the Public Sector." In *Public Management: Public and Private Perspectives,* eds. James Perry and Kenneth Kraemer. Palo Alto, Calif.: Mayfield, 1983.

Lindblom, Charles. "The Science of Muddling Through." *Public Administration Review* 19, 1959: 79–88.

March, James, and Johan Olsen, eds. *Ambiguity and Choice in Organizations.* Bergen, Norway: Universitetsforlaget, 1979a.

———. "Organizational Choice Under Ambiguity." In *Ambiguity and Choice in Organizations,* 2nd ed., eds. James March and Johan Olsen. Bergen, Norway: Universitetsforlaget, 1979b.

March, James, and Herbert Simon. *Organizations,* 2nd ed. Cambridge, Mass.: Blackwell, 1993.

Merewitz, Leonard, and Stephen Sosnick. *The Budget's New Clothes.* Chicago: Markham, 1971.

Montjoy, Robert, and Lawrence O'Toole. "Toward a Theory of Policy Implementation: An Organization Perspective." *Public Administration Review* 39, 1979: 465–476.

Morgan, Gareth. *Images of Organization.* Beverly Hills, Calif.: Sage, 1986.

Olsen, Johan. "Choice in an Organized Anarchy." In *Ambiguity and Choice in Organizations,* 2nd ed., eds. James March and Johan Olsen. Bergen, Norway: Universitetsforlaget, 1979.

Ostrowski, John, Louise White, and John Cole. "Local Government Capacity Building." *Administration and Society* 16, 1984: 3–26.

Rommetveit, Kare. "Decision Making Under Changing Norms." In *Ambiguity and Choice in Organizations,* 2nd ed., eds. James March and Johan Olsen. Bergen, Norway: Universitetsforlaget, 1979.

Stokey, Edith, and Richard Zeckhauser. *A Primer for Policy Analysis.* New York: W. W. Norton, 1978.

Wilson, James Q. *Bureaucracy: What Government Agencies Do and Why They Do It.* New York: Basic Books, 1989.

CASE 7–1   Participation in Administrative Review: A Parent's Account of Mediating with a Public School System over a Special Education Placement

Part I: Public Law 94-142—A Brief Perspective of the Law and Its Impact on Public Schools

> Nevertheless. . . . In attempting to structure an organization so that it can rationally and predictably pursue certain specified goals, the groundwork is laid for dysfunction. (Anderson 1968, 16)

On November 29, 1975, the Education for All Handicapped Children Act was signed into law. This legislation (hereafter referred to as PL94-142), along with Section 504 of the Rehabilitation Act of 1973, outlined funding provisions and detailed requirements for education programs for this country's handicapped children between the ages of three and twenty-one (currently estimated at more than 10 percent of the total school population). Any public school district that received federal funding was required to develop a special educational plan each year that detailed exactly how the law would be carried out in that particular setting.

The law recognized the fundamental rights of handicapped children and their parents or guardians by providing guidelines for such concepts as eligibility, evaluation, bias-free testing, classroom placement, and mainstreaming and for procedural rights in challenging placement. Parent and advocacy groups further supported the movement toward mainstreaming by demanding an expansion of the scope of special education and an increase in the quality of services provided by the public schools for handicapped children.

Thus, around an already cumbersome public education system, Congress flung the protective cloak of PL94-142 in an attempt to provide the battered special education subsystem protection against the harsh elements of prejudice, misunderstanding, and neglect. The new legislation inadvertently, however, exposed public school administrations to new areas of vulnerability and conflict. It created a new level of confrontation between the parents of handicapped children and public school administrators. Specifically, there has been a constant debate over the extent to which parents should be involved with the decision-making aspects of educational policy and the degree of autonomy that the school systems (teachers and administrators) should retain regarding implementation. (PL94-142) Parents, in looking out for the educational welfare of their children, are always apt to intervene directly in the educational process. No level of education, from the state department of education to the local school board to the classroom, can avoid a certain vulnerability to public pressure. Thus, school systems, as "educative organizations" are open systems that interact with their environment and reflect any significant changes in or pressures from the environment in which they exist.

> [P.L.94-142] . . . raised conflicts all along the line, from Washington to the most remote school classroom in the land [when] it sought to redefine the prerogatives of teachers . . . by mandating the inclusion of parents in a participatory role in planning individualized instruction and in a formalized appeal process. The parent—formerly an "outsider"

confined to an advisory role—suddenly became one of the "insiders" with new authority in relationship to the teacher. (Owens 1981, 7)

This change in the status of parents signals, in many ways, the loss of autonomy that schools once had in certain types of decision making. Now, with PL94-142, parents have the right to an impartial due-process hearing to resolve differences with the schools. This right can be exercised whenever the educational staff of a school system intends to initiate or change a child's eligibility, placement, dismissal, or evaluation, or the provision of a free appropriate public education; or whenever there is a refusal to initiate or change a child's identification, evaluation, placement, dismissal, or the provision of free appropriate public education. The due process hearing is a new concept for many school administrators, one that has "significant implications for school administrators in terms of time commitments, costs, non-public school placements . . . and a number of additional items" (Mayer 1982, 109). The scenario of parents pitted against school administrators is an element of dysfunction that fuels an already heated conflict. What follows is evidence that the resolution of these differences is often a convoluted process of negotiating best intentions.

Part II: PL94-142, Fairfax County Public Schools and the Triennial Review

The citizen standing at the counter of the bureau runs some risks unless he behaves in an acceptable manner. . . . The fact which he must recognize is that bureaucratic rules of conduct exist for both inhabitants and visitors. Instructions must be read, forms must be filled out and interrogations must be weathered politely. (Jansen 1978, 190)

Even without the complexity that the passage of PL94-142 added to the functioning of American public schools, the public school system in Fairfax County was one already entrenched in a high degree of bureaucratization—if for no other reason than its size. With an enrollment of close to 122,000, including approximately 13,000 special education students, the organizational structure requires a high degree of complexity. The Fairfax County Public School system is decentralized; it is divided into four areas, each having approximately forty schools. Each area has a superintendent and staff responsible for implementing instructional and pupil services programs and carrying out other routine school related functions. Also within each of the four areas is a complete special education staff that administers the special education programs and services for that area's students.

Such a large enrollment, in both regular and special education, tends to reduce the close contact between administrators and school personnel (principals and teachers), and results in procedures that are highly formalized and authority that is decentralized through specification and rules. Not long ago, I found myself "at the counter of the bureau" face-to-face with the rules, regulations, and procedures and the bureaucrats who enforced them. At that time, I attended the triennial reevaluation of our daughter's continued placement in the Learning Disabilities Self-Contained (LDSC) program in our area of Fairfax County (Area IV).

The purpose of the reevaluation (or review) is to "provide a systematic method of follow-up and reassessment of students placed in special education programs." This review is the responsibility of the eligibility and dismissal committees and determines the appropriateness of continued placement in a special education program every three years for every student in a special education program.

As the parent member of this review committee, I was acting on behalf of our daughter, who, since having been identified as learning disabled in her first year in school, had been placed in a self-contained classroom[1] for the learning disabled for the previous five years. I attended the meeting alone and was somewhat unfamiliar with the particulars of our daughter's case. Having recently attended a triennial review with my husband for another daughter, held under identical circumstances, we felt a familiarity with the general issues and problems involved and were aware of the one issue on which the outcome of this upcoming meeting would depend: the "ten-point discrepancy." According to the Fairfax County regulations, to be determined eligible for any learning disabilities program and to retain that placement, a student must demonstrate, through standardized testing, a discrepancy in performance in one or more skill areas that is "ten standard score points below the child's actual ability level." In a brief phone conversation with our daughter's teacher prior to the meeting, we were assured that the most recent testing indicated that our daughter had more than the required ten-point difference. Secure in this knowledge, and ignoring advice we had received in educational advocacy training, we decided not to attend the meeting as a two-member team.

Consequently, I was totally unprepared for the outcome of this brief meeting, held with a summer "skeleton crew" committee[2] consisting of an Area IV coordinator of special education, a placement specialist, an area math specialist (acting as an impartial observer) and our case manager—a school psychologist whose familiarity with our daughter's case was limited to whatever information he had gathered from reading her school files. On the basis of recent test results indicating our daughter lacked the necessary ten-point discrepancy, the committee ruled our daughter ineligible for continuation in the LDSC program.

Clearly, the committee pointed out, she did not meet the eligibility criteria. It was a fact that had apparently escaped the psychologist, who represented our case. His silence during the meeting indicated a general lack of concern for the findings. In his capacity as a case manager, he had neglected to inform us (the parents), prior to the meeting, of any problems we were to encounter.

Incredulous that the results before the committee contradicted those I had obtained earlier from the teacher, I quickly learned that the ten-point difference that our daughter's testing showed was actually a complete inversion of the actual discrepancy requirements. My dismay over our teacher's obvious misconception of the ten-point discrepancy issue was immediately replaced by concern over the larger problem this presented. In our daughter's case, the achievement scores (the results of academic testing) were more than ten points higher than her I.Q. score, an indication, according to the committee, that, among other things, she was outperforming herself.

This observation prompted a lively and decidedly upbeat conversation as to the extent of our daughter's success in the program and left me facing an enigma for which I had no explanation: On the basis of test scores, and in spite of teachers' written

---

[1]This commonly used special education term denotes a low-enrollment classroom in a "regular" school, usually consisting of no more than ten to fifteen students who receive all instruction in the major academic subject areas—math, science, reading, social studies, and so on in that classroom.

[2]During the months when school is in session, review committees typically consist of six to eight members, not including parents.

recommendations to the contrary, this child, who in the previous five years had never been considered capable of being mainstreamed for academic subjects in regular classes, was being dismissed from the LDSC program on the basis that "available data demonstrate extremely good academic progress; [and that] all measured academic areas are at or above measured ability level." Sensing my disbelief and concern, certain committee members congratulated me on our daughter's achievements, countering my insistence that she was ill-prepared to function in a regular classroom with assurances that my concerns were unfounded. I then pointed out to the committee the many written references to emotional/ behavioral/adjustment problems that had surfaced repeatedly in this child's written records. I further pointed out that these problems had been, only three months earlier, the subject of an intense, teacher-initiated Individualized Education Program (IEP) meeting that had resulted in a complete revision of our daughter's IEP, addressing methods for dealing with these problem areas within the LDSC setting.

Again, sensing my concern over this issue, the committee referred the case to the Emotionally Disturbed (ED) eligibility committee for further consideration, adding to their comments on the eligibility form that "a strong behavioral-emotional component remains."

In frustration, I pointed out that earlier in the year, in response to a growing concern from the teacher, we had pursued the ED placement, only to be advised by a staff psychologist and the Area IV LD specialist (also a psychologist) that based on her records and psychological testing results, our daughter was not eligible for placement in the ED program. In response, the review committee again maintained that the best course of action now would be to present our case to the ED Committee.

At that point, I sensed that if we were to lose the eligibility for the LDSC program, and not be found eligible for the ED program (the indications already being that this would happen), we would have to continue this battle up through the system. On the other hand, if I accepted this decision as it stood, we would be placing our daughter in a regular classroom without the support of any special educational services—a situation that everyone inside and outside the system had strenuously avoided for the past five years.

During this exchange of views, I was aware of some very strong perceptions that were forming. I felt certain that the members of this committee were looking at my daughter from a very depersonalized and detached point of view, and that there was virtually little, if any, evidence that this child had, in the course of a few months, become "un-LD." Further, I felt that a great deal of information relevant to our daughter's case was being overlooked and/or misinterpreted. At the very least, I felt that in the interest of strict adherence to rules, regulations, guidelines, and procedures, necessary as they were, our daughter's continuing learning problems were no longer an issue in this meeting.

To achieve their purpose that day, it was necessary for the members of the committee to resist individualized and compassionate treatment. The facts were before us and the numbers didn't add up: on the basis of objective criteria, our daughter was ineligible for continued placement. Looking at my situation objectively, I was one of many cases to be heard that day and the committee needed to find a classification or categorization for our case: their action was nothing more than an attempt at efficiency. To treat our case in any other way, at that point, would have meant increased efforts in decision-making, a slowdown in the processing of eligibility cases yet to be heard and an increase in the costs associated with such procedures.

At the end of the meeting I requested an administrative review—a special conciliatory conference—to appeal the committee's decision. Set up by the schools as a voluntary review process that "may be convened upon the prior agreement of both parents and professional staff," the administrative review is a mediation effort in the appeals process— a step before involving parents and schools in the impartial due-process hearing or in a state or federal court case.

After considerable delay, confusion, and disagreement over the appropriateness of my request, a date was set for the administrative review by the Area IV office in an attempt to bring about a resolution of the issue(s) that we faced.

Part III: Preparation for and Involvement in the Administrative Review

> An effective bureaucracy demands reliability of response and a strict devotion to regulations. . . . Such devotion to the rules leads to their transformation into absolutes; they are no longer conceived as relative to a set of purposes. . . . This interferes with ready adaptation under special conditions not clearly envisaged by those who drew up the general rules. . . . Thus, the very elements which conduce toward efficiency in general produce inefficiency in specific instances. (Merton 1957, 47)

Immediately following the triennial review, in an attempt to secure a date for the administrative review, I encountered in one administrator who had been a member of the eligibility committee (the placement specialist), a resistant attitude that was to characterize all of our future interactions. Based on our earliest (oral) communication, it became evident that this person (who would play a key role in the administrative review) disagreed with our decision to request the conciliatory review rather than to allow the case to go to the Emotionally Disturbed (ED) program eligibility committee.

In a series of "off-the-record" phone conversations, she insisted that we had no basis for questioning the triennial committee's decision. I began to feel that this opposition to our decision infringed, in some way, on our right to request the meeting—that the "grant-ing" of this right would be based on some sort of moral decision over which we (as parents) had no control. In a move to resolve this issue, I wrote to the Area IV superin-tendent, asking for clarification of the legitimacy of our request (which was confirmed in his letter of response), and thereafter limited any and all contact with the Area IV admin-istrators to written communications.

In all this I sensed that we were encroaching on sanctified territory and that our concerns as parents were being subjected to value judgments and moral scrutiny. This perception is explained, in part, by Merton's assertion that bureaucrats undergo the "pro-cess of sanctification" whereby

> through . . . emotional dependence upon bureaucratic symbols and status, and affective involvement in spheres of competence and authority, there develop prerogatives involving attitudes of moral legitimacy, which are established as values in their own right, and are no longer viewed as merely technical means for expediting administration. (1957, 54)

That the focal point for tension at this point was the interaction between the admin-istrator (the placement specialist) and the client (the parent) is not an unusual occurrence because of the "confusion of the status of the bureaucrat and the client" (1957, 56). On the one hand, I wanted to be treated as someone who had a special case and was deserving of being treated on an individual basis. On the other hand, the placement specialist saw nothing particularly special about our case and gave it the "categorical treatment" she felt it deserved. This is in keeping with the "norm of impersonality" and the "categorizing tendency" that Merton further discusses as being part of the bureaucrat's tendency toward "trained incapacity . . . in which one's abilities function as inadequacies or blind spots" (1957, 50). Thompson concurs with this, explaining that the frustrations of those who deal with organizations occur because, very often, the organization "has no program (solution) for the class of problems they represent" and therefore, doesn't know what to do. "In all of this," Thompson concludes, "the individual client . . . is treated as a problem category" (1976, 120).

This is not to say that the friction and tension didn't serve a constructive purpose. It gave us impetus to study our case in detail and to weigh the strengths and weaknesses of our arguments. From that examination, we formulated three statements that we felt summed up our position.

1. Information in our daughter's records had been overlooked in finding her ineligible for the program.

2. The committee had relied on a single assessment procedure for determining ineligibility, which violated the requirements for determination of eligibility outlined in federal regulations.

3. The referral to the ED eligibility committee was not a consideration for us at this time and should therefore not be pursued.

In addition to developing a strategy for approaching the committee, we enlisted the help of professionals who could add insight and information to our case. We contacted an educational advocate who would serve as our case manager and asked her to provide us with a report of her assessment of the differences in classroom procedures in the regular and LDSC programs, and to observe our daughter in her present classroom setting. We also asked a speech and language pathologist, currently involved in testing and working with our daughter, to provide us with the test results and a written assessment of the extent of her language problem.

As part of the preparation efforts—by this time we were into the fall school term— I contacted the LDSC teacher who had been working with our daughter since the beginning of the new school year and requested a brief oral or written statement describing our daughter's classroom performance and her views on the appropriateness of the LDSC setting. In spite of her assurances to me that she felt this was the right setting for this child, she was reluctant to become involved in the case at this point, preferring to wait until the results of current testing that she and the school psychologist were conducting were finalized. She was quite clear in explaining that she would make her official recommendation only when the testing was concluded.

As a cog in the wheels of the school bureaucracy, my request was one to which it was difficult, if not impossible, to respond. While it was evident that the teacher did not disagree with me, it became clear that I represented a "source of external pressure" for her and that as a member of the school organization, she was constrained by her internal expectations to develop and maintain the values of that group. It was an attitude that I was to confront again and would finally understand as a basis for much of the behavior of teachers and other professional staff members in formal encounters with school administrators. Since "authority resides in the rules and not in the members of the organization," the teacher merely obeys the authority that resides in the rules and thus becomes an agent, "with the rules acting as the real bearer of authority" (Anderson 1968, 25). I knew that she supported us, but realized she would be cautious about presenting testimony for us.

As the time for the administrative review drew closer, I was becoming increasingly aware of my adherence to a win-lose strategy that had not previously characterized my thinking. A win-lose attitude is exemplified by a situation in which the contesting parties see their interests as mutually exclusive and without the possibility of compromise. In this situation, one party in the conflict must fail at the price of the other's success. In spite of all that I had ever heard or felt about the school's interest in children and their welfare, I was beginning to see the school, or more accurately the system behind it, as an enemy. Individual judgment, as well as behavior and cognition, become distorted by the conflict experience. One becomes increasingly hostile to those on the "other side" and increasingly loyal to his or her own side, believing the leaders of the opposition, formerly seen as mature able people, to be irresponsible and incapable. In addition, it becomes difficult or impossible to see anything worthwhile or valuable coming from the other side, even if it agrees with one's own point of view (Owens 1981, 290). It was only with concerted effort and the perspective of those not directly involved with the case that I was able to overcome the feeling that the system was "out to get us" and that somewhere in the shadows lurked the placement specialist ready to attack.

Exactly three months after the triennial review had taken place, fifteen people filed into an Area IV meeting room to take part in the administrative review. Four were members of the Area IV Administrative Review Committee: an area administrator, an area coordinator for instruction, a staff psychologist, and a learning disabilities (LD) specialist. Those who had come to present data on our daughter's case, aside from my husband and myself, included the educational consultant and the speech and language pathologist we had hired, a family friend, our daughter's previous and current LD teachers, two school psychologists, an LD specialist, and the placement specialist (who had been on the triennial review committee). Everyone working for the school system, with the exception of the previous year's LD teacher, sat together at one end of the table; the rest of us clustered at the other end.

As members of the committee introduced themselves, I noted with interest that one member of the Administrative Review Committee, the Area IV Coordinator for Instruction, was a woman whose workshop on effective parent-school communication I had attended a year earlier. Though knowing that she did not recognize me, I immediately felt relieved. It became apparent that not everyone in the school system fit the category of a bureaucrat who would, in Merton's words, "substitute a condescending, impersonal attitude toward clients for personal consideration of individual cases, relying heavily on categories and legalistic interpretations of established procedures" (Merton, quoted in Anderson 1968, 136). I knew this person adhered to the basic principles of effective communication.

Once everyone had introduced themselves, the placement specialist (the only member of the triennial eligibility committee at this meeting), in an attempt to explain that committee's rationale for denying eligibility, immediately directed our attention to a handout taken from the Fairfax County Public Schools Special Education Regulations and read from it the eligibility criteria for the learning disabilities programs. It was as though there was a need to establish, once and for all, the rational basis for the committee's decision, to emphasize the unyielding nature of those criteria and to point out, early on, that we, as parents, basically did not have a case. She stated:

> It indicates here that in order to be eligible for a placement in a learning disabled [sic] program, the student must "a" and "b" and "c" . . . ; in other words, that's an additive definition. It isn't either/or. The child must demonstrate . . . some sort of a processing deficit in a picture of more or less average intelligence . . . and our judgment is based on test scores, not solely on test scores, but we must be able to demonstrate by means of concrete data that the child is in fact underachieving.

She continued, uninterrupted, pointing out the rationale for the committee's decision:

> It had been the committee's opinion on reading the packet [file]—and I don't think this was contradicted at the meeting, although there were a lot of cases heard that day and I don't remember all the details—that [the child's] problems were primarily social and emotional at that point. . . . Our concern was she simply didn't meet the criteria for an LD self-contained program.[3]

At this point, my perceptions of what had just been said affected my ability to sort out the facts. All I had heard was a slighting reference to the fact that the committee had "heard a lot of cases that day" and a statement that the triennial eligibility committee had not based their decision solely on test scores (which I knew not to be true). I saw these comments as further examples of depersonalized and categorical treatment of our problem. I was convinced at this point that this attitude, and only this attitude, was the basis for our conflict; that once I could expose what Ownes calls the "typical bureaucratic hardening of the categories" (1981, 286) for what it was, the issues that confronted the committee would be resolved.

At this point, my husband read the statement we had prepared, outlining the bases for our objection to the decision. He stated that much of the information in our daughter's file had been overlooked and/or misinterpreted, and that in fact the eligibility decision had been made solely on the basis of test scores, which is contrary to the procedures outlined in the regulations for determining eligibility, and that placement in the ED program was not an issue for consideration in this case.

In the hour-and-a-half that followed, everyone who was not a member of the Review Committee presented information regarding our daughter's case. Test results, classroom behavior, assessment of ability levels, classroom achievement levels, reasons for the avoidance of mainstreaming, behavior and social problems—in short, all aspects of her educational functioning—were described to the committee members.

Teacher "testimony" was presented rather hesitantly, often in subdued tones. One of the teachers was barely audible; the other spoke only when questioned by the committee. It was as though these teachers doubted the credibility of their classroom experience and observations and the validity of their test results. It became clearer to me as they presented more information that, as teachers, they experienced conflict in their roles as professionals and as bureaucrats. Neither teacher, in the presence of the school administrators, was openly and adamantly supportive of the continued placement, while in private they had been. Their ability to exercise professional discretion was curtailed by their need to main-

---

[3]Tape recording of the Area IV Administrative Review, October 23, 1981.

tain their organizational status quo. The teachers were faced with two conflicting sources of authority: one was based on professional expectations and training and was characterized by self-determination and responsibility, while the other was embodied in the bureaucratic rules and the hierarchy of the school administration. In real life, teachers often find many elements of their roles carefully specified by the rules, leaving them little or no professional autonomy, and this may lead to feelings of intense discomfort (Anderson 1968, 26). This professional autonomy was something on which we, as parents, had relied as a means of supporting the facts in the case. Much of our concern about and involvement in our daughter's continued difficulty in school had been a response to the concerns expressed by these professionals. The teachers probably understood this but felt unsure of exactly how their statements and positions would be received by their superiors.

The Area IV LD specialist was able to put to rest the issue of eligibility in the ED program. Although clearly another one of the cogs in the administration's machinery, he was able to elicit from the two school psychologists convincing testimony that according to all the testing and observations of our daughter, an ED placement was clearly not a possibility in this case.

Additional information from the educational consultant and the speech and language pathologist and our own observations of experiences with our daughter's learning difficulties all pointed to the fact that this was a child who exhibited language problems, attention deficits, and processing difficulties and that the LDSC setting was the appropriate placement. I felt confident that our case had been significantly strengthened and that what remained was the task of "softening" the LD categories for a child who, everyone admitted, "fell through the categorical cracks" of assessment. Meanwhile, the placement specialist, defending the eligibility committee's decision to the last, maintained that there had been a good case made in this meeting that the child had some problems that had perhaps been overlooked earlier and that the information presented in this meeting had not been available to the triennial review committee at the time the decision had been made.

This was, to be fair, an accurate observation: much of the information presented in this meeting had not been available to the committee when it had made its decision. However, other data, although part of our daughter's record, had been clearly outlined in numerous reports and written teacher observations, and in the interest of efficiency, had not been brought to light at the triennial review. No one at that first meeting had bothered to ascertain the reasons for our daughter's questionable and uneven educational history.

The turning point for both the meeting and my perceptions came after an interlude during which we all had reflected on the fact that the committee had "unearthed" considerable pertinent information. Acting partly on the basis that "assessments must go beyond 'single intelligence quotients' to include measures of specific areas of educational needs . . . in all areas related to the suspected disability" (Heller, Holtzman, and Messick, 1982, 37), but more importantly on the basis of what the Fairfax County Special Education regulations stipulated, the Area IV Coordinator for Instruction began an inquiry into all the areas in which the learning problems were documented and clearly evident. Even though, as a member of the Administrative Review Committee, she was bound by the same rules as all others on the committee, she was willing to encourage the group to look at the case from a different perspective.

Thus began a vigorous and concerted effort to establish the areas in which the learning problems affected academic achievement. The speech and language pathologist contributed more data that supported the discrepancy requirement. In addition, the LDSC teacher who had recently administered and analyzed our daughter's test results began participating more in the exchange of information. Gradually, with the categories or requirements becoming more pliant, this teacher revealed several subtest scores found within the recent achievement test scores that indicated the necessary point discrepancies.

Still very much aware of the necessity to adhere to the rules, and cautious as to the ramifications of the newly revealed subscores, the Area IV Coordinator for Instruction, who had become the informal leader and spokesperson for the committee, admitted that although none of the usual test scores showed the discrepancies, the committee would have to rely on the subtest scores, classroom documentation, work samples, and oral information that had emerged in the hearing.

The administrator demonstrated a flexibility and a willingness to cooperate that was atypical of the other school administrators in this conflict. By "loosening the reins" of an administrative edict while still adhering to the rules and regulations, she was able to broaden the scope of the discrepancy issue, allowing the teacher to present information that would satisfy both the goals of the committee and the county's requirements for eligibility. This collaborative effort brought on a sense of a shared ownership of the problem and resulted in resolution of a conflict that the earlier committee had not wanted to address.

After some further exchange of test result information, the educational consultant representing us gave a brief summation of our position and the meeting was dismissed. Four days later, the Area IV Administrative Review Committee sent us a letter stating that they had found our daughter eligible for continuation in the LDSC program, where she remains today.

References

Anderson, James G. *Bureaucracy in Education*. Baltimore: The Johns Hopkins Press, 1968.

Heller, Kirby A., Wayne H. Holtzman, and Samuel Messick, eds. *Placing Children in Special Education: A Strategy for Equity*. Washington, D.C.: National Academy Press, 1982.

Jansen, Robert. *The ABC's of Bureaucracy*. Chicago: Nelson-Hall Publishers, 1978.

Mayer, C. Lamar. *Educational Administration and Special Education: A Handbook for School Administrators*. Boston: Allyn & Bacon, 1982.

Merton, Robert K. *Social Theory and Social Structure*, 2nd ed. Glencoe, Ill.: Free Press, 1957.

Owens, Robert G. *Organizational Behavior in Education*, 2nd ed. Englewood Cliffs, N.J.: Prentice-Hall, 1981.

Thompson, Victor. *Bureaucracy and the Modern World*. Morristown, N.J.: General Learning Press, 1976.

Editor's Note

This is an account of one individual's experience as a client forced to appeal to the bureaucracy for special consideration. Remember that the story is told from the client's perspective and would undoubtedly be told differently if any of the other major actors in the situation were telling it. The analyst must always take into consideration the source of his or her information when looking at cases such as this. Although this case may be considered unexceptional and similar to those faced every day in the public sector, it is valuable exactly because it deals with typical situations faced by clients and officials rather than the exceptional national and international political situations, which are important but unrelated to most people's everyday world. As you go through this case, you should relate the situation and its resolution to the following questions:

1. In this case, it is obvious that the parents are from a socioeconomic class in which people are relatively knowledgeable about the procedures open for appeal when a decision goes against what they believe to be rational or just treatment. What might happen to less knowledgeable parents, and what is the responsibility of the bureaucracy to see that all avenues of appeal are available in all cases?

2. Explain the conflicts in roles described throughout the case. Can these types of role conflicts be avoided, and should they be?

3. Standard operating procedures affect an organization's capacity to imagine alternative approaches to a problem. What alternatives are considered in this case, and why are they the only ones considered?

4. Generate at least two additional alternatives that could have been used. (You may use some of the decision-making techniques presented in Chapter 7.)

5. Why is it important for the parents to show that the first decision made about their daughter was made solely on the basis of "test scores"?

6. Illustrate how the parents adopted the bureau's terminology and categories of action. Why was it necessary for them to do this? How did it contribute to their ability to change the officials' minds?

7. In what ways was the final decision a negotiated one rather than a rational one? Which model of decision making is illustrated here?

CASE 7–2   What to Do with Lawrence Livermore National Laboratory?

Introduction

The end of the Cold War has greatly reduced the role of nuclear deterrence as a part of national security policy. Coinciding with this are economic pressures from competition in the private sector and dissatisfaction with the level of the national debt, coupled with a trend in business for downsizing. Tax payers and politicians are looking for a peace dividend with corresponding reductions in the defense budget. These factors require an examination of the roles of the twenty-seven laboratories and production plants operated by the Department of Energy. Of special interest is the future of the Lawrence Livermore National Laboratory located in Livermore, California.

Background

The national government operates hundreds of laboratories and production facilities throughout the U.S. Some of these, such as the Department of Defense arsenals, have been part of government operations since the Civil War. Others, like the National Institute of Standards and Testing (National Bureau of Standards), are more recent. During World War II, a group of physicists led by Albert Einstein encouraged President Roosevelt to pursue the development of a nuclear device as a weapon. This led to the Manhattan Project, which eventually developed and constructed the two nuclear devices which were detonated over Japan.

The Manhattan Project, named for the Corps of Engineers District which was responsible for the project, not only institutionalized an organizational routine for managing complex projects, but also brought together an entire generation of physicists, astrophysicists, chemists, and engineers. Included in this group were Albert Einstein, Leo Szilard, Edward Teller, Ernest O. Lawrence, Niels Bohr, and Enrico Fermi. The Manhattan Project eventually involved research and/or production sites at Los Alamos, New Mexico; Sandia, New Mexico; Hanford, Washington; and Oak Ridge, Tennessee. Of these sites, Los Alamos, Sandia, and Oak Ridge were National Laboratories. Hanford was an electric power producer that actually had as its major function the production of weapons-grade plutonium. Highly enriched uranium was produced at Oak Ridge.

Organized to harness the organizational skills and efficiencies of private industry which had mobilized from the depression to become the "Arsenal of Freedom," the Manhattan Project was funded through the War Department and operated under a joint contract with the University of California and Bell Laboratories. These organizations were granted long-term contracts to *manage and operate* the research and development agendas and facilities owned by the U.S. government. This type of contract came to be known as an "M&O" contract and differed greatly from the operation of other federally owned and operated laboratories like the Bureau of Standards. Over time the national research facilities grew in number and in scope as they migrated from the Atomic Energy Commission (1947), to the Energy Research and Development Administration (1974–1977), and then on to the jurisdiction of the Department of Energy (1977–present).

The original weapons laboratories, Sandia and Los Alamos, were supplemented in 1952 by the creation of the Lawerence Livermore Laboratory located at a satellite facility of Lawrence Berkeley National Laboratory. The mission of the lab at Livermore was to pursue the development of thermonuclear weapons and to provide intellectual competition for the New Mexico laboratories. Sandia National Laboratory is primarily an engineering laboratory involved in the development of triggering and safety devices. Los Alamos and Livermore are the weapons design laboratories.

Beginning with 123 employees and a budget of $600,000, Lawrence Livermore National Laboratory (LLNL) grew to approximately 8,000 employees and a budget of about one billion dollars in 1992. During the ensuing forty years, the laboratory had faced potential closure, survived fizzles, and was assigned the "plowshares program" to find peaceful uses for nuclear energy. During this time it also developed the weapons system that was the backbone of U.S. nuclear deterrence throughout the Cold War, created a biomedical research base to examine the radiation effects that led to the human genome program (DNA), developed massive-parallel computing technology (the Cray Computer was developed solely to meet the requirements of the nuclear-weapons program), and it invented nuclear-powered x-ray lasers. In 1988, the end of the Cold War and shrinking defense budgets again threatened the size and formation of the weapons complex. LLNL has become a mature national laboratory engaged in government-sponsored research and development that goes far beyond the limits of weapons design. However, as the last weapons laboratory formed (1952) and as a relatively newly designated national laboratory (1980), LLNL is considered a candidate for downsizing or closing.

Issues

The issues to be considered in deciding the future of LLNL include:

Mission—If the end of the Cold War relieves the U.S. government of the need to maintain a nuclear weapons capability, then possibly LLNL is no longer needed.

Political Environment—Although Livermore depends in some measure on the laboratory for economic stimulus, many citizens there and elsewhere in California would prefer that all nuclear materials be removed from California. There is some opposition to "weapons work."

Costs—There are significant costs associated with all alternative futures for LLNL.

Alternatives—In 1992–93, several bills were introduced in Congress to create a Commission (patterned after the Base Realignment and Closure commission that was used to overcome political opposition to closure of military bases) to select Department of Energy (DOE) laboratories and facilities to be closed and/or realigned. The leaders within DOE do not believe that these decisions should be made by Congressional action.

Mission

The issue of the mission of the laboratories in general and LLNL in particular is an amalgam of topics. The core problem facing DOE, as the agent of the U.S. government that has stewardship over the majority of the Federal laboratories, is how to allocate available resources to competing uses at the national laboratories. This simple statement masks the contentious and multi-faceted problems of "What level of resources?" "For which national agenda item?" and "Which national lab is best suited for the specific tasks?"

Implicit within these issues are questions of a larger scale:

- What is the appropriate relationship between DOE and its national laboratories?
- Should nuclear weapons development and production be reassigned from civilian control to the Department of Defense?
- What consolidations are appropriate/required in the post-1992 laboratory complex, and what is the required number of separate weapons laboratories?
- How does DOE perceive the developing roles and missions of the weapons laboratories? Should the laboratories become involved in fee-for-service research and development for other parts of the government and for U.S. industry?
- How is the balance to be struck between maintaining competency in weapons design (necessary for ensuring the safety and surety of the enduring stockpile) and the provision of fee-for-service research and development resources to U.S. industry and other governmental elements.

Political Environment

The concept of a national laboratory *dedicated to environmental research and civilian energy projects* has been supported by environmental groups such as Livermore Conversion Project and other similar groups. Representative Brown's recently submitted legislation, the "Department of Energy Laboratory Technology Act" (DELTA), also contains language reflecting the desire at least to identify LLNL as a "green laboratory."

News articles in the *Washington Post* and *Inside Energy* have discussed the possibilities of such a laboratory, and Secretary O'Leary has been quoted as describing the ideas as "intriguing." The concept of an environmental laboratory is not new, and the creation of the National Renewable Energy Laboratory was partially motivated by similar objectives. Currently, LLNL is considered a prime candidate by advocates to become the green lab.

Costs

No analysis of the costs, resources, and program disturbances associated with the conversion of LLNL have been conducted. Although no formal analysis was presented, cost savings resulting from changing the status of LLNL were alluded to by all proponents and generally assumed to exist by those opposed to changes at LLNL. Cost savings were inclusive of salaries not paid, supplies not purchased, and some administrative and management costs incurred by DOE at both headquarters and field offices. Not calculated were lost tax revenues, purchases from local businesses, and costs of relocating essential functions to the laboratories in New Mexico.

Only if functions fully disappear are cost savings possible. The concept of converting LLNL from a weapons laboratory into an environmental laboratory removes weapons activities from California while maintaining the employment base devoted to more politically acceptable endeavors. This overlooks the cost of relocation of the weapons activities and the fact that environmental research represents an entirely new function. This new function would either be taken away from existing facilities or would be a "net new" budget outlay. Rather than a savings, this action would produce additional federal budget outlays at a time when the budget is already being debated on a zero-sum basis.

Alternatives

Consideration of alternatives facing DOE involves the legal constructs/mechanisms by which DOE can implement and carry out R&D activities. Discussion should be based on objective analysis of alternatives using at least: (1) costs and benefits; (2) suitability for implementation by a government agency; and (3) identification of long-term effects on DOE core missions. The following means of acquiring R&D services should be considered:

Government Owned/Government Operated—This would examine the option of moving the laboratories from contractor operation to operation by federal employees.

Government Owned/Contractor Operated—This would assess the desirability of continuing the current arrangement of contracting out the management and operation of the laboratories.

Sale—This option would call for the shedding of all assets at LLNL (and other sites) that could be sold without breaching classified secrets (there is some doubt about whether this is a realistic option given the past role of the laboratories).

Lease—The leasing of national laboratories is a possible management option available to DOE. Issues related to this option involve pricing of the lease, agency jurisdiction, further capital improvements, staffing, and last resort users of the lab.

Related to these options are the following issues:

Pricing of the Leases: The issue of pricing the lease has direct impact on the prices the lessee would charge clients and users. Options for pricing include: full-cost pricing; $1.00 a year; and bid. Arriving at a value on which to base full-cost pricing would be complicated because government finance and accounting regulations are not designed to produce the data necessary for this calculation. Also, because of the unique facilities at some of the labs, there are not "comparables" in the market place to establish a value. It is likely that full-cost pricing would price the labs out of the market. The choice of lease option would probably have to come from the other two alternatives.

Agency Jurisdiction: Currently the responsibility for the laboratory facility is under the jurisdiction of DOE. DOE is not organized or staffed to manage real property leases. Generally, property management is the jurisdiction of the General Services Administration (GSA). Transferring a laboratory to GSA would be a complex process involving such issues as environmental conditions of the site, access to special facilities, who would be considered an acceptable tenant (Would a foreign firm or a firm with foreign industrial or R&D interests be allowed to bid?), and future capital improvements.

Further Capital Improvements: Proposed capital investments at LLNL include the National Ignition Facility, additional investments in human-genome research, and additional computing capabilities. The logic of continued planning for the investments should be reexamined if LLNL's weapons mission is to be curtailed. Planning for these facilities, generally agreed to be needed for continued research in high energy physics, should be begun at alternative sites which will involve fierce competition among other national laboratories.

Staffing: Given that maintaining core competencies in specialized areas is an objective of DOE, the lease option raises the question of staffing for the new enterprise. This is an issue with all privatization options and, to a degree, with all options involving changed missions or mission focus for the laboratories. In the lease case, the government has less control and more exposure if it is required to assure that specific skills and manpower levels are maintained.

Last Resort Use: This issue revolves around the possibility of the lessor of a facility not being able to generate enough business to fully utilize the site and the expectation that DOE would be the client of last resort. Given the relatively high cost of laboratory staff, it is likely that such an enterprise may have difficulty competing against established, for-profit organizations. If such an occurrence arose, this could result in low priority work (busy work) being assigned to the laboratory in order to recover some value for funds expended. This, in turn, could result in higher costs for R&D than before the lease was renegotiated.

SOURCE: J. Kenneth Schafer, DPA. Dr. Schafer is employed by the Department of Energy. He is currently the Director, Office of National Security Policy and has served in Defense Programs and Energy Efficiency at the Department of Energy.

Editor's Note

This case addresses a decision that had to be made by the secretary of energy. This is a *simulation* of a real-life decision memo and in no way represents actual correspondence in the department. Before reading the eventual outcome of this incident, stop and think about the decision process that has to be followed in such a situation. In relation to that process, answer the following questions:

1. If you were the secretary of energy, how would you go about making a decision related to this issue? Looking at the decision models discussed in this chapter, which of them appear to be useful in describing what must be done. Which are not useful? Why?

2. Considering the factors mentioned in the decision memo, which would you consider to be the most important in making the final decision? Why?

3. What is the role of blue ribbon panels and advisory boards in the government decision processes? Is this an appropriate mechanism for government decisions? How may they be improved?

4. In a situation like this, the national laboratories supply personnel to assist in the development and analysis of options, lobby Congress, and brief the secretary directly to influence his or her decision. What are the roles of national laboratory personnel (contractors) and federal employees? How should these two parties relate to one another? What issues does this relationship raise that are appropriate to government operations including privatization?

Eventual Outcome

Between 1992 and 1995, two external review panels were convened to examine various aspects of the roles and missions of the national laboratories (these were the Galvin Task Force and the Yergin Committee, both managed under the auspices of the Secretary of Energy's Advisory Board). In addition, several internal task forces with the Offices of Energy Research and Defense Programs attempted to define the issues and formulate plans of action. Meanwhile, programmatic activities continued. DOE planning assumed program growth, funding for capital improvements, and an inclusive, continuing role for LLNL. Included in these program routines was the Programmatic Environmental Impact Statement for the National Ignition Facility that went forward to provide bases for decisions of program investments at LLNL.

The mid-term elections of 1994 resulted in a pro-defense, anti-environment Congress that appropriated a larger Defense Programs budget for the Department of Energy than was requested by the Administration. The upcoming Presidential election in 1996 was becoming a factor in decisions affecting employment and economic vitality in California, a state rich in electoral votes. In October 1995, after indicating that the National Ignition Facility (a $7 billion facility that allows for very small-scale fusion reaction to be initiated and x-rayed in a controlled environment) would be constructed at LLNL, the Secretary of Energy announced that weapons design and research would continue at LLNL and that there would be no diminishment of the mission or role of the laboratory.

Bibliography

Anders, Roger. *Institutional Origins of the Department of Energy: The Federal Energy Administration.* Energy History Series, U.S. Department of Energy, DOE/OSE-0005, November 1980.

Audit of Administration of Cooperative Research and Development Agreements at DOE National Laboratories. Office of Inspector General, U.S. Department of Energy, DOE/IG-0373, May 1995.

Buck, Alice L. *A History of the Energy Research and Development Administration.* U.S. Department of Energy, DOE/ES-0001, March 1982. (Unpublished/distributed.)

———, and Roger Anders. *Origins of the U.S. Department of Energy.* Energy History Series, U.S. Department of Energy, DOE/HR-0098, March 1995. (Draft.)

Capsule Review of DOE Research and Development Laboratories and Field Facilities. U.S. Department of Energy, DOE/ST-0002P: September 1992.

Fehner, Terrence R., and F. G. Gosling. *Coming in from the Cold: Regulations of the U.S. Department of Energy's Nuclear Facilities 1942–1995.* U.S. Department of Energy, July 13, 1995. (Draft.)

———, and Jack M. Holl. *Department of Energy 1977–1994: A Summary History.* Energy History Series, U.S. Department of Energy, DOE/HR-0098, November 1994. (Draft.)

Gosling, F. G. *The Manhattan Project: Making the Atomic Bomb.* Energy History Series, U.S. Department of Energy, DOE/HR-0096, September 1994.

Hacker, Barton C. *Lawrence Livermore National Laboratory: A Brief History.* (No other information available.)

Human Resources Management Staff. *Baseline External Assessment of DOE Efforts to Increase the Technical Capability of its Civil Service Technical Workforce in Defense Nuclear Facilities.* National Academy of Public Administration: August 31, 1994.

Lawrence Berkeley Laboratory Staff. *Energy Technology for Developing Countries: Issues for the U.S. National Energy Strategy.* LBL-28407, UC-400, prepared for the U.S. Department of Energy under Contract DE-AC03-76SF00098.

Missions of the Laboratories Priority Team. *Changes and Challenges at the Department of Energy Laboratories.* February 1994. (Final Draft.)

Secretary of Energy Advisory Board. *Task Force on Strategic Energy Research and Development. Annex 1: Technology Profile.* U.S. Department of Energy, Washington, D.C.: June 1995. (This is the Yergin Task Force.)

———. *Task Force on Strategic Energy Research and Development. Annexes 2–4.* U.S. Department of Energy, Washington, D.C.: June 1995. (This is the Yergin Task Force.)

SEAB Task Force Report on the Department of Energy National Labs. January 1992. (This is the Galvin Task Force.)

Strategic Laboratory Council of the U.S. Department of Energy Laboratories. *A Strategy for Environmental Technology and Economic Competitiveness: Commitment for Change.* January 20, 1993.

Subcommittee on Oversight of Government Management, Senate Committee on Governmental Affairs. *Inadequate Federal Oversight of Federally Funded Research and Development Centers.* July 8, 1992. (Unpublished/distributed.)

Task Force on Alternative Futures for the DOE National Labs. *Sandia National Laboratories.* April 22, 1994. (Unpublished/distributed.)

The Los Alamos, Sandia, and Livermore Laboratories: Integration and Collaboration to Solve Science and Technology Problems for the Nation. Version 3: Accomplishments Appendix. October 12, 1994. (Unpublished/distributed.)

The National Laboratories of the U.S. Department of Energy. Creating Technology for America's Energy Future. May 1993.

Chapter 8

Work Motivation

Definitions of organizations discuss "positions" and "competencies" in a very mechanistic way; however, organizations are ultimately human systems. Human beings fill those positions; human behavior is central to the functioning and effectiveness of competencies; and human motivation is the most basic psychological process in behavior. Motivation is of special consequence in *public* organizations because of the political environment and the limitations placed on actions by managers in bureaus.

The term *motivation* comes from the Latin "to move." Psychologically, human motivation pertains to internal conditions or states; it is intangible. Motivation, then, is a hypothetical construct; it is based on what we infer about internal needs and the activity or behavior consequent to them. A well-stated definition is given by Bernard Berelson and Gary Steiner: "A motive is an inner state that energizes, activates, or moves (hence 'motivation'), and that directs or channels behavior toward goals" (1964, 240).

These goals, incentives, or rewards toward which motivation and activity are directed are desired by the individual for need satisfaction. Needs are internal; incentives or goals are more external or environmentally based. For example, hunger is a need, and food is the goal. An organization that provides goals, rewards, or incentives appropriate for members' need satisfaction will be more successful in motivating workers.

A good administrator does not work alone. No manager can singlehandedly maintain a high level of organizational functioning. To achieve organizational goals, the energies and actions of others must be brought forth and directed. Because administrators usually must delegate to others to get things done, understanding the motivation processes and needs of these individuals increases both organizational and managerial effectiveness.

Motivation is an important organizational concern for several reasons: It is a factor in determining why people participate in an organization; it determines the extent to which they will allow others to direct and control their behavior; and it influences whether they strive to accomplish personal or organizational goals, or both.

The patterns of individual behavior that organizations need for effective functioning have been identified by Daniel Katz and Robert Kahn (1982). First, organizations require that sufficient personnel join and stay in the system. Second, the dependable performance of assigned roles is necessary. A third and more subtle set of organization requirements is for actions to be carried out that are not specified by role prescriptions but are needed to meet unanticipated changes and contingencies. Spontaneous innovation, cooperation with other members, and behaviors that protect and create a favorable external climate for the organization are activities of this type. Each of these organization requirements depends on somewhat different motivational patterns.

Motivation theory is characterized by a diversity of models and theoretical frameworks. Since motivation is a multifaceted concept, this diversity provides researcher, practitioner, and student with a variety of insights and perspectives to choose from or combine. There are many possible ways of grouping the numerous motivation theories, ideas, and models. In this chapter, we have chosen to organize them by four major types: content models, cognitive process theories, behaviorist theories, and bureau-based perspectives. In addition to describing the conceptual frameworks of various theories, elements allied to application—satisfaction and performance—will be included where appropriate. The bureau setting and motivation theory will also be discussed.

Content models of motivation focus on identifying the substantive nature of individual needs; in other words, they attempt to determine what motivates individuals. Cognitive process theories attempt to explain how and why people are motivated. Motivation is presented here as a complex process in which cognition—especially perception and expectation—is important. It is the interaction of these psychological variables with other factors related to the situation or environment that distinguishes process models. By contrast, internal psychological variables are excluded from the behavioristic perspective; only external factors count, mainly behavior and environmental response to behavior.

After examining these three approaches, we will consider their application to public organizations. This fourth perspective is discussed especially by Anthony Downs, whose model of motivation relates directly to bureau settings and opportunity structures. (Self-interest and personalistic goals characteristic of other theories are also included in Downs's model.) This model adds to our understanding of individual motivation in bureaus by including policy and public interest goals as well. This additional insight will allow us to consider the traditional motivation theories, and their application in the new management models like total quality management, to public bureaus.

CONTENT THEORIES

It is natural to think about motivation in content terms: What motivates us as humans? Not surprisingly, the development of motivation theory began with the substantive aspects of motivation. Ancient Greek philosophers believed that humans are hedonistic, that they seek pleasure and try to avoid pain, deprivation, and loss. These basic assumptions endured in the much later social and economic theories of John Locke, Jeremy Bentham, John Stuart Mill, and Adam Smith. Still later, the idea that motivation was based on instinct was introduced, and Freud and others proposed that unconscious desires are what motivate behavior. The modern study of work motivation is widely agreed to have begun with need or content theories.

Maslow's Hierarchy of Needs

It has become customary to introduce the discussion of work motivation theory with Abraham Maslow's hierarchy of needs. As a clinical psychologist, Maslow relied heavily on his patients' case histories; he did not use workers in an organization context to derive his needs model. His theory was not developed specifically as a model of work motivation; rather, it grew out of a more general interest in the interplay of heredity and learning in motivation. Despite this, the development of work motivation theory has been influenced greatly by Maslow's ideas (1954).

According to Maslow, individuals are motivated to satisfy unfulfilled needs. He further postulates that individual needs form a hierarchy; that is, an individual does not consider higher-level needs as important or motivating unless lower-level needs have been more or less satisfied. The five need levels in Maslow's model are physiological, safety and security, social and affiliative, esteem and recognition, and self-actualization (see Figure 8–1). The foundation or first level of the need system is hereditary, but as one moves up the hierarchy, maturation and learning are determining influences.

Physiological Needs

Our need for such things as food, water, and shelter are inborn. Although these needs are unlearned, acculturation and learning shape the manner in which they are expressed.

Safety and Security Needs

We acquire these needs or responses through experiences—being left alone, being hurt, being shaken by frightening or unpredictable events. Maslow included psychological and emotional as well as physical security needs. The order and structure of organizations, for example, may satisfy security needs of a psychological and emotional nature. Union contracts, work agreements, seniority, retirement plans, letting employees know what is expected of them, and giving them feedback on how they are doing are other ways for organizations to satisfy security needs.

Social and Affiliative Needs

We next acquire social needs as we realize that other people are important. In fact, whether we will be fulfilled or frustrated in satisfying our other needs depends on the actions and attitudes of other people toward us. Needs for love, belonging, and intimacy mark a crucial stage of human development. As the Hawthorne studies indicate, individual needs for belonging—combined with group dynamics—have a far-reaching impact on satisfaction, productivity, and control in organizations. In part, informal groups and communication networks in organizations grow out of and satisfy social and affiliative needs.

FIGURE 8–1   Maslow's Hierarchy of Needs

Esteem and Recognition Needs

These needs are often referred to as ego needs. They have to do with a desire to gain status and recognition in the eyes of others, and to have a positive self-image. This level, Maslow points out, includes both self-esteem and esteem from others. Award ceremonies, articles in agency newsletters that feature individual accomplishments, praise from a superior or peers, and the respect of other professionals are sources of such rewards in bureaus.

Self-Actualization Needs

This is the fifth and highest need level in the hierarchy. Self-actualization involves the individual's need or desire to do what he or she is fitted for. Here the self-concept or perception of self is transformed into reality through action. Performing particular activities is done for the stimulation and satisfaction of doing them; performing a given role or activity is self-rewarding. In other words, the individual finds his or her development and performance intrinsically satisfying.

A measure of the influence of a theory or idea is whether it stimulates further conceptual development, research, and application. By this measure, Maslow's needs hierarchy is an important contribution.

Although the needs hierarchy is a very general theory of motivation, practitioners and theorists alike saw its organizational significance, for in the work setting, personal needs can be translated into work motivation. The theory has both the organizational potential for satisfying individual needs and the reciprocal potential of meeting individual needs as a basis for work motivation and the achievement of organizational goals. The concept of self-actualization raised especially interesting possibilities for linking personal needs and organizational tasks and goals. And because of the simplicity of Maslow's theory and its descriptive treatment of needs, managers and organization scholars could link the needs in the model to relatively specific organizational incentives.

Herzberg's Two-Factor Theory

Frederick Herzberg's two-factor theory of motivation extended Maslow's work considerably. His theory was based on an initial study of about two hundred professional employees (engineers and accountants) in Pennsylvania firms. Hundreds of additional interviews were later conducted that included a wide variety of occupational levels, types of organizations, and cultural milieus. Respondents were asked to:

> Think of a time when you felt exceptionally good or exceptionally bad about your job, either your present job or any other job you have had. This can be either the "long range" or "short range" kind of situations, as I have just described it. Tell me what happened. (Herzberg, Mausner, and Snyderman 1959, 141)

Respondents fairly consistently associated bad feelings with factors related to the job context: working conditions, interpersonal relations, supervision, company policy and administration, salary and wages. Good feelings stemmed from a different set of factors that arose out of the content, not the context, of their work: growth, advancement, responsibility, the work itself, recognition and achievement. Factors intrinsic to the work yielded

---

FIGURE 8–2   Herzberg's Two-Factor Theory

Hygiene Factors	*Motivator Factors*
Job context	*Job content*
Policies and administration	Achievement
Supervision	Recognition
Working conditions	Challenging work
Interpersonal relations	Responsibility
Money, status, security	Growth and development

---

satisfaction; Herzberg called these *motivator factors.* The extrinsic conditions, which he termed *hygiene factors,* were linked to job dissatisfaction (see Figure 8–2).

Job dissatisfaction and the factors that cause it are different from, rather than opposites of, those causing satisfaction. Herzberg concluded that satisfaction and dissatisfaction are separate concepts and not opposite ends of the same continuum.

The motivators, analogous to Maslow's higher-level needs, increase worker satisfaction and performance. The hygiene factors, analogous to Maslow's lower-level needs, can reduce or prevent dissatisfaction, but according to Herzberg they do not lead to satisfaction. They can reduce symptoms of dissatisfaction such as absenteeism and higher turnover, but by themselves hygiene factors do not motivate workers to greater productivity. Where dissatisfaction has been prevented, people work at minimally acceptable levels to avoid job or pay loss; but motivators are needed to boost satisfaction and motivate performance.

Some later studies confirm Herzberg's two-factor theory (Herzberg 1966; Bockman 1971; Grigaliunas and Herzberg 1971); others dispute it (Vroom 1964; Schwab, Devitt, and Cummings 1971). Nevertheless, Herzberg's contributions are substantial. His studies increase the applicability of Maslow's needs hierarchy to work motivation and provide more specific descriptions of need content. The hygiene–motivator model has drawn attention to the importance of job content factors in motivation. Because these ideas gained popularity with managers, they have been applied in the workplace; for example, job enrichment, workgroup design, participative management, and various aspects of organization development rely on motivating individuals through opportunities for challenging work, recognition, respectability, and growth.

Alderfer's ERG Theory

A recent content theory of work motivation was developed by Clayton Alderfer, who, like Herzberg, bases his findings on research conducted in organizational settings (1972). Alderfer reformulates Maslow's five needs into three categories: *existence, relatedness,* and *growth* (see Figure 8–3). The theory's name is, of course, derived from these three terms. Existence needs equate to Maslow's physiological needs and in some aspects to his security needs; relatedness needs have to do with the desire for social acceptance and status in a group; and growth needs center on self-esteem and self-actualization. Alderfer's findings, however, do not point to a hierarchical ordering of needs and suggest a more complex relationship between need strength and need satisfaction. Depending on an individual's

FIGURE 8–3   Relationship Among Alderfer's ERG Needs, Maslow's Hierarchy of Needs, and Herzberg's Two Factors

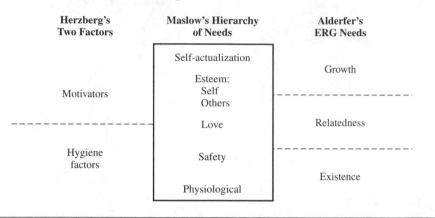

SOURCE: Fred Luthans, *Organizational Behavior,* 4th ed. (New York: McGraw-Hill, 1985): 204.

personal experiences or acculturation, for example, growth needs might take precedence over unfulfilled existence needs. Other research substantiates this conclusion, except that concern for higher-level needs tends to be precluded when lower-level needs are severely threatened (Lawler and Suttle 1972).

Interestingly, the satisfaction of relatedness needs is pivotal to interest in other needs: If these needs are satisfied, higher-level needs assume importance to the individual. Further, deprivation generally stimulates a desire for need satisfaction and promotes interest in a need, but self-actualization or growth needs can become more important as they are satisfied.

McClelland's Social Motives

David McClelland is a major critic of Maslow's work, particularly the adequacy of Maslow's conceptualization of self-actualization. Because many needs are socially acquired rather than biologically determined, they vary from culture to culture and from individual to individual. Therefore, McClelland reasoned, perceptions of actualizing one's self and reaching one's potential differ among individuals and societies. McClelland's work sheds insight into both the content of self-actualizing needs and the possible effects of these need patterns on productivity, cohesion, and conflict, as well as leader–follower relationships in the organization.

The psychological research of McClelland and his followers is based on projective techniques. People who participated in their studies were shown a series of simple but ambiguous pictures; they were then asked to write a short story about each picture. Psychologists scored and analyzed stories based on three important themes or needs: affiliation, achievement, and power.

Affiliation Needs

People with high affiliation needs desire social interaction. High-affiliation individuals want to be liked by others, and, in return, they tend to be helpful and supportive. They can contribute greatly to organizations and groups through their efforts to promote positive interpersonal relations. Conflict can be diffused through their attempts to reduce tension.

A recent review of research dealing with the "need to belong" found that:

> it seems fair to conclude that human beings are fundamentally and pervasively motivated by a need to belong, that is, by a strong desire to form and maintain enduring interpersonal attachments. . . . [There are] multiple lines between the need to belong and cognitive processes, emotional patterns, behavioral responses, and health and well-being. The desire for interpersonal attachment may well be one of the most far-reaching and integrative constructs currently available to understand human nature. (Baumeister and Leary 1995, 522)

Affiliation needs are, of course, an important reason for joining informal groups within the organization. These needs can influence both group cohesiveness and the extent to which informal group norms control a member's behavior (Cartwright 1968, 92), which, in turn, can enhance collaborative task efforts. Whether these needs are functional or dysfunctional for productivity and attaining organizational goals depends, however, on the congruence between the informal group norms and goals and those of the larger organization (Likert 1961, 31–33).

Achievement Needs

Individuals whose behavior is consistently oriented toward successful performance according to some standard of competence or excellence are motivated by high-achievement needs. People with high-achievement needs (1) like to take personal responsibility for solving problems; (2) tend to set reasonably difficult goals, preferring to take moderate risks but not gambling on long shots; and (3) want concrete feedback on their performance (McClelland 1961, 103, 205–233).

Organizations and managers who set unreasonably high standards or goals are not motivating high-achievement members effectively since the high-achievement individual's satisfaction is strongest when the goal is attainable. Nor do goals that are set too low motivate the high-achievement worker. An interesting shift is taking place in achievement motivation research: Its focus is moving from the high-achievement individual to the organizational climate and opportunity structure that encourages and rewards high achievement.

Not surprisingly, high performance is likely to be related to high-achievement needs. But as McClelland and David Winter (1971) point out, this phenomenon is contingent on organizational variables; the less bureaucratic the organization, for example, the more favorable the organizational context for high-achievement behavior.

Opinion is divided on the significance of achievement motivation for managerial effectiveness. McClelland believes that "it is fairly clear that a high need to Achieve does not equip a man to deal effectively with managing human relationships" (1970, 30). Why? Because, unlike affiliation and power motivation, which are oriented toward others, achievement motivation "is a one man game which need never involve other people" (McClelland 1970, 29). "Stimulating achievement motivation in others," McClelland concludes, "requires a different motive and a different set of skills than wanting achievement satisfaction for oneself" (1970, 30). In a reiteration of this point, some new management methods, such as total quality management, actively discourage any special rewards based on individual achievement and, instead, look to the total production system as the main basis for high achievement and quality (Carr and Littman 1993).

Other research findings reveal that leadership style and effectiveness vary with the degree of achievement need—high, moderate, or low. Unlike McClelland's image of the high-achievement individual as a loner who is not interpersonally effective, these findings suggest that high-achievement managers are optimistic about subordinates, use participative methods, and show concern for both people and production. Moderate achievers are more concerned with prestige symbols, and managers with low-achievement motivation are mainly interested in safety and security. Each tends to try to motivate his or her subordinates as he or she is motivated (Zemke 1979).

Power Needs

Greater concern for having influence over, or a strong impact on, others characterizes people with a high need for power (Veroff 1957; McClelland 1970). But people are motivated by different visions or types of power. "There are," according to McClelland, "two faces of power. One is turned toward seeking to win out over active adversaries. Life is seen as a 'zero-sum game' in which 'if I win, you lose' or 'I lose, if you win'" (1970, 36). He calls this personalized power. "The other face of the power," he explains, "is more socialized" (1970, 36). Socialized power "expresses itself in thoughts of exercising power for the benefit of others and by feelings of greater ambivalence about holding power" (1970, 36).

There are differences in the ways personalized and socialized power are exercised and in their motivating effect on followers. Acting on a need for personalized power, the leader seeks to overwhelm others, to compel their submission through dominance. This behavior may evoke follower obedience, but their passivity, or conversely, desire to resist, may be the price. McClelland notes another shortcoming of personal dominance: Although personal power may be effective in small groups, the process of influencing large organizations and groups requires more socialized forms of motivation.

Leaders who are motivated by socialized power needs are not inclined to force others to submit. These leaders are concerned with group goals, which entails not only their identification of those goals, but their promotion of the group's involvement in defining them as well. Socialized power engenders confidence in followers; they feel better able to accomplish whatever goals they share. Thus, followers feel more rather than less powerful.

In our society, we hold such a strongly negative view of power that as observers we are inclined to convert the positive face of power into a negative. That is, we believe that if the leader succeeds in an attempt to influence, that leader must have done so through dominance or manipulation. And "the more effective the leader, the more personal power tends to be attributed to him regardless of how he has achieved his effects" (McClelland 1970, 42). McClelland recognizes, however, that there is a realistic basis for this frequent misperception:

> In real life the actual leader balances on a knife edge between expressing personal dominance and exercising the more socialized type of leadership. He may show first one face

of power, then the other. The reason for this lies in the simple fact that even if he is a socialized leader, he must take initiative in helping the group he leads to form its goals. How much initiative he should take, how persuasive he should attempt to be, and at what point his clear enthusiasm for certain goals becomes personal authoritarian insistence that those goals are the right ones whatever the members of the group may think, are all questions calculated to frustrate the well-intentioned leader. (1970, 42)

Certain values in American culture may support acquiring strong personal power needs, for example, individualism and competitiveness, whereas others promote the learning of socialized power. Americans' fear of the abuse of power has led to a system of government that fragments authority. The process of exercising power requires some degree of taking into account and accommodating the goals of others—and often others' involvement in selecting and formulating those goals. This is especially germane, though problematic, in large-scale public bureaus where regulations and procedures abound, personal discretion and responsibility are curtailed, and public accountability is an enduring expectation.

Katz and Kahn's Motivational Patterns

David Katz and Robert Kahn (1982) approach motivation in organizations by looking at both individual and organizational factors. They discern different motivation patterns that combine psychologically based individual desires or values with organizational reward and control systems. Katz and Kahn identify four types of organizational incentive systems that tap into different motivation patterns and are good (or bad) for the organization in different ways (see Figure 8–4). These motivational patterns are (1) legal compliance, (2) instrumental satisfaction, (3) self-expression, and (4) internalized values.

In *legal compliance,* motivation rests on the individual's internalized acceptance of the organization's authority and rules as legitimate. The completeness and clarity of role prescriptions and organizational controls are external elements related to sustaining this motivational and behavioral pattern (legal compliance). At best, however, this incentive system is limited by its inability to motivate members beyond routine compliance with role requirements. In a sense, this system places a floor on performance levels, but it also establishes a ceiling because an "Emphasis on legalities of organizational control tends in practice to mean that the minimal acceptable standard for quantity and quality of performance becomes the maximal standard" (1982, 408).

Motivation may also be linked to behavior by *instrumental satisfaction.* Katz and Kahn identify four types of instrumental rewards: (1) general system, (2) individual, (3) approval from leaders, and (4) approval from peers.

General-system rewards come through membership and usually increase with seniority (for example, retirement systems, sick leave, cost-of-living increases). These rewards reduce turnover and are therefore most effective for retaining the organization's members. On an individual basis, they will not lead to higher quality or quantity work than is necessary to stay in the system. However, system rewards may account for differences in productivity between organizations since organizations that give better rewards than competing ones may be able to set a higher level of performance (Katz and Kahn 1982, 413).

Individual rewards, such as pay increases and promotion, are given on the basis of individual merit or performance. These rewards help attract people to the organization and hold them in it; they can also be effective in motivating members to meet or exceed

FIGURE 8–4   Motivational Patterns, Rewards Systems, and Organizational Behavior Outcomes

Incentive/Motivational Pattern	*Type of Behavior Produced*
Legal compliance	
Internalized acceptance of authority or legitimacy of organization rules, or external force can be used to compel compliance	Minimally acceptable quantity of work can reduce absenteeism
Instrumental satisfaction	
General-systems reward	Minimal quantity and quality of role performance Reduction in turnover and absenteeism
Individual rewards	Possible increase in productivity Possible reduction in turnover and absenteeism
Approval of leaders	Possible decrease in turnover and absenteeism Possible increases in productivity (or possible decreases)
Approval of peers	Possible decrease in turnover and absenteeism Possible increases in productivity (or possible decreases)
Self-expression	
Self-concept, identification and intrinsic satisfaction with the work or job itself	High productivity Decreases in absenteeism
Internalization of organization goals	
Value expression, self-identification with goals of organization	Increased productivity Spontaneous and innovative behavior Reduced turnover and absenteeism

SOURCE: Adapted from Daniel Katz and Robert L. Kahn, *The Social Psychology of Organizations* (New York: John Wiley & Sons, 1982): 398–425.

standard performance, reducing turnover, and perhaps lowering absenteeism. Where an individual's contribution(s) to a group product can be clearly differentiated, individual rewards are feasible; but where this differentiation is unclear or where teamwork receives greater emphasis, system rewards are both more advisable and foster higher identification with the organization.

Approval from leaders, with the concomitant gratification of praise from a powerful or respected person, is the third type of reward. Social approval from one's immediate workgroup is the remaining instrumental reward. Support or approval from either leaders or peers in the organization may reduce turnover. If these social relationships are unrelated to the tasks to be performed, however, they do not increase productivity or work quality.

Because motivation based on *self-expression* is internalized, performance of the role activities carries its own rewards. Self-determination and self-expression are ego-satisfying motivations; the individual is motivated to establish a positive self-concept. If successful, this motivation pattern can result in high productivity and work quality as well as personal satisfaction. Central to self-expression is intrinsic job satisfaction or identification with the work, and this is aroused and maximized when the job itself provides sufficient variety, complexity, challenge, and exercise of skill to engage the abilities of the worker. Hence the ongoing interest in job enrichment (Katz and Kahn 1982).

The fourth type of motivation extends self-expression to the *internalization of orga-nizational goals*. Here, individuals regard these organizational values or goals (which are also their personal values) as appropriate to their own self-concept. "People so motivated are usually described as having a sense of mission, direction, or commitment. In most organizations there is a small core of such committed members who have internalized the values of the system" (Katz and Kahn 1982, 362).

Partial internalization of organizational goals is more common than complete inter-nalization. Identification with general organizational values that are not unique to the specific organization is one form of partial internalization. For example, a professional such as a lawyer may internalize the values of his or her occupational specialty—but not necessarily the values of the organization or firm in which he or she exercises it. Or members often embrace the values and goals of a subsystem or unit rather than those of the larger organization. Both types of partial internalization are functional for the larger organization only to the extent that individual and group goals are congruent with orga-nizational objectives.

Three additional conditions foster organization internalization: participating in deci-sions, contributing in a significant way to organization performance, and sharing in the rewards for group accomplishment. Many organizations fail to provide these conditions, but the new participative management systems attempt to recognize and use these potential forces for employee commitment. When all is said and done, it is undoubtedly true that "the internalization of organization goals is at once the most effective motive pattern and the most difficult to invoke within the limits of conventional organizational practice and policy" (Katz and Kahn 1982, 425).

Summary

Content theory is based on individual needs, but its development has been marked by greater inclusion of situational variables and their applicability to work organizations. The content approach has branched out considerably from Maslow's hierarchy of needs.

The movement of content theory is toward a larger conceptual scope and greater usefulness for managers. A major contribution of the content approach is that its explicit treatment of needs serves to bridge the gap between individual needs and *organizationally* based incentives. Efforts to discover the links between individual satisfaction and produc-tivity and even organizational effectiveness also add to the development of work moti-vation theory and its organizational application.

Effectively linking incentives to motivation requires an understanding of worker needs and goals. Moreover, the organization must have access to appropriate resources, and managers need to have sufficient discretion or authority to make appropriate changes in reward systems—conditions that are more likely to be unmet in public than private or-ganizations. In fact, public managers may come to grief, as Cass Peterson reports, even if performance improves and the costs of rewards to employees are highly effective in or-ganizational savings and productivity.

It's Praise, Not a Raise, That's the Big Motivator

Ever since civilization removed the threat of death or starvation for people who did not work hard, managers have been arguing fiercely over how to motivate them. More pay? Sweet words? Company picnics?

A new survey by Robert Half International, a giant staffing services firm, suggests that money has lost its impact. Companies are in danger of losing good workers, the survey said, if they do not learn to nourish egos with warm adjectives and admiring nouns.

The poll of 150 executives from the nation's 1,000 largest companies found the single most common reason why employees left was lack of recognition and praise. Thirty-four percent gave that as the reason for losing workers, compared with 29 percent who cited low compensation, 13 percent who blamed limited authority and 8 percent who mentioned personality conflicts.

The Half survey adds weight to the work of scholars who have been arguing lately that the carrot-and-stick ideas ruling corporate personnel departments do little to encourage more and better work. Researchers such as Edward Deci at the University of Rochester and Mark Lepper at Stanford University say that material rewards not only do not motivate well, but poison natural motivators such as curiosity and self-esteem.

"Companies that believe money is an employee's sole motivation for working are destined to lose some of their best people," said Half, the firm's founder. "Praising accomplishments provides psychological rewards that are critical to satisfaction in any professional setting."

Lynn Taylor, a vice president at Half, said managers often think they are praising workers more often than they actually do, and are far more likely to make negative than positive comments.

Grunting "nice job" in the elevator is not a sufficient solution, she said. "They should do it in public, in front of other people as much as possible," Taylor said. "They should do it frequently, but not to the point where it is insincere."

If they don't she said, people will leave, damaging the reputation of the firm and making it more difficult to find replacements.

A 1991 poll showed that even among salespeople, allegedly fixated on cash, increased compensation was the least commonly cited reason for changing jobs.

SOURCE: Jay Mathews, *The Washington Post*, September 8, 1994: B13.

Government bureaus, in all likelihood, do not compare favorably with private firms in tangible rewards such as salaries, bonuses, advancement, and promotion. Moreover, tangible rewards are dispensed on a system basis—that is, for being a member or employee and having seniority—rather than for an individual's above average work performance. Promotion opportunities are often limited both by freezes on hiring and advancement, and by time-in-grade rules and policies.

Since tangible rewards in bureaus are in short supply and management control over them is limited, it is common practice to substitute intrinsic and recognition-type rewards such as honor boards, office- or employee-of-the-month awards, and the like. Other opportunities for intrinsic and self-actualizing rewards are more promising. For example, members of bureaus like the Environmental Protection Agency can see themselves as part of a movement for a cleaner and more beautiful environment. Internalized goals of community service can be rewarding to bureau members, especially at the local level where community needs and results are more proximate and visible.

We can point to content theory's normative significance as well. Implicit in this perspective is that organizations do not have to be hateful, punitive places to be productive. A worker's motivation cannot be reduced to money as the sole motivator coupled with an inherent dislike of work. Potentially and empirically, the substance of worker motivation encompasses a far greater range of needs and incentives that are more socially and organizationally constructive. Content theory adds a scientific basis to the belief that work organizations can be invested with humanistic values.

COGNITIVE PROCESS THEORIES OF WORK MOTIVATION

Cognitive process models and operant conditioning (which we will discuss in a following section of this chapter) currently dominate motivation theory and research. They represent a shift away from the need-based emphasis of content theory toward a focus on either information processing and cognition or situation and job environment factors (Mitchell 1982).

Cognitive process models concentrate on identifying the factors, especially cognitive variables, that compose the motivation process and on determining how and why these factors result in motivation. Their complexity results not merely from the inclusion of a number of variables, but rather from a concern with process—the relationships and interactions among variables. It is this idea of *process* in formulating models that represents a significant advance in work motivation theory.

Expectancy Models

Two streams of thought form the foundation of expectancy models: (1) the utility or rational choice theories of classical economics, and (2) the cognitive theories of psychology. Expectancy theories include both internal or personality variables and situational factors. Human beings act and choose in ways that fit their personalities and needs, while taking account of the opportunities and constraints in the situation. Expectancy theory encompasses both the emotional (feeling) and cognitive (perceiving, evaluating, learning, and so on) aspects of choice and action. People are emotional; they seek to satisfy their needs. And they are rational; they choose among alternative actions based on what they foresee as producing a satisfactory payoff.

Vroom's VIE Model

An early expectancy model of work motivation was developed by Victor Vroom (1964). The concepts in his VIE theory are valence, instrumentality, and expectancy (see Figure 8–5). Valence is the strength of a person's preference for a particular outcome. Instrumentality relates "first-level outcomes" to "second-level outcomes." The latter is the desired goal or payoff. For example, if a junior-level budget analyst perceives that

FIGURE 8–5   VIE Model of Motivation

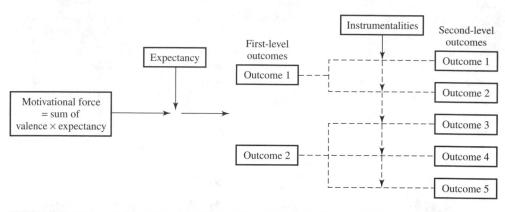

SOURCE: Adapted from Fred Luthans, *Organizational Behavior,* 3rd ed. (New York: McGraw-Hill, 1981): 187. Based on Victor H. Vroom, *Work and Motivation* (New York: John Wiley & Sons, 1964).

outstanding performance is required if she is to be promoted to a higher grade in her agency, she will be motivated to achieve an outstanding rather than an average or above-average performance. Outstanding performance is the choice among first-level outcomes that lead to the desired second-level outcome—promotion to a higher grade. If the same woman's goal were job security and she perceived that an average performance was sufficient to ensure this outcome, her choice of first-level outcomes would probably be an average performance to achieve the preferred utility or second-level outcome of job security.

The concept of expectancy relates effort to first-level outcomes. Our budget analyst's motivation—and effort—would be affected by her beliefs about her ability to achieve her first-level outcome. Motivation would be determined, in part, by whether she believed the probability was high or low that she could achieve her first-level outcome of an outstanding or an average performance. In summary, motivational force is the product of the combined variables of valence, instrumentality, and expectancy.

Porter–Lawler Model

A more elaborate model of work motivation is the Porter–Lawler model (Porter and Lawler 1968), including the refinements added by Lawler (1994). The model's major variables are effort, performance, reward, and satisfaction (see Figure 8–6).

The level of energy an individual puts into a given activity is termed *effort.* The amount of effort exerted depends largely on a combination of two factors: the value the individual places on the reward, and the perceived effort–reward probability. Effort is greater when a reward is highly valued by a worker who perceives that the probability is high that his or her effort will lead to the desired reward.

Effort is also affected by the expectancies added in Lawler's refinement: expectancy or probability that effort will produce the intended performance (E → P expectancy); and the likelihood that performance will result in a particular desired outcome (P → O expec-

FIGURE 8–6   Porter–Lawler Motivation Model

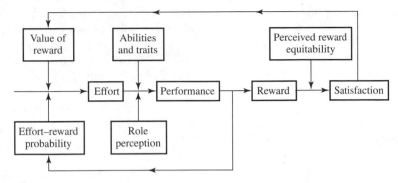

SOURCE: Lyman W. Porter and Edward E. Lawler III, *Managerial Attitudes and Performance* (Homewood, Ill.: Richard D. Irwin, 1968): 165.

tancy) (see Figure 8–7). According to Lawler, the external situation is the strongest determinant of E → P expectancies. Performance can be affected by such things as time availability, the level of cooperation necessary from others, and required procedures that may or may not be obstacles to performance. Internal factors such as self-esteem, role perception, and experiences have an impact as well.

It is important to distinguish between effort and performance: Performance is the objective result of effort. There can be discrepancies between the amount of effort expended and the effectiveness of performance; workers may expend colossal effort and still give an ineffective performance: Their abilities and skills may be deficient; their role perceptions may be inaccurate; their efforts may be misdirected—or they may have little control over the outcomes of their effort.

FIGURE 8–7   Lawler's Expectancies Refinement

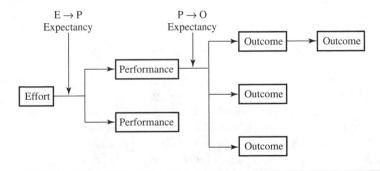

SOURCE: Adapted from Edward E. Lawler III, *Motivation in Work Organizations* (San Francisco: Jossey-Bass, 1994).

The link between performance and rewards is a central element in their theory. Rewards—and thus motivation and satisfaction—are contingent on performance. Common government practices such as automatic step increases in pay and across-the-board raises for everyone in designated job categories weaken this link because the rewards *are not* contingent on individual performance.

Porter and Lawler divide rewards into two types: extrinsic and intrinsic. Intrinsic rewards are closely tied to internal feelings and are an outgrowth of a given performance or behavior. A sense of craftsmanship or professionalism, performing up to one's capacity, and completing a challenging assignment can be intrinsically rewarding. Extrinsic rewards are external in that they come from the environment and not directly from the behavior or performance; money, for example, is an extrinsic reward.

There are numerous constraints on monetary incentives in public agencies: legal and statutory prohibitions; civil service restrictions and uniformity requirements; unavailability of funds; public opposition; and legislative reluctance to surrender control of wage increases and give supervisors and managers wide discretion. A major study of state and local government practices concluded that monetary incentives of various types are quite rare in government. Moreover, the most commonly used type, a performance-based wage increase, is weakly linked to performance owing to the inadequacies of the appraisal systems (Greiner et al. 1981, 393–395).

Promotion, another important extrinsic reward, is also comparatively limited. In a recent survey of 4,900 federal employees conducted by the U.S. Merit Systems Board, 62 percent said that they thought it unlikely that they would be promoted or get a better position if they worked harder in their present position. Responses varied among agencies, from 96 percent regarding promotion unlikely in the Office of Personnel Management to 55 percent in the Department of Health and Human Services to 29 percent in the General Services Administration (U.S. Merit Systems, Board 1984, 18).

Nonmonetary rewards, such as pins, citations, plaques, feature stories in employee publications, or a visit with an agency head pose fewer implementation problems, but no systematic studies of their effectiveness have been conducted. Many professionals and others in government agencies are motivated by the work itself or by broader public service values, but systematic studies of how this affects performance are needed here. Job enrichment is a technique associated with intrinsic rewards and satisfaction. Although public sector use of job enrichment lags behind that of the private sector, the number of public efforts has expanded considerably in recent years—more than 165 percent—with local government accounting for most of the growth (Greiner et al. 1981, 239). However, use of the technique is concentrated in police and fire agencies. Obstacles to broader use are personnel rules and job category systems, management and employee resistance, and union contracts and demands.

The work of Porter and Lawler greatly advances our thinking about satisfaction and reward–satisfaction relationships. They bring to our attention the fact that satisfaction is a cognitive state. Actual rewards only partly determine satisfaction; achieving satisfaction also depends on what rewards an individual believes are equitable for a given level of performance. Equitable reward and satisfaction levels are determined by the individual's perception of the degree to which actual rewards correspond to the perceived or expected equitable reward level; high satisfaction occurs when the reward received is perceived as equitable, and low satisfaction results from rewards that are inadequate or inappropriate based on the individual's perception of an equitable reward level.

Most previous thinking about work motivation, especially the human relations approach, assumed that satisfaction is an attitude that both precedes and causes performance. A major and revolutionary element of Porter and Lawler's theory is its proposition that performance causes satisfaction—mediated, of course, by rewards; or in any case, that satisfaction depends more on performance than performance on satisfaction.

In its complexity, the Porter–Lawler model gives us a more accurate motivation model than the comparatively simplistic content theories. The model can lead theorist and manager alike to useful insights. It depicts workers as active participants in the motivation process; they make decisions about their behavior on the basis of their expectancies about outcomes, and they choose those behaviors that they perceive they can perform. The model also encourages attention to the differences in motives among individuals.

The model's complexity, though adding to its theoretical strength, has proved a drawback to its practical application, a problem acknowledged by Lawler:

> If we try to predict a person's behavior using our model, and if we gather complete data on all his perceptions or existing relationships, we might still predict behavior incorrectly because our model would be too complex to allow for valid predictions. (1994, 60)

Equity Theory

Developed during the same period as expectancy models, equity theory is also cognitively based. Its explanation of how motivation occurs derives from cognitive dissonance and exchange theories. Stacy Adams, credited as its originator, explains the basic point of equity theory in this way: "Inequity exists for Person whenever he perceives that the ratio of his outcomes to inputs and the ratio of Other's outcomes to input are unequal" (1975, 141).

Equity occurs when the ratios of outcomes to inputs are perceived as equal:

$$\frac{\text{Person's outcomes}}{\text{Person's inputs}} = \frac{\text{Other's outcomes}}{\text{Other's inputs}}$$

Adams's terms *person* and *other* refer to any individual who perceives himself or herself as being in an exchange relationship with some other individual or group, and to other individuals or groups with whom the individual feels that equity comparisons are relevant. If individuals perceive their ratio of outcomes to inputs as unequal to those of another relevant person, they are motivated to restore equality. The strength of the motivation to restore balance is proportional to the extent of the perceived inequity.

Efforts to restore equity, Adams points out, can take many forms. Individuals may change their outputs, increasing or decreasing the quantity or quality of their work, or they might try to change their outcomes. Asking for a raise, or making one's contribution more visible might change outcomes without increasing input. Some research suggests that piece-rate workers who perceive an inequity try to improve their reward outcomes with little increase in input by turning out high-volume but low-quality products (Filley, House, and Kerr 1976, 205–206; Goodman and Friedman 1971). Other approaches may be used such as attempting to bring about changes in the other's inputs or outcomes. A more drastic response is that of leaving an organization, work project, or group for a situation perceived as more equitable (Telly, French, and Scott 1971).

Attribution or Locus of Control Theory

Attribution theory is concerned with cause–effect perceptions and behavior. Human behavior is shaped by the perceptions or attributions of causality that an individual ascribes to relevant forces in his or her environment (Kelley 1972). These forces or "attributes," may be internal, such as personal skill and effort; or individuals may ascribe causality to external forces, such as organizational policies and rules or supervisor attitudes.

Individuals perceive that their outcomes in the work situation are either internally or externally controlled. Those who perceive internal control feel they can influence their outcomes through their own skill and efforts. Those who believe their outcomes are externally controlled do not feel they can control or influence them. These locus of control perceptions (and *it is perceived,* and not actual causes or determinants that matter) affect behavior and performance.

Workers are more motivated to perform tasks well in environments where the payoff is certain and outcomes appear to be determined by their skill and performance; in this type of environment, they are more likely to perceive an internal locus of control. Workers are less motivated to high performance in situations where the outcomes or payoffs are more random, Which environment is a better description of public organizations? Is external attribution among public employees fostered by factors such as broad and sometimes contradictory goals, accountability to outside and often conflicting actors, reliance on system over individual rewards? In all likelihood the answer is yes, but further research is needed to determine both public–private differences and variations among different public contexts.

Attribution and locus of control theory can affect both worker satisfaction and management style. Internal control individuals tend to be more satisfied in their jobs than external control persons. And internal and external control followers respond differently to leadership styles. Using a locus of control measure to assess the degree to which an individual sees the environment as responding to his or her behavior, researchers found that internals were more satisfied with a participative leadership style (Mitchell, Smyser, and Weed 1975). Under some conditions, however, the nature of the task may override the relationships between participation and follower responses. If tasks are highly ambiguous or stressful, participative leadership is positively correlated with satisfaction—regardless of followers' external and internal predispositions (House and Mitchell 1974).

Terrence Mitchell and his associates investigated the way in which attribution affects management behavior, specifically leader responses to poor performance by followers (Mitchell and Wood 1979; Green and Mitchell 1979). Managers and supervisors attribute causes to poor performance. If they perceive that a subordinate's poor performance is due to internal factors—insufficient ability, effort, or attentiveness—their response tends to be punitive. But if they perceive the locus of control as external to the follower, they are more likely to respond sympathetically.

Something like an attribution process may operate on a macrolevel as well. For example, public attitudes toward bureaus and bureaucrats that hold they are ineffectual (lazy, red-tape ridden, and so on) can mean an internal locus of control is ascribed to bureaus.

This attribution makes public and political leaders all too likely to blame a bureau's inability to achieve a given level of policy result on bureau incompetence. As a result, external factors, such as unrealistic or conflicting goals, inadequate resources, insufficient time for results, and the like, go unacknowledged and uncorrected.

Summary

The basic assumption of process theory is that internal cognitive states and situational variables interact in the motivational process. The individual is an active factor, selecting behaviors based on his or her needs and on expectations about what kind of behavior will lead to a desired reward. This perspective has greatly expanded our understanding of human motivation and its complexities. Process theories provide a good conceptual grasp of how elements of internal states and behavior are related. They also offer a wide range of diagnostic and operational alternatives that can be applied to motivation, but they are difficult for managers to apply on a daily basis.

Part of the difficulty is that process theories are far more abstract than content models, making it difficult to identify specific and appropriate incentives. Further, process models not only deal with differences in individual needs, but with differences among individuals' perceptions of important elements of the situation, such as rewards, opportunity, equity, and control over outcomes. Linking the effect of specific rewards to an individual's work motivation (or satisfaction or performance) is exceedingly difficult when the effect of actual rewards is mediated by a number of subtle and internal processes of perception and expectancy. It is impractical and time consuming for managers to attempt such an assessment of employees and organizational incentives on a one-by-one basis.

For government agencies, the application of process models is difficult in other ways as well. For example, Chester Newland identifies several problems with the politically popular merit pay system. "Unless performance can be appraised well, it is impossible to relate pay to it," he points out (1984, 39). In addition, he notes that using pay to motivate performance is probably not an effective technique unless relatively large pay increases are available. Newland also cautions, in a statement prescient of later developments in total quality management and other participative methods, that individual rewards such as merit pay that focus on individually competitive behaviors "may frustrate modular and team management approaches" (1984, 39).

The two problems—rewards (their adequacy and appropriateness) and performance (its definition and appraisal)—are crucial to forging the principal link in process models: High performance results in desired and equitable rewards. The utility of rewards in bureaus is limited by constraints already discussed. Defining performance targets or goals and appraising performance are equally challenging. The link between effort and performance is stronger when performance standards or goals are clear and relatively specific.

Performance targets and their measurement are an increasing part of programs such as the National Performance Review (1993) where total organizations are being reviewed; however, the use of such tools is given mixed reviews when dealing with individuals (Deming 1986, 110). In spite of debate by scholars, the use of techniques such as MBO, employee appraisal processes, and work standards seems to be increasing in government. In such cases, there is a danger that workload rather than efficiency or effectiveness criteria may be used because of the difficulty in setting specific organization goals and breaking these down into objective specific performance measures for individuals (Greiner et al. 1981). Compared to the more specific and tangible goals of firms, bureaus pursue goals that are diffuse and conflicting, and their performance criteria are less readily defined. The link between effort and performance, and thus the expectation that given performances will produce specific rewards, is weakened by the lack of goal clarity as well as by conflicting demands. Thus the cognitive process models assume a flexibility and control over rewards that is somewhat unrealistic when applied to public managers. The next approach, behaviorism and operant conditioning, offers an alternative perspective on directly linking individual behavior and organizational incentives or rewards.

BEHAVIORIST THEORY AND WORK MOTIVATION

Motivation theory explains behavior through a broad range of internal psychological processes such as needs, expectancies, and perceptions, but such unobservable inner states are irrelevant to behavioral researchers. What an individual's motivation is, indeed, whether or not an individual is motivated, is irrelevant; from the behaviorist's perspective, only observable behavior and its consequences are important.

In a strict sense, then, behaviorist theories are not theories of motivation. However, operant conditioning and expectancy theories are related in certain important aspects despite differences in their underlying assumptions (noncognitive versus cognitive): "Both approaches argue that (1) rewards should be closely tied to behavior, (2) reward administration should be frequent and consistent, and (3) people are motivated by outcomes (expected or past)" (Mitchell 1982, 86). Thus, although their theoretical bases differ, there are parallels in the actual applications of either approach, and both entail similar practices and policies by an organization.

Behaviorist theory concentrates primarily on two factors: behavior and its consequences. Its central thesis is that behavior is caused by its contingent consequences, the essential point being that the consequence must be contingent on the occurrence of a particular behavior. Since behavior operates on the environment to produce a consequence, the term *operant conditioning* is used. It refers to the process through which behavior is learned and reinforced (Skinner 1976).

In operant conditioning, behavior is determined by four types of consequences: (1) positive reinforcement, (2) negative reinforcement, (3) extinction, and (4) punishment. Reinforcers are functionally defined by their observable effects. A reinforcer is anything that strengthens and increases a given behavior. Note how this way of defining reinforcer differs from the concept of reward in cognitive theories where a reward is that which is *perceived* to be desirable; one definition relies on the external and observable, the other on the internal and subjective. The distinction is important to an understanding of the unique perspective of behaviorist and operant conditioning theory.

Positive reinforcers are satisfying or good consequences; negative reinforcers are unsatisfying or noxious ones. Individuals repeat a pattern of behavior that elicits a satisfying consequence (positive reinforcer) or one that precludes an unsatisfying or noxious one (negative reinforcer). Thus, both positive and negative reinforcement strengthen and increase—that is, reinforce—a given behavior.

The effects of extinction and punishment on behavior are the opposite of reinforcers; they weaken or decrease a given behavior. The technique of extinction involves providing *non*reinforcement; that is, nothing must happen as a consequence of behavior. If a manager recognizes and praises those who speak up and offer ideas in meetings, for example, participation is likely to increase. Participative behavior has been reinforced. But if a manager ignores such behavior, in time followers will no longer initiate participative behavior. Human beings rarely persist in behavior that is not rewarded or, in operant conditioning terms, reinforced. Since both extinction and punishment weaken a given behavior, which technique should be used? If an undesirable behavior is relatively new, extinction may be sufficiently effective in eliminating it. But if the undesirable behavior is long-standing or very serious, punishment may be indicated despite its drawbacks.

Punishment, like negative reinforcement, involves aversive stimuli or consequences. But its effect, weakening or extinguishing a behavior, is the opposite of negative reinforcement, which, as mentioned earlier, strengthens a given behavior. Punishment, though widely used in organizational settings, has various defects and undesirable side effects. Most notable is that punishment suppresses undesirable behavior but often fails to eliminate it; when the aversive agent is removed or discontinued, the behavior recurs. Another problem with punishment is that its overall effects are hard to predict and are often dysfunctional to the organization. For example, only the particular behavior at which the punishment is directed is likely to be eliminated. Hence, an employee made resentful by punishment may retaliate by engaging in other actions that are even less desirable but harder to detect. A punitive organizational climate can result in discipline problems, low morale, and absenteeism.

At best then, punishment is limited to eliminating undesirable behavior. Its greatest drawback is that it can show an individual what *not* to do, but not *what* to do (Hersey and Blanchard 1993). Punishment can be appropriate and necessary under some conditions. For a fully effective system of conditioning to operate, however, the manager needs to then identify the desired behavior and use positive reinforcement when it occurs to increase and strengthen it in the future.

Summary

Operant conditioning is used continually in organizations and, in most cases, without organizational leaders or members having any formal knowledge of behaviorist theory. Surprisingly, the results are sometimes favorable. Unfortunately, however, inappropriate behavior is also often unintentionally reinforced (Nord 1970).

Reinforcing dysfunctional behavior in public bureaus has ramifications beyond the individual and even beyond the organization. Government budget and appropriations practices are a case in point. Ordinarily, public bureaus may not "save" or put aside surplus funds past the budget period for which they were authorized and appropriated. Such funds are to be returned to the government's general treasury. It is common wisdom among government administrators, however, that they must avoid turning back funds because legislators will conclude that the bureau can get by on smaller future appropriations. Therefore, as the end of a budget cycle approaches, unused funds are spent. Hasty expenditures on unneeded equipment and unnecessary services and travel are not desirable bureaucratic responses to legislators who oversee government agencies. Yet, by spending leftover funds, bureau officials avoid (negative reinforcement) lower appropriations in the future. Their undesirable practices are thus reinforced.

When behavior modification is used intentionally, it should be remembered that the technique is best suited to simple behaviors. Moreover, such use requires that the desired behavior be rather specifically defined and that the organization be able to provide clear and proximate rewards for individual performance. Given the ambiguity of public goals and the relative lack of flexibility and control of rewards, its systematic use in bureaus has serious limitations. On the other hand, operant conditioning offers a fresh perspective on the problem of motivating workers to perform in ways that are useful to the organization and influencing them to refrain from behavior that is not organizationally desirable.

MOTIVATION AND BUREAU SETTING

Human motivation and behavior are complex phenomena. They arise from interactions of both individual and situational variables. The bureau setting introduces distinctive constraints, values, and opportunities for motivation. Bureaus differ from firms in their personnel and reward systems, public attitudes toward the civil service, and reasons why individuals join and commit themselves. These differences do not constitute a different theory of "public" motivation, but they require changes in the interpretation of the models.

In the United States, reaction against the mingling of politics into bureau staffing and practice resulted in the establishing of a merit system to cover many bureau positions at all levels of government. Two cornerstone values of public personnel management that are part of the merit system are technical competence and equal pay for equal work.

Technical or work-related competence was established as the criteria for selection, promotion, and related personnel choices; thus, the merit system created a need to define what duties were entailed and what qualifications were required for a given position. Although clarity of job description helps limit political manipulation of positions, it can, at the same time, lead to overspecialization and narrow job descriptions. Job enrichment, or the use of an employee's "total capacity," is difficult because government managers often find that their discretion in either shifting employees or adjusting the range of tasks to match individual abilities is hampered.

Equal pay for equal work is accomplished through position classification, which organizes all positions into groups or classes based on their duties, responsibilities, and required qualifications. Again, the initial goal of equality in pay has some unintended and detrimental effects on motivation. Salaries are attached to job classifications and not to individuals. Implementing this aspect of the merit system led to job classification systems that were both highly complex and too simple. For example, all the myriad jobs in the federal bureaucracy are reduced to sixteen or so categories. Since a salary is set for each category, there is little or no flexibility around pay.

The accountability norm further complicates the merit system. For example, the evaluation system encourages supervisors to give individuals middling evaluations because very high evaluations entail extensive justification and proof, whereas very low evaluations trigger even more extensive documentation and proof because of grievance and appeal procedures.

System rewards that are based on membership or seniority in the organization predominate over individual rewards. System rewards, such as liberal vacation policies, give increases based on seniority and time-in-grade. Further, an attractive retirement system is based on membership or seniority in the system. System rewards are cheaper than monetary incentives, have lower visibility in the budget process, and thus have greater appeal to elected officials facing a tax-paying public. But system rewards are not directly related to individual performance and therefore may reduce manager flexibility in rewarding and motivating workers.

Environmental factors and external climate strongly affect bureaus' motivation and reward systems. "To the extent that the general public holds unfavorable attitudes about public employment and public bureaucracies," Perry and Porter note, "motivation-relevant employee perceptions such as self-worth and personal significance can be expected to be affected" (1982, 93).

And attitudes have not changed for the better since the early 1980s. "Bureaucrat bashing" remains a favorite political sport, and combined with the downsizing of governments (caused by everything from proposition-13-style tax limitations at the state level to budgetary deficits and philosophical restrictions at the federal level) there has been a general demoralization of government employees. Even the Clinton administration's attempt to improve the effectiveness and efficiency of government agencies has as one of its primary goals the reduction of the number of employees by rather dramatic amounts. This "disinvestment" as it is referred to by Lane and Wolf, has become a threat to what they call "governance capacity."

> The effects of continuing budgetary restrictions, antibureaucratic rhetoric, reorganizations, reductions in force, and various administrative retrenchments have adversely affected the quality of work life and sent the message that a public agency is the wrong place to invest personal energy and identity. As a result, organizational and program capacity is being lost daily as workers invest less of themselves in their work, make fewer commitments, and seek ways out of the system. (1990, 3)

Motivation theory, and its application, must be especially perceptive and sagacious in such an environment.

On the positive side, research indicates that public servants are attracted to public and nonprofit organizations for somewhat different reasons than those attracting individuals to private ones. Those who enter the public sector place less value on economic worth than those who choose the profit sector (Rawls and Nelson 1975; Rawls, Ulrich, and Nelson 1975; Gortner 1970). A desire to perform public service is cited by those entering public, but not private, careers (Gortner 1970). Some evidence points to greater security motivations among public respondents, but in other instances differences were less clear-cut (Gortner 1970; Rawls and Nelson 1975; Rawls, Ulrich, and Nelson 1975).

Studies do point to somewhat different public and private patterns of commitment. The concept of commitment has several dimensions: desire to remain a member of the organization, willingness to perform at high levels, and acceptance of organizational goals and values. Firms have considerable advantages and success in engendering commitment among their managers, whereas certain work setting and environmental characteristics of bureaus adversely affect motivation. An interesting question, for which there is no immediate answer, is to what extent the desire of public employees to function in the public service offsets the commitment-limiting characteristics of bureaus.

In a comparative study of government and business managers, it was found that an individual's perception of having contributed to organizational success had the greatest impact on his or her commitment (Buchanan 1974). Highly committed managers also feel

Some Things Never Change: At the Centennial of the Federal Civil Service, the Workers Were Under Siege

The federal civil service system marks its centennial today unhappy, unhealthy, under siege.

The assault comes from all quarters.

Even Madison Avenue has gotten into the act with advertisements for Federal Express that portray the employees of its competitor, the U.S. Postal Service, as surly, lazy, unresponsive. "The worst part of it was they were funny," said George Gould, legislative director of the National Association of Letter Carriers, whose protests helped push the hardest-hitting ads off the air.

Images have consequences. Since 1977, the lot of the federal worker has declined on a number of fronts.

—Government salaries, which by law are supposed to be kept at par with comparable private sector wages, are lagging a record 13.9 percent.

—The cost of government employee health premiums has gone up an average of 55 percent in the past two years while the benefits have been reduced an average of 12 to 16 percent.

—The jewel of the federal employees' compensation package, the retirement system, has been whittled back four of the past five years and now faces the most sweeping attack in its 62-year history.

—Since passage of the Civil Service Reform Act of 1978, designed to make the bureaucracy more responsive to political leadership, top-level careerists have enjoyed far less job security against policy or political purges.

From the viewpoint of some careerists, the loss of job protections, combined with arrival of a batch of ideologically zealous political appointees who consider the government the enemy, has been a disaster. "It has gotten to the point where many of the nation's most capable public administrators are forced into being yes-men," said Bernard Rosen, a former executive director of the U.S. Civil Service Commission. "I've never seen it so bad." All of this has taken a predictable toll on morale.

"We are the new underclass of society," said G. Jerry Shaw, president of the Senior Executives Association which represents high-ranking career bureaucrats. "People make jokes about us that they've stopped making about ethnic groups and minorities."

James Beggs, director of the National Aeronautics and Space Administration, said, "Anytime you are constantly told that you are a bunch of leeches on society, morale is bound to suffer." He worries, as do most top federal executives, that the image, pay and morale problems are leading to a "brain drain" from government.

SOURCE: Paul Taylor, "Federal Workers: Unloved and Under Siege," *Washington Post,* January 16, 1983; A1.

a sense of challenge in their jobs, experience cohesion in their workgroups, and perceive that the organization expects commitment. The substantive goals of most government agencies are diffuse, and agency effectiveness is hard to measure. As a result, the observable links between what a public manager does and the organization's success are harder to discern. Another important factor is the stability of the organization's commitment to its goals. Bureaus confront circumstances—periodic ones like elections, as well as unpredictable shifts in public and political opinion—that lead to goal instability (Buchanan 1974).

In general, studies conclude that need satisfaction (Paine, Carroll, and Leete 1966; Rinehart et al. 1969; Buchanan 1974; Rainey 1979) and commitment are higher in business organizations. Yet other studies, such as a report by the National Center for Productivity and Quality of Working Life (1978), suggest that job content and job challenge satisfy the needs of public employees relatively well: Job content satisfaction was indicated by 84 percent of managers and 64 percent of nonmanagers; job challenge satisfaction was indicated by 86 percent of managers and 77 percent of nonmanagers. The body of comparative research is still small, and it is too early to assess the degree of variation between private and public organization satisfaction or to assume that a lower level of commitment is common among public agencies.

Already, several additional factors can be identified that may give public organizations some natural advantages in the formation of high commitment levels. The more distinctive and exciting the mission of an agency, the more likely members are to develop high commitment. In the Agency for International Development, for example, managers and staff describe their agency's mission as humanitarian and important to foreign policy (Mahler 1985). The more lengthy and even hazardous the socialization, the higher the commitment level is likely to be (Van Maanen 1975a, 1975b; Kaufman 1960; Mahler 1985). A preestablished recruitment or entry pattern, reinforced by a distinctive mission, makes self-selection effective as a means of creating organizational identification and commitment (Mahler 1985; Kaufman 1960; Van Maanen 1975a).

A THEORY OF MOTIVATION IN BUREAUS

Motivation and behavior are influenced by the *public* nature of an organization, and public organizations and policy are affected by the motivation and behavior of bureau officials. Organization theories are needed that specifically address these types of organizations and behavior. A theory of motivation in public servants can be developed from the combination of the ideas mentioned earlier and their application within Anthony Downs's typology of bureau official motivation (1967, 79–111). The bureaucratic context is an integral part of Downs's model, as is the interplay between individual motivation and policy preferences.

First, it is important to remember that organizations exist for many reasons, and an excellent place to start is with the typology of organizations developed by some fellow scholars writing at about the same time as Downs. Blau and Scott (1962) note that four types of organizations exist if one refers to the relationship between the formal organization and those persons who benefit from them. These four types of organizations are (1) *mutual-benefit associations*—where the prime beneficiary is the membership; (2) *business concerns*—where the owners are prime beneficiaries; (3) *service organizations*—where the

Not a Breed Apart

People who work for the government are not a breed apart. We have the same characteristics as those who work for business. We want responsible compensation, appreciation for good work, recognition for extraordinary achievement, a decent working environment, opportunities for advancement or growth, respect as competent individuals, opportunities for our ideas and suggestions to be seriously considered, and fair treatment.

Democratic government is not just a gigantic money machine and government management is much more than personnel, procurement, and moving money around. It provides the security and stability which makes all the other nongovernment activities possible, including a free-flowing economic system, free speech, the right to be different without penalty, and the pursuit of happiness. Therefore, public employees tend to believe in their programs, become proprietary about them, take pride in public service, and deeply resent slurs about their chosen profession.

SOURCE: Eileen Siedman, "Of Games and Gains . . . ," *The Bureaucrat* 13 (Summer 1984); 4–8.

client group is the primary beneficiary; and (4) *commonweal organizations*—where the primary beneficiary is the public at large. Nonprofit organizations usually fit into group three, whereas government organizations make up most of the fourth category; however, there is spillover between these two types of organizations, and they face many of the same problems in promoting extraordinary performance. The keys to success are maintaining (1) a clarity of goals (often difficult because they are set outside the organization); (2) a reward system that encourages commitment and effort toward achieving those goals; and (3) a focus on serving clients while remembering the public interest.

In order to achieve the effort and commitment in these two types of organizations, there must be a focus on the higher rewards or satisfaction levels of Maslow (1954), Herzberg (1966), and Katz and Kahn (1982). Security is assumed in most government organizations—although cutbacks in budget and staff through the 1980s and 1990s have had a negative effect on these lower-level motivators. The workers are increasingly coming to understand the kinds of rewards available in the public sector, and the probability and fairness of their receipt on successfully carrying out their duties (Porter and Lawler 1968). Money, though not unimportant, is not the focus of most highly motivated workers outside the private sector. Interesting work, self-expression, internalization of goals, growth and development, responsibility, and a sense of achievement are the characteristics that can be affected by organizational leadership, structure, and process. These factors are increasingly the focus of motivation in most organizations, but are about the only area of flexibility to public managers and leaders. If these theories are brought together, it is possible to develop at least a rudimentary model of motivation in the public sector.

The final factor in all this, however, is the type of individual attracted to public employment. We noted earlier that those people who choose to consider public employment usually have a greater interest in serving the public interest—of doing something that helps society at large—so this gives some impetus to the preceding model. Ultimately, though, public employees, like all individuals, vary in their personalities. And we must understand that these characteristics will change throughout each individual's career as external factors change and each person goes through the various stages of life and career that we now recognize occur within each life (Schott 1986, 1987). Downs describes at least five such different sets of characteristics. What motivates each of Downs's model bureaucrats will be different.

Downs's theory of five personality types of officials is in reality a set of practical observations about motivations in public organizations. He begins with two assumptions about human nature: (1) people are rational; their behavior is directed toward goals; and (2) they are motivated at least in part by self-interest; as a result, they pursue goals that are in their own interest. But the prevalence of self-interest in the theory does not mean that officials do not take the interests of others into account; they have multiple goals, some of which are altruistic, that is, for the benefit of interests other than their own. And some goals are "mixed" in that they may be part self-interest and part altruism.

Downs says that all bureau officials have multiple goals that derive from a set of general motives: power, money, income, prestige, convenience, and security. Pride in work proficiency, personal loyalty (either to the official's own workgroup, the bureau as a whole, or to a larger entity such as the government or the nation), desire to serve the public interest, and commitment to a specific program of action are also sources of motivation. These goals or motives do not represent an individual's overall goal structure, but they do determine an official's behavior as it relates to his or her position in the bureau.

The first five motives are based on self-interest. Downs classifies the sixth, proficiency in work performance, as mixed. One's desire to serve the public interest is altruistic; one's commitment to a specific program or policy is ambiguous—it may be either altruistic, self-interested, or both.

All officials are not motivated in the same degree by all motives; rather, each individual gives greater weight to some combination of motives. Downs concentrates on five combinations, and from these groupings, he constructs a typology of officials based on their motivation structure; these officials are "ideal types." An ideal type is an abstraction in which a set of characteristics is sharpened. Oversimplification is unavoidable here, as Downs acknowledges, since no reasonable number of ideal types can "encompass the bewildering variety of personalities and characters in the world" (1994, 88).

The five types of officials are climbers, conservers, zealots, advocates, and statesmen. The first two types—climbers and conservers—are motivated by self-interest; the remaining three types—zealots, advocates, and statesmen—are mixed-motive officials. Each of these three types envisions organizational goals in terms of their perception of the public interest, and conversely, each type equates the public interest with their view of organizational goals. Their motives combine self-interest and altruistic loyalty to larger values, but the three types differ in the breadth of the larger values to which they are devoted.

In Downs's theory, as in content models, behavior is viewed as deriving from needs, goals, or motives. Motivation and behavior are also determined by environmental variables and expectancies. Bureau and position characteristics shape behavior, and the official's beliefs about the probability of attaining his or her goal are also considered determinants of motivation.

Climbers

The climber seeks to maximize his or her own power, income, and prestige by promotion, aggrandizement, and "jumping." Promotion provides the greatest personal gain and is preferred. Aggrandizement entails increasing the power, income, and prestige associated with an individual's existing position by adding new functions, control over people, or by achieving more than previous occupants of the position. "Jumping" involves moving to another organization. A consequence of jumping is that climbers in leadership situations may treat subordinates and others as pawns. And because climbers are on the move—upward in the bureau or hopping to another organization—their leadership may be sufficiently effective to produce short-term results at the expense of long-term performance and the morale of others. Bureaus' growth rates affect jumping; fast-growing bureaus attract climbers just as climbers tend to move from contracting or slow-growing organizations.

Climbers are receptive to organizational change since it can produce new opportunities for either promotion or aggrandizement. Since attachment to settled procedures and alliances is considered a hallmark of bureaucratic behavior, the climber's acceptance of risk can be useful to public managers who understand and channel it.

Conservers

These officials are motivated to maximize their security and convenience. Conservers resist change so that they can avoid any risk to their existing power, income, and prestige, and because they do not have a strong desire for more of these. Change might harm them, and they do not strongly favor its potential rewards. Thus, only changes that head off threats to their security or that make their lives easier because less effort will be required of them are welcomed by conservers.

Conservers need only maintain minimally acceptable performance levels and refrain from actions that invite failure and risk. The safety of following bureau rules, together with various personnel practices (for example, reliance on seniority, discharge only for proven cause, extensive procedural and appeals mechanisms) is usually sufficient to maintain security. Accountability and neutrality norms reinforce and give added legitimacy to the conserver's "by the book" approach.

Some officials tend to be conservers because of personality factors, but occasionally conserver behavior is created by expectancies. In the latter group are competent persons whose upward progress is barred by age, seniority, or other unchangeable traits. "In every bureau, there is an inherent pressure upon the vast majority to become conservers in the long run" (Downs 1967, 99). As a person becomes older and the expectations for substantial advancement grow slimmer, the tendency to become a conserver increases. Likewise, older and slower growing bureaus have more conservers; bureaus that rely extensively on formal rules also have more conservers.

Even climbers tend to become conservers. Changes in both the bureau's internal and external opportunity structures support and reinforce conserver rather than climber behavior. Climbers "learn" in this way to become conservers. From the standpoint of attribution and locus of control, the climber moves toward attributing external rather than internal control over rewards.

The proportion of conservers is higher at the middle levels of a bureau hierarchy than at the lowest and highest levels, and the proportion of conservers in a bureau tends to increase over time. The "closing of the hierarchy" as one advances in a career limits the chances for advancement. Most officials are required by the duties inherent in their positions to make decisions, and take the chance of making a mistake. Conservers solve the dilemma this poses for them by sticking to the rules; rules reduce the risks in decision making—and conservers are risk avoiders.

Rule following lends stability to bureau activity. It also ensures the accountability expected of officials because their positions are public, not private. But unduly rigid adherence to rules can impair bureau responsiveness and hamper efficiency with red tape. If extreme, rule following can even be dysfunctional to the accomplishment of the bureau's larger objectives and societal functions. Motivation must aim at maintaining a will to serve while recognizing the importance of security for these individuals.

Zealots

Zealots, like advocates and statesmen, are motivated less by self-interest than by higher-level needs. Even though concepts like Maslow's and Herzberg's are applicable in some measure, only Katz and Kahn's highest incentive structure directly touches on the distinctive motivation needs of these officials. The zealot perceives organizational goals and the public interest very narrowly by focusing on a "sacred" or special policy.

Because of the tremendous amounts of energy they help generate and focus in the pursuit of their sacred policies, zealots can be a significant force in overcoming bureaucratic inertia and bringing about change. This energy makes them critically important to the long-run efficiency of all bureaus. "Every bureau needs to encourage some zealots," Downs says, "and bureaus operating in rapidly changing environments need to nurture a great many" (1967, 110).

On the other hand, innovators and catalysts for change—especially zealots—generate conflict and resentment. In their willingness to vigorously attack the status quo on behalf of their policies, zealots often draw attention to deficiencies in their organizations and disseminate too much information about bureau problems and their own remedies for overcoming them. The toll that change will take on others in the organization is rarely taken into account by zealots. They are most likely to engender resentment and resistance in conserver-dominated bureaus. And, paradoxically, conservers are more effective change agents in agencies dominated by climbers and advocates than zealots since zealots tend to support only their own narrow policy and to "starve" any other developments.

Zealot behavior is not without liabilities for both the zealot and the organization. Zealots are preoccupied with their constricted concerns regardless of the broadness of their formal responsibilities and are therefore likely to be poor general administrators. They are unlikely to be found in top-level agency positions although they can be found on high-level staffs. Only when a policy with which a zealot has become identified becomes suddenly and critically significant is this type of official likely to be elevated to a leading position. To a surprising degree, then, the external political environment conditions and shapes the rewards and reinforcements for zealot behavior. If it is possible to find a way to focus the efforts of zealots on organizational goals, and in organizational processes, their internal motivaters will keep them productive and useful.

OSHA Official Airs Frustration in New Book

Edward J. Bergin is a senior Labor Department official who has chosen a unique way to challenge his superiors in the federal government. He has written a book excoriating several agencies, and the Reagan administration in general, for failing to protect the American public from pollutants.

"I'm expecting trouble, and I know I'll be subjected to tremendous pressure, . . . But I'm sick and tired of our government agencies continuing to act as if chemicals have more rights than people."

Bergin, 42, is a senior policy adviser in the Occupational Safety and Health Administration, earning about $58,600 a year. He could continue his career and retire comfortably, but he has decided to fight to revive programs, canceled by the Reagan administration, that he says are essential for the public's safety.

In 1980, Bergin participated in an exhaustive study of workers disabled by chemicals. The 138-page report estimated that nearly 2 million Americans are totally disabled by worksite chemicals, gases and dust.

"The amazing thing we found," Bergin said, "is that only one out of 20 people suffering from occupational diseases received anything from the state workers' compensation system which is supposed to take care of work-related injuries and diseases. When we looked closely at the compensation system, we found that, while it may pay for a broken leg on the job, it is designed not to pay for occupational diseases."

Yet most state laws preclude workers from suing their employers for diseases contracted on the job. "The only thing they can get is workers' compensation, but the laws are rigged to prevent them from collecting," Bergin said. He was appalled at the widespread ignorance about the compensation program, not only among workers but among physicians and lawyers, who had little or no training in toxic chemical cases.

With the Labor Department's blessing, Bergin and his colleagues designed several programs at New York's Montefiore Hospital to train physicians in recognizing and treating chemical-induced diseases. Bergin also was put in charge of a new program to teach workers in seven selected states about toxic substances and workers' legal rights.

The Reagan administration killed these programs, abolished Bergin's job and transferred him to OSHA.

"My experience convinced me that the American people were genuinely concerned about birth defects, chemicals in drinking water, toxic waste dumps and food additives," Bergin said. "I had also seen enough in my 12 years in Washington to convince me that the government was not doing its job in protecting people or the environment. I wrote my book to give people who have problems with chemicals the information they need to help themselves until the government gets its act together."

The book is a veritable training manual for workers, telling them how to make the government respond to their requests and how to find helpful information buried in government files.

SOURCE: Jack Anderson, *Washington Post,* March 14, 1981: B16.

Advocates

An advocate is motivated to promote whatever is in the best interest of the particular office he or she holds. Downs is not referring to self-interest here, but to their loyalty to the organizations in which they work (1967, 102). Certain patterns—five are identified—characterize advocate behavior.

First, advocates do not focus on only one part of their organizational domain, but rather on the overall conditions and performance that are within their purview. Consequently, they promote everything that is under their jurisdiction.

Advocates are highly partisan in their external dealings, but tend to be impartial arbiters internally. What resources and how much prestige their organization or group receives depends on their success at external advocacy, which, in turn, affects the willingness with which subordinates work for them. In their external struggles, advocates create conflict by competing and threatening the domain of others, but the other side of this conflict is that internal group unity and morale rise; members feel loyal to the advocate who champions their interests.

A third pattern is that advocates will persist in advocacy only if they believe the policies for which they have responsibility are significant and that there is a high probability that they can influence those policies. If these conditions are not met, they will not continue acting as advocates over long periods, nor will they maintain the considerable expenditure of time and energy that advocacy requires.

Fourth, advocates rather than climbers are the most aggressive and persistent sources of "bureaucratic imperialism" (Holden 1966). They support innovation and expansion by their organization, and to obtain more resources, they magnify the problems facing their bureaus. Their practice of calling attention to unfavorable conditions and deficiencies is often disturbing to their superiors and to political leaders who prefer to give the public the impression that everything is under control. Compared to climbers and conservers, whose concern is limited to their own careers, advocates see their careers and the success of the bureau as intertwined. Thus advocates develop a broad and long-term perspective toward decisions related to the agency. They are also more attentive to the long-term implications of present policy proposals.

Finally, information flow becomes specialized as a result of advocates concentrating on a particular spectrum of activities and responsibilities. Specialized and differentiated information flow reinforces an official's sense of the relative importance of the position he or she occupies and its functions. Further, an advocate is a part of and is familiar with the processes by which alternatives are deliberated and evaluated in his or her own organization. On the other hand, he or she sees only the finished reports and recommendations from other organizations or parts of the bureau and knows little about the quality of the underlying choice process. As a result, nearly every official has greater faith in the reliability of his or her own part of the bureaucracy. Motivation to advocacy behavior, Downs concludes, is supported in this way.

Special role expectations that encourage advocacy are attached to certain kinds of bureau positions:

> Because officials at all levels recognize the vital advantages of having advocates in charge of specialized bureaus, the role of bureau head (or department head, or division head, and

the like) tends to be conceived as an advocacy role by most other persons who interact
with that role, including the generalists at the top of the pyramid (such as the President).
This expectation creates a further incentive for whoever performs each such role to behave
like an advocate. (Downs 1967, 105)

In the case of bureau members and followers, this role expectation is especially strong
because the advocate's external effectiveness determines their resources and prestige.

Many rewards, both external and internal, accrue to advocates through their position
and performance. A sense of achievement often comes with the territory. Their position
in the bureau creates opportunities for influence and power. As liaison, their communications role (between their organization and the external environment) gives them visibility
and recognition, as well as information-based power. Others seek to affiliate with advocates. Advocacy and advancement are linked: The proportion of advocates increases at
higher bureau levels (Downs 1967, 109).

Many bureau factors cause officials to behave as advocates—even those who have
other psychological predispositions or motive structures. Climbers readily yield to such
pressures because they receive aggrandizement and promotion opportunities. Statemen also
perform as advocates. Conservers are less likely to be strongly inclined to assume the role,
and zealots are highly resistant to it.

Statesmen

Loyalty to a very broad conception of the public interest motivates statesmen. Attentiveness to society and the nation as a whole receives philosophical support from everyone.
Political rhetoric is filled with exhortations to public administrators to serve the interests
of the entire population; administrators, in turn, vow their loyalty to the citizenry. In reality,
however, consistent statesmanslike behavior is rare owing to the formidable obstacles in
bureau structure and other bureau characteristics. The pressures to become an advocate,
which have already been described, also operate to stifle the more diffuse altruism of the
statesman.

Officials whose behavior is statesmanlike in spite of the constraints they face, and
who forego attending to the well-being of their own bureaus usually earn the hostility of
others in their organizations. These coworkers know that if all bureaus but theirs are being
vigorously promoted, the resource allocation for their organization will suffer. It is little
wonder that statesmen are rarely promoted and are therefore more likely to be concentrated
in the lower—not higher—levels of bureaus.

Although rare, statesmanlike behavior does occur. If society's survival or that of the
overall public bureaucracy is threatened, even officials with other motivation structures
are inclined to act like statesmen. Statesmanlike behavior also comes easier in less dire
circumstances if an official's own bureau's interests are not involved.

The nature of the bureaucracy is such a powerful inhibitor on statesmanlike behavior
that under some conditions this fact of bureau life must be offset by specially structuring
some positions. An example that Downs gives is the practice of insulating certain high-
level advisory positions from the pressures of day-to-day decision making and operating
responsibilities. The relatively small number of subordinates and their expected short tenure (particularly for special task forces) probably give added leeway to statesmen.

CONCLUSION

If one theme emerges clearly from a review of the various work motivation theories and models, it is that research and application must include situational variables as well as the individual factors. Some situations elicit organizationally effective behavior; others do not. Reward systems and situational constraints in particular should be examined

Public bureaus appear to rely, for example, on security and system rewards. These types of rewards can elicit adequate role performance and reduce turnover. However, they do not promote high performance levels or activity that goes beyond role requirements. In order to heighten morale and dedication, a focus on higher-level, intrinsic factors must be developed in any motivation model for public employees.

Individual rewards would provide an alternative to system rewards if they did not pose several problems. Productivity is generally agreed to be more difficult to measure in bureaus although progress is being made. Furthermore, the cause–effect relationship between a public employee's activity and a given outcome is frequently obscure. Witness the controversy over merit pay for teachers based on pupil performance. Finally, system rewards are probably cheaper than individual monetary rewards. At any rate, some kinds of system benefits, such as generous leave and vacation policies, cost-of-living increases, and procedural protections for employees are not directly reflected in legislative budgets. Elected officials find this situation politically attractive.

Greater productivity is promoted when the content of work challenges through importance and complexity, allows for independent judgment, and offers opportunities for advancement. In order to achieve these goals, special attention must be given to the characteristics of the individuals as well as the work. Instead, specialization of tasks, rigid job descriptions, detailed rules and regulations, and required routines hinder motivation and minimize the recognition of individuality. Opportunities for promotion are often contingent on seniority and are further limited by low turnover and few openings. Actors and forces external to the public organization are frequently more powerful in shaping organization structure and procedures than bureau officials. Consequently, bureau leaders and managers have less control over factors that limit motivation than their private sector counterparts.

Motivation theories indicate that reward and performance levels can be more closely linked in other ways: These include equity of output to reward ratios, performance–reward contingencies, and operant conditioning. Here again it must be realized, in creating and implementing such reward systems, that external actors play a major role in controlling personnel policy and funds in public bureaus—and rightly so in a representative democracy.

But surely, it would seem, internalization of organizational goals is a powerful and self-renewing reward system that does not make large fiscal demands. That is true, but a cautionary note is in order. The goals of bureaus are political. They are set largely outside the organization and are the product of a political decision process. When political conflicts are not fully resolved (as often happens), these policies or goals are thrust into the bureau setting. Bureau members who are strongly identified with controversial goals run political risks, especially since the belief, however unrealistic, that public employees should be politically neutral is strongly held in our society (Thompson 1975).

Situational variables have strong and sometimes perverse influences on motivation. Public employees are subject to much disapproval often falsely placed by a public and critics who perceive them as apathetic and rule bound, yet their reward systems and environmental contexts elicit and reinforce conserver behavior. Equally frustrating and contradictory are society's expectations of public interestedness when coupled with the situational constraints confronting bureaucratic statesmen.

There is, however, room for optimism. The steady historical trend in American government has been toward a more professional and qualified public service. And despite popular perceptions or misperceptions, public employees as a group compare favorably to private ones in both motivation and productivity. Productivity and efficiency in public bureaus, however, will always require that these values be balanced by others, such as accountability and responsiveness to competing external claims.

There is a need to explore how public organizations can become more productive and effective (National Performance Review 1993). This is also important to firms, of course, but in the case of public bureaus, organizational productivity and effectiveness concern all members of the society and not just the members of a given organization. Conclusive answers and perfect solutions are too much to expect, but work motivation theory can raise useful questions to guide the efforts of scholars and officials.

FOR FURTHER READING

Motivation is an area in organization theory that is characterized by the presence of separate and distinctive theories and models rather than synthesis. The writers who have had a major impact on the field include Abraham Maslow, who in *Motivation and Personality,* New York: Harper, 1954, presents the basic argument for his hierarchy of needs model; David McClelland, *The Achieving Society,* Princeton, N.J.: Van Nostrand Reinhold, 1961, in which he begins to develop his theory of individual maturity and the social attributes of motivation; and Frederick Herzberg, *Work and the Nature of Man,* Cleveland: World Publishing, 1966, in which he develops his concepts of motivator and hygienic factors. A good example of the addition of cognition and the expectation of reward as parts of the motivation process is found in Lyman Porter and Edward Lawler III, *Managerial Attitudes and Performance,* Homewood, Ill.: Richard D. Irwin, 1968. An example of an attempt to combine and apply these various theories is found in Paul Hersey and Kenneth Blanchard, *Management of Organizational Behavior: Utilizing Human Resources,* 6th ed., Englewood Cliffs, N.J.: Prentice-Hall, 1993. One book explicitly examines the relationship between motivation and the bureaucratic environment, and that is Anthony Downs, *Inside Bureaucracy,* Boston: Little, Brown, 1967 (reissued, Prospect Heights, Ill.: Waveland Press, 1994). It is probable that a new set of literature about the impact of downsizing or rightsizing on morale and motivation will appear in the near future, and readers are encouraged to watch the appropriate journals for information on this subject.

REVIEW QUESTIONS

1. What differences are there between the content theories, cognitive process theories, and behaviorist theories of motivation?

2. How can those different theories be combined to build a more complex and sophisticated theory of motivation in individuals?

3. Explain what part of, and how, the various theories presented in this chapter are operant when considering each of the five types of individuals that Downs says exist in organizations.

4. The authors argue that motivation theories have to be interpreted and applied differently within the public sector than they are in the private sector (and that the same argument is true in the nonprofit sector). Prepare arguments both supporting and criticizing the authors' stance.

5. Consider the interactions between the motivation theories presented in this chapter and the communication and decision processes of organizations. How do they interact?

6. What impact can organizational structure and design have on motivation?

REFERENCES

Adams, J. Stacy. "Inequity in Social Exchange." In *Motivation and Work Behavior*, eds. Richard M. Steers and Lyman W. Porter. New York: McGraw-Hill, 1975: 138–154.

Alderfer, Clayton P. *Existence, Relatedness and Growth: Human Needs in Organizational Settings.* New York: Free Press, 1972.

Baumeister, Roy F., and Mark R. Leary. "The Need to Belong: Desire for Interpersonal Attachments as a Fundamental Human Motivation." *Psychological Bulletin* 117, no. 3 (1995): 497–529.

Berelson, Bernard, and Gary A. Steiner. *Human Behavior: An Inventory of Scientific Findings.* New York: Harcourt Brace Jovanovich, 1964.

Blau, Peter M., and W. Richard Scott. *Formal Organizations: A Comparative Approach.* San Francisco: Chandler, 1962.

Bockman, V. M. "The Herzberg Controversy." *Personnel Psychology* 24, no. 2 (Summer 1971): 155–189.

Buchanan, Bruce II. "Government Managers, Business Executives, and Organizational Commitment." *Public Administration Review* 34, no. 4 (1974): 339–347.

Carr, David K., and Ian D. Littman. *Excellence in Government: Total Quality Management in the 1990s,* 2nd ed. Arlington, Va.: Coopers & Lybrand, 1993.

Cartwright, Dorwin. "The Nature of Group Cohesiveness." In *Group Dynamics: Research and Theory,* eds. Dorwin Cartwright and Alvin Zander. New York: Harper & Row, 1968: 91–109.

Deming, W. Edwards. *Out of the Crisis: Quality, Productivity, and Competitive Position.* Cambridge, Mass.: MIT Press, 1986.

Downs, Anthony. *Inside Bureaucracy.* Boston: Little, Brown, 1967. (Reissued, Prospect Heights, Ill.: Waveland Press, 1994.)

Filley, Alan C., Robert J. House, and Steven Kerr. *Managerial Process and Organizational Behavior,* 2nd ed. Glenview, Ill.: Scott, Foresman, 1976.

Goodman, Paul S., and Abraham Friedman. "An Examination of Adam's Theory of Inequity." *Administrative Science Quarterly* 16, no. 3 (1971): 271–288.

Gortner, Harold F. "Student Attitudes toward Government Employment." Ph.D. diss., Indiana University, 1970.

Green, Stephen G., and Terence R. Mitchell. "Attributional Processes of Leaders in Leader-Member Interactions." *Organizational Behavior and Human Performance* 23, 1979: 429–458.

Greiner, John M., Harry P. Hatry, Margo P. Koss, Annie P. Millar, and Jane P. Woodward. *Productivity and Motivation: A Review of State and Local Government Initiatives.* Washington, D.C.: The Urban Institute Press, 1981.

Grigaliunas, Benedict S., and Frederick Herzberg. "Relevancy in the Test of Motivation-Hygiene Theory." *Journal of Applied Psychology* 55, no. 1 (February 1971): 73–79.

Hersey, Paul, and Kenneth H. Blanchard. *Management of Organizational Behavior: Utilizing Human Resources,* 6th ed. Englewood Cliffs, N.J.: Prentice-Hall, 1993.

Herzberg, Frederick. *Work and the Nature of Man.* Cleveland: World Publishing, 1966.

———, Bernard Mausner, and Barbara B. Snyderman. *The Motivation to Work.* New York: John Wiley & Sons, 1959.

Holden, Matthew, Jr. "'Imperialism' in Bureaucracy." *The American Political Science Review* 60, 1966: 943–951.

House, Robert J., and Terence R. Mitchell. "Path-Goal Theory of Leadership." *Journal of Contemporary Business* 3, no. 4 (1974): 81–97.

Katz, Daniel, and Robert L. Kahn. *The Social Psychology of Organizations,* 3rd ed. New York: John Wiley & Sons, 1982.

Kaufman, Herbert. *The Forest Ranger: A Study in Administrative Behavior.* Baltimore: The Johns Hopkins University Press, 1960.

Kelley, Harold H. "Attribution in Social Interaction." In *Attribution: Perceiving Causes of Behavior,* eds. Edward E. Jones, David E. Kanouse, Harold H. Kelley, Richard E. Nisbett, Stuart Valins, and Bernard Weiner. Morristown, N.J.: General Learning Press, 1972: 1–26.

Lane, Larry M., and James E. Wolf. *The Human Resource Crisis in The Public Sector: Rebuilding The Capacity to Govern.* New York: Quorum Books, 1990.

Lawler, Edward E. III. *Motivation in Work Organizations.* San Francisco: Jossey-Bass, 1994.

———, and J. Lloyd Suttle. "A Causal Correlational Test of the Need Hierarchy Concept." *Organizationl Behavior and Human Performance* 7, 1972: 265–287.

Likert, Rensis. *New Patterns of Management.* New York: McGraw-Hill, 1961. (Reissued, New York: Garland, 1987.)

Mahler, Julianne. "Patterns of Commitment in Public Agencies." Paper delivered at national convention of the American Society for Public Administration, Indianapolis, Ind., 1985.

Maslow, Abraham. *Motivation and Personality,* 3rd ed. New York: Harper and Row, 1954.

McClelland, David C. *The Achieving Society.* Princeton, N.J.: Van Nostrand Reinhold, 1961.

———. "The Two Faces of Power." *Journal of International Affairs* 24, no. 1 (1970): 29–47.

———, and David G. Winter. *Motivating Economic Achievement.* New York: Free Press, 1971.

Mitchell, Terence R. "Motivation: New Directions for Theory." *Academy of Management Review* 7, no. 1 (1982): 80–88.

———, Charles M. Smyser, and Stan E. Weed. "Locus of Control: Supervision and Work Satisfaction." *Academy of Management Journal* 18, no. 3 (1975): 623–631.

———, and Robert E. Wood. "An Empirical Test of an Attributional Model of Leaders' Responses to Poor Performance." In *Academy of Management Proceeding,* ed. Richard C. Huseman, (1979): 94–98.

National Center for Productivity and Work Quality. *Employee Attitudes and Productivity Differences between the Public and Private Sector.* Washington, D.C.: U.S. Civil Service Commission, 1978, as reported in James L. Perry and Lyman W. Porter, "Factors Affecting the Context for Motivation in Public Organizations." *Academy of Management Review* 17, no. 1 (1982): 89–98.

National Performance Review (U.S.) *From Red Tape to Results: Creating a Government that Works Better & Costs Less: Report of the National Performance Review.* Vice President Al Gore, New York: Times Books, 1993.

Newland, Chester. "Crucial Issues for Public Personnel." *Public Personnel Management* 13, no. 1 (1984): 15–46.

Nord, Walter R. "Improving Attendance through Rewards." *Personnel Administration* 33 (November–December 1970): 37–41.

Paine, Frank T., Stephen J. Carroll, and Burt A. Leete. "Need Satisfaction of Managerial Level Personnel in a Government Agency." *Journal of Applied Psychology* 50 (June 1966): 247–249.

Perry, James, and Lyman W. Porter. "Factors Affecting the Context for Motivation in Public Organizations." *Academy of Management Review* 7, 1 (1982): 89–98.

Porter, Lyman W., and Edward E. Lawler III. *Managerial Attitudes and Performance.* Homewood, Ill.: Richard D. Irwin, 1968.

Rainey, Hal G. "Perceptions of Incentives in Business and Government: Implications for Civil Service Reform." *Public Administration Review* 39, 1979: 440–448.

Rawls, James R., and Oscar Tivis Nelson, Jr. "Characteristics Associated with Preferences for Certain Managerial Positions." *Psychological Reports* 36, 1975: 223–244.

———, Robert A. Ulrich, and Oscar Tivis Nelson, Jr. "A Comparison of Managers Entering or Reentering the Profit and Nonprofit Sectors." *Academy of Management Journal* 18, 1975: 616–622.

Rhinehart, J. B., R. P. Barrell, A. S. DeWolfe, J. E. Griffin, and F. E. Spaner. "Comparative Study of Need Satisfaction in Governmental and Business Hierarchies." *Journal of Applied Psychology* 53 (June 1969): 230–235.

Schott, Richard L. "The Psychological Development of Adults." *Public Administration Review* 46, 1986: 657–667.

———. "Psychological Development of Adults: Further Reflections and a Rejoinder." *Public Administration Review* 47 1987: 345–346.

Schwab, Donald P., H. William Devitt, and Larry L. Cummings. "A Test of the Adequacy of the Two-Factor Theory as a Predictor of Self-Report Performance Effects." *Personnel Psychology* 24 (Summer 1971): 293–303.

Skinner, B. F. *About Behavior.* New York: Vintage, 1976.

Telly, Charles S., Wendell L. French, and William G. Scott. "The Relationship of Inequity to Turnover among Hourly Workers." *Administrative Science Quarterly* 16, no. 2 (1971): 164–172.

Thompson, Victor A. *Without Sympathy or Enthusiasm: The Problem of Administrative Compassion.* University, Ala.: University of Alabama Press, 1975.

U.S. Merit Systems Board Office of Merit Systems Review and Studies. *Report on the Significant Actions of the Office of Personnel Management during 1983,* December 1984.

Van Maanen, John. "Police Socialization: A Longitudinal Examination of Job Attitudes in an Urban Police Department." *Administrative Science Quarterly* 20, 1975a: 207–228.

———. "Breaking In: Socialization to Work." In *Handbook of Work, Organization, and Society,* ed. Robert Dubin. Chicago: Rand McNally, 1975b: 67–130.

Veroff, Joseph. "Development and Validation of a Projective Measure of Power Motivation," *Journal of Abnormal and Social Psychology* 54, no. 1 (1957): 1–8.

Vroom, Victor H. *Work and Motivation.* New York: John Wiley & Sons, 1964. (Reissued, San Francisco: Jossey-Bass, 1995.)

Zemke, R. "What Are High-Achieving Managers Really Like?" *Training: The Magazine of Human Resource Development* (February 1979): 35–36.

CASE 8–1　The Volunteer

Jessica arrived at the office at 8:40 in a rush. The party at the Gibson's the night before ran later than she expected and her daughter, Rachel, had complained of a sore throat this morning. Jessica was running late and was not entirely focused when she entered her office at the Springfield Mental Health and Rehabilitation Society. Her anxiety was further elevated when she saw Mildred sitting at the conference table waiting for her.

Mildred is a volunteer. Her husband had been a prominent attorney in town and, since his death six years ago, Mildred had turned her attention two days a week to the Society. Although she did not have any professional qualifications, mental health had been her favorite cause for most of her adult life. Although Mildred and her husband were not part of the old money scene in Springfield, she was well known and respected for taking an active role and serving on many worthwhile community projects. One of her greatest assets was her knowledge of the city's families; for instance, who had married whom and what ties they had to other families in the city. The executive director recognized Mildred's knowledge of the community's informal social structure and relied on her heavily for introductions, protocol, and an interpretation of other social subtleties.

As the Development Director, Jessica was relatively new to Springfield. She was eight years out of college, had good fund-raising experience in the University Grants Office after graduation, was active in the local chapter of the National Society of Fund-Raising Executives, and had joined the Springfield Mental Health and Rehabilitation Society when her husband completed law school and they moved to Springfield two years ago.

Jessica smiled warmly and greeted Mildred, but she thought to herself, "Mildred's help is the last thing I need today." As she hung up her coat and began to settle in, Mildred said, "I was beginning to worry about you. It is already 8:40 and you weren't here. I thought something might have happened to you."

Whether Mildred was really concerned or whether that was her way of admonishing Jessica for being 10 minutes late, Jessica was not certain. She was certain, however, that it was really irritating. If Mildred knew how much she did to keep family and work going, Mildred would be less critical. Nonetheless, she managed an upbeat, "Oh, I'm fine, just a little behind this morning because of the kids." She turned to the file cabinet, unlocked it, and pulled Mildred's working file.

Mildred went quickly to work on editing the mailing list. It was a thankless boring job, and one that was absolutely necessary. Jessica was tying to get a grant request to the Lomax Foundation and she wished the deadline was not so close. Just two more days for editing, getting the Board Chair's signature, the latest audited financial statement and the other enclosures assembled, and the letter of support from the Mayor signed. She would really have to keep her focus.

"Jessica?" Mildred asked.

"Yes."

"I think we should create a second mailing list of the people who have given to us in the past two years. If we had that information, we could send a different and more personal letter than we send to everyone else. Why, I think. . . ."

Mildred's voice was drowned out by the intercom, "Jessica, your daughter's on line two from the school nurse's office."

Jessica thought, "I can't stand it. I need someone to help me, not by dreaming up more work." She turned to Mildred, excused herself, and answered the phone. "Hello. Oh, poor dear. OK. I'll come right over and pick you up. Don't worry, I'll be there as soon as I can."

Mildred said, "That is too bad. You'll have to stay home with her now, won't you? It's too bad you don't have help. Ralph, my husband, was so good to me. We always had a housekeeper when the children were young."

SOURCE: Russell A. Cargo, Assistant Professor of Government and Politics, George Mason University.

Editor's Note

Consider the following questions about this case:

1. What role does Mildred, the volunteer, play in the organization?
2. What is Jessica's responsibility:
   a. To the organization?
   b. To her profession?
   c. To Mildred?
3. What motivates Mildred, and how would you assess the prospects for her long-term motivation based on the situation as reported in the case?
4. Prepare a plan of action for Jessica to ensure that Mildred will continue her active support of the Society.

CASE 8–2   A Problem of Motivation

Two years before, the Department of Human Services had hired six new employees with the assistance of the federal government's Work Incentive (WIN) program. Under the program, the federal government paid the employees' salaries for a six-month training period, after which the department had the option of hiring or releasing the employees based on their performance and the recommendations of their supervisors.

Julie Davis, one of the WIN employees, was placed in the Child Welfare Department. Initially she was very industrious and suggested several improvements in procedures relating to her job. She exhibited a high degree of initiative and performed her duties efficiently. After about six weeks, though, Jeff Baker, her supervisor, noticed that she was developing poor working habits, such as long coffee breaks, tardiness, and absenteeism.

Baker felt Davis's low performance had resulted from her association with two employees in the adoption unit of the department. Baker arranged a meeting with her and advised her of the unacceptability of her work behavior. He had received complaints from other employees that she was not carrying her share of the load. "Julie," he said, "generally your work has been very good but lately your job performance has not lived up to expectations. Although our standards are higher than other sections of this department, the chances for promotion and career advancement are a lot better for the hard-working employee. You can do a lot better than you have been doing!" After the session with Baker, Davis's work and behavior immediately improved. She volunteered to assist others whenever her own work was completed and quickly acquired the necessary skills for several other positions in the section. She often worked as a substitute in the absence of other employees.

At the end of the training period Baker recommended that the agency hire Davis at the level of Grade 5. The quality of her work remained consistently high and she continued to assist others willingly. Six months later, when she had completed a year with the agency, she was promoted to Grade 6 and assigned additional responsibilities. Indeed, a bright future seemed on the horizon.

About two months later, one of the employees Davis had been assisting resigned because of a death in her family. The announcement for the newly opened position emphasized it was limited to employees of the department. Since Davis was familiar with many aspects of the position, she discussed applying for it with Baker, who advised her that even though she was the only staff member familiar with the job her chance of being on the list of applicants supplied by the Bureau of Personnel was small because she had only fourteen months' experience instead of the required two years. He said she would make the list only if there were no applicants with the required experience. This was possible, though unlikely. Davis decided to apply and hope for the best. There were several applicants with the required experience and she did not make the list.

Davis's attitude changed immediately. She became irritable and her relationship with other staff members deteriorated. She developed intense feelings of insecurity. Each time a new employee was hired she felt as though she might be replaced. As a result of this constant fear she developed an ulcer. In another meeting with her, Baker reassured her of her abilities, explained the steps involved in employee termination, and outlined the grievance procedures available to employees should termination occur. Initially, she seemed to gain confidence and her work improved, though not to the level of her previous performance. Davis had become confused and felt angry toward Baker for what she considered to be unwarranted encouragement.

Since Baker felt he could no longer adequately motivate Davis, he recommended that she be transferred to another supervisor, Malcolm Tate. After a few weeks, her work performance and attitude improved considerably, and Tate soon considered her among the best employees he had ever supervised.

The problem in the department appeared to be resolved, but Tate might be faced with the same problem as Baker. In the next four months two employees under Tate's supervision were to retire. Both positions were at the Grade 7 level. Davis was now qualified for both, but there were others in the agency better qualified. Even if she made the list, there was a good possibility she would not be selected for the position.

SOURCE: C. K. Meyer et al., *Practising Public Management* (New York: St. Martin's Press, 1983): 98–101.

Editor's Note

Consider the following questions about this case:

1. Which theories of motivation seem to best describe what motivates Davis? Do you think that what motivates her might change over time? Why or why not? How has what you find motivating in your professional or academic career changed over the past three years?

2. How could her supervisors use an understanding of what motivates Davis to identify better ways to help her develop her career? What specific advice might you offer to Davis based on your understanding of what she finds motivating?

3. Are the promotion requirements in the department relevant to the work? Might someone in Davis's position feel resentful about being passed over the first time because she was ten months short of the requirement? Would you justify the requirement?

READING 8-1 Motivate Your Team

People like to work with pleasant people. You feel positive about your job when you receive compliments for your work, when others ask your advice, and when people simply know and use your name. You can motivate your team members by how you speak to them. And you can gain points for yourself by your positive communication manner.

Dr. Roger Burgraff, writing in *The Great Communicators* (Royal Publishing Co.), offers this advice on positive speech:

- Be specific. Saying, "I appreciate the great job you did on those graphics," is better than merely saying, "Good job."

- Use the person's name. Each of us likes our name linked to something positive. Saying, "Pat, thanks for coming in early to organize the meeting," is better than saying, "Thanks for coming in early to organize the meeting."

- Compare a person's activity to a higher standard. Say, "Lynn, your poster looks like an award-winner."

- Capitalize on compliments. Say, "Thanks Bob for noticing. You've made my day." *Caution:* Don't try to balance a compliment you've received by offering one of your own. It tends to diminish the value of the first compliment.

- Ask people's advice or opinion. Say, "Mary, what do you think of the proposal?" or, "We haven't heard from Mary yet. I'd like her ideas on this."

Burgraff's last point is particularly appropriate. The four most important words you can use on the job are, "What do you think?" An example that it pays off in business comes from the Marriott Corp. R. W. Marriott, chairman, cites a hotel staff member who observed a local pizza parlor making deliveries at the hotel. As a result, the hotel started offering pizzas itself and soon sold up to 100 a night through room service. Asking workers what they think pays off in credibility and business.

Use Cooperation Instead of Competition

If you want to be more productive and help your team members do the same, foster a spirit of cooperation instead of competition. People who are forced to compete against one another produce less both in quantity and quality. In competition, contestants hope to see others fail. But in a cooperative effort, team members hope to see others win—because then they win too. Furthermore, competition too often depends on gaining money and beating another person, rather than on accountability to a team leader or member.

Suggestion: Implant the team spirit. Make . . . team members feel responsible for others' success as well as their own. Give them frequent pep talks. Encourage team members to compliment each other's work. Urge them to offer each other constructive feedback that will enhance both individual and team skill levels. Build teamwork by training mentors who can help the new players when you're not available. Team members must care enough about each other and believe enough in each other to want each person to give his or her best to the team effort.

Keep People Informed

Are all of your team members getting enough information from you? And do they believe what they hear?

A Hay Research for Management survey showed that 68 percent of middle managers said they got enough information.

But the figure dropped to 60 percent for clerical staff and 54 percent for professionals. Hourly workers fared the worst, with only 47 percent saying they received enough information.

Among the middle managers, 86 percent said the information they were given was credible. Seventy-five percent of the professionals and 80 percent of the clerical workers said they believed what they heard. Hourly workers trailed again, with only 61 percent saying they received credible information.

Tip: Conduct a study of your team members. Besides asking if they get enough information from you, ask if they believe what they are getting. If they don't, ask why. Get suggestions from them on improving the flow of credible information.

Stay in Touch

Effective coaches constantly interact with their team members because they know personal contact significantly affects motivation. But effective interaction demands balance. If you limit contact, you risk missing vital information about progress and problems. If you overdo it, team members may think you don't trust them to carry the ball. To keep your balance:

- Spend about half your time keeping your finger on your team's pulse. Even if you'd like to devote more time to interaction, remember that you still need time to read, plan, and handle paperwork. If you ignore those duties, your team can suffer.

    Note: Too much contact may indicate that you're not delegating as many tasks as you should. Failure to delegate hurts teamwork because, when you delegate, you show you trust team members. And effective teamwork demands trust.

- Spread your contacts among all team members. If you favor some and ignore others, you may breed jealousy and resentment among those you don't talk to.

- Make sure you go to them more than they come to you. If you don't initiate more contacts than they do, they'll think you're not interested in how they're doing. But don't discourage them from approaching you at all or you could stifle their initiative.

- Don't set specific time limits on how long you spend with team members. Let the situation determine the length of the contact. If you find you're making many short visits, however, it could be another signal that you need to delegate more. And when the contact lasts too long, you may be overwhelming team members with more information than they can absorb at one time.

- Know when to meet face to face and when to hold a team meeting. Play this one by ear. But you'll probably find that you'll spend about half your time meeting with individuals.

Improve Morale

You also can keep yourself and your team members motivated if you cultivate at least these two traits identified in Joseph David Pincus's doctoral dissertation, "The Impact of Communication Satisfaction on Job Satisfaction and Job Performance":

- Effective communication from the immediate supervisor.
- Personal feedback from others.

The study clearly showed that employees liked their jobs more when their supervisors communicated effectively with them. And personal feedback weighed heavily in employees estimating their own job performance and being satisfied with it.

You'll also boost morale if you avoid actions that can destroy team morale. Make sure you *don't:*

- Play the autocrat. If you don't let team members take part in decision making, you violate a basic teamwork tenet. And consider this: One study found that 54 percent of all workers cherish the right to be in on decisions that affect their jobs. Among younger workers, it's 63 percent.

- Behave inconsistently. Team members want to know and must know what they're expected to do. When you keep them guessing, you breed anger, frustration, dismay, and disappointment.

- Criticize more than you praise. Most people perform well most of the time and fail to measure up on only some tasks. That would seem to indicate that you should praise them more often than you criticize them. But many traditional managers do just the opposite. Most of their comments deal with the few times workers fail. If you follow that same path, your team members may conclude that you don't recognize good work but that bad work will at least get them noticed. A team of bad workers can't win, and when they lose, you lose.

- Play favorites. Discrimination of any kind not only destroys morale but also hurts productivity. If you promote unfairly, for example, team members will quickly lose confidence in you and the promotion system. You must treat every team member as an equal partner in the enterprise.

- Resist change. When you resist change, you can ruin your team's chances to win. An inflexible coach who fails to capitalize on a sudden turnaround in the game may deny the team a chance to score.

Have a Sense of Humor

Know when to laugh at yourself. Don't take yourself too seriously and you'll boost the morale of those around you.

In fact, the right amount of humor will help you and those around you work better. Research by David Abramis at California State University at Long Beach affirms this. He found that employees who had an overall sense that work was fun reported better job satisfaction, mental well-being, job performance, social relations, and creativity than their grouchier counterparts.

Further, research by Dr. Jonathan Fry, Jr., associate professor of clinical psychology at Stanford University, provides more clues to explain why humor helps people work better.

Fry's research found that laughter produces endorphins, the brain's natural tranquilizers. Endorphins cut pain, cure tension headaches, and soothe tempers and frazzled nerves.

So humor can help you deal with pressure rather than letting it overcome you. And at times, you may find it an acceptable way to get team members to accept criticism.

Offer the Right Rewards

Like most employees, your team members will appreciate raises, better working conditions, improved pensions, and longer vacations. However, much social science research shows that these incentives don't offer the best way to motivate better performance.

Although these traditional rewards are satisfying, the research says, they typically are given at management's discretion. But the best motivation, the researchers agree, comes from something that employees can control—a sense of accomplishment, a belief that what they do matters and that their ideas count.

That's the theory. But what's the reality? Consider the [example of a] Federal Express team . . . [that] uncovered and solved a problem that was costing the company $2.1 million each year.

Few people would have been surprised to hear that the team members expected to share in the windfall. But many *would* be surprised to learn that they considered a gold quality award pin and their pictures in the employee newsletter as reward enough. That would seem to support the theory, and so would this comment from one of the team members: "It's a good feeling to know someone is using your ideas."

Accepting this motivation theory doesn't mean that you should no longer depend on other kinds of rewards to recognize team accomplishments. You should still include plaques, pins, certificates, trips, newsletter articles, dinners, and the like in your recognition program.

You can liken them to the pat on the back and words of praise a coach gives a player who just pulled off a brilliant play that won the game. The player already feels a sense of personal achievement. But that pat on the back shows the player, and other team members as well, that the coach appreciated the effort.

Recognize Off-the-Job Achievements

Most employee recognition programs focus only on rewarding achievements on the job. But to boost team spirit even more, you might want to consider expanding your recognition program to include three categories:

- First category: Achievements on the job: reaching sales quotas, being nice to customers and clients, coming up with cost-saving ideas, bringing in business and representing the organization. Typical recognition: newsletter articles, plaques, dinners, workstation displays, trips, vacations and other premiums.

- Second category: Everyday activities that make people valuable to the organization: being nice to others, answering the phone with courtesy, getting the ordinary jobs done every day and being there when people count on you. Typical recognition, gaining but still far behind: annual dinners or lunches for secretaries, evenings out at the ballpark or racetrack, annual picnics, office parties and bonuses.

- Third category: Activities and achievements away from the job that make employees local celebrities: distinguished umpiring; award-winning cooking; painting or writing; and serving on the local school board, planning board, or library commission. Typical recognition: little or none.

Recognize Secretaries

Your team's success will often depend on the vital support you get from secretaries. You'll err badly if you view secretaries as mere spectators instead of important team members. To show you appreciate what they do and to get their best efforts:

- Agree on the tasks you both feel they can perform, and give them the authority they need to do them. You'll waste your time and theirs if they must wait for you to approve every minor detail.

- Involve them in decisions. Start by letting them handle minor tasks. Once they prove themselves, let them handle more important matters.

- Seek their advice. An occasional, "What do you think of this idea?" will boost their self-esteem, and you'll often get a valuable suggestion you've overlooked.

- Treat them as you would any skilled professional, and don't waste their time on busy-work. And don't use them as gofers.

- Tap their special skills. If secretaries show they can write well, for example, give them the opportunity to compose letters rather than just typing them.

- Send them to conferences and workshops. Like you, they need the opportunity to mingle with colleagues so that they can exchange views and get ideas that will help them do their jobs better.

Be Positive

Here are some additional tips to help you motivate your team members:

- Head off problems. If you wait for something to go wrong *before* you speak up, team members may take your silence for assent.

- Ask questions. Instead of complaining that nobody ever tells you anything, seek the information you need.

- Don't play the Monday-morning quarterback role. Your comments will only make those responsible for the error feel worse. Stick to comments that can change things or avoid problems. And forget the past.

- Reassure team members. Don't make them guess how they're doing.

- Encourage risk taking. When you do, make sure team members know you won't punish them if they fail. That will reduce the fear of failure that impedes motivation.

SOURCE: "How to Unlock the Power of Teamwork" (pp. 25–29), from the editors of *Communication Briefings,* 1101 King Street, Suite 110, Alexandria, VA. 22314. 703-548-3800.

Editor's Note

Obviously, this commentary is geared toward business; however, the same motivation theories, models, and techniques often work in public and nonprofit organization life. Consider the following questions about this reading:

1. How do the management functions (communication, control, design of organizational structure, and so on) discussed in the other chapters of this book address, or have an impact on, the statements in this reading?

2. What are the basic assumptions about leadership (see Chapter 9) that are made by the author of these tips on motivation?

3. Given the special situations faced by public administrators, are all the motivational techniques discussed here available to public managers and supervisors? If not, why not? Can those techniques that, at first glance, appear not to fit the public or nonprofit sectors be adjusted or changed to make them useful and appropriate?

Chapter 9

Leadership and Management in Public Organizations

Although leadership has been studied extensively by numerous scholars and practitioners, fundamental disagreements remain about what it is; for example, whether leadership is an inborn or a learned trait is still being disputed. Despite such disagreements, there is unanimity about the need for leadership and great consternation when large numbers of relevant observers recognize its absence. When American industry's poor record regarding its international competition is discussed, a usual charge is that company officials have failed to fulfill their leadership roles. Perhaps the most damaging charge that can be made against a president is that he fails to lead the country. The attempts to "reinvent government" taking place at all levels of U.S. government start with a challenge to bring leadership to the hardworking, committed workers. At the same time, of course, a standard accusation made against public bureaucrats is that they serve as faceless functionaries and fail to seek out or elicit from themselves any leadership capacities.[1] What exactly are we getting at here?

There is a lack of agreement on specifics when defining leadership. James MacGregor Burns, in his study on leadership, found 130 definitions of the word (1978, 2). On the other hand, there is enough commonality in our understanding of leadership to enable us to carry on a meaningful discussion about it. A discussion of the subject is essential because of its centrality to success on the part of the society, the government, and the numerous constituent parts of those two "umbrella" organizations. First, we will define leadership and emphasize its existence, in similar but critically different ways, at the executive, managerial, and supervisory levels of organizational direction. Second, we will examine three major sets of theories, each of which attempts to explain how successful

---

[1] Of course, if any public bureaucrat shows signs of developing leadership capacity and using it to accomplish goals different from those desired by the critic, such skills are immediately railed against as demagoguery, and the bureaucrat is reminded that it is his or her job to carry out program functions, not to create policies or lead movements.

314

leadership occurs. Third, we will briefly explore the interrelationship between leadership and other organization theories. And finally, we will see how public organizations require a special brand of leadership that includes a healthy dose of political savvy. From all this, we will develop a picture of the successful public administrator as the leader of people in organizations immersed in a political environment.

DEFINITIONS: THE NATURE OF LEADERSHIP IN THE PUBLIC ORGANIZATIONAL CONTEXT

Even though the study of leadership has continued for several millenia and everyone believes he or she knows what it stands for, each person's definition is unique in some way. This predicament is to be expected and applauded because in a pluralist society leadership is bound to have many meanings.

> In our society, leadership is more than ordinarily dispersed. Leaders are scattered around at every level and in all segments of our national life. . . . Excessive dependence on central definition and rulemaking produces standardized solutions to be applied uniformly throughout the system. But the world "out there," the world to be coped with isn't standardized. It is diverse, localized and surprising. (Gardner 1981, 11)

Despite the truth of John Gardner's statement, we must have some common definition from which we can work; however, we must not accept that definition as all-inclusive or immutable. We will be constantly adding new insights to this first attempt at conceptualization. As a general definition, we can say that leadership involves influencing the behavior of others in any group or organization, setting goals, formulating paths to those goals, and creating social norms in the group (Lundstedt 1965).

Three Levels of Leadership in Bureaus—A Clarifying Note

Leadership occurs outside, as well as inside, formal organizations. Of course, the focus of our discussion is leadership within public organizations or bureaus, and this particular context has led to further confusion. Within a bureau, we are talking about formal positions established by the organization, or in some cases—especially at the upper levels—by the law that establishes the agency and its programs. There are three distinct kinds of positions—executive, managerial, and supervisory—that have direct involvement with bureau leadership. However, the terms are constantly used interchangeably and theories of leadership are usually discussed as if they apply equally to each level or for each type of position. Such is not the case. It is necessary to note the differences in scope and emphasis at each level or type of position and then to see how leadership relates to the separate functions. Obviously, some common factors are related to leadership anywhere and at all levels of organizations, and we shall discuss them shortly, but detailed consideration of leadership in bureaus requires us to examine its nature and function at all three levels. As we consider the three types of leadership, and to complete the picture, we must look at the fourth phenomenon, informal leadership, which occurs in every organization and must be given special consideration precisely because it occurs outside the bureau's formal structure.

Although executive, management, and supervisory positions are often discussed some-what interchangeably, and although it is admittedly difficult to describe their precise boundaries, there are differences that need to be understood since these differences result in diverse roles for the position holders and encourage equally varied opportunities for leadership. As noted before, all three positions are formally established on the basis of authority that is ultimately granted through law. Executives, however, have as part of their responsibility the establishment of the bureau's structure, including the lower positions in the agency that are then filled by managers and supervisors. Executives are expected to maintain a broad and general view of the bureau and its place within the larger political environment. They then interpret the political statements of intentions on which the or-ganization is based, which are usually vague and often contradictory, into rational goals and policies that can be used for basic guidance by those "in the bowels of the organi-zation." As the top officials, executives establish or interpret the agency's overall goals and attempt to create a general atmosphere or environment that will increase the probability of those goals being achieved. Finally, executives are expected to pay close attention to the organization's environment so that they can take advantage of opportunities that arise, protect the bureau when it is attacked or in danger, and generally represent it in the inevitable political frays.

Supervision and management occur based on authority granted by superiors within the bureau hierarchy. Thus, individuals in these positions (at least initially) depend on rules and regulations to define their power over others. Managers must interpret these goals and policies (generalized ideas) in an evermore concrete manner, into structures, procedures, and ultimately, tasks (concrete actions and products or services). General goals are interpreted to apply to increasingly smaller units of the bureau, until finally supervisors interact with individual subordinates to make sure their behavior relates to accomplishing specific organizational objectives.

Supervisors, those at the bottom of the totem pole, must focus on motivation, pro-ductivity, and interpersonal relations as they work with those most directly involved in delivering the goods or services provided by the bureau. Therefore, bureau supervisors must attempt to protect their subordinates from political pressure since these individuals usually work in some type of merit system. As supervisors attempt to do their jobs, they must work *without* some of the powers and the flexibility in applying existing powers that are usually present in the private sector because of the legal limitations placed on hiring and promotion, pay, reward for good work, and disciplinary actions. (See Chapter 8 for a discussion of the civil service system and the limits it places on those attempting to mo-tivate public servants.) Supervisors in the public sector are just as responsible for the achievement of objectives as group leaders in any organization, but they must accomplish these goals with fewer supervisory tools. Finally, those objectives, and perhaps even the routines used by the subordinates, are often established in other parts of the organization. Where executives make policy and deal with the broadest aspects of bureau life, super-visors watch and direct the work of journeymen or technical employees carrying out spe-cific tasks.

Managers operate in the middle ground between these two extremes, often being pulled in both directions by superiors and subordinates as they translate broad goals and policies into the concrete actions of organizational units and individuals (Likert 1961, 1967). Therefore, a major focus of managers is on structure and process or how the bureau can best be organized to achieve the overall goals that have been established. They do not establish the goals—that is done above them in the organization or outside of it—but they are the decisive actors in turning policy statements and broad generalizations into structure, action, and results. Managers supervise other supervisors: Though some managers may supervise some journeymen-employees, they always direct the work of some other supervisors. This means that managers are involved in directing multiple levels of an organization, which leads to an emphasis on coordination of semiautonomous units.

The fact that an individual holds a formal position in the hierarchy proves nothing about that person's leadership abilities; someone may hold any of the three positions in the organization without doing much in the way of leadership. The bureau may suffer mightily from such a fate, but it does happen regularly. It helps at all levels to use leadership skills, but the types of skills needed and the way they are applied must, of necessity, differ. We will point out some of these differences as we proceed through the rest of this chapter.

Finally, after discussing the three formal levels of leadership, we must note that leadership within an organization often comes from individuals who have no official station (although many if not most leaders hold a formal position). Herein lies the idea of the informal leader. Many people who have no formal position (such as supervisor or manager), influence behavior, goals, and procedures within the bureau. They are therefore fulfilling the role that was identified in the earlier definition of leadership even though they are doing it on the basis of something other than a formal position in the hierarchy. To understand what is going on inside the bureau, we must consider the impact of this informal leadership phenomenon along with the formal one; otherwise, we will never totally understand what is going on. Throughout the chapter, it is important to spend some time thinking about how the theories that are presented work at the organization's informal level—even if they are presented within a formal context. In most cases, the material will be equally applicable in both situations.

Defining Leadership

As we noted in the introduction to this chapter, there is no general agreement on how to define or study leadership. We can best approach the subject by taking note of the two points where there is agreement, and then expanding our ideas to include four additional concepts that are necessary for this discussion. Beyond that point lies a wealth of information about leadership that requires long and arduous study. Such study is best accomplished by courses and experience that are more narrowly defined than is our objective here, but that allow far greater detail and insight into the precise subject.

The Two Common Elements—Group Phenomenon and Influence Process

Actually, only two factors are common to all definitions of leadership. First, it is assumed that leadership is a group phenomenon; two or more people must be involved. Second, it is assumed that leadership involves an influence process; the leader intentionally influences his or her followers. This influence may take many forms (discussed later in this chapter), but whatever its source it has the same goal—rallying people together and motivating them to achieve some common goal(s). Thus, one physical condition (a group) and one process (influence) are necessary for leadership to occur.

Of course, one immediately gets into a debate as soon as causality or direction are considered in the influence process. The influence always flows from leader to group (followers). However, many researchers argue that in the influence process there is an equally important flow from followers to leaders—that the followers "grant" the leadership role to whoever wears the mantle. Within this debate are elements of both the formal and the informal side of group existence and experience. Thus, numerous additional factors may be, indeed will be, operating at the same time, and all of them must be taken into consideration; but these two factors are the only ones that *must occur* in every instance of leadership.

But what additional factors must be considered in an examination of leadership in public organizations? In the material that follows, it must be understood that each bureau has a complete set of formal leaders: Their positions are created by law or organizational rules and regulations; they have a relatively well-defined sphere of competence; and they have the right to expect a certain level of respect and obedience from those in positions below them. (See Weber's bureaucratic model, p. 58.) Bureaus have a strong formal leadership component that must be recognized as central to public organizational life. We shall focus, however, on the informal or interpersonal side of leadership because it is here that major variations occur in its study and practice. Several factors must be spelled out in more detail to discuss leadership in a truly meaningful context.

The Leader as Symbol

Leadership would not be necessary if it were not for the fact that groups have needs and goals that must be satisfied. The leader personifies the group's common purpose—not only to all who work in it, but to everyone outside it. And whether the leader has designed the goals alone or in conjunction with followers, he or she has a program in mind that will move the group toward those goals in a definite manner (Urwick 1953; Cowley 1928).

The Uniqueness of Leadership Roles

After acceptance as leader by other group members, the leadership position acquires a set of expectations and interactions that make behavior by and toward it unique and differentiated. Leaders act differently than followers, and followers act differently toward a leader than they do toward their peers. For example, leaders may vary (obviously within limits) from what is considered acceptable group behavior as long as that behavior appears to pay off for the group by helping them gain needed resources or achieve desired goals. Along with the differentiated role comes a change in expectations about contributions to the group. The leader's contribution is expected to be indispensable or of considerable consequence to the group; therefore, the group gains from accepting the individual as leader, and the leader, in return, receives a variety of opportunities and benefits that make the position challenging and worthwhile.

The Achievement of Leadership Positions

The problem with the concept just presented is that it applies primarily to leadership in organizations after someone has become leader. But an even more fundamental question is, "How was the position of leadership achieved in the first place?" There are two answers to that question. On the formal side, he or she is appointed, but to the extent that one gains acceptance beyond one's formal position, it must be gained from, or granted by, the group. On the informal side, the "leader without position" gains that status because it is granted by others. Here we are discussing that additional or informal leadership component. First, it is true that leadership is an effect of interaction—this means that leadership can occur *only if others comply*. Stogdill (Bass 1990) argues that an individual is usually given leadership status because his or her behaviors arouse expectations in group members that lead them to believe that he or she, rather than some other member, will serve them more usefully. However, it would be self-deluding to believe that leaders always gain their position through willing conferral by followers: One may also become a leader by the use of coercion or force.

The second aspect of achieving a leadership position recognizes that although leadership may be an effect of interaction, there is usually some initiation of action by the leader. Leaders generally seek their positions and then attempt to maintain them. If you wish to be a political or bureaucratic leader, you had best not wait for someone to discover and draft you, for you will almost certainly be disappointed. Leaders tend to be individuals who recognize a group need and then organize the structure and functions of the group so that the need may be met; to the extent that the leader continues to fulfill this role— which is one thing all successful leaders do—he or she will maintain the position. Further, since the leader is usually best situated to receive and interpret important information about the group, he or she has a better than average chance of perpetuating the role since knowledge is power, and power can be used to perpetuate the goal- and structure-setting apparatus in a way that protects the leader's position.

Influence, Power, and Authority in Bureau Leadership

When we start considering the initiatory aspect of leadership, we are crossing the border between group-related factors and moving to those aspects of leadership that are related to the exercise of influence. To reiterate, influence connotes the ability to get people to cooperate "because they find the goal desirable or the group or leader especially attractive." According to this view, leadership is equated with strength of personality or number of desirable traits (speech, powers of persuasion, expertise, behavior, and so on) attributed to the leader as an individual and used by that person to assume dominance over others (Weber 1947; Bogardus 1934). At a minimum, leaders attract followers to the group's goals through their words and deeds; further, leaders can gain even more loyalty to "the cause" through their charismatic qualities. The dual attachment (to cause and person) operates synergistically, thus creating combined ties that are greater than the sum of the two types of loyalty and commitment operating separately. Both J. Edgar Hoover and Admiral Hyman Rickover used charisma as well as their formal positions to gain strong commitments to their programs; hence, their personal impact on the FBI and the nuclear submarine programs were tremendous.

What we mean when we talk about gaining the support of followers to the group's goals and processes is the leader's ability to influence followers through coercive or, primarily, noncoercive techniques. Gary Yukl identifies eleven types of influence that must be used in a concerted way by a leader, only one of which is patently coercive (see Figure 9–1). An implied element of coercion exists in several of the forms of influence, but it is

---

FIGURE 9–1   Definition of Influence Tactics

Rational Persuasion: The agent uses logical arguments and factual evidence to persuade the target that a proposal or request is viable and likely to result in the attainment of task objectives.

Inspirational Appeals: The agent makes a request or proposal that arouses target enthusiasm by appealing to target values, ideals, and aspirations, or by increasing target self-confidence.

Consultation: The agent seeks target participation in planning a strategy, activity, or change for which target support and assistance are desired, or is willing to modify a proposal to deal with target concerns and suggestions.

Ingratiation: The agent uses praise, flattery, friendly behavior, or helpful behavior to get the target in a good mood or to think favorably of him or her before asking for something.

Personal Appeals: The agent appeals to target feelings of loyalty and friendship toward him or her when asking for something.

Exchange: The agent offers an exchange of favors, indicates willingness to reciprocate at a later time, or promises a share of the benefits if the target helps accomplish a task.

Coalition Tactics: The agent seeks the aid of others to persuade the target to do something, or uses the support of others as a reason for the target to agree also.

Legitimating Tactics: The agent seeks to establish the legitimacy of a request by claiming the authority or right to make it, or by verifying that it is consistent with organizational policies, rules, practices, or traditions.

Pressure: The agent uses demands, threats, frequent checking, or persistent reminders to influence the target to do what he or she wants.

SOURCE: Gary A. Yukl, *Leadership in Organizations,* 3rd. Ed. (Englewood Cliffs, N.J.: Prentice-Hall, 1994): 225.

not emphasized; in fact, the use of coercion (outside an organization, like a prison, where an individual is forced to be a member against his or her will) is an admission that the leader is authoritarian or that other forms of influence have failed. Likewise, only one of the eleven types of influence is directly related to the leader's formal position. The success of any leader depends on his or her ability to use the variety of available influences in a way that gains compliance and ensures a coordinated effort to achieve the goals of the group. The term *concerted* is used to emphasize the fact that no one type of influence always works; rather, the leader must use variations and themes on influence in a manner that meets the needs of individuals in the group, the group itself, and in many cases, the environment in which the group operates. This is no less a skill than that of a musician improvising on a theme; both require personal talent and much training and experience to carry them out successfully—and only a few people are true virtuosos.

The terms *influence* and *power* may be used interchangeably, but it is important to avoid the confusion that exists around the second term. The word *power* is used very loosely and has developed a halo of normative meanings. For example, James MacGregor Burns argues "that power as sheer domination is pervasive in this century of Hitler and

Stalin . . . as perhaps it was in every other" (1978, 52). Such statements, though true in the grossest sense of the term, cause us to lose any sense of sophistication around the use of the concept. Power must be understood in a broader context than just domination. French and Raven, for example, talk about five types of power (see Figure 9–2), only one of which is specifically based on physical or punitive forces, whereas one other (legitimate power) may include the implied threat of such force. As you can see, the powers discussed by French and Raven are subsumed by the larger list of influences developed by Yukl. Therefore, in this book, we shall use the term *power* so that it is broadly synonymous with influence, as Yukl has done in Figure 9–1.

Within public organizations, the term *authority* is sometimes used synonymously with power and must be clarified. Authority is legitimate power, or a specific kind of influence based on one's right to exert that kind of influence. It is necessary to refer to certain kinds of influence because authority is related to formal positions in organizations, and no position in a bureau gives one absolute authority over all aspects of other bureau members' lives. A formal position has a sphere of competency (Weber 1947) that places very specific limits on the authority of any officeholder. A leader, however, may have influence far beyond the authority that comes with his or her position; therefore, it is essential to look beyond grants of authority when either studying or practicing leadership.

EXPLAINING LEADERSHIP IN THE BUREAU

As soon as leadership was recognized by thinkers as a special and important phenomenon, attempts were made to define what it was and to explain why some individuals became leaders, whereas others did not. Plato, for instance, in *The Republic,* spends a great deal of time describing how carefully chosen young men should be trained so that they will have the appropriate personalities and skills to serve as leaders of the city-state. Although

---

FIGURE 9–2   The Bases of Social Power

1. **Reward Power**—based on the belief that person one has the ability to give person two pleasurable compensation for the second's obedience and loyalty.

2. **Coercive Power**—based on the perception that person one has the ability to inflict psychological or physical pain if person two is not obedient and loyal.

3. **Legitimate Power**—based on the acceptance of the idea that person one has a legal right to prescribe behavior for person two in a particular situation when that behavioral prescription is done in the proper manner.

4. **Referent Power**—based on one's psychological identification with a particular individual or group of individuals, or with a particular goal or ideal that is embodied in the individual or group.

5. **Expert Power**—embodied in a recognized skill or knowledge.

SOURCE: John R. P. French and Bertram Raven, "The Bases of Social Power," in *Studies in Social Power,* ed., Dorwin Cartwright (Ann Arbor, Mich.: 1959): Institute for Social Research, 150–167.

it was the personal aspects of leaderships that first attracted scholars' attention, they soon came to recognize the insufficiency of personality or trait theories, at which point the broader aspects of leadership theory began to receive attention. We now have a wide-ranging set of theories that attempts to explain what leadership is, and followers of these theories often claim to be able to teach one how to be a successful leader. When these various theories are combined in a comprehensive model, they do help us understand leadership far better than we have in the past. Any promise to "teach" leadership to an individual, however, must be held suspect because there are too many things we do not yet know about the subject. Moreover, there are many factors involved that cannot be controlled or "learned" through reading about, discussing, and practicing exercises derived from someone's ideas about the primary aspects of successful leadership.

So that we may create some order out of the numerous leadership theories, let us examine the material under the three related but significantly different headings discussed earlier in this chapter—executive, managerial, and supervisory leadership. Quite frankly, most of the leadership literature in generic organization theory has dealt with management and supervision, that is, the direction, coordination, and motivation of individuals and functions inside the bureaucracy. We must therefore turn to political science and its sub-disciplines of public administration and public policy for a discussion of the executive role; then we will turn to the organization theory and management behavior literature to look at the two lower levels of leadership within the hierarchy. By separating the levels or types of leadership in this way, we are not arguing that the theories presented in each section apply only at that level of the organizational hierarchy. Indeed, they cross over between levels, but the way they are interpreted and applied changes rather dramatically as we move from consideration of the executive to the manager and finally to the super-visor. Their tasks within the bureau are different because of the differences in the way the theories are useful to each type of leader in our arbitrary categories. As we look at the following material, we must remember that it can be useful to individuals at the other leadership levels while also being cognizant of the way in which it must be interpreted to "fit" those different leaders, their roles, and their functions in the bureau.

EXECUTIVE LEADERSHIP: THE SOCIAL AND POLITICAL CONTEXT

The major element added to the environment of public organizations is the political context in which they exist. Bureau executives—whether appointed from outside or chosen from within—must understand the larger context of leadership, that which goes beyond the internal functions of the organization and includes the larger social universe in which the bureau must operate. Although they cannot ignore the internal operations of the bureau, they must focus primarily on the larger institutional issues. The "coin of the realm" in the public sector is influence. Influence is gained through the skillful playing of the game called politics, and power is the reward received by the most skillful players. As has been pointed out by many students of the public policy process, bureaucrats—and especially bureaucratic leaders at the upper levels of the hierarchy—are in an enviable position as the political game is played since they have several advantages (longevity, expertise, information, and so on) that are inherent to their trade (Rourke 1984; Jones 1984; Lindblom 1993). Executive-level leaders in the public or political environment must recognize the importance of the various elements of political leadership, know how these elements can be used and misused, and then develop expertise in using them.

Of course, the use of influence (and its resulting power) operates in three different environments. Leaders obviously use these skills inside the organization. We will examine them later in this chapter, but here we will primarily note how these skills are applied within the political system and the larger social system. In the political system, several types of power are needed, depending on what part of that system is being addressed at the moment. When examining the functions of the federal agency executive, for example, political parties are important actors in the political process, as are interest groups; however, they are outside the formal paths of power and not directly related to program goals, so they often can be handled "one step removed" from the ongoing activities of the programs of the agency (for example, as important but not directly intervening variables in the ongoing process). At the same time, other parts of our federal system are often critical to the achievement of program goals. Governors and mayors are also executives in their own right at their levels of government; therefore, they must be treated as equals who have the power of life and death for many programs. Executive-level leaders must understand how these various parts fit into the larger political/administrative system, how they help guarantee the more basic democratic goals of society, and how to work with each of them.

For sophisticated political understanding to develop, however, it is essential for leaders to comprehend the larger social context in which the political activity occurs. Larry Terry refers to career executives in the public service as "administrative conservators" who must preserve and improve the institutions within which they work—from the specific organizations to the constitutional system. Conservators are guardians, individuals who preserve from injury, violation, or infraction, but who at the same time are concerned about change and reconstruction (1995, 25). In order to fulfill the roles of preservers and reconstructionists, it is necessary to understand that major social values change over time. For example, at least since the beginning of the New Deal programs of Roosevelt, a struggle has been going on between groups with different interpretations of how economic resource development and distribution should take place in society. One segment of society (made up of a variety of interest groups banded together for a wide variety of reasons) supports the handling of economic issues through the private sector, whereas another segment believes the government should play a predominant role in determining major economic questions, such as where crucial development efforts should go and how economic resources should be distributed among the citizenry. Between these two extremes are several other groups that tend to move back and forth across them, depending on the particular economic and social situation at any given time. Perhaps the proponents of governmental involvement reached their apex in the programs of the Great Society during the Johnson administration. The Republican Congress of 1995–1996 is responding to what they see as a reversal of public opinion and fighting with the Clinton administration to see who gets credit for the reduction in government "intrusion into the citizens' daily lives." Since all these changes in the attitudes of the predominant social and political coalition have occurred over time, the role of the bureaucratic leaders has shifted accordingly. Bureau executives must be sensitive to societal, political, and bureaucratic values—all of which will undoubtedly vary to at least a limited extent, but often dramatically—and then run their bureaus and tailor their own leadership roles according to the parameters created by the larger universe that they are supposed to serve.

A bureau executive may have to take a variety of external factors (factors outside his or her control) into account in making a decision about what leadership style to use. One question to be considered is "What is the political climate?" It was the impression of many public servants during the early part of the Reagan administration that the antibureaucratic climate (described as a time of "bureaucrat bashing") would make it easy for political appointees to move into offices and ride roughshod over the employees. In some cases, such as the attempt to close down the Economic Development Administration within the Department of Commerce, the administrator appeared to believe that all the employees were lazy and probably not to be trusted; therefore, he felt that the best way to shut down the program was to tear it apart procedurally and structurally. Although he ultimately failed, it was apparently his opinion that the political climate at least allowed such behavior and perhaps rewarded it. On the other hand, even though he was specifically given the task of closing the Office of Economic Opportunity, Dwight Ink, the administrator, was able to carry out the mandate to shut down the program in a way that allowed the employees to "go with dignity" and recognized the feelings of everyone related to the program. In these cases, an administrator's personal predilections probably influenced how he or she interpreted the political environment.

In another vein, at one time many public executives had very cavalier attitudes toward equal opportunity issues. Now such an attitude toward hiring, promotion, and sexual or racial harassment is a guarantee of almost instantly being in political hot water. At the same time, public opinion seems to be shifting against at least part of the affirmative action programs of the recent past and moving away from the more stringent rules established in the name of equal employment opportunity. Actions in states such as California, and in Congress, are aimed at pulling back some of the power given to affirmative action and equal employment opportunity commissions in earlier laws. The political climate is constantly in a state of change.

Another question is "What is the resource base, or the perception of the public and politicians about the availability of resources?" Not too many years ago, the public sector in the United States appeared to operate under the assumption that resources were readily available and that they would continue to grow in abundance. This attitude affected the values of many of the actors in the political arena and made growth and development of new governmental programs a goal that was accepted by both politicians and bureaucrats. Today the attitude has changed, and the values operating among politicians, citizens, and bureaucrats have changed accordingly. With the current emphasis on cutting back programs and regulations, limiting growth, and increasing efficiency, any leader who wishes to be successful must operate with an understanding of these goals.

A third question about external political factors is "What is the potential for mobilizing support for this program?" This question is another example of how political feasibility affects the style of leadership. Some segments of the political environment always seem to be well organized and easily mobilized. Business, labor, veterans, environmentalists, senior citizens, pro-choice and antiabortion advocates, and groups representing many other

The Social and Political Environment of the Public Executive: "To Trust or Not"

There is one key to (reinventing government), though it doesn't make the story simple. "We spend too much time in government . . . trying to keep bad things from happening [by issuing] rules and regulations that eventually prohibit sensible public employees from making good things happen," Bill Clinton told a group of civil servants. But the president quickly backed off, at least a little. Accountability? You bet. "[But] we don't need to overlearn the lessons of [the savings and loan debacle]," he concluded.

Congress may not see it that way. Why do twenty-three different subcommittees oversee bits of the Federal Emergency Management Agency's activities? "Congress doesn't trust anybody," says Stanford political scientist Terry Moe. "They don't want agencies to have discretion." Or as the dean of political scientists James Q. Wilson put it, in *Bureaucracy: What Government Agencies Do and Why They Do It,* "Government in the U.S. is not designed to be efficient or powerful, but tolerable and malleable. . . . Government has to be slower, has to safeguard process. . . . [It is] not hyperbole to say that constitutional order is animated by a desire to make government inefficient. . . . Government can't say yes. Government is constrained. Where do the constraints come from? Us."

Us. And long ago. In the introduction to Wilson's masterful book, he says we're welcome to skip the rest and read instead James Madison's Federalist Paper No. 51. I did. To wit: "If men were angels, no government would be necessary. If angels were to govern men, neither external or internal controls on government would be necessary. In framing a government which is to be administered by men over men, the great difficulty lies in this: You must first enable the government to control the governed; and in the next place oblige it to control itself." Hmmmm.

In fact, we're trapped on the horns of a monumental dilemma. The United States was invented *against* government. Historically we don't trust those who govern. Thus our rulers, counterpoised against each other to begin with (legislative, judicial, executive branches), create procedures to make government inefficient—so as to protect us from corruption and abuse over the long haul. . . .

Make no mistake, while most of the eight hundred suggestions (in the *National Performance Review*) appear innocent, they aren't. Collectively they depend on allowing federal employees a degree of freedom that might worry Mr. Madison. As I said to a public gathering a while back, I want my local government to be efficient, effective and swift—when *I* want approval for a plan to add a second story to my California home. But I want it to be cumbersome ("inefficient"), slow, and guard every conceivable right I can imagine, when my neighbor wants to add a floor to *his* house. Go figure.

SOURCE: Tom Peters, "Foreword." In *National Performance Review (U.S.), Creating a Government that Works Better & Costs Less: Report of the National Performance Review,* Vice President Al Gore. (New York: Plume/Penguin, 1993): xx–xxi.

Managing in the Public Sector

Public managers who have been with their chief for more than one term—perhaps for years—have developed their own views of the chief's management ability and style. Typically, however, given the limited tenure of both chiefs and managers, the public manager finds himself or herself working for a new chief—often an inexperienced one.

From the point of view of the public manager, two types of newly elected chiefs are typically encountered: the generals and the policymakers.

The "generals" know that the job has to do with running government, and that management is involved somehow with getting programs going and making things work. But this chief does not really understand the process of implementation. The general sees management as a rather simple military exercise where the general tells the subordinates and the subordinates tell the troops until something finally gets done. This chief sees the problem as one of being demanding and tough; of giving enough orders that everyone gets the message and performs. These qualities may be admirable, but they are hardly sufficient to make government work.

While the general's style may work in the military (and it sometimes fails there), it certainly does not work well in the civilian part of the public sector. In the military the commander controls all or most of the resources needed to complete the task at hand. But in the public sector the chief rarely if ever has such unilateral control. In addition, the resources public managers do control are usually circumscribed by civil service rules, union agreements, and revenue levels. Furthermore, chief elected officials have no brig for the discipline of unruly or disloyal subordinates.

The general does not realize that, in government, implementation is very tough. It is one thing to decide that prison overcrowding must end but quite another to make it happen. Nothing is more disheartening to a public manager than to deliver a particularly tough program or project in one year, only to have the chief resentful because it was not done in six months. Or worse still to have the chief announce at the outset that something will take six months when it cannot possibly be done in less than a year. Educating the "generals" about the realities of public management is an especially frustrating task for managers.

The second type of novice chief is the policymaker. For the policymaker, implementation and management are simply not considered an important part of the chief's responsibility. This chief does not really understand that he or she runs a complex organization, with money, people, and facilities which must be made to perform effectively. Policymakers typically come from legislative backgrounds—they see the job of chief as doing what they did before, only in a bigger way. The policymaker holds this view for a number of reasons: because it is more comfortable, because management may seem boring, because the chief does not really believe that anything can be done in the public sector anyway, or because the chief simply knows no better.

SOURCE: Gordon Chase and Elizabeth C. Reveal, *How to Manage in the Public Sector* (Reading, Mass.: Addison-Wesley, 1983): 27–28.

special interests in society are organized, and though each has its particular strengths and weaknesses, leaders of the public bureaucracy must reckon with varied combinations of these groups any time issues affecting their interests are involved. These groups can be mobilized to fight for or against those issues, and the bureau leader can anticipate their cooperation or resistance, as the case may be. On the other hand, some groups like welfare recipients or consumers of prescription drugs may be much harder to mobilize; thus, the leadership style used and the alternatives that are open may be limited. This does not mean that there are no opportunities to use one's leadership style and mobilizing talents; rather, it means that imagination and political savvy must be combined in finding other ways to get the important points about the particular welfare program or the process for approving new drugs across to some of the significant actors in the external environment, and that a management style acceptable to both those inside and outside the organization must be employed. In other words:

> If leaders are rigid, inflexible, and unimaginative in adjusting their preferred styles to the political challenges they face, they have very seriously limited their chances of implementing their policy options. Hence, the final—and most crucial—ingredient in effective policy implementation involves the personal component of leadership. (Nakamura and Smallwood, 1980, 167)

Although flexibility and imagination are required, it is also important to note that institutional leaders must always fulfill four functions that are integral to the leadership position. Those functions, as enumerated by Philip Selznick, are:

1. The definition of institutional mission and role (the creative task of setting goals)
2. The institutional embodiment of purpose (the capacity to build policy into an organization's social structure)
3. The defense of institutional integrity (maintaining values and institutional identity)
4. The ordering of internal conflict (reconciling the struggle among competing interests) (1957, 56–64)

In other words, leaders in the political arena must carry out their duties in a way that allows the organization to carry out its task in congruency with the environment in which it is working. Burt Nanus refers to this as "visionary leadership," and argues that:

> There is no more powerful engine driving an organization toward excellence and long-range success than an attractive, worthwhile, and achievable vision of the future, widely shared. (1992, 3)

Scholars have attempted to describe how bureau leaders accomplish this task in the implementation literature.[2] Nakamura and Smallwood, for example, point out a set of "political" problems faced by public leaders that are ignored by traditional organization theory or management behavior literature, but that cannot be ignored by the leader of a bureau. Traditional management behavior literature trends to look inward, with the emphasis on improving the internal structure and functioning of the bureau. Policy and

---

[2]By "implementation" literature, we mean that set of authors who work in the area of public policy analysis and who write on that part of the policy process that they refer to as the implementation phase. It is this part on which public administration scholars focus in their studies, except that the policy students examine the function from a political perspective rather than an organizational or managerial one.

implementation literature stresses the importance of understanding the external factors that influence a leader's ability to carry out the functions described by Selznick and Nanus. Nakamura and Smallwood argue that there are five kinds of bureau executives: classical technocrats, instructed delegates, bargainers, discretionary experimenters, and bureaucratic entrepreneurs (see Figure 9–3).

Although Nakamura and Smallwood are arguing that particular leaders tend to operate in one of these five modes, it can also be argued that successful bureau leaders adopt different styles of leadership over the years, depending on the prevailing values and assumptions of their political leaders, their clientele, the interest groups that are watching their actions, and the general public. These changes may occur gradually as the public's perception of the role of government shifts, or they may occur rapidly when a new administration comes into power. As we noted, we can certainly see change if we look back to the 1960s at Johnson's Great Society, compare it to the Reagan administration's attitude toward the role of the federal government, and then note the downsizing movement of just about all current governments and the antiregulation philosophy of the 1995–1996 Congress. The important factor, however, is the leader's ability to test and measure the political environment and then choose the leadership style that will best meet the needs of his or her bureau and of the public in general. After all, it is the public that the bureau serves.

An alternative and more traditional vision of leadership, but one that addresses an important element of being an executive in the public sector, is presented by James MacGregor Burns (1978) in his discussion of the roles of transactional leadership and transformational leadership. The more common transactional leader serves as an agent of interaction and "commerce" between the various individuals within groups and between the various groups in society. Through the control and encouragement of transactions involving resources, information, and other factors of importance to society, these leaders help keep society functioning in a relatively smooth way and ensure that goods and services are created and used in some sort of rational pattern. (No judgment is intended about the rightness or wrongness of the logic on which "rationality" is based since it can mean totally different things in different societies.)

The transformational role is the one that Burns feels is most often ignored in modern studies of leadership, and he attempts to examine this role in detail—both its positive and negative aspects. Transformational leaders help individuals, groups, and societies recognize and achieve their higher and more humane aspirations, thereby moving human understanding and enterprise to a new moral and ethical level. Although, in the total societal context, there are relatively few cases of transformational leadership, the few that exist take on significant and collective proportions historically. For transformational leaders, the time and point of action is intensely individual and personal.

> The essence of leadership in any polity is the recognition of real need, the uncovering and exploiting of contradictions among values and between values and practice, the realigning of values, the reorganization of institutions where necessary, and the governance of change. (Burns 1978, 43)

Such actions require an individual who can be cognizant of several pressures and movements at one time; further, more than one kind of ethic may be involved. Burns notes that Max Weber contrasts two types of ethics in his writing: the "ethic of responsibility" and the "ethic of ultimate ends." The last examines the leader's behavior according to its

FIGURE 9–3   Five Kinds of Policy Implementers

Classical Technocrats. Implementers have some technical discretion, but their power to make any overall policy decisions is very strictly limited.

Basic Assumptions:

- Policymakers delineate clear goals, and implementers support those goals.
- Policymakers establish a hierarchical command structure and delegate technical authority to specific implementers to carry out their goals.
- Implementers have the technical capabilities to achieve the goals.

Instructed Delegates. Implementers have more power to determine the means that will be employed to achieve the policymaker's goals.

Basic Assumptions:

- Policymakers delineate clear goals, and implementers agree on the desirability of those goals.
- Policymakers instruct one or more groups of implementers to achieve the goals, and delegate discretionary administrative authority to those implementers.
- Implementers have the technical, administrative, and negotiating capabilities to achieve the goals.

Bargainers. Implementers' power position vis-à-vis policymakers increases dramatically because they can exercise considerable clout through threats of noncompliance and nonimplementation.

Basic Assumptions:

- Formal policymakers delineate policy goals.
- Policymakers and implementers do not necessarily agree between (or among) themselves on the desirability of those goals.
- Implementers bargain with policymakers and with each other over both goals and means.

Discretionary Experimenters. Implementers experience a dramatic delegation of power away from policymakers and toward themselves.

Basic Assumptions:

- Formal policymakers support abstract general goals but are unable to articulate them clearly owing to lack of knowledge and/or other uncertainties.
- The policymakers delegate broad discretionary powers to implementers to refine the goals and to develop the means to accomplish them.
- Implementers are willing (and able) to perform these tasks.

Bureaucratic Entrepreneurs. Power is shifted to implementers because they generate and control information, have continuity so they can outlast and wear down policymakers, and have and use entrepreneurial and political skills that allow them to dominate policy formulation.

Basic Assumptions:

- Implementers formulate their own policy goals and marshal sufficient power to convince the formal policymakers to adopt those goals.
- Implementers negotiate with policymakers to secure the means necessary to achieve their own policy goals.
- Implementers are willing (and able) to carry out their policy goals.

SOURCE: Robert Nakamura and Frank Smallwoord, *The Politics of Policy Implementation* (New York: St. Martin's Press, 1980): 112–133.

adherence to "good" ends or "high" purposes. The ethic of responsibility, on the other hand, measures a set of actions by the leader, including (1) acquiring the capacity to use a calculating, prudential, rationalistic approach; (2) making choices on the basis of many values, attitudes, and interests; (3) seeing the relationship of one goal to another; (4) understanding the implications of choice for the means of attaining it (the cost for the benefit); and (5) recognizing the direct and indirect effects of different goals for different persons and interests. The most important factor is that the leader using the ethic of responsibility carries out all these calculations in a context of specificity and immediacy, and with an eye toward actual consequences rather than lofty intent (Burns 1978, 45). In our recent studies, we have tended to focus on the ethic of responsibility while ignoring the ethic of ultimate ends. In doing so, we have missed much of the importance of leadership because as Burns notes:

> For . . . leadership, the dichotomy is not between Weber's two ethics but between the leader's commitment to a number of overriding, general welfare-oriented values on the one hand and his encouragement of, and entanglement in, a host of lesser values and "responsibilities" on the other. (1978, 46)

And above all, the leader must accept and cope with ambiguity at the same time that he or she is attempting to develop and maintain overall goals for his or her followers. For, as noted by Harlan Cleveland:

> The executive's work often consists in meeting a series of unforeseeable obstacles on the road to an objective which can be clearly specified only when he is close to reaching it. He tries to imagine the unforeseen by posing contingencies and asking how his organization system would adjust if they arose. But the planned-for contingency never happens; something else happens instead. (1972, 78)

When we talk about leadership in this all-inclusive way, we must discuss personal characteristics, behavior, and environmental forces or situations.[3] Personal traits and behavior are covered in the next section of this chapter, but some specific comments related to executives need to be noted here.

Leaders of the public bureaucracy need to combine intellect and action. Too many cases can be presented of situations where individuals have operated only in one realm—to the detriment of the other. Although clear conceptualization, masterful analysis, and maximum results are all goals that are highly desirable, any attempt to achieve the ultimate level of any of these goals is liable to create "intellectual gridlock" and lead to minimal results. It takes only a few examples of agonizing and fence-sitting intellectually oriented leaders who allow the opportunity to pass by while collecting the last bit of information

---

[3]In a similar vein, but at a different level of government, James Barber (1992, 4–6) argues that a president's personality is patterned by a series of influences; this patterning is "a matter of tendencies." Three personality factors constitute the core of this patterning.

1. Style—the president's habitual way of performing his three political roles: rhetoric, personal relations, and homework. Style is his way of acting.
2. Worldview—the president's primary, politically relevant beliefs, particularly his conception of social causality, human nature, and the central moral conflicts of the time. Worldview is his way of seeing.
3. Character—the way the president orients himself toward life (not for the moment, but enduringly). At the core of character, a man confronts himself. Character is his way of judging himself and his self-esteem.

for their decision to create the antiintellectual biases and mythology that are so common throughout political society. On the other hand, there are just as many stories about the "bull in the china closet" who charges off without having done enough thinking and creates political havoc for other members of the executive because of his or her naive or uninformed action. What is needed is a leader who deals with both analytical and normative ideas, and brings them both to bear on the environment through timely action (Burns 1978).

Any leader who accomplishes this goal, however, must understand that two further factors will result from his or her actions. First, some people will not appreciate what has been accomplished; the actions will generate controversy and perhaps even hatred. Certainly, not everyone will love an intellectually active leader. This is precisely why it is so often argued that it is impossible to judge the quality of leadership given by a president of the United States until at least one generation has passed. To quote Burns:

> No matter how strong [the] longing for unanimity, almost all leaders . . . must settle for far less than universal affection. They must be willing to *make enemies*—to deny themselves the affection of their adversaries. They must accept conflict. They must be willing and able to be unloved.[4] It is hard to pick one's friends, harder to pick one's enemies. (1978, 34)

This happens because leaders must take sides. They must decide what goal they will support, what process is correct in attempting to achieve that goal, what group they will lead, and in almost every case, there is at least one other perspective—often with equally ardent supporters:

> The question, then, is not the inevitability of conflict but the function of leadership in expressing, shaping, and curbing it. . . . Leaders, whatever their professions of harmony, do not shun conflict, they confront it, exploit it, ultimately embody it. (Burns 1978, 37–39)

Political conflict, the second result of active leadership, occurs within a set of rules that helps keep it in bounds and makes it constructive for society. Bureau executives must be willing to scuffle and swap, bargain and bluff, wheel and deal, and perform all the other functions involved in the political process. And as long as the political process guarantees the rights of minorities and losers, the leader must know how to cope with both winning and losing, at least over the short run, while recognizing that political tides ebb and flow.

As an operator in a political milieu, the bureau executive must use all available resources, such as public opinion and clientele support. Thus as Wilson notes:

> To a political executive a good strategy is one that identifies a set of tasks that are both feasible and supportable—activities the organization has the capacity to engage in and that will elicit the backing of important constituencies. (1989, 207)

The leader of any bureaucracy must also recognize the limits of all forms of expertise and of his or her contacts in political offices. There are other limiting factors that prey on

---

[4]We must approach this idea from a position of moderation, and remember this caveat: The willingness to be unloved cannot be used as an excuse for riding roughshod over everyone else in the organization; the inevitability of making enemies does not justify practices that ensure doing so.

Executive Responsibility

Executive positions (a) imply a complex morality, and (b) require a high capacity of responsibility, (c) under conditions of activity, necessitating (d) commensurate general and specific technical abilities as a moral factor. . . . (I)n addition there is required (e) the faculty of *creating* morals for others. . . .

(a) Every executive possesses, independently of the position he occupies, personal moral codes. When the individual is placed in an executive position there are immediately incumbent upon him, officially at least, several *additional* codes that are codes of his organization.

(b) The capacity of responsibility is that of being firmly governed by moral codes—against inconsistent immediate impulses, desires, or interests, and in the direction of desires or interests that are consonant with such codes. Our common word for one aspect of this capacity is "dependability," by which we mean that, knowing a man's codes—that is, being aware of his "character"—we can reasonably foresee what he is likely to do or not to do, usually under a variety of circumstances.

(c) Generally the conditions of executive work are those of great activity. . . . It is clear that the higher the position the more exposed the incumbent to action imposed from numerous directions, calling for the activity of decision.

(d) The capacity of responsibility is in executive ranks rather a constant, and the tendency of activity to increase with scope of position is often controllable. The increase in complexity of moral conditions, however, is not controllable by the person affected, so that despite control of activities the burden increases from conflicts of morals as the scope of the executive position broadens. . . .

The moral complications of the executive functions, then, can only be endured by those possessing a commensurate ability. While, on one hand, the requisite ability without an adequate complex of moralities or without a high sense of responsibility leads to the hopeless confusion of inconsistent expediencies so often described as "incompetence," on the other hand, the requisite morality and sense of responsibility without commensurate abilities leads to fatal indecision or emotional and impulsive decisions, with personal breakdown and

almost all political executives, such as conflicting commitments, motives, and goals in any political administration and even within the particular administrator. A limited amount of time is given to any executive to accomplish his or her goals. Finally, bureau executives often find it extremely difficult to marshal ideological and political resources outside the immediate system; this problem appears to be increasing with the current antigovernment, antibureaucracy, single-issue sentiment, and decreasing resources. Thus, Burns is correct in saying:

> The distinguishing characteristics of executive leaders . . . are their lack of reliable political and institutional support, their dependence on bureaucratic resources such as staff and budget, and most of all their use of themselves—their own talent and character, prestige and popularity, in the clash of political interests and values. . . . Executive leaders in a power struggle may appeal to public opinion but lack the machinery to activate it, shape it, channel it, and bring it to bear on the decision-making process. Hence they . . . must

ultimate destruction of the sense of responsibility. The important distinctions of rank lie in the fact that the higher the grade the more complex the moralities involved, and the more necessary higher abilities to discharge the responsibilities, that is, to resolve the moral conflicts implicit in the positions. . . .

(e) The distinguishing mark of the executive responsibility is that it requires not merely conformance to a complex code of morals but also the creation of moral codes for others. The most generally recognized aspect of this function is called securing, creating, inspiring of "morale" in an organization. This is the process of inculcating points of view, fundamental attitudes, loyalties, to the organization of cooperative system, and to the system of objective authority, that will result in subordinating individual interest and the minor dictates of personal codes to the good of the cooperative whole.

But there is another aspect of moral creativeness that is little understood, except in the field of jurisprudence. This is the inventing of a moral basis for the solution of moral conflicts—variously called "handling the exceptional case," "the appellate function," "the judicial function." This function is exercised in the cases that seem "right" from one point of view, "wrong" from another. . . . Probably most of [these cases] are solved by substitute action, [but even in these cases] the codes governing individual relationships to organized effort are of wide variation, so that either action or failure to act in these cases does violence to individual moralities, though the alternatives will affect different persons in different ways.

[Executives are also responsible for] morally justifying a change or redefinition or new particularizing of purpose so that the sense of conformance to moral codes is secured. One final effect is the elaboration and refinement of morals—of codes of conduct. . . . That it can degenerate into mere subtlety to avoid rather than to discharge obligations is apparent in all executive experience. The invention of the constructions and fictions necessary to secure the preservation of morale is a severe test of both responsibility and ability, for to be sound they must be "just" in the view of the executive, that is, really consonant with the morality of the whole; as well as acceptable, that is, really consonant with the morality of the part, of the individual.

SOURCE: Chester Barnard, *The Functions of the Executive* (1938; reprint, Cambridge, Mass.: Harvard University Press, 1968): 272–281.

depend more on personal manipulation and executive management than on institutional support. (1978, 371–372)

Despite these limitations, executives are answerable for the health and success of their organizations. The single most important factor in determining the ability of an organization to survive and succeed, to change while continuing to meet its public mission, is the leadership of the organization. We will discuss this subject in Chapter 10; however, let us practice one of the habits needed by executives and repeat once more the central message; in spite of all the problems and limitations of working in the public sector, *leaders must create and maintain their organization's vision of its present and future.*

The executives that not only maintain their organizations but transform them do more than merely acquire constituency support; they project a compelling vision of the tasks, culture, and importance of their agencies. The greatest executives infuse their organizations with value and convince others that this value is not merely useful to the bureau but essential to the polity. (Wilson 1989, 217)

These tasks cannot be farmed out. The executives set the tone for all the organization.

Executives, however, cannot accomplish these tasks alone. They must depend on the others with official leadership positions in the hierarchical chain of command—the bureau managers and supervisors. Therefore, let us move on to leadership theories that primarily apply to those roles.

LEADERSHIP IN THE MIDDLE OF THE BUREAU: THE MANAGERS

Managers are "in the middle" in several ways. They are usually chosen from, and still belong to, the civil service; therefore, they have commitments to merit principles—but they are often directly responsible to political appointees. Although managers usually come from specialist or professional backgrounds and have been promoted because they functioned well in the organization's technical roles, they now must think as program generalists and carry out coordinative functions that do not require their original talents. Whereas those below them in the bureau focus on specific tasks or functions and those above them consider broad policy and bureau goals, managers must turn those policies and objectives into outputs by developing and coordinating structures and functions. Managers must fulfill contradictory roles: Subordinates expect them to represent their interests upward to higher officials, whereas higher officials expect them to present organizational goals downward to the workers and to see that those objectives are achieved.

In addition, middle management is the focus of much of the dissatisfaction about "bureaucratic inefficiency" that is prevalent throughout the citizenry. Since it is hard to put a value on what is done by managers, they often are the ones charged with inefficiency and ineffectiveness, and the ones cut first and most by organizations. For instance, the National Performance Review claims that by reducing the "over-control and microman-agement in government" there will be the possibility to:

> pare down the structures that go with them: the oversized headquarters, multiple layers of supervisors and auditors, and offices specializing in the arcane rules of budgeting, personnel, procurement, and finance. We cannot entirely do without headquarters, supervisors, auditors, or specialists, but *these structures have grown twice as large as they should be.* (1993, 5–6: emphasis added)

And the federal government is not alone in this attitude. In an 1995 study of 8,000 of the nation's largest companies done by the American Management Association, it was found that:

> While middle managers make up 5 percent to 8 percent of the work force, they generally account for 15 percent to 20 percent of the job losses as measured by the management group's annual survey. Last year, 15.3 percent of the layoffs were borne by middle managers, down from 18 percent a year earlier. (Franklin 1995, H6)

Because of all the countervailing forces, contradictory roles, and sequentially changing foci, managers not only are in the middle, but they have one of the most difficult jobs in the world. Likewise, management is difficult to describe and theorize about (although that has not stopped anyone from trying). Just as the position and practice of management fall in the middle, so does the study of it. Managers need to understand those on both ends of the leadership continuum, since they interact with both and must serve as a link between them (Likert 1961, 1967). Since this connection with both ends of the continuum is so important, the theories of leadership that are identified principally with the two ends—executives and supervisors—tend to apply to management as well. The obverse is also true: Those theories that focus on management spill over in both directions to a great extent; still, we can examine three major theories or models that will help clarify the manager's role in the bureau.

Manager Traits, Motivations, and Skills

Throughout this century, there has been an ongoing interest in the particular traits and skills exhibited by leaders. Originally, researchers were interested in discovering what traits were present among leaders that did not exist among followers, or which existed to a greater degree among leaders. Later research has focused on ways to select supervisors and managers or to predict managerial success. The most thorough compendium of the research on leadership traits appears in Stogdill's *Handbook of Leadership* (Bass 1981, 1990). In this volume, Stogdill surveyed 124 articles dealing with personal factors associated with leadership, all published between 1904 and 1947. He then surveyed another 163 articles that appeared between 1948 and 1970. It is useful to discuss the two studies separately because the publication of the first paper (chapter 4, Bass 1981) proved to be a:

> turning point in the study of leadership. Before this date, universal traits of leadership were emphasized. After the publication of this paper, specific situational analyses took over, in fact dominated the field, much more than argued for by Stogdill. . . . Both individual traits and situational assessments as well as the interaction between them are important, and that was Stogdill's main thesis. (1981, 43).

Even though Stogdill found little agreement among the studies carried out through 1947 (see Figure 9–4), there were some significant findings, and he classified these under the general headings of "capacity, achievement, responsibility, participation, and status." The second survey of literature on leadership (through 1970) appeared to support the generalizations presented earlier. Although a lot of new characteristics were introduced, they tended to be variations on the general concepts mentioned; the summary of that study appears to support that statement:

FIGURE 9–4   Leadership Traits—Categorized by Stogdill

1. **Capacity:** intelligence, alertness, verbal facility, originality, judgment.
2. **Achievement:** scholarship, knowledge, athletic accomplishments.
3. **Responsibility:** dependability, initiative, persistence, aggressiveness, self-confidence, desire to excel.
4. **Participation:** activity, sociability, cooperation, adaptability, humor.
5. **Status:** socioeconomic position, popularity.
6. **Situation:** mental level, status, skills, needs and interests of followers, objectives to be achieved, and so on.

SOURCE: Bernard M. Bass, ed., *Stogdill's Handbook of Leadership* (New York: Free Press, 1981): 66.

The leader is characterized by a strong drive for responsibility and task completion, vigor and persistence in pursuit of goals, venturesomeness and originality in problem solving, drive to exercise initiative in social situations, self-confidence and sense of personal identity, willingness to accept consequences of decision and action, readiness to absorb interpersonal stress, willingness to tolerate frustration and delay, ability to influence other persons' behavior, and capacity to structure social interaction systems to the purpose at hand. (Bass 1990, 87)

The level of agreement on relevant traits is low, and the findings prove useful primarily in an inductive and insightful way. No longer do scholars believe that "leaders are born," nor do they believe that there is a specific set of traits that is essential to leader success. Instead, there is agreement that the traits noted, and perhaps some others, greatly increase the probability of success as a leader.

Closely related to the trait research were some other approaches to the study of leadership that focused on the motivation and values held by managers and executives. Numerous individuals have zeroed in on managerial motivation. For example, David McClelland decided that three factors—needs for achievement, power, and affiliation—were central to the effectiveness of managers (1975; see also Winter 1973). In established bureaucracies, the dominant motive of most successful organizational managers is the need for power.[5] Along with a drive for power appears to go the self-confidence and assertiveness that are necessary to lead and control a large and complex group. The power drive, however, needs to be moderated by a sense of concern for the group, or a social sense, that generates a use of power to benefit others, and not simply for one's own advantage. A leader with a power drive that is moderated by social concern is usually more open to advice, to active participation in decisions by subordinates, to the development of clear and understandable organization structures, and therefore, to a general pride in belonging to the organization. The successful leader also has a moderate need for affiliation, in some cases only to be able to fulfill the social and public relations activities that are inherent in managerial and executive positions, but more important, because affiliation is essential to the leader's establishment of effective interpersonal relationships with subordinates, peers, and superiors. After all, commitment and loyalty tend to be reciprocal feelings.

Nor can the achievement motivation be absent. Obviously, a balance of the three drives is necessary, with the levels being determined by the situation facing the organization and the leader.

Motivation is closely related to the values held by managers; it could be argued that these values are what fuel or create motivation. Therefore, numerous attempts have been made to identify and categorize the values held by managers deemed successful. One example of such an effort is the survey developed by L. Gordon (1975, 1976). Gordon measures six major values:

- *Support:* Being treated with understanding, kindness, and consideration; receiving encouragement from other people.

- *Conformity:* Following regulation; doing what is accepted, proper, or socially correct.

---

[5]Among entrepreneurial executives, the need for achievement appeared to be dominant; therefore, achievement would probably be the motivating factor for someone successfully directing a new and struggling public organization.

- *Recognition:* Attracting favorable attention; being admired, looked up to, or considered important.

- *Independence:* Being free to make one's own decisions or do things in one's own way; experiencing freedom of action.

- *Benevolence:* Being generous and other directed; sharing with and helping those who are less fortunate.

- *Leadership:* Having authority over people; being in a position of influence or power. (Gordon 1975, 22–25)

Results regularly show that effective managers and executives tend to have higher leadership ranking and lower support, conformity, and benevolence scores. Other studies have tended to show that managers, when asked about their own values, tend to see themselves as pragmatic, identifying personal qualities such as skill, ambition, achievement, and creativity as most instrumental in achieving success (England 1967). Human relations factors, such as rationality and individuality, and ethical factors are recognized as important, but are considered secondary to the just-mentioned values.[6]

When the trait, motivation, and value concepts are combined with the specific skills needed for a particular managerial position, one has the components that are regularly considered when bureau managers are chosen. These are the factors considered important to successful management. From these basic assumptions, in fact, spring the testing procedures mentioned in Chapter 3. Assessment centers, for example, put individuals through a series of tests to determine their potential as managers because it is felt that such a multifaceted regimen is the best method currently in existence to examine the participants' traits, values, and skills.

We have found, after almost a century of research on leadership traits, that they are important, they cannot be ignored. However, other factors must also be taken into consideration. One way of recognizing and dealing with those other factors is to examine the behavior of managers and how they handle the many roles they must fulfill.

Managerial Behavior and the Fulfillment of Multiple Roles

The number and variety of tasks performed by the manager of a bureau are actually larger than our imagination allows us to perceive and comprehend. Successful bureau managers usually reach a point, when trying to describe the reasons for their success, where they can no longer verbalize their thoughts and actions; at this point, they use aphorisms such as "flying by the seat of my pants," "using my sixth sense," and "following my gut reactions." Scholars, armed with their best methodologies and the latest statistical tools, can explain only a small portion of the total behavior of managers and find little comparability between successful managers who work in the same organization or circumstance.

---

[6]All the factors discussed here ultimately seem to fall within a typology that places them into three groups—conceptual skills, technical skills, and human relations skills (Katz 1955; Mann 1965). These skills, which are closely related to individual values and personality traits, must be present in all successful bureau leaders. The situation in which the leader operates goes far toward deciding what combination of traits, values, and skills must exist for him or her to be successful. In the research, the most important situational factor appears to be the level of leadership position.

Henry Mintzberg (1973) examined much of the research that dealt with the activities of managers in a variety of organizations. From this material and his own research, he developed a group of distinguishing characteristics and roles that describe what managers do. First, he examined the roles; then he went on to describe the way they are carried out. There are ten major roles, all of which are important to, and will probably be used by, every manager at one time or another. However, the relative importance of the roles is determined by a set of factors that includes such elements as position in the hierarchy, technology involved among those being led, the "social system" or culture that exists among subordinates and peers, proximity to the organization's exterior, and danger perceived from the environment. We briefly describe these roles here, and in those cases where a role is probably more important to executives or supervisors, we note that fact in parentheses. Still, it must be reiterated that managers will be involved in all the roles to some extent.

1. *Figurehead role* (primarily an executive role). Executives and managers hold formal positions within the organization, and these positions create an obligation to participate in organizational duties, rituals, and ceremonies. These vary from signing certain documents and communications and greeting visitors to throwing out the first ball at the annual office picnic and presenting the gold watch to a colleague at his or her retirement dinner. These jobs help set a psychological tone for the bureau and the manager even though they are only peripherally related to accomplishing the objectives of the organization.

2. *Leader role* (divided between all three levels). Supervisors and managers must hire, train, direct, praise, motivate, integrate, and even dismiss employees. Executives and managers create the conditions that allow work to be efficiently and effectively done, conditions that set the "tone" of the bureau, because their style of leadership tends to permeate the organization. Therefore, the leader role is the vehicle that allows the manager to provide guidance and create favorable conditions for doing the bureau's work.

3. *Liaison role.* For a bureau to function effectively, there must be communication and coordination between the various units inside the organization and with relevant elements of the environment. This is accomplished by the manager's liaison role in which he or she establishes and maintains a web, or network, of relationships with relevant individuals and groups outside his or her particular unit or subunit. Who is relevant to a manager depends on an individual's position in the bureau. Chief executives look outward for contacts in an effort to make sure the organization has the proper linkups with other organizations and important political actors. Managers and supervisors focus on relationships that are important to their part of the organization. By making contacts, doing favors, and keeping an ear to the grapevine, each manager is attempting to sway "influential others" inside or outside the organization who, in turn, can have an effect on the success of the manager's operations. Obviously, these liaison activities are carried out in both formal and informal settings, inside and outside the immediately affected bureau.

4. *Monitor role.* Managers receive information from a variety of sources. Some is passed on to subordinates or to outsiders (other managers in the organization or relevant individuals or groups in the environment), but most of the information is analyzed in a constant search for problems and opportunities so that both external events and internal processes can be better understood. In this way, managers can immediately correct situations causing difficulty, encourage success, and prepare for future events.

5. *Disseminator role.* Since managers have access to information that is not available to subordinates, it is the manager's function to assimilate and properly interpret the information and pass it on to those who need it. Some of the information is factual: This may be passed on in its original form or may require "massaging" so that it is more meaningful to those receiving it. Other information relates to values, attitudes, or preferences of individuals and organizations that influence the manager: This information must be assimilated and evaluated regarding its importance and then passed along as mandates, goals, values, policies, suggestions, or responses to inquiries from subordinates.

6. *Spokesperson role.* Managers must serve as transmitters of information about their units to their superiors within the bureau and to interested parties on the outside. Each manager must act as lobbyist, public relations officer, and negotiator because he or she is in the appropriate formal position, has the best knowledge about his or her unit and its environment, and can guarantee that the unit speaks with "one voice" as it deals with all the other groups in the process.

7. *Entrepreneur role.* The entrepreneur role may seem at first blush an inappropriate one for a public manager, but on further consideration it becomes obvious that this role is essential in all sectors of society (Lewis 1980). As noted by Matthew Holden, (1966), there is a high degree of "bureaucratic imperialism" in public agencies; therefore, chief executives and managers must at least be on the lookout for bureaucratic marauders who may attack by snatching bits of authority and resources from their units or who may try to grab the entire operation and place it in a disadvantageous situation. By the same token, managers watch for opportunities to strengthen or expand their operation in ways that "make sense" or lead to better service for the public. Managers also act as initiators and designers of changes that are aimed at improving the situation of their units. Such changes might include the purchase of new equipment, the reorganization of formal structure, or the development of a new and needed program. Mintzberg describes the entrepreneur as a juggler. "At any one point in time he has a number of balls in the air. Periodically, one comes down, receives a short burst of energy, and goes up again. Meanwhile, new balls wait on the sidelines and, at intervals, old balls are discarded and new ones added" (1973, 81).

8. *Disturbance-handler role.* Sudden crises, such as a conflict between subordinates, a natural disaster, or the loss of key employees, take up much of a manager's time. These crises cannot be ignored, and managers usually spend so much time dealing with matters of this type that they have little opportunity to do any reflective thinking or to plan.

9. *Resource-allocator role.* Managers use their control over money, material, and personnel to guarantee their coordinative and integrative roles in the organization. In this role, the manager can determine bureau priorities and strategy through decisions about the use of resources. The role also guarantees that he or she maintains control of both specific processes and overall bureau operations by requiring his or her involvement in any decisions affecting major shifts in resources.

10. *Negotiator role.* When a manager acts in this role, he or she is probably involved because of several of the other roles noted (for example, the spokesperson and resource allocator). Managers can represent or speak for their units better than almost anyone else. For this reason, negotiations are not considered seriously underway until "the person who can make the decisions" is directly involved. Another way to note this role is through the insistence that an individual must "go directly to the top" since it is recognized that only at this level can bargains be struck and commitments made. Although the scope and type of negotiations change at different levels of an organization, anyone in an executive or managerial role is involved in the negotiating role.

The roles all exist, but the decision regarding what combination of roles is important at any one time and how much emphasis to place on them is something that can often be decided only by managers after they have examined the major factors impinging on both them and their unit. Once those matters have been decided, the roles are enacted through a set of managerial work activities. But everyone in a bureau is active (even if not always in constructive ways), so the problem is to define how managerial activities are unique. Mintzberg again devised a set of distinguishing characteristics, or characteristics that were more descriptive of how managers spent their time in comparison to other members of the organization. It should be noted as we begin this discussion, however, that in each case the characteristics connote degree; that is, they are not a description of activities that were unique to managers and nonexistent among other bureau members. Mintzberg identified five major characteristics, four of which we describe next.

1. *Work pace.* Managers tend to work without a break, at a grueling pace, for long hours, and even take work home with them. Two factors may explain this characteristic. Individuals who have reached managerial positions tend to be embued with the work ethic and to find their primary self-gratification through their work. Second, since they have trained their minds to search for and analyze information related to their work and their organizations, they find it nearly impossible to turn off their minds when they close the office door.

2. *Activity duration and variation.* Managers tend to engage in a wide variety of activities that occur, one could say, almost at random, with each receiving only a brief burst of attention before the next impinges on the manager's consciousness. Most activities take only a few minutes and very few—approximately one-tenth—require more than an hour. The frequent changes of subjects, and the importance of the matters, require that managers shift focus and mood constantly. This characteristic becomes even more pronounced when an individual operates at the lower management levels.

3. *Action rather than reflection.* Managers seldom engage in general planning, abstract discussion, or reflection; instead, they tend to gravitate toward the active aspects of their jobs. Although they enjoy nonroutine activities, they do not like ambiguity and therefore prefer well-defined goals and functions. Specific rather than general or ill-defined issues gain most managers' attention, and they focus on current rather than older information.

4. *Communication media usage.* (This characteristic is essential to several of the roles mentioned earlier.) Managers use five major methods of obtaining and dispensing information: written messages, scheduled meetings, unscheduled meetings, observational tours, and telephone messages. Each medium is used for a slightly different set of purposes, but any method that allows oral communication is preferred. Managers in every study are found to spend a majority of their time in oral communication, with two-thirds of that time spent either on the telephone or in unscheduled meetings. From what was noted in the second and third characteristics, we can conclude that these contacts tend to be varied and of short duration.

Managerial Style

So many roles and behaviors are involved in managing that it is hopeless for an individual to have to think about the process and make carefully considered decisions about which role and which behavior fits each arising situation. The world moves too fast. Before all the possible combinations can be considered, the situation changes, and the process of analysis must start over. In such a case, the manager suffers from "role behavior gridlock." Consequently, the individual develops a general management "style"—or a habitual way of performing—that includes a particular style for the most common bureau situation and a set of standard responses or styles for the most common crises or recurring phenomena that require special attention. These styles quickly become known to other actors in the bureau, especially the manager's subordinates, and one can commonly hear people say, "Boy, the boss is going to blow her stack when she finds out about this" or "No matter what the crisis, the boss always keeps the group focused on the agency goals." Styles become important because they give critical cues to everyone, in and outside the agency, about what the manager's values and perspectives are and how the actors in the unit should proceed.

When managers' roles and behaviors and the characteristic ways (styles) used to fulfill those roles are combined into a single equation, it becomes obvious that the task of management in a bureau is incredibly complex. On top of all this, the manager is the linchpin that holds together the upper and lower levels of the bureau. Therefore, the manager is truly the person in the middle. With it all, many managers are successful, and one of the major reasons is that these individuals have been able to make the transition from technician and professional to coordinator, communicator, and fulfiller of all the other management functions. Along the way, they have usually passed through the supervisory ranks. Good supervision leads to good management, and successful supervisors—with continued growth and training—often become successful managers. This is true because the managerial position requires perspectives and skills that are simply "another step forward" on the continuum between supervisors and executives.

The Manager's Mission

I can remember, when I first became administrator of the New York City Health Services Administration (the first nonphysician to hold that position), that I would call in my commissioners and senior managers and ask them what they'd been doing—what their agencies or units or programs had been up to in the last few weeks or months or years.

Some of these senior officials would start by telling me how many meetings they had attended, how many memos they'd written, how many staff they'd hired, and similar benchmarks of bureaucratic activity. I'd look at them and say: "But whom did you make healthy today (or last week, or last year)? Did you make anybody in New York healthier—and how do you know?"

In short order people came to realize where I wanted my emphasis—not on the mechanics of running public agencies but on the outcome of the services we were there to deliver. It's not that I didn't understand the importance of dealing with the chief, overhead agencies, and the rest of the characters in our daily fare; it's just that I wanted the right perspective—I wanted my managers to be conscious of the fact that we were there to make people healthier, and not to lose sight of that fact in the daily squabblings that we all had to endure.

No one can predict with certainty what will make a good public manager. No single combination of education, experience, personality, and talent will make the same person a great commissioner of welfare for New York City and a smashing water and sewer director in Seattle. Each state, city, county, and township has a unique set of political, social, and economic challenges to which an aspiring public manager must adapt.

But . . . there are predictable problems, dilemmas, conflicts, and confrontations that are sure to occur at some point, to some degree, in every public manager's life. And one thing . . . is certain: a manager's view of his or her mission will be the key to success in the public world.

Charisma, rhetoric, and good public relations, while sometimes crucial to a particular problem or issue, are not sufficient to sustain a public manager. Performance—the ability to deliver against multiple odds, and to deliver quickly and consistently—is what matters.

If a manager's mission is to promote a given politician or a particular ideology but services are poorly managed and people (our clients) are poorly served, then what is the point? As manager, your mission must be first and foremost, to make government work—to decide what values you have, how they relate to government's role, how that translates into government programs, and how you can make those programs work. With that perspective in hand, an aspiring or a veteran manager can make judgments about where to work, whom to work for, and how to tackle the environment.

Sitting behind the desk, meeting with interest after interest, fighting against another round of red tape with the budget bureau, and listening to one more lecture from a twenty-two-year-old on the governor's staff, all make maintaining perspective a challenge in itself. Public management is not a profession for the faint of heart, for those who want always to be loved and admired, or for those who think there is nothing to running the public's business but a little common sense and acumen. It is tough work, and its rewards are often ambiguous, but they are by no means nonexistent.

SOURCE: Gordon Chase and Elizabeth C. Reveal, *How to Manage in the Public Sector* (Reading, Mass.: Addison-Wesley, 1983): 177–179.

LEADERSHIP AT THE INDIVIDUAL AND GROUP LEVEL: THE SUPERVISORS

At the productive heart of the bureau, the groups that are "getting the work done" are led by supervisors. Supervisors are not usually involved in making policy for the bureau or even in establishing the coordinative structures. Rather, supervisors have three major focuses in all of their activities: production, maintenance of individual morale, and maintenance of group cohesiveness. Higher officials decide what is to be done and how the bureau will be structured to accomplish those goals; the supervisor makes sure that the particular tasks and goals of his or her group are completed properly and productively. Although supervisors must organize and coordinate their groups, the main talents they need are a combination of the skills used by their subordinates and the ability to work with those subordinates on an interpersonal level. Since they are usually chosen from the workers, supervisors can be expected to possess the requisite technical skills; thus, the area of expertise that must be either present or quickly developed is the interpersonal.

Supervisory Behavior

Much of the research on group leadership—often referred to as the Ohio State University studies—has focused on what Stogdill defined as *consideration* and *initiation of structure*.

> *[Consideration]* describes the extent to which a leader exhibits concern for the welfare of the other members of the group. The considerate leader expresses appreciation for good work, stresses the importance of job satisfaction, maintains and strengthens self-esteem of subordinates by treating them as equals, makes special efforts to help subordinates to feel at ease, is easy to approach, puts subordinates' suggestions into operation, and obtains subordinates' approval on important matters before going ahead.
>
> *[Initiation of structure]* shows the extent to which a leader initiates activity in the group, organizes it, and defines the way work is to be done. The initiation of structure includes such behavior as insisting on maintaining standards and meeting deadlines and deciding in detail what will be done and how it should be done. . . . Particularly relevant are defining and structuring the leader's own role and those of subordinates toward attaining those goals. (Bass 1990, 511–512)

The two behaviors almost always happen together: Both are present and active at the same time. In fact, other behaviors (noted in the section on managers) are obviously involved, although to lesser degrees, and the success or failure of a supervisor depends on the mixture of behaviors that is appropriate to the situation at hand. Still, these two factors are especially important, and studies of the relationship between consideration and initiating structure (Fleishman and Harris 1962; Skinner 1969) showed that supervisors high in consideration experienced fewer grievances and lower turnover among their subordinates than supervisors who emphasized the structuring of behavior. Finally, these researchers found that in those situations where a substantial amount of structuring was required, a high level of consideration alleviated much of the dissatisfaction. Therefore, to maintain standards and productivity while minimizing subordinate dissatisfaction, it is essential for supervisors to use behavior that emphasizes both factors. (In the public sector, where other tools are often unavailable to supervisors because of civil service limitations, a judicious combination of both factors becomes exceedingly important.)

Although this research was impressive and met the test of common sense, there were mixed findings when it was tested by other researchers. There is a question about whether the findings can be generalized to other kinds of leaders or to subordinate behavior in anything but a production situation. Nevertheless, the idea behind the consideration and initiating structure relationship has been the basis for several important management and supervision theories or models now used widely throughout the Western world. However, when these models are examined, it becomes apparent that in addition to style, another factor must be considered to understand what supervisors do in the real world. That factor is "the situation." The situational concept also applies to the other levels of bureau leadership, of course; we discussed it earlier. But it is a central concept in most modern models of supervisory leadership, so we must look at it closely.

Situational Theories of Group Leadership

Supervisory styles change dramatically depending on the time and place where they are applied. No leader is going to respond to all situations in the same way; nor would such behavior be productive. Instead, the response will be determined by how three questions about the individual leader and the group are answered: (1) What are the important factors that must be taken into consideration if a particular individual is going to be successful in leading this group? (2) How many of those factors can be combined and still be manipulated by the individual who is attempting to lead? (3) How does the leader keep track of newly developing factors that may prove important to leadership success? Supervisors are human beings, with all the limitations inherent in the species. They can deal with only a limited number of factors, and the real world is far more complex than any model. That is at least part of the reason why the leadership models that researchers have developed are relatively simplistic. When applying any model to a real situation, the important thing to accomplish is the selection of the "right" factors for inclusion in the model and then to develop a way to deal with the constantly changing environment. Most of the existing models start with the two factors in the Ohio State University leadership studies and build from there.

One popular model for supervision of both individuals and groups is known as the "managerial grid" (Blake and Mouton 1994).[7] The grid is based on the overlaying of two dimensions of behavior—"concern for people" and "concern for production"—that are very similar to consideration and initiating structure. A grid is used for two reasons: First, managers cannot be realistically dichotomized in description; and second, managers cannot always operate the same way. Leadership behavior depends on the situation being faced, and more than one set of behaviors exists and needs to be used as the situation changes. According to the managerial grid, the goal is a supervisor who is sensitive to the need for production while emphasizing a concern for people. Blake and Mouton (1985) assert that:

> The (team management) theory of managing presumes a necessary *connection* between organizational needs for production and the needs of people for full and rewarding work experiences. The leader's desire is to contribute to corporate success by involving others so that they too may contribute. Such a "can-do" spirit is contagious, inspires a "win" attitude in others, and promotes enthusiasm, voluntarism, spontaneity, and openness. Contributions with caring in the sense of a genuine desire to help others reach their highest potential is basic to creativity, commitment, and cohesion. (82)

---

[7]The grid deals with management at all levels of the organization, but it focuses on the functions that we have identified as primarily supervisory.

Achieving such a relationship with subordinates creates the feeling of a common stake in the outcome of their endeavors and allows for a much higher chance of success in achieving the organization's goals and its continued existence over the long run.

Another of the better known of the situational theories of leadership is the contingency model proposed by Fiedler (1964, 1967). By having the leader rate, on a bipolar scale containing several items about personal characteristics, his or her *least preferred coworker* (past or present), an LPC score is developed that Fiedler believes can be interpreted to predict supervisor effectiveness. (Individuals who are critical of their least preferred co-worker receives low LPC scores, and those who are tolerant receive high ones.) Although the interpretation of LPC scores has changed several times over the years, the situational variable involved has remained constant. The factor around which the LPC scores and leader effectiveness revolves is the extent to which the situation gives a leader influence over subordinate performance. The level of influence is measured according to three criteria:

1. *Leader–member relations.* If leaders enjoy the loyalty and support of subordinates, enthusiastic compliance with their wishes and orders usually follows. The opposite can be expected if attitudes and feelings toward the leader are reversed.

2. *Position power.* If leaders have substantial power built into their position, they can use it to reward and punish compliance or noncompliance with wishes or orders. If leaders do not have such power, they must rely on other sources of influence to gain compliance.

3. *Task structure.* If tasks are highly structured, standard operating procedures exist, finished products or services are clearly defined, and the quality of work done by subordinates is clear, so control and guidance are easier. If task structure, procedures, and end products are not so clear, the leader can have less control, give less guidance, and workers can find more ways to circumvent the leader's wishes and orders.

Fiedler goes on to argue that when situational control is either very high or very low, based on these three criteria, an individual with low LPC scores will be more effective, whereas in a situation with intermediate levels of situational control, supervisors with high LPC scores will be more successful.

The factor that most interests us at the moment is the introduction of situational variables into a discussion of what might be the appropriate behavior for a group leader. Fiedler verbalized in his theory what had been recognized for a long time but had not been dealt with in a formal way: Proper leader behavior must be based on an evaluation of the situation in which it occurs.

Another theory that introduces a situational component into the determination of supervisory behavior is that of Hersey and Blanchard (1993), who use a task-behavior–relationship-behavior matrix (like the one we discussed in the last section) and introduce a specific situational variable into the model. The situational variable is follower *maturity,* which appears to be borrowed from McClelland's discussion of the high achiever where he defines the concept as "the capacity to set high but attainable goals (achievement motivation), willingness to take responsibility, and education and/or experience" (1961, 161).

According to Hersey and Blanchard, the combination of behaviors—relationship *and* task oriented—requires changes of supervisors as the maturity level of subordinates increases (see Figure 9–5). The task-oriented behavior steadily decreases as subordinates achieve higher levels of maturity. On the other hand, the relationship-oriented behavior increases as subordinates advance from immaturity to a moderate level of maturity. Then, as subordinates move on to a higher level of maturity, the amount of considerate, supportive, consultative behavior is reduced as the leader delegates responsibility and increases the independence of the worker. Mature workers, because of their initiative, self-confidence, and commitment, do not need much supportive behavior from their superiors.

Perhaps the supervisory model that uses the most comprehensive set of intervening variables[8] is the "multiple linkage model" of leader effectiveness developed by Gary Yukl. Yukl looks at an extensive set of situational variables that affect individual and group performance as well as the ability of the supervisor to influence the intervening variables that determine that performance. As a first step in the model, Yukl presents factors that influence group performance. These include:

1. *Subordinate effort.* The extent to which subordinates strive to attain a high level of performance and show a high degree of personal responsibility and commitment to task objectives.
2. *Subordinate ability and role clarity.* The extent to which subordinates understand their job responsibilities, know what to do, and have the skills to do it.
3. *Organization of the work.* The extent to which effective performance strategies are used by the group to attain its task objectives and the work is organized to ensure efficient utilization of personnel, equipment, and facilities.
4. *Cooperation and teamwork.* The extent to which group members work together smoothly as a team, share information and ideas, help each other, and feel a strong identification with the group.
5. *Resources and support.* The extent to which the group has the budgetary funds, tools, equipment, supplies, personnel, and facilities needed to do the work, and necessary information or assistance from other units.
6. *External coordination.* The extent to which the activities of the work unit are synchronized with the interdependent activities of other subunits in the same organization and those of outside organizations (e.g., suppliers, clients, joint venture partners), thereby avoiding unnecessary delays, disruptions, and wasted effort (1994, 295–296).

The performance of individual subordinates depends on the first four factors, and the performance of the group as a whole is related to the next two. All six factors interact to determine the levels of individual and group commitment, morale, and productivity, and the factors are themselves influenced by a set of intervening variables that Yukl classifies in three categories.

The first category of variable directly affects one or more of the six factors spelled out, thus indirectly influencing individual or group performance. Examples of this type of variable are the formal reward system, the intrinsic motivating potential of a task, the level of formal role prescriptions, the budgetary and resource allocation system, and the size of the work group. The second type of variable affects the relative importance of the six

---

[8]Obviously, no set of variables is ever complete, but it is possible to spell out several of the more important ones, thus taking them into consideration.

FIGURE 9–5   Situational Leadership

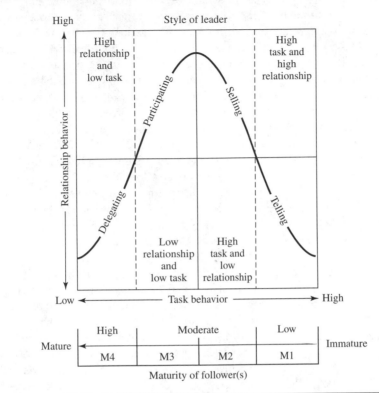

SOURCE: Paul Hersey and Ken Blanchard, *Management of Organizational Behavior: Utilizing Human Resources,* 6th ed., © 1993, p. 197. Reprinted by permission of Prentice-Hall, Inc., Englewood Cliffs, New Jersey.

factors to the group. Technology, for example, may change and increase or decrease the task skill needed by workers or the amount of time required to give subordinates feedback if they are doing something either well or poorly. If few supplies, equipment, and support services are required by a task, then such factors will not be important. Finally, the third type of situational variable in Yukl's model deals with organizational constraints on leader actions to alter directly the intervening variables (1994, 295). The ability of a leader to act is constrained by such factors as position in the hierarchy, ability to control rewards and punishments, and discretion over work assignment, procedures, and resources.[9] (The third factor focuses on constraints of special importance to public organizations.)

---

[9]Other researchers, especially Kerr and Jermier (1978), have discussed these intervening variables under the heading of "substitutes for leadership." These substitute variables tend to negate the leader's ability to influence follower satisfaction or performance. Several of these factors (well-trained and experienced workers, professional orientation on the part of workers, intrinsically satisfying work, methodologically invariant tasks, close-knit and cohesive work groups, organizational rewards that are not within the leader's control, and so on) have been discussed at other points throughout this chapter and book. Gulick (1937) also dealt with this idea when he noted that coordination (read leadership) could occur through "the dominance of an idea," which could lead to a singleness of purpose in the minds and wills of those working together as a group so that each group member would, of his or her own accord, fit his or her task into the whole with skill and enthusiasm.

From the set of factors influencing group behavior and the interacting situational variables, Yukl has developed a set of what he calls "fourteen middle-range behavior categories" or practices (Yukl 1994, 69), grouped under four "primary processes in managing" (43) that are appropriate for use in different situations (see Figure 9–6). Here we see what may be the most complex formal model of situational leadership behavior that has been developed to date. It uses the same approach as the other theories mentioned, but increases the complexity, sophistication, and delicacy of the calculations that must occur. In each case, the supervisor, manager, or leader is expected to evaluate the situation (set of circumstances related to the internal and external forces acting in or on the organization) and the existing characteristics of the organization (the strengths and weaknesses associated with the organization's members, resources, processes, and objectives), after which a decision is made about what behaviors of leadership (style) are appropriate at this time. That decision must look at both the short- and long-term effects of the style and balance its costs and benefits. (Obviously, each style has a variety of specific component behaviors attached to it; these are developed from the theories related in the other chapters of this volume.) In the meantime, the leader must have a built-in barometer that is constantly measuring reactions to the current style and predicting when it is time to reinvestigate the situation or change the style of leadership that is in use.

At the upper levels of a large organization, the evaluation of the situation will lead to a general style that will probably evolve slowly. Frequent and dramatic changes are liable to create chaotic conditions because any shift in leadership style can only be adjusted to gradually. A dramatic change may be required in case of a crisis; however, such a change is usually carried out with assurances that the new emphasis meets the crisis and will be "the norm" for some time, or at least until the crisis is surmounted. At the lower levels of bureaucracy, the supervisor must increasingly consider group *and* individual situations, and at this level the diversity and frequency of change in style increases because of the higher volatility in situations involving smaller numbers of individuals. Although workers still feel a need for continuity and focus or direction from their leaders, there is also a need for superiors to recognize and react to the changing situations faced by their subordinates. Herein lies the key to the situational approach: The leader must respond to the needs of the organization and subordinates; subordinates should not have to analyze and react to the changing whims or mood of superiors. Although an individual must have a variety of leadership styles that can be called into action as situations change, subordinates must be able to expect consistency in the way any particular recurring situation is met by their superior.

The situational approach to leadership is generally accepted as the most appropriate way to deal with the problem or challenge of managing the modern public bureau. No other way to manage has been discovered that allows one to deal with the innumerable cross pressures that exist in the public sector. How else can a bureau leader take into account the individual, organizational, and political demands that must all be considered as one attempts to achieve efficiency and effectiveness?

CONCLUSION

After looking at much of the literature about leadership and applying it to public sector organizations, it becomes obvious that the process is cyclical. Although different aspects

FIGURE 9–6   Yukl's Categories of Managerial Practices

Making Decisions

Planning and Organizing: Determining long-term objectives and strategies, allocating resources according to priorities, determining how to use personnel and resources to accomplish a task efficiently, and determining how to improve coordination, productivity, and the effectiveness of the organizational unit.

Problem Solving: Identifying work-related problems, analyzing problems in a timely but systematic manner to identify causes and find solutions, and acting decisively to implement solutions to resolve important problems or crises.

Consulting: Checking with people before making changes that affect them, encouraging suggestions for improvement, inviting participation in decision making, incorporating the ideas and suggestions of others in decisions.

Delegating: Allowing subordinates to have substantial responsibility and discretion in carrying out work activities, handling problems, and making important decisions.

Influencing People

Motivating and Inspiring: Using influence techniques that appeal to emotion or logic to generate enthusiasm for the work, commitment to task objectives, and compliance with requests for cooperation, assistance, support, or resources; setting an example of appropriate behavior.

Recognizing: Providing praise and recognition for effective performance, significant achievements, and special contributions; expressing appreciation for someone's contributions and special efforts.

Rewarding: Providing or recommending tangible rewards such as a pay increase or promotion for effective performance, significant achievements, and demonstrated competence.

Building Relationships

Networking: Socializing informally, developing contacts with people who are a source of information and support, and maintaining contacts through periodic interaction, including visits, telephone calls, correspondence, and attendance at meetings and social events.

Managing Conflict and Team Building: Facilitating the constructive resolution of conflict and encouraging cooperation, teamwork, and identification with the work unit.

Developing and Mentoring: Providing coaching and helpful career advice, and doing things to facilitate a person's skill acquisition, professional development, and career advancement.

Supporting: Acting friendly and considerate, being patient and helpful, showing sympathy and support when someone is upset or anxious, listening to complaints and problems, looking out for someone's interests.

Giving-Seeking Information

Monitoring: Gathering information about work activities and external conditions affecting the work, checking on the progress and quality of the work, evaluating the performance of individuals and the organizational unit, analyzing trends, and forecasting external events.

Clarifying Roles and Objectives: Assigning tasks, providing direction in how to do the work and communicating a clear understanding of job responsibilities, task objectives, deadlines, and performance expectations.

Informing: Disseminating relevant information about decisions, plans, and activities to people that need it to do their work, providing written materials and documents, and answering requests for technical information.

SOURCE: Gary A. Yukl, *Leadership in Organizations,* 3rd ed. (Englewood Cliffs, N.J.: Prentice-Hall, 1994): 69–72.

of the leadership role are emphasized at the three levels of the organization, all are important at each level. Even those individuals not in formal positions may often hold informal leadership roles because they have some of the characteristics that we have ascribed to leaders or they fulfill some of the functions needed by the group. Fulfilling a leadership role in the public sector is often a doubly difficult job because of the factors from the political environment that must be added to the calculation. And, of course, action must be taken in many cases without time for calculation. Being a successful executive, manager, supervisor, or even informal leader is not an easy task; it is simply a task that must be done if the public bureaucracy is to carry out its mandate of serving the public and helping maintain the democratic system. If the leader is able to overcome the difficulties, carry out the tasks, and make the significant value choices that are inherent in the position, then he or she embodies the leader role and can look forward to success and a feeling of deeply satisfying accomplishment. When the political environment, the technology, the group dynamic, the economic situation, or some other similar factor in the equation shifts, the process of analysis, understanding, choice, and action must begin anew. The reward to successful leaders is the challenge.

FOR FURTHER READING

The major compendium of leadership theory over the years, which is useful as a place to start when doing any research on the subject, is Bernard M. Bass, *Bass & Stogdill's Handbook of Leadership,* New York: Free Press (Macmillan, Inc.), 1990. Perhaps the best "classic" work on leadership, and one that is well worth rereading occasionally, is Chester Barnard's *The Functions of the Executive,* Cambridge, Mass.: Harvard University Press, 1938. (A thirtieth anniversary edition of this book was published in 1979.) A major work that tries to deal with political leadership by combining psychological, social, and cultural perspectives is James MacGregor Burns, *Leadership,* New York: Harper & Row, 1978. James Q. Wilson, in *Bureaucracy: What Government Agencies Do and Why They Do It,* New York: Basic Books, 1989, does a masterful job of presenting the problems faced by individuals at each level of leadership presented in this chapter when he discusses the behavior of "Operators," "Managers," and "Executives" in different sections of his book. When examining the managerial level within the organizational hierarchy, the place to start, because of its examination of the multiple roles of the manager, is Henry Mintzberg, *The Nature of Managerial Work,* New York: Harper & Row, 1973. Several major attempts to explain supervision of individuals or workgroups exist. Two are suggested here because of their use of multiple variables in analyzing the organizational environment and developing a supervisory style. They are Paul Hersey and Kenneth H. Blanchard, *Management of Organizational Behavior,* 6th ed., Englewood Cliffs, N.J.: Prentice-Hall, 1993; and Gary A. Yukl, *Leadership in Organization,* 3rd ed., Englewood Cliffs, N.J.: Prentice-Hall, 1994. Two excellent sources for examining the complexity of views existing in relation to leadership are Barbara Kellerman, *Leadership: Multidisciplinary Perspectives,* Englewood Cliffs, N.J.: Prentice-Hall, 1984; and Jameson Doig and Erwin Hargrove, *Leadership and Innovation: A Biographical Perspective on Entrepreneurs in Government,* Baltimore, Md.: Johns Hopkins University Press, 1987. Finally, a fascinating, easy-to-read book that draws from science and the emerging field of chaos theory to look at leadership has been written by Margaret J. Wheatley and is entitled *Leadership and the New Science: Learning about Organization from an Orderly Universe,* San Francisco: Berrett-Koehler, 1992.

REVIEW QUESTIONS

1. Consultants and scholars agree that leadership is the critical element that pulls together all the other aspects of organizational life (covered in Chapters 2 through 8). Why is this so? Within the public bureau, is the leader as important in determining success as in a private organization?

2. What are the major differences in the tasks or functions of individuals operating at the three leadership levels of the organization?

3. Explain how contingency theory, or "the situation," helps determine an individual's style of leadership. Does situational theory work at all levels of the organization? Is the leader's style determined by the situation, or can the leader control the situation?

REFERENCES

Barber, James D. *The Presidential Character: Predicting Performance in the White House,* 4th ed. Englewood Cliffs, N.J.: Prentice-Hall, 1992.

Bass, Bernard M. *Bass & Stogdill's Handbook of Leadership: Theory, Research and Managerial Applications,* 3rd ed. New York: Free Press (Macmillan, Inc.) 1990.

_____, and Enzo R. Valenzi. "Contingent Aspects of Effective Management Styles." In *Contingency Approaches to Leadership: A Symposium Held at Southern Illinois University,* Carbondale, eds. James G. Hunt and Lars L. Larson. Carbondale: Southern Illinois University, 1974.

Blake, Robert R., and Jane S. Mouton. *The Managerial Grid III.* Houston, Tex.: Gulf Publishing, 1985.

_____, *The Managerial Grid.* Houston, Tex.: Gulf Publishing, 1994.

Bogardus, Emory S. *Leaders and Leadership.* New York: Appleton-Century-Crofts, 1934.

Burns, James M. *Leadership.* New York: Harper & Row, 1978.

Cleveland, Harlan. *The Future Executive.* New York: Harper & Row, 1972.

Cowley, W. H. "Three Distinctions in the Study of Leaders." *Journal of Abnormal and Social Psychology* 23, 1928: 144–157.

England, George W. "Personal Value Systems of American Managers." *Academy of Management Journal* 10, 1967: 56–68.

Fiedler, Fred E. "A Contingency Model of Leadership Effectiveness." In *Advances in Experimental Social Psychology,* ed. Leonard Berkowitz. New York: Academic Press, 1964.

_____. *A Theory of Leadership Effectiveness,* New York: McGraw-Hill, 1967.

Fleishman, Edwin A., and Edwin F. Harris. "Patterns of Leadership Behavior Related to Employee Grievances and Turnover." *Personnel Psychology* 15, 1962: 43–56.

Franklin, Stephen. "Shear Persistence: Corporate America Keeps Downsizing." In *The Washington Post,* October 29, 1995: H6.

French, John R. P., and Bertram Raven. "The Bases of Social Power." In *Studies in Social Power,* ed. Dorwin Cartwright. Ann Arbor, Mich.: Institute for Social Research, 1959: 150–167.

Gardner, John W. *Leadership, a Sampler of the Wisdom of John W. Gardner.* Minneapolis: Hubert H. Humphrey Institute of Public Administration, University of Minnesota, 1981.

Gordon, Leonard V. *The Measurement of Interpersonal Values.* Chicago: Science Research Associates, 1975.

———. *Survey of Interpersonal Values: Revised Manual.* Chicago: Science Research Associates, 1976.

Gulick, Luther. "Notes on the Theory of Organization." In *Papers on the Science of Administration.* eds. Luther Gulick and Lyndall Urwick. New York: Institute of Public Administration, 1937.

Hersey, Paul, and Kenneth H. Blanchard. *Management of Organizational Behavior: Utilitizing Human Resources,* 6th ed. Englewood Cliffs, N.J.: Prentice-Hall, 1993.

Holden, Matthew, Jr. "'Imperialism' in Bureaucracy." *The American Political Science Review* 60, 1966: 943–951.

Jones, Charles O. *An Introduction to the Study of Public Policy,* 3rd. ed. Monterey, Calif.: Brooks/Cole, 1984.

Katz, Robert L. "Skills of an Effective Administrator." *Harvard Business Review* 33, 1955:33–42.

Kellerman, Barbara, ed. *Leadership: Multidisciplinary Perspectives.* Englewood Cliffs, N.J.: Prentice-Hall, 1984.

Kerr, Steven, and John M. Jermier. "Substitutes for Leadership: Their Meaning and Measurement." *Organizational Behavior and Human Performance* 22, 1978: 376–403.

Lewis, Eugene. *Public Entrepreneurship: Toward a Theory of Bureaucratic Political Power.* Bloomington: Indiana University Press, 1980.

Likert, Rensis. *New Patterns of Management.* New York: Garland, 1987. (Reprint of original published by McGraw-Hill, 1961.)

———. *The Human Organization; Its Management and Value.* New York: McGraw-Hill, 1967.

Lindblom, Charles E. *The Policy-Making Process,* 3rd ed. Englewood Cliffs, N.J.: Prentice-Hall, 1993.

Lundstedt, Sven. "Administrative Leadership and Use of Social Power." *Public Administration Review* 25, 1965: 156–160.

Mann, Floyd C. "Toward an Understanding of the Leadership Role in Formal Organization." In *Leadership and Productivity; Some Facts of Industrial Life,* eds. Robert Dubin et al. San Francisco: Chandler, 1965.

McClelland, David C. *The Achieving Society.* Princeton, N.J.: Van Nostrand Reinhold, 1961.

———. *Power: The Inner Experience.* New York: Irvington, 1975.

Mintzberg, Henry. *The Nature of Managerial Work.* New York: Harper & Row, 1973.

Nakamura, Robert T., and Frank Smallwood. *The Politics of Policy Implementation.* New York: St. Martin's Press, 1980.

Nanus, Burt. *Visionary Leadership: Creating a Compelling Sense of Direction for Your Organization.* San Francisco: Jossey-Bass, 1992.

National Performance Review (U.S.). *Creating a Government That Works Better & Costs Less: The Report of the National Performance Review,* Vice President Al Gore. New York: Plume/Penguin, 1993.

Rourke, Francis E. *Bureaucracy, Politics, and Public Policy,* 3rd ed. Boston: Little, Brown, 1984.

Selznick, Phillip. *Leadership in Administration: A Sociological Interpretation.* Berkeley, Calif.: University of California Press, 1984. (Originally published by Harper & Row, 1957.)

———. *TVA and the Grassroots: A Study in the Sociology of Formal Organizations.* New York: Harper & Row (Torchbooks), 1966. Originally published by the University of California, Berkeley, in 1949.

Skinner, Elizabeth W. "Relationships between Leadership Behavior Patterns and Organizational-Situational Variables." *Personnel Psychology* 22, 1969: 489–494.

Terry, Larry D. *Leadership of Public Bureaucracies: The Administrator as Conservator.* Thousand Oaks, Calif.: Sage, 1995.

Urwick, Lyndall F. *Leadership and Morale.* Columbus: Ohio State University, College of Commerce and Administration, 1953.

Weber, Max. *The Theory of Social and Economic Organization,* trans. and eds. A. M. Henderson and Talcott Parsons. New York: Oxford University, 1947.

Wilson, James Q. *Bureaucracy: What Government Agencies Do and Why They Do It.* New York: Basic Books, 1989.

Winter, David G. *The Power Motive.* New York: Free Press, 1973.

Yukl, Gary A. *Leadership in Organizations,* 3rd ed. Englewood Cliffs, N.J.: Prentice-Hall, 1994.

READING 9–1 Distinctions Between Managers and Leaders

- The manager administers; the leader innovates.
- The manager is a copy; the leader is an original.
- The manager maintains; the leader develops.
- The manager focuses on systems and structure; the leader focuses on people.
- The manager relies on control; the leader inspires trust.
- The manager has a short-range view; the leader has a long-range perspective.
- The manager asks how and when; the leader asks what and why.
- The manager has his eye always on the bottom line; the leader has his eye on the horizon.
- The manager imitates; the leader originates.
- The manager accepts the status quo; the leader challenges it.
- The manager is the classic good soldier; the leader is his own person.
- The manager does things right; the leader does the right thing.

SOURCE: Warren Bennis, *On Becoming a Leader* (Reading, Mass.: Addison-Wesley, 1989): 45.

Editor's Note

Consider the following questions about the preceding statements:

1. What are the values and assumptions, made by the author, that might underly these statements? Are those values and assumptions right/correct or wrong/incorrect? Does the political environment of the bureau affect the validity of the values and assumptions?

2. When looking at each comparative statement, can you refer to any theories or models presented in this chapter that help explain the points being made by the author? How do those theories or models clarify the meaning of the statements?

3. Can you refer to any theories or models in prior chapters that help explain the points being made by the author? Again, how do those theories or models help clarify the meaning of the statements?

CASE 9–1   A Plethora of Problems

The Graphics and Photography Division of Midstate University provided services for the academic, business, and maintenance divisions of the institution. It was divided into five units: Graphics Production, Printing and Duplicating Services, Photographic Services, Equipment Maintenance and Distribution, and Educational Films Library. The division employed twenty-five staff people full time and from fifteen to twenty students part time.

The division was not happy. The unit supervisors were empire builders of the first order who jealously contended for more funds and more employees. Meetings of unit heads with the division director were marked by bickering and there was little cooperation among the units. Because there was little esprit de corps among the division administrators, there was likewise little among the employees.

The director of the division was Dr. Olaf Johanssen, a likable man who in the fifteen years he had held his position had been generally viewed as a weak administrator. Now sixty-three years old and planning to retire at sixty-five, Johanssen had increasingly relaxed his control over the division, leaving administrative and personnel matters chiefly to Lester Best, the assistant director

Best, who was thirty years old, had held his position for five years and was extremely eager to get ahead. To his superiors, he had always shown a respect that bordered on servility, but with his coworkers he was thoughtless, tactless, inconsiderate, and arrogant. He had a campus reputation as a womanizer and his relations with women staff members were marked by sexual overtones.

Difficult personnel problems had arisen particularly in the Photographic Services unit, supervised by Jerome Christianson, and in the Equipment and Maintenance unit, supervised by Donald Waterman. The smallest unit of the division, Photographic Services employed three people and usually one or two students. Christianson, age thirty-one, was highly qualified in education and professional experience for his job. He had begun work for the unit six years before as a Photographer I and within a few months had been made supervisor. Because of cuts in appropriations throughout the entire university, a promotion for Christianson was not immediately foreseeable and his pay increases had not kept pace with the cost of living.

Because Christianson's unit was small, he had closer contact with his staff than most supervisors. A principal personnel problem had involved John Bishop, twenty-eight, who had worked as a Photographer I for ten years. He was married and had two children but difficulties in his home life interfered with his work.

Three years before, Bishop's work became so poor because of a family crisis that Christianson attempted to have him dismissed after first discussing the matter with Johanssen. After the termination procedures were well underway, Johanssen told Christianson to halt the proceedings, explaining that he thought Bishop now saw how matters stood and would improve his work. "We shouldn't be too severe with him," Johanssen said. "After all, he has a wife and children to support." Bishop's performance did improve for a time, but it never became entirely satisfactory. Recently it had again become so poor that Christianson had to mention it to him. Upon Christianson's recommendation, Bishop and his wife sought out a marriage counselor, but if his home life improved it did not show up in the quality of his work.

Another personnel problem for Christianson concerned Andrew Polk, age twenty-six, the newest employee in the unit. Christianson and Polk had been good friends for several years. A former newspaper photographer, Polk took a job as a photo lab technician to earn money while doing graduate work in journalism at the university. Polk's work was decidedly superior and he was well liked throughout the division. Early in his employment Polk was called upon by the assistant director, Best—who was acquainted with his work as a newspaper photographer—to take pictures, assignments that were not included in his job description. He received overtime pay for these special assignments.

Toward the end of Polk's six-month probationary period he discussed the possibility with Christianson, the Photographic Services supervisor, of being raised to the Photographer I level. Often called upon to perform Photographer I duties, he felt he should receive overtime pay commensurate with that rank when taking pictures. Christianson agreed and told him: "Best is using your talents as photographer but he isn't paying you the Photographer I scale. I think he should. Why don't you ask him about raising your salary?"

The next day Polk was in the main office picking up his mail when Best approached him about another assignment. Polk replied, "I'd be glad to help you out, Lester, but I feel it's only fair that I get paid overtime on the Photographer I scale rather than the lab-technician scale."

Best, surprised that a person still on probation would make pay demands, protested: "But you forget that during your interview we stated that from time to time you would be asked to perform overtime duties."

"Well, I remember that Johanssen did say I would be asked to on occasion," Polk said, "and I'm willing to do so. However, he made a point that he didn't want me doing the work of a photographer because others might complain I wasn't hired for that type of work. I'm willing to do the work. I'd just like to get paid for it."

"Well, we will just have to see about that," Best said and walked away in a huff.

Next morning Christianson was called to Johanssen's office, where he found the director and Best awaiting him. Johanssen said that Best reported that Polk had been insubordinate and that he should be reprimanded by Christianson.

Christianson returned to his own office and explained to Polk that he was to do whatever was asked of him. "I know it isn't fair," he said, "but that's the way this place works. Maybe after a few months I can get you raised to Photographer I."

During the next four months, Polk performed all tasks requested by Best and Johanssen without complaint. Both he and Christianson kept a record of extra duties performed to use as "ammunition for a promotion" when additional funds became available for another Photographer I position.

Meanwhile, Donald Waterman in the Equipment and Maintenance unit had been having problems. Now sixty years old, Waterman had worked in the division for eighteen years. He planned to take an early retirement "because this damn place will never shape up."

Three weeks before, one of Waterman's technicians resigned because he was "tired of waiting for two years for a promotion from Johanssen." Five days before the effective date of resignation, the division director raised the position from Electronics Technician I to a II. The office rumor was that the promotion was pushed through to make the position more attractive and easier to fill, since the university's salary scale made it difficult to hire technicians.

Hired for the job was Roscoe Flinch, age forty-two, a TV repairman, who in accepting had negotiated a deal by which he would receive a raise after his first month of employment. This speedy raise would give him a salary $1500 higher than that received by Waterman after eighteen years of service. Waterman was furious and exclaimed on first learning about it: "How can I supervise him when he makes more than I do?" He was so nettled that he determined to take it easy during the two years before he retired.

A few weeks later employees were surprised to observe Flinch taking pictures of various activities of the division. Andrew Polk was curious and asked him, "What are you doing? I didn't know you were a photographer."

Flinch grinned and said, "Best wants some pictures for a slide show illustrating the services the division provides and asked me to prepare them."

Polk went to Christianson's office and told him of the project. Angrily Christianson rushed to Johanssen's office and confronted him. "What the hell is Flinch doing with a camera?" he asked. "He's not working in the photography unit."

"Well, he is working on a slide show for us," Johanssen said.

"That's what I hear. Why wasn't I told about the project and why wasn't the photography unit given the job?"

Passing by the open door of the office, Best heard Christianson's protest and quipped: "Maybe he is interested in photography, Jerome." Christianson realized he was a victim of another of the division's unaccountable administrative procedures and, too overwhelmed to say more, returned to his own office. He had lost another skirmish in the civil war being waged in the Graphics and Photography Division.

SOURCE: C. K. Meyer et al., *Practicing Public Management* (New York: St. Martin's Press, 1983): 33–36.

Editor's Note

Consider the following questions about this case:

1. There seem to be a number of problems revealed in this short description of life in the Graphics and Photography Division. Examining not only the theories and models in this chapter on leadership, but those in the prior chapters, identify at least four dimensions of problems in this case. What are the most important sources of these problems?

2. How would you characterize the administration of the division? How would you characterize Johanssen's leadership style? Best's style?

3. Contrast the implicit theories of human nature that characterize the four administrators in the case. Which are the more appropriate assumptions under the circumstances? The least appropriate? Why?

4. If you had been brought in to replace Waterman, what would you do in response to a situation such as the one described involving Flinch? Why?

5. If you were Johanssen's supervisor in the university, how would you respond to reports of events such as those described in the case? What would you do?

Chapter 10

Organization Change and Development

"But in time nothing can be without becoming."[1] The recognition of this fact has made organizational change perhaps the most popular field of study among students of organization theory during the last three decades. Although change is constant, even if not constantly noticed, the more common opportunities for development in organizations—and for the people who populate them—occur during the times of periodic crisis and change in the life of such institutions. Of course, this opportunity is not always grasped by those in positions to do so, and crisis can lead to the collapse and decimation of an organization just as quickly as it can lead to growth and dynamism. (*Growth* does not always denote "increase in size"; it can also mean "development or evolution from a lower or simpler to a higher or more complex form, thus an increase in wisdom or capability in dealing with one's surroundings.") The result depends on the intelligence, wisdom, and flexibility of those in leadership positions, and in the willingness and ability of organization members to follow those leaders. Decimation may be the more common result, although it may not lead to the organization's disappearance, but rather to banality, subsistence, and an inability to fulfill its function.

We are beginning to understand how to cope with, even to take advantage of, organizational change. There is a growing body of literature about understanding both change and organizational responses to it. In fact, with our increased understanding that organizations can influence change and control how it affects them, "controlled change" is a concept that is increasingly being discussed. Therefore, throughout this chapter, we will talk about "planned" and "unplanned" change. Unplanned change (change that occurs outside the control of the organization) is a major area of concern: It includes almost all external and many internal factors, and takes up much of the time of top management in any organization. Of special interest to public managers is the political environment; however, numerous other factors are of importance. From among these numerous forces for unplanned change, we will focus on economic trends, sociological shifts, political evolution, and technological breakthroughs. These four are central to understanding the current public organization's environment and must be considered as we try to make change work

---

[1]Ursula K. LeGuin, *Tehanu: The Last Book of Earthsea*. New York: Bantam Books, 1990, 12.

for the organization; they will be the center of our discussion on unplanned change toward the end of the chapter. First, however, we will look at several types of planned change.

In the next section, we will discuss the way that some of the major organization theory schools approach change and some of the questions that these approaches raise. Then we will examine several of the techniques that are currently used to attempt planned change in organizations. Third, the constructive use of conflict, which is an inevitable part of change, must be considered. A brief discussion of conflict in organizations must, therefore, be included as part of looking at change and conflict in the bureau's environment. Finally, it is essential to examine the impact of the environment around public organizations and to discuss ways that bureaus may take advantage of the unplanned but ubiquitous changes in the environment.

THEORIES ABOUT CHANGE

Every school of organization theory has its own set of assumptions about the meaning of change and its objectives or ends. The objectives, in turn, lead to assumptions about the process involved, or when, how, and why change occurs. Before examining these schools of theory, however, we will look briefly at some of the general objectives that surround the idea of organizational change or that are basically accepted by all students of change.

Although the literature about change in organizations takes numerous forms and discusses widely divergent issues, it is possible to summarize many of the commonly accepted goals under five topics.

1. It is generally agreed that bureaus should be able to adapt to external change in the political, social, economic, or technological environment; the corollary to this idea is that bureaus must be able to create new knowledge, processes, or technology. (It is often difficult to tell precisely whether a current process is necessary or is simply justified because it exists—that is, is taking place.)

2. A general call for greater rationality in decision making exists in organizations. Improved decision making can take many forms, however, and what is meant by rationality varies depending on the type of organization being discussed and, when dealing with public organizations, both the political and managerial philosophy of the critic.

3. The goal of these schemes for improving management or for changing any aspect of the bureau's structure or process is to improve efficiency and effectiveness. In the public sector, lacking a clear goal such as "profit," the definitions of *efficiency* and *effectiveness* will differ among competent observers, but it is around these basic concepts that much of the debate about "what should be done" will occur.

4. The goal of change efforts carried out by many social scientists is to reduce "organizational pathology." Pathology here refers to "deviation from propriety or from an assumed normal state." Having established what they believe is "proper/normal" behavior in groups, the social scientists are attempting to correct deviations from that behavior, improve human development or human relations within the organization and beyond, increase members' motivation and commitment,

reduce alienation, and increase freedom (autonomy or self-determination) among organization members.

5. To at least a limited extent, these goals are also involved in attempting to reduce conflict or redirect it in constructive ways. This applies to conflict both within and between organizations. Some conflict can be eliminated, but much of it is not only inevitable but useful when directed toward appropriate channels and controlled in ways that keep it from diverting the individuals involved from the bureau's goals.

The various organization theories that have been prominent over the years have all addressed at least some of the goals presented here. However, these theories have either left out important elements or have stressed select factors. Change theorists attempt to deal with all five goals at once.

When we look at decision-making theory, for example, it is obvious that the rationalist and incremental theories each deal with only a few of the five goals, but neither deals with all of them. The rationalist theory focuses on greater rationality and improved efficiency and effectiveness, but fails to recognize the importance of being able to adapt to external change, reduce organizational pathology, or reduce and redirect conflict. In fact, adapting to external change and reducing conflict are the major points stressed in the incrementalist model of decision making. Change theorists would argue that all five factors must be given *proper,* not necessarily *equal* (depending on the situation), emphasis for an organization to successfully achieve its objectives efficiently and effectively. If we look at any of the other special areas of organization study (motivation, control, communication, leadership, and so on), we can see the same kind of partial attention to all five goals in most popular theories. The organizational change literature attempts—with differing levels of success—to develop a more universal theory.

CHANGE AND THE PUBLIC ORGANIZATION'S EXTRA DIMENSION

When discussing theories of organizational change as they relate to public administration, it is necessary to add one particular value that influences both the process and the result of change: responsiveness of the bureaucracy to the citizen. This value is usually discussed in the context of a continuum that stretches from *accountability* to *responsibility* (see Figure 10–1). One's view of whether public organization members must adhere strictly to the law and to the orders of superiors (accountability) or must be responsive to the needs of their clientele or their personal moral code and do "what is right no matter what the law says" has a tremendous effect on how one sees the need for and the goals of change. Everyone can agree that change is needed to achieve greater efficiency, but the concept of effectiveness has very different meanings to people at different ends of the continuum. *Effectiveness* refers to the impact of a program or process, and to evaluate it there must be some consensus about both long- and short-term goals, with one of the long-term goals being the preservation of our democratic form of government. The debate between those holding different views about bureaucratic responsiveness often becomes a confused discussion that includes the program's immediate results, the properness of the procedures

FIGURE 10–1   Continuum from Accountability to Responsibility

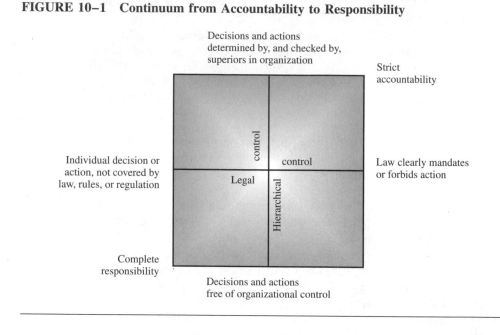

being used, the attitudes of the bureaucrats implementing the program, and the impact of all these factors on the more basic question of how all this correlates with the basic goals of maintaining our social system and strengthening democracy.

Those who are committed to the idea of accountability will place following the letter of the law above such factors as individual freedom of action within the bureaucracy; for them, the important issue is to ensure that the bureaus remain within their sphere of competence and power and that the duly elected representatives of the people make the law. Where making public policy is at issue, it is the elected officials, and not the bureaucrats who must be responsive. In some situations, the goals of bureaucratic accountability and individual freedom within the bureaucracy will conflict, and though individual happiness and the development of each person's full potential are valid goals, accountability must take precedence. For accountability advocates, organizational change must always be designed with this priority in mind.

Those who are committed to the idea of individual responsibility to one's own moral code or to one's clientele are not necessarily arguing against accountability; they simply believe that it is achieved in another way. They argue that the long-range goal of maintaining (they would probably argue "of achieving") democracy is best served when public administrators are sensitive to the needs and desires of those they serve. This goal will be best reached when public organizations are receptive to change and when individuals within organizations are free to contend with others about appropriate goals and procedures. Only by changing public bureaus in ways that will allow more freedom, both inside the organization for individual members and outside for the organization as an entity representing the interests of its clients in the political world, can accountability truly be achieved. For those holding this view of public organizations, change takes many forms, including reshaping organizational cultures and depending to a much greater extent on the sense of responsibility felt by public servants.

These two interpretations of change—accountability and responsibility—influence any discussion of the subject within public sector organizations; therefore, they will reappear throughout the rest of this chapter.

PLANNED CHANGE

Change is an inherent and ubiquitous fact of life for any organization. If this were not so, we could simply program the activities of organizations and not worry about most of the problems that we have discussed throughout this book. Things are changing, however, both inside and outside the organization; this is just as true for the public bureau as it is for the private corporation. Great efforts are being made to increase the area of planned change for organizations, which is the goal of theorists as they go about the systematic study of organizations. The first step is obviously that of description, but the final product, if definition and description are successful, is the prediction of events and prescription of ways to handle them as they occur—or better yet, in some cases to correct or change elements within the organization in advance so that advantage may be taken of opportunities or problems avoided.

The area of planned change appears to be growing, especially as we develop greater capacity for collecting, storing, and using information. Information that applies to the external environment does not necessarily allow planned change; rather, it allows a quick reaction to indicators of change that are constantly monitored. Thus, quicker reaction is assured, but the knowledge gained through the information revolution does not allow most organizations to control that environment.[2] Information about the internal operation of the bureau, such as the greater understanding of the interrelationship between organizational structure and the functions of production and management, and an equally important growth in our knowledge about the way individuals function in bureaus allows us to plan change. Coincidentally, we can argue that planned change occurs in three major areas of bureau life: behavior and values, structure, and process and technology. Each of these will be considered briefly here, and each deserves additional attention from those who wish to develop an in-depth understanding of them.

Planned Change in Behavior and Values

The area of planned change that has attracted the most interest during the last three decades is organization behavior, whose fundamental elements include individuals in groups,

---

[2]One of the worries expressed by critics of developing megaorganizations (both national and international) is that these organizations are so large and powerful that they control a dominant proportion of resources (finances, material, personnel, and so on) and information about events in their area of activity. The monopoly on resources and information may give these organizations the ability to control what is normally considered activity outside their jurisdiction, but that has an influence on their functions. The danger, of course, is that the organizations will make decisions about events occurring outside their immediate boundaries that are "best" for them but damaging to society as a whole.

groups combined into organizations, the actions of individuals and groups in organizational settings, and, by inference, the values that are the basis for action by both individuals and groups. This area of study or action, known as "organization development" (see Figure 10–2):

> is a long-term effort, led and supported by top management, to improve an organization's visioning, empowerment, learning, and problem-solving processes, through an ongoing, collaborative management of organization culture—with special emphasis on the culture of intact work teams and other team configurations—utilizing the consultant-facilitator role and the theory and technology of applied behavioral science,[3] including action research. (French and Bell 1995, 28)

According to its practitioners, organization development (OD) is *applied* organization theory and behavior, drawn from sociology, psychology, cybernetics, political science, and other related fields. Thus OD, in its broadest sense, can be considered the applied side of the basic research that has been ongoing in the social sciences—at least that part of the social sciences related to organizational phenomena (Argyris and Schon 1978). (OD detractors would call this a self-serving and inaccurate description.) The field has developed from two important techniques that came into existence separately but were ultimately recognized as complementary. Around those techniques, a whole set of other tools was developed that allowed individuals to understand better the structures, processes, culture, values, and behavior within organizations. Once these factors are understood with a degree of clarity, it is possible to plan ways to change one or more of them.

The first of the two techniques is *laboratory training,* an unstructured small-group situation in which participants learn from their interactions and from the evolving group dynamics. This type of training began around 1946 and resulted in people acquiring greater sensitivity to group dynamics and a better understanding of the values that underlay personal and group behavior. The laboratory-training groups, or T-groups, comprised strangers who came together temporarily for the experience and learning that could be gained. However, it was extremely difficult to take the personal and interpersonal skills that the trainees learned back to the workplace. This type of training was often characterized by confrontation and open expression of feelings, and carrying such behavior back to an environment where others were not used to, or capable of dealing with, such openness was very dangerous. To apply the learning in the more permanent and complex organizations, it was discovered that "teams" drawn from the organization had to be involved, or that groups of people who worked together or regularly interacted had to be included if the learning was to be applied and retained over any length of time. The earlier type of training for individuals is still available, but today, when laboratory training is used in complex organizations, it is usually carried out in a less intensive manner and on a rather extensive and inclusive basis.

---

[3]Two terms require definition for the reader who may be new to this field. A "consultant-facilitator" is a third party to the organizational unit being considered who can operate as an objective, noninvolved consultant on *ways to accomplish the desired change in processes.* Consultant-facilitators are neutral about the goals of the organization. "Action research" refers to a model of research involving several steps that are used cyclically: (1) a preliminary diagnosis of the issue or problem being examined; (2) data gathering from the client group; (3) data feedback to the client group; (4) data exploration by the client group; (5) action planning (what the client group will "do about it"); (6) action; and (7) repetition of the process after the action is put into effect. For further information about this definition and the general area of organization development, see French and Bell (1995), which offers a good overview of the field.

FIGURE 10–2 Distinguishing Characteristics of Organization Development

1. OD focuses on culture and processes.

2. Specifically, OD encourages collaboration between organization leaders and members in managing culture and processes.

3. Teams of all kinds are particularly important for task accomplishment and are targets for OD activities.

4. OD focuses on the human and social side of the organization primarily, and in so doing also intervenes in the technological and structural sides.

5. Participation and involvement in problem solving and decision making by all levels of the organization are hallmarks of OD.

6. OD focuses on total system change and views organizations as complex social systems.

7. OD practitioners are facilitators, collaborators, and co-learners with the client system.

8. An overarching goal is to make the client system able to solve its problems on its own by teaching the skills and knowledge of continuous learning through self-analytical methods. OD views organization improvement as an ongoing process in the context of a constantly changing environment.

9. OD relies on an action research model with extensive participation by client system members.

10. OD takes a developmental view that seeks the betterment of both individuals and the organization. Attempting to create "win-win" solutions is standard practice in OD programs.

SOURCE: Wendell L. French and Cecil H. Bell, Jr., *Organization Development: Behavioral Science Interventions for Organization Improvement* (Englewood Cliffs, N.J.: Prentice-Hall, 1995): 33.

The second technique that was essential to the beginning of OD as a recognized method of changing values and behavior was *survey research and feedback*. This approach can be traced to the opening of the Survey Research Center at the University of Michigan although its roots go back somewhat farther. The validity and use of survey research and feedback depended on the development of carefully constructed questionnaires that could be given to all respondents, the use of probability in choosing samples, and the careful coding of responses so that results could be fed back to the participating groups (which could be part of or an entire organization). In this way, participants could find out, through a process that guaranteed anonymity, what people believed and felt about the organization, its objectives, and its members' values and behavior.

From these two basic techniques—laboratory training and survey research and feedback—a multitude of programs have sprung into being, all of which attempt to intervene in the ongoing organization (thus the name OD interventions) and to change the structure, processes, behavior, or values of individuals and groups (see Figure 10–3). These interventions are put into eight groupings by Golembiewski, Proehl, and Sink according to the level of complexity and subtlety required in applying them.

1. *Process analysis activities,* or applications of behavioral science perspectives to understand complex and dynamic situations. These perspectives can be very simple, for example, as in routine retrospection among task group members who ask:

FIGURE 10–3   Underlying Values and Assumptions of Organization Development

1. **Assumptions about people as individuals:**

   Individuals desire personal growth and development if the environment is supportive and challenging.

   Most people are willing to make a higher level of contribution to attaining organizational goals than is permitted by the environment.

2. **Assumptions about people and leadership in groups:**

   One of the most psychologically relevant reference groups for most people is the workgroup (both peers and superiors).

   Most people want to be accepted and to interact cooperatively with more than one small reference group (including the workgroup, family, personal friends, and so on).

   The formal leader cannot perform all the leadership and maintenance functions in all circumstances; hence, the informal part of the organization is important in groups because different individuals must perform a variety of leadership roles.

   Suppressed feelings and attitudes adversely affect problem solving, personal growth, and job satisfaction.

   The level of interpersonal trust, support, and cooperation is much lower in most groups than is either necessary or desirable.

   The solutions to most attitudinal and motivational problems in organizations involve alteration of mutual relationships by all parties in the system. (Attitudinal and motivational problems are "transactional.")

3. **Assumptions about people in organizational systems:**

   Since organizations are characterized by overlapping workgroups, the leadership style and climate of the higher team tend to be transmitted to lower teams.

   "Win–lose" conflict strategies between people and groups are not optimal in the long run in solving most organizational problems.

   Time and patience are important in changing organizational values and behavior because such changes take a long time.

   For any changes to be sustained, the total human resources system (appraisal, compensation, training, staffing, job, and communications subsystems) must change appropriately.

4. **Assumptions about values held by members of the client organization:**

   Members believe in both collaborative efforts and the end products of the organization.

   The welfare of all organization members is important, especially to those people having the most power over others.

5. **Assumptions (values held) made by behavioral science change agents:**

   Organized effort exists to meet the needs and aspirations of human beings.

   Work and life can become richer and more meaningful, and organized effort more effective and enjoyable if feelings and sentiments are permitted to be a more legitimate part of the culture of organizations.

   Equal attention must be given to research and action applying the research.

   The goal of organization development is to utilize human resources more effectively. Power equalization and the democratization of work environments may be important but are not exclusive issues in this regard. Better utilization of human resources should increase everyone's power.

How do we feel about what we just did? The perspectives also can be complex, as in seeking to understand interpersonal conflict as an expression of differing predispositions among actors about and toward administration.

2. *Skill-building activities,* or various designs for gaining facility with behaviors consistent with OD values, as in giving and receiving feedback, listening, and resolving conflict.

3. *Diagnostic activities,* which often include process analysis, but which also may employ interviews, psychological instruments, or opinion surveys to generate data from and for members of some social system. These data get fed back into the system to serve as the raw material for action research sequences: diagnosis, prescription of changes, implementation, and evaluation.

4. *Coaching or counseling activities,* which seek to apply OD values in intimate situations, as between a pair in conflict in an organization via "third-party consultation."

5. *Team-building activities,* or efforts to increase the efficiency and effectiveness of intact task groups. Variants may use T-group or sensitivity-training modes, as well as one or more of the other activities listed here.

6. *Intergroup activities,* which seek to build effective and satisfying linkages between two or more task groups, such as departments in a large organization.

7. *Technostructural activities,* which seek to build need-satisfying roles, jobs, and structures. Typically, these activities rest on a "growth psychology" such as that of Maslow, Argyris, or Herzberg. These structural or policy approaches—job enlargement, flexi-time, and so on—often are coupled with other OD activities.

8. *System-building or system-renewal activities,* which seek comprehensive changes in a large organization's climate and values, using complex combinations of the seven activities sketched, and may take three to five years to implement (Golembiewski, Proehl, and Sink 1981, 680).

There is much debate about the validity and success of OD; nonetheless, the field has had a tremendous impact on what is believed possible in planned change of individuals' and groups' values and behavior in formal organizations. Golembiewski and his compatriots argued that after "toting up the score" for about a decade, more than 80 percent of the 270 interventions carried out in public agencies (for which they found published materials) "had at least a definite balance of positive and intended effects" (1981, 681). Although the results of this study must be viewed with a great deal of skepticism (because of the authors' bias, the weakness of the methodology, the tendency for only successful experiments to be reported, and the tendency for the reporters to interpret results in the best possible light since they are usually also the initiators of the interventions), they still present evidence that OD can be successful, and that planned change in behavior and values can occur in some instances within the public sector.

Fifteen years after Golembiewski and his compatriots examined the success of OD in public agencies, there is little question that such activities have an important impact on those organizations. In Washington, D.C., there are major efforts to apply most of the methods noted here, and total quality management, which uses many aspects of organization development in its regimen, has adherents throughout government as well as business. There is an increasing emphasis on "system concepts," and the recognition that all the various parts of the organization and its environment interact. The other major factor that must be recognized, according to the disciples of systemic change in organizations, is that causality is not always simple and direct: Interactions may be quite complex and seemingly unrelated sequentially on a first, cursory examination, thus requiring rather sophisticated analysis in order to uncover the interconnectedness (Senge 1990).

In addition, there is an increasing emphasis on culture and values as the core factors in determining the success of organizations over time, and the ultimate goal of those who work to create what are often now called "learning organizations" is to create a culture that guarantees common understanding of the goals of the organization and then allows open questioning of assumptions, actions, and the consequences of both. Likewise, it is recognized that there are distinct stages of "growth" that occur along the way to becoming a learning organization (see Figure 10–4).

If an organization achieves the third level of development, then Senge says that it, and the people in it, become able to understand the world and how the organization can create its future instead of "just surviving" in its world. Through analysis, adaptation, and "generative learning" (learning that enhances the ability to create), the organization can become an active partner in defining and developing its role in the larger world (Senge 1990, 14).

There is a danger of overselling what can be done in the public bureau, however. Even when a public organization accomplishes the goals of organizational change and growth, there is no guarantee that it accomplishes the ends desired by the larger society or by those chosen to represent that society. In addition, there is a fine line between attempting to motivate workers by helping them change their values and behavior and manipulating workers through skillful external control and maneuvering of rewards and

---

FIGURE 10–4   Stages in Developing Learning Capacities

Stage One: New Cognitive, Linguistic Capacities
People see new things and can speak a new language. This allows them to see more clearly their own and others' assumptions, actions, and consequences of both. Typically, they find it hard to translate these new cognitive and linguistic competencies into fundamentally new actions. They may begin to behave differently, but the basic rules, assumptions, and values are the same.

Stage Two: New Action Rules
As old assumptions "loosen" in response to the cognitive insights of Stage One, people begin to experiment with action rules based on new assumptions so they can see what they yield. They may need to rely on the new language to produce new actions, and they will find it difficult to access or string together new rules when under stress.

Stage Three: New Values and Operating Assumptions
People can string together rules that reflect new action values and operating assumptions. They can enact these rules under stress and ambiguity, continuing to aid their own and others' learning. By this stage, people will have adapted the rules into their own particular model, speaking in their own voice.

SOURCE: Peter Senge, *The Fifth Discipline: The Art and Practice of the Learning Organization* (New York: Currency/Doubleday, 1990): 377.

values to get them to do what others want them to do. Thus, when TQM or any other organizational change technique is applied, it is essential to understand the difference between motivation and manipulation.

A second problem is that even when techniques of change are applied in an appropriate manner, there is the possibility of "fade-out" as time passes, the immediacy of the training and learning decreases, and new actors enter the bureau. All this means that there must be a long-term commitment to the process and to the maintenance of the new system once it is in place. Long-term change and maintenance, however, can be very difficult to carry through in the public sector since people tend to have relatively short attention spans and elected leaders move in and out of office rapidly and at inopportune times. For example, many major organization change activities take several years to accomplish, but elections take place at more frequent intervals than the period normally allocated for those interventions. Furthermore, there is no guarantee that one group of elected officials, who are supportive of the activity, will still be in office when the activity reaches its critical later stages. Just when the chance of success seems strong, for example, a new city council may be elected that is indifferent or unsympathetic to the efforts, and a lot of work must go into "selling" them on the idea or finding ways to neutralize their influence on the bureaucracy. (How much can the bureaucracy be protected from the elected officials, however, before the traditional and important concept of control of government by elected representatives is undermined?) In spite of all the effort, it is not uncommon for the officials to refuse cooptation and to demand that other management styles or processes be used. Just as the Clinton/Gore effort to improve the productivity of the national bureaucracy seems to be working, along may come a Senator Phil Gramm, who as part of his run for the presidency declares that the National Productivity Review is "too little too late" and that hundreds of thousands of additional government workers should be removed. What impact does such political posturing on the part of candidates have on the morale of public employees and their willingness to participate in efforts at public bureau change? In such circumstances, the work of "improving the workforce" or of "better serving the customer" may be undone completely or may have to be started again at a later date.

The turnover of appointed officials is often greater than that of politicians, so there is great difficulty in establishing enough continuity to accomplish most long-term goals. Political appointees know that they are probably going to be in office for a very short time, and they are interested in seeing goals and objectives established that will allow them to leave some imprint on the bureaucracy and on the programs being delivered to the public. For them, success must be measurable by at least the next election and perhaps within eighteen months (when they expect to resign and move to another position either in government or private industry).

Finally, planned organizational change in values and behavior is precisely the area where the issue of accountability becomes paramount. As we noted in the prior section of this chapter, to what degree the public bureaucracy should be "democratized" is debatable. It may be appropriate to increase trust and participation in the bureau's operations; such a step may improve efficiency and effectiveness. But is there any guarantee that the changed culture will increase responsiveness to the political leaders and to the bureau's goals? Or is there any guarantee that the bureau members will understand how the bureau's goals fit into the larger social and political fabric? And will these new values and behavior lead to activities that undercut or ignore bureaus' accountability to external parties?

During the 1970s, for example, it was argued that public bureaucrats should be leaders in the reformulation of public policy (Dvorin and Simmons 1972). Although the bureaucracy is an important actor in the overall policy process, the extent to which the bureaucracy should publicly proclaim its role and demand a position of leadership can be vigorously debated. Bureaucrats tend to have a strong commitment to their agency, their program, and their clientele; thus, it is difficult to know if they can see "the big picture" (politically, economically, or socially) in the same way that people in more generalist positions do. The ultimate question, then, is: Is it possible to change civil servants' values and behavior within the organization, and guarantee that those changes will not have deleterious effects from the perspective of members of the larger political system? Experts in the field answer with an unqualified yes, but many politicians may not be convinced.

However that particular debate is settled, it must be remembered that though values and behavior may play an important role in the overall change and development of public organizations, they are only one part of a larger mosaic. The other parts must also be considered if any meaningful picture of what occurs as society and technology make new demands of government is to be developed. Therefore, it is time to move on to the second of the three aspects of planned change that we must consider.

Planned Change in Structure

Structure plays two roles in the process of planned change. First, much of the planned change that occurs is in the area of structure. When it appears that an organization must change, an obvious place to look is at its structure; in many cases, doing so is appropriate because structure can influence the organization's ability to carry out all the other functions of management. In fact, newly appointed leaders in public organizations will routinely examine the structure; that is their way of trying to make an immediate and lasting impression on the system.

Second, in order to deal with this demand for planned change, most modern organizations of any size have established planning offices in their central headquarters. It is the job of these offices to look into the future and envision the programs, policies, and structures of the bureau in a way that will allow the leaders to plan any changes that may be necessary. For example, the Internal Revenue Service (IRS) has an office that has as one of its primary functions the prediction of the impact of the information revolution on the way the IRS will do its work in the future. Many local governments have planning offices that specifically deal with the physical development of the community; any of these offices can show you their models of "the community of the future" as they envision it. Both kinds of offices—those dealing with physical planning and those involved in structural or procedural planning—are an accepted part of the successfully functioning public organization.

Within bureaus there is much discussion of creating more fluid and responsive structures and processes through flattening hierarchies, developing teams, creating quality circles, focusing on clients as customers, and in general applying the new social science technologies. Chapter 4 describes traditional and contemporary approaches to planned organizational design: The central point here is that the political benefits and drawbacks of each of the design approaches discussed in that chapter must also be recognized. Gawthrop (1983) points out that there are four approaches to organizing for change: (1) organizing for control, (2) organizing for bargaining, (3) organizing for responsiveness, (4) and organizing for analysis. Different structures help accomplish whatever major objective is paramount for the leader or legislature establishing or changing the bureau. Each of Gawthrop's approaches results in a different structure; it is also important to remember, however, that all of them exist in every bureau to some extent. We are simply stating that one will be preeminent.

The focus of current political efforts toward organizational change is on downsizing and especially the reduction of "middle management"—a phenomenon that may be defined differently by various participants in the debate. The major emphasis seems to be on efficiency, the lowering of "bureaucratic costs" in government; however, at some point the issue of effectiveness must also be considered. Notice that efficiency is not specifically one of the four reasons Gawthrop gives for structural change. Control may include the idea of checking for efficiency, but effectiveness is of equal importance in the concept. Reduction in the size of governmental bureaucracies, especially middle management positions, may make sense, but it should make sense in the larger context of all four factors mentioned by Gawthrop, or the unanticipated consequences of the reductions may be amazing and require quite a bit of readjustment of earlier actions.

Organizing for Control

This approach is central to the overall idea of bureau existence. To guarantee that the bureau's objectives are being achieved—which is the responsibility of every public manager—control mechanisms must exist. The typical hierarchical structure is central to control; through its use, there is always someone who is responsible when things go right or wrong. If change creates problems that must be dealt with, there are people responsible for making whatever organizational adjustments are necessary. Whether they fail or succeed, they can *supposedly* be held responsible and acknowledged for their effort in an appropriate manner. "Supposedly" is emphasized because there are numerous discussions of the shortcomings of the accountability system and the unanticipated consequences of these shortcomings.

Another aspect of control is equally important and must be discussed in the context of the issue of change. Most organizations have particular parts of their structure that are especially sensitive to, and need to be protected from, change in the environment. James Thompson (1967) argues that the structure of a complex organization specifically takes this part of the system into account when he notes that "boundary-spanning units" protect the technological core from environmental buffeting (again described in Chapter 4). The part of the bureau that cannot operate efficiently under the pressure of change or constant surveillance from a "fickle public" is protected by the structure in a way that allows its vital function to be carried out in a steady or "private" manner, thereby guaranteeing the efficiency (and let's hope the effectiveness) of overall bureau activity. Steady operation requires the guarantee of resources necessary to that operation, whether the production of a material good, the delivery of a particular service, or the handling of a procedure. Public organizations attempt to accomplish this goal by ensuring the flow of necessary resources through long-term appropriations, the charging of fees, special arrangements with influential constituents or consumers of the service or product, or by the guarantee of resources to that part of the bureau before other parts are considered. In other words, the bureau attempts to cushion the vital part of the structure from the exigencies of the political environment. (Private organizations often attempt to achieve this protection through vertical or horizontal integration. Perhaps some of the steps taken by bureaus can be likened to those of private sector corporations.)

Similarly, the protection from constant observation and the "kibitzing" that may accompany it is accomplished through structures that remove the decision-making process from the public's view. This may be accomplished through the use of executive sessions, closed-door negotiations, the use of security classifications to inhibit the release of information, the claim of "professional privilege," and other devices aimed at limiting public disclosure. Particular segments of bureaus are established to help clarify where such processes are possible and legal, and to aid all other parts of the agency in using these processes properly.

This particular aspect of public organizational operation often becomes the center of controversy, however, since those protected functions are precisely the ones that interested outsiders often want to influence or observe. It is toward these aspects of bureau operation that sunshine laws, sunset laws, and time limits on appropriations are aimed, thus forcing these activities into the limelight and the political fray when bureaus feel that such attention—and the inevitable uncertainty that goes with it—limits the agencies' ability to function in a rational, efficient, and effective manner.

Whatever the control issue may be, emphasis on it tends to give special power to those with formal positions of authority in the hierarchy. This power is also supported by legal mandate as established by the legislative body and ratified by the chief executive. Therefore, control with its concomitant power is always present in public agencies, probably to a greater extent than is usually true in the private sector.

Organizing for Bargaining

This approach requires that people with the appropriate expertise in both the politically and technically relevant areas be available in the bureau; that these people (whether lawyers, scientists, social scientists, or politicians) be placed in positions where they can carry out the required negotiations and at the same time have the ear of the bureau's decision makers (if they are not the decision makers themselves); and that they be protected (by their position descriptions or by knowledgeable and sympathetic superiors) from negative reactions to the wheeling and dealing (as long as it is within the bounds of propriety) that is inherent in such a role.

Organizing for Responsiveness

This approach requires that the structure allows appropriate external forces (clients, professionals, legislators, and so on) to be involved in the decision making related to the fulfillment of organizational objectives. Thus, the bureau must create structures that allow participation by outsiders, both in the establishment of priorities and procedures and in the judgments about success in accomplishing the objectives. The phrase "maximum feasible participation" that was used during the 1960s in the Johnson administration's War on Poverty programs led to the development of new structures, especially at the local government level, that guaranteed citizens in the area affected by a program a chance to have some say about how and where federal money was spent. Obviously, this changed the power relationships within the bureaucracy as well as between the bureaucracy and those it served. Responsiveness will always create this type of structural change, and the accompanying trauma and insecurity that those not committed to the concept will feel.

One example of an attempt to organize for change that involves the desire to increase responsiveness within the public agency is the creation of citizen boards to work with the bureau. Such boards have existed at all levels of government since the War on Poverty. However their major impact has been at the local government level. Two types of citizen boards exist (not including the formally elected councils): advisory boards and review boards.

Obviously, advisory boards get involved at a much earlier point in the policy process. Therefore, it is to be expected that they have greater ongoing influence over the daily operations of an agency and that the agency's managers will pay closer attention to the ideas, wishes, and suggestions of the board members. A review board can also have an important impact on an agency, especially if the board and the agency develop either an advocative or adversarial relationship. The important factor to consider here is the way the involved bureaus handle the creation of these new entities that can have a tremendous negative impact on the agency or, in many cases, serve a useful function in responding to and anticipating change in the environment. Successful structuring within an agency involves making sure that the organization recognizes and respects the existence of the citizen board; this usually means that those holding top leadership or managerial positions in the agency work with the board and see it as a useful entity. An agency of any size will usually create within its formal structure an office whose primary function is to work with the citizen board, thus ensuring that the board and the agency receive the information to which they are entitled. The other members of the bureau are often told that communication with the citizen board should be carried out through the appropriate channels. At the same time, the leaders of the agency recognize that the citizen board plays a valuable role in communication from the citizenry to the agency and vice versa. Whatever the final results, the successful use of citizen boards requires that their existence be recognized within the formal and informal structure of the public agency. Structural change is necessary to use the citizen board to deal, in an even better way in the future, with the phenomenon of change.

Organizing for Analysis

This final approach puts those with technical and analytic skills in places of influence with respect to information and decision making. Formal authority may have little impact in such an agency. Individuals who are traditionally "staffers," with all the drawbacks inherent in such positions, may find themselves in the sometimes frightening situation of playing major roles in deciding the priorities and processes that ultimately influence the agency's fate. Although the organization's structure need not reflect the analysts' increased power, its *formal* structure will probably change over time to reflect the changing status and roles of the various actors. One of the focuses of the next section of this chapter is a more detailed discussion of the problems related to organizing for analysis.

Planned Change in Process and Technology

Technological change, especially its scope and speed, has moved from "news" to "accepted way of life." During the 1970s, 1980s, and 1990s, Alvin Toffler (1970, 1980, 1995), John

Naisbitt (1982, 1994), and Thomas J. Peters (1994) have made a handsome living by writing about and defining the ideas of the technological society—explaining what has happened in the last few decades and predicting what the future will be like as the new technologies take root and flourish in society. Much of this discussion of change is educated guesswork (though admittedly good in many cases), but it points out how much change is a constant in determining the way organizational objectives are set and met. Instead of attempting to note and discuss all the various technological and procedural changes that have occurred, are occurring, or may occur, we will focus on a few of the ways in which organizations respond to changes in process and technology. Chapter 4 describes the structural responses to technological changes, but organizations respond in other ways as well. As we discuss this issue, it is essential to note that we cannot do so without referring to the types of planned change (behavioral and value change as well as structural change) that were discussed earlier in this chapter.

Perhaps the most cohesive set of skills regularly applied to the problems of procedural and technological changes come from a set of quantitative and qualitative techniques that are commonly referred to as systems analysis. These techniques have as their roots or beginnings a field of study in the biological sciences where it became obvious that a single organism or phenomenon could not be studied in a vacuum. In biology, each organism is part of a much larger system (for example, the food chain), and to understand individual parts of the biological world, it is necessary to comprehend how many seemingly disparate elements interact over a wide geographic area or a long time (Boulding 1956).

The same general principle applies to the study of organizations. Systems analysts, in the study of organizations, assume that multiple factors must be considered whenever anyone is interested in understanding or changing organizational structures or processes (see Figure 10–5). Although the systems approach will never preclude the need for experience and personal insight, the quantitative and qualitative managerial techniques developed by management analysts, operations researchers, and decision and information scientists help reduce the public manager's reliance on intuition by pointing out unexpected

---

FIGURE 10–5   Systems-Analysis Techniques

Technique	*Description or Purpose*	*Level of Complexity*
Bayesian analysis	Analysis of conditional probabilities based on subjective probability estimates. Used to predict the probability of the occurrence of future events	Moderate
Decision trees	Analysis of branching choice possibilities, focusing on the value of each outcome weighted for the probability of its occurrence. Used to assess alternative courses of action involving several branching decision points	Moderate

FIGURE 10–5   *(continued)*

Technique	Description or Purpose	Level of Complexity
Dynamic programming	Analysis of the occurrence of an event based on the occurrence of events immediately prior to the target event. Used to structure solution sets to complex problems	High
Flowcharting	Simple graphic representation of the elements, processes, and linkages in a system. Used to model the "flow" or progression of activities within a system	Low
Game theory	Analysis of the probability of outcomes in a competitive choice situation. Used to construct models of alternative outcome possibilities in a conflict situation	Moderate
Inventory analysis	An analytical method of projecting demand for resources under conditions of uncertainty. Used to estimate the demand for resources in a system	Moderate to high
Linear programming	A technique (may use graphs) used to select the optimum mix of resources in a project. Used to plan resource allocation in a project	High
Markov process	A technique used to determine the probability of achieving alternative outcomes based on prior event probabilities. Used to model system performance probabilities	Moderate to high
Program evaluation and review technique (PERT); critical path method (CPM)	A technique to map the utilization of time to complete parts of a project. Used to plan for the timing of a project and estimate ways of reducing total project time through the strategic allocation of resources	Low
Payoff matrixes	A technique used to evaluate alternative strategies under various conditions. Used to evaluate action alternatives when implementation circumstances are not certain	Low to moderate
Queueing theory	A technique used to analyze waiting times for service in a system. Used to model resource demands on a system	Moderate to high
Simulation	Techniques that provide quantitative analysis of the performance of interrelated variables in a system. Used to model system performance under varying conditions	Moderate to high
Time-series analysis	A technique employing linear regression to evaluate variable relationships over time. Used to model future system performance based on past system performance	Moderate

SOURCE: Prepared by John Ostrowski, Associate Professor of Public Administration, California State University, Long Beach.

consequences, sharpening goals, clarifying processes, and generally disciplining managerial thinking. According to exponents of systems analysis in the public sector:

> The entire intellectual orientation is toward explicit conceptual models of phenomena relevant to that purpose [stated in the prior sentence]. There are models that aid the detection of problems, models that aid decision making, and models that aid the institutionalization of the decisions or designs chosen in response to the problems recognized. Our logic is in the first place cybernetic and, as a consequence of our concern with models, structuralist. Additionally, we tend toward the normative/idealistic rather than the descriptive/realistic. We are concerned with how things are organized, but at least as much with how things might be organized. (White et al. 1980, 9)

The application of such approaches to public organizations is very difficult—more difficult in many cases than is so for private industry. Businesspeople do not have to include, in any major way, the political environment as they calculate the optimal way to structure their offices and plants; nor do they have to worry about the outside world involving itself in their processes of production (unless they are polluters or other rogue operations). Not so for the public manager, as is noted by White and his compatriots:

> Public management is a political process in which the political demands, internal and external, are concerned with how the services are produced as well as with their characteristics as end products, and with who gets the services as well as with how much is produced. This situation is much more complicated than that of a business, where the customers have only begun to express a concern with the processes of production (and even then their concern is usually expressed through government agencies rather than directly to the producer). (1980, 4)

At the opposite end of planned change at the procedural level, the focus of attention becomes the individual job and the flow of work within an agency. The major developments in this area are job enrichment and moving from individually defined jobs to teams. To improve employees' satisfaction and quality of work, their jobs are being restructured so that they are not so repetitive and fragmented—the tasks performed by an employee are *enriched*. Where in the past a social worker may have been involved in only one major aspect of a client's case, he or she may now handle the entire case. It is hoped that this approach will allow the caseworker to use all of his or her skills to make the work more interesting. At the same time, it is hoped that the broadening of the caseworker's scope in the process will improve the quality of the counseling and aid received by the client because it makes it possible for the caseworker to consider all aspects of the client's problems and the interrelationship of the pieces as decisions are made about the situation. An accountant may be given certain accounts to administer rather than having responsibility for only one step in the accounting process; or a park grounds keeper may be given a small park to maintain rather than being in charge of mowing or tree trimming.

In each case, the important element is the attempt to remove the monotony from work and to allow workers who wish to do so the chance to use all of their skills or develop new ones. And, of course, leaders plan all changes in techniques or procedures with the ultimate end of improving the bureau's overall performance.

Likewise, the use of *teams* is meant to make workers more satisfied with their work while improving the quality of the "product" delivered by the organization. The idea has been around for some time and is at the center of the matrix organization structure presented in Chapter 4. Further impetus came from the emphasis on quality circles and other participative management concepts related to total quality management. In addition to gaining the pooled knowledge, it is believed that teamwork leads to greater commitment to the goals of the organization. Of course, the success of this concept depends on how the idea is carried out. Michael Schrage argues that:

> most companies simply assign people to teams and expect those selected to be ready, willing, and able to collaborate. The belief is that any group of people within the organization can be assembled into a team where the whole is greater than the sum of the parts. (1995, 222)

If top management knows its individuals very well, that plan may work; however, there are numerous ways of setting up teams, and every situation calls for a unique procedure for creating working groups.

The concept of teams means more than putting a group of people together to work on a project. According to Katzenbach and Smith, "A team is a small number of people with complementary skills who are committed to a common purpose, performance goals, and approach for which they hold themselves mutually accountable" (1993, 45). That short definition includes several specific factors that often take a good deal of time and effort to achieve; in order to achieve these factors, the authors present a set of questions (see Figure 10–6) that must be answered affirmatively before the designation of "team" fits any group that is working together. As they answer these questions, special problems often arise for public administrators. These problems are related to the political environment within which the bureau or nonprofit organization operates.

The introduction of new techniques automatically means that procedures will change, and the opposite is usually—though not always—true. As computers came to play an increasing role in organizational activity, procedures changed accordingly. Now, with the permeation of microcomputers, even faster and greater changes are occurring in the structure and procedures of public agencies (see Reading 10–1). With the introduction of teams, the communication, decision making, and "product delivery" procedures change in an organization.

Concomitant with such changes come alterations in values and behavior. The roles of workers are changing, with less division of labor along strict substantive and procedural lines. Top management can now prepare, send, and receive messages quickly and efficiently, cutting out the middle steps of dictating, typing, and mailing information. Of course, this means that managers must get rid of their aversion to keyboards, which is based on an attitude of superiority toward secretaries and, at the same time, a fear of the technical knowledge required to do this supposedly demeaning work. Likewise, managers must also change their attitudes toward status in organizations because different individuals will step into and out of leadership roles during the development and delivery of program goals, whether they are concrete products, social services, or intellectual property. This kind of fluctuation can lead to role ambiguity, at least in the short term, and the necessity of playing different parts in relatively short periods in the larger organizational scenario.

Technology has helped create the environment that allows rapid change in roles and the building of teams with large pools of commonly shared information because microcomputers can make available to individuals throughout the organization information that was once the private domain of top management. Thus, the sacredness of position is going to be harder to protect because much of the deference to superiors has been based on the supposition that those above "have better information than their subordinates." Such may not be the case with the new information technology. Deference to superiors may be based, to a much greater extent in the future, on proven performance in the job as perceived by

---

Fewer Secretaries on Hand
to Celebrate Their Day

Della, Perry Mason's secretary, is dead. But it's no big mystery who did it. . . . (T)he letter-taking, coffee-fetching, hatted-and-gloved Dellas in our offices grow fewer and fewer. The perpetrators? Everything from downsizing to the spread of computers to the belief that fetching coffee is exploitive.

But while many people . . . know that the traditional secretary has gone the way of the milkman and the corner newsboy, the full contours of the trend are less well understood. The old-time secretary hasn't exactly disappeared, for instance. She has split in two. . . . (T)he modern secretary faces a dual path. One road leads to a dynamic super-secretary who takes on many more managerial responsibilities. The other ends up as a temporary office clerk hired on the cheap to do only mundane tasks.

"In some companies, secretaries are both appreciated more and given new skills and opportunities," said Ellen Bravo, executive director of 9 to 5, National Association of Working Women. "In other companies, they are shunted down into 'paper towel' jobs—jobs that are disposable and can be done by anybody."

Ms. Bravo, whose organization represents about 15,000 women, said that because of these diverging trends some secretaries now run the corporate committees that they used to take minutes for. But others, caught in the staff reductions of the 1990's, have lost their regular salaries and benefits and can get only temporary or part-time work.

Cristine A. Jackel, who has spent more than 24 years as a secretary, is one of the lucky ones. As the profession has evolved, her job has gotten bigger rather than smaller.

In 1971, as an 18-year-old graduate of Bartlett High School in Webster, Mass., Mrs. Jackel went to work for Cranston Printworks, a manufacturing company in Worcester. She used an electric typewriter to put out memos on onion skin paper. "We didn't even have white out," she said.

Now 42, Ms. Jackel is assistant to the president of the Paul Revere Insurance Company. Also in Worcester. She is still a secretary but with a smarter title and greater responsibilities.

"I sit in on the president's staff meetings not to take minutes but because I am part of the team," she said. "The secretaries and the assistants serve as part of the staff. We have really been empowered with a lot more authority."

---

subordinates who are relatively well informed about the bureau's internal and external situation. Authoritarian management styles may be much harder to camouflage and justify because information on which decisions are based will be much more readily available to all participants in the agency, and it will become increasingly normal for others than "bosses" to play the role of group leader based on expertise. Thus, such things as management style and motivational techniques will be influenced by the new "hard" and "soft" technologies that are currently gaining widespread use. And we cannot even imagine some of the techniques that will exist in the near future.

One of the important questions that public administrators must face is the effect of these new technologies on the ultimate objective of serving the citizenry at large. How,

She does her work on a computer and her memos are distributed to the company's offices across the country by E-mail and by fax. If her boss goes to the cafeteria, he offers to bring her coffee.

But, whether their jobs have grown or shrunk, all modern secretaries share another trait: there are fewer of them. As more executives use their own computers, secretaries have become much scarcer in the United States over the last two decades. According to the Bureau of Labor Statistics, the 3.4 million secretaries in the country last year comprised 2.8 percent of the work force—substantially down from the 3.7 percent they constituted in 1974.

That drop often means multiple bosses. In today's office, only the highest-ranking executives still have their own personal assistants.

And the drop in secretaries has tracked a corresponding fall in use of that term. For many people, secretary is a sexist or degrading word; preferred substitutes, said 9 to 5's Maripat Blankenheim, are executive assistant, administrative assistant and clerical staffer.

"In some corporate cultures," she said, "you will be corrected if you ask for someone's secretary."

The Katharine Gibbs Schools never had to worry about names; "secretary" never appeared in its title. But the profession's evolution has made a big mark on something much more central to the school's mission: its curriculum.

"Even 10 years ago, shorthand was the matrix of our curriculum," said Ms. McDonough, noting the school has 6,000 students at seven campuses in the Northeast. "But now," she said, "the emphasis is on keyboarding and English. The instantaneous communication of modern technology has increased the value of these skills," she explained.

Classified notices prove the change. Ads that in the 1960's looked for "bright-eyed lassies" now demand expertise in word processing and spreadsheet skills.

As those ads also suggest, secretaries of the past were perceived as much as office decoration and romantic prospects as business resources. But if today's executives were to treat secretaries as if they stepped out of "How to Succeed in Business Without Really Trying" . . . they might be accused of sexual harassment. The ideology of the modern office is business, all business.

SOURCE: David M. Herszenhorn, *The New York Times,* April 23, 1995: Sec 3 Financial Desk, p. 15.

for instance, does the increasing use of computers affect law enforcement? First, the types of crimes that are occurring are changing rapidly; now crimes are not only committed "on the street" but also on "the information superhighway" created by the Internet. Therefore, the skills needed within the law enforcement profession are changing just as rapidly. Second, the ability of law enforcement agencies to deny individuals their civil rights is greatly enhanced by the sophisticated new equipment; at the same time, new definitions of "civil rights" must be developed for the new technologies. Therefore, officials must be deeply committed to the basic tenets of democracy and aware of both the short- and long-term results of the use of new technologies on those basic values. The type of law enforcement agency and officer that must exist in the future is dramatically changed by the

FIGURE 10–6   Questions Related to the Formation of Teams

Answering the [following] questions can establish the degree to which your group functions as a real team, as well as help pinpoint how you can strengthen your efforts to increase performance. They set tough standards, and answering them candidly may reveal a harder challenge than you may have expected. At the same time, facing up to the answers can accelerate your progress in achieving the full potential of your team.

1. *Small enough in number:*
   a. Can you convene easily and frequently?
   b. Can you communicate with all members easily and frequently?
   c. Are your discussions open and interactive for all members?
   d. Does each member understand the others' roles and skills?
   e. Do you need more people to achieve your ends?
   f. Are sub-teams possible or necessary?

2. *Adequate levels of complementary skills:*
   a. Are all three categories of skills either actually or potentially represented across the membership (functional/technical, problem-solving/decision-making, and interpersonal)?
   b. Does each member have the potential in all three categories to advance his or her skills to the level required by the team's purpose and goals?
   c. Are any skill areas that are critical to team performance missing or underrepresented?
   d. Are the members, individually and collectively, willing to spend the time to help themselves and others learn and develop skills?
   e. Can you introduce new or supplemental skills as needed?

3. *Truly meaningful purpose:*
   a. Does it constitute a broader, deeper aspiration than just near-term goals?
   b. Is it a *team* purpose as opposed to a broader organizational purpose or just one individual's purpose (e.g., the leader's)?
   c. Do all members understand and articulate it the same way? And do they do so without relying on ambiguous abstractions?
   d. Do members define it vigorously in discussions with outsiders?
   e. Do members frequently refer to it and explore its implications?
   f. Does it contain themes that are particularly meaningful and memorable?
   g. Do members feel it is important, if not exciting?

4. *Specific goal or goals:*
   a. Are they *team* goals versus broader organizational goals or just one individual's goals (e.g., the leader's)?
   b. Are they clear, simple, and measurable? If not measurable, can their achievement be determined?
   c. Are they realistic as well as ambitious? Do they allow small wins along the way?
   d. Do they call for a concrete set of team work-products?
   e. Is their relative importance and priority clear to all members?
   f. Do all members agree with the goals, their relative importance, and the way in which their achievement will be measured?
   g. Do all members articulate the goals in the same way?

5. *Clear working approach:*
   a. Is the approach concrete, clear, and really understood and agreed to by everybody? Will it result in achievement of the objectives?
   b. Will it capitalize on and enhance the skills of all members? Is it consistent with other demands on the members?

FIGURE 10–6 *(continued)*

    c. Does it require all members to contribute equivalent amounts of real work?

    d. Does it provide for open interaction, fact-based problem solving, and results-based evaluation?

    e. Do all members articulate the approach in the same way?

    f. Does it provide for modification and improvement over time?

    g. Are fresh input and perspectives systematically sought and added, for example, through information and analysis, new members, and senior sponsors?

6. *Sense of mutual accountability:*

    a. Are you individually and jointly accountable for the team's purpose, goals, approach, and work-products?

    b. Can you and do you measure progress against specific goals?

    c. Do all members feel responsible for all measures?

    d. Are the members clear on what they are individually responsible for and what they are jointly responsible for?

    e. Is there a sense that "only the team can fail"?

SOURCE: Jon R. Katzenbach and Douglas K. Smith, *The Wisdom of Teams: Creating the High-Performance Organization* (New York: HarperBusiness, 1993): 62–64. Copyright © 1993 by the President and Fellows of Harvard College. All rights reserved.

technology developing around them. To quote an anonymous police chief responding to a questionnaire about the problems faced by police executives:

> The most challenging aspect of a police administrator's job is leading an organization through necessary change, a half step behind the society we interact with. We cannot be pace setters for societal change yet must adjust to it rapidly in order not to lag too far behind. (Witham 1985, 124)

Another example of technology's impact on public administration can be seen by looking at how changes in information systems affect the concept and practice of citizen participation. The impact of changing information technology on citizen participation may be dramatic. For instance, cable television allows citizens to observe the debates of governmental bodies—from Congress to the local library board—and some technologists argue that direct democracy could become commonplace by letting citizens vote on almost any issues that face the community. However, the kind of civic participation that would be required by such procedures is not now part of most citizens' values and behavior. Thus, the results of such procedures may be quite skewed and even damaging to the community if ways are not found to guarantee the appropriate use of the technology. Citizens' values will have to change, but how is such change accomplished without the use of manipulative strategies that could have serious long-term implications about the continued guarantee of individual rights and liberties? The danger of manipulation does not suggest that such procedures cannot be developed; it does argue that finding solutions to such problems is extremely difficult and requires special creativity if these technologies are to be appropriately applied to larger social and political questions. The second question—how increased citizen participation might change the public bureau's functioning—is an issue that can be raised here, but not answered.

Finally, in looking at the changes in social technology and their impact on public administration, what if teams are created and the members of organizations begin to have an increasing impact on the decisions and processes of organizations? Will public administrators remain the *servants* of the people? What is to guarantee that the tenets of public choice theory do not become true and that the members of the organization act in their own interest instead of the public interest? This question strikes close to the issues raised in "public administration ethics," and though no final answer can be presented here, it is an issue that has been debated regularly by earlier scholars such as Dwight Waldo (1948) and Paul Appleby (1952), and more recently by writers such as John Rohr (1989), Terry Cooper (1991), and Harold Gortner (1991). If the public choice advocates are correct, and individuals ultimately always act in their own self-interest, the debate may be futile, and the development of new social and technical procedures may make democracy more difficult to maintain. But if we accept the idea that individuals do respond to the general obligations of citizenship—and public servants to the peculiar requirements of their career (especially that of acting in and for the public interest)—then the proper implementation and direction of new organizational change techniques is an important issue that must be studied carefully, but may ultimately help maintain the democratic system even when threatened by new social and technical pressures. As part of the inculcation of these new ways of working in organizations, we must stress:

> the need for deep commitments by our public officials to civic virtues, democratic values, and constitutional procedures. . . . [T]he traditions of republicanism, democracy, and constitutionalism ground the common values of the cadre of civil servants that we need today as they did the corps of expert administrators envisioned by Woodrow Wilson. (Garvey 1993, 220)

Change and Conflict

Finally, one area where there is an attempt to control and make change positive within organizations is the area of conflict analysis and management. Although conflict management has been inherently a part of public management, its recognition as a specific field of analysis, theory, and practice has primarily occurred during the last decade. In 1925, Mary Parker Follett was arguing that:

> As conflict—difference—is here in the world, as we cannot avoid it, we should, I think, use it. Instead of condemning it, we should set it to work for us. Why not? What does the mechanical engineer do with friction? Of course his chief job is to eliminate friction, but it is true that he also capitalizes friction. The transmission of power by belts depends on friction between the belt and the pulley. The friction between the driving wheel of the locomotive and the track is necessary to haul the train. All polishing is done by friction. The music of the violin we get by friction. We left the savage state when we discovered fire by friction. We talk of the friction of mind on mind as a good thing. So in [organizations], too, we have to know when to try to eliminate friction and when to try to capitalize it, when to see what work we can make it do. (Graham 1995, 67–68)

Over the last decade, special efforts have been made within a variety of public organizations to understand and guide conflict into positive, constructive, collaborative activities. Specific groups have been set up to deal with interpersonal conflicts within agencies, and managers are given training on handling intergroup and interorganizational problems. And, especially in the area of regulation, officials are looking for ways to constructively resolve long-standing conflicts between groups in the community and between governmental agencies and interest groups of all kinds rather than just assuming that those conflicts are inevitable and eternal.

Critical to the study of conflicts in and between organizations is the definition of what we are examining. It was assumed for a long time that conflicts occurred because of different beliefs or different desired results that were part of a zero-sum game—only one side could win and the other must lose. The newer definition of conflict accepts differences in beliefs and desired ends, but argues that by getting both sides to understand and lay on the table their beliefs and desires it is often possible to arrive at what Mary Parker Follett called an "integrative solution" (1995, 68–86). In an integrative solution, both sides are able to find a place for their desires so that neither side has to sacrifice those factors nearest and dearest to their hearts. However, the analysis, understanding, and negotiation processes have usually changed the priority listing of the conflicting groups as part of the conflict management process.

Of course, the political system is itself a structure established to allow the civilized and productive resolution of conflicts that cannot be settled at lower levels of the society. However, the focus of conflict analysis goes beyond understanding of conflicts and looks for ways to allow conflict to be used productively and to be turned into collaborative, joint problem solving that can be useful to all sides (Burton 1990). Likewise, it is recognized that conflict and change are inextricably bound together—one seldom happens without the other. As L. David Brown notes:

> Change is often closely tied to conflict. Sometimes change breeds conflict; sometimes conflict breeds change. Effective conflict management is often critical to constructive change processes. Change is important if inequitable and unacceptable conditions exist for some party, but so too there is a need for order, consensus, and common goals *within and between organizations and between organizations and the public they serve* in an open society. (1983, v)

Public organizations must play an important part in the larger social and political conflicts. Unless individuals within the bureaus understand the dynamics of the conflicts within which they are major actors and know how to turn negative feelings toward more constructive paths, they may easily exacerbate the problems they are mandated to fix. Ultimately such action, taken in ignorance, can be destructive to the total fabric of society. Often that destructiveness occurs because there is no understanding of the different cultures that may exist in the conflicting groups. Wallace Warfield addresses this problem by suggesting that, in many cases, a third-party intervenor skilled in public-policy conflict resolution may be needed in order to help the two sides work through the misunderstandings. Warfield notes, for example, that:

> Low-power cultural groups, who have traditionally been kept away from the negotiating table, see the origins, processes, and outcomes of conflict through the lens of values that have historically shaped their relationships with the dominant culture. They bring different voices to the negotiating process that often do not fit the protocols of interest-based bargaining. At the same time, public organizations are complex entities that have cultures of a different kind. . . . When these forces are joined in conflict, the third-party intervenor must find a way to bridge the cultural gap. Frequently, this means playing an interpreter role for one side or both, in a way that provides a context for the actions and language of the opposing side. (1993, 190)

Attila the Hun on the Art of Negotiation

Negotiation is one way antagonists try to resolve conflicts. Attila the Hum offers some advice on this skill and how to use it to *"win"* when negotiating—which may or may not always fit the needs of public administrators. (Editor's note.)

"The techniques of negotiation are not easily taught. It is for both Hun and chieftan to learn skills useful in negotiating. These are mastered only through understanding gained by experience. . . . Now I give to all assembled my counsel, in the hopes that it will serve to add to your wisdom and your expertise in the leader's vital art of negotiation.

- Always maintain the diplomatic initiative in all negotiations. Be on the offense always— never lose contact with your enemy. This will place him in a lesser position, and you will have the upper hand.

- Always negotiate at the lowest level possible. This will serve to resolve small things before they grow out of proportion and make negotiating impossible.

- Never trust negotiation to luck. Enter every session armed with knowledge of the enemy's strengths and weaknesses; knowing his secrets makes you strong and allows you to better deceive him as to your ultimate goals.

- Keep negotiations secret! They must be conducted in private. . . . Only the policies should become public knowledge. How they are negotiated should remain confidential, saving a loss of face.

- Time is your ally when you're negotiating. It calms temperaments and gives rise to less-spirited perspectives. Never rush into negotiations.

- Never arbitrate. Arbitration allows a third party to determine your destiny. It is a resort of the weak.

What is sought in conflict *management* is a "balance of conflict": Too little conflict leads to complacency and no desire for change or to the inability to face issues of friction, imbalance in distribution of costs and benefits, or other factors that may, when not noticed and dealt with early, become issues of bitter hostility and confrontation at a later date.

Within bureaus, the "culture" of the organization is dramatically affected by the types of conflicts that occur between individual members and between groups. All efforts at changing the values of the group, improving intraorganizational cooperation and collaboration, focusing attention and getting agreement on the goals of the bureau, and attempting to improve overall efficiency and effectiveness will depend on developing an acceptance of conflict as a normal individual or organizational phenomenon and learning to deal with it constructively. Used constructively, conflict can be a powerful tool for clarification of individual, group, and organizational values, ideas, and actions and the development of greater understanding and collaboration between all the actors. When conflict is recognized as a normal factor in organizational life, it can be calculated into the set of variables that can be dealt with on a regular basis. If conflict in organizations is not recognized and dealt with, it is one more "external factor," discussed later in this chapter, that randomly influences bureau functionality.

- Never make negotiations difficult on immediate, lesser points, at the cost of a greater outcome. Acquiescence on lesser issues softens the spirit of your adversary.
- In negotiation you must take well-studied risks. Try to foresee all possible outcomes to determine those that will yield favorable results.
- Be aware of the temperament in your foe's camp. Take advantage of troubles and turmoils that arise during negotiations.
- Never overestimate your own adroitness. You may simply be negotiating with a weak opponent. Though fortuitous, this will not always be the situation.
- Never intimidate.
- Honor all commitments you make during negotiations lest your enemy fail to trust your word in the future.
- Remember, agreement in principle does not dictate agreement in practice. It does, however, serve to save face at the moment.
- Be bold in facing the inevitable. Acquiesce when resistance would be pointless or when your victory can be gained only at too high a cost. Of this you may not approve, but it is your duty to do so for the good of all Huns.
- Be keenly aware of time. Present appealing alternatives that are appropriate to your opponent's situation at the moment of your negotiations. Otherwise, he will dismiss your propositions.

Now, you mighty chieftains must come to an understanding of a final simple fact. It is never wise to gain by battle what may be gained through bloodless negotiations. Reserve the potential loss of your warriors for great causes not attainable without waging battle."

SOURCE: Wess Roberts, *Leadership Secrets of Attila the Hun* (New York: Warner Books, 1987): 82–85.

The Continuing Debate over Planned Organizational Change

The discussion up to now has focused on a general theory of organizational change and the techniques used in accomplishing that change; however, we must not be lulled into believing that there is agreement on what the results of change should be. There are alternative models for organizational behavior and values, structure, and process. Not everyone wants the organization to look or act the same. It is important to recognize the existence of a variety of models to see the choices that exist and the results that may ensue from the adoption of any of these models in the public sector. After all, each model is based on a different set of assumptions about organizational objectives, the role of public bureaus in society, and the ways people are expected to function in them.

In our earlier discussion of control (both in this chapter and Chapter 6), various systems of participatory control were discussed, including workers' councils (Tannenbaum et al. 1974) and quality circles (Ouchi 1981). We pointed out that the justification for these different participatory systems varied from implementing particular aspects of Marxist philosophy to practicing humanist psychology; in addition, these systems varied according to the culture of the particular country or society. Therefore, when one speaks about participatory management systems, it is necessary to spell out exactly what type of system is being referred to and what the objectives in using that system may be.

If the objective of the participatory system is to improve control, the type of participation encouraged may be quite different from that sought when the objective is to improve overall efficiency or effectiveness. Still another type of participation may be encouraged if the objective is to increase member identification with the particular bureau. In each case, the point at which participation is encouraged may also change. If improved control is the goal, participation may be encouraged only after bureau objectives and plans have been completed, and the participation may occur only in specific areas of organizational activity. But if the goal of the participation is to increase member identification with the bureau, there may be an attempt to involve members as quickly as possible in the definition of bureau goals and plans so that they will have a sense of "ownership" in those important organizational elements. Of course, there is always the problem of deciding the degree to which the members of a public agency should set their own goals or whether they should be set by duly elected representatives of the people. It is even possible to question how much leeway bureau members should have in establishing their own procedures; the answer appears to be determined primarily by the way in which we perceive human beings in general. "Can or cannot people (as bureaucrats) be trusted to care about the constitution, due process, efficiency and effectiveness, and their fellow man, and will that care show in the way they do their work?"

Each of the approaches to participation results in a different structure. If identification with the organization is important and participation in the establishment of goals and procedures is encouraged, an agency creates strong communication circuits that work both up and down. These circuits will be apparent in the organization's structure, and those offices that play an important role in the communication system will be given higher status and protected so that they can function without feeling threatened by either internal or external forces unsympathetic to the organization's established philosophy. It is very likely that such an organization will have a relatively "flat" hierarchy. On the other hand, if the primary goal of the organization is control, no matter how much participation is encouraged, the organization will undoubtedly have a "taller" hierarchy with a greater number of managerial layers. Similar differences can be found for almost any organizational goal and the type of structure and processes occurring because of that primary goal.

Another factor that influences the structure of public organizations, determines whether or not they should change, and decides how that change should take place is directly related to the type of service that organizations deliver and the structure required to carry out that service. Many organizations in the public sector were originally set up to deliver specific concrete products. The early role of the government was primarily helping to tame the wilderness and aiding in the creation of our industrial might; highways had to be built, harbors had to be developed, and floods controlled. Much of government had an "industrial look" to it. The organizational structure and process emulated that of business.

Later, government became much more involved in the delivery of services to citizens and to other organizations existing in society.[4] Service organizations have a different con-

---

[4]All the roles discussed here have always existed in government and still do. It is important to remember, however, that the level of importance for each has changed dramatically at different points in our country's development.

figuration than organizations of an industrial, product-oriented nature. In fact, many of the tensions existing in government are related to the misunderstanding that occurs when one judges the performance of a service organization by production organization standards. Many people have not yet recognized the difference between the two, especially politicians who try to apply standards of efficiency taken from industry to government programs such as Aid to Families with Dependent Children or Medicare.

Another developing governmental role that has created much controversy is the function of regulation. In our interdependent world, it has been determined by the legislature that certain business communities need to be regulated either because of inefficiency or failure in the normal market processes. Regulatory activities have a dynamic all of their own, and it is impossible to judge the efficiency or effectiveness of such organizations by any industrial standard. Questions of due process, equity, and public interest are paramount in these activities instead of simple measures of the number of cases handled or pieces of paper pushed. Careful understanding of the goals for which these organizations were established, and the dynamic of the process over time, are critical in making judgments about change in objectives, organizational culture, structure, and process.

A new major role in government is that of information broker or "information organizer." In this role, a bureau's main mission is the collecting, analyzing, using, and dispensing to appropriate others of information generated and needed throughout major sectors of society; and the information is needed simply to keep the government, or the social or business sectors of society, functioning effectively in our highly technological and interdependent world. If the bureau is not directly furnishing this service, it is often regulating that part of society that is collating and delivering the information. This new type of bureau requires a completely different set of knowledges and skills; the structures of authority, communication, and decision making, and the procedures followed in carrying out its mission are quite different from those of the three types of organizations noted earlier. Because of the immense amount of expertise required and the phenomenal rate at which the technology and external demands change, these organizations often assume the characteristics of the temporary organization discussed in Chapter 4. The nature of these organizations is often highly disquieting to politicians since it makes it hard for them to maintain political control over such dynamic activities. The governmental policymaking machinery is deliberately structured to operate slowly through a coalition-building process that requires special majorities to achieve temporary closure on any issue. Bureaus at the forefront of technology may change structures, processes, and even objectives several times in the span of time that their legislative masters require to make policy. And while this is happening, these new technologies and the organizations using them are often capable of carrying out activities that could be quite injurious to the health of our democratic system. This situation places many public managers and executives in positions where they must make serious ethical and political decisions about what are and are not appropriate behaviors, procedures, and objectives for their agencies.

Finally, there must not be a mistaken idea that change is necessarily "good." There is no one model or structure of organization that is "right" and that should be always sought; no particular structure is guaranteed to be better than another. Instead, the decisions concerning what is appropriate for a bureau, what change is necessary, and what the new structures and processes should be must be made after careful consideration of the environment in which the agency is working and what its goals are. At that point, decisions can be made about the necessity of change and what the goals are for that change. In many cases, the alternative models (to the one existing at the present time) are not improvements. Any attempt to create change in an organization without carefully weighing all these issues opens one to the charge of being "in favor of change for change's sake," or being enamored of the excitement of change rather than interested in accomplishing preordained goals. Such a charge, if true, is very damning; if untrue, the charge is still damaging and must be immediately rebutted by a careful enunciation of the goals of the change. Everyone may not agree with the goals, but at least one is able to refute the charge of thoughtlessness. That is vital to success. It is also vital to know if insufficient thought has gone into the process so that the process can either be halted or corrected before serious damage is done to the bureau. The final decision about what structure is "correct" or "better" for public organizations can be made only by some combination of politicians, bureaucrats, clients, and other interested parties in the political or administrative process.

UNPLANNED CHANGE

Outside the bureau, the political, economic, and social characteristics of our society are constantly changing. Other countries also play an important role in influencing activities in our government. For example, our perception of the military might of the Soviet Union and its interest in using that military strength to foment trouble around the world had a dramatic impact on the amount of resources that were available for other activities within our government. With the end of the cold war, it was expected that the government should have a "peace benefit" that might help in other government programs; however, such a surplus did not appear, and the political mood changed to one of cutback and reduction of the government's role in society, so the international changes were offset, as far as government programs were concerned, by social value changes. The oil crisis of the 1970s created an upheaval throughout our society that affected all types of public and private organization policies, structures, and procedures. Whether the crisis was or was not a manufactured one, it pointed out inevitable long-term problems and choices that would have to be made at some point in the future. Neither government nor industry has been the same since that time. We may question whether the Pony Express was efficient and effective (historical debunkers argue that the Pony Express was romanticized, and not nearly as efficient as we are led to believe), but there is no doubt that the completion of the railroad and telegraph systems across the United States rendered the Pony Express obsolete. Good or bad management was not the central issue.

Likewise, the civil rights movement, which reached a peak of activity during the 1960s, changed the way in which all organizations (public and private) conducted required personnel activities as employees were hired, trained, and promoted. Affirmative action and equal employment opportunity programs were central to all personnel functions in public organizations. Now an effort is being made to reduce or stop affirmative action programs at the federal level, California has done away with some of its affirmative action programs, and as of January 11, 1996, the governor of Louisiana mandated an end to those same programs—arguing that even Martin Luther King would support his action. Managers inside individual bureaus cannot control these forces, but must react to them in the best possible way. No matter how effectively and responsibly a bureau is managed, the

La. Governor Bans Affirmative Action: Legislature Must Agree; Republican Says King Would Share Stance

Gov. Mike Foster signed an executive order today to halt affirmative action programs in Louisiana state government, but he acknowledged it will have little practical effect unless the Legislature backs him up.

On his fourth day in office, Foster also said he was proclaiming Monday a state holiday in honor of slain civil rights leader Martin Luther King Jr.—and he declared his belief that King would have opposed affirmative action programs.

"King sort of believed like I do on that," Foster said. "I can't find anywhere in his writings that he wanted reverse discrimination. He just wanted an end to all discrimination based on color."

Foster, a white Republican, defeated Rep. Cleo Fields, a black Democrat, in a November runoff and was sworn in Monday. One of his main campaign issues was his opposition to government programs giving preferential treatment on state contracts to benefit women and minorities.

He acknowledged today that his order cannot stop affirmative action in any program funded with federal money or any state affirmative action program specifically protected by state law.

Foster said that probably would include nearly all state programs.

"To tell you the truth, I'm not sure what impact it will have right now," Foster said of his executive order. He noted, however, that it includes a "reporting requirement so the agencies can let us know what is covered by the law."

Foster said he hopes to eliminate all state-funded affirmative action programs and set-asides by abolishing the laws in a special legislative session expected to begin in late February or early March.

"It's what I said in my campaign," Foster said today. "I just think reverse discrimination is wrong."

In California, Republican Gov. Pete Wilson last year led efforts to end affirmative action in the University of California system and also abolished affirmative action advisory boards for a handful of state agencies under his control.

Also in California, an effort is underway to let state voters decide whether to end affirmative action programs.

"They have the initiative in California to bypass the Legislature. That's what I want to do for Louisiana voters," Foster said. "When they think an issue is important enough and the Legislature doesn't address it, they can put it on the ballot for a vote."

Under Louisiana law, the governor gets some discretion in which days to designate as legal state holidays but must choose the Rev. Martin Luther King Jr.'s birthday at least once every two years.

In the past eight years, Foster's two predecessors never left the day off the list of state holidays.

SOURCE: Guy Coates, *Washington Post*, January 12, 1996: A11.

next election may bring into office a president who believes that his or her mandate includes a charge to do away with a program that is an important part of that bureau. Likewise, nonprofit organizations must react to changing priorities among the general public and the legislative bodies that constantly affect the functions of public service organizations.

Perhaps the whole concept of workforce diversity is a good example of external changes that require response within organizations. The various changes in demography related to race, ethnicity, gender, and other factors that have occurred regularly in our society have led to bitter disputes and numerous laws. This is an area that was always changing more than was realized. The magnitude of change in organizations of the future was forcefully spelled out in *Workforce 2000: Work and Workers for the 21st Century* (William and Packer, 1987). Now it is a problem, or opportunity, that plays a central role in much of our social and political consciousness. Affirmative action and equal employment laws have tried to deal with these changes, but the only way to really deal with current changes in the workforce is to specifically face the issue of diversity that exists, and will increase, in organizations as in the larger society. Specific efforts must be made to establish some way of handling the changes that diversity brings. The values, goals, and processes related to workforce diversity must be established by political decision makers and public administrators—in collaboration with organization members and the larger society. Those who argue for "diversity programs" do so because they believe it is easier to deal with such issues when the organization acts proactively rather than reactively (Golembiewski 1995). Public leaders, in this case, are attempting to plan for external forces over which they may have little control, but which they know are existent and bound to have an effect on overall success of their organizations (see Figure 10–7).

Inside the bureau, unplanned changes may not be of the same magnitude, but they are just as important when they occur. The loss of a critical employee during a period of peak activity may cause temporary backlogs in the processing of cases, slow down the decision-making process, or delay experiments that are underway. The breakdown of equipment can have the same types of effects. For example, perhaps the most common complaint currently heard in large offices is that work is delayed because "the computer is down." Numerous activities of both employees and management also have "unanticipated consequences"; and these unforeseen results of what are thought to be planned changes often create serious problems for everyone involved.

Change in the Political System: The Focus for Public Organizations

Unplanned change requires quick and appropriate reaction; thus, organizations must maintain the flexibility to respond to it. Those that do can prosper; those that do not can expect hard times. Public organizations must be aware of all aspects of their environment, but their attention is primarily focused on one area. All public agencies have one overwhelmingly important characteristic that colors all thought about change. Bureaus are inextricably bound up with the political system and the variations in public opinion and policy that are a constant part of political life. The bureaus' original broad objectives are established in the whirlwind of political, public-interest group, and legislative activity; even though administrative leaders form these relatively malleable objectives to the advantage of the

FIGURE 10–7 Major Sources of Advantage and Disadvantage in Managing Diversity in the Public Sector

1. *Legal:* failure to manage diversity will result in high costs of litigation as well as of adverse judgments by the courts.

2. *Costs:* the costs of doing business will be higher with failure to manage diversity—communication will be more difficult, employee involvement will be reduced, relationships will be strained if not adversarial, and so on, as organizations become more diverse.

3. *Intergroup Conflict:* a special case of costs, with broad implications for the quality of working life, labor-management relationships, the quality of unionization—conflict will be greater where managing diversity is less successful.

4. *Attractiveness to Potential and Actual Employees:* failure in managing diversity will be a major disincentive for existing as well as potential employees, which is of special significance in the public sector which has well-known disadvantages in recruitment and retention. This attractiveness holds not only for minorities, who will form large portions of the pool of employees, but also for others interested in a public work force that "looks like America."

5. *Attractiveness to Budgeting Authorities:* government agencies derive their life's blood from complex executive-legislative views of requests for appropriations, and poor performance in managing diversity may well become a growing factor in adverse reviews.

6. *Attractiveness to Clientele or Customer:* unsuccessful diversity efforts may well have direct implications for how an agency serves its clients or customers. The latter will become increasingly diverse over time, their needs presumably will be more accessible to diverse work forces and managements, and the comfort level for both service provider and client/customer should increase.

7. *Attractiveness to Managers and Executives:* more managements are not only tasking subordinates with diversity goals, but performance on those goals is taken into increasing account re promotions and salary judgments.

8. *Creativity and Problem-Solving:* many observers argue that organizations successful in managing diversity will bring broader perspectives, different experiences, and lessened attachment to past norms and practices, all of which can be expected to have a positive effect on creativity and problem-solving.

9. *System Flexibility:* agencies with successful diversity efforts will be more accustomed to dealing comprehensively with a changing environment, and hence more fluid and perhaps less standardized, as well as arguably more efficient and effective in responding to environmental turbulence.

10. *System Legitimacy:* success in managing diversity is associated with core values in our political and social philosophy, and hence that success also should have regime-enhancing tendencies.

11. *System Image:* successfully managing diversity provides another opportunity for government to exercise leadership as model employer.

SOURCE: Robert T. Golembiewski, *Managing Diversity in Organizations* (Tuscaloosa: University of Alabama Press, 1995): 47.

organization, there is only so much flexibility in the available interpretation. Similarly, the physical resources and political support for programs change as time goes by, sometimes dramatically but always inevitably, and the changes are often totally unrelated to success or failure in meeting the stated objectives. Public administrators must recognize this ubiquitous change in the environment and learn how not only to survive, but to turn this environmental characteristic into a useful tool when it is appropriate to do so. The important task is to recognize the appropriateness of manipulating the environment since there are times when a program is no longer wanted or needed by the citizens that it supposedly serves. When this is the case, it is essential to arrange a decent and timely organizational death. In many instances, however, bureaus are simply experiencing the normal swings of the public opinion pendulum, and popular and unpopular programs will trade places in the polls after an unspecified period. Such is the nature of the political world.

The important things for members of public organizations to remember are that (1) any particular period in the life of an organization is probably temporary; (2) each period creates opportunity for at least one of the types of change that have been discussed earlier in this chapter; and (3) all changes must be planned with the assumption that unless the change is occurring in a crisis situation the basic objectives of the organization remain the same or change only slightly. This means that the proposed changes must fit into the overall goals, and change is only justified if it improves the bureau's ability to meet those goals.

Public administrators must have both a short- and long-term outlook as decisions about the necessity and feasibility of change are considered. It is essential to think how a particular change—in design, process, or values and behavior of members—will work in the present situation. It is also necessary to realize that the political environment may change tomorrow, or most certainly in a few years, and either the anticipated change will have to fit a new set of demands or be easily adjusted. Quick fixes often portend future difficulty that is exacerbated rather than alleviated by the instant solution that fails to calculate future costs.

The biggest problem in this area is that many decisions that affect the bureaucracy are made outside it, and thus the bureau leaders have no control over an initial externally made decision about change. If a governor decides to run for national office and, as part of her campaign, promises that the number of public employees in the state will decrease during her term of office, the public managers do not have any say over that initial decision; the governor will mandate staff cuts in state agencies. The problem for the manager is to find a way to turn this externally mandated change into a positive action within the agency. One possibility is to use this mandate as the impetus for carefully studying the organization's functions, structures, and processes to see if changes can be made that will increase the efficiency and effectiveness of the operation while adhering to the political leader's orders. If such new procedures can be found, it is possible to use the external pressure as one form of justification for the changes that should ultimately be valuable to the organization anyway. This is a variation on the saying that "necessity is the mother of invention."

Normally, there are groups of clients and interested citizens who support any new program as it starts (Downs 1967); public administrators must turn to these people as a new program gets underway. It is also essential to recognize that many of the initial supporters will lose interest as time goes by, or that they will disagree with the way the program is run and therefore stop supporting it as ardently as they originally did. In our political system, almost every program or policy can expect to have a group of dissenters or opponents who will look for an opportunity to attack and destroy or to change the current program for one that they want.

The wise public administrator, therefore, will attempt to build bridges to new groups that will take the place of those that he or she lost, or will help balance the growing number of opponents. In addition, the leader will look ahead for situations that will probably bring out the opposition or allow the organization to advance its cause; both will inevitably occur. Then the leader has compromises or new proposals (including adjustments to, or new, objectives) that can be brought to bear on the situation. Thus, what may appear to be a compromise or a retreat may in fact be a change for the organization that has been planned and waiting in place for just such a situation so that it can be presented when the time is ripe.

Long-term changes, however, can be very difficult to implement in the public sector because people tend to have relatively short attention spans and elected leaders move in and out of office rapidly and at inopportune times. Therefore, it may be necessary to find a way to divide long-term goals into a series of short-term, easily identifiable, and supportable projects or modules that will ultimately achieve the bureau's long-term goals but will also allow those who must operate under shorter time constraints a sense of achievement as they observe what has been accomplished during their tenure. This approach matches in many details the argument presented by students of decision making: Major decisions may be accomplished through a series of incremental ones as long as there is some general agreement on objectives. Strategy and tactics become important in organizational change in the public sector just as they are important in any other decision-making situation.

CONCLUSION

What we finally have in public organizations is closely akin to the dialectical process (thesis, antithesis, synthesis). Bureaus exist with certain mandates from the political leaders; they try to carry out those mandates in particular ways. In the political world, it is normal to expect opposition; after all, that is why an issue is handled in the political world. There is no way to achieve unanimity on what objectives or procedures should be. From the constant tension that is generated around the public programs, there arises a stasis or balance in which the bureau operates—but that stasis is temporary. A compromise or synthesis exists because of that momentary balance. Once the balance shifts, the bureau has to develop a new modus operandi to meet the new situation. This is a never-ending struggle. Usually, society is shifting slowly enough so that the adjustments can be made relatively easily, almost without being noticed, and without discomfort to organizational members, clients, and interested parties who are not directly affected. However, inevitably, there are times when the changes are uncomfortable and even threatening to some or all of the actors in the process. It must be remembered that the synthesis that results is developed from opposing views.

All this is painful because public organizations represent the institutionalization of power in society. Those who "win" in the political process get to decide the goals, structure, and procedures used by the bureaus that carry out their policies. Luckily, these decisions are incremental, as is their implementation; nonetheless, an examination of the governmental bureaucracy gives us a very good picture of who in society has won and lost over the last few decades. Political dilemmas are generated by change in the bureaucracy, especially if that change comes from within the bureaucracy. Who has the "right" to change the way things are done? How will changes affect the balance of power within society? Can dramatic, internally generated change occur without affecting the balance of accountability and responsibility within the bureaucracy, and will that change have an effect on the democratic principles on which our government is established? There are no easy answers to these kinds of questions, yet answers are essential. None of these questions rules out change within the public bureaucracy; they simply point out the difficult issues that must be faced as we confront the inevitable.

FOR FURTHER READING

Although they are popular and simplistic writings on a very complex subject, it is still worthwhile to look at the works of Toffler and Naisbitt, not as actual pictures of what will be, but as interesting examples of attempts to think about how society, technology, organizations, and individuals will change over the next few decades. Therefore, when dealing with change as a generic subject, see Alvin Toffler's series of books, starting with *Future Shock,* New York: Random House, 1970, and going through (at the moment) *Creating a New Civilization: Politics of the Third Wave,* Atlanta: Turner, 1995. John Naisbitt's books, *Megatrends: Ten New Directions Transforming Our Lives,* New York: Warner, 1980, and *Global Paradox: The Bigger the World Economy, The More Important Its Smallest Players,* New York: W. Morrow, 1994, likewise deal with the subject of global change. When looking at organization development and change, it is necessary to begin by understanding what is meant by organizational culture, and this idea is well presented from a diverse set of viewpoints by Peter J. Frost et al., *Organizational Culture,* Beverly Hills, Calif.: Sage, 1985. Finally, to develop a good overview of organization development from both the philosophical and procedural perspectives of reputable practitioners, one should read Wendell L. French and Cecil H. Bell, Jr., *Organization Development: Behavioral Science Interventions for Organization Improvement,* 5th ed., Englewood Cliffs, N.J.: Prentice-Hall, 1995. A critique of two technocratic disciplines—the managerial and policy sciences—and their role in what the author believes is an increasingly undemocratic decision process is presented by Frank Fischer, *Technocracy and the Politics of Expertise,* Newbury Park, Calif.: Sage, 1990.

A recent book dealing with the general question of diversity in the workforce is edited by Martin M. Chemers, Stuart Oskamp, and Mark A. Constanzo and entitled *Diversity in Organizations: New Perspectives for a Changing Workplace,* Thousand Oaks, Calif.: Sage, 1995. Robert T. Golembiewski specifically deals with the issue of *Managing Diversity in Organizations,* Tuscaloosa, University of Alabama Press, 1995.

In the area of conflict analysis and management, one of the first books to weave conflict dynamics into the analysis of organizational phenomena was Anthony Downs, *Inside Bureaucracy,* which has been reissued by Waveland Press of Prospect Heights, Ill., in 1994. L. David Brown, in his book *Managing Conflict at Organizational Interfaces,*

Reading, Mass.; Addison-Wesley, 1983, argues that organizational efforts are hampered by either too much or too little conflict. Step-by-step guidelines for managing or mediating conflict in a variety of public policy issue areas are spelled out by Susan L. Carpenter and W. J. D. Kennedy in *Managing Public Disputes: A Practical Guide to Handling Conflict and Reaching Agreements,* San Francisco: Jossey-Bass, 1988.

REVIEW QUESTIONS

1. Look at each of the types of change discussed in this chapter, and note how they might interact or each influence the other.

2. The 1990s appears to be the decade of "downsizing" or "lean and mean" organizations. At the same time, there is a stress on "serving customers" and on working as teams to increase "efficiency and effectiveness" in public and nonprofit agencies. How do these forces fit together with the types of changes discussed in this chapter? What will public and nonprofit organizations look like after they have been acted on by all these forces? Especially think about (1) work settings, (2) hierarchies and managerial roles, (3) the role of "contractors as staff," (4) the changing roles of nonprofits and governmental agencies, and (5) the impact of all this on careers in these sectors of the society and economy.

3. Look back at Figure 10–5 and think about each of the questions raised. What concepts, theories, and models, discussed earlier in this book, serve as assumptions in forming each of the questions?

REFERENCES

Appleby, Paul H. *Morality and Administration in Democratic Government.* Baton Rouge, La.: Louisiana State University Press, 1952.

Argyris, Chris. "Today's Problems with Tomorrow's Organizations." *Journal of Management Studies* 4, 1967: 31–55.

———, and J. Schon. *Organizational Learning: A Theory of Action Perspective.* Reading, Mass.: Addison-Wesley, 1978.

Baber, Walter F. *Organizing the Future; Matrix Models for the Postindustrial Polity.* University: University of Alabama, 1983.

Boulding, Kenneth E. "General Systems Theory—The Skeleton of Science." *Management Science* 2, 1956: 197–208.

Brown, L. David. *Managing Conflict at Organizational Interfaces.* Reading, Mass.: Addison-Wesley, 1983.

Burton, John. *Conflict: Resolution and Prevention.* New York: St. Martin's, 1990.

Cooper, Terry L. *An Ethic of Citizenship for Public Administration.* Englewood Cliffs, N.J.: Prentice-Hall, 1991.

Downs, Anthony. *Inside Bureaucracy.* Boston: Little, Brown, 1967. (Reissued, Prospect Heights, Ill.: Waveland Press, 1994.)

Dvorin, Eugene, and Robert Simmons. *From Amoral to Humane Bureaucracy.* San Francisco: Canfield, 1972.

French, Wendell L., and Cecil H. Bell, Jr. *Organization Development: Behavioral Science Interventions for Organization Improvement,* 5th ed. Englewood Cliffs, N.J.: Prentice-Hall, 1995.

Galbraith, J. *Organization Design*. Reading, Mass.: Addison-Wesley, 1977.

Garvey, Gerald. *Facing the Bureaucracy: Living and Dying in a Public Agency*. San Francisco: Jossey-Bass, 1993.

Gawthrop, Lewis C. "Organizing for Change." *The Annals of the American Academy of Political and Social Science* 446, 1983: 119–134.

Golembiewski, Robert T. *Managing Diversity in Organizations*. Tuscaloosa: University of Alabama Press, 1995.

Golembiewski, Robert T., Carl W. Proehl, Jr., and David Sink. "Success of OD Applications in the Public Sector: Toting up the Score for a Decade, More or Less." *Public Administration Review* 41, 1981: 679–682.

Gortner, Harold F. *Ethics for Public Managers*. New York: Greenwood Press/Praeger, 1991.

Graham, Pauline. *Mary Parker Follett—Prophet of Management: A Celebration of Writing from the 1920s*. Boston: Harvard Business School Press, 1995.

Hunsaker, P. L., W. C. Mudgett, and B. E. Wynne. "Assessing and Developing Administrators for Turbulent Environments." *Administration and Society* 7, 1975: 312–327.

Katzenbach, Jon R., and Douglas K. Smith. *The Wisdom of Teams: Creating the High-Performance Organization*. New York: HarperBusiness, 1993.

Knight, Kenneth. "Matrix Organization: A Review." *Journal of Management Studies* 13, 1976: 111–130.

Landau, Martin. "On the Concept of a Self-Correcting Organization." *Public Administration Review* 33, 1973: 533–542.

Naisbitt, John. *Megatrends: Ten New Directions Transforming Our Lives*. New York: Warner Books, 1982.

_____. *Global Paradox: The Bigger the World Economy, The More Important Its Smallest Players*. New York: W. Morrow, 1994.

Ouchi, William. *Theory Z: How American Business Can Meet the Japanese Challenge*. Reading, Mass.: Addison-Wesley, 1981.

Peters, Thomas J. *The Pursuit of Wow! Every Person's Guide to Topsy-Turvy Times*. New York: Vintage, 1994.

Rohr, John. *Ethics for Bureaucrats: An Essay on Law and Values,* 2nd ed. New York: Marcel Dekker, 1989.

Schein, Edgar. *Organizational Psychology,* 3rd ed. Englewood Cliffs, N.J.: Prentice-Hall, 1980.

Schrage, Michael. *No More Teams! Mastering the Dynamics of Creative Collaboration*. New York: Currency/Doubleday, 1995.

Senge, Peter M. *The Fifth Discipline: The Art and Practice of the Learning Organization*. New York: Currency/Doubleday, 1990.

Tannenbaum, Arnold et al. *Hierarchy in Organizations*. San Francisco: Jossey-Bass, 1974.

Thompson, James D. *Organizations in Action*. New York: McGraw-Hill, 1967.

Toffler, Alvin. *Future Shock*. New York: Random House, 1970.

_____. *The Third Wave*. New York: Morrow, 1980.

_____. *Creating a New Civilization: Politics of the Third Wave*. Atlanta: Turner, 1995.

Waldo, Dwight. *The Administrative State: A Study of the Political Theory of American Public Administration*. New York: The Ronald Press, 1948; 2nd ed. New York: Holmes and Meier, 1984.

Warfield, Wallace. "Public-Policy Conflict Resolution." In *Conflict Resolution Theory and Practice: Integration and Application,* eds. Dennis J. D. Sandole and Hugo vander Merwe. New York: Manchester University Press, 1993: 176–193.

White, Michael J., et al. *Managing Public Systems: Analytic Techniques for Public Administration*. No. Scituate, Mass.: Duxbury, 1980. (Paperback reprint: Lanham, Md.: University Press of America, 1985.)

William, B. Johnston, and Arnold E. Packer. *Workforce 2000: Work and Workers for the 21st Century*. Indianapolis: Hudson Institute, 1987.

Witham, Donald C. *The American Law Enforcement Chief Executive: A Management Profile*. Washington, D.C.: Police Executive Research Forum, 1985.

READING 10–1   End-User Computing in the Public Organization: Realities of Organizational Life in the Information Society

During the last quarter century, the United States has been transforming itself from a nation dedicated and driven by industry and manufacturing to a nation increasingly dependent on the processing of information. At the heart of this dramatic change is the device we've come to know as the Personal Computer, or PC. First seen as a hobbyist's tool in the late 1970's, PCs now play a dominant role in the functioning of both public and private organizations in the U.S. Unfortunately, the explosive pace of adoption of new computer-based technologies brought with it significant changes in the way organizations operate but not an inherent *understanding* of the impact of the technology on the form and function of the organization. In organizations increasingly dependent on computers, it is critical that managers understand not only the hardware and software of the computer but also its impacts on the personal and institutional dynamics of the organization. This essay considers a number of impacts stemming from the new computer technology on organization structure and design, management and control, communication, decision making, and motivation and work habits.

To understand the impacts of computers on the public organization, it is first necessary to understand a little about the nature of the "computer revolution" in the public-sector organization. Computers are not new to the public sector. From the "hollerith cards" used at the turn of the century for census data analysis, to the use of electronic cipher machines during World War II, to the development of the COBOL programming language by Grace Hopper of the Navy, computers have been an integral part of many aspects of government operation. In fact, during the first half of the 20th century, governments, particularly the Federal government, led in the development of computing technology. This leadership began to fade when computers entered the mainstream of business during the 1950s and 60s. By the early 1980s, governments found themselves no longer in a position of leadership in the development and use of computing technology, but rapidly being left behind by the explosion of computer power in the private sector.

A critical juncture was reached in the early 1980s when the PC began to be accepted by the private sector as a tool of business. The tremendous influence of IBM, with the introduction of the IBM PC, effectively legitimized the personal computer in the business world. The growth of computer usage in the private sector since that event has been nothing less than explosive. During the 1980s and early 1990s, the numbers of PCs in use doubled, tripled, even quadrupled each year. From an exotic plaything, the PC rapidly evolved into the preeminent type of computer used in business.

In the public sector, however, the in-roads made by personal computing technology were not as great or as rapid. Even today, governments strive to catch up to a technology that appears to evolve at light-speed. Both the initial reluctance to accept the new technology and the subsequent rush to adopt it, have put tremendous pressures on public organizations—pressures that, even now, are only barely being explored and understood. What no one doubts, though, is that computing technology, in particular end-user personal computing technology, is having a tremendous impact on the public organization.

The reason that PCs are having such a tremendous impact on the public sector organization is simple: flexibility. Since the PC is physically located in the individual user's work space, can run a multitude of varying software applications, and can be customized to fit specific needs, the machine provides the user with a flexibility unheard of in older mainframe and mini-computer systems. PCs can be linked together to form *local area networks* allowing the direct passing of information from machine to machine without the production of paper output. In this way entirely new *electronic mail* communication networks are created, including the world-wide "Internet" which permits near instantaneous exchange of communication and information across the entire globe. The PC can be used by the manager to compose memos, monitor the progress of a project, or prepare an agency budget. Information can be transmitted over phone lines from field offices to headquarters and vice versa. Modifications to planned expenditures can be instantaneously evaluated.

Flexibility in design, usage, and applications are the reasons why PCs offer the potential for dramatic increases in productivity. Of course, improperly managed, unsecured, or poorly designed PC systems also hold the potential for significant problem generation within the organization. Let us look now at a few specific impacts of PCs on the public organization.

Organization Structure and Design Impacts

The computer, and particularly the PC, offers the potential for revolutionizing the design of the traditional organization. Instantaneous communication networks, direct information access, and a dramatically expanded capacity for information processing are all products of computerization that offer the potential for radically altering our perception of the needs of organization design.

Perhaps the greatest impact on organization design is felt in those organizations that have been in existence for some time. When introduced into an established organization, the PC frequently obviates the need for certain aspects of the existing organization structure.

For example, one of the original Weberian concepts of the bureaucratic organization is the division of labor, which is seen in the organizational approach to the production of memos, reports, or other documents. In the old style organization the task of document production is spread among several individuals, from the manager or analyst handwriting or dictating the first draft, to the typist who produces the document, to the clerk who reproduces the document, to the courier who distributes the copies, to the filing clerk who files a copy for future reference.

In an organization with a PC local-area network, the tasks outlined above can be substantially redefined. Since the analyst or manager responsible for producing the initial draft of the document is working on a computer using a word processing application, the traditional job of the typist becomes superfluous. Distribution is handled electronically via e-mail (electronic mail), as is the addition of the document to the organization's computerized data-base. On the surface then, it appears that the PC obviates the need for the typist, courier, and file clerk. In terms of the traditional job descriptions of those occupations, that is true.

The PC-supported organization, however, creates demand for new or substantially redefined occupational categories, such as document-control editors who insure that the documents produced directly by managers and analysts do not proceed with spelling, grammar, or other errors. Data-base management clerks are needed to see that new information is properly integrated into the organization's data-base, which must be properly designed and updated by a data-base analyst. In addition, the use of a computer network requires support personnel that are responsible for the function and upkeep of both the computers and the network to which they are linked.

As this example suggests, one of the most significant impacts of PCs on organization design is not necessarily the elimination of jobs, but the substantial redefinition of employee tasks. In an existing organization, the large-scale introduction of end-user computing can have a significant dislocating effect on the nature of the existing job positions in the organization.

Moving from the traditional set of job position categories to new information-processing-based classifications has important implications for the structure of the organization. For example, new job-task requirements do not match traditional position descriptions. In civil-service-oriented public organizations, this presents a potential for significant difficulty in: (a) obtaining authorization for nonstandard positions; and (b) dealing with employees filling the existing positions. Since the newly-defined job categories require expertise substantially different from the traditional positions, existing employees may no longer be qualified or capable of carrying out their new job responsibilities. The frequent result of efforts to reclassify positions to more accurately reflect the technology-based elements of the job is significant employee resistance, which may range from simple protests and grievances up to deliberate acts of sabotage.

Even if employee resistance to changing the structure of the organization is discounted, the task of redefining existing positions is not easy, particularly since the rapid advance of technology means that even more changes will be required in a relatively short period of time. Unfortunately, the reluctance of many public organizations to embrace the new computing environment forces them into a perpetual game of catch-up, in some organizations this translates into a kind of organization *du jour* where there is little, if any, long-term position stability. For the existing organization, then, the introduction of PCs requires careful analysis and planning to insure that the revised job structure is both appropriate and flexible enough to deal with additional rapid changes in technology.

When the managers of an organization make a decision to implement a large-scale PC network or operations system, they must "freeze" the technology at some point in order to implement it. The problem is that, very likely, by the time the implementation is complete, it is also outdated and inefficient compared to new technologies. There is a real danger that realizing this occurrence of instant obsolescence results in a tendency to procrastinate in hopes of not missing the "next breakthrough." Compound this problem with the considerable time required to thoroughly analyze and redefine position categories in any organization of even moderate size and the reluctance of many organizations to adopt new technology is understood.

Since any kind of substantial restructuring is inevitably in conflict with organizational production guidelines, the tendency is to implement the computer system piecemeal, as a kind of "maximin" approach that seeks to avoid the commitment to fading technology. The result is an organization structure that is unbalanced, with pockets of high technology side-by-side with offices modeled on traditional concepts. It is not difficult to picture the productivity nightmares faced by such organizations. The resulting bottlenecks, delays, and re-do's can effectively stifle any anticipated productivity increases.

In a broader sense though, how does the implementation of PC-based computer systems and networks affect the actual structure of the organization? Rather than adopt the traditional "pyramid" structure grounded in traditional bureaucratic theory, the techno-organization appears much flatter and more amorphous. Networking and electronic communications obviate the need for many of the intermediate layers of the traditional organization. Information transmission is virtually instantaneous, as is the potential for communication and feedback. Organizations committed to computer technology and networking find increasing amounts of flexibility in employee assignments since the concept of "workgroups" in the techno-organization refers almost exclusively to functional groupings, not physical ones. Released from the bounds of physical proximity, the new-style organization can be physically spread over significant distances. Some employees may even telecommute, working from home or a satellite office, physically very remote from the core-organizations. Essentially, the new organization structure becomes defined by function rather than place, dramatically increasing both task and employee flexibility.

The whole concept of organization structure defined by span-of-control, formal communication channels, and hierarchy of command falls by the wayside in the techno-organization. Replacing it is a structure based on as-needed functional groupings, frequent and rapid reorganizations, and significantly greater employee autonomy. For many public organizations, it also means significantly increased stress levels, downsizing of permanent employee forces and uncertainty about future stability, or even existence.

PC Impacts on Management and Control

There are two schools of thought on the impacts of PCs on management and control in the organization. The "Orwellian" school sees the PC as a tool for absolute management control, the "Gatesians" (from Bill Gates, founder of Microsoft and leading PC visionary) see the computer as a mechanism for enhancing creativity and individuality in the organization. Both sides make persuasive cases.

Those who see the PC as the tool of ultimate control base their contentions on the use of personal computer technologies as perfect auditors. Software is readily available to record and keep track of every use to which the computer is put. From the number of words typed per minute, to the duration of time lapses between keyboard accesses, to the precise type of work being performed, the PC can be used to monitor the performance of the individuals using it. The advantages that the PC offers in a Theory X-type management environment are substantial. As long as employees are conducting their work on the computer, the manager has complete oversight capability. In a networked environment where systems are linked together, the employee would not even be aware that the observation was occurring.

As might be expected, this Orwellian view of the control capacities of PCs prophesies the almost total abridgment of the right to privacy for any employee working in a computerized environment. This is especially true of the public employee. With the increasing pressures on public organizations to increase productivity while reducing costs, public managers may find the PC a tempting device for both setting and reviewing the performance standards of employees. In the case of dismissal for incompetence or just plain slowness, the PC could provide very precise evidence.

Beyond the intra-organizational control possibilities, the computer can also serve as a tool for legislative or legal review. Networked systems can be programmed to watch out for unauthorized or personal communications, identify non-approved software or the use of personal software. E-mail messages can be scanned for improper phrases. Without proper limiting safeguards, public employees could find their every action subject to multiple layers of scrutiny.

The impacts of this kind of control are substantial. It is not difficult to envision the substantial psychological complications which could arise from constant productivity monitoring. Creativity would be stifled since the risk of failure would be enormous. Employee paranoia could lead to a "by-the-book" approach that precludes individual initiative and actually results in reduced productivity due to prolonged periods of decision making and requirements to take all questions through formal channels. It is a fact of organizational life that many of the routine decisions are handled outside of the formal managerial and communication channels. In the Orwell PC-based organization, this option would be foreclosed.

Those who argue on the other side of the issue reject the Orwellian position as a practical impossibility in a democratic society. In their view, the introduction of PCs into the public organization offers the possibility for dramatically enhanced productivity while obviating the need for many managerial activities.

Rather than serve as a controlling force in the organization, the PC frees the employee to engage in more creative and individual enterprises. Since much of the routine detail-work in the organization will be automated, the requirement for close supervision by managers to insure accuracy and quality will be substantially reduced. The PC makes it possible to redefine the notion of the office or work space to accommodate telecommuting and other non-traditional work situations. The flexibility inherent in telecommuting and cyber-tasking frees up the employee from the rigid business-day schedule and makes it possible to establish very individualized work hours, the ultimate in flex-time.

Taking the view that the PC will act as a liberating force in the public organization means that significant redefinition of managerial responsibilities is in order. One obvious requirement is that managers must understand how PCs may be used in the organization. Traditional education for public managers does not prepare a manager for the concepts of networking, telecommuting, or distributed processing. This is not to suggest that all managers must become computer technicians, rather they must develop an understanding of the *uses* of the new technologies and the *impacts* of those technologies on both the workforce and the way the organization functions.

Managers in the micro-equipped office must learn to cope with a double-edged sword. The computer presents the manager with a tool that can be used for extremely oppressive management as well as a means to enhance the personal freedom and creative individuality of the employee. Like any other tool, the computer is a tool that can be used by management for both the benefit and the detriment of the organization's employees. A key problem with the use of computer technology, however, is that many managers do not have a complete understanding of either the function of the technology or the effects of applying (or misapplying) the technology.

A final comment is in order regarding the role of managers in a PC-equipped organization. Current experience indicates that the manager in the computerized organization will have to possess more of a technical background than is required in the traditional organization. While it is not necessary for every manager to be a PC expert, the nature of decentralized PC use requires that there be some point-of-use expertise in dealing with simple problems relating to both the hardware and software. In this area, perhaps more than any other affecting management, is the greatest resistance seen. Many managers still perceive the PC as being a tool for those of clerical or secretarial rank; managers manage people not machines. As the computer replaces many of the basic office functions and forces redefinition of positions, the requirement for the manager to become directly involved in the design, implementation, and operation of the PC system will increase. For middle managers who survive the downsizing and job redefining process, the future is likely to require a more technical orientation, as well as the ability to effectively coordinate the use of individuals and computers.

Impacts on Communication

The impacts of PC usage on both intra- and inter-organizational communications are tremendous. Rather than attempt an inevitably incomplete laundry list of those impacts, this essay will consider two of the most relevant to the public manager.

As Herbert Simon and others have suggested, one of the ways to improve organizational effectiveness is to improve the vertical communication system within the organization. The theory behind this suggestion is that information which travels accurately and rapidly up and down the organizational chain-of-command enhances the ability of the organization to carry out its functions. The PC, when linked in an organizational communication network, provides the elements for a super-efficient communications system. The key is that the computer-based communication network offers instantaneous transmission of precise information.

No longer is communication filtered, delayed, modified, or stopped at various levels within the organization. An electronic memo distributed on the communications network arrives at all of its destinations simultaneously, in the precise form it was sent. Communication up the organization structure moves directly from sender to intended receiver without passing through intermediary levels where changes can be made or communication halted. Obviously, the PC-based network eliminates the need for complicated formal communication channels. While this speeds up the communication process in the organization and insures the accuracy of that communication, it also poses a few problems.

Students of organizational communication know that much important communication in an organization occurs informally. Informal communication tends to be faster, more direct, and less procedurally cumbersome than traditional formal communication procedures. These advantages are essentially the same as implied for PC-based information networks. The question arises, then, of how computerization of much of the communication in a bureau will affect its informal and interpersonal communication processes.

While each organization is likely to react somewhat differently to increasing computerization of communication due to organizational culture, two general avenues of response are available. Either the computerization of communication will increase its effectiveness by augmenting informal networks, or an increasing reliance on computerized communication networks will inhibit informal communication and force a "formalization" of much of the communication occurring in the organization.

The first response is more likely to occur in an organization where computer-based communication is established on a flexible basis and great efforts are made to safeguard the privacy of communication. If the employees of an organization perceive that the communication network is secure from snooping by managers and the rules for using the network are neither too restrictive nor too cumbersome, then the use of the network is likely to be perceived as beneficial and useful. This is not an easy state to achieve. With the ever-expanding links of the Internet reaching into more and more organizations, control of outside personal communications conducted during business hours can become a problem. Implementing a policy banning such communications, aside from being almost impossible to enforce, may also suppress internal informal communications.

Establishments which follow this approach must be tolerant of the inevitable gossip and rumors that appear on the network. However, even these forms of communication can prove valuable in the organization, and the computer networks can also serve as quick and authoritative rumor control centers.

Organizations which implement a tightly controlled and restrictive communications network may find that it actually inhibits the free exchange of information. A common reaction to the use of computerized information networks is fear that whatever is entered into the network will be stored on file and may be later recalled and used against the sender. If this practice of total recall is followed, users of the system will tend to provide only the most routine and insignificant messages for transmittal. No one wishes to be held accountable for an inappropriate or misguided comment that was "captured" by the network. The result of this approach is frequently a system that dramatically fails to live up to its potential and may actually serve to inhibit communication in the organization.

A second major impact of computer-based communication on the public organization concerns security of information. Information security—who has access to what and how to prevent unauthorized access—is both an intra- and inter-organization problem.

Within the organization, there are major questions to be resolved concerning the access to organizational information. For example, in smaller organizations, it is not uncommon for both the organization's administrative information (personnel files, payroll information, etc.) to reside on the same computer or network as the productive information (resource data-bases, reports, statistical information). While an analyst has a legitimate reason for having access to the data-base, there is no reason for that person to have access to payroll records (and very good reasons why s/he should not have access). The problem, then, is how to control access to this sensitive information. Use of passwords and other "soft" security devices are notoriously ineffective in deterring the dedicated individual. Physically limiting access may preclude legitimate use. Clearly, the organization that moves to computer-based information systems must consider the security implications in such an installation.

The public organization, in particular, faces a number of very complicated issues relating to computer-based communication of information. A major issue is the type of information that should be made available "online." In other words, what, if any, of the information compiled by the public organization should be electronically accessible by the public. Should a taxpayer be able to use his home computer to dial into the local government's property tax assessment data-base and review his property assessment? If that information is available by mail or in person on an on-demand basis, should it not be available electronically if the citizen has computer communication capability? If such information is made available electronically, how will access be controlled or monitored? How will individual privacy be maintained?

While public access to government information is still in its infancy, the rapid growth of the Internet and other public-access electronic networks insures that this issue will grow rapidly. The technology exists to offer government information directly to individual citizens or private companies through phone-linked computer connections and the number of citizens with access to such information expands on a daily basis. The issues surrounding such transfers are very complex and delicate. Consider though, that beyond the security, access, and privacy issues, there are a number of public managerial concerns involved. Who will monitor such systems? Will staff be required to provide online help? Who will settle disputes over access or investigate privacy infringements?

These and other issues require that the manager of the computerized public organization must have a good background in the issues surrounding the implementation of electronic communication networks and be trained in implementing solutions to the potential problems outlined above. How many current public managers have such training? How many public management education programs are providing it?

Decision-Making Impacts

In the modern organization, computers frequently serve as aids to decision-making. Computers are not yet capable of replacing the human element in complex decisions, rather the analytical strengths of computing systems lie in their ability to organize, process and "model" complex decision situations. For this reason, the use of PCs and other computing systems in decision-making situations in organizations is often referred to as *decision support* and the computing systems used to provide such support are termed *decision support systems* (DSS).

PCs are generally recognized as the technology responsible for popularizing managerial decision support systems. DSSs have been used in mainframe computer environments since the 1960s. To use these systems, however, required an extensive knowledge of computers and programming and the results produced required considerable interpretation. With the advent of the personal computer, DSS moved from the cloisters of Management Information Systems control centers to the manager's desk.

The first uses of PCs for decision support grew out of the use of spreadsheet programs such as VisiCalc. These programs, which duplicated the accountant's spreadsheet on the computer's video screen and allowed extensive manipulation of numerical information, encouraged the manager to examine several alternatives in a decision situation, modelling "what-if" cases to select the best option. With the advent of current generation spreadsheets such as Microsoft Excel, Novell Quattro Pro and Lotus 1-2-3, these programs have gained the ability to produce presentation-quality graphics, organize and manipulate data-base data, and provide the user with an impressive array of built-in functions for complex statistical, mathematical and financial operations.

Beyond spreadsheets, a growing array of DSS-type applications continues to expand the definition of the DSS. For example, "idea processor" software is available to assist small (or large) groups in focusing on analysis for very complex problems. These "front-end" programs are complemented by decision-aiding software packages designed specifically to guide users through processes designed to produce high-quality, substantiated decisions. At the leading edge of DSS are the *expert systems* programs which combine extensive data-bases of knowledge drawn from experts in a specific field with query programs based on sophisticated logic, decision-rules and "inference engines." These programs are designed to augment the decision maker's abilities by providing "expert" advice on the issue at hand.

There is a general belief among decision makers that any decision that is supported by quantitative analysis is inherently a better decision than one based on subjective evaluations. The PC DSS provides the means for analyzing quantitative information in ways never before possible. The result is a strong tendency to want to structure decisions to take advantage of the number-crunching capacity of the computer.

To be able to effectively utilize the DSS, one requires the basic decision information be in a form that can be manipulated by the decision support package. Thus, organizations which implement PC-based DSSs require that the information gathering functions of the organization be realigned to facilitate the use of the DSS. Emphasis is placed on collecting and storing quantitative information. If care is not exercised and the limits of a quantitative DSS not observed, the use of valuable but qualitative information in decision making may be overlooked.

In any case, there is a clear trend towards the use of computer-based DSSs in organizations. To effectively use a DSS, like any other quantitative analysis tool, requires extensive training and knowledge of the limits of the techniques being used. The implication for professional managerial education is that new managers will be expected to know how to manipulate the formulas and templates required to effectively use the DSS. Unfortunately, the traditional training in statistics and mainframe data analysis do not necessarily carry over to the use of the new computer-based decision tools.

The use of micro-based DSSs in public organizations offers a number of implications for the structure and operation of those organizations. As suggested in the first section in this essay, positions and functions in organizations which rely on the computer extensively must be organized around information processing tasks that crosscut traditional job categories. Public employees must be trained and retrained to facilitate the collection, cataloging, extraction, and analysis of information with the new technologies. Managers take on tasks once reserved for statistical analysts and accountants and therefore must have a far more extensive knowledge of analytical techniques and how to apply them. The expectations of decision makers increase. Analysis must be supported extensively and justification given for foreclosing options not pursued.

The PC-based DSS offers the advantages of faster, more carefully analyzed, and more comprehensively justified decisions. These gains, though, come at a price. Even though the DSS facilitates the analysis of information, more work is needed to make a decision, not less. More information must be gathered, categorized, and analyzed than could possibly have been used with a more traditional approach. Use of the DSS tends to replace group judgements with multi-dimensional computer-based analysis (and that has both good and bad points). Finally, like all other quantitative analytical techniques, DSSs are subject to abuse and manipulation so care must be exercised in the use of the results gained from their application. G.I.G.O. (garbage in, garbage out) must be a real concern when using the DSS.

An implication which underlies the use of the micro-based DSS is that the preferred model for decision making in the organization is the rational model. As history has taught us, that is not always the case. The rational decision-making model is most appropriately used in limited cases where all of the components are known and understood and a single-best solution is possible. In many organizational situations, the circumstances do not fit these criteria. Unfortunately, there is a tendency to try to fit the problem to the solution since the use of quantitative analysis and justification "looks" more professional and impressive. Forcing problems into predefined solution models does not, however, produce good decisions. Fortunately, the latest generations of DSS-type programs offer analysts and decision makers a broader array of "fuzzy" or qualitative options for decision analysis. These options significantly increase the range of problems addressed in the organization that the computer may be able to assist in solving.

As the power of PCs increases, they are starting to be used as aids in heuristic decision situations. New software is developing around concepts in artificial intelligence that allow the decision maker to use the computer to assist in the evaluation of qualitative as well as quantitative information. The goal of much of this research is the development of expert systems that are capable of replicating the logic and analytical processes of a human expert in a specific field. For example, in recent years several medical software diagnostic programs have been developed that analyze a patient's symptoms and medical history and produce a diagnosis. These programs do not take the place of the physician, rather they provide additional information which enhances his or her ability to make correct diagnoses.

Expert systems are moving rapidly from the corporate boardroom to the offices of the public bureau. Programs designed to deal with hazardous materials management, land-use planning, utility-grid planning, and contracts negotiation are finding a ready audience in public organizations seeking to improve the quality of decisions made under increasingly strict resource availability. As suggested earlier, managers need to be prepared to deal with this new technology both as users and recipients.

While none of the computer-based decision-assisting strategies discussed in this essay will supplant careful, well-reasoned efforts by decision makers, they can provide ways to enhance both the efficiency and effectiveness of decisions. The key is the knowledge of the user. Managers and other decision makers must have a clear understanding of the strengths and weaknesses of decision-aiding programs prior to their use. It is easy to "blame the computer" for a poor, incorrect decision. The fact remains though, it is always up to the human decision maker to accept or reject the information provided by the program.

Impacts on Motivation and Work Habits

For the most part, the human animal seems to be resistant to change. Perhaps nowhere has this resistance been more evident than in the attempt to introduce PCs into organiza-

2. Should politicians and appointed leaders fear or cheer the growth of information availability to all members of the organization and, to a great extent, to the general public?

3. Consider other functions of the organization, such as leadership, decision making, and communication, and determine the impact of the information revolution on these aspects of organizational life.

4. What is the impact of the information revolution on the new attempts at creating customer- or client-centered organizations with greater quality in services? Return to this question after reading Case 10–1.

CASE 10–1 Challenges of Applying a Process-Improvement Technique in Public Agencies

Plans are being made by the Higher Education Manufacturing Process Applications Consortium (HEMPAC) to apply its process improvement technique in organizations other than manufacturing firms. Before addressing the feasibility of applying the technique in public agencies, some background is necessary on HEMPAC and the process improvement technique it uses.

HEMPAC

The Higher Education Manufacturing Process Applications Consortium (HEMPAC) was formed in 1993 to provide a process improvement service to small (fewer than 500 employees) manufacturing companies in Minnesota. A second goal of HEMPAC is to improve manufacturing education in Minnesota's public colleges and universities.

Organizations that belong to HEMPAC (see Figure 1) are from three sectors: education, business and government. Education-business-government partnerships have had a successful history in the United States since business-funded agricultural experiments began at state-funded Land Grant colleges established under the 1862 Morrill Act. In the latter part of the current century, focus has shifted from agriculture to other industries.

Because the organizations in HEMPAC are working together to address an issue that is too complex for any of the organizations to address alone, HEMPAC may also be called a collaborative alliance (Gray 1989). In HEMPAC's case, the educational organizations are needed in the collaborative alliance as sources of personnel and training, and 3M Company is needed as the source of the productivity improvement process on which HEMPAC's technique is modeled. The role of a small manufacturing firm in the collaborative alliance is to represent clients served. The two government agencies provide advice and financial support.

In 1993, following a successful pilot program funded by the Minnesota Job Skills Partnership, HEMPAC was awarded a $2.53 million cooperative contract with the Department of Defense under the Technology Reinvestment Project (TRP). This post–cold war program was developed to assist defense-related industries in making the transition to the manufacture of "dual use" products that are useful in both commercial and defense applications. As with many business assistance programs, the core goal of the TRP is

---

tions. Although several terms have been used to describe the reaction of some employees to PCs such as "computer-phobia," "PC-anxiety," and "compu-fear," the basic reaction is that the employee fears s/he cannot cope with the new technology and will, therefore, become obsolete.

Since the trend toward automation in the public organization is not likely to wane in the near future, the issue of computer fear is a very real and significant concern for public managers. From now until the turn of the century, those who deal with computers in the public sector can be classified as part of the *transitory workforce*. This means that most individuals working in public organizations entered public employment prior to the extensive use of computers. These individuals must be retrained and equipped to deal with a radically new technology. Overcoming initial resistance and fear is a major component of this retraining.

It is possible to view the fear of computers as the product of two sub-concerns: fear of an inability to learn the new technology, and fear of replacement. It is unfortunate that our society has had a tendency to portray computers and robots in popular literature as frequently malevolent and somehow anti-human. As computers have moved from the pages of science fiction to the desk of the average office worker, the negative conception of computers has translated into the very real fear of the machine.

Now, organizations are faced with the difficult task of overcoming this fear in their employees. Some individuals find the transition easy, others find the process far more difficult. This disparity, compounded by the basic fear, results in a number of costly problems for any organization introducing PCs into the workplace. For example, the pace at which individuals learn to use computers varies widely. The consequence of this is that vast disparities in productivity will occur for some time after the introduction of computers. For those on the high end of the learning curve, there is a common perception that they are shouldering an excessive amount of the workload. For those at the low end of the learning curve, there is fear that they will lose their jobs due to their inability to keep up.

Motivating each of these groups to continue to perform at their best potential is a difficult and subtle management problem that is not normally covered in traditional management education. Consider one other product of the learning-curve problem. What does one do with the employee who either cannot or refuses to learn the new technology? Dismissal? Transfer? Whatever course of action is taken, there are likely to be adverse consequences for either organizational productivity or employee morale. Finding the fine balance point for the needs of the organization *and* its employees is not an easy task.

Beyond employee resistance to computers, another problem which affects employee motivation is the environment in which the computers are used. In order for an employee to effectively use a PC, there are a number of environmental factors such as lighting, eyestrain, posture and seating, and noise that must be considered. Taken together, these problems are covered by the field that has come to be known as *ergonomics*.

Using a computer requires the user to adopt a posture and body position that is different from that taken when working at a typewriter or flat desk. The video display of a PC is far more subject to glare and improperly located lights than a typewriter or piece of paper. Improper ergonomics can result in very real physical problems—from headaches and backaches, to eyestrain, to nausea, to dizziness. Therefore, to maintain employee morale and motivation, care must be taken to design the computer work space with great care and concern for human engineering. Unfortunately, many organizations pay little more than lip-service to these requirements. The consequent loss of employee work days and productivity is frequently blamed on the "evils" of the technology when the reality is the failure of management to provide a proper environment for the use of the technology.

A corollary to the ergonomics issue is one of worker health. Although the results of studies have varied, there is general concern that working for long periods at computers may have harmful health effects, particularly for pregnant women. Unions have picked up on this issue and proper ergonomic design of work space and health quality assurance programs are becoming strong negotiating issues for union and management. Organizations desiring to implement computer systems must do more than plop the machines down on employee's desks. In many cases an extensive redesign of the work space may be needed to accommodate the new technology in a healthful environment.

Of course, one way for an employer to avoid the expense of office redesign is to allow employees to work at home. One very clear impact of computers in the public organization is the redefinition of work habits. Earlier in this essay, the term *telecommuting* was used to describe the use of a home computer to conduct work while remaining at home or at a satellite location. This is but one of the ways that the flexibility of computers will lead to new work habits. Basically, an employee who uses the computer to do his or her work need no longer be bound in either time or location to the traditional office working day. Once freed of the traditional 9-to-5 routine, computer-using employees are free to work a schedule that best suits their temperament and natural rhythms—even if that means working at 3:00 A.M.

Increasing numbers of organizations are establishing work-at-home programs for employees. The advantages to such programs are increased flexibility in working hours and reduced commuting costs, organizational overhead and work space requirements. Telecommuting opens up new labor markets such as the disabled, and part-time workers who are unable or unwilling to leave their homes. In the information society, the concept of the workplace is undergoing dramatic changes. Telecommuting, e-mail, faxes, teleconferencing and remote computer access are all non-traditional work technologies that make moot the requirement for employees to spend all their working time at a desk located in a traditional office. Into the 21st century, the real office may consist of a laptop computer, cellular fax modem/video phone and portable printer, all in use at the beach, on a mountaintop or even in one's kitchen.

Not everyone sees the advent of telecommuting and the flexibility of computers as benefits. Labor organizations argue that by employing part-time telecommuters, organizations are taking jobs away from full-time workers. In the New England area, unions are using old "cottage labor" laws designed to regulate textile sweatshops to stop companies from undertaking telecommuting programs. Since telecommuting and the use of other computer-based technologies requires some degree of technical competence which favor younger, more computer-literate employees, accusations of age and sex bias are also being raised. It seems inevitable that these issues will continue to grow in importance over the next several years.

From a management perspective, increased flexibility in work time and location gives rise to questions concerning control, accountability, and responsibility such as those discussed earlier. To be effective, telecommuting and other non-traditional, computer-based work environments must be based on a significant amount of trust from management and self-direction from the employees. For some, the temptation of working at home, with

virtually no supervision, may lead to procrastination, sloppy work, or even no work at all. Once again, new rules and managerial approaches will need to be created and implemented to deal with the new circumstances.

Preparing for the Future

Throughout this essay, the point has repeatedly been made that the manager in a bureau which extensively uses computers requires knowledge and expertise that is still not a common part of most public management education programs. In the information society the manager of a government agency or other public organization must be able to deal with technological issues that did not exist even a few years ago. Traditional training in management theory, decision making, organization structure and design, and communication stops short of dealing with many of the issues raised in this essay.

While it may seem that public administration educational programs need only emphasize statistics and computers more to account for current deficiencies, that approach proves far from a satisfactory solution. Unfortunately, most current research methods, statistics, and computer use courses still focus on technology that was in vogue during the 1960s. Few managers today will ever find it necessary to use a computer for statistical analysis or write a filing program in FORTRAN or COBOL. The real skills needed concern the use of application programs, not programming languages, and small computer systems and networks, not traditional mainframes.

Even with the proper technological preparation, the manager in a computer-intensive organization is still inadequately prepared for the psychological and human-dynamics issues endemic to the use of PC systems. Proper training for microcomputer management must include knowledge of the human dimensions of the new technologies. As suggested earlier in this essay, many of the real managerial issues surrounding PCs stem not from the hardware or software but from human interaction with the system. Clearly, the techno-organization manager must be better equipped to deal with these issues than his or her predecessors. The bottom line is that introducing computers into the public organization increases the complexity and difficulty of the manager's tasks. The new technology offers tremendous promise for increasing organizational efficiency and productivity. This promise will not be achieved unless public managers are prepared to deal effectively with the technological and human dynamic changes which are part of the information revolution.

SOURCE: Dr. John W. Ostrowski, Associate Professor, Graduate Center for Public Policy and Administration, California State University Long Beach.

Editor's Note

The technological area is perhaps the fastest changing aspect of public organization life. At the same time, it is interconnected with all the other aspects of bureau life that we have discussed.

1. What impact does changing technology, especially the rapidly increasing flexibility and power of personal computers and the development of the Internet, have on the structures and procedures of public organizations?

CASE FIGURE 1   Organizations Represented on HEMPAC Board

Six Minnesota public colleges and universities:
Alexandria Technical College
Anoka-Hennepin Technical College
Pine Technical College
St. Cloud State University
St. Cloud Technical College
University of Minnesota Duluth

Two businesses:
3M Company—A Fortune 500 firm headquartered in St. Paul, Minn.
Atscott Manufacturing Co.—a job shop representing HEMPAC clients

Two state-supported agencies:
Minnesota Job Skills Partnership—an arm of Minnesota's Department of Trade and Economic Development that funds projects that create jobs
Minnesota Technology, Inc.—a non-profit corporation that assists Minnesota manufacturers through funding from the State of Minnesota and the National Institute of Standards and Technology (NIST)

economic development by preserving or even increasing the number and pay levels of jobs provided by affected companies. From 1994–97, with TRP support, HEMPAC is conducting projects in 36 Minnesota companies of 25–500 employees to test its productivity improvement process as a way for companies to become more efficient and able to adapt to changing market conditions. A significant part of the project is a special study being conducted by the University of Minnesota Duluth to determine if the process can be initiated successfully in very small companies of fewer than 25 employees. Four "microprojects" are being conducted.

Manufacturing Improvement Process

The productivity improvement process provided by HEMPAC is modeled on Optimized Operations (02), a technique that is the property of 3M Company. Optimized Operations was developed in the 1980s by 3M to meet several challenges in its plants, including waste reduction, improved efficiency, quality and safety. Newly hired manufacturing control engineers attend a two-month training program in Optimized Operations, after which they serve as team members on 02 projects. In its Optimized Operations unit, 3M employs manufacturing engineers, trainers and project advisors. Some 400 projects have been conducted by 02 teams in 3M plants around the world.

The adaptation of the 02 process that is offered by HEMPAC is called the *Manufacturing Improvement Process* (MIP). The MIP process has the following key components:

- Reliance on the scientific method for identifying root causes of problems and effective solutions
- Use of teams to conduct projects
- Emphasis on continuous quality improvement
- Training company employees in skills that are essential to the success of their MIP project

- Reliance on process improvement tools such as Just-in-Time (make orders for materials and components a function of production line needs), constraints management (identify and control bottlenecks in production line), changeover reduction (reduce time needed to change tools on machines in line to manufacture a different product) and quality function deployment (define quality throughout the steps of a production process as a function of customer expectations)
- Emphasis on development of human relations skills
- Handoff of the MIP process by the HEMPAC team to company employees
- Iterative nature of MIP that allows it to be integrated into the culture of a company and used repeatedly to address additional problems as they emerge

The Manufacturing Improvement Process can be diagrammed as shown in Figure 2.

CASE FIGURE 2   Elements of the Manufacturing Improvement Process

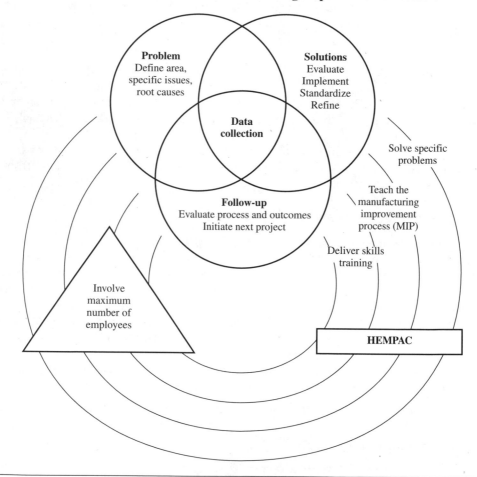

SOURCE: Steve Thieman and the Standard Iron and Wire Works, Inc. MIP Team.

Project Selection

Companies are selected for HEMPAC projects on the basis of need, ability to benefit and readiness to engage in such a process. Readiness is the factor most difficult to judge. It is evaluated on the basis of perceived attitudes of management and workers toward change, their current involvement in change processes, their motivations for choosing MIP as a route to improvement, the company's prior efforts at improvement and reasons for their success or failure, the degree of authoritarian management in place at the plant and willingness of management to listen to workers.

Project Personnel

Once a company is selected, a team is formed to conduct the six-month MIP project. The MIP team usually consists of five members:

- Team facilitator
- Two student interns
- Two company employees

When 3M company conducts an Optimized Operations project, the team facilitator is a 3M engineer who has completed an 02 training program. When HEMPAC conducts a MIP project, the team facilitator is a faculty member from one of the six HEMPAC institutions who has attended 3M's 02 training or the Summer Institute that HEMPAC conducts to train MIP project facilitators. An effort is made to match the experience and skills of the assigned facilitator with the needs of the particular project and company.

Two students enrolled in HEMPAC colleges in engineering, business, computer science, or technology-related fields also serve on the team. The interns are responsible for many of the positive outcomes of the MIP projects because they have up-to-date knowledge of improvement processes, they usually are young and relatively inexperienced—and, therefore, non-threatening—they find the shop floors interesting and regard workers as expert sources of information, and they are willing to ask endless questions. They usually keep journals of their experiences and may have to complete other assignments as well, since most of them use the project as a required internship that counts for credit toward their degrees.

In addition, the company selects two people to be assigned to the MIP team full time for the six months of the project; often one is from middle management and the other from the shop floor. After learning the MIP process during the early part of the project, they gradually take over until at the end of the project the faculty facilitator is merely observing and the company employees have assumed all facilitator functions and responsibilities. Projects are set up this way so that company employees learn how to conduct them on their own and can undertake additional MIP projects after HEMPAC facilitators and staff leave the plant.

Cost Sharing

The cost of each project is shared by the company and the federal cooperative contract, the latter paying the salary of the project leader (up to $30,000, including fringe benefits, for six months) plus $12,000 for 120 hours of company-wide, on-site training related to the success of the project. The company pays the student interns ($10 per hour) and provides a meeting room for the team. Both HEMPAC and the company provide the team with a computer and supplies.

Stages in a MIP Project

Management tells the MIP team the aspect of the business on which to concentrate, but team members decide the goals of their project and design it. Projects focus on improving plant processes and can range across the company from sales to design and engineering to production.

Usually, data collection to identify root causes of problems extends through the second month of the project. At that time, a "baseline review" is conducted, at which team members present to a gathering of company employees and HEMPAC board members and staff the data they have collected and analyzed to reveal root causes of problems. During the subsequent four months, solutions to these problems are identified, tested and implemented, and reports are prepared.

Six months is a long time and a great deal can be accomplished by a five-person project team working full time for that period. The project team reports weekly to a guidance team that includes owners or managers of the company. Presentations are formal, with overheads and other illustrations, because management seems more responsive to routines and practices that they use themselves in staff meetings and that are used by the consultants they hire. Faculty members and students are accustomed to this presentation format, but it can place great stress on workers from the production floor who may view public speaking as worse than death. Care must be taken to help prepare anyone who feels insecure about presenting because success of the MIP project depends upon management learning to listen to employees who never before had voices. If those voices are disorganized or illogical, management is given a reason to ignore presentations and perhaps the entire project.

Every week to ten days projects are visited by HEMPAC's assistant director to make sure they are proceeding satisfactorily. Learning teamwork can be difficult and advocating and adapting to change is always painful. Frustration and anxiety sometimes run high. Team members spend long days "just thinking" and the physical inactivity attendant upon this can be extremely difficult for production floor workers to bear, being accustomed to constant movement. Management often is threatened by the team making decisions. "Why are we needed?" they may ask themselves. Often, management is too autocratic to accept team decision making and just as often workers are unwilling to accept the responsibility. "What's in it for me?" both groups ask. Not everyone welcomes flattening the hierarchy.

At the end of a project, a final review is conducted to which management, workers, HEMPAC board and staff members and other guests are invited. As with the baseline review, the final review is a formal presentation with all team members discussing how analyses were undertaken, what problems and solutions were identified, how solutions performed in trials and how they were integrated into operations. Usually, a project gives rise to other projects that can be immediately begun by new teams led by the employees who served on the original MIP team.

Every project at every company follows the Manufacturing Improvement Process, yet every project differs in goals, data collected, improvement tools applied and results. Throughout the process, evaluations are conducted. The 120 hours of company-wide training are conducted by faculty members from HEMPAC colleges on subjects related to the success of the MIP project. Such training nearly always includes units on basic subjects such as the scientific method, team building, communications skills and adapting to change.

Project Results

Figure 3 shows results of some 1994–95 MIP projects:

Project Description 1: Hibbing Electronics Corporation

Hibbing Electronics Corporation is located in Hibbing, Minnesota and employs 470 people. The company manufactures circuit boards and electronic subassemblies for instrumentation, computer, telecommunications and industrial uses. The focus of the MIP project was to improve machine run time in the surface mount area, reduce the lead time required for scheduling, produce a more efficient floor plan, reduce cycle times, and streamline and reorganize the handling of materials from the dock to the machine. By improving layout of the plant and flow of materials, the company was able to show a 50% improvement in machine operations, including the time required for the "booking to start of run" segment, and a 25% reduction in total cycle time. Seven project action teams remain in place, and the company continues to evaluate and reposition material on the shop floor to maximize material flow and reduce cycle time.

CASE FIGURE 3   Some Results of 1994–1995 MIP Projects

Quantitative

- $15,000–$35,000 annual savings in raw material costs
- $37,000–$54,600 annual savings in labor costs
- 39–90% reduction in order processing time
- 10% reduction in inspection hours
- 50% reduction in scrap rate
- 50–112% increase in throughput
- $7,500 monthly savings due to increased accuracy of production
- $200,000 savings due to improved process control
- 250% production increase of parts from 400 to 1,000 per hour
- 50–75% reduction in changeover time

Nonquantitative

- Development of written procedures for inventory management
- Development of pricing system that accurately reflects company costs
- Increase in company morale
- Development of method sheets for jobs on shop floor
- Development of procedures for operation of production areas

---

SOURCE: Developed by John Olson, HEMPAC.

Project started June 6, 1994 and ended January 17, 1995.
Project leader: John Voss, University of Minnesota, Duluth.
Source: Kendall & Powers, 1995.

Project Description 2: Standard Iron and Wire Works, Inc.

Standard Iron and Wire Works, Inc., which employs 175 people, has three locations, in Alexandria, Sauk Centre and Monticello, Minnesota. One division of the company produces hand rails, decorative weldments, and other steel, non-structural parts of buildings. The second division creates steel parts for industrial and agricultural equipment. The MIP project began by improving documentation to the shop floor and expanded to include most of the information flow through the company. A feedback system team was established to monitor work on an operation and work order basis. A reengineering team developed an improved method for creating and monitoring routings to the shop floor. A third team worked on organization and flow of raw material. Benefits of these efforts included greater understanding of company information systems, team building, and emphasis on quality and planning.

Project started March 27, 1995 and ended September 21, 1995.
Project leader: Steve Thieman, St. Cloud and Pine Technical Colleges.

Project Description 3: W. F. Scarince, Inc.

W. F. Scarince, Inc. is located in Sauk Rapids, Minnesota and has 40 employees. The company produces items requiring high tolerance welding. The MIP project focused on inventory management, information flow, production planning and process analysis and design. Results included a $37,000 savings in labor associated with searching for raw materials, development of an information team that has created manuals for training on its computer system, determination of plant utilization efficiency and capacity rates, 112% increased throughput of one CNC burning machine, and increased communication and job awareness throughout the organization.

Project started June 1, 1994 and ended December 15, 1994.
Project leader: Dr. Warren Yu, St. Cloud State University.
Source: Kendall & Powers, 1995.

Project Description 4: Ceramic Industrial Coatings

Ceramic Industrial Coatings is located in Osseo, Minnesota and employees approximately 50 people. CIC was started in 1976 and is one of the largest manufacturers of paint and coating products in the upper Midwest. The mission of the CIC team was to increase CIC's competitiveness by reducing the cycle time associated with the paint production process. Results of the project included a 39% reduction in cycle time, a 23% reduction in late batches, a 49% reduction in "X" batch (ruined during production) yield and 72% reduction in "X" batch cost (waste).

Project started July 11, 1994 and ended January 11, 1995.
Project leader: Lynn Smaagard, Anoka-Hennepin Technical College.

Project Description 5: Granite Gear

Granite Gear is located in Two Harbors, Minnesota and has 27 employees. It manufactures high quality outdoor recreation equipment. The company needed assistance in adjusting its operations due to a tremendous growth in sales, from $42,690 in 1986 (startup year) to $785,713 in 1995. The MIP team initiated this process by improving the production of large *Round Rock Solid Compression Stuff Sacks*. To accomplish this goal, the team analyzed cycle time from customer order to customer receipt, production scheduling, production design and inventory control. Because of the high volume and basic design of Rock Solids, improvements developed should apply to other Granite Gear products.

Project started June 5, 1995 and ended November 22, 1995.
Project leader: Dr. David Wyrick, University of Minnesota, Duluth.
Source: Kendall & Powers, 1995.

Leader Training

One of the early tasks of HEMPAC was to begin to train faculty as leaders of MIP projects. The 3M Company trained HEMPAC's first eight leaders. Since then, HEMPAC has conducted two Summer Institutes at which additional leaders were trained. An employee from each company that has completed a MIP project also is invited to attend the Summer Institute to renew MIP skills (see Figure 4).

CASE FIGURE 4   HEMPAC Summer Institute Topics

HEMPAC and MIP Orientation
SPC Toolbox and Applications
MIP Project Tours
Brainstorming
Design of Experiments
Decision-Making Tools
Evaluation Tools
Benchmarking
Leadership Theory
Team Building: Leadership-Facilitation
Coaching
Changeover Reduction
HEMPAC Project Startup
Human Relations Issues
Project Leadership
HEMPAC Resources
Team Building: Conflict Resolution
Stages of Problem Solving

Team Building: Goals and Roles
JIT Simulation
Project Scheduling
Improving Receptivity of Change
Process Mapping
Cost of Quality
Project Management Theory
Material Flow and Plant Layout
Team Building: Meetings
Quality Function Deployment
Cell Manufacturing
Ergonomics
Constraint Management
MIP Project Challenges
Effective Presentations
Effective Communication
Project Transfer and Continuation

The Summer Institute curriculum has been patterned after the 02 curriculum used at the 3M Company but modified to serve the needs of the small manufacturing company. Instruction has come from trained MIP leaders, 3M Company, HEMPAC member institutions, and consultants. The Summer Institute lasts five weeks and uses 60-hour MIP miniprojects at local manufacturing companies to provide attendees with the opportunity to practice immediately what they are learning.

By the time the Department of Defense's Technology Reinvestment Program support ends in 1997, HEMPAC will have used the Manufacturing Improvement Process at small manufacturing companies of different sizes, products, initial manufacturing cultures, management structures and styles, employee background skills, competitive positions, labor–management relations, and technological capabilities. From this experience, HEMPAC is documenting the MIP process and developing standard MIP materials to guide and evaluate project activities. An oversight structure is being developed to select companies for MIP projects, monitor progress and document outcomes, including long-term gains by the companies. HEMPAC's goal is to develop a proven process that can be used by companies across the United States.

Relation of MIP to Total Quality and Learning Organizations

Figure 5 shows the relation of MIP to *total quality* (adaptive) and *learning* (change-anticipating) organizations. The Manufacturing Improvement Process, as most frequently used by HEMPAC, can be classified as a total quality approach. The technique is generic in nature, however, and can be used as effectively in anticipating and avoiding problems as it can in resolving them. Luthans, et al. view learning organizations as embodying total quality core values to which are added characteristics that distinguish the learning organization. MIP is a tool sufficiently strong to be useful in the broader venue of the learning organization.

CASE FIGURE 5   Relation of MIP to Total Quality and Learning Organization Theories and Practices

Luthans, Hodgetts and Lee (1994) stated ten core values that characterize a total quality (adaptive) enterprise:

Customer-driven	Prevention, not detection
Leadership	Management by fact
Full participation	Long-range outlook
Reward system	Partnership development
Reduced cycle time	Public responsibility

Regarding learning (change-anticipating) organizations, the authors identified five additional characteristics:
Intense desire to learn (anticipating change)
Values emphasize shared values and system thinking
Strong commitment to generating and transferring new knowledge and technology
Use of dialogue, scenario analysis and process reengineering as specific techniques
Openness to the external environment

MIP Project Challenges

Any MIP project faces innumerable obstacles in every project phase. Some of the most common problems include:

- Convincing authoritarian management to listen to employees regarding needed process changes, but not to use employees' ideas without giving them credit
- Losing momentum before changes are implemented
- Choosing team members who lack the knowledge or skills to contribute to the project or are unwilling to accept responsibility for recommending change
- Encountering union leaders who believe that team activities threaten their power
- Jumping to the solutions phase of the process before collecting and analyzing data to reveal root causes of problems
- Neglecting to spend sufficient time in team formation and cultivating efficient operation

The Manufacturing Improvement Process is a generic technique that should be applicable in a variety of situations. In discussing its use in organizations other than manufacturing, MIP will be called PIT (for *Process Improvement Technique*) to avoid confusion, although its basic steps will remain unchanged. As with MIP, a key in applying PIT in any organization is to conduct an initial project likely to have significant results. Initial success will make it easier to branch out into other parts of the organization with additional projects. For example, a PIT project conducted in the business office of any public university is likely to produce significant savings. With this success to cite, efforts to improve processes in the administrative and teaching sectors of the university would stand better chances of success.

In any case, processes should be selected for improvement that (a) promise opportunities for significant savings; (b) are relied upon heavily so that changes have noticeable impact; (c) take into account the unique challenges intrinsic to the business or company so that the initial PIT project can be used as a model for projects elsewhere in the organization; and (d) can be subjected to measurement, in some sense, so that progress can be clearly and accurately described.

Challenges of Applying PIT in Public Agencies

Modifications of PIT

Changes in PIT that could be necessary in applying the process in a public agency include:

- Need for qualitative as well as quantitative approaches to address problems that do not lend themselves to scientific analysis or measurement
- Reliance on professional or other skilled individuals to address particular issues instead of teams—because of tradition, cost or other factors
- Definition of continuous quality improvement that makes sense in the context of the problems being addressed
- Identification of process improvement tools appropriate to the context

Differences Between Public Agencies and Manufacturing Companies

In applying PIT in the public administration area, attention must be paid not only to concerns intrinsic to the PIT approach, but to differences between public agencies and manufacturing companies that influence the outcomes that are possible.

1. Difference in Product

In manufacturing, customers receive a physical product. Some public agencies also provide a visible service or product, such as welfare checks or road maintenance. Because other public agencies provide less tangible services, such as developing policies and making rulings, their customers may not be aware of being affected by what they do.

2. Definition of Customer

In manufacturing, receipt by a customer of a product can occur at several stages in the manufacturing process inside a company or across a supply chain (in which a series of value-added procedures are performed on an item) as well as when an item reaches a customer in the broader marketplace. A public agency likewise may have customers internal to it or in fellow agencies, in addition to customers or clients in the public it serves. Its key customers, however, are those in the legislative or executive branches who have the power to shrink the budget or duties of the agency. To ensure that their agency remains viable, therefore, employees may not believe they can afford to allow other client or consumer satisfaction to drive their behavior.

3. Drivers of Change

Change in manufacturing is driven primarily by market forces such as price and sales volume, which depend on customer satisfaction. These elements are not germane as drivers of change in public agencies unless major budget cuts have occurred, reorganization is demanded or election campaigns precipitate change.

4. Difference in Goals

Private companies worry about profit, which is affected by productivity. Public agencies are less concerned with productivity and worry instead about accountability. Whether statutory authority authorizes actions is of prime concern, not efficiency, effectiveness or worthiness of objectives in the eyes of consumers.

5. Rule Making and Review

Rules that are followed in achieving accountability and review procedures often are established by law. Therefore, if a better way (more efficient, less expensive) of conducting a process can be identified, adopting it may be excruciatingly difficult, involving waiting for a legislative session to occur, extensive lobbying and significant expenditure of resources. In many states, a statutorily mandated rule-making process also exists, entailing public hearings, time consuming legal proceedings and negotiations to take into account concerns of regulated industries.

6. Reward Systems

In private industry, rewards depend on helping an organization meet its profit goals. Rewards include raises, promotions and "perks." Employee reductions are rewarded because they save money for the company. In public agencies, either by statute or union contract, rewards such as promotions, bonuses and merit increases sometimes are prohibited. Rewards instead may include longevity and meeting criteria of legislatively-mandated promotions and salary increments. Building a bigger staff may lead to promotion, if position depends on number of persons overseen.

7. People Involved

Entrepreneurs are attracted to the opportunities and rewards offered by business. They tend to be constrained by statutory requirements, however, with the result that people who survive in a public agency tend to be those who are more comfortable with regulations and routines. Entrepreneurial behavior may be encouraged in "re-invented" organizations, but more often than not is punished in public agencies because it challenges the status quo and the maintenance behavior that is rewarded.

Applying PIT in Public Agencies

Given all of the above constraints, can PIT be applied effectively in a public agency? Adjustments can easily be made (and indeed are currently made in MIP projects) to offset difficulties inherent in the PIT process by including appropriate qualitative approaches, assigning pieces of the issue under consideration to be studied by appropriate professionals not part of the project team, defining what is (or should be) meant by "continuous improvement" in the particular organization being examined, and identifying appropriate tools to improve the processes that are being addressed.

While public and private bureaucracies can be stifling, it must be remembered that the purpose of their procedures and measures is to ensure fair and equal treatment under the law. Furthermore, in many public agencies, a surprising degree of freedom to be entrepreneurial exists, if one is willing to invest time and effort in identifying problems that cry out for resolution, in building broad-based support for clearly-defined changes that promise to be fruitful in finding ways to encourage fellow employees in ways not prohibited by statute or union regulations, and, most important, in caring deeply about outcomes. With energy and persistence, a way can always be found to transform a "can't do that" culture to one that asks, "How can this best be done to serve our customers?" One effective strategy is to convince the prime sponsor of an agency, such as the governor or chair of a legislative committee, to lead in advocating change. Efforts of an elected official of high rank can result in shifting a degree of emphasis from accountability to efficiency or from centralized control and authoritarian leadership to decentralization and broader participation in deliberations, decisions, problem solving and planning.

In sum, it bears repeating that the Manufacturing Improvement Technique is a generic approach that can be modified to particular needs of projects in a variety of settings. Practitioners in fields infrequently addressed by scientific analysis may understandably have reservations concerning the approach. Results can be useful, however, and that fact should be sufficient to convince many public agency employees to grant it a fair trial.

SOURCE: Dr. Mary Powers, Director, Higher Education Manufacturing Process Applications Consortium.

References

Gray, B. *Collaborating: Finding Common Ground for Multiparty Problems*. San Francisco: Jossey-Bass, 1989.

Kendall, L. A., and Powers, M. F. *HEMPAC: Improving Manufacturing and Manufacturing Education*. Paper presented at the World Conference on Engineering Education, St. Paul, Minn. October, 1995.

Luthans, F., Hodgetts, R. M., and Lee, S. M. "New Paradigm Organizations: From Total Quality to Learning to World Class." *Organizational Dynamics*, 4, 1994: 5–94.

Editor's Note

In this essay, Dr. Mary Powers, the director of the HEMPAC project, describes one procedure established to bring about change (in both efficiency and effectiveness or quality) in private sector manufacturing organizations. She also points out some of the major problems faced when attempting to change the focus of the process from private to public organizations.

1. Examine the issues that Dr. Powers notes when discussing the problems faced in public organizations. What impact do these issues have on the probable success of total quality management in public organizations? Can you add any more issues *within the public organizations* that must be faced to those she mentions?

2. What political or environmental factors will decide the ultimate fate of programs such as this that try to improve quality or effectiveness in public agencies.

3. This is an interesting exercise that will help you better understand the Process Improvement Technique.
   a. Choose a process that should be improved from an organization familiar to you—where you work, attend class, are entertained, purchase food or other goods, or obtain medical care or other services. Map that process. An easy method of process mapping is to write elements and subelements of the process on self-adhesive notes that can be rearranged and added to until the process is described clearly.
   b. How would you proceed in attempting to improve the process you have mapped in question 3a? What challenges would you face?

Name Index

Subject Index